The
Concordia Pulpit

for 1935

Volume VI

EDITOR-IN-CHIEF
PROF. MARTIN S. SOMMER

St. Louis, Mo.
CONCORDIA PUBLISHING HOUSE
1934

PRINTED IN U. S. A.

CONTRIBUTORS TO THIS VOLUME

Prof. W. Arndt
Rev. H. W. Bartels
Rev. J. W. Behnken
Rev. Aug. F. Bernthal
Rev. C. J. Beyerlein
Rev. H. J. Bouman
Rev. L. Buchheimer, Sr.
Rev. H. W. Degner
Rev. K. H. Ehlers
Rev. Wm. H. Eifert
Prof. Theo. Engelder
Rev. Fr. Evers
Rev. A. Fahling
Rev. R. Grote
Rev. A. H. Grumm
Rev. W. H. Hafner
Rev. G. E. Hageman
Rev. J. H. Hartenberger
Rev. F. A. Hertwig
Rev. W. E. Hohenstein
Rev. Geo. Hoyer
Rev. Otto H. Hoyer
Rev. A. Jordan
Rev. O. C. J. Keller
Rev. C. J. Killinger
Rev. A. C. Klammer
Prof. H. A. Klein
Rev. J. G. Kleinhans
Rev. Alb. J. Korris
Rev. H. Kowert
Rev. K. Kretzschmar
Prof. O. Krueger
Prof. Theo. Laetsch

Rev. Titus Lang
Rev. W. F. Lichtsinn
Rev. L. A. Linn
Prof. W. A. Maier
Rev. E. F. Manske
Rev. A. W. Meyer
Rev. G. Mieger
Prof. J. T. Mueller
Rev. O. C. Mueller
Rev. A. E. Neitzel
Rev. F. Niedner
Rev. W. Nordsieck
Prof. W. G. Polack
Rev. A. F. Pollex
Rev. J. A. Rimbach
Rev. E. L. Roschke
Rev. O. H. Schmidt
Rev. E. Schnedler
Rev. G. W. Schoedel
Rev. P. Schumm
Rev. W. A. Setzer
Rev. G. H. Smukal
Prof. M. S. Sommer
Rev. F. C. Streufert
Prof. H. Studtmann
Rev. E. F. Tonn
Rev. W. F. Troeger
Rev. G. A. Troemel
Rev. C. A. Weiss
Rev. F. Wessler
Rev. O. W. Wismar
Rev. Geo. Witte
Rev. H. M. Zorn

BETTER PREACHING.

It is the duty of a minister to strive to improve in preaching. St. Paul tells Timothy that he is to study and to give himself wholly to his duties in order that his advancement, progress, and improvement may be evident to all, 1 Tim. 4, 16.

It is a mistake to believe that a minister will improve in preaching as a matter of course as he continues to preach. If a clergyman does not watch over himself, he will deteriorate instead of improving. There are forces at work within and without us which would impede our way, corrupt our manner, and hamper us. Christians do not become better Christians by simply letting nature take its course, and preachers do not become better preachers by simply letting themselves take the course of least resistance. Improvement in preaching requires effort, and it is distinctly God's will that His ministers make this effort.

Nor is it a secret how this is to be done. The minister improves by increasing, first, in godliness, secondly, in knowledge, thirdly, in physical ability. We need not speak of those to whom the hearers may say, "What you are speaks so loud that we cannot hear what you say." Every minister who knows anything of the Bible knows that God admonishes the preachers: "But thou, O man of God, flee these things and *follow after* righteousness, godliness, faith, love, patience, meekness; fight the good fight of faith," 1 Tim. 6, 11. 12. The preacher is not to be a sign-post, pointing the right way, but not going that way himself; he is to be an ensample to the flock, 1 Pet. 5, 3. The preacher especially is to follow the example of Paul and other godly men who have shown us the way in righteousness and purity of living.

However, the official duties of a pastor require that he have the abilities required of one who is to hold the office of this good work of being a bishop of the flock of Christ, 1 Tim. 3, 1. He should therefore also do what St. Paul told Timothy to do — *give attention to reading,* 1 Tim. 4, 13. And is there any question what he should read? He should read God's Word, that is, he should study the Bible. What a wealth of truth, what a power of sanctification, what spiritual treasures, what sources of life, and life more abundant, are found in the sacred pages! The better a man knows his Bible, the better he will preach. Not very long ago we heard a preacher hold the attention of his audience during a rather long

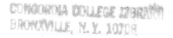

sermon; and when we searched for the cause of the interest which the hearers evidently felt in all that the man said, we discovered that it was his skill in quoting examples, illustrations, and proof from the sacred pages. We could write pages upon pages on this subject; however, we are not writing to entertain our readers, but to give hints to those who are willing to follow them. Continue, my brother, to study the Bible systematically, or if you have not done so before, take it up now and let your constant prayer and sighing to God be: "Lord, open Thou mine eyes that I may behold wondrous things out of Thy Law," Ps. 119, 18.

Then the preacher ought to read other good and reliable literature. We are not to despise the gifts that God has given to His Church in giving them men like Luther, Chemnitz, Gerhard, Walther, and a host of others too many to mention. Certainly no one will expect me to give a list of worth-while theological books; but let me suggest that the old Latin and German literature of the Church contains very valuable, interesting, and impressive material. There are the Confessions of our Church and the commentaries, sermons, and monographs written by devout and learned men, who gave themselves wholly to the study of the oracles of God. Every page of this literature enriches the intelligent reader. Just in passing we will also call attention to the good *histories* that have been written, from which much valuable information and illustration of divine truth may be culled.

But we must hurry on to another matter that is not to be neglected. Speaking (preaching is one species of speaking) requires physical strength, exertion, and control of those organs which enter into the production of voice. We remember hearing a young man preach his last sermon. At that time he was a consumptive and died a few months after delivering this farewell address to his congregation. It was very painful to listen to the poor young man. He was scarcely able to finish, and he never preached again. That man was godly, sincere, and learned, but it was a task to listen to him. All were relieved when he finished. He lacked physical strength and control. Preaching requires that the physical organs which are used in public utterances be healthy, strong, and under proper control. Lawyers and statesmen and others who must speak in public study what is called elocution. They do it to receive a corruptible crown. Should we not do our utmost in the service of the King of kings and Lord of lords? The old argument which St. Augustine used still holds true: "Those who defend falsehood and wish to deceive mankind enter the conflict fully armed with all the weapons of rhetoric, oratory, and elocution. Shall the defenders of the truth stand naked against their enemies?"

No one would expect us to offer anything like a complete curriculum for physical training in public speech, but we would call attention to the following essential points: The speaker should be natural. By *natural* we do not mean that he should speak in the way in which he is accustomed to speak. That may be very unnatural. Through sin we have all become corrupt. By *natural* we mean that the expression, intonation, modulation, strength, force, pause, pitch, must be *in accord with the sentiment which we wish to express.* Take the following sentence: "Woman without her man is an animal." If you through modulation and pause speak this sentence in this manner: "Woman without her man — is an animal," you malign woman and make an enemy of every woman in the audience. But pronounce the sentence in the following manner: "Woman! — without *her* — man is an animal," you praise woman highly. In both sentences the words are exactly the same, but your intonation, your pause, your modulation, make the difference.

There are thousands of orthodox preachers in the world, but why is it that some of these cannot hold the attention of a small audience while others are listened to with interest for a half hour or more by thousands? The difference is in their delivery.

Cicero tells the following story about Aeschines. This Greek orator, after being thoroughly vanquished by his opponent Demosthenes, felt so ashamed of himself that he left Athens and went to Rhodes. The people of Rhodes had heard of the wonderful speech which he had made at Athens and requested him to read it to them. He read it to them. Then they asked him to read also the speech made by his opponent Demosthenes. Aeschines read that speech also, and we are told they all admired the wonderful oration of Demosthenes. Then Aeschines said to them: *"Quanto magis admiraremini si audissetis ipsum."* Cicero, after telling this story, reminds his readers that much depends upon good delivery, since the same speech, if delivered by a different man, seems to be an entirely different speech.

In delivery two things are to be avoided: slovenliness and affectation. For the first of these the German have an adjective; they call a speaker who is guilty of it *maulfaul.* Shakespeare condemns it in the words of the Danish prince: "But if you *mouth* it as many of our players do, I had as lief the town-crier spoke my lines." The other fault is affectation. But the subject is too large to be dealt with even briefly in this place. Let us, however, keep in mind that the Master whom we serve and the purpose which we have in view require that we do our very best. Plain, simple speech, well, exactly, and properly spoken, is very effective. Oliver Wendell Holmes also called attention to this when he said: —

> Speak clearly, if you speak at all;
> Carve every word before you let it fall.

Do not take it for granted that you speak well and distinctly. Make sure that you do by reading or speaking in the presence of one who understands his business and have him give you directions for improving also in this respect.   MARTIN S. SOMMER.

TABLE OF CONTENTS.

SUNDAY MORNING SERVICES.
Outlines on Series of Old Testament Lessons.
Adopted by the Synodical Conference.

CONFESSIONAL ADDRESSES.

MID-WEEK SERVICES.

SUNDAY EVENING SERVICES.

Index of Scripture-Texts Treated.

Topical Index.

Angels, 277.

Blessings Bestowed on Us, 490; Preservation, 105; Grace, 106; Peace, 107; how We Keep His Blessings, 490.

Busybodies, 413.

Charity, 108.

Children and Christian Education, 26; Children of God a Peculiar Race, 63; Blessedness, 152.

Christ. What Think Ye of Christ? 308; Sinless Perfection, Absolute Truthfulness, 318; the Infallible Teacher, 460; Isaiah's Vision of Calvary, 268; Burial, 383; the Redeemer Lives, 75; Ascension His Coronation, 273; Melchizedek a Type of Christ, 68.

Christians, the Blessedness of, 83.

Christmas, the Light of, 229.

Church, the Holy Christian, 293; Enemies, 302; the Church of the New Testament, the Glory of God's House, 14; Foundation, 18; Corner-stone, 19; the Lutheran, 298.

Church-work, when Successful, 36.

Comfort of Faith, 328.

Confession of Christ. Peter's Denial, 396; Confession of Sin: Joseph's Brothers, 190.

Corner-stone of the Church, 295. 296.

Covenant, the Better, 44.

Cowardice of Peter, 396.

Creation. God Our Creator, 87; Reveals the Glory of God, 29.

Days Are Numbered, 499.

Dependence upon God, 59.

Devil Tempts to Sin, 54; Struggle against, 49. 50.

Discouragement, 405.

Divisions because of Christ, 223.

Doubt of being Saved, 330; Overcome by Faith, 56.

Education of Children, 26; Christian Education, 439.

Enemies of the Church, 303.

Envy, 313.

Faith. Grace the Foundation, 373; the Comfort of Faith, 328; the Prospect, 331; Fiery Trial, 184; Overcomes All Doubt, 56; Enables Us to Give Obedience to God, 57; is Blessed by Grace, 58.

Faultfinding, 409.

Fear, Anxiety, Threaten Progress, 405.

Forgiveness of Sins. David, 82; Forgive Thy Brother, 191. 192.

Friends of God and Mankind, 93; an Example of Friendship, David and Jonathan, 193.

Gift of God, the Holy Spirit, 102.

Glorification of the Believers, 349.

God. "I Am that I Am," 126; God's Glory Revealed in Creation, 29; What God has Done for Us, 72; God's Faithfulness, 217; Almighty Power, 238; Constant Watchfulness, 239. God's Word; cf. Word.

Godly and Ungodly People, 176.

Grace, 106. 107; Woe unto Those who Spurn God's Grace, 417.

Harvest, 489.

Heaven. That Better Land, 492; Hymns of Joy and Praise, 122.

Help Comes from the Lord, 238.

Hereafter. Prepare for It, 234.

Home of the Ungodly and Godly, 353. 358.

Hope, Rejoice in, 482.

Hymn of the Church Triumphant, 120.

Hymns: Jesus Shall Reign, 370; Now I have Found the Sure Foundation, 373; Whatever God Ordains Is Good, 376.

Hypocrisy, 398. 128.

Idol Baal, 162. 163; Idolatry of Israel, 140; Nebuchadnezzar's Image, 185.

Impulsiveness of Peter, 393.

Jesus. Melchizedek a Type of Christ, 68.

Judge Not, 409.

King of Glory, 3.

SUNDAY MORNING SERVICES.

OUTLINES
ON SERIES OF OLD TESTAMENT LESSONS.

ADOPTED BY THE SYNODICAL CONFERENCE.

First Sunday in Advent.
Ps. 24.

Advent has come again, with its cheering message and joyful
spirit. Whereas on the last few Sundays we looked backward on the
church-year that was drawing to a close, on its problems, blessings,
and responsibilities, we now look forward to Christmas with its grand
message. Four Sundays and four weeks to prepare for the great event,
even as mankind had 4,000 years to wait and prepare for the coming
of its Redeemer. He is of course, and should be, the center of all our
Advent and Christmas preaching. Our text calls Him —

The King of Glory.

1. Who Is This King of Glory?

A) *The Lord of Hosts, Strong and Mighty.*

a) There is a striking similarity between the aspirations of most
of the nations of the earth in these troubled times and the Advent
message. Everywhere in the world political, social, and economic
conditions have become chaotic and well-nigh unbearable. In such
a situation people instinctively look forward to the coming of a strong
man, a leader, who shall restore order and bring about better conditions. In our day they call such a man or leader a dictator. In
ancient times they would call him a king. Carlyle says that the
original meaning of the word *king* was *canning, i. e.,* a man who can
do things.

Now, the spiritual condition of mankind after the Fall certainly
was very pitiful. Considering their own resources, they were helpless.
Then at least some of them began to look for a hero who should help
them out of their misery. This hope was not an empty dream like the
expectation of a "golden age" entertained by some heathen poets, but
a well-founded hope, founded on the promises of God, *e. g.,* Gen. 3, 15,
Gen. 49, 9. 10, Is. 11, 10. All these contain the idea of power and
strength, and this is also very beautifully brought out in our text.

b) In reply to the question Who is this King of Glory? is He an
able man? the answer is given: vv. 8. 10. And if the further question
is asked: Has this King given any proof of His ability? has He
already accomplished something? the answer is: "He hath founded
the earth upon the seas and established it upon the floods."

The King of Glory, then, is He who has founded the earth, the

Creator of the universe. By His Word He has called all things into
being. The vastness of the visible creation, the broad oceans, the
great plains, and the lofty mountains testify to the power and might
of their Maker. The forces of nature and the great stores of energy
in coal-beds and reservoirs of oil are likewise proofs of the omnipotence of God. The orderly arrangement of this world, particularly
such things as the regular change of time and season, bears witness to
the omniscience of the Lord. All this creation He holds in the hollow
of His hand; it is all His, because He has made it, v. 1.

But these things are only the hem of His garment. Suppose we
knew no more of Him. Then we should have a beginning without end
and purpose. Suppose God had withdrawn from all contact with His
creatures and left us to our own thoughts and imaginings. What
would we think of Him then? He would be to us an unknown being,
a being far removed from us and far above us, possibly a strict judge
to whom we are responsible.

B) *The God of Our Salvation, Holy and Merciful.*

a) There is more to the glory of God than His creative power
and wisdom. "God is a spirit, and they that worship Him must worship Him in spirit and in truth." With Him the greatest values are
spiritual values, and the virtues which He prizes most are spiritual
virtues.

His kingly crown is holiness,
His scepter, pity in distress.

The *holiness* of God is the perfection of His will, in consequence
of which everything that He wills is for that very reason good and
everything contrary to His will is for that very reason evil. This
holiness is revealed in the Scriptures, Ex. 15, 11, Is. 6, 3, Rev. 15, 4. It
is most perfectly revealed in "the express Image of His being," the
Lord Jesus Christ, John 1, 14. God's holiness is the guarantee that
His government will always be right. It causes men and angels to
worship Him and to make Him the pattern which they seek to imitate.

b) That is the will of God with respect to those of His creatures
whom He has endowed with a soul. They are to stand "in His holy
place," to live in communion with Him, to serve Him with holy works,
and to find their greatest happiness in such communion and service.

But, alas, an enemy has come and desecrated and defiled the work
of God, has deprived men of their original holiness, poisoned their
nature with sin, destroyed their happiness, and plunged them into
misery, despair and death.

What a contrast between the holy God and His sin-cursed creatures, between what man should be and what he is! Shall this contrast
last forever? God forbid!

That is the very essence of the Advent-message. The King of
Glory shall come in and restore to men holiness and the blessed communion with God.

c) Is this worth while? Sin and all its awful by-products —
ignorance, hopelessness, despair, and death — He will utterly abolish
and usher in a reign of holiness, knowledge, hope, happiness, and life.

> No more let sins and sorrows grow
> Nor thorns infest the ground;
> He comes to make His blessings flow
> Far as the curse is found.

Will He be able to accomplish all this? Once more I point you
to the text, vv. 8. 10. The Lord of hosts, strong and mighty, the God
of our salvation, holy and merciful, will take charge of the war in
which we have been defeated, and He will win the victory. No enemy
shall be able to withstand Him. Ps. 118, 15. 16. — The question naturally suggests itself: —

2. How Is This King to be Received?

A) *With* Sincere *Faith.*

a) V. 7. These words are like a clarion call. Let every man,
woman, and child heed them. Open your hearts, homes, and churches
to the King of Glory.

There are those to whom this message means nothing. They ask
the question "Who is this King of Glory?" sneeringly and hatefully.
The reason for this is that they have no faith at all. They despise
Christ and His kingdom, His doctrine, and all His works. What can
He do for us? they ask. He was rejected of men and crucified. "There
is no form or comeliness that we should desire Him." His holiness
and righteousness do not interest us; His grace and mercy we neither
need nor desire; we will not have this one to rule over us. They are
of course excluded from Christ's kingdom, having excluded themselves.

b) V. 3. Who receives the King of Glory in a manner which will
please Him?

The Jews had settled this question long ago. They thought that
as children of Abraham, members of the chosen people, having Moses
and the prophets, Temple, priesthood, and sacrifice, they, and they
only, would stand in the holy place of the Lord.

Roman Catholics likewise think this question is settled. Have
they not the largest crowds, the most magnificent buildings, the most
splendid ceremonies, the most perfect organization, and the merits of
unnumbered saints? In their opinion they, and they only, will stand
in the holy place of the Lord.

c) But what says the text? V. 4. The person with a *sincere faith*
shall be privileged to receive the Lord.

Is your faith of this kind? Are you interested in just one question: How can I be saved? Is that your reason for being a church-
member? Or is it just a matter of habit and custom, or, worse still,
do you seek to derive some temporal advantage from your connection
with Christ? Then you do not "come into court with clean hands."

Do you give a whole-hearted loyalty to Christ? Or is your heart divided and are you inclined to listen to the voice of false prophets, who have "sworn deceitfully," *i. e.,* used the name of God falsely?

A sincere faith is a faith like Mary's of Bethany, who sought the one thing needful; a faith like Paul's, who considered all thing dross just so he might win Christ; a faith which says: —

> Thou, O Christ, art all I want;
> More than all in Thee I find.

B) *With* HUMBLE *Faith.*

a) Your soul must not "be lifted up to vanity." The Lord cannot and will not tolerate pride and self-righteousness. It must be a faith like St. John's, 1 John 1, 8. 9; a faith which says: "In my hands no price I bring, Simply to Thy cross I cling."

b) It must be a faith which says, Lord, thou requirest a pure heart; my heart is not pure. Do Thou, then, create in me a clean heart and renew a right spirit within me.

Conclusion. — The King of Glory does not demand anything from His subjects which He is not ready to give to them first. He will kindle such a sincere and humble faith in them. By His Spirit He will help our infirmities and make of us such people as shall be worthy to stand in His holy place. Be ready, then, to receive Him with a sincere and humble faith.

> Redeemer, come! I open wide
> My heart to Thee; here, Lord, abide!
> Let me Thy inner presence feel;
> Thy grace and love in me reveal.

W. NORDSIECK.

Second Sunday in Advent.
Deut. 18, 10—22.

Rom. 15, 4. These are the introductory words of to-day's Epistle. Certainly the prophecies of the Old Testament are not without importance. They well deserve to be studied carefully, particularly since we can study them in the light of fulfilment. It is foolish and wicked to wish to discard the Old Testament, as some suggest. Our text is a prophecy concerning Christ by the most prominent leader of the Old Testament and the mediator of the Old Testament Covenant.

The Great Prophet Foretold by Moses.

1. He is to Be Like Moses.

A) *Like Moses in Divine Authority.*

a) Both were divinely commissioned. Moses at the end of his career recalled that memorable day forty years ago in the wilderness of Midian when the Lord had appeared to him in the burning bush, Ex. 3, 9. 10. The Lord had disclosed to him His secret name, Ex. 3,

13. 14, and had given Him as a proof of his divine commission the power to work miracles, so that he might be able to convince friends and to confound enemies. (Mention the most important of these miracles, Ex. 4, 1—9.)

Christ was like Moses in this respect. Vv. 15 a. 18 a a prophecy perfectly fulfilled. The New Testament emphasizes the fact that God *sent* Christ into the world, Gal. 4, 4; John 12, 45; Luke 4, 18. Likewise He had the power to work miracles, Matt. 11, 3—5. His crowning miracle, His own resurrection, is the final and conclusive proof of His divine commission.

b) Both Moses and Christ had to vindicate their divine authority over against false prophets and impostors. Moses forbids his people to have any dealings with them, vv. 10—12. These are heathen abominations, but they are still practised in our times. In our enlightened age, men and women still listen to witches and observers of times, to consulters with familiar spirits, to fortune-tellers and spiritualists. Christ likewise had to wage unceasing warfare against false prophets. The New Testament repeatedly bids us be on our guard against them as against ravening wolves. Vv. 20. 21. How shall we recognize false prophets? By their life; does it conform to the Law of God? By their doctrine; does it agree with the Gospel? And a further test is mentioned in the text by which we may know them as impostors, v. 22. Let these founders of new religions, such as Mrs. Mary Baker Eddy and Mr. Joseph Smith, show that they were divinely commissioned by rising from the dead. Let the Russellites and others who have repeatedly foretold the exact day of the end of the world make good on their prophecies; then we will look further into their doctrines. Until they do so, we will continue to rely on the Old and New Testaments of the inspired Scriptures; we will continue to sit at the feet of Moses and Christ, of whom we know that they were divinely commissioned.

B) *Like Moses in Bearing a Divine Message.*

a) The chosen people were to be established not only as a nation, but as a Church. They needed a lawgiver. Through Moses they received a complete system of civil, ceremonial, and moral laws. These laws were not devised by Moses himself in the manner of other lawgivers of whom history tells us. They were given to him by God "through the ministration of angels." Of every one of its injunctions and prohibitions, of the most minute rules and regulations, he could say: "Thus saith the Lord."

b) Yet Moses, contemplating this marvelous, magnificent, and perfect system of the Law, is moved by the Holy Spirit to prophesy the coming of another Prophet, who shall bring an equally divine message, 18 b. c. Not the same message; this Prophet is not to be another preacher of the Law. A second prophet of the Law was not needed, for Moses had taught the Law fully. This prophecy can refer only to Christ, for the other prophets, who reiterated and restored the Law, were not equal to, but inferior to, Moses in dignity.

c) Behold, then, Christ, the second great Prophet, coming with a revelation from God which Moses had not given to men. Not human thoughts, opinions, and conclusions, not uncertain hopes and promises, but a message direct from heaven, John 12, 49. 50.

d) Moses prophesying of Christ, Christ referring back to Moses for confirmation. Picture to yourselves the scene on the Mount of Transfiguration, when these two met face to face. Moses and Christ, each the representative of a covenant, bearers of Law and Gospel, the whole counsel of God. Do you appreciate the greatness of God's gift, who has not left us to grope in the dark, but has given us His Word? Ps. 119, 105. Would you know the holy will of God? Then do not listen to those who teach for doctrines the commandments of men, but go "to the Law and Testimony." Would you learn the gracious will of God? Then do not follow the thoughts of your own heart, but go to Christ with His everlasting Gospel.

2. And yet in Spite of This Similarity This Prophet Is Greater than Moses.

A) *This is Shown by the Difference in Their Doctrines.*

a) Compare these two teachings and study them. One of the worst mistakes any one can make who would understand God's way of salvation is to confuse Law and Gospel.

The Law *demands.* It was designed to control your whole life, what you are to do, say, think. It says, This is right, do it; and again, This is wrong, thou shalt not do it. There is no comfort in such commands and orders. — The Gospel *gives.* It shows that the treasures of the kingdom of God, life and salvation, are not to be earned by our own efforts and works, but that we are to receive them as a free gift of God. Jesus bids you come to Him and receive from His hand grace for grace. Therefore Christ is greater than Moses.

b) The Law *condemns.* It reflects the perfect holiness of God and sets it up as a standard for your conduct, Lev. 19, 2. Have you in your life, in your attitude, in your actions, lived up to this standard? Have you kept the Law, kept all of it, kept it always, kept it perfectly? If not, you stand condemned, without any if or but, Deut. 27, 26. There is no comfort here, but only terror and despair. — How different the message of Christ, the Gospel. It *saves,* John 3, 16. 17. But what of your sins? Matt. 9, 2; John 1, 29b. What about the righteousness which you lack? Is not Christ's name *the Lord our Righteousness?* There is nothing in the Gospel that is not comfort, hope, and joy. Therefore Christ is greater than Moses.

c) Even in His dealing with those who reject His Word the Lord shows that the Gospel is greater than the Law. Those who disobeyed the Law were to be punished by the civil government. Not so with the Gospel. It is to be preached, and its regenerating power is to be brought to bear on the hearts of men. But if they will not accept it, if they stubbornly resist and finally reject it, they are not to be punished by the hands of men. The Lord Himself will deal with them and call them to account, v. 19.

So the message of Christ is sweeter and better than the message of Moses. In fact the Law was intended by God to be preliminary and preparatory, Gal. 3, 24, but the Gospel is eternal.

B) *This Difference has Ever been Recognized by God's Children.*

a) The *children of Israel* were told that the Law of Moses was not the final revelation of God. They looked for a gentler and more gracious word, v. 16. They did not, and could not, clearly express their wishes, but the Lord knew, v. 17. Cf. Acts 15, 10b.

b) *Moses* would be the last man to deny the superiority of the great Prophet who should come after him. He knew that his covenant would end some day and that the kingdom of Christ would take its place. He knew that he himself would have to be saved by Christ. On the Last Day, when all knees shall bow and all tongues shall confess that Jesus is the Lord, you will find Moses in the forefront of those doing homage to the Savior of the world.

c) Do *you* appreciate the preciousness of the Gospel? Does its sweet message strike a responsive chord in your heart? Do you hunger and thirst for the righteousness which you could not possibly achieve by your own efforts, but which Christ has earned for you and offers to you? Then accept Him as your Prophet and Savior, the only one who can show you the way of salvation. Rejoice, especially in the Advent season, in the fact that He has come, the great Prophet foretold by Moses, has come with His divine message of grace and pardon, and that He still comes to you in His Word and Sacrament.

W. NORDSIECK.

Third Sunday in Advent.
Is. 61, 1—3.

No wise teacher is ever afraid of repeating himself. The average mind requires a repetition of truth again and again before it can make this truth its own. One coat of paint is not enough; it soon rubs off. Therefore Paul writes: Phil. 3, 1. Certain substantial foods are needed daily for the body if it is to grow, thrive, maintain strength and energy. Likewise a certain substantial food, the age-old, never-changing Gospel, for the soul if it is to grow in grace and knowledge. So we offer in our services not novel entertainment and passing thrills, but thorough instruction in Law and Gospel to the upbuilding of faith and growth in holiness of life.

The message must ever be the same if we are to achieve this end, but the images and pictures which enable us to visualize it will vary to lend a touch of freshness to the spiritual meal we offer. Thus Christ; *e. g.,* Sermon on the Mount, parables; cf. also Matt. 13, 52. Thus the apostles and prophets. Example in text. Wealth of expression in prophetic form, offering marvelous blessings, a beautiful Gospel. Very fine Advent message. Let us concentrate our attention on one of these many expressions.

"I will Give unto Them Beauty for Ashes."

1.

A) "Unto them that *mourn* in Zion," v. 3, the poor and afflicted people of God, the believers, especially in the New Testament Church. Cf. Luke 4, 21, where Christ applies these words to His day. a) The meek, v. 1. Usually means patient upon suffering injuries; opposed to revengeful, irascible. Here: afflicted, distressed, needy, borne down by calamity of any kind. LXX and Luke 4, 18: "poor." — b) The broken-hearted, v. 1, those deeply afflicted and distressed for some reason, *e. g.,* sin, captivity, loss of relatives, friends, etc. — c) Summarizing: Those facing sorrows caused by battles of life, disappointments, discouragements, poverty, bereavement, death; tempted to worry and forget God; struggling in solitude because brethren, relatives, friends, have — and at times God seems to have — forsaken them; with sorrows arising from lack of faith in God; with grief because of waywardness of heart, its proneness to sin; with lack of faithfulness to God and His Word and other sins oppressing the conscience, whose accusations make them miserable and unhappy; sorely vexed by Satan, who seeks to lead them from their moorings of faith to despair, shame, vice, etc.

B) Unto them that are *captive,* v. 1, *i. e.,* under captivity of sin, and *bound,* v. 1, *i. e.,* under bondage to Satan and hell. The Law is ready to condemn them, sin their executioner, death their judgment. Bound and captive before, but preaching of Law or adverse circumstances have made them conscious of it now. In good days their man-made scheme of happiness seemed to hold, but with the rift in the rainbow, with the storm threatening destruction, this scheme and philosophy of life failed them. They look death and hell in the face and see no escape. Like man on a sinking steamer with all life-craft gone; one hour ago safety, now death and no escape. Death has them in their power all the time; but they had not realized it until all human props were knocked away from under them. (Hymn 310, 2.)

To men in such a predicament is offered, if they but accept it in faith, "beauty for ashes."

2.

A) *"Beauty,"* v. 3, a symbol of joy. So used in Scripture from description of Eden, Gen. 2, 9, to that of the heavenly city, Rev. 21, 21; associated with Old Testament service: ornate Temple, splendor of service and of garments of priests and high priests, choirs of many voices, singing of beautiful psalms, etc. Here "beauty," v. 3, means turban of happy bridegroom. Marriages were customarily held in home of groom, to which bride was previously brought by the groom's friends or her servants. The groom, distinguished by tiara, would start from home of friend along dark streets with his attendants to meet the bride in his home. On roofs of houses women would look for light of procession and herald approach of groom with joyous shouts. Arrived at home, he entered, closed the doors, and the festivities commenced, the tiara, or turban, on his head ("beauty" in our text) symbolizing this joy of the marriage-feast.

B) *"Ashes,"* v. 3, a symbol of sorrow, grief, humiliation. Common for orientals to cast dust and ashes upon their heads or sit in ashes in time of mourning, Neh. 9, 1; Job 2, 8; Jonah 3, 6. No law, but outburst of oriental people's impassioned temperament. Nothing seemed more appropriate than ashes to symbolize sorrow.

C) *"Beauty for ashes,"* joy and happiness for sorrow and grief, spiritual joy for spiritual sorrow; for it is of these the text speaks. No promise of God to His children there will be *no* ashes. In world of sin we must expect sorrow. But beauty *for* ashes, joy *for* sorrow. To afflicted and distressed and needy good news of help and deliverance, v. 1; to the broken-hearted consolation, v. 1; Ps. 147, 3; to sin's captives, bound by Satan and hell, liberty and opening of prison, v. 1; to the mourning comfort, v. 2. Battles of life leaving you bloody, child of God? Here strength to carry on, balm to heal all wounds. Discouraged, disappointed, sunk in poverty? Here new hope and courage. Forsaken and alone? Here companionship, fellowship, sustaining love. Bereaved or facing death? Here assurance of resurrection and life, freedom from fear even in death's dark vale. Heart wayward, conscience-stricken? Here power to overcome temptation, here relief from burden weighing heavily upon you. Bound by sin, death, and hell? Here righteousness to satisfy demands of Law, merit to stay all judgment, freedom from executioner, deliverance from every foe. Marvelous gift. Possible? Yes, note the Giver.

3.

A) *I* will give. "He has sent *me*," v. 1. Isaiah is certainly not speaking of himself. He was indeed anointed as prophet *of God* to bring Judah consolation, temporal, 2 Kings 18, 19; Is. 4, 2—6; 29, 1—8; 43, 1—13; spiritual, Is. 1, 18; 9, 2 ff.; 53: Even Grotius, after remarking on Is. 61: "Isaiah here speaks of himself," adds:

"But in him we see not an obscure image of Christ." But Isaiah does not speak of himself. Neither he nor any other merely human prophet could of himself give men truly spiritual joy for spiritual sorrow. Isaiah tells of this joy, but points to another as giver. Show vanity of placing trust in human helpers, especially in spiritual needs: sin, death, etc.

B) *I* will give. Christ, *the* Prophet, Deut. 18, 15, God's Son, Matt. 17, 5; Heb. 1, 1. 2, is speaking. Cf. Luke 4, 18—21. Anointed by Holy Ghost, v. 1, at baptism and thus set apart for mediatorial office, He began to preach. Subject: He Himself. Other prophets told of light, He is the Light; told of help, He the Helper; told of Redeemer, He the Redeemer. He is the Word made flesh, John 1, 14; fulfilling all righteousness, Matt. 3, 15; giving His life a ransom for many, Matt. 20, 28; reconciling the world unto God, 2 Cor. 5, 19; making believers heirs of God, Gal. 4, 7. "If God be for us . . . give us all things," Rom. 8, 31. 32. In Him all promises of God yea and Amen, 2 Cor. 1, 20. Our Strength, Phil. 4, 13; Rest, Matt. 11, 28; Provider, Helper, Matt. 14, 17 ff.; 10, 29—31; Mark 4, 39; ever present Companion, Matt. 28, 20; Ressurrection and Life, John 11, 25 (Lazarus); Good Shepherd, Ps. 23; Advocate and Mediator, Rom. 8, 34; 1 John 2, 1; stilling voice of the Law against us, Gal. 3, 13; freeing us from sin, 1 Pet. 1, 18. 19; overcoming Satan and death, Heb. 2, 14. 15; our Victory, 1 Cor. 15, 55—57: Fully able to give beauty for ashes. Is He yours? Do you receive these gifts from Him? Mark well the manner in which he offers them.

4.

A) Will give *not by means of the Law*. Prophets of old were preachers of righteousness, Elijah, 1 Kings 21, 17—23; Jeremiah, chap. 5—12; Isaiah, chap. 1, 2—17, denouncing sin with fiery eloquence, in telling terms pressing home God's wrath, consequences of unrepented and unpardoned sins. Jesus was greater as a preacher of the Law. Showed deep spiritual meaning, Matt. 5—7; note 7, 28. 29. Sin black and devilish in contrast with His Word and life, *e. g.,* on Calvary (contrast between His actions and prayer and those of foes). In withering, scorching terms He denounces sin and speaks of God's wrath, Matt. 23, 13 ff. Surgeon's knife wounding to restore health. That not manner of giving beauty, but preparation. No beauty without ashes for sinner, no true joy without sorrow, or penitence.

B) Will give *by means of Gospel*, v. 1. "To preach good tidings." (LXX: "to preach the Gospel.") That is mark of His Messiahship, Matt. 11, 5; that only means He relied on to convey to men the grace He was to merit, to give beauty for ashes. Cf. John 3, 1—18; 4, 1—42 (note vv. 26. 42); 17, 17; Matt. 13, 1—23; 9, 2. Therefore Paul says: Rom. 1, 16; 10, 1—15; 1 Cor. 2, 2; Peter: 1 Pet. 1, 23; James: chap.

1, 18. Men by nature inclined to trust in marching armies, powerful navies, political parties, great legislative power, their own strength, wisdom, influence, to obtain beauty for ashes. Christ rejected all these as means to that end. Through Gospel alone would He find entrance into men's hearts, engendering faith and bringing forgiveness, love, hope, strength, joy, deliverance from bondage, eternal life. (Stress need of knowledge of and faithfulness to Gospel especially in our day.)

Conclusion. — Theme repeated. Christ's offer to us to-day. Millions have accepted the gift and many of them were crowned with this beauty in eternal glory; others still in this life, but blessing Christ for the joy and happiness He has given and is giving them. But millions still in ashes to-day; many remaining there forever. What about you? To-day this gift offered again. Take heed lest to-day's offer spurned rise up on the Last Day to condemn you. Hymn 138, 5. ARNOLD H. GRUMM.

Fourth Sunday in Advent.
Hag. 2, 6—9.*

Reading Old Testament prophecies, *e. g.,* Hag. 2, 6—9, the thought comes at times, Did Old Testament saints have a clear picture in their minds of the Savior, His person, His work, His Church? We to-day can understand these prophecies in the light of fulfilment. Having beheld the original itself, we can readily perceive the prophetic picture's taking definite shape with each additional brush stroke of prophecy. (Carry thought out briefly, if desired.) But Old Testament saints did not have this advantage. We have the body to judge shadow by; they had only the shadow to judge the body by, we the fulfilment, they mere symbols and types (Temple, sacrifices, etc.).

Nevertheless Old Testament saints found in these prophecies a sure foundation for their faith in the Redeemer and in His kingdom, just as we have to-day in the prophecies concerning the end of the world and eternal salvation a sure foundation for a living hope of an inheritance laid away for us. Consider the picture Eve had of her Savior ("I have gotten a man, Jehovah," Gen. 4, 1, exact translation) on the basis of the first promise, Gen. 3, 15; or Jacob, Gen. 49, 10 (Shiloh, Prince of Peace) and v. 18; or Job, chap. 19, 25—27; or Daniel of the "kingdom," Dan. 7, 14.

Despite this sure hope, however, these Old Testament saints longed for the day of fulfilment, when faith might be changed to clear sight and hope to complete possession. Do we living in the day of fulfilment long as fervently for the Savior and His kingdom that have appeared? Do we acknowledge with grateful hearts the unmerited blessing of our greater privilege? Let us seek to recapture this eager,

---

* For exegetical treatment cf. *Theol. Monthly,* Dec. 1931, p. 920.

burning longing of the saints of old and prepare ourselves to come with hearts filled with gratitude to worship our new-born Savior and King. This is an appropriate time to do so. How? By studying and applying the Advent prophecy contained in our text, which speaks to us of —

The Latter and Greater Glory of God's House.

1. What Is This House of God?

A) The occasion for this reference. Haggai had successfully prevailed upon the returned exiles to take up again under Zerubbabel and Joshua the building of the Temple in Jerusalem, which had been abandoned for about fifteen years due at first to the enmity of the Samaritans and later to the indifference of the prospering Jews, Ezra 5 and Hag. 1. The work barely under way, the superstructure slowly beginning to rise upon the foundation previously completed, comparisons are made between the first glory of "this house" and its present, seemingly inferior, glory, Hag. 2, 3. (See also Ezra 3, 1 ff.) To encourage the workers seems necessary.

B) The prophet presents this Temple as the type of one whose glory shall be greater, v. 9: "The latter glory of this house shall be greater than the former" (*Stand. Am. Bible*). (This translation is preferable to the one in our A. V. Note v. 3: "Saw *this* house in *its* first glory." In harmony with this v. 9 should be: "The *latter* glory of *this* house." The prophet sees but *one* Temple, *one* Church, always continuing through all changes of time. V. 9, literally: "Great shall be the glory of *this* house, the latter before the former.") He is speaking of the New Testament Church. Cf. Eph. 2, 21; 2 Thess. 2, 4; Rev. 3, 12 for a similar usage. See also Heb. 12, 26—28, where part of this prophecy (v. 6) is quoted and referred to the destruction of heaven and earth on the Last Day, when Zerubbabel's Temple will have been out of existence for many centuries and only the "kingdom which cannot be moved" will remain.

C) Note the Old Testament prophets' use of *Temple, Zion, Jerusalem* (Heb. 12, 22. 23) as types of the New Testament Church; all prophecies concerning the latter are couched in figurative language. Noting this, we shall be kept from falling into the error of the chiliasts, who force a literal meaning on these figurative passages, obscuring the intended meaning (visible reign of Christ on earth, Jerusalem the capital, restoration of the Jews, etc.). Taken in their intended sense, these passages offer comfort and joy to us, as we see pictured there the glory of the New Testament Church, often hidden from us by the cross resting on it.

2. What Is This Latter Glory with which God's House is to be Filled?

A) The Jews of Haggai's day thought of outward glory, of gold and jewels, which the Temple formerly had and now lacked. The later Jews had similar thoughts; so Herod sought to win their favor by adding such glory. He built a temple so beautiful that it ranked among the world's wonders: white marble, covered with heavy plates of gold in front, rising above its marble-cloistered courts below; a snow-covered mountain; a conspicuous and dazzling object from every side, begun 19 B. C., finished 64 A. D., six years before its destruction. Gold and silver in profusion. That was not meant by Haggai, v. 8. A mere passing glory, which God could give immediately in such measure as to excel all other buildings ever erected if that were all that were needed to make the Temple worth while and glorious. — Warning: Do not overemphasize outward glory of the church: building, liturgy, etc. Dangerous. Beauty in place; ugliness not necessary. But this not the real glory, just the setting.

B) Text speaks of inward, hidden glory.

a) V. 7: "The desirable ones," the precious ones. (This singular noun is taken collectively because the verb "shall come" is in the plural. Cf. Job 1, 14, where "oxen," a singular noun taken collectively, is construed with the plural; Ezra 4, 4; et al. Therefore this translation is preferable to "Desire of Nations," referred to Christ, a noun that cannot be taken collectively and therefore demands a singular verb.) These "desirable ones" are the chosen ones, the elect, in whom God has pleasure, Ps. 16, 3. So Septuagint: "the elect of all nations." Cf. Rev. 21, 26: "And they shall bring the *glory and honor* of the nations into it" (the heavenly Jerusalem, the Church Triumphant); v. 27: whose names are written in the Book of Life, a Scriptural term for elect. Cf. also Rev. 21, 15. However, not only into the Church Triumphant, but also into the Church Militant. Rom. 8, 30: "predestinated," "called," "justified," "glorified"; the last visibly in heaven, but real glory here already, though hidden. Redeemed, washed in blood of Lamb, holy before God, precious to Him, His jewels by grace. Cf. Eph. 5, 25—27.

b) "Of all nations," v. 7. Just a few Jews returned and rebuilt the Temple, Ezra 2, 64. 65. Ten tribes gone, most of Judah's strength dispersed, many a slave people. New Testament house to consist of men and women and children of *all* nations. What a gathering of people! Note the preparations to make this possible, v. 7: "I will shake all nations"; v. 6: "It is a little while." Think of wars of Persians with hundred thousands in battle (about 500 B. C., "little while"); Grecian wars: Athens, Sparta, Thebes; Syrians, Phenicians, Bactrians, Parthians, Macedonians under Alexander the Great, Seleucidae in Egypt and Syria, then the Romans, East and West. The result: Nation after nation, coming into closer contact with Jews, hears of Jehovah. By-product of this shaking: Greek language becomes the world language, to serve as the medium for the general spread of the New Testament with its universal Gospel. Commerce, road-building, brought nations closer together, enabling Gospel-messengers to speed from East to West, from North to South. Note Christ's command: Matt. 28, 19; Acts 1, 8. Pentecost. Activities of twelve apostles; Paul; later missionaries to Northern Europe, to America, Africa, Asia, etc. "All nations." Activity of Bible societies. Universal Church.

c) "I will fill this house with glory," v. 7. In v. 6, quoted Heb. 12, 26. 27, we are told of the shaking of heaven and earth and sea at the coming of the Last Day. The shaking of the nations, v. 7, ordered world affairs so that the messengers of Christ could proclaim their tidings to many nations, and the house of God was filled with people of all nations. Elect, one after the other, being gathered in as time draws to its close. Temple being completed, Eph. 2, 19—22. When last stone is placed, scaffolding of world torn down, and the true glory of the temple revealed.

C) Blessed he whose name is written in the Book of Life. Have you hearkened to the Gospel call? Are you one whom God has changed and made His child? Who has no part in the glory of this house, will have part in the shame and everlasting contempt of the devil's abode. No other alternative. And you who are by God's grace such a chosen and precious one, be comforted, despite trials, crosses, fightings and fears within, without; yours is the true glory, hidden, some day to be revealed. Do you appreciate? Are you grateful? Doing what you can to fill His house with glory, to bring others in from all nations under the sun?

3. Why will This Latter Glory Be Greater?

A) Presence of God symbolized by the cloud of glory that overshadowed the Tabernacle, Ex. 40, 34, and Solomon's Temple, 2 Chron. 7, 1—3, God communing with Moses from above the mercy-seat between the two cherubim, Ex. 25, 22, still dwelling there in Solomon's Temple in the days of Hezekiah, 2 Kings 19, 14. But the Ark of the Covenant and the mercy-seat, symbols of Jehovah's presence, no longer in the Temple in Haggai's day. Even that symbol gone. Temple and sacrifice remained, Word of Prophecy present.

B) But in midst of the New Testament Church no longer symbol and type of prophecy, but God Himself in the form of His only-begotten Son, our "Peace." V. 9: "I will give peace." Not temporal, but spiritual and eternal peace. Old Testament saints had peace with God through the promised Messiah, 'tis true; but New Testament saints have the promised Messiah, who is called "Peace." "Peace" because He is the "Prince of Peace," Is. 9, 6; because His kingdom is a kingdom of peace, Is. 11, 6—9; 52, 7; Zech. 9, 10. Gideon, Judg. 6, 24, called his altar "Jehovah-shalom," the Lord is Peace. Jacob calls the Messiah "Shiloh," the Prince of Peace. Peace is an essential characteristic of the Savior, and Eph. 2, 13. 14 the apostle says of Him: "He is our Peace." Men, unhappy because not at peace with God, desire such peace, though they cannot analyze their desires. When Jesus and His work is offered and accepted, His reconciliation, 2 Cor. 5, 19. 21, these desires are fulfilled. A child feels that its wants are taken care of when food and drink are offered, though it may not be able to explain why it cried for them. Jesus is the only Peace between God and men. If any man becomes one of the "desirable ones" of God, it is alone through the effort and grace of the God-given Peace. He it was that made Old Testament saints precious before God through the redemption He was to accomplish, just as He does with the New Testament saints. In this there was no difference in glory between the Old Testament and the New Testament Church. But in this was the latter glory of God's house greater than the former that into the New Testament Church the promised Christ Himself has come, bringing peace on earth to men. No longer in symbol and type, but in reality, is God's Peace dwelling among us, exalted, sitting at God's right hand, present with us always even unto the end of the world. That makes the latter glory greater than the former. Matt. 13, 16. 17; Heb. 11, 13; 1, 1 ff.; John 1, 16.

Is Christ your Peace? Does He still all your longings? If not and you are longing for that which leaves you unsatisfied, what then? A Christmas without Christ in your heart is like a cross without the Savior, a hope without heaven, a soul without salvation. We are by God's grace born into that period of time when the latter glory of God's house is greater than the former, when the Christ has come and our redemption is accomplished; yet —

> See, how we grovel here below,
> Fond of these earthly toys;
> Our souls, how heavily they go
> To reach eternal joys!

How shall we escape if we neglect so great a salvation? In this pre-holiday rush let us for the sake of our souls take time to find God's own Peace. ARNOLD H. GRUMM.

Sunday after Christmas.

Is. 28, 14—19.

The Christian Church has many enemies. It has had them in all ages, but they never have been more dangerous than in our age.

It is true that the enemies of the Christian Church no longer persecute the Christians in so bloody and cruel a manner as was the case during the early Christian era (the ten great persecutions, 64—311 A. D.). The enemies of the Christian Church have learned something since that time. They have learned that the blood of the martyrs is the seed of the Church; that the Christian Church could not be destroyed by bloody persecutions. They have also learned that it could not be destroyed by atheism and agnosticism (Voltaire, Paine, Ingersoll, Marx, and others). The enemies of the Christian Church now use different methods and tactics in order to eradicate it. They try their very best to destroy it by unionism, Liberalism, Modernism, etc. They endeavor to make Christians believe that all true Christians are narrow-minded, bigoted, and illiterate people; that they are not "up to date"; that they are "harmless fools" for accepting the teachings of the Holy Scriptures; and they advise all Christians to make use of their common sense, to get away from the Bible doctrines, and to turn their backs upon the Christian Church. They boast their own learning and science, so called, and tell Christians that, since they are living in the twentieth century, they must no longer hold fast to what people believed in olden times. For this reason the enemies of the Christian Church to-day are more dangerous than they were in bygone centuries. Yes, they have been more successful by using the weapons of ridicule in their foolish and ungodly endeavors. (Call attention to the sad fact that many young Christians at colleges and universities are leaving the Church and their dear Savior because they put more faith in the words of spiritually blind men, evolutionistic and atheistic professors and teachers, than in the infallible Word of God, etc.)

Shall we, dear fellow-Christians, renounce the faith of our youth, the faith of our God-fearing fathers and mothers, as so many are wont to do in our day and in our country? Surely not. We have not the slightest reason for doing that; for the Christian Church is in reality the most glorious institution in this world; it cannot be destroyed, but according to Christ's promise will abide; even the gates of hell shall not prevail against it, because it is built upon a foundation that cannot be moved. This foundation was laid by God Himself, as we see from our text. Let me, then, call your attention to —

The Immovable, Sure Foundation upon which the Christian Church is Built.

Our text assures us —

1. *That It is Built upon the Rock of Ages, the Divine-human Savior of the Sinful, Lost World;*
2. *That All Those are Immeasurably Blessed who Rest Their Faith in Him.*

1.

Text, vv. 14. 15. With these words the almighty God defies the enemies of His Church; He laughs at them, mocks them, Ps. 2, 4. He tells them by the mouth of His prophet Isaiah: v. 16. With these defying words He tells them that He Himself, He, the Omnipotent

One, is not only the Designer, but also the Builder of His Church. "Behold," says He, "I lay in Zion for a foundation a Stone, a tried Stone, a precious Corner-stone, a sure Foundation." He builds His Church upon the immovable, sure foundation that cannot be destroyed; for He builds it upon the Rock of Ages, the very Messiah, Savior of the sinful and lost world who is both God and man. Therefore the great Apostle Paul writes to his fellow-Christians in Corinth: 1 Cor. 3, 11. Jesus Christ, the Savior of the world, is the Stone, or Rock, whom the builders, the unbelieving Jews, have rejected. But God is going to make the Savior the Head of the corner, Ps. 118, 22; Matt. 21, 42; Mark 12, 10; Luke 20, 17; Acts 4, 11; Rom. 9, 33. The Lord God calls the foundation of the Christian Church a stone, or rock, because it is immovable, ever-abiding. Every structure must be built upon a sure, solid foundation; otherwise the strong winds and the floods will easily destroy it or wash it away, Luke 5, 48. 49. How much more, then, is it necessary that the Christian Church be built upon an immovable, sure foundation because all kinds of storms and floods dash against it! These storms and floods are temptations, crosses, tribulations, persecutions, etc. In Jesus Christ the Christian Church has such an immovable, sure foundation, which cannot be moved, a foundation that shall never pass away, though heaven and earth shall pass away. Though the enemies be ever so numerous and powerful, ever so cunning and cruel, they shall never be able to destroy it. The fact is rather: vv. 17—19. Yes, the Lord God shall break all the enemies of His Church in pieces, etc., Is. 30, 14; but the Christian Church shall abide, even as Jesus Christ, its sure Foundation, shall abide forever, being the same yesterday, to-day, and forever, Heb. 13, 8.

This, my fellow-Christians, is not a *vain boast,* but a *divine fact,* and for this very reason God calls the foundation-stone of His Church a *tried Stone.* Jesus Christ, the Savior of mankind, was tried in many different ways and under the most severe circumstances; but He at all times stood the tests. Many sinners have tried to find true happiness and bliss in the gaining of temporal, earthly things; others have endeavored to persuade themselves that there is no God, no heaven, no hell, no Judgment to come, and no eternity; still others have sought to gain everlasting life by all kinds of self-devised and self-satisfying works and merits of their own. But the results were always the same: disappointments, dissatisfaction, and finally despair; they never found peace of conscience, rest of soul, and true happiness of heart. No, they always finally realized that they were deluded, fooled. Many therefore have bitterly regretted and denounced their own follies and have deplored that they had deceived themselves. But can you mention one, yes, only one, poor sinner who ever was sorry for having embraced Jesus in true faith? No, you cannot; for there is none such in this whole world. Call to your memory all *true* Christians, true believers in the Savior, whom you have seen on their death-beds; search the books of history, both old ones and new, and see whether you can find one who on his death-bed regretted having put all his trust in Jesus Christ, the Savior of sinners. Not a single true Christian throughout all the ages has ever given utterance to such a regret. To Him, the Seed of the Woman, our fallen parents in Paradise took their refuge, and they found comfort and hope in Him. In Him Noah and his household found a mighty Helper during the time of the most destructive Deluge. With Him Abraham, Isaac, and Jacob, and all other true believers in the Messiah found peace when the end of their earthly pilgrimage was at hand. He was the only hope of the patriarchs, the joy of the holy apostles and of all those who looked for a deliverer from their temporal and spiritual ills and tribulations. Through His saving Gospel untold numbers of heathen people, who by nature were dead in trespasses and sins, found life and forgiveness and were eternally saved. Indeed, Jesus Christ proved Himself to be the Savior of all those who ever came to Him in their distresses of body and soul.

God furthermore says of Jesus in our text that He is a *precious Stone.* Jesus is more precious than heaven and earth; for in Him dwelleth the fulness of the Godhead, Col. 2, 9. In Him are hid all the treasures of wisdom and knowledge, Col. 2, 3. He is the image of the invisible God, Col. 1, 15. What could be more precious than He! But not only is His person so precious, but also the gifts and blessings which we obtain through and by Him. He is the Savior of us all. Through Him we receive forgiveness of sin, life, and eternal salvation. Without Him all of us would forever have to suffer the torments of hell. He has made us heirs of God and His joint heirs.

Pray, tell me, dear fellow-Christian, what could be more precious to us than Jesus, the dear Savior? Ask the harassed, vexed man Job, over whom all the heavy storms of disaster broke loose like a mighty hurricane and who trusted in the promised Redeemer as his Deliverer? He will answer you, What He was to me no human tongue can adequately describe; He is too precious for human tongue to tell. Ask Mary Magdalene, what Jesus was to her. She will tell you, He was my precious Savior. Ask, dear fellow-Christian, all believing Christians who lamented over the demise of one of their loved ones, What was Jesus to you? They will answer, Oh, He is so gracious, so precious to us that words fail us to describe it to you. His love, His grace, His loving-kindness is past finding out. Throughout all eternity we shall not grow tired in praising Him for the precious and abiding comfort that He showered upon us. (See also Rev. 5, 12.)

Finally God says of Jesus that He is the *Corner-stone,* which holds together the foundation. By the preaching and teaching of His Gospel He gathers His elect from all four corners of the world and unites them in one faith, one hope, and one chain of eternal happiness, Eph. 4, 4. 5.

I ask you, dear fellow-Christians, Is not Jesus Christ a most precious Corner-stone of His Church? God Himself says of Him that He is the sure Foundation of His Church, which cannot be destroyed, but abides forevermore. Need we, then, fear the many and powerful enemies of the Christian Church? (See Ps. 46.) Oh, blessed, forever blessed, are all those who rest their faith in Him! Of this I shall add a few remarks in the second place.

2.

V. 16b: "He that believeth shall not make haste." He who believes in Jesus Christ confesses: Christ Jesus became true man and suffered and died for all sinners. By His sacrifice He has reconciled all sinners to God and procured for them perfect righteousness. He also very graciously invites all poor sinners to come to Him, Matt. 11, 28—30; John 6, 37; 3, 16. Therefore I am persuaded that I am saved, too, that I shall not perish, but have everlasting life in heaven.

What a contrast between a believing Christian and an unbeliever! While an unbeliever and infidel must ever and anon ask himself, What will become of me? What will happen to me after I have departed this life? Where shall I finally go? The true believer can give a correct answer to all these questions from God's Word. And if a true believer must suffer all kinds of crosses, trials, and tribulations, if he is also ridiculed and derided by unbelievers and scoffers, he can truthfully say: Micah 7, 8. The true believer is sure that his God and Savior will not leave nor forsake him, Heb. 13, 5; Josh. 1, 5. If he is sick, yea, even sick unto death, he is not afraid, knowing that he need not fear temporal death because eternal death has no power over him; he is confident that Jesus will take his soul into His bosom as soon as it has left the body and that on the Last Day He will raise it up and unite it again with the soul, and not only that, but that He will give him a glorified body, Phil. 3, 21; 1 Cor. 15, 44. (Hymn 535, 5; 559, 7. 8.) Yes, he that puts his trust in the Rock of Ages will abide forever; he will not make haste; he will not be put to shame; for the promise of the Lord Is. 49, 23b will be fulfilled in him.

God grant for the sake of Jesus Christ, the Rock of Ages, the sure Foundation of His Church, that every one of us by true faith may cling to Him in life and death and thus receive the end of his faith, eternal life! Amen.   J. H. HARTENBERGER.

Epiphany Sunday.

Is. 60, 1—11.

Epiphany is one of the oldest of the festivals of the Christian Church. It was celebrated since the second half of the second century. At first observed by the Eastern, but soon also by the Western Church. Called Epiphany because at first held in commemoration of the baptism of the Savior. At Christ's baptism the voice of His Father was heard, "This is My beloved Son," etc., Matt. 3, 17, which confirmed as an established fact the epiphany, *i. e.,* the appearance or manifestation, of the promised Savior. Since it was at first thought that Jesus was baptized on His thirtieth birthday, Epiphany served the combined purpose of celebrating both the birth and the baptism of our Lord and Savior. Later on the Western Church observed Epiphany in commemoration of the coming of the Wise Men from the East, whereas the Eastern Church continued to observe it as the day marking the baptism of Jesus. And thus it is to this day.

Almost from the very first the Epiphany Festival was called the *Christmas of the Gentiles,* since the Magi were the first among the heathen to come to the new-born Christ-child and accept Him in faith as their Savior. When the Magi from the far East came to Bethlehem, the time was at hand in which the prophecy of our text was in the process of being fulfilled. With the incarnation of the Son of God that Light which was to enlighten also the Gentiles had made its visible appearance on earth. Immediately this Light began to attract those who were still in spiritual darkness. And following upon Pentecost, when through the preaching of the holy apostles the powerful rays of this Light began to illumine the whole world, the forces of the Gentiles, great multitudes of them, were attracted to the Savior.

We, too, who are descendants of Gentile nations, have been attracted by this Light; our heathen ancestors were brought to faith in the Son of God, the Light of the world. We, too, bask in the saving Light which appeared at Bethlehem almost two millenniums ago. "The glory of the Lord" is risen also upon us, its radiance suffuses us with heavenly brightness. Oh, how we should thank and praise God for His great mercy! Coupled with our joyous expression of gratitude, however, should be a lively realization of the duty incumbent upon us of sharing our blessings with others.

The First Epiphany the Manifestation of Christ to the Gentiles.

It reminds us —

1. *Of the Wondrous Grace of God that has Come to Us;*
2. *Of Our Solemn Duty to Share This Gracious Blessing with Others.*

1.

Our text contains a prophecy of the great prophet Isaiah, who lived about seven hundred years before the birth of Jesus Christ. Isaiah is rightly called the Evangelist of the Old Testament; for his prophecies concerning Christ, the Messiah, are very numerous, accurate, beautiful, and pointed.

As Isaiah foresaw the monumental struggle and victory of the Redeemer on Mount Calvary (53d chapter), so he also visioned the precious booty, or spoil, the reward and fruits, of that mighty conflict. Standing on Mount Zion, his prophetic eye beholds the darkness disappearing, giving way to a bright light suddenly arising over yonder hill of Golgotha and enfolding Mount Zion with a splendor never seen before by the eye of man. Warmed by the pleasant rays and with quickened heart-beat, he raises his prophetic voice to describe that which he has seen, unto the Zion of the Old Covenant, the Church of God. (Text.)

At the time of Isaiah's prophecy, conditions in the Old Testament Church were very sad and deplorable: idolatry, dead formalism; all but a small remnant had fallen away from God, etc. Cf. chap. 1, 8 ff.

Conditions in the Church similar at the time when the Light of the World arose in Bethlehem. "Darkness covered the earth and gross darkness the people." Spiritual darkness enveloped the heathen world. The heathen despised and rejected even the natural knowledge of God, until God finally gave them up to uncleanness and vile affections. Cf. Rom. 1, 18 ff. The most shocking immorality, debauchery, profligacy, lewdness, was practised openly; even the gods of the heathen were regarded as not being innocent of such vices. — Darkness enshrouded also Israel, the Covenant people, from among whom the Messiah was to come. Most of the Jews worshiped God only outwardly, not with their hearts; mere external observance of Jewish ceremonies; the prophecies and promises concerning the advent of the Messiah were interpreted carnally, so that the great majority of the Jews awaited, and longed for, a temporal ruler from the house of David, an earthly deliverer from the cruel bondage of the Romans. Pitifully small was the number of true Israelites, who yearned for the "Consolation of Israel": Zacharias, Elisabeth, Mary, Joseph, Simeon, Hannah, the shepherds of Bethlehem's hills, mostly poor, unknown, uninfluential people. This faithful remnant the prophet urges to rise and shine, proclaiming unto them: "Thy Light is come, and the glory of the Lord is risen upon thee." Yes, he exhorts them: "Lift up thine eyes round about and see," etc., v. 4 ff. Indeed, still greater, more wonderful tidings he has for them; for great multitudes of heathen, including many mighty princes and kings, shall be converted; the abundance of the sea (chiefly along the shores of the Mediterranean Sea) and a mighty multitude from every land shall come, bring rich gifts, and show forth the praise of the Lord.

What a great, truly wonderful, and glorious vision of the prophet! His words drip with exultation, joy, ecstasy. His heart overflows with heavenly rapture. He seeks to impart his heart's overpowering joy and delight to the Church of the Old Covenant. He ardently desires that she, too, may rejoice and exult jubilantly with hymns of praise and thanksgiving to the good and gracious God. To the Old Testament Church the prophet in our text portrays the picture of the Church of the New Covenant. And the picture he presents is not an illusion; it is a true, vivid, accurate portrayal of the New Testament Zion, the Christian Church. Isaiah's prophecy was fulfilled; his vision became a reality.

The Light of Bethlehem's manger, which was to be a Light also to the Gentiles, has proved to be the true Light of the world. Countless immortal souls in every part of the world have been drawn to it out of the darkness of heathenism. Soon after this true Light came into the world to "light every man," John 1, 9, the Magi from the East came to Bethlehem and reverently knelt before Him, worshiped and adored Him. After the first Christian Pentecost, when the apostles carried the light-bringing Gospel into many parts of the world, souls from the Gentile nations far and near came to this Light in ever-increasing numbers. By the end of the first century a half million people are said to have been converted to the Savior. From decade to decade, from century to century, their number has grown, often by leaps and bounds. To-day the number of Christians is estimated at over a half billion. Thus "the forces of the Gentiles," as the prophet foretold in our text, have been attracted to the Church of God.

By the grace of God we, too, are numbered among these. It was not always thus. There was a time, a thousand years since, when those whom we call our forebears, were not Christians, but heathen, without light, without hope, without God. "Dark as their densely bounded forests was the spiritual condition of our forefathers, the Germanic, Teutonic tribes, a race, barbarous, hateful, hating one another, reveling in drunkenness and violence, their form of religion a worship of imaginary deities, with rites of foul and bloody idolatry too revolting to be mentioned." (Describe briefly the missionary activities of those who brought the Gospel to the Germans.) Later, when the Gospel was hid, almost extinguished, by Rome, God sent Dr. Luther. — Also we Lutherans of America have been enlightened by the Light of Bethlehem. The services of two men are outstanding in this respect, namely, of Henry Melchior Muehlenberg in the eighteenth and Dr. Walther in the nineteenth century. Yes, in America we not only possess the light of the Gospel in its truth and purity, but we also enjoy religious liberty, equaled in very few other lands.

Epiphany reminds us of this undeserved grace and blessing of God. How much reason we therefore have to thank and praise! — However, this festival reminds us also of the fact that it is our duty to share our blessings with others.

2.

Text, vv. 1. 2. — The prophet exhorts the Church of the Old Covenant not only to arise and to look about, but also to *shine,* to be a light unto others; for *"thy light is come, and the glory of the Lord is risen upon thee."*

What does the prophet mean to tell the Church of God with these words? He means to say: Hear and behold, thou Zion of the Lord! Since thy Light, the Messiah, has come and the glory of the Lord has risen upon thee, get thee up into the high mountain, lift up thy voice with strength, and proclaim the acceptable year of the Lord; proclaim the advent of the Lord; call upon all men to prepare themselves for His coming; preach repentance. And by adding the words, "For, behold, the darkness shall cover the earth and gross darkness the people," he reminds the people of God that the great majority of men are still without the true Light and must forever remain in spiritual darkness unless the light of the Gospel is brought to them.

And in order to spur the Old Testament Church on to greater activity, to shine brightly, to send out powerful beams of light, the prophet promises the most glorious success. Text, vv. 3—11.

This precious promise is most assuredly meant also for the Church of the New Testament to the end of days. Let us bear this in mind on this Epiphany Festival, the blessed day of the manifestation of Christ to the Gentiles. We, too, are to shine; we, too, are to be a shining light to others. We have the privilege and duty of carrying the saving light of the Gospel into the darkest corners of the earth, into the gloomy haunts of heathenism, so that many may be attracted to the Light of Bethlehem, come to the knowledge of the saving truth, and be saved. (Speak very briefly on the Missionary Forward Endeavor and encourage the members of your congregation to become active in this God-pleasing movement. Adduce statistics of conditions at home and abroad. Mention obstacles hindering a concerted missionary forward movement. Make a fervent appeal for greater mission-mindedness, for more ardent, consecrated, zealous participation in cooperative mission activity. Hymn 484.)

J. H. HARTENBERGER.

First Sunday after Epiphany.

Ps. 78, 1—7.

Of the childhood of our dear Lord very little is known. With His parents He had to flee to Egypt. Afterwards He lived with them in Nazareth. Then history is silent on the life of the Christ-child. Of His whole life from His flight into Egypt until His baptism by John the Bible records but one incident — His appearance in the Temple at Jerusalem at the age of twelve years, where His parents found Him sitting, as St. Luke tells us, "in the midst of doctors, both hearing them and asking them questions."

This incident in the life of our Savior is of great importance to us. On the one hand, it is a beautiful example for all children; on the other hand, it shows all parents how they should bring up their children. We need but look at the twelve-year-old Christ-child and hear the words: "And He went down with them and came to Nazareth and was subject unto them," and: "Jesus increased in wisdom and stature and in favor with God and man"; I say, we need but look at the Christ-child as He sits in the midst of those doctors in the Temple and hear these words penned by St. Luke regarding Him, and we shall surely wish and say from the depth of our hearts: O that our children were like unto the Christ-child! This is a desire quite natural for all Christian parents, especially in our days, when the bringing up of children is so difficult and by many parents is so shamefully neglected. The text before us gives us occasion to speak on the bringing up of children.

Children Should be Brought Up in the Nurture and Admonition of the Lord.

Let us learn —

1. How This is to be Done;   2. Why It should be Done.

1.

The psalmist in our text first of all bids God's people of his days to pay attention to what he will say in this psalm, v. 1. It is something of the utmost importance, something that pertains to the eternal welfare of your children. Hence listen and take to heart what I say.

And so, my dear friends, I would now also ask you to pay close attention to me and take to heart what on the basis of this text I am about to say to you on the bringing up of children.

Children are by nature under the wrath of God, Eph. 2, 3; they are by nature sinful, Ps. 51, 5, flesh born of the flesh, John 3, 6. They must therefore be brought to the knowledge of their sinful state and their damnableness because of it; and then they must be told of the Savior of sinners, who is also their Savior; they must be instructed in the way of salvation through faith in this Savior; they must be brought up in the nurture and admonition of the Lord. How is this to be done?

a) By certain means, vv. 2, 3, "the dark sayings of old, which we have heard and known and our fathers have told us." What is meant thereby? Old sayings with a wonderful hidden meaning; sayings proclaiming the wonderful works of God, vv. 4. 7; sayings that have come down to us from the fathers. What is meant thereby? Nothing but the Word of God, the Law and the Gospel. This is the means by which our children are to be brought up. The Bible is the means by which our children are to be brought up so that they will know, and believe in, their Savior and serve God, live a godly life here in this world and after this life obtain life eternal through Jesus Christ, their Redeemer. Especially should they learn the old sayings with a wonderful hidden meaning which tell them of the wonderful works of God, of all that God has done for the salvation of mankind. This they must be taught with all diligence.

b) By whom must this instruction be given? By the fathers, vv. 5. 6. The fathers, or, we may say, the parents, are to instruct their children in the one thing needful. Of old this was done by careful transmission from generation to generation. Hence also the command in Deut. 6, 7. The same command holds good for all fathers, or all parents, of to-day, Eph. 6, 4; Col. 3, 21. By careful instruction in the Word of God they are to make known to their children the wondrous works of God. Indeed, a solemn duty! The parents, it is true, are also to see to it that their children receive the necessary instruction in the various branches of secular knowledge. But even the best education in these branches would be of little or no benefit to them if they would forget Ps. 111, 10; Job 28, 28; 1 Tim. 4, 8. Here, too, apply the words of warning of our Lord Matt. 16, 26. The best education for our children is the education in matters that are of eternal benefit to them. Learn what they may, if they learn not the fear of the Lord, they will perish for lack of knowledge. Happy hours indeed and pleasant evenings for children as they sit at their parents' knees and listen to their instructions as to things eternal!

Are we always mindful of this duty toward our children? And do we always faithfully and conscientiously discharge it?

2.

But *why* should children be brought up in the nurture and admonition of the Lord? V. 7: "That they might set their hope in God"; *i. e.,* that they might learn to know Him and through faith in Him, their Lord and Savior, finally reach their eternal home. "And not forget the works of God." Nothing is more easily forgotten by sinful man than what God did and does for him. It is even so among men;

deeds of love and kindness are soon forgotten. Much more so, however, are the deeds, the works, of God forgotten. Hence we must again and again be reminded of them. And especially should Christian parents remind their children of them lest they be forgotten by them; what God has done for them should be deeply impressed upon their minds and hearts, so that afterwards they will be able to tell them to *their* children, v. 6. And "keep His commandments." The children must be shown that out of gratitude to their gracious God they should lead a godly life, show forth their faith in their manner of living, do what is pleasing to their dear Savior, whom they love, avoid what is displeasing to Him because they do not wish to offend Him, confess Him in word and deed, and thus press toward the goal for which they were created, their eternal home.

Surely great reasons for bringing up our children in the nurture and admonition of the Lord. To our children belongs the kingdom of heaven, Mark 10, 14. They were redeemed, purchased, through the precious blood of Christ, the Son of God, that they might enter the kingdom of heaven. To this end they were baptized and born again. And for the kingdom of heaven they are therefore also to be trained and brought up. To them belongs the kingdom of heaven, and they belong into the kingdom of heaven.

May God help us always to do our duty toward our children!

H. A. KLEIN.

Second Sunday after Epiphany.
Ps. 104, 24—35.

The psalm from which our text is taken begins with the words: "Bless the Lord, O my soul." We indeed have great reason to bless, to praise, our Lord, to sing hymns of praise and thanksgiving to Him for His loving-kindness toward us, the children of men, for what He has done for us. We have reason to praise Him for what He has done for us in regard to our eternal salvation. Just think of it! We had forsaken our good God, we had turned our backs to Him, we had become His enemies. His love toward us we had shamefully trampled under foot and were heedlessly speeding toward eternal perdition. But what did He do? Did He leave us to our doom? He might have done so. This would not in the least have harmed Him, would not in the least have impaired His eternal glory; it would have been our just due. But instead, what did God do? He opened a way of pardon and salvation for us, sent His own Son to the earth to redeem us, to rescue us from eternal perdition, and to prepare for us the way to our eternal home. Surely great reason for us to praise God, to sing unto Him. (Hymn 310, 1. 5.) Great indeed is the loving-kindness of God and His glory as manifested and revealed in the work of redemption.—

But great is His glory also as revealed in the works of creation, and also for this we have reason to praise and worship Him. Our text speaks of —

The Glory of God as Revealed in the Works of Creation.

Let us learn —

1. That God Indeed Revealed His Glory in the Works of Creation;
2. Whereunto This Truth must Induce Us.

1.

a) The glory of God is revealed in His works, which we behold on and within the earth. In v. 24 the psalmist extols the glory of God as revealed in the works of creation. And the works of creation indeed reveal His glory. Let us look at some of the works mentioned in our text. V. 24: "O Lord, how manifold are Thy works!" The works of the Lord are not only many in number, but they are manifold, of a great variety. Just think of the variety of the works of God as we find them in the mineral, vegetable, and animal kingdoms. Great and manifold indeed and innumerable, Ps. 40, 5. "In wisdom hast Thou made them all"; all have been brought forth by the incomprehensible wisdom and power of God, Ps. 136, 5; Prov. 3, 19; Is. 10, 12. When man makes something and then looks it over, he often finds this or that fault in it; but when God had finished His works of creation and looked them over, He saw that all were good, Gen. 1, 31. Not even infinite Wisdom could find any fault in them. "And the earth is full of Thy riches." Our God is not parsimonious; He did not give an insufficient supply to man of all that He created, but a great abundance. The earth is a rich storehouse of all that man and beast need for the sustenance of life.

b) The glory of God is revealed in the works we behold in the sea, vv. 25. 26. Men are continually engaged in exploring the sea, the ocean, in studying the animals inhabiting it. But the animals of the sea cannot be counted; they are innumerable. Everywhere in the sea there are moving things and animals, small and great, tiny creatures and great mammals, which live and play and wander about amid the waves. And the ships not to be forgotten! "There go the ships." The sea, the ocean, is traversed by ships "that do business," Ps. 107, 23; Ezek. 27, 9. So also on the sea, the ocean, we find men. It is the highway of nations and unites, rather than divides, distant lands. What glory of God revealed in all this!

c) The glory of God is revealed also in His work of preservation. V. 27: "These wait all upon Thee." They all look to the Lord for their sustenance, Ps. 145, 15; Job 38, 41. What an immense household to take care of! And God does take care of it. "That Thou mayest give them their meat in due season." Whatever all are in need of is given them by God, and He gives it to them when they are in need of it. "He cares for us by day and night, All things are governed by His might." But they must work for it. V. 28: "That thou givest them *they gather.*" God gives it, but they must put forth efforts to get what they need. All animals and birds have to work in order to obtain food. And so must man. But nevertheless it is true that our heavenly Father feeds all. "Thou openest Thine hand, they are filled with good." Ps. 145, 16; 136, 25; 147, 9. God opens His hand; *i. e.,* He gives unto all living creatures what they are in need of. If He would not open His hand, death and starvation would be the result. Yes, v. 29: "Thou hidest Thy face, they are troubled." If God hides His face from His creatures, hides it in anger, if He does not open His hand, does not give them what they need, but frowns upon them, they are filled with terror, and they are terribly perplexed, Ps. 30, 7; Deut. 31, 17. And: "Thou takest away their breath, they die and return to their dust." If the Lord does not permit them to breathe, then all vitality is gone, and the body crumbles back to the earth, from which it was originally taken. In God all things live and move and have their being, Acts 17, 28. We live only as long as God permits us to live, until He bids us die, as even the little sparrows, which fall not to the ground without our Father in heaven, Matt. 10, 29. And on the other hand, v. 30: "Thou sendest forth Thy Spirit, they are created; and Thou renewest the face of the earth." By the Spirit of God creatures come forth and have their living, Job 33, 4. The Holy Spirit, together with the Father and the Son, is the Creator and Preserver of heaven and earth, Ps. 33, 6; Gen. 1, 2. The Spirit of God, who created at first, creates new life to this day. The work of creation was finished in the first six days of the world, but the work of creation is renewed every day, and the work of preservation goes on and continues to the end of the world. In fall and in winter the earth, as it were, goes to sleep, which makes it appear worn and old; but how readily does the Lord awaken it with the voice of spring and deck it anew with the beauty of youth!

Ah, great indeed is the glory of God as revealed in the works of creation! May we often ponder upon this! The more we do this, the greater and more glorious our God will appear to us, and we shall be constrained to praise and glorify Him.

We shall consider in the second place whereunto this truth must induce us.

2.

It must induce us to praise and glorify God, to praise and glorify Him who has so gloriously revealed Himself in the works of creation, vv. 31—35. These words are words of praise, words in which the psalmist gives vent to the thoughts of his heart about the greatness of God. V. 31: "The glory of the Lord shall endure forever." Though everything passes away, His glory will not pass away. He will still be glorious when "the earth and all the works that are therein shall be burned up," and He therefore deserves to be praised without ceasing. And "He shall rejoice in His works." The Lord, who after the six days of creation rested and, as it were, rejoiced because He saw that everything was very good, still to-day in a measure rejoices in the works of creation as far as they are the works of His hand. And if He rejoices in them, we ought surely also to rejoice in them and thank and praise God for having created them and having placed them at our disposal, for our sustenance and our delight. V. 32: "He looketh on the earth, and it trembleth; He toucheth the hills, and they smoke." How often did the earth tremble in earthquakes, and the hills, the mountains, the volcanoes, smoke, vomiting forth torrents of lava! And this, too, must induce us to praise Him, our God, who with a single look is able to do this; it must induce us to stand in holy and reverential awe before this our great and majestic God. And we ought to sing unto Him all our lives, v. 33. Even if He visits the earth in earthquakes and eruptions of volcanoes, He is still our God, my God, in whom we have our being, and is worthy of all praise and honor and glory, is worthy to be forever exalted and extolled in the songs of all redeemed mankind. And especially we Christians must not forget nor neglect this. We know and believe: John 3, 16; and: Rom. 8, 32. How could we keep silent? We know Him to be our God, who means well with us, even if at times He, as it were, hides His face from us and frowns upon the earth. We must praise and thank Him also for the evil days which He permits to come upon us because we know: Rom. 8, 28. And to sing unto Him and to praise Him will the longer, the more be a pleasure to us. V. 34: "My meditation of Him shall be sweet; I will be glad in the Lord." The more we meditate over, and think of, God and of what He did and still does for us, the sweeter such meditation will become to us, and the more delighted we shall be thus to survey His works; and it will be a source of joy to us to think of God. And "what the heart thinketh the mouth speaketh." We shall sing to our Lord. (Hymn 62, 1. 3.) And in thus singing to the Lord, the psalmist in v. 35 gives voice to the desire that there would be no more sinners on the earth, that all sinners were consumed and be done away with, and that all human beings would join in the praises of God, and God could again look on His works, as He did immediately after He had created them, before they had been marred by sin, and see and behold everything to be very good.

May we never forget to praise our good Lord for His wonderful works! May we never be slow in doing so! He is our great God, who always means well with us, who has created everything for our benefit and enjoyment and therefore is surely worthy to receive glory and honor and power. Hence: Hymn 65, 1. 6.   H. A. KLEIN.

Third Sunday after Epiphany.
Dan. 6, 10—23.

Shall I turn to the right or to the left? — How often we come to the crossroads on life's pathway, to the parting of the ways! We ought to, we must, decide, and yet our weak flesh shrinks from the decision. Shall we, then, plunge ahead without any regard for the consequences or pursue a policy of vacillation, procrastination, waiting for something to turn up that will make the decision easier for us? Shall we like Balaam obey at first, but then hope that circumstances may change, so that the Lord will speak to us again and permit us after all to do what He had at first forbidden?

Let us never forget that we are Christians and that God *has* spoken to us, once for all time, in His Word. If we hesitate at all, it must be only because we are not yet sure of His holy will. As soon as we have ascertained and know what He would have us do, the only thing that remains for us to do is to obey. Dire consequences may result if we disobey, 1 Sam. 13, 8—13; 15, 17—23.

Above all things we dare not permit the will of man to oppose the will of God. God has spoken, and we know it; but now men speak to us and expect us to follow *them*. It takes Christian courage to say no, and we are sorely tempted to disregard the will of God. How may we be strengthened to decide aright? The lesson before us will help us. It provides what we need. It calls to us: —

"Dare to Be a Daniel!"

1. By Obeying God rather than Men;
2. By Quietly, Calmly Trusting to God's Protection.

1.

a) Daniel knows the will of God, for God has been in communication with him at Babylon during the reign of Nebuchadnezzar, of Belshazzar, and now of Darius. Though far from home, among an alien, heathen people, he has not forgotten the lessons imparted to him in his youth and earlier manhood. Therefore the present dilemma does not cause him any dismay. He knows and so is able to think quickly and to decide correctly.

What a valuable possession for the Christian! If knowledge is power, then Christian knowledge is certainly an accomplishment to be coveted, Prov. 8, 10. 11. Men wonder why we spend so much time on the Christian nurture and instruction of our young in our Christian day-schools, in catechetical instruction, etc. But do we deserve the encomiums heaped upon us? We have the apostle's injunction, Eph. 6, 4; however, do we all live up to it as we should? We need more Daniels, who make it their business to keep on learning the Lord's will and who pray: —

> O that the Lord would guide my ways
> To keep His statutes still!
> O that my God would grant me grace
> To *know* and do His will!

Cp. Ps. 32, 8; 25, 4. 5; 119, 12. 66; 143, 10; Prov. 4, 5.

b) Daniel knew what had been done behind his back. King Darius had made Daniel the highest of his three presidents, v. 2, and intended to honor him still more, v. 3. The other presidents and the princes were filled with envy and sought to pull Daniel down. They inquired carefully whether Daniel had not perhaps failed in his duty toward the king. But as Daniel knew his duty toward God, he knew also that God makes and unmakes kings and that he must be loyal to Darius and render him due obedience, Rom. 13, 1. The wicked plotters learned that their efforts in this direction were futile, v. 4; and so they devised greater mischief. They knew of Daniel's allegiance to His God and felt sure that he would obey the Law of his God, v. 5. — Men are quick to see whether we are in earnest with our profession of faith and adherence to Christian principles, and they like to try us out. We must therefore know our ground and stand firm, Eph. 4, 14. In this case the enemies of Daniel were convinced that he would stand by the precepts of his religion, and so they planned to make him commit an act of disobedience to his king and thus endanger his life, vv. 6—9. The blind despot was flattered to think that for thirty days he was to be worshiped as God. He was ignorant, not only of the right, but also of the cunning of his advisers. He signed the decree, signed away the life of his best friend and adviser.

c) When Daniel heard of it, he knew at once that his sovereign would carry out the decree and that his life might be at stake. He had not forgotten the similar experience of his three friends under Nebuchadnezzar, chap. 3, and did not indulge in illusions.

Nevertheless he mapped out his course of action without delay; for he knew the will of God and was determined not to act contrary to it. We are told, v. 10, that he worshiped God and prayed as heretofore. He did this openly, in the sight of men, v. 11, to testify to the fact that we must obey God rather than men, that man in matters of religion or conscience must not be bound by anything but His Word.

O Christian, in like circumstances you must do the same thing. When the evil moment comes, face the issue squarely. Do not confer with flesh and blood and then cower and shrink from doing the will of God in the face of danger. Never forget that you are a child of God. God is the Sovereign to whom you owe your first allegiance. You are fortunate in possessing Christian knowledge above many others; act according to it. If you are not quite sure of your ground, then inquire of God, Acts 9, 6, consult His Word, Ps. 19, 7; 93, 5; consult your pastor or some other seasoned Christian friend.

If in a given case you know that it is your duty to obey God, do not temporize, procrastinate, or seek evasions, as did Balaam of old. And do not whimper and complain that it may hurt your business, cost you your friends or even your life if you put your religion first. Think of those Christians of the early Church who would not deny their God, even when they were told that they would be burned at the stake or thrown to the lions if they would confess Christ as their Savior. Think of Luther at Worms, where soon after his bold confession of the truth he was declared an outlaw; then study his battle-hymn of the Reformation. Think of the apostles, who had been clapped into prison and who therefore realized the danger they were in and yet made their courageous confession, Acts 5, 29.

Dare to be a Daniel. Learn where duty lies. Think straight, act upon convictions which you have gained from the Word of God. Do not fail to pray regularly that God may guide and strengthen you to do what is right.

2.

Or do you still feel that the ordeal will be too much for you? Then know that God protects those who obey Him. Trust Him! Trust Him implicitly!

a) Daniel was caught in the net his enemies had spread for him, and they now become base informers. They first reminded the king of the decree which he had signed and said that he must not change it, v. 12. They knew that he held Daniel in high esteem, and feared that he might want to retrace his steps when he would see what they had in mind. Then they brought their accusation against Daniel, v. 13. Note that in doing so, they added a falsehood: "He regardeth not thee, O king." This need not surprise us, for we cannot expect the enemies of the truth to be truthful nor to understand the demands of the Eighth Commandment.

When the king was informed, there was a rude awakening, v. 14. He blamed himself for his folly and considered ways and means of preserving Daniel's life. But in vain; for as he had been a weakling in yielding to the blandishments of his wicked advisers, so now he was a moral coward. He was fully persuaded that he ought not to molest Daniel, but he lacked the courage of his conviction. When he could hold the princes off no longer, v. 15, he gave the command that faithful Daniel should be thrown into a den of hungry lions.

Learn from all this that faithfulness to your God may rouse the enemies of the truth to persecute you with word and deed. Some of them will basely plot your downfall and make no secret of the matter;

some will show you a smiling face and pose as your friends and well-wishers because in their hearts they know that you are in the right; cf. King Agrippa, Acts 26, 28 ff. Yet they fail you in the crucial moment. Do not lean on such broken reeds.

What, then, would you do if your very life were in danger? You are to follow the example of Daniel, of Shadrach, Meshach, and Abednego, Dan. 3, 17. 18, and to obey the words of Jesus: Matt. 10, 28. Render implicit obedience to God, and let Him decide whether it is better for you to live or to die a martyr's death. Trust the Almighty; for: Luke 1, 37.

b) When you have learned to resign yourself entirely to God's holy will, you will also believe that He can hold His protecting hand over you in the hour of need. Consider Daniel's further experience. The king worried so much about David that he would not eat, and no sleep came into his eyes at night, v. 18. In the morning he went to the den of lions and found Daniel unharmed; Daniel ascribed his deliverance to God, vv. 20—22. He then had Daniel taken out of the den and his enemies thrown in, who were devoured at once, v. 24. Cp. Esther 9, 24. 25. Only too often the enemies of the truth are "hoist with their own petard."

To what do you attribute Daniel's preservation? To the favor of the king? Darius is but an instrument in the hand of God to thwart the wicked designs of the princes and presidents. Read v. 23 b for the correct answer.

Daniel's is not an isolated case. His three friends were saved from the fiery furnace, chap. 3, 26; Peter and other apostles were freed from prison, Acts 4, 21; 12, 7—10; 16, 25 ff.; Luther went unscathed. When a man obeys God, he may count on His protection. The lives of His saints are in His hands.

Dare to be a Daniel, prudent, fearless, obedient to God, trusting firmly in the promises of your God. Rom. 4, 20. 21.   C. A. WEISS.

Fourth Sunday after Epiphany.
1 Kings 19, 9b—18.

God has graciously made us members of His kingdom through faith in Christ Jesus, and therefore we have the certain hope of eternal life, John 3, 16. 36a; Mark 16, 16; 2 Tim. 4, 18. Again, God graciously keeps us in the Kingdom of Grace, the Church here on earth, in order that we may glorify His holy name, among others, by laboring diligently for the salvation of our unconverted fellow-men, Matt. 28, 19. 20; Mark 16, 15.

The first of these two statements will be granted readily enough by many of us; we all want to go to heaven. But what about the second? When we are asked to sound the Gospel trumpet, that sinners may hear and heed and come into the kingdom of God, do we always respond with alacrity as did the Apostle Paul, Acts 16, 10 ("immediately"), or do we not often frame weak excuses? Where is the missionary zeal of the fathers, where the true Epiphany spirit? We hear of open doors, but do we always go in? We have trained mission-workers standing idle in the market-place, but we do not hire them. Are we, then, not guilty of doing the work of the Lord negligently? Jer. 48, 10; cp. margin and Luther's rendering.

We are Christians; we love the Gospel; we have in the past taken an active interest in the work of the Kingdom; but is it not a fact that to-day many have become indifferent, weary in well-doing, despondent, following a policy of defeatism? And nevertheless we complain that our Church is not growing, that our church-work does not prosper as it formally did.

The lesson before us is an antidote against negligence and despondency in doing the work of the Church, because it points the way to success. Let us seek an answer to the question: —

When May We Hope for Success in Our Church-Work?

1. When We Labor with Unflagging Zeal;
2. When We Put Our Trust Solely in the Lord and in His Promises.

1.

a) We are to *labor* in God's kingdom, not to idle away our time, not to take it for granted that there will be others to perform the service. The kingdom of God is not built by drones and shirkers. If we want our church-work to succeed, we must be actual church-workers and heed the earnest warning given us in Amos 6, 1. But is it not a fact that many of our efforts are so feeble that they do not deserve the name of labor? Do we not sometimes work at cross-purposes, because we do not inform ourselves sufficiently about the needs of the Church? There may be feverish activity in many directions, and yet, when we sum it all up, the result is negligible. Our efforts are to be spent in the actual upbuilding of the Kingdom, and God does not permit us to offer substitutes. If we desire success, we must work for Him.

Learn from Elijah. God called him to labor in the Northern Kingdom, the kingdom of the ten tribes, under the reign of the wicked King Ahab and his even more wicked wife Jezebel. Imagine what a task it must have been to teach Israel what the sin of idolatry involves, to testify in private and in public against the worship of the false god Baal, chap. 17, 1; 18, 19 ff. With singular courage and in no uncertain terms he announces the wrath of God over the murder of Naboth both to Ahab and Jezebel, chap. 21, 17 ff. Meanwhile he conducted a school of the prophets and instructed others to carry on the work of the Lord in Israel, 2 Kings 2. Read the history of his life, and you cannot fail to see that Elijah was a faithful church-worker.

When God made us Christians and thus called us into His vineyard, he called us to work in it, Matt. 20, 1 ff.; 21, 28 ff. There is so much to be done that all hands should keep busy, not only the prophet, but also the people. The Law and the Gospel must be preached, men must be taught the way of salvation, our prayers and our offerings dare not be overlooked, and personal mission-work is to be done, John 1, 45. 46. Hymn 476. May we never be found idle! John 9, 4.

b) We are to labor in God's kingdom with unflagging *zeal*. If we labor as mere drudges, there is always danger of our growing weary and of giving up entirely. Zeal indicates that we are devoted to our work because we want it to succeed, that we are filled with enthusiasm, with fervor, with a holy fire, with eagerness to do the holy will of God. Such zeal is commended, Gal. 4, 18; it is catching, it rouses our fellow-Christians to action, 2 Cor. 9, 2; it keeps us on the alert against the evils that would hinder the work of God's kingdom, Ps. 119, 139.

Look again at Elijah. Can there be any doubt as to where he stood in the matter? He could truthfully claim for himself, v. 10: "I have been very jealous [zealous] for the Lord God of hosts," and in v. 14 he repeats the above assertion without fear of reproof. Follow him to Mount Carmel, chap. 18, where he will not rest until he has exterminated the 450 prophets of the false god Baal, v. 40, and has forced Israel to acknowledge that the Lord is God, v. 39. That was true zeal, not a blind, carnal enthusiasm, — the impulses of our flesh can only work havoc in the Church (Carlstadt), — but a fervor that is engendered by prayer, vv. 36. 37, and prompted by a correct knowledge of God's holy will. Picture him as an energetic, fiery character, ready to move quickly, direct in his speech, gifted with strength and endurance.

We are to be like Elijah; for men such as he can do great things in the kingdom of God. St. Paul was like him; his missionary zeal has never been equaled. Cp. Acts 18, 5. 28; 16, 10 ("endeavored"); 1 Cor. 9, 16. We cannot but think also of Luther, who worked so zealously to restore the Church to its pristine apostolic purity. Above all we think of Jesus, of whom "it was written [Ps. 69, 9], The zeal of Thine house hath eaten Me up," a zeal which He showed not only in the cleansing of the Temple, John 2, 13—17; Matt. 21, 12. 13, but throughout His ministry.

Pray God to grant you the unction of the Holy Spirit that you, too, may be filled with a fervent zeal to labor for the upbuilding of His glorious kingdom.

c) We ought to labor with *unflagging* zeal. It is ours to labor, but God's to grant success. To our disappointment the results do not always correspond to the amount of labor expended. Peter preached on the first day of Pentecost, and three thousand souls were added to the Church, Acts 2, 4; a little later we read of five thousand. But St. Paul preached just as fervently at Athens, yet the results were rather meager, Acts 17. When success does not show in our church-work within a reasonable length of time, we are tempted to become disheartened. Then the fire dies down, our zeal abates, "our devotion dies." Our text is to warn us against this.

Here is where Elijah failed at one time. He was human; he had worked hard for the Lord, but could not see that he was making any headway. So he became discouraged and said in effect, What's the use? Vv. 10. 14. He gave up his work for the time being to become a hermit in the wilderness, to live in a cave. But could he work and hope for success there? Notice the gentle rebuke that lies in the Lord's repeated question, vv. 9. 13: "What is there for you here, Elijah?" The prophet, as a teacher, must be among the people. There he is needed, to warn and to threaten, to instruct and to comfort; in the wilderness he cannot count on success.

You have seen Christian men and Christian churches thus dispirited, discouraged, and you knew at once that they could not hope for success at this rate. What a pity to labor zealously for years in the kingdom of God and then to give up, just because we do not seem to be making much headway, possibly none at all. Humanly speaking, what would have become of that little band of Saxon immigrants in the year 1839 when their leader went wrong if Dr. Walther and his colaborers had given up in despair? Cp. Gal. 5, 7; 1 Cor. 9, 24.

God is gracious to his disheartened servant Elijah. He applies the needed tonic and sends him back to his work, commands him to continue it with his old-time zeal. Let us, too, look up to God when our ambition lags; for He can rekindle the sacred fire, Ps. 27, 1.

2.

a) We must learn to put our trust *solely* in the Lord and in His promises. This means that we are not to rely on our own efforts nor to expect to build God's kingdom by methods of our own. All that we can do is to labor faithfully and zealously according to the will of God; the success, the blessing upon our efforts, can come from Him alone, 1 Cor. 3, 6.

Elijah had pursued a certain fixed course in his dealings with Israel. In the very nature of the case he had been compelled to operate largely with the thunder and hammer of the Law, and he could not understand why this stern preaching did not prove more effective. In his impatience he declared that he had labored in vain, v. 10:

"I, even I only, am left." He needed a lesson on the nature and limitations of the Law, and so the Lord led him to Mount Horeb (Sinai), where the Law had been given under Moses. Elijah was told to stand upon the mount, and the Lord passed by, v. 11. 12a, with a demonstration similar to the one that took place when the Law was first given, Ex. 20, 18. When it is stated that the Lord was not in the wind nor in the earthquake nor in the fire, we are to understand that the Law cannot convert the sinner, and Elijah was to learn that he had made a serious mistake if he had relied upon his preaching of the Law to turn Israel.

"The Law is good," 1 Tim. 1, 8; but notice that Paul at once adds, "if a man use it lawfully." It is needed to break the stubborn heart of the sinner, and we must be just as faithful as Elijah in applying it. If we fail to do so, we are not faithful laborers, and God will withhold His blessing from us. But if we think that by preaching damnation to sinners, we have, as it were, offered our contribution and that this ought to prove equal to the occasion, we are again sadly in error.

b) If we really expect to succeed in our church-work, we must rely entirely upon the Lord and His Holy Spirit to bless our feeble efforts. After the mighty wind, the earthquake, and the fire there came to Elijah a still, small voice, v. 12 b; and the Lord was in that voice, which symbolized the gentle, sweet voice of the Gospel. If we proclaim the Gospel just as faithfully as we do the Law, there *will* be blessed results. The Law kills and condemns, but the Gospel gives new spiritual life. It warms the cold heart of the sinner by pointing him to Jesus, the Savior of sinners, and thus converts him.

Can you still doubt? Will you not put your trust in the Lord and in His promises? Rom. 1, 16; Is. 55, 10; Heb. 4, 13. Even where it seems to fail because we cannot look into the hearts of men, the Word of God has done, and is still doing, its work. For his comfort and encouragement Elijah was told in v. 18 that there were seven thousand in Israel who had not committed the sin of idolatry. Elijah, who undoubtedly had proclaimed also the Gospel, now could not but see that the Lord had been working with him and had blessed his zealous labors beyond his fondest hopes. And so, when the Lord commanded him to go back to his work, he did not hesitate, vv. 15. 17, even though this included continued preaching of the Law, namely, God's announcement of the impending doom. When he was told to anoint his successor, v. 16, he understood that the Lord intended to carry on the work; and he was obedient to Him and absolutely trusted in Him.

As *we* work in the kingdom of our God, let us also look for success to God alone. God gives us the work we are to do, but forbids us to worry about the results. We also have His gracious promises; in these we must rest content, 1 Cor. 15, 58; 2 Cor. 1, 20.   C. A. WEISS.

Fifth Sunday after Epiphany.

Gen. 11, 1—9.

The punishment that followed the building of the Tower of Babel, Luther considers a calamity more damaging than that of the Great Flood. For the Flood destroyed only the people of one age and time, while the judgment visited upon the people of Babylon continues to affect the peoples of all ages and countries to the end of time.

Yet the same folly is reenacted over and over again with similar results of multiplied and ever-continued confusion of men and destruction of their best interests, socially, politically, and spiritually.

As we view the history of nations and of individuals, of governments and of churches, we observe the same godless attitude, bringing about the same dire consequences: alienation, strife, discord, wretchedness, in State and Church.

Surrounded on all sides by evidences of this world-wide folly, we ought to recognize the lesson we are to learn lest we add to our own as well as to the world's troubles.

Lest We Rebuild the Tower of Babel,

1. Let Us Beware of the Sinful Folly that Prompted the Building of This Tower.

Sin makes fools of men. It was thus with the building of the Tower of Babel. That was one of the greatest follies ever attempted by man. What particular iniquity may have led to, and paved the way for, this folly?

Undoubtedly the *prosperity and easy life* that these people enjoyed in the fertile plains of Shinar had something to do with it. Abundance and riches have turned the hearts and heads of many from the Lord to foolish and disastrous schemes, Prov. 30, 8. 9; Luke 12, 20. Should we not do a little searching of our own hearts along these lines? 1 Tim. 6, 6—10.

Again, these people had plainly become guilty of *inappreciation and abuse* of the precious gift of language oneness. Instead of using this powerful medium for the purpose of edifying, instructing, and strengthening one another in the ways of the Lord, they used it to unite their efforts in opposition to the Lord and to spread false doctrine and wickedness. Christians must be careful to make proper use of, and not to abuse, the good gifts of God, 1 Cor. 7, 31. Many of the abominable things in this world are directly traceable to this sin. Cf. Rom. 1, 23 ff.; 13, 14.

However, the real cause underlying the folly that proved so disastrous was the utter *disregard* of these people *of the precepts and commandments of God.* Ham, Noah's son, set the evil example. He had mocked and shamefully despised his father. Nor did the curse which descended on him for this bring him to his senses. Instead, he left the parental roof, disassociated himself from his God-fearing brothers, and continued to pursue his wicked course. As was to be expected, the children followed in the footsteps of their godless father. Nimrod, by his tyranny and oppression, became the terror of the land. — Contempt for parental authority is the outstanding sin of the youth of to-day. Let our children and young people beware. Prov. 30, 17. — Then there is this *separating of oneself from the congregation of the Lord* and seeking the companionship of the children of this world, membership in ungodly societies, and undue intimacy with the churchless and those of a false faith. All of this is ruining the spirituality of many, 1 John 2, 15; 2 Tim. 4, 10; Ps. 1, 6.

Above all, these people openly *revolted against God*. They cared nothing for His Word. The promises of the Messiah were foolishness unto them. The solemn warnings of Noah they laughed to scorn. When a person begins to despise the Word, to leave his Savior, to frown upon the admonition and reproof of faithful pastors and teachers, he not only falls from grace, but commits foolish and unreasonable things, which are destructive also to his temporal happiness, Hos. 4, 6; 2 Thess. 2, 10. 11; Ps. 14, 1.

Finally, the sin of these people was *pride and haughtiness*. They would set themselves up to become the lords of the earth. They conceived the notion of building a tower, a monument to themselves, that they might perpetuate their name and establish a world center around which all future activity was to revolve and from which authority and world control should emanate. They recognized the tremendous advantage and power of language uniformity. By this undertaking they aimed to preserve it to their own selfish purposes. The top of the tower was to "reach into heaven." Not possibly so much to provide a place of refuge and safety in case of another world catastrophe as rather to eliminate the distance between heaven and earth, between God and man. God was to come down from His throne; man was to be His equal. The same old story: "Ye shall be as gods," Gen. 3, 5. — Pride and self-conceit has been the downfall of many. Not only has much folly followed in its wake, but also untold heartache and disaster. Faith cannot thrive in a proud heart, Luke 1, 52; Is. 13, 11; Prov. 16, 18. Many of the schisms in churches were brought on by pride.

Lest we rebuild the Tower of Babel, let us in the second place ponder —

2. The Disastrous Consequences of the Building of That Tower.

God will not be mocked. He will not give His glory to another. He resisteth the proud. He confounds His enemies. So here.

a) V. 5. *God descends, i. e.,* takes note of the doings of the builders of that tower. They had become carnally secure, believing that God was either unaware of what was going on or unconcerned about their undertaking or impotent to prevent it. Such is Satan's master scheme of deception. He causes his victims to assume that sin goes unnoticed because they perceive no sign of immediate punishment; yea, they imagine that their abominable acts are condoned or connived at.

What folly! While they are hard at it, God looks on, takes note of, makes ready to put an end to, their godless undertaking. No, God will not always remain silent. He may delay and grant the sinner time and space for repentance; but ignore wickedness, never! Ps. 50, 16—22. He may wait until the day cools, as in Adam's case, or until the sinner has filled his cup to overflowing, as in the case of the pre-Deluge world. But all the while He descends and observes. The sinning of sinners is done in the very presence of God.

b) V. 6. "Behold"; it is with evident regret that the Lord finds it necessary to interfere with, and punish, the doing of the children of men. The wickedness of man is, as it were, a sad surprise to the Lord. The terrible demonstration of divine wrath in the Flood had so affected God Himself that He, in His great compassion, had resolved not to visit another Flood upon man. His rainbow stood in the sky, a symbol of His grace and mercy. And yet, within so short a space of time this flagrant disregard of His power, His long-suffering, His unmerited grace. The Lord is pained; yet punish He must, and punish He will. Gal. 6, 7.

While there is a warning in this for all men, there is at the same time comfort for God's people. His Church may at times seem to be downtrodden and doomed to destruction. The godless element may appear to have the upper hand. All efforts at evangelization appear to be futile. The masses laugh to scorn the faithful warnings of God's people. But here we learn that our regrets and griefs cannot be more keen than His. May His Church persevere in spite of all discouragements! God will avenge her wrongs.

c) Vv. 6. 9. *God punishes.* He confounds the speech of those people. Within the twinkle of an eye their laborious schemes collapse. Their efforts suffer an abrupt termination. They are put to shame and disgrace. For all times to come their haughty scheme stands exposed as a most fallacious undertaking.

However, they are not the sole sufferers. Rather, they have brought upon the world another catastrophe. The chasm between peoples has become greater. Lack of understanding begets coldness, antagonism, hatred, envy, strife. Here the very foundation was laid for greater world troubles. Brotherliness was practically wiped out. Selfishness received new impulses. The glorious one-family spirit gave way to clannishness, isolation, exclusiveness, aloofness.

Worse, however, than these social disruptions was the spiritual bereavement that followed in their wake, the difficulty that now arose to retain and maintain the spiritual treasure of the pure Word, the promulgation and spread of the Gospel. Nor was it long before this became universally evident. As the various tribes collected themselves and departed, each going its own way, their sinful inclinations and tendencies multiplied, and the vast majority drifted off into the darkness of unbelief, despair, and other great shame and vices. Truly, a sad sequel to a godless undertaking. What a forcible warning to us!

Lest we rebuild the Tower of Babel, let us finally note —

3. God's Gracious Effort to Help These People.

a) The Lord did not destroy those people, much as they had deserved it, but remembered His promise to Noah, Gen. 9, 9—17. He confounded their speech merely to bring them to repentance. Yea, the tower itself, or whatever remained of it, its very ruins, were a standing call to repentance, Ps. 103, 8—14; Rom. 11, 22; Acts 17, 30.

God continued to proclaim the Messiah to them. Not long after this happening He gave the promise of the Redeemer of mankind to Abraham, Gen. 22, 18, and repeated it again and again, also to Isaac and Jacob. He admonished them: Jer. 51, 6. He pleaded with them: Ezek. 33, 11. He assured them: Jer. 29, 11. 13. 14.

God is very much concerned that the diversity of tongues should not bar any of the nations of the earth from the salvation merited for all mankind by the Savior of sinners. His disciples on Pentecost received the gift "to speak with other tongues," Acts 2, 3, and He grants His Church diversity of languages in order to bring together again what has become separated. The different languages may remain, but the scattered people are brought into His fold. The Gospel unites them in unity of faith and doctrine. There can again be oneness of spirit. Ultimately, in heaven, He will also restore unity of language. And in all this God would use us as His instruments.

b) Our God-given commission is to be workers together with God in this effort. How?

By preaching the Gospel to *all* people, irrespective of language, race, or color, Matt. 28, 19. 20, supporting the various missions, maintaining Christian schools and colleges; by making diligent use of all modern means of communication and contact: the press (church-papers and Christian literature), the radio, etc.; by fostering the unity of spirit in our congregations and preventing or correcting dissension and strife in our own midst, Jas. 3, 14. 16; Zeph. 3, 9.

Conclusion. — The story of the Tower of Babel will ever stand as a solemn warning against contempt of the Word of God, haughtiness, worldly-mindedness. May we heed the warning! More specifically, however, it challenges our most determined and consecrated effort to bring to a distracted world that peace of God in Christ Jesus which unites men in the fellowship of one faith, etc., Eph. 4, 5. 6.;

Gal. 3, 28, and which at last will become the "bond of perfectness," Col. 3, 14, namely, when, with the last vestige of Babel's curse forever effaced, a vast congregation "out of every kindred and tongue and people and nation" will sing with one accord the new song to the Lamb that was slain, Rev. 5, 9. 10, and has given them, in a fuller and more glorious sense, to "reign on the earth" and "made them a name," inscribed on the everlasting pages of the Book of Life.

H. STUDTMANN.

Septuagesima Sunday.

Jer. 31, 31—34.

Our text speaks of covenants. A covenant is an agreement, or compact, entered into by two or more parties for purposes of mutual fidelity and good will.

Covenants are frequently mentioned in the Old Testament. We read of solemn contracts made between Abraham and Abimelech, Gen. 21, 22; Jacob and Laban, Gen. 31, 51; David and Jonathan, 1 Sam. 18, 3; etc.

More especially do the Scriptures speak of God's covenants with his people. The suggestion of such a covenant in every instance originated with God. God pledged His faithfulness, His gracious assistance, His blessing, to the children of men. Cf. Gen. 6, 18; 9, 19; etc.

Such a covenant is distinctly expressive of God's condescending solicitude for the temporal and eternal well-being of His helpless and skeptically minded people. For God's promises indeed needed no solemn confirmation on His part to make them reliable and valid. Yet, in order to invite and encourage men's fullest trust in His unwavering desire for their salvation, God pledges Himself by sign and token, as man to man, to do unto them as He has promised.

Of such covenants two are outstanding. One of these covenants served to comfort, direct, and guide His people during the era of expectant hope in the Messiah to come. While, however, its underlying principle consisted in the promises of the prophets, its characteristic features were expressed in terms of laws and regulations as promulgated on Mount Sinai. This is commonly referred to as the Old Covenant, or the Covenant of the Law. — The other divine covenant is the covenant of the New Testament dispensation, established in the fulness of time and based solely on the redemption through Christ Jesus, with perfect freedom from all regulatory mandates. This the prophet calls the New Covenant.

The Better Covenant.

1. The Old Covenant Was a Good Covenant.
2. The New Covenant Is a Better Covenant.

1.

The Old Covenant was a good covenant, Heb. 9, 1.

A) It was founded on God's loving-kindness, on His tender mercies, Is. 54, 10.

a) It was not so that the patriarchs of old were to merit God's blessing or earn His salvation by keeping His laws and statutes, Gal. 3, 11.

b) Also in the Old Testament God's children were led to place their hope of eternal life on the unmerited grace of God in the promised Messiah, Gen. 49, 18; 32, 10; Is. 45, 24; Dan. 9, 18, the same as we, Gal. 3, 6.

B) It was a covenant of great glory, 2 Cor. 3, 7.

a) Given amidst signs of awe-inspiring majesty, Deut. 33, 2.

b) Ordained by angels in the hand of a mediator, Gal. 3, 19.

C) According to this covenant the Lord led His people with loving concern for them.

a) V. 32. He "took them by the hand" and led them as a father leads his children, Deut. 1, 31; 32, 10. 12.

b) Out of bondage (Egypt) into the land of freedom and plenty, ever protecting them against the treacherous assaults of powerful enemies, Josh. 21, 43—45; giving them victory over their agressors, Ps. 105, 14; ever repenting of His anger when He permitted Gentile nations to lead them into captivity, Ps. 106, 45.

D) Yet this covenant was, and of necessity had to be, adapted to the time in which, and to the conditions under which, it obtained as well as to the framework on which it was built.

a) The *time* was the prefulfilment dawn, comparable even to the night, Is. 21, 11. 12, with all the disadvantages of prevailing dusk. Compared with "the great plainness of speech" in the New Testament, Moses "put a veil over his face," as Paul puts it, 2 Cor. 3, 13. Little wonder that the prophets were required to search diligently "what or what manner of time the Spirit of Christ which was in them did signify," 1 Pet. 1, 11.

b) The *conditions* to which the Old Covenant had to apply itself were those of infancy and childhood. It therefore assumed the rôle of a schoolmaster. Though children of God and heirs of the riches of the household of God, the fathers were "under tutors and governors until the time appointed," Gal. 4, 12. Hence the many and burdensome statutes that prescribed for them their course of conduct and action, the manner of their worship, etc., until the people, smarting under the severity of such ordinances, carried on with sighing: Ps. 14, 7. Not surprising that Israel yielded to its inborn frailty and became guilty of ever-recurring infractions, v. 32b, although the Lord was "an Husband unto them," who with tender solicitude for His betrothed would keep His people close to His side, faithful to Himself, as He was to them, and at a safe distance from false gods, whose idolatrous worship was so enticing to the flesh.

c) The *framework* finally of the Old Covenant was the Ceremonial Law of continual sacrifices, which in spite of their daily repetition could avail nothing of themselves, Heb. 10, 4, and because of their merely typical values only served to intensify the longing for the God-appointed High Priest and the real Paschal Lamb.

Thus, the Old Covenant was a good covenant, yet not "faultless," Heb. 8, 7. In spite of its good intentions it could convey neither the determination to will nor the strength to do the things necessary to keep the covenanters within the grace of its promises. And therefore, "because they, the people, continued not in His covenant," the Lord was obliged "to regard them not," Heb. 8, 9, to withhold from them the full covenantal blessings. Hence it was that the Lord by His prophet promised "to make a New Covenant with the house of Israel and the house of Jacob," *i. e.,* with His spiritual Israel. And

2.

This New Covenant is a better covenant.

A) Better because of its *permanency.*

a) "I will make a New Covenant," such are the prospects which the Lord holds out to His people. "In that He saith . . . made the first old," argues the writer to the Hebrews, chap. 8, 13. There was both a necessity and a general desire for this transition from a temporary to a permanent covenant. Alien forces from without and evil elements from within were harassing God's people, the former knocking at the very gates of the earthly Jerusalem, the latter threatening complete disintegration of the spiritual Jerusalem. As a result of both Israel-Judah faced humiliation, decimation, and forfeiture of God's covenantal graces.

b) But Israel was to lift up its head in joyful anticipation. *"Behold,"* the Lord tells them. That is to say: Take new courage and give heed to what I have to say. *"The days come,"* etc. The exact time is not specified. Yet, the event is certain. Four times in as many verses the assurance "saith the Lord" is added. And that New Covenant will be lasting, "once for all," Heb. 10, 10, final. There will be nothing to add, nothing to change, because it is "perfected forever," Heb. 10, 14. In fact, the solemn warning is issued: Gal. 1, 8; Rev. 22, 18. 19.

B) Better because of its *character.*

a) The New Covenant will not deal with, nor stress, externals. Statutes and ordinances will cease, Gal. 4, 25. 26; John 8, 36; Gal. 5, 1; Col. 2, 16.

b) It will be spiritual. Not engraved in stone, but put "in their inward parts" ("mind," Heb. 8, 10) and written "into their hearts," so that from a better understanding will result a more profound knowledge, Eph. 4, 13. 14; from a truly filial love will flow a more ready compliance with God's will, Ps. 110, 3; from heartfelt gratitude will proceed a more active obedience of faith, 2 Cor. 5, 14; John 5, 3.

C) Better because of its *ministration.*

a) The ministration of the Old Covenant was limited to mediators, priests, and high priests, Heb. 8, 4. 5.

b) Under the New Covenant all believers are "a royal priesthood," 1 Pet. 2, 9; Is. 54, 13. "They shall teach no more," etc., v. 34, not in the sense that teaching will be unnecessary and dispensed with. This passage is not a charter for an uneducated ministry, as some fanatics have surmised. But, due to a greater measure of the Spirit's enlightenment, direction, and guidance, there will be a greater and deeper Christian knowledge and understanding, 1 Cor. 2, 10; 1 John 2, 20. "They shall all know Me," etc. Walking in the sunshine of the full day, Is. 60, 1; John 1, 5, "the earth shall be full of the knowledge of the Lord," Is. 11, 9. "From the least to the greatest." Cf. Joel 3, 1; Ps. 8, 2. Our Christian schools.

D) Better because of its *extent.*

a) The Old Covenant was made with, and primarily was the prerogative of, "the seed of Abraham." The Jews were the foremost beneficiaries because they were the chosen people, Ps. 135, 4.

b) The New Covenant is universal. "Every man — his neighbor; every man — his brother," v. 34. Cf. Gal. 3, 28; Is. 60, 5. 6; Matt. 28, 19.

E) Better because of its *dispensation.*

a) The Old Covenant functioned by proxy, so to speak. There was purification and cleansing by blood, and it had to be, Heb. 9, 22. But it was the blood of animals, which could not atone for sins, Heb. 10, 4. 1.

b) Of the New Covenant the Lord promises: "I will forgive," etc. In these words our text reaches its jubilant climax. Unconditional pardon, complete redemption, full atonement, and therefore all-sufficient grace and eternal salvation are held out. And all this because: Heb. 9, 11. 12. 15, so that: Acts 13, 39. This, the Lord avers, "is My covenant to them when I shall take away their sins," Rom. 11, 27.

c) To make assurance doubly sure, the Lord has given to His Church, under His hand and seal, as it were, the "testament in His blood," 1 Cor. 11, 25. "Thus of His fulness have all we received, and grace for grace," John 1, 16.

Conclusion. — Surely rejoicing belongs to the people of the New — and better — Covenant. "Let us, then, draw near," etc., Heb. 10, 22 ff. And may we manifest a new and better zeal in bringing the excellency of the New Dispensation to the attention of men everywhere, so that in the fullest sense of the term "God will be to them a God and they to Him a people." H. STUDTMANN.

Sexagesima Sunday.
1 Sam. 17, 42—51.

The solemn Lenten season is fast approaching; only ten days more, and Lent will be here. Then we shall not only contemplate the fierce struggle our Savior had to undergo in order to gain our freedom from sin and its dread consequences, but we shall learn to realize, perhaps more than we have in the past, that we, too, must fight if we would win and wear the victor's crown; that we must suffer with the Savior here if we would be glorified with Him there, Rom. 8, 17. On His way to Jerusalem He Himself significantly said to His disciples: "Behold, *we* go up to Jerusalem"; not I alone, but we, you and I together; and the disciples, sensing that nothing pleasant was awaiting them there, "were amazed and, as they followed Him, they were afraid," Mark 10, 32.

In our text we have —

A Type of Two Great Struggles.

1. The One the Savior Had for Us;
2. The Other We Have as We Follow Him.

1.

A) a) Vv. 4—7. 41. The giant in armor, ready for battle.

V. 42. David was a contemptible little antagonist in the sight of the giant, an easy mark, so to speak, a trifle girlish, unused to battle and not at all to be feared. The giant looked upon him with disdain. Nay, more, the giant began to curse and revile David and sought to intimidate him with loud-mouthed boasting, vv. 43. 44.

b) David realized full well that in himself he was no match for the giant, that he was very weak and unskilled in the art of warfare, all out of proportion to the giant. But he did not trust in himself, as the loud-mouthed boaster did; he trusted in the Lord of hosts. And this his trust in God made him very bold: vv. 45—47. Marvelous words, these; a paean of victory, a song of triumph, sung before the battle.

Nor was it idle boasting as was that of the giant; for: v. 48. What sublime courage! What holy zeal! "Hasted," "ran," vv. 49—51a. He defeated the giant with the latter's own weapon, v. 51. Yes, great deliverance was wrought in Israel that day, and "all the assembly knew that the Lord saveth not with a sword and spear; for the battle is the Lord's."

B) In like manner Jesus, the great Son of David, slew the hellish Goliath and wrought great deliverance for us all.

a) Satan is a mighty warrior of old. He delights in murder and bloodshed. And he is heavily armed. Eph. 6, 11. 12; John 8, 44.

> Deep guile and great might
> Are his dread arms in fight;
> On earth is not his equal.

b) Jesus seemed weak by comparison. When Satan met Him in the wilderness, He had fasted forty days and forty nights, and physically He was very weak indeed. And when the two clashed in Gethsemane, the Savior was lying prostrate, "a worm and no man." See Him "sorrowful and sore amazed and very heavy," writhing in agony, praying: "Father, take away this cup from Me; nevertheless not what I will, but what Thou wilt." And Satan, beholding this, no doubt treated him with supreme contempt, with utter disdain, and greeted Him with loud-mouthed boasting and cursing, Ps. 22, 7. 8. 13. (See the Passion-story concerning the scorn heaped upon the Crucified One.)

But Jesus prayed. He trusted in God. (See Pss. 69 and 22; also Passion-story.) He sought and received strength from on high. "There appeared unto Him an angel from heaven, strengthening Him." Hear the loud cry He uttered in His dying moments. Hear Him triumphantly exclaiming: "It is finished!" The great work of redemption is finished. "Father, into Thy hands I commend My spirit." — Ah, the Serpent had bruised His heel, but He had crushed the old Serpent's head. "Not by might nor by power" (of an army); "the Lord saveth not with sword and spear," but by the blood and death of the Son of God.

c) And oh, what deliverance He thus has wrought! We need no longer fear the gates of hell; for all our sins are atoned for, they are all forgiven. God's wrath has been fully appeased, and He is all grace toward us. Death has been utterly abolished, and life and immortality have been won for us. Satan is conquered, utterly defeated. Yea, the risen Savior descended into hell and spread consternation among the Serpent's brood, triumphing over all our infernal foes. The gates of hell are closed, and the gates of heaven are opened wide.

Now let Israel shout in appreciation of this deliverance; let them obtain and enjoy it through sincere repentance and faith in the Savior, and then let them "arise" and "pursue the Philistines."

We have in this text a type of another struggle, the one *we* have as we follow Jesus.

2.

A) Having failed in his struggle with Christ, Satan now takes issue with Christ's followers. He strives with might and main to keep the redeemed from reaping the fruits of their redemption. And here, too, he is a wily, crafty foe, one who delights in murder and bloodshed, and a powerful antagonist withal, Eph. 6, 12. "Deep guile and great might," etc. "Your adversary, the devil," etc., 1 Pet. 5, 8.

B) In this battle he often applies the same tactics he used in his struggle with Christ. He bullies the Christians; he does a lot of loud-mouthed boasting and scoffing. Think of the boasting of his minions, the self-styled scientists, who have long since decried the Bible as a book of fables and trumped up "the assured results of scientific research." Think of the false religions and false doctrines with which he has swamped the Church: Catholicism, Modernism, Unitarianism, Mormonism, Christian Science, lodgism, etc. Think of the blight of unionism and the isolating of those who cling to the truth, by combining their opponents into a vast army of Philistines. The devil, too, takes the same delight in murder and bloodshed to-day that he did in days of old. The persecutions of the ancient Church have been matched by the persecutions under the Papacy and the more recent ones, in Russia, for example. See Rev. 20, 8. 9 a.

C) And oh, how weak we Christians are in ourselves! "The spirit indeed is willing, but the flesh is weak." Peter and his two companions slept instead of watching and praying. Peter denied, and all the disciples forsook the Master and fled; they were offended because of Him. *We* often fail to watch and pray, neglect the Word of God, forget to watch our step, walk right into temptation, and then lack the power to overcome it. Yea, we, too, are offended in Jesus because He does not always answer our prayers at once and in the manner in which we would have them answered. Yes, Satan has a powerful ally of our own flesh and blood.

D) However, thank God, we may say: "Your adversary the devil, . . . *whom resist steadfast in the faith.*" Yes, steadfast in the faith. Do not trust in your own self, but *do* trust in the Lord of hosts. Trust in His promises, of which the Bible is full. And obey His precepts and His promptings. And fight under His command. "Put on the whole armor of God," etc., Eph. 6, 11. 13—17. Say unto Satan: "It is written." Do not argue with the devil, but smite him with the Word of God. Hymn 276, 3.

Yes, "resist the devil, and he will flee from you." "A mighty Fortress is our God," etc. Amen.   J. A. RIMBACH.

Quinquagesima Sunday.
Jonah 3, 1—4, 11.

This week we enter upon one of the holiest seasons of all the year, the solemn season of Lent. Lent commemorates the suffering and death of the Son of God. — The suffering and death of the Son of God is a mighty call to repentance. We Christians are commanded to carry that call into all the world, and we must heed that call ourselves. The world needs repentance badly, and so do we.

This twofold truth is brought out with remarkable clearness and emphasis by this text from the Book of Jonah. Let us consider this text and observe —

1. *How Jonah, at God's Behest, Preached Repentance to Nineveh;*
   2. *How God had to Preach Repentance to Jonah.*

1.

a) God had commanded Jonah to go to Nineveh and preach repentance. But Nineveh was a heathen city, and Jonah was a Jew. Should he, being a Jew, preach repentance to the heathen? Could there be such a thing as *repentance* among the heathen? Was not Israel God's chosen people, chosen from among all the nations of the earth? Yea, worse than that. Jonah knew that God was "a gracious God and merciful, slow to anger, and of great kindness, and [that He] repented Him of the evil," chap. 4, 2. Jonah *feared* that Nineveh *might* repent, and then God would show them mercy; and surely those heathen were not worthy of such a thing, were they? So Jonah sought to escape from the Lord, and instead of going to Nineveh and preaching repentance, he went to sea, boarding a ship bound for Tarshish. God had told Jonah to go East, and Jonah went West!

b) Well, he didn't get very far. God sent a raging storm after him, and the ship on which he had taken passage seemed doomed. Finally he confessed his guilt, and at his own suggestion he was cast into the sea, whereupon the storm abated and Jonah went to the bottom of the ocean. But God commanded a great fish to swallow Jonah, and he was in the fish's belly three days and three nights. And oh, Jonah repented and prayed to God out of the fish's belly, and God spoke to the fish, and it vomited out Jonah upon the dry land.

c) Now God commanded Jonah "a second time, saying, 'Arise, go unto Nineveh, that great city, and preach unto it the preaching that I bid thee.' So Jonah arose and went to Nineveh according to the word of the Lord." He did not follow his own inclinations this time, but obeyed the Lord. Now, Nineveh was "an exceeding great city of three days' journey." It took a man three days to walk around it. "And Jonah began to enter into the city a day's journey, and he cried and said, 'Yet forty days, and Nineveh shall be overthrown.'" For a whole day Jonah went about in Nineveh and preached repentance. He told the people that they were sinners, great sinners, idolaters, wicked people, and that, if they did not repent and turn to God, the true God, the God of Israel, they would be damned eternally; also their city would be laid waste. But Jonah told the people more than that. He told them that God was merciful and forgiving for the sake of the promised Savior and that, if they believed in Him, they would receive forgiveness and be saved. And while Jonah did not look for such an outcome or even wish it, the people of Nineveh "believed God." They repented and proclaimed a fast. Even the king and his noblemen humbled themselves and really and truly repented, vv. 6—9. "And God saw their works that they turned from their evil way; and God repented of the evil that He had said that He would do unto them, and He did it not," v. 10.

d) Oh, what joy! The Word of God is preached just a little,

just a few short days, in a great, great city, steeped in heathenism from time immemorial, and the whole city, as it were, repents and believes God and is spared. The very beasts cry unto God after a fashion, v. 8, and God hears their cry, vv. 4. 11. True, the repentance of the people does not seem to have been of very long duration, and later Nineveh was actually overthrown. But for the time being a great number of people repented, and some at least remained penitent and died in the faith and were saved. See Luke 11, 32. That they really repented appears also from v. 10a. Those were works of true repentance. Cp. Joel 2, 12 and Is. 58, 6. 7; as also the king of Nineveh had said, Jonah 3, 8b.

e) Oh, how may we account for this astounding occurrence, that a whole big city, at least a very great number of the inhabitants of a big city, which had been steeped in heathenism for centuries, turned to God on hearing repentance preached for a few short days? Matt. 12, 41 the Savior tells us: "They repented *at the preaching of Jonas.*" The Word of God — and that is what Jonah preached in Nineveh — has the power to soften the hardest heart and to work true repentance. We have this selfsame Word of God, and we are commanded to preach it to the world to-day. The present-day world is steeped in the same sins to which the people of Nineveh were slaves: idolatry and violence toward its fellow-men. (Point out.) Let us Christians preach repentance to the world, and our preaching will bear fruit; not in the same measure always as did that of Jonah, but it will bear fruit. God Himself says so Is. 55, 10. 11.

Astounding as this occurrence was, there is something in this text that should be far more astounding to us, and that is Jonah's attitude toward this very miracle which God's grace wrought through his preaching and God's attitude toward Jonah. Let us take up the second part of our text, chap. 4.

2.

V. 1 (lit.: "It was a great evil to Jonah" that Nineveh repented and was spared). Vv. 2. 3. How strange! Was that a thing to be displeased at, a thing to move one, a prophet of God at that, to wish he were dead? Oh, the depth of iniquity of the human heart, even in a child of God! For Jonah was a child of God still; he still prayed, and the Lord did not deal severely with him, not at all. He said very mildly: v. 4. Jonah certainly thought he did; for: vv. 5. 6. ("Gourd" is a sort of wonder-tree; it grows very quickly.)

But now listen: vv. 7—9. Oh, the perversity of man's heart! How is it possible for a human being whom God has shown such exceedingly great mercy, whom He has saved from destruction with a mighty hand, and whom, in spite of His very recent gross disobedience, He has used to perform such a precious work, — how is it possible for such a man to be angry with God and to quarrel with Him? If it were not plainly stated here in the Bible, we should never believe it. — Ah, it is *our* heart that God portrays in His portrait of the heart of Jonah. The prophet Jeremiah says: chap. 17, 9. Thus God says of every human heart, of your heart and mine. How often have we cried to God in our distress and implored Him to help us; or fervently thanked Him for some recent deliverance and vowed that henceforth we would faithfully serve Him; and, lo! scarcely had the word been uttered when our old discontent and faultfindings and doubtings returned and took possession of our soul, and we wished we were dead! Surely it is not Jonah's heart merely that is shown us here, it is our very own. Jonah's case is simply cited as an example. And the picture is painted in such glaring colors in order "that we may learn to look with terror at our sins, and to regard them as great indeed, and to find joy and comfort in Him alone, and thus be saved through such faith."

These sins of Jonah were not sins of malice, but sins of weakness. So with all Christians. The spirit indeed is willing, but the flesh is weak. We often think of sins of weakness as being *weak sins,* insignificant little mistakes. But here we see that oftentimes these sins are very formidable, and if it were not for the fact that God's grace knows no bounds, not one of us would be saved.* Surely we must all live in daily repentance, and grace must be our only plea. Mark how gently God deals with His erring child, vv. 9—11. That is all. To this question Jonah makes no reply. How could he? What could he say? Luther: "Here Jonah is silenced, being convicted by his own findings. And thus it is in every case where a man undertakes to quarrel with God and to criticize His justice and His wisdom. Therefore let us rejoice in His grace, revealed to us in His holy Word. Let us praise and thank Him for that great treasure. But as for judging God, let us humbly place our finger upon our lips in this life lest we be made speechless in the world to come." Yea, let us learn from this text to look with terror at our sins and to regard them as great indeed and to find joy and comfort in Him alone and thus be saved through such faith. Let us seek and find salvation wholly and solely in the blood and death of the Son of God.   J. A. RIMBACH.

First Sunday in Lent, Invocavit.
Gen. 3, 1—15.

The first part of this Bible-passage takes us back to that blissful period in the history of our race before sin had entered the world. It is difficult for us to imagine a world without sin. We are so used to living in a sinful world, and everything in our experience is so contaminated by sin, that it is hard for us to realize what the world

---

* See an excellent paper on the Book of Jonah in *Proceedings of Michigan District*, 1910.

would be like if there were no sin. There would be no hate and no revenge; no crime and no prisons; no police and no courts; no poverty and no unemployment; no hospitals, no funerals, and no cemeteries; it would be a different world if sin and its dire consequences were absent. Sin brought about the greatest change in the history of the world. People like to study the factors in history that bring about great changes. It will therefore be interesting and instructive to study this text; for it tells about the beginning of sin in the world.

Three Important Truths Concerning Sin.

1. The Devil Tempts to Sin.   2. Man Commits Sin.
3. God Forgives Sin.

1.

The devil plays his part in sin by tempting man to sin. Created a good angel, the devil fell and was cast out of his heavenly habitation, Jude 6. He is God's enemy and plots the ruin of God's creatures. He is diabolically cunning. Note his methods in the Bible-story before us. He is a spirit, but assumes a visible form to approach man; he chooses the form of an animal, not of a common animal, but of the most subtile animal, endowed with wisdom, so that man will be more inclined to listen to the words of temptation. Note also the devil's deep guile. He knows that God had forbidden man to eat of that certain tree and that dreadful punishment was sure to come if they would disobey Him; but the devil begins to sow the seed of doubt and misbelief: Did God really say that? And did He mean just exactly that? No, you will not die, you will be like God; you will not lose by eating of the tree; on the contrary, you will gain.

Thus the devil comes to man in most alluring guise, making his wares seem attractive and desirable; he accommodates the temptation to the nature of the person tempted. If a man leans to pride, the devil will tempt him to win fame by sinful means; if he craves luxury, the devil will put sinful gain before his eyes. And what lying promises the devil makes! Eve was made to believe that she would have a great gain through sinning; and she received only a terrible loss. So the devil deceives man. He tempts a person to steal, promising riches and pleasure, and the thief receives the due punishment; he tempts another to evil lust, to drunkenness, to any sin, and promises enjoyment and happiness, and the cheated fool who listens to the false promises reaps only ruin. The devil always cheats; he promises good value and pays in base coin. See how he cheated Saul, David, Judas. Read your newspapers; they are full of accounts of people who believed the devil, committed sin, expected gain, and experienced loss. And when Judgment Day comes, the gates of hell will close upon many to whom the devil promised gain from sin and who lost their souls by the wiles of the deceiver. Surely the Bible's forceful description of the devil as a "murderer" and "devourer" (John 8, 44 and 1 Pet. 5, 8. 9) is apt, and it is the greatest wisdom to turn from temptation and to believe no lying promise of the devil.

2.

A second truth with respect to sin is that man commits sin. Looking again at our text, we find Eve listening interestedly to the words of the Tempter. She knew God's will; but she thought, What if these honeyed words of the serpent were really true? May we not try the forbidden fruit, just once? Adam and Eve had it in their power to resist the Tempter; in their breast beat no weak, sinful heart like ours; yet they listened to the Tempter and took of the fruit. And the Bible rightly puts the blame for sin on man, Rom. 5, 12.

Thus sin, beginning in Satan, crept to man; and in the succeeding generations of men on earth all were sinful; Adam begat a son in *his* likeness, Gen. 5, 3. Cf. Ps. 51, 5; Gen. 8, 21; Ps. 14, 3; Is. 64, 6. Man enters this life with original sin, and he passes through this life committing actual sins. In his unregenerate state man's condition and life are wholly sinful, and he is incapable of anything good in God's sight; regenerate man is able to avoid many of the grosser sins, but still commits sins daily through the weakness of his flesh, Phil. 3, 12; Ps. 143, 2.

And although man commits sin, he always tries to extenuate his guilt. When confronted with his misdeed by his Creator, Adam put the blame on Eve, and she blamed the serpent. King Saul blamed the people for his sin, 1 Sam. 15, 15. We hear people blame their sin on heredity, on society, on environment. While there are often contributing circumstances, man is himself responsible for the sins he commits; and he must expect punishment for his sins at the hand of a holy and just God, who is rightly offended. Punishment came to the first sinners; punishment must be expected by all sinners. The punishment is a guilty conscience, the feeling of guilt and shame, God's wrath and displeasure, temporal death, and finally eternal damnation.

3.

What a fearful prospect for the sinner! Enough to drive one to despair. But from the third truth in respect to sin we derive much comfort: God forgives sin. Let us not misunderstand: God does not condone or ignore sin. God hates sin and threatens to punish all that transgress His commandments. It is quite evident from the text that God punishes sin. The serpent is cursed, Adam and Eve are driven out of the Garden, death enters the world. God continues to punish sin: Sodom, Israel, Jerusalem, etc. But although God does not condone sin, He does forgive sin. The last verse of our text contains the first prophecy of the Redeemer, who, it was promised, would crush the Serpent's head. The trembling pair could expect nothing but condemnation for themselves and their children; now they have new hope and faith: God would forgive sin for the sake of Jesus, the promised Redeemer of the world. And that is our own comfort and assurance by faith, that God forgives our sins for the sake of Jesus Christ, 1 John 1, 7b.

Thus we have considered three important truths concerning sin. Let us guard against the devil, who tempts us to sin; let us watch our own lives lest we commit sin; let us thank God that in His mercy He forgives sin. Let us believe the precious Gospel: John 3, 16.

FREDERIC NIEDNER.

Second Sunday in Lent, Reminiscere.
Gen. 22, 1—19.

If for some reason you would wish to enumerate your possessions, beginning with the most important and valuable, I wonder what your list would look like? There are people who make such an appraisal of their possessions, perhaps at the end of a year or at another time. And in making a list of their possessions, they draw a true picture of their inner selves. If they place at the head of their list their money, securities, houses, and land, or their home, wife, and children, or their health, or their good reputation, they are revealing what possessions they value most.

Those of us who would set down as their supreme possession our Christian faith would thereby reveal their Christian character.

In order to realize more fully the value of our Christian faith, let us study this story from the life of Abraham as a lesson concerning —

Faith, Our Supreme Possession.

1. It Overcomes All Doubt.
2. It Enables Us to Give Obedience to God.
3. It is Blessed by the Abundant Grace of God.

1.

Let us first note how faith enabled Abraham to overcome all doubt. Abraham was a man of God and walked before Him. All his ways were directed by God. At God's command he left his father's house and his country to dwell in another land. Because the king of Egypt took away Abraham's wife, God plagued the Egyptians; when Abraham was childless, God promised him a son; a great nation should come from him; the Redeemer should be of his seed; God gave him great riches; angels visited his home. (See Gen. 12, 13, 15, 18.) Abraham enjoyed God's favor to a very high degree. He worshiped his Lord and served Him. He was a true believer in the promised Messiah (John 8, 56) and had peace with God.

And now into this serenity came the crushing command of God, v. 2: Slay thy son, thine only son, whom thou lovest, and burn him as a sacrifice to Me, thy loving God! Can you picture the heart of Abraham when he heard this command? Do you not think that doubt and despair might have filled his heart? He might have thought: And this is a God of love and mercy? What a fool I have been to trust in Him! All that I believed is false. From now on I am through with God and prayers and trust! Abraham *might* have thought thus, but he did not do so. No word of doubt comes from his lips. His faith enabled him to overcome all doubt.

Are we not also sometimes assailed by doubt and despair? We have faith in God; we believe that He loves us. But then we are sorely tried; perhaps we are stricken with illness; unfortunate circumstances deprive us of our possessions, and we get into dire straits; perhaps death knocks at our door and takes away a beloved child, husband, or wife. Then the whisperings of doubt may come: Does God really care? Is He a God of love and mercy? God has forsaken me. I am done with the church, prayer, Communion, service. I will no longer believe.

Such thoughts may assail a Christian; but his faith will overcome them. Faith will say: God has shown me such great love; above all He has sent Jesus into the world for me; I can still believe that He loves me and that He cares, Rom. 8, 32. With such a faith Abraham overcame his doubts; and with our faith we can overcome doubt and despair, 1 John 5, 4. We see clearly that faith is our supreme possession.

2.

The second reason why we call faith our supreme possession is that it enables us to give obedience to God. What a task Abraham had! Surely it was hard for him to obey God. He might have said: That is murder; I cannot and will not do it. Take all my silver and gold; take a thousand sheep of my flocks; but I will not give my son. I cannot break the heart of Sarah, the lad's mother. And, Lord, how canst Thou ever make good Thy promises of the Redeemer?

So Abraham might have said, but he did not say it. He rose up early to obey lest his resolution waver. He took wood and fire and a knife. He might purposely have left these at home and then found it impossible to sacrifice his son.

You may say it took great will-power to do this. I say that it took more than will-power; *it took faith.* Abraham believed that God would make His promise good in some way, Heb. 11, 19. He believed that he should obey God's command and not reason out the probable results.

Such is the power of faith. We know the commandments. But how hard it often is for us to obey! How hard to keep our hearts from loving, and trusting in, the things of this world! How hard for you children and young people to obey your parents in all things! How hard for you to remain pure in body and mind! But your faith will enable you to obey God. You will think of God's love and of the atoning work of your Savior, and you will say: All this He did for me, — I shall live my life for Him, 2 Cor. 5, 15. — Once more we learn that faith is our supreme possession.

3.

A final reason: Faith is blessed by the abundant grace of God. Note the outcome of the story. When Abraham's obedience was proved, God halted his actions; a ram took the boy's place; and God gave Abraham the wonderful promise: vv. 16—18. Abraham realized again the love that God bore to him, and he heard again the wonderful promise of the Redeemer.

And our own faith will thus be rewarded: we shall see the fulfilment of every promise of God and finally the fulfilment of His gracious promise that whosoever believes in Jesus shall be saved.

Surely we see now that faith is our supreme possession. Let us keep our faith, strengthen it through Word and Sacrament, and pray that we may never lose it; for our faith is indeed our supreme possession.   FREDERIC NIEDNER.

Third Sunday in Lent, Oculi.

Ps. 25.

David, the most famous king of Israel, the leader and champion of the Lord's Church and people, it is who wrote the words of our text, the Twenty-fifth Psalm. Since the day the prophet Samuel had anointed him king of Israel, the Spirit of the Lord was upon him. He had a marked talent for poetry, music, and song, and the Holy Spirit qualified, animated, inspired, and taught him to write psalms, spiritual songs, to be used at public worship.

The history of David's life is very interesting — shepherd, musician, champion, courtier, poet, warrior, king. His experiences therefore were manifold, and they are frequently reflected in his psalms, which reveal him to us wrestling with difficulties, distresses, doubts, and fears, out of which he emerged again and again by grasping, and clinging to, the gracious promises of the Lord. For this reason these psalms are a priceless treasure to the afflicted and tried in all ages. Thus this Twenty-fifth Psalm is a prayer the key-note of which we find in the words, "O Lord, I trust in Thee; I wait on Thee."

David's Prayer: "O Lord, I Trust in Thee; I Wait on Thee."
This is —

1. *An Avowal of His Utter Dependence upon God;*
2. *An Expression of His Implicit Trust in God's Gracious Promises.*

1.

A) The prayer of David: "I trust in Thee" (vv. 2 a. 20 b); "I wait on Thee" (vv. 5 b. 21 b), is an avowal of his utter dependence upon God.

a) Vv. 4. 5. He expresses dependence upon God for *knowledge, counsel, and guidance.* Is it not strange that David acknowledges dependence upon God for knowledge, counsel, and guidance? Was he not a man of intelligence, of knowledge, of keen understanding? Was he not a wise judge with varied experience? Was he not a prophet of the Lord Jehovah and the author of many psalms? Do not his psalms show his clear knowledge of God, His majesty, providence, government, etc.; his knowledge of the person, work, struggles, victories, blessings, etc., of the Messiah; of the nature and purpose of His kingdom? Do not his psalms prove his clear understanding of God's ways and paths, and do they not offer sound counsel, etc.? No one in Israel had a better knowledge and understanding than David, and yet, he does not imagine that his knowledge and understanding were complete or that his psalms were the product of his own mind; but candidly he avows his dependence upon God's teaching for knowledge and guidance. He prays that the Lord would preserve and increase in him an ever better understanding of His truth and His ways, so that His truth would not merely convince his mind, but live in his heart, rule and govern his life, direct his plans and steps, that it be the foundation of his faith and hope and the unfailing counselor and guide in his life; that the Lord's truth be a lamp unto his feet and a light unto his path, the path of cheerful obedience, which is a path of peace, a path of light, a path on which the beams of divine favor are ever poured in living luster. Prov. 4, 18.

b) Vv. 7. 11. 18 b. David expresses his dependence upon God *for the pardon of his sins,* v. 17: his natural depravity; v. 7: the sins of his youth; v. 18 b: all sins of his life. He considers his sins a very real and a serious matter. His sins, even the sins of his youth (particularly his grievous fall), filled him with humiliation and sorrow; they were ever before him, haunting him, troubling his heart and mind, and wounding his spirit. His sins were his heaviest burden, he could not forget them, so that in the midst of his recital of the Lord's gracious promises he interrupts himself by crying out: "O Lord, pardon mine iniquity, for it is great." — But why did David permit his sins to trouble him? Was he not a man of piety? Had he not done great things for the Lord's Church and people? Had not the Lord called him "a man after His own heart" and selected him to be one of the fathers of the Messiah? True. But David knew that all this could not atone for his guilt. He realized the exceeding guilt of sin; he knew that he had sinned against God, his heavenly Father, etc., had offended Him and provoked Him, etc. In his helplessness, etc., he avowed his utter dependence upon God for the forgiveness of his sins.

c) Vv. 2. 19. Here David avows his dependence upon God *for the deliverance from his enemies,* afflictions, distresses, etc. Is it not strange that David should depend upon God for the deliverance from his enemies? Was not David a man of rugged vitality, of dauntless courage, of great resourcefulness? Had he not as a youth faced a bear and a lion and slain them single-handed? Had he not slain Goliath? As king of Israel, was he not the brave and brilliant chief of a formidable, undefeated army, who had defeated and subdued the nations round about? Why did he not employ his power to destroy and crush his enemies who were defaming and slandering him, scheming and plotting against him to bring about his downfall and ruin? Why did he endure their treachery, hatred, and cruelty, etc.? Because he feared God, who had said: "Vengeance is Mine; I will repay," Deut. 32, 35, and because he considered what he suffered from them a well-deserved chastisement for his sins. He did not resort to revenge, but was meek and forgiving toward his enemies, 1 Sam. 24, 10 ff.; 2 Sam. 26. Yea, he besought God to keep him in uprightness and integrity, v. 21, that he might not give his enemies any provocation, but fear the Lord, walk in His ways, and in all things retain a clear conscience. Depending upon the Lord, he prayed: vv. 2. 19. And since his enemies were at the same time the enemies of the Lord's Israel and Church, whose leader and most prominent member he was, so that Israel's welfare and peace was intimately connected with that of his own, he added: "Redeem Israel, O God, out of all his troubles," v. 22.

B) Do all people follow the example of David? Do they lift up their soul to the Lord, trust in Him, wait on Him, avow their utter dependence upon Him, etc.?

a) Can it be possible that any person with the least spark of intelligence should not notice and feel his dependence upon God? But, alas! most people in their spiritual blindness, contemptible self-importance, and self-sufficiency do not recognize the need that God teach them His truth and His ways, pardon their sins, and deliver them from their enemies, sorrows, etc. The truth that they are dependent upon God for every real good, necessary for the welfare of body and soul, is offensive to their unconverted nature. Their natural pride revolts against it, and they consider it humiliating and debasing to wait on God in all conditions, circumstances, and relations of life.

1) They do not wish that God should teach them His truth and paths. They do not want to be dependent on God for *knowledge, counsel,* and *guidance.* Not to speak of those outside of the Church, are there not multitudes of professing Christians who do not want to recognize the Bible as the absolute authority in all matters of doctrine and faith and the infallible and all-sufficient guide on the path of life? Are there not entire church-bodies that claim to have the right in matters of doctrine to follow their own reason or their own convenience? They say there are things in the Bible which we may accept or reject. Is not that one of the saddest features in many of present-day church-bodies, that they boast possession of the Bible while the authority of the Bible is boldly set aside? Is it not a very popular notion that it is of little consequence what people believe, provided they are moral, honest, charitable, etc.? All this sounds plausible enough; but what will it lead to? To get rid of God's teaching, rid of the Bible, rid of Christ, rid of God. They do not want God to teach them His truth and ways. But if the Holy Ghost does not make us know, does not give us the certainty, that the Bible is the divine truth, nothing and nobody can. If God does not teach us His ways and paths, we shall choose the wrong paths, which end in darkness, misery, and destruction.

2) Moreover, how many are there in Christendom who do not realize their dependence upon God for the *pardon* of their sin! Only too many know nothing of their natural depravity; the sins of their youth they consider a laughing matter and their countless other sins trifles, mere human foibles and shortcomings. They do not see the need of repentance and pardon. Others imagine their sins will be blotted out by forgetting about them, etc. Many others trust to their civic righteousness, etc., to get forgiveness for them, to square their guilt. They do not pray: vv. 7. 11. 18.

3) Finally, how many are there who do not notice their dependence upon God for deliverance and relief from enemies, afflictions, etc.! They depend on their own efforts, apart from God, human agencies, etc. They resort to revenge, force, violence, treachery, etc., to subdue and ruin their enemies, etc. In afflictions, sickness, bereavements, they depend upon their friends, etc., or turn to fatalism, etc., v. 22. The devil, the world, and all false churches are enemies of the Lord's true Church. John 15, 18—20. Etc.

b) How is it with us? Do we unreservedly acknowledge our dependence upon God for, etc.? Do we lift up our soul to God and pray: "O Lord, I trust in Thee; I wait on Thee"?

2.

A) David's plea: "O Lord, I trust in Thee; I wait on Thee," is, furthermore, an expression of implicit trust in the gracious promises of God. If David had not known these promises, or if God had not given such promises, it certainly would have been presumptuous for David to expect knowledge, guidance, pardon, and deliverance from God. What did David do? He recites God's promises, vv. 6—15. He reminds the Lord of His promises. David did not think that God's precious promises were not meant for him or that they are not dependable and trustworthy. On the contrary, he made the proper use of them by trusting in them with implicit confidence.

a) Relying on God's promises, he prays for *knowledge,* etc., and feels assured that this will not be in vain, vv. 8. 9. 12. Ps. 32, 8: "I will instruct," etc.

b) Trusting in the Lord's promises, David prayed for *pardon* and forgiveness and felt assured that his trust in God would not meet with disappointment, but that the Lord would wipe out the sins of his youth and his transgressions, pardon his great iniquity, and forgive his sins, vv. 7. 11. 18. David says *"for Thy name's sake";* that means that God had promised that the Messiah would make atonement and complete satisfaction for all sins and that God would for the Messiah's sake forgive the sins of all those who repent and cling to the Messiah as their only Savior. To them that fear the Lord, v. 14, to the penitent, He will reveal and make clear the *secret,* the secret of the Gospel, the secret of the doctrine of justification by grace, through faith. He will show them the covenant of His grace, make them partakers of Christ's redemption through faith, and thus imprint upon, and write into, their hearts His covenant, and let them experience the power of it. John 7, 17: "If any man will do His will," etc.

c) Also in his trust in, and dependence upon, the Lord for *deliverance* from the cruelty and hatred of his enemies, from afflictions, distresses, etc., David relied confidently upon the Lord's promises, vv. 13. 15.

B) Did David's trust in the Lord's promises meet with disappointment? Certainly not. The promises of God are certain of fulfilment. Is there anything more certain than a promise of God? Is. 54, 10; 55, 3; Matt. 24, 35. The Lord heard David's prayer and gave him knowledge, guidance, pardon, deliverance; He kept him in His Word and faith unto his end, etc., Ps. 18, 18; 32, 5. 10; 103, 2—6. The Lord cannot and will not change or repudiate any of His promises, Ps. 33, 4; Num. 23, 19. *For His name's sake* and His truth's sake He will not go back on any of His promises, etc., and will not put to shame those who trust in them.

C) Oh, let us follow David's example! Let us lift up our soul to the Lord of our salvation and beseech Him —

a) To grant us *knowledge* and understanding of His Word and will and to *guide* us in His ways, Jas. 1, 5. The Lord is willing and ready to give us true knowledge and guidance. The question is, Are we ready to receive it? David says, v. 9: "The *meek* will He guide in judgment," etc. Are we truly meek? Are we ready humbly to accept God's teaching and cheerfully to follow His guidance? Are we reading and hearing the Word of God in uprightness of mind and honesty of purpose? If so, the Lord will surely, etc. Col. 1, 10. 11.

b) Relying on God's gracious promises, let us pray Him for forgiveness of all our sins. David relied on the promises of God that He would forgive sins for Christ's sake, whose coming was still *in the future;* how much more willing and ready should *we* be to rely on His promises, knowing that Christ has completely finished His work of redemption by His atoning death and sealed it with His glorious resurrection! We have many more promises for pardon than David, 1 John 2, 12; Eph. 1, 7; etc.

c) Relying upon the Lord's gracious promises, let us pray Him for deliverance from afflictions, distresses, etc., and from every evil, Is. 41, 10 ff.; Ps. 91, 9—16; etc. Promises respecting protection of the Church and deliverance out of all her troubles, trials, etc., Ps. 46; 2, 4. 5; Matt. 16, 18. Let us rely on the Lord's gracious promises with childlike confidence, and He will not let us be ashamed, etc. The merciful and faithful God grant, etc.   FRED EVERS.

Fourth Sunday in Lent, Laetare.
Deut. 7, 6—11.

The Bible teaches God's children to be humble and to think very little of themselves. We find such statements as these: Matt. 20, 26. 27; 23, 12; Phil. 2, 3; Jas. 4, 6. We need to keep all this in mind in order that we may remain in right relation with God at all times and inherit the blessings of His kingdom hereafter.

But quite as often the Bible speaks of God's children in very complimentary terms, ascribes to them a unique distinction, promises them a glorious future, and thus causes them to think highly of themselves. This, too, is important and therefore worthy of earnest consideration. The text offers a striking instance.

God's Children a Peculiar Race.

1. They Prove that They Are Such;
2. They Show What should Follow.

1.

Background and connection. — The children of Israel, after their forty years of sojourning in the wilderness, had at last arrived on the borders of the Promised Land. The serious business of conquering, and taking possession of, their prospective homeland was before them. But previous to organizing the people for the campaign of conquest, Moses considers it important to put them through

a final course of instruction and inspiration in order to deepen their
spiritual life and to confirm them in the way of godliness. He introduces his series of discourses, as we read in the chapters preceding our text, with a brief, but gripping survey of the long and
arduous journey through the wilderness. He then proceeds to re-
state for the benefit of the new generation the laws and ordinances
given on Mount Sinai forty years previously. He also adds such
statutes and commandments as will be required to govern their
future life in the land of Canaan and will insure for them continued
divine favors and blessings. Among these statutes is the one given
in the verses preceding our text, vv. 2. 3. 5.

And now the text, its facts and teachings, v. 6. There is
a striking emphasis on the fact that Israel is a peculiar people, chosen
of God, "holy," cleansed, purified, accepted, segregated as in a class
by itself. A repetition of statements made on previous occasions,
Ex. 19, 5. 6; Lev. 26, 12. Cp. also Deut. 4, 6—8.

This distinction was Israel's not because of personal merit, moral
excellence, national superiority. How wayward, disobedient, and
stubborn they had been and still were! Deut. 9, 6. 13. 24. God had
made the choice of His own free will, being moved only by His grace
and mercy, and in faithfulness to the promises given to the fathers,
vv. 6—8. Cp. Is. 41, 8; Ps. 135, 4; Deut. 10, 15; 14, 2; Luke 1,
70—73.

The Lord's inward resolve had led to visible action. Having in
His mind lovingly singled out for Himself a special people, God had
proceeded to gather and segregate them. The process of separation
had been begun in the case of Abraham, Gen. 12, 1. 2. 4. In Egypt,
Israel had lived in a separate province. Then came the great delivery
and the exodus. Note that the Israelites were set apart not only
inwardly, spiritually, but also locally, physically, v. 8 b. Note also
that mere numbers meant nothing to God in the process of selection
and segregation, v. 7 b.

We bring the lessons of the story up to date. — In general, Israel
a type of God's people in every nation and age. Its history illustrates the career of the Church of Jesus Christ. God's ways with
the Israelites and their attitude and behavior toward Him reflect the
mutual relations of the Lord and His people in all generations. Hence
the lessons of the text are timely and apply to-day. Rom. 2, 28. 29;
9, 6—8; 15, 4; 1 Cor. 10, 11.

God's real children are those who by faith have accepted the redemption perfected by Jesus Christ and offered in the Gospel, John
1, 12. 13; Rom. 8, 14. 16; Gal. 3, 26. Like Israel of old they have been
delivered out of bondage and are now on the way to the eternal land
of promise, Col. 1, 12—14; Heb. 13, 14. Blessed are all they who

are counted among God's people. Are you among them? Make sure to-day.

The children of God are *a peculiar race,* newly born, distinctive in character, of superior standing, separated from the world, walking their own way, prepared for a signal glory, 1 Cor. 6, 11; Eph. 2, 19. 22; John 15, 19; Jas. 1, 18; 2 Pet. 2, 9. Their apparent lowliness, humility, weakness, are merely the elements of a present disguise, 1 John 3, 1. 2, inevitable concomitants of their wilderness journey. Their true character, already apparent to God and His angels, will be manifest to all eyes when the Lord will come to lead His people to the land of eternal glory.

All this is *not the achievement of human endeavor,* nor is it a reward of merit or service. Among individuals and nations on earth there are those who in temporal affairs rise to the level of a unique excellence and distinctiveness through sheer power of will, effort, efficiency, and accomplishment. But no one has ever become one of God's peculiar people in that way, for the simple reason that mankind is by nature under the curse and every man's just desert is not commendation, but condemnation, not distinction, but extinction, Ps. 130, 3; 143, 2; Is. 64, 6. It is God's free grace alone that redeems, elects, calls, converts, preserves, and glorifies human souls and gathers them into the spiritual fellowship of God's peculiar people, John 15, 16; 2 Cor. 3, 5; Eph. 2, 8. 9; 2 Tim. 1, 9.

Let it be borne in mind that number and size play no part in the establishment and extension of God's kingdom here on earth. While God "will have all men to be saved" and His wish is that His "house may be filled," it is also a divinely revealed fact that comparatively few will be saved, which is due to man's wilful unbelief. No one must be disturbed by the fact that God's people while in this world will always be "a poor small crew."

Are you a member of God's holy nation? If not, you are still an alien. Pitiable state! Do you want to continue in it and take the inevitable consequences? God is calling, inviting, urging you to-day, Is. 55, 1—3; 2 Cor. 6, 17. And if to-day you are privileged to count yourself as one of God's peculiar people, do not glorify yourself, but praise the grace of God, which has made you what you are and given you what you have, 1 Cor. 15, 10; 2 Cor. 3, 5.

2.

What, now, should follow?

It is important that those who have become God's peculiar people learn to keep themselves as such.

Moses, in the text before us, does not merely wish to point out a gratifying fact, an existing happy condition; he is especially interested in inducing His people to hold fast what is already theirs.

We read: vv. 6. 9—11. Being a special people, the Israelites were to keep themselves as such and to become confirmed in their unique relation to God and in their loyalty to Him. This would imply conscientious separation from those who lived away from God. It is to this that the "for" of v. 6 refers. Going back, we read: vv. 2—5. Other references: Ex. 34, 12—16; Judg. 2, 2; 1 Kings 11, 2. It would also imply that the people through diligent teaching, such as is given by Moses in our text, be kept in constant remembrance of their status before God and of His relation to them, v. 9 a, and that, in addition, they walk in His ways and serve Him faithfully all their days, v. 11. If these things were lost sight of, a wayward, unfruitful, rebellious Israel would soon learn to its bitter cost that God will not permit Himself to be mocked, that His justice will avenge the spurning of His love, and that then every appeal to a privilege once enjoyed will avail nothing, v. 10; Matt. 3, 9; John 8, 33. 39. 40. 44; Rom. 9, 7; Gal. 3, 7. It soon becomes apparent, and later history confirms it, that the Israelites remained God's peculiar people as long as they were loyal to the covenant He had made with them, but lost their standing with Him and among the nations on earth whenever they became indifferent and disobedient.

These lessons are timely and necessary to-day. The children of God dare never forget what a precious privilege is theirs to be God's peculiar people, 1 John 3, 1. It is indeed of vital importance that they become confirmed in the keeping of what they have. Rom. 11, 17—22; Phil. 2, 12; Rev. 3, 11. What does this imply, and why is it necessary?

It implies that Christians be not identified with unbelievers, that the disciples of truth must have no fraternal communion with the children of error. This is supported clearly and emphatically by passages such as Rom. 12, 2; 2 Cor. 6, 14—18; Rom. 16, 17; 2 Tim. 3, 5. All this applies not only to general intimate companionship with the world and to membership in erroristic churches, but also to identification with lodges and other antichristian organizations and to so-called mixed marriages. If separation was important in the days of Israel, why should it be less important to-day? True, the world condemns such a policy; even many so-called Christians strongly censure it. But this, instead of causing compromise or surrender, must rather induce God's peculiar people to become the more loyal and devoted to their Lord and His cause and the more single-hearted and unyielding in their policy of separation. It is far better to bear the world's ostracism for a time than be eternally disowned by God Himself, Matt. 10, 28.

In order that the children of God may deepen their knowledge and become confirmed in the practise of these things, there must be constant teaching and preaching of divine truth. Not only must every new generation be taught to "observe all things," but those, too, who have once been duly taught must be kept in constant remembrance of the things they have learned in order that they may at all times "earnestly contend for the faith which was once delivered unto the saints," Jude 3. It should go without saying that this must include not only adults, but especially also the little ones; for: Prov. 22, 6. Cp. also Deut. 6, 6. 7; Eph. 6, 4.

Then, too, God's children will give evidence of their status as a special people by walking in God's way and serving their Lord. This will include, in general, careful avoidance of those things that are contrary to the divine will and incompatible with the Christian profession as well as diligent participation in worship, zealous activity in church-work and charitable endeavors, liberal giving, and other forms of the godly life, Matt. 5, 13—16; 1 Pet. 2, 11. 12; Ps. 1. In particular it includes the establishment and extension of God's kingdom among men. It is characteristic of God's peculiar people to be vitally interested in the spiritual welfare of others and to desire the privileges they enjoy for all those who do not yet possess them, John 1, 35—46. Church exclusiveness and religious snobbery are foreign to the character and life of God's spiritual Israel. The more truly "peculiar" God's children are, the more thoroughly and universally inclusive they will be, Acts 10, 28. 34. 35.

And, finally, the reason why all we have heard should be conscientiously heeded is this, that God will not permit us to keep what we do not appreciate, make use of, and share with others. The privilege of being God's peculiar people can be lost; the Jews lost it. Let us be warned; for: Matt. 25, 24—30; Heb. 6, 4—8; 2 Pet. 2. 20. 21.

God's peculiar people, a blessed race! Happy here, to be glorified hereafter. Praise the undeserved mercy of God if you are counted among them. Hold your privilege in high esteem; "walk as the children of light"; "be ye separate"; help to win others. And may He who has begun the good work in you perform it unto the day of Jesus Christ! K. KRETZSCHMAR.

Fifth Sunday in Lent, Invocavit.
Gen. 14, 8—20.

"First in war, first in peace, first in the hearts of his countrymen," that was the rare distinction to which the first President of our country attained. We highly honor the memory of this great man, and his name is famous far beyond the boundaries of our country.

And yet, if we may attempt a comparison at all, those words of high praise might have been applied to Abram in our text in a much higher degree. What a man of peace! See chap. 13, 8. 9. And yet, when the emergency arises, he is also ready to strike a decisive blow of war with such undaunted courage that it might have put the greater war heroes in the shade, vv. 13—16. Nor was he prompted by avarice or ambition, but solely by the principle of charity, *viz.*, to help his brother and neighbor in need. "Never was a military expedition undertaken, prosecuted, and finished more honorably than this of Abram's." No wonder that even the envious king of Sodom went forth to pay him his respect. But we must remember that Abram besides and above all was a special favorite of God.

Could there have been a more distinguished and a more respectable person in all the land of Canaan than Abram? And yet there evidently was. Melchizedek appears on the scene, who from what we know from our text and from Scripture otherwise outranks Abram. This Melchizedek is so honorable because he was a type of the most honorable person that ever appeared on earth, our Lord Jesus Christ. Let us now under the guidance of the Holy Spirit observe: —

Melchizedek a Beautiful Type of Jesus Christ, Our Savior.

We note,

> 1. *His Mysterious Person,*   2. *His Exalted Office.*

1.

When Abram with his little band of servants and allies, after vanquishing the victorious armies of four kings and taking heavy spoils, descended on his return into the valley of Shaveh, a royal reception was awaiting him. The king of Sodom came out to meet him. But this royal greatness did not seem to mean so much to Abram; it was another king, Melchizedek, upon whom Abram evidently looked as a person deserving of high respect. That this Melchizedek typifies the mysterious greatness of the person of Jesus Christ appears —

a) From what our text reports about the extraordinary person of Melchizedek. Abram is great, but he is blessed by Melchizedek, v. 19. "And without contradiction the less is blessed of the better," Heb. 7, 7. Again, Abram paid tithes to Melchizedek, v. 20. The Levitical priesthood, descended from Abram, received tithes from Israel. But this priesthood, being yet in the loins of Abram, itself paid tithes to Melchizedek in Abram, Heb. 7, 9. 10. What a dignity, then, must rest on this Melchizedek! Melchizedek, however, is but a type of Christ, Ps. 110, 4; Heb. 7. Abram is great, but Melchizedek is greater. How great is, then, the person of Christ, of whom Melchizedek is but a type and a shadow! This becomes evident especially —

b) From a circumstance which our text passes over in silence, but which later holy writers have interpreted. Melchizedek suddenly appears in the history of Abram, and just as suddenly he vanishes again. Though he is such an extraordinary person that even Abram pays him homage and subjection, yet Scripture remains silent about his genealogy.

For ages people have asked, Who is this Melchizedek? Some, among them even Luther, have thought him to have been Shem, who in patriarchal fashion may have presided over the people of God in those days as king and priest. As far as time is concerned, this is well possible; for Shem outlived Abram by thirty-five years. But why should his name here be changed? And how shall we explain his being a king in Canaan at this time? Others have held that this Melchizedek was Jesus Christ Himself, who appeared to Abram here in an assumed human form, similarly as He appeared to him later as the Angel of the Lord. But while this opinion may seem to have some support in Scripture, it does not agree with Heb. 7, 3: "made like unto the Son of God." (*Simile non est idem.*) Then Christ would have been a type of Himself, which is absurd. Nor does David in Ps. 110, 4 declare that the Messiah is Melchizedek, but a priest after the order of Melchizedek. There are still other conjectures uttered about the person of Melchizedek, but they have even less ground than those just mentioned.

Evidently God in His Word left the person of Melchizedek shrouded in mystery for a definite purpose, *viz.,* that he might all the more strikingly be a type of Jesus Christ, whose generation none can declare. Thus Scripture remains silent about Melchizedek's father and mother in order that he might fittingly foreshadow Christ, who according to His human nature, being born of a pure virgin, Luke 1, 34, was without father and according to His divine nature, being born from the Father from eternity, John 1, 14, was without mother, Heb. 7, 3. Scripture mentions nothing about the commencement or the termination of Melchizedek's office that he might all the better prefigure Him who has no beginning and no end, the eternal Christ, Ps. 110, 4; Heb. 13, 8; 1 Tim. 3, 16 a. There is nothing said about the descending of Melchizedek's priesthood to him from another nor from him to another, which is to indicate that Christ has neither predecessor nor successor, being made higher than the heavens, Heb. 7, 26.

What a beautiful type of Christ is Melchizedek! Here the wonderful person of our Savior, in whom singularly the human and the divine nature are mysteriously united, is prefigured in the mysterious person of Melchizedek. How wonderful must be our Savior to project His shadow so far ahead! How glorious — He towers above the greatest of the great of God's people! Such a Savior is surely fitted for the highest office.

2.

Melchizedek appears at once as a servant of the most high God in a particular sense, vv. 18—20, and so is a beautiful type of Christ also in view of His exalted office.

a) He is not here expressly called a prophet, but he performs prophetic functions. He solemnly declares the most high God the Possessor of heaven and earth, thus proclaiming the sovereign power of the Creator. In saying, "Blessed be Abram of the most high God," he no doubt also made a reference to the promised Seed with which God would bless Abram. And in his publicly praising God for the victory granted Abram over his enemies we may even see an allusion to the work of the Spirit. — So Jesus Christ, the Only-begotten, out of the bosom of the Father, has declared the true God unto men, John 1, 18. In making Himself known as the Son of God and the Savior of the world, He has revealed to men that hidden knowledge of God by which alone man can be saved, John 17, 3; 14, 6. The entire work of Christ had but this purpose, to make known the glory of God, John 17, 4 ff.

b) Melchizedek is expressly called a priest of the most high God, v. 18. A priest's office had to do with the offering of gifts and sacrifices for sins, Heb. 5, 1. No offering is mentioned here of Melchizedek (for evidently he brought forth bread and wine as a refreshment for Abram and not as an offering to God); but no doubt, being called a priest, he did what the office required, *viz.,* brought sacrifices to reconcile God to sinners. And his "Blessed be Abram of . . . God" involved prayer and intercession. — So Christ is our true High Priest, Ps. 110, 4; Heb. 7, 26. 27; 9, 11—15. Christ offered Himself up for our sins once for all times, Heb. 10, 14. 18; 1 Pet. 2, 24; Rev. 5, 9. On Good Friday we see this great High Priest bringing the supreme sacrifice on the altar of the cross, entering by His own blood into the Holy Place of heaven, obtaining an eternal redemption for us, Heb. 9, 12. All the offerings of the Levitical priesthood and even that of Melchizedek received their power and value from this perfect sacrifice. While Christ sojourned upon earth, He repeatedly interceded for men, Luke 23, 34; John 17, etc. Now that He is at the right hand of God, He still intercedes for us with His heavenly Father, 1 John 2, 1. 2.

Abram was a priest, and yet he and in him all the sons of Levi and Aaron submit to the preeminence of Melchizedek's priesthood. Therefore Christ, the antitype of Melchizedek, must have the most exalted priesthood.

c) Melchizedek was a king, v. 18. So is Jesus Christ, Ps. 2, 2. 7. And He is the King of kings, Lord of lords, 1 Tim. 6, 15, King over all, Ps. 103, 19, and He rules forever, Ps. 145, 13. Melchizedek signifies king of righteousness. In this he is a beautiful type of our divine King, who is declared "the Lord Our Righteousness," Jer. 23, 6. Not only has He a right to bear this title, not only is He righteous in His judgments, but He has also wrought for us perfect righteousness through His active and passive obedience, Rom. 3, 25. The Gospel is His royal manifesto, proclaiming and offering this righteousness to all His subjects, Rom. 1, 17; 2 Cor. 5, 19. As Melchizedek was the king of Salem, which denotes peace, so Jesus Christ is the Prince of Peace, Is. 9, 6. All that accept the righteousness which He offers in the Gospel have peace with God, Rom. 5, 1; true peace in the world, John 14, 27; comfort in affliction, Phil. 4, 7; finally the peace of eternal rest, Heb. 4, 9. His kingdom of peace includes all that hear His voice, John 18, 37. While He rules all things for the best of His kingdom, the Church, by His mighty power, His own people will be guided by His gentle voice, John 10, 27. 28. These He finally translates into His Kingdom of Glory, 2 Tim. 4, 18.

What a beautiful type of our Lord Jesus Christ is Melchizedek, also in respect to His exalted office! Abram, also a servant of the most high God, bows to Melchizedek's exalted office. How excellent, then, must be the office of Christ, of whom Melchizedek is but a type! As Abram paid tithes of his spoils to Melchizedek, so let us pay Christ the tithes of a humble, submissive, obedient faith and thus avail ourselves of the benefits of His exalted office.   H. W. DEGNER.

Palm Sunday.
Psalm 8.

(NOTE. — The best commentary on Ps. 8 is the New Testament; without it much would remain obscure. But in the light of such references as Heb. 2, 6—9. 14. 15. 17. 18; 1 Cor. 15, 27; Matt. 21, 16 we discover it to be a beautiful Messianic psalm, glorifying the Son of Man, Jesus Christ, who through humiliation and exaltation became the Savior of fallen man. The theme of this psalm therefore is not so much the glory of the Creator as that of the Redeemer.)

"The heavens declare the glory of God, and the firmament showeth His handiwork." With radiant clearness and brightness the glory of God is written upon the broad expanse of the sky. We also find many things reflecting the glory of God as we look to the earth at our feet. But there we also see everywhere the ugly traces of sin: tares among the wheat, sun-parched fields, worm-eaten apples, death and decay. However, if we look upwards, how imposing the vast azure canopy of heaven! How wonderful the brilliant luminaries in the distance! How beautiful even the shading clouds, tinted and gilded by the glistening rays of the setting sun! Nothing mars the beauty of the glory of God as we look heavenward. And therefore our text declares that the Lord has set His glory above the heavens, v. 1 b.

And yet, this point our psalm would bring out by way of contrast. God has revealed His glory in an even higher degree upon earth, among sinful men. This glory, the glory of the Redeemer, indeed is not so readily noticed as that which is written upon the heavens, the glory of the Creator. In fact, it is not visible at all to our human gaze. But God's Word, especially the words of our text, reveals to us this unrivaled glory. In pointing this out to us, our text comes forth as a mighty appeal to all the people of God: —

Extol the Lord for the Excellency of His Name in All the Earth as Your Redeemer!

1. Extol Him for What He has Done for You.
2. Extol Him for What He would Do by You.

1.

A) In the beginning God laid His glory upon man as upon no other creature upon earth; for He created him in His own image and made him lord over all things on earth, Gen. 1, 26—28. "The enemy and the avenger," v. 2b, of God, seeking revenge for being reserved in everlasting chains under darkness unto the Judgment of the great day, Jude 6, turned upon man, tempted him to sin, and so sought to destroy the glory which God had laid upon the crowning work of His creation. And man suffered himself to be misled and so to be deprived of the divine image, Gen. 5, 3; Col. 3, 10; Eph. 4, 24, including his honor, glory, and dominion. Man now even had become God's enemy, Gen. 6, 3. 12; Rom. 8, 7, a child and servant of the devil, 1 John 3, 8, and subject to damnation, Gen. 2, 17; Eph. 2, 3. Who could care any longer for a creature that had so shamefully forfeited its marvelous prerogatives as man had done? V. 4.

B) Wonder of wonders! The Lord was yet mindful of man and visited him in His grace, v. 4. By the redemption of the entire lost and condemned mankind the Lord revealed such an excellent name on earth that even the angels desire to look into this mystery of divine love, 1 Pet. 1, 12.

a) The Lord became incarnate, the Son of Man. Cp. vv. 4. 5 with Heb. 2, 6—9, also with Matt. 21, 16; 18, 11. What an honor for us that the Lord assumes our nature!

b) The incarnate Lord humiliated Himself to the deepest depths of misery and digrace, v. 5a. (We follow Calov, Stoeckhardt, and others in translating: "Thou hast for a season let Him fall short of God," *i. e.,* "of the intercourse and presence of the world-ruling Deity in His glory, which the angels, as the inhabitants of heaven, always enjoy.") This is manifest in those five stages which our Second Article enumerates, but is particularly pronounced in His God-forsakenness, Matt. 27, 46, and ignominious death on the cross, Phil. 2,

5—8. Cf. Heb. 2, 9, where evidently "made a little lower than the angels" (the inaccurate LXX rendering of Psalm 8, 5 a) is explained by "the suffering of death."

c) After His deep humiliation the Son of Man was exalted, vv. 5 b. 6, being crowned with glory and honor, etc., 1 Cor. 15, 27. His exaltation followed upon His humiliation in accordance with the eternal counsel of God revealed in such prophecies as Ps. 8, Is. 53, etc., which teach that Christ through suffering must enter into His glory, Luke 24, 26.

d) This incarnate Lord, the Son of Man, was all men's Substitute. "That He by the grace of God should taste death for every man," Heb. 2, 9 b. The Son of Man, Jesus Christ, has fulfilled the Law for every man, Gal. 4, 4. 5; He suffered death and thereby destroyed the power of the enemy, the devil, and set all men free, Heb. 2, 14. 15. And as He was delivered for our offenses, so He was raised again for our justification, Rom. 4, 25. God has exalted our Substitute, Phil. 2, 9—11; Eph. 1, 20—23, for our benefit. In Christ the recovery for all lost honor, glory, and dominion is assured for the entire human race.

C) In His Word, *e. g.*, in our text, God has graciously revealed to us His excellent name on earth as the Redeemer, so that we do not only say "O Lord," but with personal confidence in Him also confess: "Our Lord," etc., v. 1 a. By this gracious self-revelation God kindles faith in our heart, by which we appropriate to ourselves all that the incarnate Lord did for us. Thus a beginning of the renewal of the divine image is made in us. By faith in Christ we have not only dominion over "sheep and oxen," etc., but also over sin, world, and death, 1 John 5, 4, yea, even over the world to come, Heb. 2, 5.

Let us extol our Lord for the excellency of His name as our Redeemer. He has done much for us as our Creator. But had He done no more, we should have lived but a short time here on earth and then have perished forever. Through the redemption of the Son of Man, however, more has been regained than the first man ever lost. Hymn 101.

2.

But our text offers even another truth that should impel us to extol Him.

A) From our psalm it is very evident that "enemies," yea, that particularly *the* enemy," is still, even now, at work on earth, v. 2. And from other passages of Scripture we know that not only "all the world lieth in wickedness" (in the Evil One), 1 John 5, 19, but that this enemy's rage is particularly directed against the people of God, the believers, 1 Pet. 5, 8. 9. (Compare also the history of Job.) And the devil is a very dangerous adversary, Eph. 6, 12.

> Deep guile and great might
> Are his dread arms in fight;
> On earth is not his equal.

He is bent upon the utter destruction of every child of God. And we know from Bible history and from experience that only too often he achieves his purpose. Think of Judas, Demas, and many that have been baptized and confirmed at our altars and to-day are in the enemy's camp or have gone to their place. Cf. John 6, 66.

B) But now notice what the Lord would do by us: "Out of the mouth of babes and sucklings Thou hast ordained strength because of Thine enemies that Thou mightest still the enemy and the avenger," v. 2. Him who is the mightiest on earth, the Prince of this World, the Lord proposes to bring to fall, nay, He will even silence him, by the frailest specimens of mankind, by babes and sucklings. "He hath scattered the proud in the imagination of their hearts. He hath put down the mighty from their seats and exalted them of low degree," Luke 1, 51. 52. See also 1 Cor. 1, 26—28. Special reference is here made to the "mouth" of babes and sucklings to indicate that by the prayers proceeding from the lisping, stammering mouths of frail human beings the arch-enemy's power is brought to naught. The almighty Redeemer can make the feeblest manikin so strong that but a sound from his lips can cause the old growling, roaring Lion to hush and be still.

> One little word can fell him.

So then, after all, the will of God can and will be done on earth.

C) How does the Lord make it possible to do these great things through men, even the weakest? The babes and sucklings of the people of God, to whom God has made known His excellent name as Redeemer, are meant here. By the rite of Circumcision the name of the Redeemer in the Old Testament was, and by the Sacrament of Baptism in the New Testament is, implanted into the hearts of even very small children, God Himself working faith in their hearts. And every one who believes in the Savior, be he young or old, need but in prayer touch upon this mighty name of the Savior, and the devil and all his helpers become powerless; for in this name the devil recognizes his Conqueror. By faith in Christ we become devil-tamers and world-conquerors. If we believe in our Savior, nothing shall prevent us from gaining the victory over all enemies and so finally obtaining the glory, honor, and dominion in the world to come through our Lord Jesus Christ. 1 Cor. 1, 27. 28; 1 John 5, 4; Is. 54, 17.

How excellent is the name of our Redeemer! Extol His wonderful name on earth, ye babes and sucklings as well as ye grown men and women, ye children as well as ye aged; for the Lord is your Strength and your Salvation. Hymn 478.   H. W. DEGNER.

Easter Sunday.
Job 19, 23—27.

This is the day which the Lord hath made;
We will rejoice and be glad in it.
The Stone which the builders refused
Is become the Head of the corner.
This is the Lord's doing;
It is marvelous in our eyes.

Hallelujah! Christ rose from the dead! He is risen, He is risen indeed! What joy entered the sorrowing hearts of the disciples when this blessed conviction came over them! He lives! At first this blessed truth came into their darkened souls like the early dawn of the morning. But as the angels preached at the open tomb, as one visitor after another came back from the garden of Joseph of Arimathea and proclaimed the joyous message, and as the risen Lord Himself appeared to them time and again, this conviction shone into their hearts more and more unto a perfect Easter Day. Every first day of the week, every Sunday, was for them and is for us an Easter celebration. Even in the twilight of Old Testament prophecy we hear a child of God in glorious Easter anticipation sing an Easter-song out of the depths of adversity and suffering. Our text is an Easter-song out of the depths, an Easter triumph in the midst of what natural man will always call defeat. It has echoed and reechoed through the ages. It has been put into songs and hymns. It has been carved upon millions of tombstones. It has cheered millions of weary souls through dark and somber valleys. It is preached from thousands of pulpits on this Easter Day. Our Easter text! "Oh, that my words were now written! Oh, that they were printed in a book, that they were graven with an iron pen and lead in the rock forever!" Vv. 23. 24. Oh, that God the Holy Spirit would write them indelibly into your and my heart this Easter morning!

"I Know that My Redeemer Lives! What Comfort This Sweet Sentence Gives!"

1. He Lives.   2. I shall Live.

1.

Who lives? Job sings an Easter-song out of the depths. All other helpers had failed him. His children were dead. His fortune was gone. His friends, even his wife, turned against him, vv. 14—20. "They whom I loved are turned against me." "Familiar friends have forgotten me." "My kinsfolk have failed." His health was gone. "My breath is corrupt; my days are extinct; the graves are ready for me," Job 17, 1. At the brink of the grave, when even his closest earthly friends forsook this man of sorrows, he turns in triumphant faith to *one* — "my Redeemer." *Goel* = my Blood-relative, who takes my part against the enemies that are killing me. My Avenger, my Vindicator, who conquers my killers. When in the times of the Old Testament a person was slain, his nearest of kin took up his cause, pursued the killer, and slew him. This man was called the *goel.* Job knows of a *Goel,* a Blood-relative of his, who will take up his cause when his kinsfolk have failed; a *Goel* who will conquer over and kill death. "He shall stand at the Latter Day upon the earth" as Victor over death. This *Goel* is none other than the resurrected Christ. "Thy Redeemer, the Holy One of Israel," Hos. 13, 14. A Blood-relative of Job — true man. But a Redeemer, who is far more than man, a Redeemer from death — also true God. He is also *our* Redeemer.

This *Goel,* Redeemer, *lives.* He came back to life. During the past Lenten season we saw our Redeemer in the throes of suffering and death. He took up the battle with the enemies of our soul, sin, death, and the power of the devil. We saw Him sink into the jaws of death. Triumph in the camps of the enemy in Jerusalem and in hell. The enemies in Jerusalem are not so sure about victory: "Sir," they say to Pilate, "we remember that that deceiver said while He was yet alive, After three days I will rise again. Command therefore that the sepulcher be made sure until the third day." The third day came. The dawn of Easter. Guards had been stationed about the grave. A vivid recital of the Easter-story in Matt. 28. — And thus He is *my* Redeemer. My *Goel* is my Substitute. Jesus for me. His battle with my foes is *my* battle; His victory is *my* victory. St. Paul says: *"I* was crucified with Christ." *"We* are buried with Christ." My sins were buried when Christ was buried. I rose with Christ. His resurrection is the absolution pronounced by God over a world of sinners, for whom Christ was made to be sin. The "Peace be unto you!" of Easter is not conditional. It declares no armistice. It contains no if's. "My Redeemer" — He and He only is my Redeemer. The glorious Easter fact is the *seal* of God upon the redemption wrought by His beloved Son.

He lives! There is no fact of sacred and secular history better attested than the fact that He who was born in Bethlehem, grew up in Nazareth, suffered in Gethsemane, at Gabbatha, and upon Golgotha, died and was buried by His friends in Joseph's tomb, on the third day rose again from the dead and now lives and reigns. They who before Easter fled and were afraid to die with Him after Easter went out and preached of Him and suffered and died for His sake. For a dead Christ? a Christ who had told them time and again: "On the third day I will rise again," and then did not keep His promise? Never! Never will a man die for such a cause. Long before Easter,

Job sees, his eyes of faith see His resurrected *Goel,* and he rejoices in complete and absolute certitude: "I *know,*" etc.

Skepticism and unbelief have always assailed this salient fact of our Christian faith: "On the third day He rose again from the dead." The guards began to preach against it on Easter morning. But the Old Testament prophesied it, and the New Testament has recorded the fulfilment of this prophecy. Thousands have died for this faith. Millions have died confessing this faith. Every Christian is a living proof of the truth: He lives; for "Christ liveth in me." The living Word of the living Christ is the one great power of God unto salvation.

"I know," "my Redeemer." He was delivered for *my* offenses and was raised again for *my* justification. Personal faith!

2.

I, too, shall live. "The graves are ready for me." "The wages of sin is death." "It is appointed unto men once to die." It has been stated that "there is nothing more certain for us than that we must all die, but there is nothing more uncertain than the time when, the place where, and the manner in which we shall die." But there is for us, thank God, something more certain than that we shall die, and that is that we shall *live*. This certainty is wrought and nourished in our hearts by the living Word. "I know that ... He shall stand at the Latter Day upon the earth; and though after my skin worms destroy this body, yet in my flesh shall I see God." As my Redeemer triumphed over death when death seized Him, so He will triumph over death when death seizes me. Job sees himself dead and buried and his body returned to the dust. The whole earth he sees as one vast graveyard. On this graveyard my *Goel* will stand, stand as Victor on the Last Day, stand triumphantly. For "in my flesh shall I see God," and this will come to pass "after ... worms destroy this body." The children of God in the Old Testament believed in the resurrection of the body and the life everlasting. Martha had been taught by the Old Testament Scriptures, and she tells Jesus at the grave of her brother: "I know that he shall rise again in the resurrection at the Last Day." Impossible? Job: "Though, ... yet!"

"The hour is coming," John 5, 28. "Ye shall live also," John 14, 19; 11, 25. 26. And all "because I live." "I know that," etc. "What *comfort* this sweet sentence gives!" Not only live, but live with God. "See God." "Mine eyes shall behold." No cloud any more between God and His children. No more sin. No more pain and suffering. "I shall be satisfied when I awake with Thy likeness." Ps. 17, 15. To see God is to know God. All questions will be answered.

Imagine the joy of Mary and Martha when Jesus raised their brother from the dead for another span of life in this vale of tears. They took their brother home. Celebrated the anniversary of his being raised. But they knew that they must part again. Others were glad, too, to see Lazarus again. If you had come to Bethany after the resurrection of Lazarus and had asked some of the friends of Mary and Martha, "Why are you so joyful?" they would have answered, "Because our good friend came back from the grave." But if you had asked Mary and Martha, "Why?" they would have answered, "Because *our brother* rose again." If I could tell you on this Easter Day, "Your brother rose, your mother lives, whom you have mourned as dead," what joy would fill your heart! But He who is far more to you than your mother, brother, or darling child, your and my Redeemer, lives. For where would our mother, our brother, and all our loved ones be who have died in the faith if Christ had not risen from the grave? We would all be lost. "Then also they which are fallen asleep in Christ are perished." "But now *is* Christ risen from the dead," 1 Cor. 15, 20.

God grant that all of us who are gathered here on this Easter morning may on the Last Day join the great throng gathered before the throne of the Lamb, singing the resurrection song: "Death is swallowed up in victory," 1 Cor. 15, 54. Amen.   F. A. HERTWIG.

First Sunday after Easter, Quasimodogeniti.
2 Sam. 12, 1—10. 13. 14.

The Word of God is a light. Light reveals and heals. It reveals God's holy and just will; it reveals man's disobedience. It also reveals God's mercy and grace.

The Bible is not a book which misrepresents. Different from story-books, which hardly ever are true to life. The stories told from the life of individuals and nations in our Bible are true, true to life. The Bible shows the heart of fallen man and the resultant sin and iniquity without shading the truth in any point. It never flatters fallen man. You will look in vain for a glorification of the sinful nature of man in the sacred pages of Holy Writ. It gives merciless publicity even to the sins of God's own children. A truly revealing light. Such revealing light does not flatter. It is not welcomed by those who love darkness rather than light. This frank revelation of sin has given great occasion to the enemies of the Lord to blaspheme, v. 14. Some years ago an American journal of some importance offered valuable prizes in a contest of original poetry. Lo and behold, the judges gave first prize to a "poet" who had written a most disgusting and suggestive lampoon entitled *King David*. The satire dealt at great length on the immoral relations of David and Bathsheba, constantly interweaving in a most cunning and devilish manner quotations from the psalms of David. It is true what Nathan said to David: "Thou hast given great occasion to the enemies of the Lord to blaspheme." But be not deceived, God is not mocked. While such frank revelations of sinful man's depravity will continue to be a stumbling-block to the ungodly readers of the Bible, children of God see in them a warning flash in which they clearly read and reread the divine lesson: "Let him that thinketh he standeth take heed lest he fall." But we have in the sacred stories of the fall and rising again of Peter and of David above all the mellow revealing and healing light of God's mercy and grace. Sweet Gospel! Surely these happenings as recorded for us by the Spirit of Purity are to us clarion calls to repentance, to a life of repentance. The story of the fall and rising again of King David does not give us occasion to blaspheme in secret joy and laughter, but it is for us —

A Most Solemn Call to Repentance.

For it reveals —
        1. Sin,   2. Grace.

1.

This story of David's fall exhibits to us the sinful, deceitful heart of man and God's holy wrath over sin. — David had been victorious in many a hard-fought battle. As a shepherd boy he slew a lion and a bear that had stolen lambs from his father's flock. He slew Goliath, the Philistine, in the name of the Lord of hosts. Time and again he had conquered the enemy nations that had troubled Israel and tried to subjugate it. He was now, by the grace of God, king of Israel and was ruling the united nation with great wisdom and bringing order out of chaos. But in the midst of victory there came a day of sad defeat for this great king. While his armies were courageously hammering at the gates and walls of Rabbah, "David tarried still at Jerusalem." And enjoying a life of ease, he lost a decisive battle against the enemies of his soul. An idle brain again became the devil's workshop. The soldier of God was not watchful over his own heart, and the devil of lust conquered. He who had conquered all the enemies of the realm was conquered by the enemy within. While he was walking on the flat roof of his palace at eventide, he spied a beautiful woman taking a bath in her garden. It was the wife of Uriah the Hittite. And while Uriah was valiantly fighting for his king, this king and Uriah's wife fell into the power of the devil. "Be sober, be vigilant!" Bathsheba soon notified her royal paramour that she was with child. And what did David do? He immediately set to work with all sorts of schemes to hide his sin from the public. He did not seem to be concerned about his breaking away from God. His chief worry was: "What will the people say?" The devil said: "Cover up!" He called Uriah home from the field of battle; but Uriah was too good a soldier. The devil whispered: "Dead men tell no tales!" David sent Uriah back sealed instructions to Commander Joab: "Place Uriah in the forefront of the hottest battle, and then retire ye from him that he may be smitten and die." Out of adultery came murder. One sin begets another. One lie must be covered up with another, etc.

King David had departed from the Lord. For one entire weary year he went about with the sins of adultery and murder upon his guilty conscience. He had departed into a far country of unbelief, of impenitence, away from all that makes life worth living: the peace, joy, and rest of a pardoned soul. Of this terrible state of impenitence, of warfare against God, David speaks in Psalms 6, 32, and 51. "When I kept silence, my bones waxed old through my roaring all the day long. For day and night Thy hand was heavy upon me, my moisture is turned into the drought of summer." One year of agony, one year of "I am weary with groaning! I water my couch with tears." "The wages of sin," etc. "Cursed be," etc. He who had won many battles and was considered a hero in Israel had lost the battle with his own deceitful self. Oh, what an enemy we have within us! How often has this been the case in the history of the human race! And David continued his evil fight. There was enmity in his heart against the Lord. He fought off the approaches of his God. "The heart is deceitful above all things and desperately wicked; who can know it? I, the Lord, search the heart." God seeks the erring sinner. Thus He sought fallen man from the very beginning in Paradise. Peter. Luke 15. God visits fallen David through His prophet Nathan. His minister. Thank God for that office!

V. 1: "The Lord sent Nathan unto David." God sends His minister to the erring. Woe if the erring say: "That is none of your business!" "He that despises you despises Me."

Nathan came prepared. He knew what God had against his king, and he told David without fear or favor. Nathan told a story, a parable, which struck the heart of the sinner. (Tell the touching story of the cruel rich man who took away the pet lamb of his poor neighbor and feasted himself and his guests with it.) When Nathan had finished his recital, David was filled with rage, v. 5. Without another word from the lips of the prophet he pronounced judgment upon "the man that hath done this thing." "Surely die!" He was ready to send out his executioners. Yea, he took a solemn oath: "As the Lord liveth, the man that has done this shall surely die." He had no pity for such an abominable wretch. He shall not see another sundown and no longer breathe the air in my kingdom. Away with such a man!

Oh, if people would only know themselves as God knows them! Instead, we are constantly denouncing others. Picture this scene, one of the most dramatic and impressive in sacred history. With a face crimson with anger and wrath over that cruel sheep-stealer, King David shouts so that his palace reverberates and Bathsheba (the human sheep which he had stolen and ravaged) could hear it: "As the Lord," etc. "Because he had not pity." Call the executioners. — At that moment Nathan raises his hand and interrupts further maledictions of his king. He points his finger, not in the direction of some street in Jerusalem where this damnable wretch might be found and hanged; he points it straight at his king and says: *"Thou* art the man!" You are the man whom God has blessed so signally among men; He has established your throne and given you all that your heart desired, given you the happiest home in Israel. And what have you done? How have you repaid your Lord? Broken up the happy home of one of your humble subjects. You are the man! You are the sheep-stealer! You are the lamb-killer! Your anger over the man without pity is just a dim reflection of the anger in the heart of the holy and just God over your sin. The judgment which you have pronounced just now you have pronounced upon your own life. "Thou art the man!" Vv. 7—10. You have pronounced your own doom. "Thus saith the Lord God of Israel." — God give us men who, like Nathan and John the Baptist, will go out and tell sinners, tell without fear or favor: "Thou art the man." "It is not lawful." "Thus saith the Lord God." "It is wrong for you to sue for that divorce." "It is wrong for you to remain a member of that lodge." Etc. Yes indeed, people will listen to us when we tell them from the pulpit. But let me come down from this pulpit into your home, into your palace, and tell you, "Thou art the man," and how will you accept such work of love? Like Herod or like David? Such a preacher is sometimes referred to as a "man who has the knack of making enemies." The greatest work of love which I as your pastor can do for you is to seek you when you are straying away from the fold and to bring you back to it.

2.

David was moved to sincere repentance by the words of his pastor. He confessed his sins before God and men, v. 13. Penitential Psalms. No excuses. No mention of extenuating circumstances. No blaming of others. Deep sorrow, which often came back in later life. "I have sinned against the Lord." Against Thee, Thee only, have I sinned and done this evil in Thy sight." All sins, those against the first and also those against the second table of God's holy Law, are sins against

God. Only that realization is real sorrow over sin. "I am sorry that I have sinned against God." If that sorrow is absent, there is no real sorrow over *sin*. So much that is called sorrow over sin is in reality selfishness or self-pity. Sorrow of the world is sorrow unto death.

It was the grace and power of God which through the spoken words moved the heart of David to sincere repentance. God sought him. God found him. And now, out of the same mouth which but a few minutes before had proclaimed the wrath and judgment of God upon his sin, David now hears those wonderfully soothing words of absolution: "The Lord also hath put away thy sin," v. 13. "There is forgiveness with Thee." David received this word of forgiveness as from God Himself and in no wise doubted, but firmly believed that his sins were forgiven by God in heaven. The peace of God again entered his weary soul. David's Son and David's Lord is the Lamb of God, which taketh away, etc. He it is who has given the power of imparting the forgiveness to sinners when He said: "I will give unto you the keys . . .; whosesoever sins ye remit," etc.

Though his sins were put away by the Lord, David could not forget them. He often remembered them in deep humility. He had many, many reminders: the child begotten in adultery died, and the peace and tranquillity of his home and country was often disturbed, as Nathan had foretold. The sins which he had committed against others were committed against him. Civil war and bloodshed, vv. 14. 10. 11. But these reminders were not acts of God's punishing justice; they were chastening rods in the hands of the Father. They were consequences of sin, but no longer punishments for the child of God who had again been received into grace.

This story of David's fall and rising again has always given great occasion to the enemies of God to blaspheme, but to thousands of alarmed souls it has shown the way back to the peace of God which Christ brought from the grave for all sinners. David: "Then will I teach transgressors Thy ways, and sinners shall be converted unto Thee." One cannot understand what was going on in the heart and home of King David, one cannot understand those psalms of David, if one has not learned to know sin and grace. The one monstrous evil is sin. The one great blessing is the removal of sin or grace. And the one great knowledge is "the knowledge of the glory of God in the face of Jesus Christ," 2 Cor. 4, 6.

> Jesus sinners doth receive.
> O may all this saying ponder
> Who in sin's delusion live
> And from God and heaven wander.

Amen.   F. A. HERTWIG.

Second Sunday after Easter, Misericordias Domini.
Psalm 23.

"The Lord is good to all, and His tender mercies are over all His works," Ps. 145, 9. "He maketh His sun to rise on the evil and on the good and sendeth rain on the just and on the unjust," Matt. 5, 45. Whether men are conscious of, and thankful for, His goodness or not, the Lord is good to all. Yes, sometimes the lot of the unbeliever in this present life seems more desirable than that of the Christian. Often he is more prosperous, has less sickness, and finds his path much smoother than the believer. Besides afflictions common to all men the disciple of Christ is called upon to bear the cross of Christ (ridicule, scorn, persecution). This leads enemies of the Church of Christ to conclude: It does not pay to be a member of the Church. We fare better than do the Christians. Cp. Ps. 73.

Nevertheless it is true: Only the Christian can be truly happy; only he fares well in time and in eternity. He enjoys the best of care and infinitely greater blessings than those who reject the Lord's salvation. Our psalm pictures the lot of the Christian. What a precious hymn it is! How many tears has it dried! How many hearts has it filled with confidence! How many fears has it dispelled! May it lead us, too, to a better understanding and a greater appreciation of—

The Blessedness of Christians.

1. *The Lord Is Their Shepherd.*
2. *He Feeds, Leads, and Protects Them.*
3. *They will Dwell in the House of the Lord Forever.*

1.

David by inspiration of the Holy Ghost wrote this psalm. David himself had been a shepherd. He was taking care of his flock when the Lord sent His prophet to anoint him king of His people. This psalm seems to rise directly out of his own experiences. He says, — and every true Christian will happily say it with him, — "The Lord is my Shepherd."

Who is this Lord? It is Jehovah, the living God, Father, Son, and Holy Ghost. The God who "was in Christ, reconciling the world unto Himself." The Lord to whom David turned when he had fallen: "Deliver me from blood-guiltiness, O God, Thou God of my salvation," Ps. 51, 14. He is not only the One who has created man, but the One who has redeemed him. Of Him the psalmists say: He shall suffer, die, rise again (Ps. 16. 22), ascend into heaven (Ps. 47), and sit at the right hand of God (Ps. 110). This Lord is speaking in to-days Gospel-lesson, John 10, 11: "I am the Good Shepherd. The good shepherd giveth his life for the sheep." Of this Lord, David and every Christian says: "The Lord is my Shepherd."

If the Lord is the Shepherd of all believers, then they are His sheep. How did this come about? Did they choose this Shepherd, because they knew how greatly blessed are the sheep of His flock? No. "They were dead in trespasses and sins," "by nature children of wrath," Eph. 2, 1—3. He has chosen them, John 15, 16. "You hath He quickened," Col. 2, 13. What a blessing: to the dead He gave life! The "great love wherewith He loved us, even when we were dead in sins," moved God, "who is rich in mercy," to quicken them ("by grace ye are saved"), Eph. 2, 4—5. The grace of the Lord has made them members of His flock and taught them to say: "The Lord is my Shepherd."

Friend, are you a member of the Lord's flock? Does not the love, goodness, and mercy of this Good Shepherd move you to turn to him in repentance and faith?

2.

Knowing who this Lord, their Shepherd, is, is it any wonder that Christians continue with David: "I shall not want"? How could they lack anything that is good?

V. 2: "He maketh me to lie down in green pastures." He gives them all that they need for the support and wants of the body, according to His promise: "Seek ye first the kingdom of God and His righteousness, and all these things shall be added unto you." The Christian looks upon all earthly things he receives as gifts from the hand of God. But these temporal blessings the Lord showers upon all men. The green pastures in which He provides food for His own are the means of grace, His Word and Sacraments. The Word of Life kindles faith and nourishes this new life in them. This Word is a *green* pasture, never parched, never consumed, always in rich abundance. We have these green pastures to-day. Oh, let us not look for "something better"! Let us feed in them, lie down in them, abide in them.

"He leadeth me beside the still waters." There are standing waters. They corrupt and gather filth. There are troubled seas, their waves rising high. Great floods rush down to the sea. But the waters to which the good Shepherd leads His sheep flow gently and softly. They are the streams of His grace, flowing in the Gospel. In the green pastures beside the still waters the sheep receive all the gifts of God's love procured for man by the Shepherd Himself.

V. 3: "He restoreth my soul." Sin is a heavy weight, a burden upon the soul; the afflictions of this world cause the spirit to droop. "He restoreth the soul," He relieves it of its burden and lets it taste the sweetness of His love in adversity. He regenerates the poor, sinful soul.

"He leadeth me in the paths of righteousness." He *leads!* Like a shepherd, he chooses the path. The sheep may not think this path the best, but it is. The paths where danger threatens the sheep are avoided. The sheep know that this is true, that His path leads to heaven, and that all things must work together for their good; therefore they place complete confidence in the Shepherd and follow Him also when the countryside through which He leads takes on a rougher appearance. Rom. 8, 32.

V. 4: "Yea, though I walk through the valley of the shadow of death." Yes, "we must through much tribulation," etc. The path to heaven often leads through dark valleys. The sun is hidden from the traveler's eyes; deep darkness surrounds him; death casts its shadow across the way. Sickness visits the Christian; old age creeps upon him; by reason of sin he is a dying man. But though death is the king of terrors to others, it is not that to the Christian. It is in reality but a shadow. "The shadow of a serpent will not sting nor the shadow of a sword kill." Christians are not led into the valley to stay, but merely to walk through. The Shepherd will not lose them in the valley, but will safely lead them to the other side. "I will fear no evil, for Thou art with me." He is ever at their side. "Thy rod and Thy staff, they comfort me." The Lord's power, coming to them through the means of grace, sustains and protects them and offers the right consolation in every trouble.

V. 5: "Thou preparest . . . runneth over." Enemies surround the Christian. The devil, the world, and his own flesh seek his destruction, but the Lord sets a table before him in spite of all his enemies; *i. e.,* the Christian is secure and sure of refreshing and satisfying joys after all afflictions. The Lord "anoints his head with oil"; he is a welcome guest at the feast God has prepared for him. "His cup runneth over." The spiritual blessings God pours into his cup fill it, yea, cause it to run over; he shares it with others.

My friends, does the Lord take care of His own? Through the means of grace He gives them all that they need for time and eternity. How necessary these means of grace! How important to use them diligently!

3.

The Lord being my Shepherd, "surely goodness and mercy," etc. The Lord leads His Christians upon the path to heaven. Let them turn about and look back. What do they see? The goodness and mercy of God is following them. The goodness and mercy which pardons, protects, supplies them with all they need for body and soul. The path turns to the right, turns to the left, passes through dark places, over high mountains, — goodness and mercy are still there. We grow older, sickness and weakness come, death approaches; but all the days of our life "goodness and mercy" follow us. "Surely." As sure as His promises.

"And I will dwell in the house of the Lord forever." He is mine, and I am His. With Him will I remain. His own I shall be forever. Here on earth He has made me His own and has kept me with His flock; when this life is ended, He will move me into another world, where I shall dwell in the house of many mansions forever. Fulness of joy and pleasures forevermore await me in heaven, Ps. 16, 11; 17, 15.

Can you afford to stand idly at the wayside and see the happy flock (numbering millions) led by the Shepherd passing by? Soon they will be around the bend and out of sight, and the opportunity to join them gone. Oh, seek the Lord while He may be found! Call upon Him while He is near! Acknowledge your sinfulness, ask Him for forgiveness, and cast yourself upon His mercy! He will not reject you. You will receive His pardon. He will be your Shepherd, and verily you shall not want.   OTTO H. HOYER.

Third Sunday after Easter, Jubilate.
Psalm 100.

Luther says in the explanation of the Eighth Commandment: "We should fear and love God that we may . . . speak well of our neighbor." Forgetting his faults and frailties, we are to discover his good points and speak of them, praise his good qualities, and also show our appreciation of any assistance or service he may render. Surely it is considered almost self-evident among men that those who receive favors from others show gratitude. —

No one has a better right to expect praise and thanksgiving from men than God. There is no goodness, love, kindness, mercy, anywhere to be compared with His. If we are to speak well of those who have some good traits and to be thankful that they show it in their actions, how much more should we "praise God, from whom *all bless-ings* flow"! To men we may owe much, but to the Lord we owe infinitely more. "In Him we live and move and have our being," Acts 17, 28. It is not at all surprising that David says: "I will bless the Lord at all times; His praise shall continually be in my mouth," Ps. 34, 1.

May to-day's meditation cause us to see what David saw: that we have every reason to praise and thank the Lord! This psalm calls upon all people to come into the presence of the Lord with praise and thanksgiving. We are thus offered the theme: —

Praise and Thank the Lord!

1. The Lord Is God, Your Creator;
2. The Lord Is a Wonderful Savior;
3. His Goodness, Mercy, and Truth Are Everlasting.

1.

There are people who deny the existence of God. *We* call them atheists; *God* calls them fools. "The fool hath said in his heart, There is no God," Ps. 14, 1. They deny the existence of God; the fool says in his heart, there is no God. But do you think that even the fool believes it? All men, whether they have the written revelation of God or not, know that a God exists, Rom. 1, 19. 20. But all men do not worship the same God. They sing the praises of, and bring offerings to, many gods (sun, moon, stars, rivers, mountains, ancestors, etc.). We cannot join them. There is but one God, Deut. 6, 4. Nations of the earth, before ye make preparations to act upon the admonition of this text, "know ye that the Lord (Jehovah), He is God," v. 3. There is no other God. This God, Jehovah, says Is. 45, 18: "I am the Lord, and there is none else," and v. 21: "There is no God else beside Me, a just God and a Savior; there is none beside Me." This is the God who says to *all* men: "Thou shalt have no other gods before Me."

"Know ye that the Lord, He is God." Ps. 148 calls upon the angels, sun, moon, and stars, the heavens, snow, mountains, all creatures, to sing His praises. Is. 42, 8: "My glory will I not give to another, neither My praise to graven images." Know ye this, all ye lands, and "make a joyful noise unto the Lord; serve the Lord with gladness."

What reasons have we to come before His presence with praise and thanksgiving? V. 3: "It is He that hath made us and not we ourselves." How, then, did all nations come into existence? There are many legends about this. They are all human inventions. Some men live as if they had made themselves; they call themselves "self-made" men. The truth is: The Lord has made them. He deserves praise and thanksgiving for man's existence. The Lord has made us, the men and women of the twentieth century. Yes, my friends, the Lord has made us who are assembled here this morning. The Lord has made me. He has given me a body wonderfully constructed, a soul that shall never die. Luther attempts to bring home to each individual what it means to him that God has given him existence: "He has given me my body and soul, eyes, ears, and all my members, my reason, and all my senses, and still preserves them." Let me stop you at just one of these gifts to-day; that gift is your reason. Do you know what a sound mind is worth? A man who has lost the gift of sight knows the value of a seeing eye. If you have the opportunity to visit a hospital for the insane, do so. You will know what it means: God has given me a sound mind. You will know that "the Lord is good," v. 5. Look about you and see the many other gifts that God has showered upon you. Do not these many gifts move you to come

into His presence singing His praises? Will they not turn your
thoughts to Him and move you to thank Him?

The Lord has made you, and it is the Lord who keeps you alive.
"He upholds all things by the word of His power." The fact that you
are alive shows that the Lord is active in your behalf. He has not
forgotten you. Without Him you could not exist. Only in Him
can you live and have your being. Thank Him for having created
you; thank Him for sustaining your life. Ps. 103, 1—3.

2.

"We are His people and the sheep of His pasture." By physical
birth we come into the kingdom of darkness, the kingdom ruled by
the prince of this world, because our parents are the children of fallen
Adam and Eve. The subjects of this kingdom end in everlasting
darkness. No man nor angel can save them. Now, the psalmist says:
"We [the Christians] are His people," the Lord's. No longer in the
kingdom of the devil, but children of God and "sheep of His pasture."
We have been transferred from the kingdom of darkness into the kingdom of light. And this we owe to the Lord. It is His work from
beginning to end and in all its parts. 2 Tim. 1, 9; John 15, 16.

He Himself became man to prepare salvation for us and all men.
A full pardon, forgiveness for all transgressions, peace with God, life
eternal, all this He earned for men. He became their Savior. He
erected His courts among men, in which these things necessary for
salvation could be offered and distributed to men. In these courts
His Word is now proclaimed: Repent and believe in the Savior Jesus
Christ, and thou shalt be saved. And: Those who believe in the Son
have everlasting life. The places where this Word is preached thus
become the Lord's gates to heaven. Men, all unworthy of salvation,
unable to save themselves, are saved by His grace without money and
without price. Should not all nations "enter into His gates with
thanksgiving" to seek the salvation prepared for and offered to them
and thankfully accept it? Surely all men have great reason to thank
and praise the Lord.

But we, the Christians, have still greater cause to sing His
praises. For "we are now His people, the sheep of His pasture."
Only believers in Christ, true Christians, can apply these words to
themselves. And they can do it only because God has made them
what they are, and not they themselves. As God has made us, as He
has given us our natural life, even so He has made us His people and
the sheep of His pasture, has given us spiritual life. As men cannot
create themselves, so they cannot give themselves spiritual life. "It
is God which worketh in you both to will and to do of His good
pleasure," Phil. 2, 13. God has turned us, has drawn our hearts to
Jesus, 1 Cor. 12, 3. "We are sheep of His pasture." In this pasture

(the means of grace), always green, always nourishing, He feeds us. By His power we are kept through faith unto salvation, 1 Pet. 1, 5. Let us enter into His gates with thanksgiving, and into His courts with praise! O all ye Christians, you who are God's people and sheep of His pasture, be thankful to Him and bless His name. Come into His courts and "make a joyful noise unto the Lord." God does not want sad, long, gloomy faces in His temple. He wants His people to be a happy people, Phil. 4, 4. Let us, then, come into His presence with singing and serve Him gladly. Let us tell the nations of the wonderful things God has done for us and, moved by gratitude, run the way of His commandments.

3.

Finally, also the fact that the goodness, mercy, and truth of God are everlasting should induce us to sing His praises and should fill our hearts with gratitude towards Him. The text says: "The Lord is good." He is the Fountain from which all that is good flows. "The Lord is good to all," Ps. 145, 9. We know that He has been good to us in the past. We have to confess that "He has richly and daily provided us with all that," etc. He has guarded and protected us. And what a blessing that He has redeemed us and brought us to the Savior! Now, the Lord, our God, is not subject to change. He is the same yesterday, to-day, and forever. Good in the past, good now, good in the future. Let us thank Him.

"His mercy is everlasting." He keeps us in existence, feeds, clothes, guards, and protects us "purely out of fatherly, divine goodness and mercy, without any merit or worthiness in us." It is His mercy in Christ Jesus, our Savior, that moves Him to forgive our transgressions. What if He should cease to be merciful! Let us thank Him that His mercy endures forever. We daily sin much, it is true, but we can also daily find forgiveness. What a blessing to all poor sinners!

"His truth [faithfulness] endureth to all generations." His Word will ever be reliable. All generations will find that He keeps His promises. Of Abraham He promised to make a great nation. Now, Abraham and Sarah grew old and had no child. But God kept His promise. All the Messianic prophecies were fulfilled. "His faithfulness endureth to all generations." Here is a guaranty that we, too, may safely rely upon all promises He has given us. And so we trust in His promise: "By Him [Jesus] all that believe are justified," Acts 13, 39; John 3, 15. We believe in Him now and rely upon His word "He which hath begun a good work in you will perform it until the Day of Jesus Christ," Phil. 1, 6. He will come again to "receive us unto Himself," and He will lead us into the heavenly mansions, where a place has been prepared for us, John 14, 2. 3. Hymn 62, 14. 15.

OTTO H. HOYER.

Fourth Sunday after Easter, Cantate.
Jer. 15, 15—21.

In the 10th chapter of the Gospel according to St. Luke we find the well-known account of our Savior's visit in the home of Mary and Martha. The story is brief and simple, and its significance is obvious. While Martha was cumbered about much serving, Mary sat at Jesus' feet and heard His Word. Martha desired that Mary assist her in attending to the Master's bodily comforts. However, Jesus made use of the opportunity to show that, after all, only one thing is needful — His Word. God's Word is all-important.

Fifteen hundred years later we find Martin Luther, a twenty-year-old student, at the University of Erfurt, in Germany. For the first time in his life he finds a complete Bible. How eagerly he scans its sacred pages! How engrossed he becomes in the story of young Samuel! How earnestly he desires to possess such a Book! Throughout the remainder of his life this Book, because it is the Word of God, is of paramount importance to him. Diet at Worms and Marburg Colloquium. Last year we commemorated that outstanding event in modern history when Luther gave to the world his complete translation of the Bible. Luther learned to say with Samuel, "Speak, Lord; for Thy servant heareth." Both in questions of doctrine and in the application of doctrine to life, God's Word was to Luther all-important.

We are to-day addressing Christians. Christians know that without the revelation of God's will to mankind we would be most miserable. We would not know the true God. Without God's Word we would know nothing of our blessed Lord and Savior and of the blood that was shed for our sins. We could have no certain hope regarding life or death. But we are happy and thankful; for God's Word has revealed to us who God is and what He has done for our salvation. And yet, my friends, do we always consider the Word of God to be the one thing needful? Is it to us the most important thing in life? For our instruction, comfort, and inspiration let us to-day go back in spirit to an Old Testament period, to the time of the prophet Jeremiah, and learn of —

The Importance of the Word of God in the Life of Jeremiah.

Jeremiah found in the Word of God

1. The Bread of Life;   2. An Anchor and a Stay;
3. A Lamp unto His Feet.

1.

Jeremiah, who lived about 600 years before Christ, says in our text, v. 16: "Thy words were found, and I did eat them." Although God had, through Isaiah and other prophets, previously warned the Jews, had extended to them most loving invitations, and had given to them most glorious promises concerning the Messiah, most of the people appeared to care nothing for the Word of God. It was indeed a dreadful time. Sunken in materialism and indifferentism, like the foolish rich man in the parable, the Jews were satisfied to feed their souls with earthly things; they were content to eat, drink, and be merry. As for himself, the prophet says that he found, and did eat, the words of God. He made them his own, digested them, so that they became, as it were, part of his life and being. They were welcome to him as food to the hungry, and he admitted them to his understanding and heart, imprinted them on his mind. His words remind us of Deut. 8, 3, where Moses says: "Man doth not live by bread only, but by every word that proceedeth out of the mouth of the Lord doth man live." Also quoted by Jesus. St. Peter, writing to the Christians of his day, speaks of God's Word as spiritual food when he says: "As new-born babes desire the sincere milk of the Word that ye may grow thereby." Cf. Ezek. 3, 1—3.

And what was the effect of this "eating of the words of God"? V. 16 b: "Thy Word was unto me the joy and rejoicing of mine heart." Jeremiah took pleasure in the words as a hungry man finds satisfaction after he has partaken of food. They were agreeable to him, and whatever God said to him brought him pleasure. He was glad to know and to do God's will; for it was to him, as with Jesus, meat and drink to do the will of Him that had sent Him, John 4, 34.

There is plenty of heart-hunger in the world to-day. And how vainly men try to satisfy the longing of their hearts! Some follow the numerous fantastic and fanciful isms. The road to Endor is crowded when people no longer listen to God. Cf. 2 Kings 1, 1—4; Acts 17, 21. But human philosophies and superstition bring only disillusionment and often despair. Others seek happiness in riches; but if these could satisfy, wealthy people would be happier than they are. Still others follow the will-o'-the-wisp of pleasure; but instead of finding contentment, the devotees of pleasure are ever seeking new forms of entertainment and amusement. Rev. 3, 17. 18. Compare, if you will, the dominating avarice of the miser and the affected gaiety and morbid restlessness of the worldling with the "peace of God which passeth all understanding" as we find it in the simple, devout Christian and decide for yourself which is best. There may be substitutes for the daily food we now use for our bodies, but there is no substitute for the food required by the soul. Only the Word of God can supply this need. Let us therefore feed upon the Word; let us diligently hear it, read it, and study it. (Hymn 2, 2.)

2.

Jeremiah found in the Word of God an anchor and stay in the troubles of life. Life is often likened to a sea, which is sometimes calm and peaceful and at other times stormy and tumultuous. In the storms it is necessary to have an anchor and a stay. Jeremiah was perplexed and troubled, v. 18. Gentle and tender by nature, it was his mission to announce a hard and dreadful judgment to his people. Nor would he have anything to do with the scoffers and mockers. He was compelled to forego the pleasures of youth, v. 17. Persecution followed him. Like Paul, centuries later, he was abused and insulted. The enmity to which he fell victim on account of his declaration of nothing but the truth he deeply felt. Add to that his anxious concern for the welfare of his people, and we can well understand the misery of body and soul of which we get a glimpse when he feels as if God had forsaken him.

However, Jeremiah does not altogether despair. Out of the depths he cries unto the Lord, v. 15. He has found an anchor and a stay. From the many promises of God he has received divine assurances of help, chap. 1, 8. 10. God will help. And even though his wound seem incurable and his pain perpetual, he need not give up hope. God will not be to him as a liar or as waters that fail. God is not a man that he should lie. The fountain of life will never be diminished. God's ways may be past finding out, Ps. 73; Rom. 11, 33; but the prophet can rest assured that God will not leave him nor forsake him.

What comfort for us to know that when troubles come, when God's dispensations perplex us, when all earthly helps fail, God sees us and knows all about us! It is a matter of comfort to Christians to know that, whatever ails us, we have our God to go to, before whom we may spread our case and to whose omniscience and grace we may appeal. He is ready "all our sins and griefs to bear." Often the storms of life are sent in order that we might come closer to Him. He would have us cast all our cares upon Him. He has promised to be with us alway. May we learn from the godly prophet that at all times God will be our Anchor and Stay. "Earth has no sorrow that Heaven cannot heal."

3.

The prophet found in God's Word a lamp unto his feet.

A lamp shows us the way lest we go astray or stumble. Jeremiah needed light to direct him in his perplexed state of mind. And even though his cry to the Lord reveals much human frailty, God graciously directs him on the right way. God tells him, v. 19, to return, to become reconciled to his work, Jonah 4, 4. He is not to doubt the Lord's interest in his work. He should continue to preach the Word. In doing this he must "take forth the precious from the vile." Amidst all the wicked there are still many precious souls, about which he must be concerned. He shall let the wicked return to him, but he is not to return to them. The prophet must rightly divide the Word of Truth, Law and Gospel. And he must not compromise with falsehood and unbelief. Further to strengthen the prophet and to illuminate the way for him, God promises to grant success to his labors, vv. 20. 21. He shall be as God's mouth, God's ambassador. What an honor! God will restore to him tranquillity of mind. He shall be like "a fenced brazen wall," v. 20, and the enemies will not be able to prevail against him. God will finally preserve him to his heavenly kingdom. If God be for him, who can be against him? Josh.1, 5—9.

The Word of God is a lamp also unto our feet. God has told us all we need to know, from cradle to grave. He convicts us of sin and tells us of sin's dread consequence, Rom. 6, 23. But He also points us to the Savior, John 14, 4; 3, 16. He leads us in the path of righteousness, Ps. 23, 3; Titus 2, 12. He warns against compromise with evil, 2 Cor. 6, 14—18. He brightens the gloom of sadness, Matt. 11, 28. He lights up our death-bed, Ps. 23, 4, and even sends forth rays of light to give us a glimpse of the harbor of heaven, John 14, 2. 3. We never need dwell in darkness or be uncertain about the way if we will follow the light of God's Word. "Once when the famous Faraday was lying ill, his physician found him in tears, with his arm resting upon the table, on which lay the open Book. 'I fear you are worse,' said the physician. 'It is not that,' said Faraday, with a sob, 'but why will people go astray when they have this blessed Book to guide them?'"

Concluding, my friends, we ask once more, What does the Word of God mean to you? Pray God that it may be also unto you the bread of your soul, your stay and anchor, the lamp unto your feet, your choicest possession, your greatest joy, and the most important thing in your life. (Hymn 119.)　　　G. WALTER SCHOEDEL.

Fifth Sunday after Easter, Rogate.
Gen. 18, 16—33.

A winsome word — friend. One of God's choicest gifts to mankind — friendship. — The word brings up two conceptions. Friends are joined together in intimate, loving campanionship. And he is my friend who has my best interests at heart. The word fittingly describes

The Relation of the Christians to God and to All Mankind.

1. The Christians the Friends of God.
2. The Christians the Best Friends of Mankind.

1.

Friends of God! Abraham "the friend of God," Jas. 2, 23. "Ye are My friends," John 15, 14. 15.

1) *The Lord has chosen us for His friends and holds friendly intercourse with us.* How shall we account for that? He saw us disgraced, corrupt, hateful, and bestowed His friendship upon us, Ezek. 16, 8. How shall we account for that? He bestowed His grace

upon us in the Beloved, Eph. 1, 6. (R. V.) How shall we account for that? It pleased the Lord to look upon us from eternity with the favor of His grace and to make us His own. Nothing in Abraham to gain for him God's eternal favor. "I know him" — I have chosen him from eternity as My friend. "Ye have not chosen Me, but I have chosen you," John 15, 16. It is a miracle of unfathomable grace that Christ calls us His friends, that He washed us from our sins, brought us to the Father.

God holds friendly intercourse with us. Friendship of David and Jonathan. They lived together as one. The Lord God sitting at table with Abraham and revealing His inmost thoughts to him. God loves the company of His believing children. Deut. 4, 7: "so nigh unto them." Through Word and Sacrament He comes close to them. John 14, 23: "Keep My words . . . make Our abode with him." Closer to us than our dearest earthly friend; with us to allay our fears, to relieve our wants, waiting for His friends to come to Him for help. His home always open to them; yea, He makes His home with them. Jesus loved Martha and her sister and Lazarus, loved to tarry in their cottage, John 11; Luke 10, 38 f.

And He reveals His inmost thoughts to His friends. He makes them His confidants. "Shall I hide," etc. Amos 3, 7; John 15, 15. The unbelievers do not know and cannot know the mind of the Lord. The Christians have received God's Spirit and know His mind, Ps. 25, 14; 107, 43; Hos. 14, 9. God revealed His will to Abraham by word of mouth, to us by Scripture, Ps. 147, 19. Great and wondrous thoughts fill the mind of God. Holiness and justice. Grace and loving-kindness. And these thoughts He communicates to men. The unbeliever scorns them. The Christian understands them. Friends understand one another. The Lord delights to commune with His friends and to discourse intimately with them (as with Abraham on the terrible judgment descending on Sodom), on the salvation His loving-kindness has prepared for all the nations of the earth.

2) *The Christians enjoying the privileges of friendship.* Abraham importuning his Friend. He asks favors again and again and yet again. Holy shamelessness of faith. Bold, because he knows the goodness and truth of the Lord. Our petitions a delight to the Lord, Prov. 15, 8. He asks us to pray and assures us that for Jesus' sake our prayers are acceptable, Matt. 7, 7—11; John 16, 23 f. The insistent pleading of the Syrophenician woman, Matt. 15, 22 f.; of the widow, Luke 18, 1 f. "As dear children ask their dear father." Unworthy of God's favor, Dan. 9, 18. Jesus gained us God's full favor. Therefore: Heb. 4, 16. It was not in Jonathan's heart to refuse David anything. Hymn 395. In this cold, selfish, unloving world there is Jesus dwelling in the homes of His friends, there are the Christians finding sweet solace in the arms of their Friend.

3. *The Christians living up to the duties of friendship.* V. 19: God lovingly chooses Abraham to be the teacher of his family and the world, to declare God's holiness and mercy to men. That duty devolves upon all the friends of God, 1 Pet. 2, 9. The world does not know God, slanders, reviles Him. It is the part of friendship to make known the true character of the friend. Jonathan would not have his friend slandered. Our chief business in the world is to publish the praises of the Lord. A duty which is a sweet privilege. We cannot keep silence. He has done so much for us. We must tell our neighbors of it. God has chosen us to be His own that we should sing the praises of Him, our dearest Friend.

How utterly the world misjudges the situation! These Christians, representing the foolish things of the world, etc., this foolish, backward generation, they are exalted above princes and kings — God's friends and intimates. We ourselves often fail to realize what it means to us. Are we friendless? Hymn 395, 3. We cannot accomplish much in the world? Our lives mean so little to us? 1 Pet. 2, 9: "Chosen generation . . . that ye should show forth the praises," etc.

We are God's friends, and because of that we are *the best friends of mankind.*

2.

We keep ourselves aloof from the world, Jas. 4, 4. And still we are the best friends mankind has. None so concerned with the welfare of men as the Christian. To none the world owes so much as to these despised Christians.

1) *The holy sympathy and divine compassion of the Christians for their fellow-men.* Abraham's attitude towards Sodom. Col. 3, 12. The compassion of Christians stirred to the utmost depth by the miserable condition of their neighbors, the doom of eternal damnation. The sympathy of the unbeliever a carnal affection; does not extend to the real need. The Christians have the mind of Jesus, "the merciful and faithful Priest," Heb. 2, 17. Eph. 5, 1. 2. Theirs is the true humanity. The daughter of the Syrophenician woman had no friend like her mother, who loved her indeed. The woe of the miserable world touches the hearts of the Christians, who are like their God and Savior. Jesus the great Philanthropist, Titus 3, 4.

2) *The Christians are the great benefactors of mankind.* a) *They are the teachers of the world.* Men need to know above all else what sin means, what grace means. The Law and the Gospel are made known to men through the Christians. My best friend is he who reproves me for my sin, he who gives me the assurance that God has forgiven me my sins. The Christians, discharging their duty towards their Friend in heaven, publishing His holiness and His mercy, thus perform the greatest act of friendship in the interest of the world.

Preaching the Gospel by word and deed, they are the salt of the earth, Matt. 5, 13, and the saviors of many.

b) *The Christians are the conservators of the world.* World preserved for the sake of the elect, Matt. 24, 14. And many a city doomed to destruction is spared for the sake of the Christians in it. "I will spare all the place for their sakes." Zoar saved because of Lot's presence there, Gen. 19, 19—21. Sodom's doom restrained till Lot's departure, Gen. 19, 22. Nabal spared for Abigail's sake, 1 Sam. 25. Is. 65, 8: "There is a blessing in it." The Christians a blessing to their community.

c) *The Christians the world's intercessors.* They stand between the world and God's wrath. Abraham making use of his relation to God in behalf of Sodom. The intercessory prayer of the Christians of weight with God, Jas. 5, 16 f. Six times the Lord graciously acceded to the request of Abraham. There comes a time when the grace of God, persistently spurned, gives place to the final wrath, the judgment of obduration sets in, and intercession is no longer in place; but aside from that situation the intercession of God's friends for mankind moves God to suspend His judgment against the wicked and to bless the words of His children. Paul relies upon his brethren to support his work with their prayers, 2 Thess. 3, 1. Temporal blessings come upon the world because of the intercession of the Christians, 2 Tim. 2, 1 f. And the prayers the Christians offer in great heaviness and sorrow for their unbelieving neighbors, Rom. 9, 1 f.; 10, 1 f., are not in vain, Ex. 22, 9—14; Ps. 106, 23; 1 John 5, 15. 16. Barren fig-tree, Luke 13, 6—9. Christ intercedes for the sinner, Luke 23, 34; Is. 53, 12. The effectual fervent prayer of the righteous for the sinner, one with Christ's prayer, availeth much.

The Christians the world's best friends. For they are God's friends, enlisting the power of God in behalf of their fellow-men. Esther, loving her nation, beloved of the king, saved her people from annihilation.

In distress the world looks to the counsels of the great for help. In reality it is the Christian people that direct the affairs of this world and bring God's blessings upon the entire earth. "Through their prayers the Christians, as instruments of God, preserve and govern the entire world, as Luther says 8, 350: 'For the Christian's sake God gives and preserves to the world all that it has. The Christians are altogether helpers and Saviors of the world. All that the world has and does it holds of these beggars, who have nothing and yet possess all things.'" (F. Pieper, *Chr. Dog.,* III, 98.) Luther: "Who, then, can comprehend the lofty dignity of the Christian? Through his kingly power he rules over all things, and through his priesthood he is all-powerful with God, because God does the things which he asks and desires." (19, 998.)

Jesus Christ is the best Friend of mankind, and He would have His Christians acquit themselves as the best friends of mankind. "I sought for a man among them that should stand in the gap," Ezek. 22, 30. And shall he say: "I found none"? The world needs us. Let us not desert it. The Lord stood by us in our need, and we shall stand by our fellows in their need. God richly blessed us in Christ, and He tells us: "Thou shalt be a blessing," Gen. 12, 2.

TH. ENGELDER.

Sixth Sunday after Easter, Exaudi.

Is. 55.

One of the leading bodies of water mentioned in Biblical history, especially in the story of God's chosen race, is the Red Sea. We see 600,000 Israelites, men, on foot, besides women and children, flocks, and herds, very much cattle, a long caravan, leaving Egypt, and bound for the Promised Land. They are now drawing nigh unto the Red Sea. Behind this Israelite host we see another great army, Pharaoh, his 600 chosen chariots, and all the chariots of Egypt, and captains over every one of them — an immense army. It is also bound for the Red Sea. When the children of Israel reach the Sea, Moses, at God's command, stretches forth his hand over the sea, and the waters are divided. Israel goes forward; a wall of water on their right hand and on their left, they walk upon dry ground. The Egyptian army follows. The pillar of fire separates the two hosts. The Egyptians follow to the midst of the sea after Israel. Israel reaches the other side of the Red Sea. Suddenly the massive walls of water move, crumble, fall, return to their old bed, and cover the Egyptians. All the host of Pharaoh that came into the sea after Israel was drowned; there remained not so much as one of them. Israel was saved.

There are other waters flowing on this earth, infinitely more important, infinitely more glorious, infinitely more salutary. These waters are the waters of which our text speaks, the waters of salvation, the Gospel of the risen and ascended Savior, Jesus Christ. Upon this subject we shall meditate to-day.

Come Ye to the Waters of Salvation.

1. *These Waters Are Free and Satisfy.*
2. *These Waters are being Drunk and Refresh Many Nations.*

1.

The waters of which our text speaks, the waters of salvation, are *free* and *satisfy*, vv. 1. 2. There is no charge, no exchange of goods necessary, nothing; all is free, v. 1. All is to be had without money and without price. Just as God has given to man the physical, material waters, the oceans, the seas, the rivers, and refreshing springs, freely and without any cooperation on the part of man, just so the heavenly Father dispenses these spiritual waters, Christ and His salvation. All has been prepared, prepared by God. The spiritual waters are God-made and God-given. Take, for example, Adam and Eve after the Fall. They had sinned. They were polluted. Yet they knew not where to betake themselves in their distress. They fled. They knew there was something wrong. Their conscience was alive and accused them. But nowhere could they find peace for their souls. God had to come. God had to act. God had to give. And God did act, Gen. 3, 15, freely.

That is the deplorable condition of man by nature. He flees. He does not come to God. God must come to him. Gasping and famishing humanity, in spite of outward progress, science, invention, culture, and the like, does not know where to go. 1 Cor. 2, 14: "The natural man," etc. Rom. 8, 7: "The carnal mind," etc. As Isaiah looks into the future and announces the appearing of the great Light, he attempts to arouse the New Testament Church to action with the words: "Arise, shine; for thy light is come, and the glory of the Lord is risen upon thee. For, behold," he continues with lamentable words, "darkness shall cover the earth and gross darkness the people," Is. 60, 1. 2. In another Bible-passage this same prophet writes (Is. 9, 2): "The people that walked in darkness have seen a great light; they that dwell in the land of the shadow of death, upon them hath the light shined." "Foolishness," "enmity against God," "darkness," "the shadow of death," these and countless similar Biblical expressions vividly impress upon us the deplorable condition of man by nature. Natural man knows not the free waters of salvation.

Take the example of the Ephesians at the time of the Apostle Paul. Ephesus at that time was a well-known city. It was a center of Greek education and culture. Yet when Paul, the messenger of Christ, entered that city with his Gospel-preaching, the Book of Acts (chap. 19) tells us that there was a great confusion. "The whole city was filled with confusion." The cry was raised: "Great is Diana of the Ephesians! Great is Diana of the Ephesians!" Not Christ, the Savior of the world, was worshiped, but a heathen goddess, Diana. And when converts for the Christian religion were gained in that city, the people brought books together, books of curious arts, and burned them. The price of them was fifty thousand pieces of silver (about $10,000), — indeed not a small sum. Ephesus, a seat of culture and education, one of the leading cities in Paul's day, was steeped in idolatry and its concomitant, the dark arts. "Without Christ, aliens from the commonwealth of Israel, foreigners, strangers, having no hope, without God in the world." They knew not the free waters of salvation.

They knew certain waters. Man knows certain waters. But these waters do not satisfy. They may momentarily satisfy the body, but they cannot satisfy the soul. Listen to the words of our text: v. 2 a. — In these days of physical needs and spiritual distress many look upon gold, the gold or silver standard, riches, as the panacea for the ills of man. But, my friends, gold, riches, cannot satisfy the soul of man. Solomon writes Prov. 23, 4. 5: "Labor not to be rich. . . . Wilt thou set thine eyes upon that which is not? For riches certainly make themselves wings; they fly away as an eagle toward heaven." They are not dependable. Many examples in our days corroborate this statement. Our Savior says: "Lay not up for yourselves treasures upon earth," etc., Matt. 6, 19. Examples of robberies, thefts, ransom money. One gains, the other loses. A constant change. No rest.

Other waters. Some turn to their own works and deeds for soul satisfaction. Luther, for example, before the Lord through His Word opened his eyes. His monastic life. No relief. No satisfaction. No rest for the soul. The heathen in foreign lands. Their sacrifices and self-imposed tortures. All human efforts are in vain.

You can spend your money, you can spend your labor, mental and physical, for this and similar bread, but satisfaction you will not reap. Christ alone is the Bread of Life, Christ alone is the Water of Life. That water is given freely. It also satisfies. Matt. 11, 28. 29. He tells the woman at Jacob's Well: John 4, 13. 14.

Come therefore, one and all. No one is excepted, no one is excluded. V. 1: "every one." Take without money and without price and let your soul delight itself in fatness. Come!

2.

There are other reasons why we should not neglect so great a salvation. Our text tells us that many shall drink and shall be refreshed. V. 5: "Nations that knew not thee shall run unto thee." The prophet speaks of the coming of the Gentiles into the holy Christian Church. That was the glorious theme of many Old Testament passages. In various figures the prophets spoke of this great miracle of God. Read Is. 54, 1—3; 56, 3—8. Not only the house of Israel, not only descendants of the Jewish race, but also the Gentile race, sons of the stranger, the eunuch and others, will be called, will drink. Is. 49, 22. 23: "Kings shall be thy nursing fathers and their queens thy nursing mothers." Gen. 26, 4: "In thy Seed shall *all the nations* of the earth be blessed." Is. 60, 1—11. And through the mouth of Malachi, the last prophet of the Old Testament, the Lord said: "From the rising of the sun even unto the going down of the same My name shall be great among the Gentiles; and in every place incense shall be offered unto My name and a pure offering; for My name shall be great among the heathen, saith the Lord of hosts." Now turn to the

New Testament, to words spoken by Jesus. In the Gospel-lesson of the Good Shepherd, John 10, 16: "other sheep." Jew and Gentile, converted, shall enter the great fold. When the centurion came to Jesus and made his noble confession, Jesus marveled and said, Matt. 8, 10—12: "Many shall come from the East and West and shall sit down with Abraham and Isaac and Jacob in the kingdom of heaven. But the children of the Kingdom shall be cast out into outer darkness; there shall be weeping and gnashing of teeth."

Mark well these last words about the children of the Kingdom. Therefore our text: v. 6: "Seek ye the Lord," etc. You have this message. You have these waters. Do not despise them. The Master has ascended into heaven. He has withdrawn His visible presence. Nevertheless His words shall not pass away. "He that heareth you," etc., Luke 10, 16. The prophetic office of Christ. Drink! Come! For: vv. 8—11. God will abundantly pardon. His Word shall not return unto Him void.

These waters refresh, vv. 12. 13. Cf. Is. 35. The apostles in prison; yet: Acts 4, 23—30. The early Christians, persecuted; yet: Acts 4, 32—35. Paul, stoned, etc. (2 Cor. 11, 25); yet: Rom. 8, 31—39. Joy! Ask our city missionaries. (Cf. *Luth. Witness,* Nov. 21, 1933, pp. 391. 392.) Include also our missionary to the tubercular sick in the Adirondack Mountains of New York State. His pastoral visits; many beds; joy! He brings Christ, the Living Water, to these perishing souls. Without these wells of living waters this world would indeed be one large waste, or desert. An oasis where Christ's message of salvation is proclaimed.

We have these living waters. Have *you* tasted them? "Ho, every one that thirsteth, come ye to the waters, and he that hath no money; come ye, buy and eat; yea, come." Do not hesitate, do not linger, do not wait. The message is true. Your God says so, and He cannot lie. "Buy wine and milk without money and without price." Forgiveness of sins for *all.* Come!   A. F. POLLEX.

Whitsunday.
Ezek. 36, 22—28.

To-day we are celebrating one of the three great and joyous festivals of the Church. On each of these festive days we speak and sing of the wonderful works of God, of those works by which and through which God has blessed and is still blessing us.

I shall not estimate the importance of each of these days in comparison with the other. You know something of the joys of Christmas, of its glory and its blessing. Hymn 151.

It is but a few weeks ago that we tasted the joy and peace of Easter. Hymn 218, 1. 2. Ps. 118, 13—24.

Now, it is true, if there were no Christmas and Easter, there could be no Pentecost. But, on the other hand, it is also true that, if there were no Pentecost, we could know nothing of the joys of Christmas and the peace of Easter. God grant that the blessed message of each of these days may always continue to the end of your lives to be the joy of our hearts!

There is need for such a prayer; for the powers of darkness would rob us of these rich blessings of God; especially would the spirit of error take from us the great and priceless blessing of Pentecost Day. And I repeat, if the blessing of Pentecost Day is taken from us, the other gifts of God cease to bless us personally. Without the Gift of Pentecost we could have neither a single Christmas carol nor a single Easter hymn, nor could we sing them. Let us therefore on this joyous day give attention to that of which the prophet in our text also speaks in sublime, incomparable, and beautiful words: —

The Wonderful Blessing of Pentecost.

Concerning this subject the prophet in our text answers three questions: —

1. *Who Bestows This Blessing upon Us?*
2. *What Is the Precious Nature of This Gift and Blessing?*
3. *How does This Blessing Enrich Us?*

1.

a) At first sight it may seem that it makes very little difference who gives us a gift, if the gift is precious in itself. But it is only at first sight that it may so appear. After all, it makes a great difference who gives us a gift. God had commanded the Jews to bring burnt sacrifices, first-fruits, and the offerings of the harvest; but after these Jews, through their sin, had become hateful to God, God refused their gifts. He told them: Is. 1, 11—15; cf. Prov. 28, 9. And God has told all men that He does not want their praises and prayers if their persons are not pleasing to Him, Prov. 1, 24—31. At one time, when a man offered Peter money, Peter in very forcible language refused the money, Acts 8, 20. It was not because Peter thought that the money in itself was a poor or evil gift. That money of Simon's was just as good money as any that existed at that time; but Peter did not want this money from Simon as long as Simon was what he was.

Yes, it makes a difference from whom a present comes. The Bible forbids us to take presents from certain people, namely, from those who wish to give us presents in order to bribe us. And does it not make a difference whether a bride receives flowers from her bridegroom or whether they are given to her by some other person? Do we not treasure a prayer-book or Bible which a dear father or mother has given to us because of the giver?

b) Now, this Pentecostal blessing of the Holy Spirit is a gift of God, and that makes the gift so precious. God is the One from whom all blessings flow. If we are children of God, God is our dear heavenly Father; no one is more dear to us, no one more loved by us, no one closer to us, than God. To no one do we owe so much gratitude, to no one are we so greatly attached in heart and mind and soul as to our dear Father in heaven, from whom all our blessings come. The smallest of our blessings, the greatest of our blessings, they all come from Him. He spared not His own Son, but delivered Him up for us all. And that is the same dear, precious Father in heaven who gives us the Pentecostal blessing. In explicit words our text calls attention to that. (Note the pronoun of the first person, especially in vv. 25 and 26.)

God promised us this Gift in the Old Testament, Prov. 1, 23; Joel 2, 28; Is. 44, 3; Zech. 12, 10. In the New Testament Jesus repeated and emphasized these promises, John 15, 26; 16, 7b. In each case we are assured that the Giver of this Gift is God Himself. And the very fact that God in the Old Testament makes so much of this Gift and emphasizes the fact that He, the Lord of lords and King of kings, the Creator of heaven and earth, is the only One who is to bestow this Gift, shows us and indicates to us what a very precious Gift this is. No man in his own powers, no Church, no king, can bestow this Gift if God does not bestow it. Just as God gave us His beloved Son to be born of a woman, to assume flesh and blood, just as God alone could raise His Son from the dead, just so God alone can give us this precious Gift of Pentecost.

c) Note also what it is that *moved* God to give us this Gift, v. 22. Not our merit, but His truth and faithfulness.

Application. — We ought therefore to be impressed to-day with the truth that we cannot of our own reason or strength give to ourselves the Holy Spirit. He, the Giver of all our gifts, is the only One who can bestow this Gift upon us. Let us be sure always to receive it from Him, even as our Savior has impressed this upon us in these words: Luke 11, 13. Let us in this connection also not forget that every good gift and every perfect gift cometh down from above, from the Father of lights. God gives no poor, shabby gifts. And this is one of the gifts which He especially emphasizes and recommends to us.

2.

But not only does the *Giver* of this Gift insure its preciousness, but our text tells us also of its priceless *nature*. *What is the nature of this Gift?* Our text tells us: It is God's own Spirit, v. 27a.

a) It is not some material gift. True enough, God does give us material gifts, food and drink, clothing and shoes, house and home, wife and children, fields, cattle, and all our goods; indeed, this whole world and the sun which blesses us during the day and the stars which twinkle at night, these all are the gifts of God. The government that protects us, the friends who cheer us, our loved ones who bless us, all these are God's gifts. And we certainly should appreciate these gifts and thank God for them.

b) But this Gift of Pentecost is something greater than all these. Even though you had all those earthly blessings of which I just spoke, if you are without the Pentecostal Gift, you are poor indeed. Even though you have no friends, no relatives, and are otherwise poor, even if you are without health, if you have this Gift of Pentecost, you are by this Gift alone a world-conqueror, and a kingdom and a throne are awaiting you. For the Gift of Pentecost is *God's own Spirit,* is God *Himself.* Could God give you anything richer than Himself, than His own Holy Spirit?

Consider also that by the Gift of Pentecost God's Holy Spirit enters your heart. And that is the Spirit of Truth, John 15, 26. Through Him you can know all that may be known of God here in this world. Oh, how puzzled and confused, how perplexed and troubled, are many people because they do not know the truth! But God, through this Gift of Pentecost, gives us His own Spirit of Truth, who guides us through the Word of Truth (John 17, 17) into all truth. Thereby He does not only, like some earthly teacher or philosopher, expound a theory. No, by this Gift He persuades us fully of the truth that we are sinners, Rom. 3, 23, and of the truth that Jesus is our Savior, John 3, 16. Oh, there are many false prophets and spirits in the world! Indeed, Satan himself transforms himself into an angel of light, 2 Cor. 11, 14. And this deception is not an insignificant matter. These deceptions mean our temporal and eternal ruin; for Satan is a liar and a *murderer* from the beginning, John 8, 44. There is only one way of escape from these murderous and ruinous deceptions, and that is through the Gift of Pentecost. In this way the Spirit of Truth enters into our heart, leads us into all truth, reveals to us all deceptions, protects us against all falsehoods. What richer gift could we desire than this? Oh, let us pray for this Gift, let us ask God to bestow it upon us in richer measure! Luke 11, 13. And for this purpose let us be sure to use God's Word daily; let us crowd His courts that He may bestow this Gift upon us through His Word, for this Gift is given through the Word of God, Acts 10, 44; Gal. 3, 5b; 1 Pet. 1, 12.

3.

But the preciousness and worth of this Gift of Pentecost is seen also very clearly from *its effects in us and upon us.* And our text calls attention just to this point. It answers for us the question: *What does this Gift of Pentecost achieve in us and for us?*

a) The first thing that is mentioned in our text as an achievement of this gift of the Holy Spirit is this, v. 25: "I will sprinkle clean water," etc. It effects *cleansing*. Through the Holy Spirit we receive forgiveness of our sins. Our sins are washed away. We are pardoned and forgiven in the sight of God. We were scattered among the heathen, and we were of the heathen and the pagans, but by the Holy Spirit God gathers us, takes us from among the heathen and the unbelievers and the wicked, gathers us into His own holy land, into His holy Church, into His family, His forgiven and pardoned and adopted children, so that we are now a chosen generation, a royal priesthood, a holy and peculiar people, just as the prodigal son was received into the home and to the bosom of his father.

b) But not only does this Gift bring to us cleansing and forgiveness of sins; it also *changes our nature*. Text: "I will take away the stony heart out of your flesh and will give you a heart of flesh." Without the Holy Spirit our heart is a stone; there is no spiritual life in us; we are dead in transpasses and sins. Just as corruption, filth, parasites, and scavengers live upon a dead carcass, so all manner of sins and vices live in an unconverted person. But by the Holy Spirit this dead body is brought to life. Cf. Ezek. 37, 1—14. The holy life of God comes into us, our hearts are made alive with faith, with love, with hope, with courage, with all spiritual gifts, heavenly virtues, and activities.

We see that in the lives of the saints. What a shameful person was Paul before his conversion, and what a saint be became by the gift of the Holy Spirit! What was Peter when Satan had driven out the Holy Spirit from his heart and he fell into grievous sin? But what a beautiful testimony issued from that man when the Holy Spirit came upon him! How desperate was David when Satan gained the victory, caused the Holy Spirit to depart from him, and made his heart a cesspool of iniquity! But when the Holy Spirit reentered the heart of David and abode in it again, what words of precious content from him, words that we sing continually in our churches and never tire of repeating in our private devotions! What a monster of folly, of superstition, and of self-righteousness was Luther without the Holy Spirit! But what a brilliant light among Christians and preachers and teachers of the Church did he become when through the Gospel the Holy Spirit entered his heart and enlightened his soul! Every unconverted person is a cursed being, a burden unto himself, and a center of infection to others; but let the Holy Spirit enter such a person, and from a monster of selfishness and iniquity he is transformed into a saint, into a child of God, into a center and fountain of blessings to himself and to others. John 4, 14.

Do you not see what a very, very precious Gift this Gift of Pentecost is? The Gift of Pentecost, that is the Gift you need for your soul; that is the Gift which your children need; that is the Gift which your wife, your husband needs; that is the Gift which we need here in our church. Oh, let us pray for that Gift — and be sure that God wants to give that Gift to us. Come, then, to that fountain from which this Gift flows into our souls, the fountain of God's holy Word. Hymn 257. S.

Trinity Sunday.
Num. 6, 22—27.

To-day the Christian Church celebrates the festival of the Holy Trinity. While at the other church festivals we meditate upon some great *act* of God, we on this day emphasize a *fact,* a fact that is basic for our faith. This fact is the doctrine of the "Holy Trinity, the undivided Unity," one God, existing in three distinct Persons — the Triune God. This is the God of the Bible. "The Lord, our God, is one Lord," Deut. 6, 4. This one God exists in three distinct Persons, Father, Son, and Holy Ghost, Matt. 28, 19. Three Persons, one God, the Lord Jehovah. Never did the Father have self-existence without the Son and the Holy Ghost or the Son without the Father and the Holy Ghost or the Holy Ghost without the Father and the Son. — This is the God in whom we believe, whom we worship and adore, the God of all ages, the God of the faithful in the Old Testament and the God of the Christians of the New Testament, the God "from everlasting to everlasting." This doctrine of the Triune God will always be and remain a mystery to our thinking. However, it is not taught in the Bible for the purpose of furnishing food for human speculation, but to furnish food for our faith, that we may learn to *know* this God, and to know Him as the Source of all our blessings, material and spiritual, temporal and eternal. These blessings, which are to be appropriated by faith, are mentioned in our text.

The Threefold Blessing Bestowed by the Holy Trinity: —

1. Jehovah's preservation by the Father;
2. Jehovah's grace by the Son;
3. Jehovah's peace by the Holy Ghost.

1.

Our text, the Aaronic blessing, not only reminds us of the Holy Trinity, but also assures us of the fact that the God Jehovah has blessings in store for us, blessings to be conveyed to, and appropriated by, His children. "On this wise ye shall bless the children of Israel, saying unto them, The Lord bless thee and keep thee." The Lord is our Keeper. "The Lord shall preserve thy going out and thy coming in from this time forth and even forevermore," Ps. 121, 8.

It is not by accident that the universe came into existence; this was done by the design and the creative power of God. It is not by accident that the world is existing unto this day; this is done by the design and the preserving power of God. So a child of God will not only confess, "I believe that God has made me and all creatures," but will confidently add, "and still preserves us." Every one of God's children is under the providential care of an almighty, all-wise, ever-present, good, and benevolent heavenly Father. Had not the children of Israel experienced all this in their wide and varied career? In years of depression and want God provided for them through Joseph; after years of oppression He delivered them through Moses; in their long and trying journey in the wilderness He guided and protected them; He fed them day by day and even sweetened the bitter waters of Mara that they might again be refreshed; He granted them victory upon victory over their enemies and finally gave them possession of the Promised Land.

And Israel's God is also our God. Under all the varied conditions and circumstances in our lives the Lord, Jehovah, is our Keeper. In our occupation and profession, in hours of happiness and in times of grief, in sickness and in health, when we labor and when we rest, by day and by night, from the time of our coming into this world to the day of our departure, the Father in heaven will never depart from us nor forsake us. "He richly and daily provides me with all that I need for this body and life, He defends me against all danger, and guards and protects me from all evil."

Why, then, worry? Many a pleasant day is spoiled by unnecessary worrying. How much health and happiness have we wrecked by needless worry! Mothers worry from the time that their boys or girls go to school until they return, imagining all manner of untoward happening and danger which may befall the little ones. Fathers and mothers worry when sons and daughters leave the parental roof to go out into the world. — Why not bid them a cheerful good-by, which means, "God be with you," and commend them to a Father's care? Matt. 6, 32 b. (Other examples may be adduced.) "Cast all your cares upon Him, for He careth for you." "The Lord bless you and keep you." Be assured of Jehovah's preservation by the Father, who for Jesus' sake is your Father.

2.

For Jesus' sake God is your Father. Our text continues: "The Lord make His face shine upon thee and be gracious unto thee." This is the second blessing — Jehovah's grace by the Son.

Ever since the fall of man there has been a disturbing element in the world — sin. Sin is disturbing as to its nature and as to its consequences. Sin is opposition to God, rebellion against Him and His holy will; sin is transgression of the commandments of God;

sin is the direct opposite of the very essence of God. And the consequences of sin are unspeakably sad. Sin severed the happy relation that existed between God and man; thus we lost the concreated righteousness and incurred God's wrath and displeasure, temporal death, and eternal damnation.

Man was at variance with his Maker. And what could man do to redeem himself and reconcile a just and holy God? As far as man was concerned, the situation was utterly hopeless.

But God in His infinite love and mercy found and furnished a ransom: His only-begotten Son. Before the gates of Eden had been closed, a ray of hope was shed into the gloomy hearts by God's promise of the Woman's Seed. Through the mouth of prophecy the promises of a Helper, a Savior, were multiplied. The entire cult of Israel was centered in a vicarious atonement, and with eager expectation God's children accepted the promise and looked forward to the time when the "salvation of Israel would come out of Zion." To them the frowning countenance of an angry God was changed as often as they heard the oft-repeated benediction: "The Lord make His face shine upon thee and be gracious unto thee."

And now that Messiah has come, we of the New Testament can rejoice with the apostle: "The grace of God that bringeth salvation hath appeared to all men," Titus 2, 11. "When the fulness of the time was come, God sent forth His Son, made of a woman, made under the Law, to redeem them that were under the Law, that we might receive the adoption of sons," Gal. 4, 4. 5; 1 Tim. 1, 15. Now we can bask in the sunshine of the grace of the reconciled God in the face of Christ Jesus. How wonderful is the assurance of Jehovah's blessing by the grace of the Son!

3.

The last of the threefold blessing of the Holy Trinity we find in our text in the words: "The Lord lift up His countenance upon thee and give thee peace," Jehovah's blessing by the peace of the Holy Ghost.

Peace — what a wonderful word, what blessings contained in the promise of peace, in the assurance that we are to be *possessors* of peace! It is that peace of which the angels sang when Christ, the Savior, was born, that message of peace with which the risen Lord greeted His disciples. This blessing of peace is the positive assurance that God is at peace *with us*. Not because there was a truce or treaty on the part of man, but because "God was in Christ, reconciling the world unto Himself," was peace established on the part of God. But notwithstanding the fact that God's love to sinners is universal and that the grace of salvation is here for all, there are so many who on their part are never at peace with God. God who has done so much *for* us must also do something *within* us if the peace of God is to fill our hearts. And just this is the work of the Holy Ghost. Creating faith in our hearts through the Gospel and thus enlightening our hearts that we see Jesus as our Savior, the Holy Ghost gives this wonderful peace and enters into the heart of every believer.

Many in Israel obstinately resisted the Holy Ghost, and for the same reason many in our day never come to the realization of the blessings of peace with God. To His children God gives the blessed assurance that "we have peace with God through our Lord Jesus Christ." Yes, "the Spirit itself beareth witness with our spirit that we are the children of God." So there is really nothing to fear; our sins are forgiven, and God is our Friend. Fearlessly we face the future. Even death cannot but bring us everlasting peace. God's countenance is lifted upon us. Another glorious victory, another sinner won for the kingdom of heaven.

Friends, as you have heard the words of the Aaronic blessing in the past, so you will hear them again and again in the future. Take into your homes, into your hearts, into your lives, the threefold blessing of the Holy Trinity!   J. G. F. KLEINHANS.

First Sunday after Trinity.
Prov. 11, 23—31.

Our text is taken from the book of the Bible known as the Proverbs of Solomon. By some these proverbs have been looked upon as brief and pithy statements of wisdom and experience for the direction of human life, but, after all, as the products of human reason, often lacking truth and reliability. That is an entirely erroneous view.

In this Book of Proverbs we have not only the popular sayings of a man whose very name is so closely connected with wisdom, Solomon, the son of David, the king of Israel, but *the inerrant truth of the Spirit of God,* by whose inspiration also these maxims were written as words of divine wisdom and truth, worthy of solemn meditation by the Christians of the New Testament as well as by the believers of Solomon's days. Being the Word of God, these proverbs do not only give sound instruction for the proper conduct in the lives of men, but the same Spirit who inspired them has the power to change the heart and to attune the will of man to the wisdom of God.

Our text speaks of the selfishness of the wicked in his attitude toward his fellow-men and the charitable disposition of the righteous toward his neighbor.

Selfishness — Charity.

1. A Warning against the Selfishness of the Wicked.

2. An Encouragement for Charity as Practised by the Righteous.

1.

Selfishness is the fundamental sin of the wicked; it is the very opposite of love of God and therefore also the opposite of love of the neighbor. The thoughts, desires, and love of the selfish man are centered in himself; he lives only to benefit himself. A number of the detestable outgrowths of this vice are mentioned in our text and condemned in no uncertain terms.

V. 24b: "There is that withholdeth more than is meet, but it tendeth to poverty." In order to be able to withhold, one must possess, and possession is not in itself sinful. But the craving of the selfish person is to hold and withhold "more than is meet." Dives withheld; while faring sumptuously every day himself, poor Lazarus was left to the dogs. The pleas and the tears of those in want, the cries and sighs of the orphans and widows, do not touch the heart and do not open the hand of him who withholds more than is meet. But "it tendeth to poverty." How literally true these words are has been experienced by many a man in our days; and oh, how poor the soul that forgets to do good and to communicate and to bring the sacrifice so well pleasing to God!

V. 26: "He that withholdeth corn, the people shall curse him." Here we have another example of selfishness. Does it not tend to show the wickedness of the selfish heart that the same speculative manipulations in practise to-day obtained in the days of Solomon? While the producer must sell, often even below the price of production, the unscrupulous speculator "withholdeth corn," the very necessities of life, in order to prey on the ultimate consumer. And "the people shall curse him." The cry of the oppressed is a denunciation of the practises of the greedy, and the curse of God rests upon him; for "woe to him that increaseth that which is not his!" Hab. 2, 6.

V. 27b: "He that seeketh mischief, it shall come to him." What a man soweth, that shall he reap. Sow the seed of evil or injury, and evil and injury will be the reward.

V. 28: "He that trusteth in his riches shall fall." When a man succeeds in this world, we say that he has been blessed with riches. And indeed it is not God's purpose that riches shall be a curse to man. It is quite a different matter to be blessed with temporal possessions and to *trust* in riches. Such trust is idolatry, and he who will not trust in God will find that his idols will miserably fail him, will give no support when help is most needed, and will not be able to keep him from falling.

Now let us follow the selfish man into his home and family. V. 29: "He that troubleth his own house shall inherit the wind." He wants every one and everything in his house to exist merely for his service and welfare; he insists on being the household god, who must be worshiped by all; he is the cause of continued annoyance, a source of untold trouble and mischief, dreaded by all, loved by none. But he "shall inherit the wind." His gain shall be nothing, "and the fool shall be servant to the wise of heart." Yes, verily, he that exalteth himself shall be abased.

2.

Let us now turn to a more pleasant view of the picture. Our text is also an encouragement for charity as practised by the righteous.

Righteousness is the opposite of self-righteousness. The righteous man does not claim to be righteous because of any goodness or worthiness in himself. In God's sight men are righteous if they have appropriated the righteousness of the Redeemer by faith. "Abram believed in the Lord; and He counted it to him for righteousness," Gen. 15, 6. Cf. Gal. 5, 4. 5. But a necessary fruit of faith is the righteousness of life, true godliness. "Faith worketh by love, Gal. 5, 6. Love, charity, the benevolent disposition to promote the well-being and comfort of others, is a characteristic of the righteous. His righteousness will therefore become evident also in his attitude toward his temporal possessions, as described in our text.

V. 24: "There is that scattereth and yet increaseth." He who is open-hearted will also be open-handed; sincere love of his fellow-man makes a man generous and liberal, willing to distribute his goods. Knowing that he is but a steward over what he possesses, the liberality of the believer merely is honesty toward God and honesty toward his neighbor. To hear the plea of the needy is an appeal to the heart to which the self-sacrificing giver will cheerfully respond. "God loveth a cheerful giver," and "he that scattereth" nevertheless "increaseth." Charity never impoverishes. On the contrary, the kindness of the righteous will be amply rewarded by the bountiful blessings of God; for "the liberal soul shall be made fat, and he that watereth shall be watered also himself," v. 25. This finds expression in the beautiful words of St. Paul: "He which soweth sparingly shall reap also sparingly, and he which soweth bountifully shall reap also bountifully. And God is able to make all grace abound toward you that ye, always having sufficiency in all things, may abound to every good work," 2 Cor. 9, 6. 8. Let us not be inclined so much toward ownership as rather toward stewardship, and we shall be richly compensated by the munificence of God.

Charity also finds its reward in the good will and gratitude of those who have been benefited. While the avarice and greed of the speculator and hoarder invites the curse of the people for withholding that which is necessary for life, "blessing shall be upon the head of him that selleth it," v. 26. To live and to let live is the policy followed by the man whose actions are motivated by neighborly love.

The righteous man never wearies in well-doing, but "diligently seeketh good and procureth favor," v. 27. Instead of trusting in uncertain riches, a believer will strive to "do good, to be rich in good works, ready to distribute, willing to communicate," 1 Tim. 6, 18. A life so spent is well-pleasing to the Lord. That man shall "flourish as a branch," v. 28, receiving his vigor and spiritual vitality from trusting in the living God.

V. 30: "The fruit of the righteous is a tree of life; and he that winneth souls is wise." The righteous man can always and under all conditions of life be depended upon to bring the fruit of a living tree. In the home, in his community, in the church, he will be a source of blessings; his greatest ambition will be to win souls for the kingdom of God, John 4, 14; 15, 5. 16.

V. 31. If such a man who is favored by God and is a blessing to all who come in contact with him is subject to the trials and crosses here upon earth, how terrible will be the punishment of the wicked and the sinner! Truly, the opening verse (23) has properly introduced the sentiments of truth and wisdom of our text: "The desire of the righteous is only good; but the expectation of the wicked is wrath." 2 Cor. 5, 15; Gal. 6, 2. 10.

May the Spirit of God ever guard us against the foolhardy confidence of finding reward in a life of selfishness and greed and evermore teach us to seek satisfaction in filling our lives with that charity which is kindled and kept ardent by the fire of God's infinite mercy and love!   J. G. F. KLEINHANS.

Second Sunday after Trinity.
Judg. 2, 1—12.

"Come, for all things are now ready." This invitation in the Gospel for to-day may be called the greatest invitation in the world. It bids sinners to enter into the kingdom of God. God is in earnest; He would have all men to be saved, 1 Tim. 2, 4.

Why don't all people accept this invitation? Why is it rejected by so many even in our days? Why are so many excuses offered for declining it?

"Marvel not if the world hate you." The word "world" in this sentence from to-day's Epistle denotes the unbelievers. Why should the unbelievers hate us? We pray for them, warn them against dangers; we invite them to our churches. Jesus commands: "Go ye, etc., Mark 16, 15. In the name of the Triune God we offer not what everybody wants, but what everybody needs. It is necessary that we ourselves hear this again and again. This strengthens us in our faith and increases our joy and activity in the "work of the Lord," 1 Cor. 15, 58. Our text explains this mystery as far as we should know it here. It is therefore not only a necessary, but also a welcome word of God. It presents: —

God's Covenant of Grace.
1. What It Is;   2. What It Requires of Us.

1.

"I will never break My covenant with you," the Angel of the Lord, God Himself, said to the children of Israel when He appeared unto them from Gilgal to Bochim. He refers to previous appearances, "I said." God frequently speaks of His covenant in the Bible, especially in the Old Testament. The word is used about three hundred times in the Bible. The Bible may be called God's covenant with the human race. *Covenant* means a promise, an agreement; it is an agreement between two or more persons. In our text God speaks of the most important, the most necessary covenant that can be made, of God's covenant with man for time and for eternity.

To make this covenant with man, it is necessary that God reveal Himself, His promises, to man, declare the purpose of this covenant, what it is. The purpose is to save sinners. The foremost questions of life: Who is the true God? How can we be justified in His sight? How can we serve Him? cannot be answered by all the accumulated wisdom and experience of the bygone centuries. No progress has been made by man apart from divine revelation in regard to the answer to these questions. Nothing has ever been invented by man to improve the soul of man. The abuse of many of our inventions and discoveries has aggravated the problem of sin. The problem of sin, its essence, its treacherous work, its disastrous results, all this is the hopeless problem of the human race left to itself. God in His mercy has provided a solution for the problem of sin, a plan of salvation, which He clearly reveals in the Bible, 2 Tim. 3, 15—17, a covenant with the sinner.

God's covenant is a covenant of grace, the promise of forgiveness of sin, the assurance that we, who are condemned by His holy Law, who are "lost and condemned creatures," are justified not by our own works, but by grace, for Jesus' sake, through faith. There is only one way of salvation, the way of grace for Jesus' sake, Acts 4, 12. He, true God, the Son of God, from eternity is the promised Savior. The sins of the world were imputed to Him. He is man's Substitute before God. By fulfilling the Law of God, by suffering the punishment of our sins as our Substitute, He finished the work of our salvation, He saved us. He obtained grace for all. Through faith in Him we receive forgiveness of our sins, are justified in the sight of God; in the moment when we believe we are received into His covenant of grace, we are children of God and heirs of everlasting life.

How blessed, therefore, is the sinner who says: "I believe in Jesus, I accept God's offer of grace"! And how miserable is the sinner who says: "I do not believe, I reject His covenant"! How righteous and just before God the believer, who says: "God be merciful to me, a sinner"! How wretched the unbeliever, who says: "I need no mercy, I am 'working out' my own salvation, yes, 'I thank Thee, God, that I am not as other men are,'" etc.! Luke 18, 11.

In regard to this covenant of grace, God says in our text: "I will never break My covenant with you." What an assurance! What a comfort! We daily sin much and indeed deserve nothing but punishment. We pray: "Forgive us our trespasses, as we forgive those who trespass against us." The believer keeps God's covenant with him; the unbeliever breaks it. Man may break this covenant; God never. No man would accept the covenant, 1 Cor. 12, 3, no man could keep this covenant, if God had not provided the means of grace, through which the Holy Ghost works, "strengthens and preserves us steadfast in His Word and faith unto our end." It was ever so. In the Old Testament the means of grace were the Word of God, Gen. 3, 15; Acts 10, 43; Circumcision, Gen. 17, 7; and the Passover, Ex. 12, 21. 23. 24. In the New Testament the means of grace are the Word of God, Rom. 10, 17; Matt. 28, 18—20; the Sacrament of Baptism, Mark 16, 16; and the Sacrament of the Altar, Matt. 26, 26—28; 1 Cor. 11, 23—25. The purpose of the Sacrament of Baptism, the purpose of preaching, teaching, memorizing, reading, and hearing the Word of God is twofold, namely, to bring us to faith and to keep us in it; the purpose of the Sacrament of the Altar is to keep us in faith. Through faithful use of them God gives us grace and power to keep His covenant.

2.

What does God's covenant require of us? God sets forth the requirements that are to be observed. "He hath showed thee, O man, what is good; and what doth the Lord require of thee but to do justly, and to love mercy, and to walk humbly with thy God?" Micah 6, 8.

"Why have ye done this?" The Angel of the Lord, who appeared to the children of Israel and asked them this searching question, also reminded them of God's covenant with them, of His special promises unto them for their life on earth, the land sworn unto their fathers, the leading of them from Egypt to Canaan, the Promised Land, of His command that they make no league with the "inhabitants of the land," the heathen, and that they "throw down their altars," as well as of their disobedience, their sins, against God's command. The children of Israel repented immediately, wept, brought sacrifices, called the name of the place "Bochim," which means weepers. The message of the angel of the Lord and the response of the children of Israel show how important and how necessary the requirements of God's covenant are, how faithfully they should be observed.

"Why have ye done this?" This question God also directs to us. He reminds us of His covenant with us, of our faith in the Triune God, Father, Son, and Holy Ghost, of the Sacrament of Baptism, the Sacrament of the Altar, the preaching of His Word, the promises of His grace, of our confirmation vow, of living in daily repentance and

faith, Ps. 2, 12; 1 John 1, 8—10. Under the leadership of Satan the
unbelievers of to-day wield their "deep guile and great might" against
God and His covenant with the believers, seek to entangle them in
a league with them, to seduce them to commit idolatry with them.
Hatred, opposition, persecution. It is estimated that there are about
two billion people living in the world to-day. Through modern inventions and discoveries the teeming millions of this world have been
brought nearer to each other, and the danger to believers increased,
Mark 13, 22. God commands us who believe to go forth and preach
the Gospel to every creature, to fear neither devil nor unbeliever, but
to trust in God's grace and power, to enter into no compromise with
unbelief, never to surrender to it. Many churches which formerly
preached the Triune God have surrendered to unbelief and no longer
proclaim God's truth. In our churches many individuals who vowed
to be "faithful to the Triune God," to "suffer all, even death, rather
than fall away from it," to "conform all their life to the rule of the
divine Word," etc., have become unbelievers, persecute believers, and
wilfully transgress God's holy Law. Why have they done this? —
What are we doing to rescue them, to prevent others from breaking
God's covenant? Who of us is innocent, without any sin, in regard to
this deplorable situation? Who is without blame in regard to the sins
of other people? Certainly the question of the Lord "Why have ye
done this?" reminds us of the need of daily repentance and faith, of
watching and praying, carefully studying the requirements of God's
covenant with us, and should impress upon our hearts once and for
always that through the means of grace God grants us new power for
the requirements of His covenant.

Neglect of the means of grace is ruinous, vv. 10—12. How was it
possible for another generation to arise "which knew not the Lord nor
yet the works which He had done in Israel"? How was it possible for
them to serve the idols of the heathen? How is it possible to-day?
How may it be prevented? "Beware of false prophets," Matt. 7, 15;
1 John 4, 1; Rom. 16, 17. "Be not unequally yoked together with unbelievers," 2 Cor. 6, 14—18. Use the means of grace to resist successfully the encroachments of unbelief, false belief, unsound tendencies
of the "religious" world to-day. "It is written" — with this weapon
of God's holy Word we triumph over all our foes, Matt. 4, 1—11. Be
not alarmed over the opposition and denunciation of unbelief, over its
claims of superor wisdom. "For what if some did not believe," etc.?
Rom. 3, 2. 3. — "Behold, therefore, the goodness and severity of God,
etc., Rom. 11, 22. Hymn 306, 3.

God's covenant is made and kept and its requirements observed
the world over by many believers to-day. Record given in our text
regarding the children of Israel, vv. 7—9. In spite of inhabitants who

were "thorns," in spite of idols who were "snares" to them, they served the Lord many years. The example of Joshua and of the elders. In every generation and under most adverse circumstances God's covenant has been kept by His believers. In days of special trials, persecutions, we, too, can keep it and should "live peaceably" with all men, if possible, overcome evil with good, Rom. 12, 18—21, "seek peace," 1 Pet. 3, 11, etc. Daniel in the lion's den, Dan. 6; the three men in the fiery furnace, Dan. 3; Abraham, Gen. 22. In the history of our Synod, our congregation, individual lives. Hymn 445, 5.

Let us thank God for His covenant with us, faithfully use the means of grace, the Word and the Sacraments, to keep it, learn its requirements, and live according to them from day to day, until we rejoice in heaven with all those who have been saved by this covenant of grace, God's one and only way of salvation. Let us vow new devotion, homage, and loyalty to the Triune God and serve Him with gladness. "He has made a covenant with His people, has given Himself for their Portion, His Son for the Price of redemption, His Spirit for their Guide on the way, His earth for their accommodation by the way, His angels for their guard, the powers of darkness and death for their spoil, everlasting glory for their crown." (Adapted from Richard Alleine.) "Persecution has not crushed it; power has not beaten it back; time has not abated its force; and, what is most wonderful of all, the abuses and treasons of its friends have not shaken its stability." (Horace Bushnell on Church.) Hymn 411.

HENRY KOWERT.

Third Sunday after Trinity.
2 Chron. 33, 9—16.

"Likewise there is joy in the presence of the angels of God over one sinner that repenteth." This "one sinner" is a monument of the grac of God. Other sinners have read it and rejoiced; angels read it and sing. They sing at the new creature that comes from the hand of God, the repentant sinner, as they sang on Creation's morn; they sing for joy that the repentant has escaped a terrible doom and laid hold of an eternal bliss. But their song is chiefly a hymn of praise to God, who is so full of grace that, when He sees a sinner fall, He cannot let him lie, but urges him to repentance and faith that he might be saved, — another monument of the grace of God.

There is joy in heaven. That word makes the devil a liar. It is a lie when he says to the sinner: Your death-warrant is signed; you are lost. It was a half-truth when he said to Cain: Your punishment is greater than you can bear. He "spoke of his own" when he pointed out to Judas the rope as the only consolation for him. He hides the greatest power that was ever conceived, the grace of God. "Jesus Christ is able to save them to the uttermost that come unto God by Him, seeing that He ever liveth to make intercession for them." "Where sin abounded, grace did much more abound." That grace follows the prodigal to the far-off country and urges him to go to his father and to confess to him: "I have sinned." That grace enters Simon's house and lifts the great sinner through her tears to forgiveness. That grace has established a monument for itself in the greatest apostle, once Saul, now Paul. "For this cause," says Paul, "I obtained mercy, that in me first Jesus Christ might show forth all long-suffering," 1 Tim. 1, 16. That grace plucks the malefactor, all but consumed, out of the fire, covers his sin, and invites him to paradise. These are all monuments of the grace of God. A monument is a permanent reminder of things that should not be forgotten. Monuments are erected for us to behold and inscriptions chiseled into them for us to read. The inscription on every monument of divine grace reads: "Where sin abounded, grace did much more abound." Such a monument is Manasseh. He belongs in the list of those who sinned greatly and yet found great mercy.

Manasseh a Monument of the Grace of God.

1. Manasseh Lost.   2. Manasseh Saved.

1.

Manasseh was a son of pious Hezekiah. He was born during the respite years which God gave Hezekiah after he had been sick unto death. Much was expected of him. The pious father certainly did not neglect to educate his son properly, especially since he was born after his miraculous healing and his wonderful delivery from Sennacherib. Manasseh was twelve years old when his father died, old enough to remember the piety of his father and the prayers of his mother. If, in addition, his mother was the daughter of Isaiah, as some suppose, we have ideal conditions for a son who would "do right in the eyes of the Lord and walk in the ways of David, his father."

But Manasseh did evil in the sight of the Lord. What his father had torn down he rebuilt, and what his father had built he tore down. We cannot imagine a greater contrast between father and son than this. Manasseh himself became an idolater; he reared up altars for Baalim, made groves, worshiped the host of heaven, and walked in all the abominations of the heathen, observing times, using enchantments and witchcraft, choosing familiar spirits and wizards as his guides instead of the prophet of God, shedding innocent blood till he had filled Jerusalem from one end to the other, 2 Kings 21, 16; indeed, he sinned so much and so abominably that his sins and trespasses were tabulated in the sayings of the seers, v. 19.

All of this in spite of a good father and a godly mother. The piety of the father does not save the son. "We have Abraham for our father." Sunday-school and parochial school are no cure-alls. "I was baptized a Lutheran," — but what are you now? The reputation of the father is a good recommendation in business; but the faith of the father is no passport into heaven for the son. Often sons of worthy parents are most ungodly. It is a notorious fact that men who go wrong after a good training are often more wicked than others. Examine the leaders of infidelity to-day and see how many come from good families; of old, Samuel's sons, Absalom, Jacob's sons. — Shall we quit our Christian training? Not by any means. Intensify it. Train the children even longer than before. Will such love's labor be lost? Vv. 12—16 would undoubtedly never have been written had it not been for Manasseh's early training. God's seeds sprout slowly at times, sometimes as late as on the gallows, Luke 23, 42.

Manasseh was exceedingly sinful. He built altars in the house of God, altars for all the host of heaven in the courts of the Temple; he placed a carved image in the Temple. He did not retire into his private chamber to pray to his god, he did not conceal his idol in his closet; "he was born with a brazen forehead and lifted his face to heaven with insolence and impudence"; he put his idols into God's Temple, insulted God to His face, challenged God directly. "Who is the Lord that I should obey him?"

There is no greater rogue than a Christian who has fallen away, 2 Pet. 2, 20—22; Luke 11, 26. His bad conscience drives him to extremes. He becomes possessed of an enmity against God and all godliness. When he curses, he curses loud. When he preaches, he does it from the housetops. Why, for instance, do modern Liberalists not keep their infidelity to themselves? Why must they shout it? They have no rest; must bring it into the Christian Church; deny Jesus from the pulpit; insult God in the clergy gown; carry their idols into the chancel. — Paul had more success among the Gentiles than among the Jews. Mission-work harder among "former Lutherans" than among the unchurched. — Example, environment, temptation, no excuse for backsliding. God's Law knows no mitigating circumstances. Christianity is a matter of the heart and should never be influenced by locality or opinion of others. Lot was faithful in wicked Sodom, Joseph in wicked Egypt, Obadiah in Ahab's court, Shadrach, Meshach, and Abednego in idolatrous Babylon. God counts our faithfulness in trying circumstances all the higher, Rev. 2, 13; but He never excuses sin on account of them, Prov. 1, 10. — Resist the beginnings. Once the camel's head is in the tent, you will soon be without.

Manasseh led others into sin. That is the height of ungodliness. He caused his children to pass through the fire. He made Judah and

the inhabitants of Jerusalem to err. Great opportunity as king to lead
his people aright. — As the king, so the people. Manasseh had received
a great trust from God. Misused it. When any of the ungodly went
forth to war against God, he led them. Priests of infidelity were
proud to say, The king is on our side. How readily the son, Amon,
followed the father into sin! But, alas! Amon did not follow him by
later repenting of his sins.

No true Christian lives for himself. It is not a trifling thing to
be a church-member. A member of the Church of Christ should be
a model after whom others may pattern. He is responsible not only
for himself, but also for those who see and hear him. The greater the
prominence of the Christian among his fellows, the richer his gifts and
intelligence, the greater is his influence as a leader, but the greater
also the destruction he can cause by leading them a wrong path.
Offenses. Your curse word leads others to say, If he can do it, why
not I? Your dishonesty sanctions his dishonesty in his mind. Oh,
that we would always keep our brethren in mind when we live and
speak before them! One word of doubt causes a doubt in the brother's
heart, and long after the doubt has vanished from your mind, it still
gnaws in his. You as a leader in the Church, to whom others have
a right to look for guidance, speak as though there were no harm in
the world's fashions and ways, no harm in going to see scenes that
are immoral, to minister a little to the flesh, to read literature that is
spicy and salacious, to whirl a bit in the dances of the day. Let us
sift our conduct and speech; we are our brother's keepers. Responsibility of parents, teachers, pastors, elders, leaders among the young
people — their "hero." — Modernist preachers again: The most prominent preachers in the country fill the church page. What responsibility to lead others! Again, canvassers with heretical and impure
literature, Matt. 23, 13; 18, 6. — Manasseh is a lost and condemned
sinner.

There is a Manasseh in every one of us. Is it too harsh to say:
We are lost and condemned sinners? Danger of minimizing our own
faults, 2 Kings 8, 13; Luke 18, 11. Sin is in our heart, Prov. 22, 15;
John 3, 6. Insinuation of the devil: Your sins are but little lapses.
Principle the same — disobedience to God. Whether Adam stole the
Garden of Eden or took only of the fruit of one tree, the disobedience
is the same. Little sins required the same sacrifice of Christ as great
ones; little sins also condemn; little sins harden the heart more than
great ones; whereas great sins often cry for repentance and press
a tear into the eye, little ones frequently go unrepented and cause the
heart to become calloused. Rather: Ps. 51, 5—7; 32, 5. If we would
compare ourselves with Manasseh, we need but go into our private
room, my soul and I, and talk to each other. We need but direct our

ears to the wall of our heart and listen; examine the filthy corners of our soul; probe the unspoken words that lie within our heart; go to the bottom until our little sins become so great that we realize that they, too, have killed the Son of God. Then we shall find a Manasseh in every one of us.

2.

Manasseh was lost in sin, but he shall be saved. God does not desire his damnation, Ezek. 33, 11; 1 Tim. 2, 4; 2 Pet. 3, 9; Matt. 23, 37. He calls him to repentance, v. 10. He threatens to send such evils that both ears of him who heareth it shall tingle; to wipe Jerusalem as a man wipeth a dish, 2 Kings 21, 10—15. He sends the severest chastisements, v. 11. Jerusalem is taken, Manasseh is bound with fetters, and is carried to Babylon.

No less does God desire us to repent. He calls us by the same Word. Often He sends auxiliaries to His call: the husks to the prodigal, bitter shame to the great sinner, a cross to the malefactor, blindness to Saul, a cockcrow to Peter, sickness, death, and depression to us. By means of these He knocks at our door.

And now we see what God can do. No longer the proud Manasseh, no longer a blasphemer; we now see him on the cold floor of the prison, on his knees and crying: O Lord, wilt Thou have mercy on a wretch such as I am? V. 12. — Manasseh's repentance is sincere. He comes to the Lord just as he is, v. 12; Ps. 51, 4. He has no excuses to offer. His sins are his own. He greatly humbles himself before the Lord, as his sins are great, v. 12; Ps. 32, 5; he trusts in the mercy of "his God," v. 12; Dan. 9, 18; Luke 18, 13. Undoubtedly he himself caused his many sins and transgressions to be entered into "the book of the kings of Israel." They were his confession. Read the prayer of Manasseh in the Apocrypha. Whether this apocryphal record is genuine or not, the sentiment of that prayer was Manasseh's prayer, especially the last part: "I have sinned, O Lord, I have sinned, and I acknowledge my transgressions. But I pray and beseech Thee, release me, O Lord, release me, and destroy me not with my transgressions. . . . For Thou art God, the God of them that repent, and in me Thou wilt show all Thy kindness."

Manasseh became a monument of the grace of God. "This greatest sinner, this man who trampled on his father's prayers, who had wiped from his brow the tears which had been shed there by an anxious parent, who had stifled the convictions of his conscience and had gone to an extremity of guilt, in bold, open, and desperate sin, yet this man was at last, by divine grace, humbled and saved." (*Spurgeon*.) God accepted him, v. 13; John 6, 37; Is. 42, 3. He forgave his sins. He restored him to the throne.

Manasseh showed an active faith. He offered peace-offerings and thank-offerings. These typified the Messiah. Manasseh believed in

the Savior. He built again what he had torn down, abolished the
idols which he himself had carved, removed the desecration which he
had wrought in the Temple by cleansing it and established the true
worship again, admonished Judah, whom he had seduced, to return to
the service of God, and took a live interest in the welfare of his people,
vv. 14—16. And so there was joy in heaven.

This monument of the grace of God was erected for us. Let us
read it. Shall we, in turn, be monuments of His grace to those who
shall come after us? 1 Tim. 1, 16; Is. 1, 18. (Hymn 99.)

GEORGE HOYER.

Fourth Sunday after Trinity.
Isaiah 12.

The prophecies of Isaiah deal not only with those events which
were to take place in the days of this prophet, chap. 37, 33, but point
also to what was to occur far beyond his own time. There is a decided New Testament ring to many of the passages in his book, so
that he has rightly been called the Evangelist of the Old Testament.
He knew of the forerunner of the Savior, John the Baptist, chap.
40, 3; he frequently speaks of the coming of Israel's great Deliverer,
chap. 9, 6. 7, even announcing that the Messiah should be born of
a virgin, chap. 7, 14; in the wonderful 53d chapter he describes the
Passion of the blessed Redeemer and its precious fruits so clearly that
the passage might have been penned by one standing at His cross.
In glowing, picturesque language he portrays the beauty of the Zion
of the New Testament, chap. 35; and like John the Divine, more than
seven hundred years later, he has visions of the new heavens and the
new earth, to be called into being when time shall have ceased, chap.
65, 17. So also in the text before us we hear an echo of the hymn
of joy and praise that will rise from the lips of the perfected saints
on that great day when the Church of God on earth will have become
the Church Triumphant in heaven.

The Hymn of the Church Triumphant.
1. A Hymn of Joy.   *2. A Hymn of Praise.*
1.

The careful reader of the prophets will find that it is not unusual
for them to use important events in the nation's history as types of
what is to happen to the spiritual Israel, the Church of God, in later
times. Thus when the Syrian army was threatening Jerusalem in
the days of King Ahaz, the prophet, in the name of the Lord, promised
relief, but used the occasion to speak of a greater deliverance, when
"a virgin shall conceive and bear a son and shall call His name
Immanuel," chap. 7, 14. — In Isaiah's day the kingdom of Assyria

was a constant menace to the peace of its neighbors. For perhaps six hundred years it had been, with but brief interruptions, the leading power of the East, and powerful nations had been compelled to submit to its yoke. Nor were Israel and Judah spared, and in the hands of God the kings of Assyria became a scourge for the punishment of God's people. God was indeed angry with His people, v. 1, when, following their wicked kings, they forsook the living God and worshiped heathen idols.

Yet the Lord was not unmindful of the covenant which He had made with Abraham and his seed forever, and He sent Isaiah to speak words of comfort to the harassed Jews and to predict the utter downfall of the proud Assyrian conquerors, chap. 10, 12. The prophecy was fulfilled when about hundred years later the Assyrian empire was definitely conquered by the combined forces of the Medes and Babylonians.

But here again, while speaking of the destruction of Assyria and the restoration of Israel, the prophet sees farther into the future and in spirit beholds David's great Son, who will effect a deliverance from enemies more to be dreaded than any earthly foe and rescue His people from sin and all its dreadful consequences. "There shall come forth a Rod out of the stem of Jesse, and a Branch shall grow out of his roots," chap. 11, 1. He tells of the Redeemer's work, the blessed state of the believers, the true Israel, under His reign, and looks forward to the time when all the Church's enemies, of whom Assyria is but a type, shall forever have been vanquished. Then the Church shall rise triumphant and enjoy peace and security everlasting; and "in that day," v. 1, the halls of heaven shall ring with the hymn of the redeemed, a hymn springing from joy unmixed with sorrow and sadness. "With joy shall ye draw water out of the wells of salvation," v. 3.

As a wanderer through the hot and parched desert is transported with joy when he finally reaches the oasis and can quench his burning thirst in the shade of spreading palms, so the delight of the saints of God in heaven will be unbounded as they drink deeply of the inexhaustible joys prepared for them by the Lord Jehovah. Ah, how different that joy will be from that which in our short-sightedness we here so often seek to draw from "broken cisterns, that can hold no water," Jer. 2, 13!

Certainly, the members of the Church of God do not wait until they have reached their eternal home before opening their lips in hymns of joy; for God is constantly affording them occasions here below to sing for gladness. When the formidable host of the Egyptians, following hot upon the heels of the fleeing children of Israel, had by a mighty act of God perished in the waters of the Red Sea, the joy of God's people at this deliverance broke forth in the glad notes of Moses' song, Ex. 15, 1 ff. Many of the psalms of Israel's poet-king radiate the holy joy of a heart that has found peace and comfort in the Redeemer. The overflowing happiness of Mary, chosen to be the mother of God's own Son, found vent in the glorious Magnificat. Shouts of joy rent the air as Israel's King rode into Jerusalem on Palm Sunday. The apostles and their congregations sang psalms and hymns and spiritual songs. (Mention Luther's hymns, etc.) And what beautiful hymns of praise in our hymnal! Indeed, the humblest believer, if he but takes time to reflect, will find abundant reasons for joyful songs.

But, alas! our hymns of joy here on earth are not unmixed with sadness. Ever and anon a mournful note creeps into David's glad rejoicings. Hardly had the echo of the virgin's exalted strains died away when she must hear from Simeon of the sword that will pierce her soul; and who of us has not experienced again and again the quick change from singing lips to weeping eyes? Our hymnal also contains plaintive melodies and the mournful tunes of the afflicted.

But all will be different in heaven; for there no shadow of fear, no trace of weakness, v. 2, will dim the beauty and rapture of our singing; for "they shall hunger no more, neither thirst, . . . and God shall wipe away all tears from their eyes," Rev. 7, 16 f.

And well may the saints in the heavenly Jerusalem sing for joy; for the burden of their song will be "salvation." Three times the prophet mentions it in the text in quick succession. They will not tire of singing in ever new variations of how God sent His own Son to "turn away His anger," v. 1, at sin and sinners, which otherwise would have barred them forever from the joys of heaven and consigned them to the agonies of perdition. Gone will be the sadness caused by the power of sin and the weakness of our faith in the Savior; gone the sorrow that arises in us from the knowledge that our service of God is beset with so many imperfections; gone everything that might detract in the least from complete enjoyment of the blessings of eternal salvation. Our joy will be perfect because it has been prepared by the Lord Jehovah, v. 2. Ps. 17, 15. God speed the day when we shall reach the place where "innumerous choirs before the shining throne," etc. Hymn 559, 8.

2.

But not only will surpassing joy mark the hymn of the Church Triumphant, heaven also will resound with the praise of Him who is the Author of its joys, vv. 4—6.

Praise of God is an important function of a Christian in this life, and the more fully he realizes what God has done for him, the more eagerly will he tell the glad news to others, proclaim the name of the Lord among his fellow-men, and declare His doings among the people. He is a poor Christian indeed who does not constantly feel the urge to fill the earth with the glory of the Lord by making known with every means at his disposal the excellence both of the power and of the mercy of God. A Christian speaks indeed of the greatness of the Creator as shown by His marvelous works in the realm of nature, Ps. 8; 104, 24; but more eloquent does his praise become when he rehearses that work of God in which His glory shines even more brightly than in the marvels of creation, namely, the redemption of sinners by the blood of the Son of God, which is so wonderful as to excite the astonishment of the bright spirits of heaven, 1 Pet. 1, 12; Ps. 36, 7. — And the Christian's purpose in thus praising God before his fellow-men is to set as many as possible on the road of faith that leads to the happiness of paradise, 1 Pet. 2, 9.

Alas that our sinful heart does not grasp to the fullest extent the excellency of God's work in preparing salvation for us through the work of His Son! Alas that as a consequence our praise of Him to others is often so cold and indifferent and that our hymns of praise are lacking in warmth and not always ringing with a conviction that would draw sinners irresistibly to the wells of salvation! Is. 40, 9. Hymn 79.

At best our praise of our God and Redeemer here on earth is but the faintest hint of the anthems of praise that will rise from the Church Triumphant in heaven. Then its purpose will no longer be to make known the name of the Lord in all the earth; for this will have been accomplished, v. 5 c. All will acknowledge, whether with joy and praise or with weeping and gnashing of teeth, the greatness of the Holy One of Israel, v. 6. One thing only will our paeans of praise have in view: to laud and magnify the glorious name of the Lord Jehovah. Not only shall we hear again that celestial hymn that broke upon the midnight clear when Jesus Christ was born; not only shall we, as did St. Paul when he was caught up into paradise for a brief period, hear unspeakable words, which it is "not lawful for a man to utter," 2 Cor. 12, 4, but we shall join the angelic hosts in the new song before the throne of God and the Lamb: "Hallelujah! For the Lord God omnipotent reigneth," Rev. 19, 6.

Let us, in anticipation of the joys that await us, go through life rejoicing even in sorrow, praising God even in afflictions, knowing that our path leads to the abode where —

> Through all eternity to Thee
> A joyful song I'll raise;
> But, oh! eternity's too short
> To utter all Thy praise. (Hymn 72, 5.)

ERWIN SCHNEDLER.

Fifth Sunday after Trinity.
Ex. 3, 1—15.

The standard Gospel-lesson of to-day tells of the disciples' miraculous draught of fishes. Overcome by the flash of divine glory issuing from the humble Son of Man, Simon Peter fell down at Jesus' knees, saying: "Depart from me, for I am a sinful man, O Lord," Luke 5, 8. But the miracle was the forerunner of something far more important, the call to apostleship: "Henceforth thou shalt catch men," Luke 5, 10. — In our text we also have such a manifestation of God's glory on the occasion of the calling of Moses to lead the children of Israel from the servitude of Egypt to the freedom of Canaan.

The Manifestation of God's Glory at the Calling of Moses —

1. In the Miraculous Manner of His Appearance;
2. In the Gracious Promise to Deliver His People;
3. In the New Name by which He is to be Called.

1.

The unveiled glory of God may not be gazed upon by sinful man without instant destruction; for God dwelleth "in the light which no man can approach unto; whom no man hath seen, nor can see," 1 Tim. 6, 16. Cf. Ex. 33, 20 (God's words to Moses): "Thou canst not see My face; for there shall no man see Me and live." Some few favored men of God had a closer and more intimate vision than others and were overwhelmed: Moses, Isaiah, Paul, John the Apostle.

God therefore manifests His presence to men in a manner that they may bear. — Moses had spent forty long years, an exile in the land of Midian, whither he had fled from the wrath of Pharaoh, who sought his life for having slain one of the Egyptians. He whose youth had been spent under promising auspices at a monarch's court has now descended to the level of a humble shepherd. He is eighty years old and possibly has resigned himself to spending his declining years far from his own people.

Then one day the Lord appeared to him in the miraculous manner described in the text, v. 2. While He is called the Angel of the Lord, He is in the rest of the narrative referred to as the Lord and calls Himself the God of Abraham, of Isaac, and of Jacob. So it was the Angel of the Covenant, the Second Person of the Holy Trinity, the Son of God, appearing here to Moses. Cf. Gen. 22, 11. 12. 15. 16.

As soon as Moses was apprised that it was the Lord speaking to him from the burning bush, he was filled with fear, v. 6. No matter in what manner the glorious presence of God draws near to man, the first reaction is always fear. Elijah did not quail before the great and strong wind that rent the mountains; the earthquake did not alarm him, nor did the fire frighten him, but when he heard the "still, small voice" of the Lord, he wrapped his face in his mantle, 1 Kings 19, 12 f. The vision of the thrice holy God vouchsafed to Isaiah in the Temple filled the prophet with terror: "Woe is me! for I am undone. . . . Mine eyes have seen the King, the Lord of hosts," Is. 6, 5. Cf. also Rev. 1, 17; Judg. 13, 22.

God does not appear to us in such visions; still we can see His glory all about us, proclaimed by the marvelous works of creation. Sun and moon and stars, mountains and hills and valleys, streams and lakes and oceans, the changing seasons, the teeming life on the land, in the air, and in the sea, all these eloquently preach: Glorious is the Lord, our Maker! Ps. 19, 1—6. And if we accustom ourselves to see the power and wisdom of the Creator in all His marvelous works, a feeling of awe will creep over us, and standing even before the humblest work of God, we shall be in the mood to do what the Lord bade Moses do: "Put off thy shoes from off thy feet, for the place whereon thou standest is holy ground," v. 5. And we shall be moved as was the poet to say: Hymn 72.

2.

Great, however, as is the glory of God in the realm of nature, it shines more brightly still in the work of redemption. God's greatest glory consists in this, that He devised means to bring sinful mankind, estranged from the Creator, back to Himself. To believing eyes and ears the story of how God by His Word called the earth and all its marvels into existence is not half so wonderful as the account which tells that "God was in Christ, reconciling the world unto Himself, not imputing their trespasses unto them," and that "He hath made Him to be sin for us who knew no sin that we might be made the righteousness of God in Him," 2 Cor. 5, 19. 21. Nowhere does God appear so glorious to the believer as in the record of how His promises of salvation and deliverance have always been kept.

After making His presence known to Moses in the burning bush, which nevertheless was not consumed by the flames, the Lord tells Moses of His plans for Israel, vv. 7—9, and the words must have fallen like sweetest music on the ears of this exiled Israelite. For he knew at first hand the oppression under which his countrymen were laboring. The miracle of the burning bush must have been forgotten and the glory of God appeared to Moses far greater as he heard that the promise given to Abraham and his seed centuries before had not been set aside, but was about to be fulfilled.

More wonderful still it must have seemed to Moses that he of all men should become the instrument in the hands of God to accomplish the delivery of Israel from the house of bondage. To thousands of the younger Israelites he would be altogether unknown, and the older ones may have forgotten him. His early attempt to alleviate the distressing lot of his countrymen, Ex. 2, 11 ff., had ended in failure, and well might he exclaim: "Who am I that I should go unto Pharaoh and that I should bring forth the children of Israel out of Egypt?" V. 11.

Great and glorious the Lord must have appeared to Moses in these promises to deliver Israel from the house of bondage; more glorious still when they were fulfilled, Ex. 12, 51. And when later Moses, grown bold by long and intimate communion with God, expressed the wish to see His glory, the Lord answered: "I will make all My *goodness* pass before thee," Ex. 33, 19. And so it was; as He passed by, He proclaimed: "The Lord, the Lord God, merciful and gracious, long-suffering and abundant in goodness and truth, keeping mercy for thousands, forgiving iniquity and transgression and sin," Ex. 34, 6. 7.

While God's children do not fail to sing of God's glory as evidenced in His creation, Ps. 104, their hymns rise to loftier heights when redemption from sin and death and hell is the theme. The deliverance of Israel from the tyranny of Egyptian kings but foreshadowed the greater salvation, which the Son of God, here speaking to Moses, was to work out for all men in the fulness of time. That was the big theme of the prophets of old, 1 Pet. 1, 10 f.; that was the burden of the prayers of faithful Israelites, Ps. 53, 6; that was the subject of David's welcome to the King of Glory, Ps. 24, 7—10; and looking back on the fulfilment of all of God's glorious promises for their salvation, the saints standing before the throne of the Lamb in the heavenly Jerusalem will sing a new song to the glory of the Redeemer, Rev. 5, 9. 12. 13.

3.

Having received the commission to become Israel's leader and to bring his suffering countrymen the glorious promises of deliverance, Moses still hesitates. Will the Hebrews believe him? Who, shall he say, sent him? The almighty God? The heathen round about might have used a name like that in speaking of their idols. So Moses asks what he is to say in reply to the question which he anticipates from his kinsmen. And the Lord thereupon designates Himself by a new name which also manifested His glory: "I AM THAT I AM," v. 14. This was indeed a new name, as the Lord Himself said when a little later He renewed the ancient covenant with Israel: "I appeared unto Abraham, unto Isaac, and unto Jacob by the name of God Almighty, but by My name *Jehovah* was I not known to them." Ex. 6, 3.

As it is impossible for the human mind to grasp the essence of God, so human language is altogether inadequate to convey an idea of what God is. In answer to this question the Word of Truth simply tells us: God *is* and thereby expresses the eternity of God, Ps. 90, 2;

John 8, 58, as well as His immutability, Ps. 102, 27; Heb. 13, 8. And because He is eternal and unchangeable, His glorious promises will endure. God faithfully kept the promises made to the patriarchs; and how often in later years, when the burden of his position as political and religious leader of Israel seemed intolerable, Moses must have taken strength from the assurance: "Certainly I will be with thee," v. 12.

We are sometimes apt to be dazzled by the glory which some of our fellow-men attain here on earth; yet how fleeting is such splendor and how easily changed to shame and disgrace! But "Thy name, O Lord, endureth forever," Ps. 135, 13. Let us thank God that our eternal happiness does not depend on the shifting, uncertain favor of any human being, but rests on the great I AM, whose attitude toward His creatures never changes, whose loving-kindness is the same toward us as toward Abraham and Moses, whose promise "I will be with thee' accompanies us through life as it did the great heroes of faith in the Scriptures, and who is leading us, as He guided Israel from Egypt to Canaan, to our home above, to be partakers of His glory and to bask in the bright sunlight of His presence forevermore.

Let us seek to fill the earth with the glory of God by telling men of His wonderful works, not only and not chiefly as Creator, but as Redeemer from sin, by proclaiming His wonderful name to all nations and peoples and tongues, 1 Pet. 2, 9; Matt. 5, 16. Then we shall perform the same office as the bright spirits of heaven, who continually stand before His throne and sing: "Holy, holy, holy, is the Lord of hosts; the whole earth is full of His glory." Is. 6, 3.

ERWIN SCHNEDLER.

Sixth Sunday after Trinity.

Gen. 4, 3—16.

Text a picture of horrible wickedness. Crime of the deepest black. Cain, the first son born to the sinners driven from Paradise, becomes the murderer of his own brother. Picture sorrow and grief. Seed of the Serpent. And what a short and sudden step down from the enjoyment of the forbidden fruit to Cain's gruesome deed! And we know that God hates wickedness. God is not a God that hath pleasure in wickedness; neither shall evil dwell with Him, Ps. 5, 4. And Cain went from wickedness unto wickedness. A hypocrite. God's warning. But Cain despised, was defiant, would not repent, lied to the Lord Jehovah, and finally killed. Thus did Cain go from iniquity unto iniquity. His end was despair, destruction of body and soul in hell. The ungodly are like the chaff which the wind, etc. Ps. 1, 4—6.

What a warning! We all need it, 1 Cor. 10, 12. Woe unto them
that go "in the way of Cain"! Jude 11. Let us hear and heed this
warning.

Beware of Going in the Way of Cain.

That is —

1. Beware of Hypocrisy;   2. Beware of Despising God's Warnings;
3. Beware of Letting Sin Rule over You.

1.

A) Text takes us back 6,000 years, to the first family on earth.
Because of the Fall, God had sent Adam and Eve forth from the
Garden of Eden to till the ground from which they were taken and
which had begun to yield thorns and thistles. Gen. 3. The Bible is
silent on the tears they shed when they established their home. But
on some things the Bible cannot remain silent. It reports the birth of
their children Cain and Abel; see context. "And in process of time
it came to pass," etc., vv. 3. 4a. Shows what the faith and life of
Adam and Eve was. There was contrition, godly sorrow. They lead
a life of repentance and in the fear of God; believed in the coming
Redeemer; drew near to God in sacrifice that demanded life for
atonement. That was the sign of God's presence. See Luther, St. L.,
I, 320 ff. By it they came to God, just as we, the children of God to-
day, draw near to God through the sacrifice that was slain on Calvary's holy mountain. Yes, that is the old, old religion. No man
could make or give it; it was given of God. And in this way Adam
and Eve brought up their children. See the text again. There is no
doubt that Cain was at first a believer. Even now he brought an
offering and still belonged to the visible Church. He was still religious, for no man brought up in this way will fall in such a manner
that he will forthwith cast all aside with one fell swoop. But Cain
was going a doubtful and precarious road. Gradually he had drifted
away from the faith of his father. He was going a self-chosen way.
In fact, he was becoming a hypocrite. He dissembled before his
parents. There was no self-examination. There was no repentance.
Cain denied the guilt of his own person. He underestimated the
misery of his sinful condition. He needed no atoning sacrifice, no
expiation, no reconciliation. In a foolhardy, impertinent, saucy, and
self-righteous manner he came to God, not to receive, but to give, not
with an atoning sacrifice, but with a gift-offering. The heart of his
religion, faith, was dead, gone. While Abel, the believer, brought "of
the firstlings of his flock and of the fat thereof," Cain went to no such
trouble and expense. In short, Cain had only the form of godliness,
he denied the power thereof. He was an unbeliever, his faith was
gone, he was a hypocrite. Therefore: vv. 4b. 5. "Fire" — see Luther,
I, 308.

B) Be warned. Beware of this way of Cain. Beware of hypocrisy. Prove your own selves. See whether you are in the faith.
You come from a Christian home. Have had Christian instruction
and training. Advantages of a Christian day-school. You come to
church, sing, pray, and bring your offerings to the altar of God. Beware of mere formality. Mere formality stifles faith, destroys spiritual life, or is already deadness, is hypocrisy, is going in the way of
Cain. Cp. Gospel for the Sixth Sunday after Trinity. Also Matt. 23.
Hymn 83, 10.

2.

A) V. 5 b: "And Cain was very wroth, and his countenance fell."
God warned Cain, as He warns all. We are not told how this warning came; perhaps by direct revelation, maybe through Adam. See
Luther, I, 320 ff. God reminded Cain that he was not doing well,
was not good, not pious and God-fearing, and therefore not acceptable.
He told him that he could be and would be accepted if he did well,
i. e., if he lived the life of a genuine believer. Faith in the Redeemer
alone makes acceptable before God. Note the care and compassion of
God, pastoral, in seeking to win, etc. The questioning: "Why art
thou wroth?" "And why is thy countenance fallen?" Come to Me
as a penitent sinner, seeking grace and salvation; and seek that by
faith in the coming Redeemer. God also warned Cain of temptations
in store. He told him that sin was at the door, was lying in wait like
a wild animal, suddenly to pounce upon him with all its fury and terrible consequences. (G. St., B. G. A. T., p. 7.) But these warnings
were not heeded. They fell on deaf ears. God rejected his offering,
but Cain did not repent; instead he went on in his wickedness. It is
true he again talked to his brother Abel, v. 8; but if it was a friendly
talk, it was hypocrisy and pretense, for his heart was full of envy,
anger, hatred, wrath. All the (pastoral) care of the heavenly Father
went for naught. Cain showed on every hand that he would not be
warned. He would not do the will of, nor walk in the ways of, the
Lord, but would continue to do his own will and walk in his own way.

B) Be warned. Beware of this way of Cain. Beware of despising
the warnings of God. God continually warns all of us. He is doing
so now by this. He warns especially those who, like Cain, have, etc.
He warns by the voice of conscience within us, and He warns by His
Word from without. He warns by parents, pastors, teachers, etc. He
wants to save. He is not willing that any should perish. He warns
against hypocrisy, against all sin, against unbelief. Despise not the
warnings of God. Do not let them fall on deaf ears. Heed the voice
of your conscience. Accept the admonitions of parents, pastor,
teacher, etc. Not to hear and heed them is to go in the way of Cain,
and that is going the way of destruction, as the text will further show.

3.

A) V. 8. Cain slew his brother. Instead of ruling over sin, he allowed sin to rule over him. Of his own free will he became the servant of sin. Under the circumstances it need not surprise us that Cain murdered his own brother. By his refusal to be warned and to repent he himself invited the beast to pounce upon him. He who allows sin to rule over him carries within himself the potentiality of the meanest and lowest of crimes. The Spirit of God and His protecting power is not with the servants of sin, Jas. 1, 14. 15. But once more God came to Cain in an endeavor to save him. He severely reproved Cain for his awful crime, v. 9 a. But note again the question, pastoral care, of the Lord. But Cain is still stubborn, defiant, obstinate. He lies to the Lord Jehovah. Lies accompany sin as a shadow. It is another sign of impenitence. But his sin is known. Must not God know it? He tells him that He does. His brother's blood cried from earth to heaven. Note three times "brother." God makes a threat that the earth is not henceforth to yield her strength to his tilling; he must become a fugitive and and a vagabond on earth. But Cain is still defiant. He will not repent. For reasons of His own God provided for Cain's safety from avengers. A special mark and sign was put upon Cain. But even this favor made no impressions on the impenitent man. Finally Cain's defiance turns to despair. He refuses to believe in the bounteous grace of God. He dreads the consequences of his sin more than the loss of God's favor. Despair, the deepest essence of impenitence, makes the loss of soul irreparable. See v. 13. Cain is now far, far, away from God. He leaves also the company of believers, v. 16.

B) Beware of this way of Cain. Beware of a wilful service of sin. Finally spells destruction of body and soul. Jas. 1, 14. 15. See Rom. 6, 12. 13. 16. Also the Epistle-lesson for this Sunday, Rom. 6, 3—11. Let no one think that the devil always gets his victims by one fell blow. No; he often prepares them gradually for the fall and perdition. Hypocrisy, carelessness, indifference to, despisal of, God's warnings, callousing to sin by the service of sin. Saul a case in point. As we read the last verse of this text, who is not reminded of what is said of Judas in John 13, 30 and Matt. 27, 3—5? Oh, beware of going in the way of Cain. 1 Cor. 10, 12. If any one here is already on that way, repent. Abhor that way and turn to Jesus, the Savior of sinners, who has borne our griefs and carried our sorrows and whose blood speaketh better things than that of Abel, Heb. 12, 24. (Read Luther's exposition of this text, Vol. I, 320 ff.)   A. C. KLAMMER.

Seventh Sunday after Trinity.
1 Kings 17, 1—16.

Few names have such a halo of glorious association surrounding them as that of Elijah. He appears suddenly and disappears miraculously. In the whole range of history there is scarcely another quite so stern, rugged, mysteriously grand, and impetuous a character. In certain elements he resembled Moses under the Old Testament dispensation and John the Baptist under the new. The highest compliment ever paid John was, when, preaching in the wilderness, with his hairy garment around him and his eloquent voice causing, through the Holy Spirit's power, thousands to repent and even the king to tremble on his throne, Jesus said: "This is Elias which was for to come."

The mission of Elijah was to reprove and punish King Ahab; for under him and his idolatrous and wicked wife, Jezebel, Israel had reached a depth of depravity which it had never attained before. The whole land was given over to idolatry, the altars of the true God were overthrown, and those of Baal, the sungod, were set up in their stead. Faith and loyalty to the true God had so completely died out that Elijah, so far as he could see, was the only one left who loved and worshiped the Lord God Jehovah. A peculiar phase of the apostasy of Israel, under the leadership of Ahab and Jezebel, was the adoption of the Phenician worship of the material elements which produce rain and dew, while the God that made them was forgotten. While Ahab was congratulating himself on the success of his policy and leadership, suddenly there appeared before the king and queen, perhaps as they were enthroned in their palace, this messenger of the God whom Israel had forsaken to thunder out this curse: "There will be no dew nor rain these years but according to my word." "Let the house of Ahab and all Israel know that the living God, the Creator, is superior to His works, and He will restrain both dew and rain, and all the world shall know that He is God."

His approach is sudden, his disappearance is just as sudden. Where is he to go? Ahab will seek his life. Where shall he find sustenance? When the heavens are shut up by the word of the Lord, what will become of the prophet who declared that word? Will he not suffer from the drought in common with the sinners on whose account the dew and rain are restrained? Will not a demoralized people resent their sufferings upon the man of God and aid Ahab in seeking his life? The prophet's God knows all and is equal to all emergencies.

1.

"And the word of the Lord came unto him saying, Get thee hence and turn thee eastward and hide thyself by the brook Cherith that is before Jordan. And it shall be that thou shalt drink of the brook; and I have commanded the ravens to feed thee there."

"The Word of the Lord is right, and all His works are done in truth." The rainy season came, and the sky above continued cloudless, blazing like burnished brass with the red glare of the fiery sun. Month after month no dew drop sparkled on the withered grass; the fountains refused to flow, the rivers dried up in their beds, and grim, gaunt famine began his desolating march across the land. The grass had become blackened and was destroyed, as if some prairie fire had passed over it with its scorching breath. Then the cry awoke in the palace and was echoed in every quarter of the land: "Where is Elijah the Tishbite?" They sought him east and west and north and south; they sought him in the towns and in the desert, on the mountainsides and in the lonely places; in Gilead and Judea, in Israel and Zidonia, wherever they heard that any one answering to the description of his person had appeared, there Ahab sent messengers in the hope of getting the prophet into his possession. But all search was in vain. Elijah was safe, hidden away by God.

"So he went and did according to the word of the Lord; for he went and dwelt by the brook Cherith, that is before Jordan." He did not go there because he was afraid of anything that might be done to his person because of the bold message which he had carried to Ahab in God's name, but because God sent him there; and in taking up his abode in that rocky cavern, he served his Master as faithfully as he did when he entered the palace of Jezebel to confront the king or when he stood on the summit of Carmel and put to shame the worshipers of Baal.

"And the ravens brought him bread and flesh in the morning and bread and flesh in the evening; and he drank of the brook." The Lord God never sends a man to a warfare on his own charges. If He sets one on a pilgrimage, He will put a staff into his hand and will support him in the way. If He calls one to suffer for His sake, He will sustain him by His grace and cheer him by His favor. If He requires one of His children to do a certain thing, He will provide for him the resources which are needed for the doing of it. There may have been no miracle in the continuance of the mountain torrent; this appears from the fact that by and by it failed. But it continued to flow long after the other brooks had dried up. And this stream, which ran so long, was in a hidden retreat, where no one would think of seeking the prophet.

But more wonderful is the latter part of the promise: "I have commanded the ravens to feed thee." Ravens are unclean creatures. They are insect-feeding, carrion-eating birds, themselves fed by the special providence of God. Yet God commands these otherwise unclean creatures to bring Elijah food; for the instincts of all creatures are in His hands. He restrained hungry lions from harming Daniel and instructed a fish how to behave toward Jonah and another to lift a piece of silver from the bottom of a lake and then fasten upon a hook. "Is there anything too hard for the Lord?" "Never have I seen the righteous forsaken nor his seed begging bread." In the barren wilderness He gave bread from heaven. "In the days of famine they shall be satisfied." Elijah had called a famine upon the land and broken the whole staff of bread; but he himself had enough. God spread for him "a table in the wilderness," and almost in the presence of his enemies. The stars shall fall from their courses, but he shall have enough. It has been thought by some that the ravens brought him bread and meat from Ahab's own table. It would have been so had it been necessary. He only received a small supply of food each time the ravens appeared; so though he had no lack, he had no profusion. He had "daily bread" — for "the morning and the evening are one day." Even he must walk by faith and learn "to take no thought for the morrow."

"And it came to pass after a while that the brook dried up because there had been no rain in the land." The ravens bringing Elijah food and the brook furnishing him with water whispered to him of the care of God and of the provision made by a Father's love. When he drank, he drank in faith. He drank in the firm faith that God was interested in him, was watching over him, was ready to supply all his needs. But one morning as he visited the brookside, he was struck by the fact that the little stream was more hushed and subdued than it had been. And there came to him the startling realization that the water of the brook was failing. It was a bewildering experience. Every day he noted that the waters were falling more and more. Then there came a day when he made his way to its banks and found it altogether dry. There was no water, only parched, glittering sand.

Why did the brook dry up? It did not dry up because God had forgotten His prophet. It did not dry up because God was so busy governing the universe that He allowed all thought of Elijah to be crowded out of His mind. You and I forget sometimes, but God never does. He is great enough to light suns and fashion stars, but He is also great enough to stoop to the humble task of clothing the lily. He is not too busy to sit by the sick-bed of the sparrow and to think upon the day of its death. And be sure of it that whatsoever of seeming harm has come to you or to this prophet did not come because of the forgetfulness of God.

God allowed the brook to dry up because He had other plans for His faithful prophet. Over yonder at Zarephath was a poor widow at whose skirts a hungry child was plucking. She was a widow who was not only sorely in need of material bread, but more sorely in need of the Bread of Life. God sent His prophet to find sustenance there.

She was a blessing to him, and he became a far greater blessing to her. "All things work together for good to them that love God." They are defeated by no disaster. They are conquered by no calamity. There is absolutely nothing that can come to them that God cannot cause to work for their good.

2.

"And the word of the Lord came to him [Elijah], saying, Arise and go to Zarephath, which belongeth to Zidon, and dwell there; behold, I have commanded a widow woman there to sustain thee." A new trial for his faith. To obey this command required that he cross the entire tract of Israel lying between Jordan and the Mediterranean Sea, that he should go to the territory of Ethbaal, the idolatrous father of wicked and vindictive Jezebel, and that even there he should be cast on the support of a woman whose natural breadwinner and protector had been stricken from her side. It did not seem a very inviting prospect, but it was God that gave him the command, and so "he arose and went to Zarephath."

"I have commanded a widow there to sustain thee." That does not mean that the word of the Lord came to her as it did to Elijah himself, but simply a similar mode of speech, as in the case of the ravens, that God would sustain the prophet through her instrumentality. In the course of divine providence Elijah would be supported by a widow in Zarephath. But how was he to know to which of the widows of the city he was sent? It does not appear that any information was given him on this point until he reached the gate of the town. As he approached the entrance into the city, he saw a woman gathering sticks, and under the guidance of the Spirit he approached her and asked her if she would kindly "fetch him a little water in a vessel that he might drink." He had walked a long way; it was a time of drought, and he was exhausted after such a long journey. It was natural therefore that he should make such a request. But water was a scarce commodity just then, and the woman might have been excused by many if she had declined to comply with the request of a stranger. She went, however, to do as he had asked; but while she was going, he called after her and said, "Bring me, I pray thee, a morsel of bread in thine hand." This, however, seemed more than she could bear; so she revealed a terrible depth of distress by saying, "As the Lord, thy God, liveth, I have not a cake, but a handful of meal in a barrel and a little oil in a cruse; and, behold, I am gathering two sticks that I may go in and dress it for me and my son that we may eat it and die." Here indeed was extreme misery. "Surely," the prophet might have said, "this is not she to whom I am sent." But he did not say that; he saw in her the very person for whose deliverance he had so opportunely come. So he said to her: "Fear not; go and do as thou hast said; but make me thereof a little cake first and bring it unto me and after that make for thee and thy son. For thus saith the Lord God of Israel, The barrel of meal shall not waste, neither shall the cruse of oil fail, until the day that the Lord sendeth rain upon the earth."

"Make me thereof a little cake first." As she heard these words, she might have felt disposed to say: "How dare you ask that of me? Here I have left only a meal for myself and my son, and you, an entire stranger to us both, ask that I should make a cake for you!" But the promise with which the prophet closed his petition took care of her misgivings. Elijah virtually said, "If you make this cake for me, God will provide for you through this terrible drought. And believing in God's willingness and ability to keep His promise, she at once went and did as the prophet had requested. And God kept His word; for "the barrel of meal wasted not, neither did the cruse of oil fail, according to the word of the Lord which He spake to Elijah."

Now, in conclusion, what are a few lessons from this amazing story?

a) The first thing that strikes us is the minuteness of God's daily providence. The Redeemer Himself has said that "a sparrow shall not fall to the ground without your Father." This narrative exemplifies that divine assertion in such a manner as almost to stagger our intellect. And this minute providence is the same to-day. It is as true now as it was then that God is "above all, and through all, and in you all." He is "not far from every one of us." He is on every side of us. His providence encircles us with His protection and guides us with His wisdom. What a comfort there is in the assurance that God is with us and for us, so that each of us can sing with David: "I am poor and needy, yet the Lord thinketh on me," especially since God's provident love is based upon His mercy in Christ Jesus, Rom. 8, 32.

b) In the second place, we learn here that, no matter how small our resources may be, we can still do something for God if we have but the will. This poor woman could scarcely have been in more destitute circumstances. She was at the point of starvation, and yet by her unselfish liberality with what she had she was honored of God to sustain His prophet for perhaps two years, besides having all the necessities furnished for herself and her son. Never let any one say: "I am of no use in the world; I can do no good; I am too poor to render any service." The little we have becomes much in the hands of God. Think of the lad's loaves and fishes in the hands of the Savior. An ox-goad in the hands of Shamgar; a bone in the hands of Samson; lamps, pitchers, and trumpets in the hands of Gideon's three hundred; a sling and a stone in the hand of David. Under

God's grace and power our weakness will be our strength, so that like Paul we shall say: "When I am weak, then am I strong."

c) Our doings for God should go before our devotions to ourselves. The world's maxim is: "Take care of yourself first." The Christian principle is to merge self in Christ. God requires the firstfruits. It will not do merely to serve ourselves and give the surplus to Him. We must serve Him and advance His cause even if we should be required like this poor woman to eat a smaller cake ourselves, and to give a smaller portion to our families. There is no faith exercised in giving to God only what we can spare after we have served ourselves. Faith will, like this poor widow of Zarephath and the poor widow at the Temple treasury, give all, if need be, to God and look to Him for continued supply.

d) In giving thus to God, we are so far from losing anything that we are rather actually gaining. What God gets from us, His children, He repays with an abundant increase. This woman gave one meal to the prophet, and God sustained her for two years. This is ever the divine law — we get by giving. We must sow if we would reap; we must open our hearts in love to others if we would have God's love shed abroad in our souls. It will not do, however, for us to have regard to the reward. We are to "do good and lend, looking for nothing again"; and then it is that our reward will be great, and "we shall be the children of the Highest."

e) Lastly we learn that God's help is often delayed until the very last, to make us realize all the more that, when relief comes, it comes from Him. Not till the brook was quite dried up, did the Lord make provision for Elijah; and the widow was preparing her last meal when Elijah came. "Man's extremity is God's opportunity." It was in the fourth watch of the night, when the disciples were worn out by their long toil in rowing, that Jesus came walking over the sea to their assistance. It was after Lazarus had been buried four days that Jesus came to help His friends at Bethany. Let us therefore not despair, no matter how dark the outlook may be. It would indeed be a sad thing to be in perplexity with no God to fall back upon; but while we have Him saying to us, "I am thy God," all is well. But sad, ineffably sad, it is when a man has nothing but earthly things to sustain him. The day will come when the brook will fail him and the barrel become empty; and what shall he do then without God?

> Leave God to order all thy ways
>   And hope in Him, whate'er betide;
> Thou wilt find Him in evil days
>   Thine all-sufficient Strength and Guide.
> Who trusts in God's unchanging love
> Builds on the Rock that naught can move.

W. A. SETZER.

Eighth Sunday after Trinity.
Jer. 23, 21—32.

You and I, dear hearer, have two kinds of enemies — open foes and secret, deceitful adversaries. Just as Jesus was opposed by declared enemies (John 8, 48) and secret traitors (Matt. 22, 16; Luke 22, 21. 22), so we are surrounded by both of these. Among the most harmful, dangerous, and treacherous of these are the men who come to us telling us that they are *messengers of God,* whereas they are the most vile deceivers. At times the Bible calls these men "false prophets," at other times they are called "hirelings," "vain talkers and deceivers," and "heretics." One of the most apt names given to these treacherous persons is "wolves in sheep's clothing."

Here permit me to ask you a question: "Do you think that your Good Shepherd, Jesus Christ, would warn you so earnestly against these men if you were in no danger at all of being deceived by them? I trow not.

But you may now ask: How shall I guard myself against these insidious foes?

This very question is answered in our text.

Three Marks of Religious Deceivers.

1. They are Not Sent by God, but Come of Their Own Accord.

a) The first mark of a wolf in sheep's clothing is the one mentioned in the first verse of our text, v. 21.

But how do we know that a prophet is sent by God? At one time God often called a preacher of His Word directly, *e. g.,* Moses, Isaiah, Paul, etc. But at present God calls and sends our pastors through the call extended to them by the church. That custom began even in the days of the apostles, for we read that the disciples chose Matthias to be numbered with the eleven apostles, Acts 1, 21—25. We read also that the disciples at Antioch, guided by the Holy Spirit, ordained and chose and sent Barnabas and Saul to go forth and proclaim the Gospel in other places. Even so Paul told Timothy to commit the doctrines which he had heard of Paul to faithful men who were able to teach others also, 2 Tim. 2, 2. The same Apostle Paul writes to Titus that he, the apostle, had for this very cause left Titus in Crete that Titus should ordain elders in every city. This practise we have followed in the Lutheran Church down to the present day. God wants to make known His will concerning His pastors and shepherds through the flock. That man, therefore, whom the Christians of a congregation have called to preach God's Word to us, he is the one whom God has sent to us with His Word.

b) The false prophets, the deceivers in religion, are neither called by the congregation, nor are they sent with a message from God. As our text states, "yet they run." God did not speak to them, and yet they come and pretend to be God's messengers.

There were many of these in Old Testament times. Some of them even performed miracles, Deut. 13, 1—3. Moses had to warn his people against them again and again. In later years they increased; they were especially common in Samaria. At all times these hirelings have come to live upon the flock of Jesus. They never ask, What does God want? Does God send me? Their question is, How may I reap riches, renown, honor, power as a religious teacher and leader. Let us note that the Lord Jesus calls our attention to the fact that these men often appear among us in sheep's clothing; that is to say, they have all the appearance of belonging to the flock of Christ. They *run,* they are full of zeal; they *teach,* they seem to have authority; the world hears them, they are popular. Who can deny that we have such in Christendom to this very day? Let us be warned. It is the voice of the Good Shepherd saying to us, Beware!

The second mark which our text points out as a characteristic of these religious deceivers is this: —

2. They do Not Preach God's Word, but Their Own Dreams.

a) Some of these deceivers tell us outright that the Bible is an antiquated book and that there are new revelations. They make no secret of it that they do not agree with all things in the Bible; either they claim that they have received a new message from God, or that through scientific or philosophic reasoning they have discovered the truth about this matter and have a *new message for a new day.* These people try to substantiate their claim by telling us that mankind has made advances and that we can no longer accept in simple faith what our ancestors accepted thousands of years ago. Let us remember: however many changes there may be and however many new discoveries, there are some things which do not change. Our multiplication table has not changed one whit since the beginning of the world. When Adam lived, twice two was four, and twice two is four to-day, and twice two always will be four. And just so the fundamental revealed truths of God's Word are eternally the same. No philosophy, no reasoning, no science, can change these eternal truths.

b) Another class of deceivers claims to be in full agreement with the Bible; in fact, they claim to be teaching the Bible. But they pervert the Word of God, teaching Eddyism, immersionism, Romanism, or other rationalistic and fanatical teachings which they try to grace with Scriptural phrase and pious-sounding vanities. These people at times say much in honor of the Lord Jesus. They may call Him Lord; they may call Him a divine man; they may promise us great results from their preaching; they may even perform lying miracles. But let us beware; let us keep in mind what God told His people

Israel in the Old Testament, Deut. 13. Even though such men perform miracles, we should not follow their false teachings. Also in our
day the messenger of God is not to be tested by miracles, but, as our
text states: "He that hath My Word, let him speak My Word faithfully. What is chaff to the wheat? saith the Lord," v. 28. Let us
always be ready to use the proper criterion, the measuring-rod of God:
"To the Law and to the Testimony; if they speak not according to
this Word, it is because there is no light in them," Is. 8, 20. Cf. John
8, 31. 32.

O how many deceivers of this kind there are in the world! Centuries ago our fathers uttered the complaint: —

> Those haughty spirits, Lord, restrain
> Who o'er Thy Church with might would reign
> And always offer something new,
> Devised to change Thy doctrine true." (Hymn 110, 6.)

How many "new" isms have come since that day! Let us pray God
daily that He would keep us in His Word and truth, so that we may
ever recognize and love the voice of our Good Shepherd alone.

But is it of such great importance that we avoid every religious
error? Indeed it is. Our text points out a third mark of religious
deceivers.

3. They do Not Profit the People, but Cause Them to Err, v. 32.

God's Word is a word of salvation. Just as God Himself has
provided for our body the proper food and drink, so in His Word He
has given the proper food and drink to our souls. There is no fanaticism, there is no deception, there is no superstition, in God's Word.
In His holy Law, God makes known to us the exact nature of sin.
He does not tell us just how to fold our hands, what kind of clothing
to wear, whether to kneel or to stand up, but He tells us to love God
above all things and to love our neighbor as ourselves. He denounces
those people who pay tithes of mint and cumin and forget the
weightier things of the Law, judgment, mercy, and faith. He condemns those who make clean the outside of the cup and of the platter,
while within they are full of extortion and excess, Matt. 23, 23—25.
Do you not see how Luther was made to err by false teachers when he
was told he must take the vows of the cloister, he must fast and bring
the sacrifice of the Mass for his sins? That false teaching of the Law
would have made of Luther a hypocrite, a fanatic, and perhaps driven
him insane. And no one knows what fearful error, what mischief,
what harm, has come through the false teaching of the Law among
men. Not only the Inquisition of Rome, but also the Puritans of the
New England States and other fanatics have brought shame, misery,
and gloom upon mankind, in part, even eternal damnation, through
their errors and tyranny.

Worst of all, however, is this, that the Gospel is not preached in its truth and purity. God wants us to become rich through the Gospel. In His Gospel He gives us the unsearchable riches of Christ, forgiveness of sin here and the inheritance incorruptible, undefiled, and that fadeth not away in heaven. False teachers, religious deceivers, cheat us out of our inheritance and our spiritual riches. Oh, let us beware lest the glad tidings, which God intends for all men, be perverted, adulterated, corrupted, by the foolish surmises, conjectures, and errors of these religious deceivers! How happy was St. Paul in the truth of the Gospel when he exclaimed: Rom. 8, 31—39! How happy was he who could with full confidence say: Hymn 325, 1. 2!

Let no one deceive you with vain words, my dear hearers. No, and even though an angel from heaven proclaims any other Gospel to you than the unsearchable riches of Christ, be not deceived; cling to your Savior, hold fast that which you have, that no man take your crown!   S.

Ninth Sunday after Trinity.

Ex. 32, 1—14.

Our text tells of an incident which occurred during Israel's journey from Egypt to Palestine. The history of that pilgrimage is not only intensely interesting, but also very instructive and profitable. The difficulties, the struggles, the sufferings, and the battles which those wanderers experienced all in turn claim our attention. But most impressive of all is God's wonderful providence, which guided these people, protected, fed, and preserved them. It is God's purpose and will that the story of this pilgrimage should never be forgotten. Therefore Feast of Tabernacles and frequent rehearsal in Old Testament, e. g., in Deut. and Psalms. Therefore Paul also in New Testament calls attention to the occurrences and appeals to all Christians to heed the admonitions, 1 Cor. 10, 11. Would that Moses could have told more of the godliness and faith of Israel! But as it was, there is many a record of Israel's sin. Such is the one to which our text refers.

Israel Commits Idolatry.

1. How did That Happen?

a) It was not the first sin which these people had committed while fleeing from Egypt. Even in Egypt they murmured and complained when they should have given thanks, Ex. 5, 20. 21. Again, when they had traveled but a short distance, Ex. 14, 10, and at other times.

How ungrateful is man! How rebellious!

b) Now that Moses had gone up to the mount to receive the Law from God, the children of Israel became impatient, v. 1. And at once there were those who suggested that God had forsaken them, that they must provide for themselves. And, of course, if God had left them, they must have some god. They called upon Aaron to make them an idol. And Aaron was too weak to resist their sinful proposal. He made them a *man-made* god.

That is the course which leads away from God to ever darker sin. First *dissatisfaction* with God's Word and ways, then one sin leads to another, till man does not even hesitate to commit the most vile wickedness. Cf. John 6, 60—66; 12, 4—6; 1 Sam. 13, 7—14. Be warned! Let us daily pray: Ps. 139, 23. 24.

2. Why Was Israel's Sin So Shameful and Damnable?

Because it was gross idolatry. Idolatry is that sin whereby men substitute something in the place of the true God. Now, there is nothing higher, more majestic, or more adorable than the true God, Ps. 47; Ps. 100; Ps. 139, 1—12. And in place of this God, men choose the vilest objects: devils, 1 Cor. 10, 20; animals, Rom. 1, 23. — What a shameful sin!

When we to-day hear of people in pagan lands building temples to elephants, snakes, and monkeys, we stand appalled. But these poor heathen were never taught the truth. How much worse is idolatry when found among people who know the truth and have often experienced God's help! Such were these Israelites. What faithful instruction they had received! What wonderful deliverance and guidance of the true God! Luke 12, 47.

However, let us not imagine that *we* are in no danger of committing idolatry. Right here in this Christian country thousands, yea, millions are living in a more refined form of this sin without in all cases being convinced of it. All those who fear and love any one or anything more than they fear and love God commit this sin of idolatry. All those who place their confidence and trust in anything more than in God are idolaters. In this way many make a god of mammon, Matt. 6, 24; of their own bellies, Phil. 3, 19; of their parents or children, Matt. 10, 37; of their country, Acts 4, 19; of honor among men, John 5, 44, etc.

How shameful is this sin by which man prostitutes his most precious and costly possession to fornication with an idol! And yet, how common is this sin! Who is entirely free from its pollution? Should we not cry out, O God, have mercy upon us? By this sin we incur God's displeasure, for He is a jealous God, Ex. 20, 5. Text, v. 10.

Men speak much of unfairness and sin against our neighbor; and it is true, the sins against our neighbor are not small matters. But the fact that by sin we insult God, we transgress His commandments, we defy Him, we rebel against His authority and government, makes our transgression all the more heinous and the punishment all the more severe. Let us therefore ask, —

3. How was Israel Delivered from the Guilt and the Curse of This Sin?

a) Many of these Israelites were not delivered. They would not repent of their sin; and when Moses came down from the mount, he had those who either did not participate in this gross iniquity or repented of it slay those who continued in this sin, so that in one day three thousand of them died and perished in their iniquity, v. 28.

Just so to-day many live and die in this sin of idolatry. However much we testify against it, the hearts of these people cling to idols. In their eyes God is a negligible quantity or even a non-existent; but they have an exaggerated view of money, pleasure, honor, and other ambitions. They will not hearken to the warning voice of the preaching of repentance and are therefore like Dives. They go where there is howling and gnashing of teeth.

b) But not all Israelites perished because of this sin. Thousands of them repented, came to God, and with Moses begged the Lord to remember His covenant with Abraham, Isaac, and Jacob. And God was merciful unto them and forgave them. He did not blot them out, but again showed them His favor and received them as prodigals who repentingly returned to Him.

That is the only way in which we also may be delivered from this guilt and iniquity — by repentance, by turning to God, by pleading the covenant of His grace. 'Tis true, this sin of idolatry fully deserves God's wrath, displeasure, temporal death, and eternal damnation. The Lord, however, is not willing that any should perish, but that all should come to repentance. You also, my dear hearer, know very well that this sin has taken possession of you again and again. You know that you have loved the creature more than the Creator; you know that you have trusted in temporal power, in earthly friends, more than in God. Remember, "If we say we have no sin, we deceive ourselves, and the truth is not in us"; but if we confess and forsake our sin, God will have mercy upon us. The blood of Jesus Christ is so precious that it also cleanseth us from this sin. Let us therefore, as long as the day of God's grace lasts, as long as the gate to His kingdom is open, plead for God's mercy: "God be merciful to me, a sinner." Let us rejoice in His grace, in the efficacy of the blood of Jesus Christ, and let us earnestly pray that God would give us strength and power to conquer this sin, so that our hearts may be freed more and more from this vile pollution of idolatry and that we may worship none but the Lord, our God, and serve Him alone, so that we can truthfully say with the psalmist: "Whom have I in heaven but Thee," etc., Ps. 73, 25. 26; that we may say with Joseph: "How, then, can I do this great wickedness and sin against God?" Gen. 39, 9; that we may say with Job: "Though He slay me, yet will I trust in Him," Job 13, 15.   S.

Tenth Sunday after Trinity.

Deut. 4, 23—31.

V. 6 of our text-chapter: "a wise and understanding people."
If Israel would give diligent study to the statutes and judgments
which the Lord had taught them through Moses, then they would
commend themselves to the neighboring nations as "a wise and
understanding people." Moses exhorts the people to walk in all the
ordinances and commandments of God. That will secure them God's
blessing.

"The fear of the Lord is the beginning of wisdom." God has
manifested His grace and love to men. It is an act of wisdom to take
heed of all His mercies. The people who have received mercy and
have experienced the goodness of the Lord should show their gratitude
by rendering obedience to Him. If we neglect to do that, if we are
disobedient people, then we shall forfeit all those favors which God
has intended for us.

But who are the wise and understanding people? Our text gives
the answer.

Who Are the Wise and Understanding People?

1.

The children of this world have a wrong conception of wisdom
and understanding. They consider it wise to do anything that may
add to their own comfort and enjoyment. They disregard God's
Law and will entirely, even considering it to be a hindrance to their
progress. Whatever men may find to be of advantage to their material
welfare, that they will pursue. They even look upon the Christians,
who for conscience' sake will avoid certain things and who seek to
please God, as foolish and deluded people. Sin in their sight is
only a trivial thing. "What difference does it make in the end whether
men obey God's will or not?" As long as they get out of life what
they possibly can, they think they are acting wisely.

But listen to the advice which Moses, the servant of the Lord,
gives to the people v. 23: Take heed unto yourselves; forget not the
covenant of the Lord; do not follow after false gods. It is true, the
majority refused to heed this solemn admonition. How often did
they turn away from their covenant Lord and worship at the altar
of idols! How often did they provoke their Lord to anger! Heaven
and earth are called upon to witness against them, v. 26. The children
of Israel soon experienced how true it was what their leader said:
v. 24. God fulfilled all the threatenings announced to those rebellious
and ungrateful people. Oh, that they had remained a wise and
understanding people! To forsake God and disregard His will was
their greatest folly. Their departure from God was at the bottom
of all their misery.

A very timely admonition for the people of our day. How many still care for God and His Word? In the days of prosperity one could notice the spirit of pride on all sides. Our American people exalted themselves. "Look at the wonderful country we have built up." "We are the greatest people among all nations." "Behold, how wise and understanding we are!" Our people worshiped at the shrine of their pet idol. Mammon was their god. Very few ever thought of giving honor to the heavenly Father, from whom alone every good and perfect gift comes. Who deemed it necessary to give any attention to the important matter of religion? Nor have things changed much for the better in the past years, in which the proud and the wise of this world were humbled. We do not see that the people are turning to God in great numbers, that they are seeking to walk in the commandments of God. Oh, the terrible folly! If you think it is wisdom to follow the ways of the world, then Satan has deceived you. God's attitude toward the disobedient never changes. V. 24 is still true in our modern age. Our departure from God and disrespect of His holy Word is the underlying cause of all the trouble in the world to-day. True wisdom demands that we realize and acknowledge that fact.

To show that it is not wisdom when people forsake their God and forget His statutes, call attention to the terrible judgments which the Lord pronounced upon the Jews in the Gospel-lesson for this Sunday. The Jews neglected the time of their gracious visitation. "The way of the ungodly shall perish," Ps. 1, 6. Eternal ruin and misery are the fatal consequences of disobedience. Wise and understanding people will heed the warning.

2.

Vv. 29. 30. The certain benefits and advantages of obedience. — Moses reminds the people that true prosperity will depend on their piety and their loyalty to God. If they seek the Lord, they will find Him and enjoy the land of inheritance. Even when because of their grievous waywardness they have suffered the great tribulation of the captivity, if then they will turn to the Lord and obey His voice, He will accept them again as His children. God is merciful and faithful, v. 31. He will never forsake those who put their trust in Him, Ps. 51, 17.

This is true at all times, and it applies to nations as well as to individuals. "Godliness is profitable unto all things." This does not mean that true Christians and servants of God will never have to suffer trials and tribulations. It will always remain true: "We must through much tribulation," etc. It may even seem at times as though the ungodly were the favored in the land and the Christians the sufferers. But we must not allow ourselves to be deceived by appearances. While the children of God may be deprived of some of the comforts and joys of life, they rejoice in the possession of the gifts which God bestows in His mercy. They have the assurance that for Christ's sake God has pardoned all their sins, that in Christ they have peace with God. Rom. 8, 38. 39.

Why should Christians be envious of the foolish when they see the prosperity of the wicked? Ps. 73, 3. Follow the example of the psalmist, and you will receive wisdom and understanding, Ps. 73, 16. 17. Let us learn to say: v. 23.

Yes, consider the end; then you are wise and understanding people. When you see the apparent happiness of the ungodly and you are tempted to compare therewith the lot of the believers, consider their end. You do not say when the sun rises in the morning, "This has been a fine day," but you wait until the sun has set. You do not judge a painting by the first strokes of the brush, but you wait until the painting is finished. Think of the ungodly man lying on his death-bed. His gaiety, his pleasures, his riches, are all gone. There is no hand to guide him through the valley of the shadow of death. He must sink into the night of gloom and despair. Then behold the man who has trusted in the mercy of God. He knows that his merciful and faithful God will not forsake him even in the last and greatest tribulation. "God knoweth the way of the righteous." The righteous man is like a tree planted by the rivers of water. "His leaf shall not wither." Lifting his eyes heavenward, he can say: Whether I live, I am the Lord's; whether I die, I am the Lord's, Rom. 14, 8. Cf. Ps. 23.

Those are the wise and understanding people who have learned to know God as their merciful Father in Christ. They consider it joy to render obedience to Him. That will secure to them peace, prosperity, and happiness. Hymn 83, 5. GEO. MIEGER.

Eleventh Sunday after Trinity.
Micah 2, 7—13.

A most deplorable condition existed in Israel at the time of which our text speaks. The people opposed the messages of God's prophets. Many despised the Word of Truth and endeavored to silence the faithful ministers. When a prophet censured them or corrected their faults, they turned away from him. They wanted prophets who would flatter them notwithstanding their sins and say "smooth things," Is. 30, 10. Many actually demanded that the prophets proclaim what they desired to hear. They wanted men who would not disturb them in their security.

We have similar conditions in our age. What type of ministry is considered popular to-day? A ministry that tells people the truth, censures the sins of the people, calls men to repentance, or the ministry that proclaims "smooth things"?

Let us thank God for the faithful ministry that He has given our Church. Let us not oppose the prophets that bring God's messages. Messages from them will bless us.

The Messages that will Do Thee Good.

1.

V. 7. In the Old Testament, God gave His words into the mouth of His prophets. Those men came to the people and introduced their message with the words: "Thus saith the Lord." The prophet Micah, standing before the people in our text, makes an appeal to the experiences of the generation of the upright. Did not God's words do good to them that walk uprightly? They can supply the answer themselves: "Yes, certainly they did." Why, then, are they opposing God's words? They also knew that the doings which had been going on in the land were not God's doings. The Spirit of God was not with those unprincipled prophets who preached to "itching ears." They were depriving themselves of the benefits which were designed for them by the Word of God.

In like manner true Christian ministers to-day should always proclaim God's words. Those are the messages that will do the people good. What are men benefited by those pastors who preach human wisdom or by those who even associate themselves with the sins of the people by merely glossing over the wickedness of men? "Thus it is written," should be the motto for all those who are called to preach. Then their messages will ring with authority and be of benefit to the people. — Much of our modern preaching is similar to that of the prophets mentioned in v. 11. They have "a spirit of falsehood" and are deceiving the hearers for the sake of personal gain. How much of God's Word is still being preached from the modern pulpits in our land? There is no need of going to church in order to hear the discussions on politics, social reform, how to prevent wars, etc. You can read about those topics in daily newspapers and in magazines. If ministers resort to all modern pulpit tactics, that is their doing and not the Lord's. Our ministry must remain "the ministry of the Word."

2.

The ministers of God are also to proclaim a message that will not be so flattering to the hearers. Micah's message to the people in vv. 8. 9. Here he directs attention to his hearers' grievous sins. Like enemies at warfare they committed ravages against men, women, and children. Fearlessly the prophet of God reproved them for the frauds they had practised against their fellow-men. We can well understand why they opposed the faithful ministry of this prophet. The preaching of God's Law was not to their liking.

Likewise our preaching must contain the stern rebukes of God's Law. That message is necessary if people are to be brought to the knowledge of their sins. It may hurt the pride of the people when the search-light of God's Law is directed against them, when their sinful ways are exposed and condemned. But dare messengers of God omit doing this and so be like "blind watchmen or dogs that cannot bark, lying down and loving to slumber," Is. 56, 10? What would you think of a physician who would hesitate to perform a painful operation if that operation could save the life of his patient? Ezek. 3, 17—19.

The majority in Israel did not accept the message of their true prophets and heed their warning. They had to suffer the consequences. The Assyrians came and took their land from them, v. 13. They had to go out of their own gates and suffer themselves to be led into captivity. That was the Lord's judgment upon the sins of the people. — This is written for our warning. To-day, when you hear God's voice, harden not your hearts. There will be a day of reckoning. Woe to the man that falls into the hands of the righteous Judge!

3.

V. 10. Another message that will do thee good. "Arise ye and depart." Quit this world; prepare to leave, for this is not your rest. Canaan, the land of milk and honey, was still in this world. It was polluted by the sins in this world. Being attached to it, living entirely for it, could only bring destruction.

This may be applied to our present estate in the world. This world is not our portion, but merely a land through which we are to pass as we seek "our better country," that city fair and high which is eternal in the heavens. "We have here no continuing city," etc. "This is not our rest"; not only not because these things are fleeting and must be left behind, but also not because there is so much corruption in the world. Unless we diligently avoid the pollution, we shall be destroyed with the world. "Be not conformed to this world, but be ye transformed by the renewing of your mind," Rom. 12, 2. Let us also ponder Phil. 3, 20, which will arouse anew a fervent longing in our hearts for heaven, our home. 1 John 2, 15—17.

4.

The heavenly home is guaranteed to us by the message of God's mercy. After pronouncing God's judgment upon the unfaithful and disobedient people, the prophet comforted "the remnant in Israel," v. 12. If they will heed the words of God and serve their covenant Lord in true faith, God will number them among the sheep of His fold. "I will gather them together as the sheep of Bozrah." Bozrah was the capital of ancient Edom. The literal meaning of the word is "stronghold." God will put a hedge around the sheep of His pasture. They shall be safe in His care and protection. Ps. 23.

All this was accomplished when Christ by the Gospel gathered together in one all the children of God that were scattered abroad and united both Jews and Gentiles in one fold and under one Shepherd. It will reach its final consummation when Jesus shall come again to gather His elect from the four winds. An innumerable multitude has already been gathered, the redeemed that are making a joyful noise unto the Lord, v. 12.

Let us value the messages of God when they are brought to us. If we accept the offers of His mercy, God will help us through all the difficulties in the way and at last take us unto Himself. Never despise "the messages that will do thee good." Hymn 119, 4. 5.

GEORGE MIEGER.

Twelfth Sunday after Trinity.
Ex. 34, 29—35.

The two chief doctrines of the Bible are the Law and the Gospel. It is of paramount importance to understand each and not to commingle them. If they are not properly understood and not carefully distinguished, the whole Bible becomes an obscure book, a book full of contradictions. "Rightly divide the Word of Truth," says Paul to his colaborer Timothy. The ministers of the Word, in preaching and teaching, must make a definite distinction between Law and Gospel, and the hearers should observe and heed this distinction. Therefore the apostles do not become weary in expounding the Law and the Gospel to their congregations, to show them the marked difference of each, and to point out to them the functions of each. Thus the Apostle Paul gives a clear and explicit discourse on the Law and Gospel in 2 Cor. 3, 4—11. He speaks of the glory of the Law and the glory of the Gospel and shows his fellow-Christians how much more glorious the Gospel is than the Law.

Our text speaks of the glory of the Law. If the Law is properly understood the glory of the Gospel will also become clear to us, and there will be no danger of commingling one with the other. Let us, then, under the guidance of the holy Ghost, at this time consider —

The Glory of the Law.

1. Its Source;   2. Its Effect;   3. Its Duration.

1.

The Law is of divine origin. It is God who has given man the Law. Rationalists claim that what Christians call the Law of God has really come about by a long process of evolution. Gradually, they say, as man evolved into a rational being, he also became a moral being; he learned more and more to discern right from wrong and finally he systematized his knowledge and experiences and made an ethical code that is generally acknowledged by all nations as the Moral Law. According to evolutionists, man is responsible for his transgressions only to himself and to the community in which he is living. These perverted thinkers belong to the class of which divine wisdom says: Ps. 14, 1.

The inerrant Word of God says: God, who created man, has also given His Law to him. At the creation of man He inscribed His Law into his heart. Man is responsible to his Creator for all his thoughts, words, and actions. When our first parents transgressed God's commandment in the garden, they knew they had done wrong; for they hid themselves from God; and later, when called to account, they tried to exonerate themselves by putting the blame on others. Through sin the clear knowledge of the Law became obscured in the heart of man and to some extent was wiped out; but there are still remnants of the Law in natural man, as is clearly seen in the case of pagans, whose conscience will either accuse or excuse them for the things they have done or said, Rom. 2, 14. 15.

God is the Author and Giver of the Law. This is clearly shown in our text. We read that Moses came down from Mount Sinai with the two tables of the Testimony (Law) in his hand. This was the second time he came down the mountain with the commandments. The first time he descended the mountain, he saw the children of Israel worshiping a golden calf, whereupon he threw the tables on the rocks, thus breaking them, and punished the idolaters. Then the Lord said to him: vv. 1. 2. When Moses had done this, the Lord said: vv. 27. 28. Every one who believes the Bible to be God's inerrant Word will accept also the words recorded in this chapter and acknowledge God to be the Author of the Law.

Because God is the Author of the Law, the Law cannot but be glorious. Everything that comes from God is glorious. As heaven and earth, the handiwork of God, so also the Law of God is full of His glory. Its commands reveal His holiness and power; its threats, His divine justice and vengeance; its promises, His truth and goodness

The glory of the Law was brightly mirrored in Moses. When he came down from the mountain, his face shone. It had a remarkable luster, so that the people of Israel could not look upon his face. This shining face of Moses was a reflection of the splendor of God and His divine Law. So great was the splendor that Moses had to put a veil over his face when he conversed with the people.

My friend, ponder this lesson well. It is the great, majestic God, the Creator of heaven and earth, your Creator, who speaks to you in the Ten Commandments which you have learned in your childhood days. You are responsible to God for everything you think, say, and do. God demands that all your acts, words, and thoughts be in perfect conformity with His holy Law. Keep in mind the awful majesty and glory of the Lord revealed to you in His commandments, Jas. 4, 12.

2.

Let us continue and learn what effect the glory of the Law has upon men. When our first parents transgressed the command of God, fear befell them. They did not dare to step before the holy and righteous God. They tried to hide from Him. When the Lord on Mount Sinai proclaimed the Ten Commandments to the children of Israel, they were filled with fear and dread and fled from the mountain, calling out to Moses: Ex. 20, 10. And when Moses came down from the mountain with the Ten Commandments of God and the people saw the luster in his face, they were again filled with fear and did not dare to come near him. So the glory of the Lord does not gladden or soothe sinful men. It fills them with fear and terror. And what else can be expected? Every sentence of the Law is a thunderous "Thou shalt" or "Thou shalt not." Man, hearing these commandments, is smitten in his conscience; he knows he has not kept them. Out of his heart, etc. Matt. 15, 19. The Law accuses him of a whole catalog of sins in thoughts, words, and deeds and pronounces the penalty for each, death and damnation. "The letter killeth," says the apostle. The Law mercilessly condemns every transgressor, Deut. 27, 26.

What grievous error many are making! They want to gain God's favor and their salvation by the works of the Law. They imagine God to be an indulgent father, who does not notice or condones the failings and shortcomings of his children. Or they think their good works and virtues will blot out their transgressions. What a folly! They do not understand the holiness of God, nor do they perceive the inability of their sinful nature to meet the requirements of the Law. Have they forgotten what the Scriptures say of them and their works? Gen. 8, 21b; Rom. 7, 18; Jas. 2, 10; Ps. 143, 2.

Are you, my friend, also given to the illusion that you can gain God's favor and a place in heaven by the deeds of the Law, by your good works? Then know that every one of your evil thoughts, every one of your sinful words, and every one of your unjust acts is so loathsome and so detestable to the holy and righteous God that all the good deeds which you may bring before Him for your justification will avail nothing in His sight. The Law must strike terror in your heart, so that you have to exclaim: Alas, my God, Thy Law condemns me; my sins are great! I have deserved Thy wrath and displeasure, temporal death, and eternal damnation. It remains forever true: "By the deeds of the Law can no flesh be justified."

3.

But let us now hasten to the third part of our discourse and consider for our comfort the duration of the glory of the Law. The luster in Moses' face did not remain. It faded away after he had imparted the commandments to the people. Later on, when he went into the Tabernacle and stood before the Lord with an uncovered face, it shone again so that he had to veil it when he spoke to the people. But the luster again passed away from his face. This we also learn from St. Paul in 2 Cor. 3, 7. 13. And the apostle applies the passing of the splendor of Moses' face to the passing of the glory of the Law. The Law should not always exert its condemning power on man. When it has brought man to the knowledge of his sins; when it has shown him his inability to keep the commandments; when it has terrified him with the threat of God's punishment, with eternal death and damnation, then it has done its work, its office is fulfilled. Then another glory shall be revealed to the alarmed sinner, a glory that is greater than the glory of the Law — the glory of the Gospel, the joyous tidings of the grace of God in Christ Jesus. The children of Israel also beheld this glory in the promises of the Messiah, and it was symbolized in their burnt offerings. We behold the glory of the Gospel in the fulfilment of the promises, in our Lord Jesus Christ, Gal. 4, 4. 5; 3, 13; 2 Cor. 5, 21.

Indeed, Christ is the end of the Law for righteousness to every one that believeth, Rom. 10, 4. My friend, what you could not do, namely, fulfil the Law, your Lord and Savior has done for you. He is your proxy. This is the saving truth the Gospel proclaims to you. Therefore fear not; but firmly believe in Him, and His merits are yours. And this life-giving Gospel will give you strength joyfully to serve your Lord, Luke 1, 74. 75.

God grant to us all a true knowledge of our sins and a blessed knowledge of our Savior and our salvation!   E. F. Manske.

Thirteenth Sunday after Trinity.

Ex. 20, 18—24.

In the Holy Scriptures the true believers of the Old and New Testaments are called the sons and daughters of God, God's children, Is. 43, 6; 1 John 3, 1; Gal. 3, 26. These are very precious names. They assure the faithful that God is their beloved Father. They may with all boldness and confidence look up to Him and communicate with Him as dear children with their dear father. If men realized what a privilege this is, they would eagerly seek to become such children of God. And we Christians, if we were to dwell upon this thought, should be far happier and more courageous than we are. Let us therefore now meditate upon the text which pictures to us —

The Blessedness of the Children of God

1. In the Old Testament;   2. In the New Testament.

1.

It may seem strange to speak of the blessedness of the children of God in the Old Testament when we take notice of their situation as described in the context. From it we learn that the children of Israel after three months' journeying in the wilderness came to Mount Sinai. There God told them through Moses to wash their clothes and sanctify themselves and be ready for the third day. When this day came, they went, by the command of Moses, to the foot of the mountain. Looking up the mountain, they saw a thick cloud and lightnings, and they heard thunderings and a voice of the trumpet that waxed louder and louder. The whole mountain quaked. Suddenly they heard the voice of the Lord. He proclaimed to them the Ten Commandments. When the children of Israel heard the voice, heard the commands of God, they were terrified; they could endure it no longer; they thought they would die. The demands which the Lord made and the manner in which He made them known filled the people with fear and terror.

Nor were these all the commandments which the children of Israel had to obey. Reading the chapters following our text, we find laws concerning holidays, and sacrifices, and purifications, and meat, and drink, and garments — laws, laws, almost without end. Can it be possible that people burdened with such a load of laws be happy and feel blessed? Did they not have to live in constant fear of transgressing some of these commandments and incurring God's displeasure and punishment?

Nevertheless the children of Israel were a blessed people. 430 years before this event on Sinai, God had appeared to their ancestor Abraham and given him this promise, "In thy Seed shall all nations of the earth be blessed," Gen. 22, 18. In this promise, God pointed to a Savior, a Helper for all men. This Helper will bring peace and rest, blessing and salvation. This promise assured Abraham that God is merciful and gracious. The old patriarch believed this promise with all his heart, and God counted this faith to him for righteousness. Now, God had not disannulled His gracious promise when He appeared on Mount Sinai and gave the Law. Every one in Israel, as he stood there at the foot of the mountain terror-stricken by the Law, should rejoice in the gracious promise of the Seed of Abraham and believe in God's mercy and blessings. This the Lord Himself indicates in our text. He speaks of "burnt offerings and peace offerings." Now, what else were these offerings but types and images of the promised Seed of Abraham, the Lamb of God, who by His self-sacrifice should take away the sins of the world and bring all nations God's blessings? The Lord furthermore states: v. 24b. In all His revelations God has gracious intentions with His children. He comes not to condemn, but to bless them. Of His mercy and loving-kindness He later on reminded Moses on Sinai. Testifying of Himself, He said: Ex. 34, 6. 7a. For the sake of the Seed of Abraham, whom the Lord had already promised as the woman's Seed to our first parents in Paradise and of whom the prophets in the subsequent centuries prophesied to the people, God forgave all sins and iniquities and offered and sealed to His people blessings and salvation. Because of this promise, which the children of Israel were to believe and accept, they were truly blessed.

But why, then, did the Lord give the Law to His people? Moses answers this question, saying to the children of Israel: v. 20. God gave His people the Law not that they should by the works of the Law obtain salvation, but to prove them, to test them, whether they were true and faithful to Him. They should thereby prove and test their own hearts and acknowledge their transgressions of God's Law. They should know that they because of their sins and iniquities deserved no blessings whatever, but God's curse, death, and damnation. They should repent of their sins, ask God for forgiveness, and rejoice in His free gift of the promised Seed of Abraham. If God had not given them the Law and by it revealed to them their natural depravity, the sinfulness of their heart, their inability to gain salvation by their own deeds, and His displeasure over every transgression, they would never have repented of their sins nor have had any desire for the promised Seed and God's forgiveness and blessings. What Moses said the apostle also confirms in his Epistle to the Galatians. Chap. 3, 19 he also asks the question "Wherefore, then, serveth the Law?" and he answers: "It was added . . . promise was made." Furthermore God gave the Law to His people that His fear might be before their faces, that they sin not, v. 20b. When the children of Israel by the Law have come to the knowledge of their sins, repented of them, and received forgiveness, they should withstand their sinful propensities and lead a life pleasing to God. They should not make unto them gods of silver and of gold, but worship Him, the only true God, fear and obey Him, and sin no more.

All those in the Old Testament who thus understood rightly the Law of God and His gracious promises were happy and blessed. Think of the expressions of happiness and blessedness in Pss. 103, 32, 23, 119, and others. Are these not wonderful expressions of blessedness? Jesus calls the believers of the Old Testament happy John 8, 56. There are millions living in the New Testament who are not as happy as Abraham. God forbid that we belong to these!

2.

Let us now also look at the blessedness of the children of God in the New Testament, to whom we should belong. Since those days when God proclaimed the Law from Sinai thirty-five centuries have passed over this world. During that time many things have happened. The chief among them is the glorious fulfilment of the promises which the Lord had given to His children in the Old Testament. Hymn 146, 2. In the fulness of time the promised Helper and Redeemer came upon earth. It was the Son of God Himself. He became man and lived as man among men. Jesus Christ, true God and man, was the woman's Seed; He bruised the Serpent's head, destroyed the works of the devil. He was the promised Seed of Abraham; through Him all the nations of the earth are blessed. To His disciples He at one time said: Luke 10, 23. 24. Indeed, their eyes were blessed to see the great redemption wrought by their Master's holy life and by His innocent and bitter suffering and death. Their ears were blessed to hear the precious Gospel of the forgiveness of sins, of deliverance from death and devil, and of the eternal salvation for all that believe and accept Him as their Savior. If God's children in the Old Testament were blessed, our blessedness in the New Testament is greater. They were living in the starry night of the promises, waiting anxiously for the dawn of day; we are enjoying the cloudless day and bright sunshine of the glorious fulfilment.

And what about the Law of God? Does it not concern us? Mark well, my friend, the Ceremonial Law, which the Lord gave to His people in the Old Testament, the laws concerning holidays, sacrifices, meat, drink, purifications, and the like, the Redeemer has entirely abolished; for they were types and shadows of Him and His redemptive work and were fulfilled by His coming. Therefore the apostle says: Col. 2, 16. 17; Gal. 4, 10. 11. The Moral Law, the Ten Commandments, our Redeemer has not abolished. He has fulfilled it for us and thereby secured for us a perfect righteousness before God; He also has suffered the penalty for our transgressions of the Law and thereby removed from us the curse of the Law, so that it no longer can condemn us, Rom. 8, 1a. But because of the sinfulness of our flesh and the temptation of the wicked world and the devil the Law has still an office to perform. It is to prove us. It shows us our transgressions, our sins; it reveals to us that we have deserved neither grace nor favor of God, but His wrath and displeasure, temporal death and eternal damnation, and that this punishment will be meted out to us if we remain in our sins. The Law terrifies us so that, when the Gospel is preached to us, we seek refuge with Jesus Christ, whose blood cleanseth us from all our sins. Being in Christ, we crucify our wicked flesh with its lust; we endeavor to keep it in subjection; we desire not to sin any more, but to live before God in righteousness and purity. Here the Law shows us how to serve God; it leads us to know what are truly good works.

Indeed, the children of God in the New Testament are truly blessed. God comes to them with His means of grace, His Word and Sacraments, and offers them peace and rest for their souls. Their Lord and Savior has given them the assurance: Matt. 28, 20; 18, 20. In all vicissitudes of life every child of God in the New Testament can joyfully exclaim: Rom. 8, 31—39; and in death: 1 Cor. 15, 55 b—57.

Do you belong to the true children of God? If not, why not? Delay not; now is the accepted time. And you who for years have enjoyed the blessedness of the children of God, hold fast what you have.

Thanks be to Thee, Father of our Lord and Savior Jesus Christ, for Thy merciful blessings. Unto Thee be praise and glory forever and ever. E. F. Manske.

Fourteenth Sunday after Trinity.
Num. 21, 4—9.

An occurrence of unusual significance is related in our text; it is frequently referred to in the Old Testament; in the New Testament Jesus, speaking to Nicodemus, a Pharisee, directs attention to it in the words: "As Moses lifted up a serpent," etc., John 3, 14. 15. Paul: "Neither let us tempt Christ, as some of them also tempted and were destroyed of serpents," 1 Cor. 10, 9.

According to the words of Jesus our text points to the first recorded curse of God upon the devil and His first promise to Adam and Eve after they had sinned, Gen. 3, 14. 15, and to the fulfilment in Jesus. According to the words of the apostle our text serves also as a warning against tempting God. The Gospel-lesson for to-day reminds us of this sin. Only one of the ten lepers who were healed by Jesus returned to thank and to serve Him. Jesus therefore exclaims: "Were there not ten cleansed? But where are the nine?" We are frequently in danger of tempting God and should carefully guard against committing this sin. Under the guidance of the Holy Ghost therefore, etc.

The Sin of Tempting God.

1. *Our Text Describes This Sin and Its Results.*
2. *Our Text Points Out Safeguards against It.*

1.

A nation is on its journey from one country to another; God's chosen people are traveling from Egypt to Canaan, the country promised to their forefathers. Under the leadership of Moses they are returning to their promised inheritance. 430 years the descendants of Abraham, Isaac, and Jacob had lived in Egypt; many years they had been enslaved there. More than 600,000 men with their wives and children ("the entire number of the people may well have exceeded 2,000,000 souls"; Kretzmann's *Popular Commentary*) had received their marching orders from God through Moses and Aaron. In a unique and remarkable way God manifested His presence to them "by day in a pillar of a cloud to lead them the way and by night in a pillar of fire to give them light," Ex. 13, 21. 22. Forty years were required for this journey. The Lord provided them with manna and protected them against the perils on the way. He never forsook them. They, however, frequently lost courage, became disheartened, and tempted God. On the occasion narrated in our text they tempted Him in a very alarming way. V. 5: "And the people spake against God," etc. Shameful accusations against God! What base ingratitude and vehement insinuations against the Lord and His leadership by His own people! He whom they had promised love and loyalty, worship and obedience, whose praises they had sung so frequently, was now denounced by them. A large number of this nation in revolt against its God, in open defiance against His leadership. His guidance was condemned, His benign providence bitterly assailed. God was tempted by His people!

Why, we ask, this change of heart toward God and His leader? V. 4 we read: "The soul of the people was much *discouraged*." They were traveling at this time on a roundabout, circuitous, route; Moses had asked the king of Edom for permission to travel through his land, but permission had been refused. Moses earnestly entreated the king again for permission and added assurances of special consideration, including payment for water; but all to no avail. Instead of granting permission, the king of Edom went "against the children of Israel with much people and a strong hand." At Mount Hor, Aaron, the high priest, died; Eleazar was appointed in his place. Thirty days the children of Israel remained at Mount Hor to mourn over the death of Aaron, and then they continued their journey. When King Arad, the Canaanite, heard that they were coming, he fought against them. A glorious victory over this new enemy was won by the children of Israel in answer to their prayers. After traveling on for a while, they began to question God's wisdom, mistrust His guidance, and discourage one another; they became despondent, the soul of the "people was much discouraged," and they tempted God.

We, too, are God's people. By the grace of God we are journeying to our eternal home, to heaven, 1 Pet. 1, 3. 4. We are "strangers and pilgrims on the earth," Heb. 11, 13. God is gracious to us for Jesus' sake, "daily and richly forgives all sins to us and all believers," guides and protects us, and provides for us. In many perils He has graciously preserved us. Through the Word and the Sacraments He preserves and strengthens our faith. In our worship in church His Word is proclaimed to us every Sunday, and in our family worship at home His Word is read; we pray to Him for grace and guidance. We thank and praise, serve and obey Him. In our Christian joy we sing: "Now thank we all our God," etc. (Hymn 64.) We jubilantly exclaim: Ps. 103, 1—5; 116, 12. "We are His people," etc. (Hymn 78, 2.)

And we who are God's people are earnestly warned in our text against tempting God. After warning believers against committing this sin, the apostle continues in a few verses after our text with the solemn admonition: "Let him that thinketh he standeth take heed lest he fall," 1 Cor. 10, 12. When our hearts are troubled with thoughts like these: "Does God love me? Is He really guiding me? Why is the wicked person often prosperous (Ps. 73)? Why are there so many sorrows and disappointments in life? Can I believe that I am a child of God, that He is gracious to me? Has He not forgotten me?" when such questions torment us and we do not earnestly contend against them, we grieve our heavenly Father, we tempt Him, and are in danger of forsaking Him. If we try to defend an error with God's Word, Matt. 4, 6, if we purposely sin to win in business, to gain honor and power, to obtain personal enjoyment and gratification, we tempt God. There is no day on our journey to heaven in which we are not confronted with dangers to tempt God; there is no experience in life, no joy, no sorrow, no success, no failure, that may not be abused and lead to tempting God. The devil, the unbelievers, and our sinful nature, our Old Adam, frequently assail and entice us to tempt God. Some of the greatest scoffers in the world to-day belonged to God's people years ago, rejoiced in worshiping and serving Him, but now use the Word of God to denounce, accuse, blaspheme, and tempt God publicly. Most of them began to tempt God in a quiet, timid way. However disguised and cunning the sin of tempting God may be in its growth and power, however timid or bold it may be, however learned and courageous it may appear to be in the opinions of some people, its consequences are ruinous. The result described in our text is unusual and sudden and demands special attention.

V. 6. "And the Lord sent fiery serpents among the people, and they bit the people, and much people in Israel died." This action of God reminds one of the words: "Be not deceived, God is not mocked," Gal. 6, 9. It clearly shows that God is zealous of His honor and that this unusual way of dealing with the sin of tempting Him is to be a warning to the end of the world. The consequences of this sin are God's wrath and displeasure, increasing danger of non-repentance, of abounding in wickedness, and of God's eternal punishment, Rom. 1, 18—25; Matt. 7, 13; Is. 66, 24.

Again and again we are warned in the Bible against tempting God, Deut. 6, 16; Matt. 22, 18; Acts 5, 9; 1 Cor. 10, 9; Heb. 3, 9.

God, who in His Word describes the sin of tempting Him and its results and warns us against it, also most graciously provides the necessary safeguards against it which we are to use every day.

2.

V. 7: "We have sinned, for we have spoken against the Lord and against thee." Thus the children of Israel confessed their sins. They repented.

True repentance is a safeguard against tempting God. When we sincerely repent of the sin of tempting God and ask Him "for the sake of His infinite mercy and of the holy, innocent, and bitter sufferings and death of His beloved Son, Jesus Christ, to be gracious and merciful to us," this implies that we "purpose to amend our sinful life," to watch carefully over our sinful heart also in regard to this sin. Yea, in the very act of tempting God in thought, word, or deed we should immediately bethink ourselves of the great sin we are committing and remember the look that Jesus gave Peter to bring him to repentance or call into remembrance some special passage of God's Word rebuking that sin. However, we must never consider our sin too great to be forgiven, nor, on the contrary, so small that it need not be forgiven or that we may delay our repentance. Repentance is obedience to the pleading of the Holy Ghost and dare not be postponed. In the tears of penitent Peter we see a beauty, a power, a glory, that was of special significance. True repentance is a safeguard against tempting Him who forgives us, Rom. 6, 1. 15; Luke 19, 8; John 8, 11.

V. 7: "And Moses prayed for the people." This was done according to their urgent request that he pray unto the Lord to remove the serpents. God told Moses to make a fiery serpent and to lift it upon a pole and promised life to every one that was bitten if he would look at it.

Prayer is another safeguard against the sin of tempting God. In our prayer we ask God for help and strength; in special trials we beseech Him to grant us special power; and God answers our prayer. We are also to pray for others, knowing that others, too, are in danger of tempting God, 1 Pet. 5, 8. 9, and that God exhorts us to pray for them, 1 Tim. 2, 1. The example of Jesus, Luke 22, 31. 32. The Lord's Prayer is intercessory from beginning to end. In it we pray for one another and with one another. God strengthened Elijah by assuring him that seven thousand were still faithful in Israel, and He told him that he was not to die at once in answer to his prayer for death, but that He wanted him to continue to render service of great importance, to live with and for the remnant of believers in Israel,

1 Kings 19, 4. 18. Prayer is a powerful safeguard against the sin of tempting God.

Another safeguard lies in the knowledge obtained from the study of God's Word what our needs are from day to day, what special dangers confront us and what opportunities are offered us. God's plan for preserving the life of the Israelites was to be made known to them. Ignorance of His plan meant death. A knowledge of the Bible, faithful searching of God's Word, is thus inculcated in our text; it is demanded by Jesus, John 5, 39, and enjoined in many places of Holy Writ. The experience of Christians the world over attests to the value of a thorough knowledge of the Bible. What a comfort there is and what power in many Bible-verses and Bible-stories if we make proper use of them; also in *hymns.*—Each Israelite had to look at the brazen serpent for himself or herself. To every one the brazen serpent was to be a special reminder of God's wonderful promises concerning the promised Savior from sin. "The just shall live by his faith," Hab. 2, 4. Justification, sanctification. The skilful use of the Word of God by Jesus in every temptation by the devil. Matt. 4: "It is written." Know your Bible, study your Catechism; use them for the proper evaluation of the occurrences of the day and for progress in sanctification. Tremble not, fear no ill, at the thought of devil, world, and flesh. One little word of God can fell the devil. "A mighty Fortress is our God." (Hymn 273.) "Have we trials and temptations?" (Hymn 395, 2.) A mother wrote into the Bible which she gave her child: "Either this book will keep you from sin, or sin will keep you from this book." Ps. 119, 9; 2 Tim. 3, 15—17; Hos. 4, 6. Fellowship with Christians, Acts 2, 42; reading of the *Lutheran Witness* and of other publications of our Synod. The reading of a short biography of a country pastor influenced young Walther to study theology and to become a pastor. Gratefully and prayerfully let us use all opportunities for better appreciation of God's Word and its value as a safeguard against the sin of tempting Him.

Our present age with its mockery of things holy and righteous, its ridicule and vituperation of the grace of God in Jesus Christ, its boasted pomp and glorification of human reason, and its appalling works of iniquity requires unremitting zeal, consecration, and determination to resist the opposition of devil, world, and flesh on our journey and faithful use of the means of grace, Rom. 1, 20; 2 Tim. 3, 13. God grant that we earnestly take to heart the lesson of our text. Trusting in God, we can say with the Apostle Paul: Rom. 8, 38. 39. Amen. HENRY KOWERT.

Fifteenth Sunday after Trinity.

1 Kings 18, 21—40.

Among the hills of the Holy Land Mount Carmel stands out with special prominence. (Describe Mount Carmel, especially the southern extremity of the range, the natural amphitheater which was so admirably suited for the great occasion of which our text tells, which lends to Mount Carmel its peculiar significance.) Mount Carmel stands to-day a constant monitor, needed as much to-day as in those days of yore. For there was held an assembly at which issues were decided that to the end of days will arise in the lives of people and will call for a decision. Would to God that now the same decision were made that was made on the memorable day of the story of our text! To this end let us consider the narrative of —

The Great Convocation on Mount Carmel.

1. *The Situation which Brought It About;*
2. *The Vital Issues which Called for a Decision;*
3. *The Majestic Vindication of Jehovah at This Assembly.*

1.

A) Evil days had come upon Israel. We know how wonderfully God had led this people, how He had raised the erstwhile nomadic tribes to the dignity and splendor of a world power under the great kings David and Solomon. We know especially the merciful purpose of God to have this people to bear, to guard, and to promulgate the promises of the world's Savior. Then came the revolt of the ten tribes under the weak and wicked Rehoboam and the setting up of the Northern Kingdom of Israel.

But Israel had revolted also from Jehovah. From the time that Jeroboam had set up two golden calves at Bethel and at Dan, 1 Kings 12, Israel had gone from bad to worse, and the character of one king after another is summed up in the ever-recurring sad refrain: "He did evil in the sight of the Lord." But in King Ahab, son of Omri, wickedness reached its height. Of him the sacred chronicler says: "And Ahab did more to provoke the Lord God of Israel to anger than all the kings of Israel that were before him," 1 Kings 16, 33. Ahab, long faithless to Jehovah, had a mind for earthly glory and power only. And for the purpose of satisfying his all-consuming ambition he sought advantageous alliances with neighboring heathen nations. Particularly, to establish an alliance with the wealthy and powerful Zidonians, he had married the wicked princess Jezebel and had introduced the iniquitous Baal-worship of the Zidonians. Baal (look up in Encyclopedia), together with the female counterpart Ashtoreth, was the idol to whom productiveness, good crops, material wealth, etc., were ascribed and all the carnal pleasures that wealth enables one to indulge in. With diabolical fanaticism Jezebel set about introducing the pagan religion in Israel, importing priests of Baal by hundreds, setting up his altars everywhere, and mercilessly persecuting all who opposed.

Unmistakably Jehovah had registered His disapproval. By a long drought the land had been reduced to famine and starvation.

It was at this time that Elijah the Tishbite was sent by God once again to reprove Ahab and to demand of him a gathering of all Israel, together with the priests of Baal, on Mount Carmel that there he might have an opportunity to call the wayward people to repentance. And before the dauntless courage of Elijah, Ahab wilts and obeys.

B) *Application.* — Alas, that this situation presents itself over and over! How many who have experienced the wonderful mercy of God, who by Baptism were made children of God and heirs of heaven, who vowed and renewed allegiance to their Savior, have sooner or later cast off that allegiance and worshiped the Baal of this world! How many have yielded to the lure of material wealth and made the dollar their God or would not let fidelity to Christian principles stand in the way of sinful pleasures or the achievement of some carnal ambition! What inroads the Baal of lodgery and false religions has made upon the ranks of God's people! This situation calls for a searching self-examination. Does God occupy our hearts or Baal? Oh, let us, too, humbly join that throng on Mount Carmel's heights and listen attentively to the fair presentation of the most vital issues, issues as vital to-day as they were then!

2.

A) "How long halt ye between two opinions? If the Lord be God, follow Him; but if Baal, then follow him." From this ringing appeal of the prophet we see that the great masses of Israel had not intended entirely and openly to cast off their allegiance to Jehovah. They still professed to be God's people. But they had sought to compromise between God and Baal. In their spiritual blindness and corruption they had attempted the impossible, *viz.,* to harmonize the service of the true God with the service of Baal. Elijah points out the impossibility of this and the abomination of their attempts. Fairly and squarely he places this issue before the people: Is Jehovah God, or is Baal? They must make a choice. And according to their choice undivided allegiance must be given either God or Baal. Nor had Elijah left the people in doubt as to what depended upon this issue and their decision. Attempts to evade the issue, or the choice of Baal, had brought misery upon the land and would finally bring eternal woe.

B) This issue is ever with us and demands a choice from every heart: God or Baal. The story of the great convocation is especially meaningful to those who still profess allegiance to the Triune God, maintaining the outward appearance of Christianity by membership in the visible Church, etc., but who secretly in their hearts worship Baal, the idol of Mammon, of sinful pleasures, etc. St. Paul shows the utter futility of all attempts to harmonize the worship of God and Baal. "Be ye not unequally yoked together with unbelievers. For what fellowship hath righteousness with unrighteousness? And what communion hath light with darkness? And what concord hath Christ with Belial? What part hath he that believeth with an infidel? And what agreement hath the temple of God with idols?" 2 Cor. 6, 14 ff. Cf. also 1 John 2, 15. No, you cannot harmonize the true God and Baal. You must face the issue squarely: Is Baal God or Jehovah? Can the things symbolized by Baal give you true happiness? Can they comfort you in the days of trial? Can they help you in the hour of death? Can they give any assurance of a blessed hereafter? If so, then follow after them, wholly and openly. Then openly embrace the philosophy: "Let us eat and drink and be merry, for tomorrow we shall die."

On the other hand, consider the question: Is the Lord God? Is God as He has revealed Himself in all creation, above all is the Triune God, who has revealed Himself in the Bible as our Creator, Redeemer, and Comforter, the God to whom we are accountable, the one Lawgiver who is able to save and to destroy, Jas. 4, 12? Is He God who in Christ Jesus revealed unfathomable love for a world of sinners and provided their one salvation? Then, as you value your soul, follow Him! Then eagerly, cheerfully yield yourself to Him with your whole heart and with an undivided love and loyalty.

God grant that this latter may be the choice of every one before whom the issue is so placed! To this end let us note, finally, the majestic vindication of Jehovah at the great convocation on Mount Carmel.

3.

A) Baal an Impotent Idol.

a) Picture the vast assembly on beautiful Mount Carmel. There was the king, proud and haughty, surrounded by his courtiers. There, in proud array, in gorgeous vestments, the 850 priests and prophets of Baal. Then, in almost endless numbers, the people of all Israel, filling the vast natural amphitheater. Finally, there came, alone, Elijah, fearless and undaunted, the courage of faith and the conviction of truth in his heart.

Without delay, determination in his bearing, Elijah proposes the test between God and Baal, vv. 23. 24. His proposal is accepted, and the test is on. The priests of Baal are given every advantage. The very nature of the test was in their favor, for fire was the element over which Baal was supposed to have peculiar power. They are given first place and permitted to arrange everything to their liking.

But what a dismal failure attended Baal and his priests! V. 26. In holy, stinging irony Elijah tells them: v. 27. And spurred on by this taunt, they spend their last frantic efforts in pleading with their idol for a vindicating response. But "yet there was neither voice nor any to answer nor any that regarded." Finally, exhausted, panting, bleeding, they must concede the dismal failure of Baal.

b) Thus Baal has ever been a colossal failure, and they are duped who follow after him. Never have the things symbolized by him satisfied a human heart. On the contrary, Baal has ever exacted a fearful toll from all his followers. Disappointment, misery of every description, follow in his wake. And oh, for that final disillusionment which awaits those who persist in following him to the end! It seems that the very days through which we have been passing are but a reenactment of Baal's failure on Mount Carmel, these days in which Baal-worshipers have seen their fortunes swept away in a night, have seen opulence succeeded by poverty, wild pleasures by misery and despair. Many worshiping fame are relegated now to contempt and oblivion. And have not the many vain frantic efforts to remedy things, the confusion in high and low places, often vividly reminded us of the frantic yelping of those priests of Baal to their idol? There was no voice nor answer, neither then nor now. For *Baal is not God.* And God forbid that he be our choice!

B) Jehovah the True God.

a) But now came Elijah's turn. He is divinely sure of his God. Therefore, having prepared his sacrifice, he has it flooded with water, etc. Then he turns to his God in this prayer: Vv. 36—38.

And lo! In a twinkling, in glorious vindication of Jehovah, "the fire of the Lord fell and consumed the burnt sacrifice, and the wood, and the stones, and the dust, and licked up the water that was in the trenches." Little wonder that after this majestic and conclusive vindication the people fell on their faces in humble, penitent worship and then sent up the mighty shout: "The Lord, He is the God!" V. 39.

b) Thus, over and over, with overwhelming power and majesty, by the sheer power of His divine love, our God has proved Himself the one true God. All history attests the blessing that the Gospel, the proclamation of His love in Christ, has ever wrought. Uncounted human hearts have experienced His saving power. And think of the crowning evidence, the resurrection of Jesus Christ from the dead. As in majesty on Carmel's heights Jehovah accepted Elijah's sacrifice, so in love He proved by the resurrection of Jesus Christ from the dead that He had accepted the great sacrifice of His Son, brought as the atonement for the sins of the world. Contemplation of Christ's resurrection as the fullest vindication of our faith in the God of the Bible, the God of the Gospel, cannot but bring to our lips the exultant shout: "The Lord, He is the God!" Upon Him our hope of salvation is immovably founded.

God grant that we may ever unhesitatingly make the choice of Israel on the day of its great convocation on beautiful Mount Carmel, so that finally, etc.   AUG. F. BERNTHAL.

Sixteenth Sunday after Trinity.
2 Kings 5, 8—19 a.

"God will have all men to be saved and to come unto the knowledge of the truth." To that end He gave to the first world the Gospel of the Seed of the Woman; to that end He spared Noah in the Flood, that after its subsidence he might continue as a preacher of righteousness; to that end He called Abram and made him the father of a nation that was His peculiar people, a people to whom He entrusted His oracles, His promises of the Messiah; to that end He sent forth, in the fulness of time, His only-begotten Son, Jesus Christ, who suffered and died on the cross for the redemption of men; to that end He established His New Testament Church and gave her the great command to preach the Gospel to every creature; to that end He often employs wonderful ways with the individuals, as exemplified in Naaman, of whom our text treats.

The Wonderful Ways of God with Naaman.

1. God Puts a Bitter Drop into Naaman's Cup of Happiness.
2. He Sends a Little Slave Girl into His Home to Be a Preacher.
3. He Crushes His Proud Spirit and Gives Him the Spirit of Trust.
4. He Again Removes the Bitter Drop.
5. He Makes Him His Grateful and Conscientious Servant.

1.

In order to understand our text, we must page back in the life history of Naaman. Naaman was the captain of the host of Syria. He was the commander-in-chief of his king's mighty army. He had won many a battle. He was great, mighty, exalted, rich, and a favorite of his mighty king. He was happy. But into his cup of happiness the Lord put a bitter drop; for Naaman was a leper.

In the eyes of men that was a dreadful calamity; it spelled Naaman's doom. But in the gracious providence of God it was to serve for the healing of his soul. If Naaman had not become leprous, he would never as far as we can see have come to the knowledge of, and faith in, the true God.

Naaman evidently had come in contact with Israel in more than one conflict on the field of battle. He must have learned something of Israel's religion; but he did not pay the slightest attention to it. He was perfectly satisfied to be as he was, until God laid His heavy, yet merciful, hand upon him.

So many an individual to-day, although coming in contact with the religion of Jesus Christ in many a way, does not react to it in the smallest degree. He is enjoying life and is satisfied. But then God in His grace and mercy puts a bitter drop into his cup of life. It may be sickness, grief, or some other misfortune. Now he is dissatisfied; now he realizes his own helplessness; now he is groping for deliverance. He does not see it, but God has devised ways and means for his rescue. Gen. 42, 21.

2.

While Naaman was tasting that bitter drop in his cup of life, having no hope of ever ridding himself of it, God sends His messenger to him. And who is this messenger? Is it some celebrated and mighty prophet, who, in a way, may be said to be on an equal footing with this great and mighty Naaman? Not at all. It is a little Jewish slave girl who was taken captive in war and was made an attendant of Naaman's wife. Pitying her master and ardently desiring his recovery, she said in the hearing of her mistress: "Would God my lord were with the prophet that is in Samaria! For he would recover him of his leprosy." Naaman grasps at this last straw of hope, and with a letter from his king, and carrying with him much gold and silver, he repairs to Samaria.

In a similar manner God has since that day sent some seemingly insignificant messenger of hope to many an individual. It may have been only a humble Christian who chanced to visit him in his misfortune; it may have been only a Christian girl nursing him in a hospital that spoke a few words about the Great Physician; it may have been only a little, humble tract which spoke of the crimson remedy that cleanseth us from all the leprosy of sin that put him on the road leading to the true God. Cf. 2 Kings 7, 3—16.

3.

Naaman came to Samaria, but he came with a proud and haughty spirit. God, however, crushes that proud spirit and gives him the spirit of humility and trust.

When Jehoram, the king of Israel, read the request of the Syrian king in behalf of his great captain, he thought it was an adroit pretext to start a war, since every man knew that no mere human being, even though he was a king, could cure any one of leprosy.

But while the king of Israel was at a loss as to what he might do in this case, God's prophet Elisha sent him a message; "Let him come now to me, and he shall know that there is a prophet in Israel."

So Naaman came with his horses and with his chariots and stood at the door of the house of Elisha. He expected the prophet to come out and give him all the honor due his rank and position. Instead, however, Elisha sends a servant out to him, who tells him: "Go and wash in the Jordan seven times, and thy flesh shall come again to thee, and thou shalt be clean." Now Naaman was wroth; his pride was deeply wounded by such treatment. He left in a huff and said: "Behold, I thought he will surely come to me and stand and call," etc., vv. 11. 12.

So it is with many a man to-day. When he hears from a humble prophet or preacher of the Lord that all he is to do is to repent of his sins and believe in Christ, who suffered and died for him in order that he might be saved, he will take umbrage at it; it is all too simple. (That is what offends some in the Sacraments — water; bread and wine.) He has his own ideas as to the way he might be saved, e. g., through his own righteousness, good works, sufferings, and sacrifices. And so, in the carnal pride of his heart, he often turns away from God's saving hand just as did Naaman.

But while Naaman turned away from the prophet and the prophet's God, God did not turn away from him. He had Naaman's servants talk to him. They reminded him that it was the prophet, the prophet of God, who told him what to do. If the prophet had bidden him do some great thing, would he not have performed it? "How much rather, then, when he saith to thee, Wash and be clean?"

Now Naaman becomes humble, He goes down and dips himself in the Jordan seven times according to the direction of the man of God. God had given him the spirit of trust and faith.

Thus God still does with proud and obstinate man. He does not change His way of salvation to meet the approval of human reason, but by means of His almighty Word He changes the proud heart of man. He opens his eyes to see that, if He is to save, He must save in His own way, that this is the only way. Thus man finally yields and accepts God's gracious offer of free salvation through Christ; he penitently acknowledges that the leprosy of sin has made him entirely helpless, and in childlike faith and trust he plunges into the crimson flood of the Savior's precious blood. And the result?

4.

After Naaman, trusting in the promise of God given him by the prophet, dipped himself seven times in the Jordan, "his flesh came again like unto the flesh of a little child, and he was clean." The bitter drop that had fallen into his cup of happiness was miraculously removed.

It is even so with the individual sinner. Having dipped himself in true faith in the crimson flood of Jesus' blood, he becomes clean of the leprosy of sin; for the blood of Jesus Christ, God's Son, cleanseth us from all sin. That bitter drop of his absolute guiltiness and damnability in the sight of God, that bitter drop of terror in view of the holiness and righteousness of God, that bitter drop of the fear of death and eternal damnation, all this is removed from his heart, and the joyful assurance that for the sake of Christ God is his gracious, merciful, forgiving, and loving Father now fills his cup of life.

5.

Finally God does one thing more — He makes of him whom he has brought to faith in Christ a grateful and conscientious servant.

Naaman, seeing what God had wrought, returns to Elisha. He now stands humbly before him, openly confesses God by saying: "Behold, now I know that there is no God in all the earth but in Israel," and offers the prophet a "blessing," a rich donation of gold and silver, as a reward. Knowing the weak state of Naaman's faith, Elisha does not accept any gift. Naaman is to know that the grace and mercy of God are free; they cannot be bought or paid for. Elisha is satisfied with the evidence of Naaman's gratitude.

But now Naaman begs for two loads of earth from which he desires to build an altar in his home country and upon which he intends to bring burnt offerings and sacrifices, no longer to other gods, but unto the Lord. The fact that his altar was to be built from Israel's soil was to be an external proof that he had definitely and absolutely broken with the idols and the worship of his people. But there is one thing that still worries him. He remembers that, as his king's personal attendant, he must go to the temple of the god Rimmon, where his king worships, and as the king bows down, he must also lower his body to support the king, not indeed to worship Rimmon, but to serve his royal master. Will that be wrong? Elisha says, "Go in peace." If you make yourself clear on that point, if everybody will know that you have forsaken the idols and are a true worshiper of the true God, then this service which you are giving to the king will be properly understood. Thus God made Naaman His grateful and conscientious servant.

God does so with every one whom He has cleansed by the blood of Jesus from the leprosy of sin. He brings about a realization in such a man's heart that he owes his eternal healing solely to God's grace and mercy, and for that he is grateful. Like Naaman he is willing to give liberally to the cause of God's kingdom, to show in every way, also externally, that he is serving the true God only, and he conscientiously avoids any compromising situations. — Am I, are you, such a servant? God grant it for Jesus' sake. Amen.   L. A. LINN.

Seventeenth Sunday after Trinity.
1 Sam. 15, 13—26.

In his farewell address to the elders of the church at Ephesus, Paul said: "I have not shunned to declare unto you all the counsel of God." He had preached to the Christians at Ephesus the Law of God in all its severity and the Gospel of Jesus Christ in all its sweetness. Thus they had been made Christians, children of God, and heirs of life eternal. But after they had become such, another important duty over against them devolved upon Paul, a duty that he discharged with no lesser fidelity than the preaching of the gracious counsel of God for their salvation, and that was the duty of warning them against the sin of back-sliding, against apostasy, which would cause them to lose all they had gained by faith in Christ Jesus. Paul says Acts 20, 31: "Therefore watch and remember that by the space of three years I ceased not to warn every one night and day with tears." And so to-day it is the foremost duty of a Christian preacher to declare "all the counsel of God" to his hearers. He is to preach to them the holy Law of God that they may realize their most wretched condition, their being children of wrath by nature and subject to death and eternal damnation. But then he is to proclaim to them the Gospel of Jesus Christ, who redeemed them by suffering and dying for them, that by gracious illumination of the Holy Spirit faith in their Savior may be kindled in them.

In addition to that a Christian preacher must also warn those who have become Christians against apostasy, against turning away from God and His Word, lest they lose the salvation which once had been theirs by faith in Christ Jesus.

This morning's text, which portrays to us the conduct of King Saul and its dire results, contains such a warning. Let me, then, present to you —

The Conduct of Saul as a Warning to Us.

We shall center our attention

1. On the Conduct of Saul; 2. On the Warning It Contains for Us.

1.

Saul, by the command of God, was made the first king of Israel. At first he was a true and faithful servant of the Lord, and the Lord blessed all his endeavors, especially granting him many victories over the enemies of Israel, and established him as a mighty monarch. His enemies feared him, and his people honored and obeyed him. Instead of remaining humble, however, and thanking God for his successes and for his elevation to the throne of Israel he gradually became proud and disobedient to the Lord. While still worshiping Him externally, his heart was far from Him.

This deplorable fact is demonstrated by his conduct as described in our text. God had given him an explicit command to exterminate, utterly destroy, the inveterate enemies of Israel, the Amalekites. Saul gathered an army of 210,000 men and smote the Amalekites. But he disobeyed the command of God in part; he did not "destroy utterly," but kept Agag, the king, a captive, evidently for the glorification of his own power, and many sheep and oxen, doubtless for the gratification of his own greed.

For his disobedience he is called to account by Samuel at the direction of God. And what does he do? Does he humbly and penitently confess his disobedience? Not in the least. The first thing he does is to add a lie to his infraction of God's command; for he says to Samuel in feigned piety: "Blessed be thou of the Lord. I have performed the commandment of the Lord." Samuel, however, is not deceived by his pretended piety; he says to him: "What meaneth, then, this bleating of the sheep in mine ears and the lowing of the oxen which I hear?" Dead sheep and oxen make no noise. Saul is caught in his lie.

Does he perhaps now make a clean breast of his disobedience? Alas, no. He tries in a cowardly manner to put the blame on some one else; he says: "The people spared the best of the sheep and of the oxen to sacrifice unto the Lord, thy God."

Samuel justly disregards this flimsy excuse, adorned with pious cant, and proceeds to tell Saul the judgment of the Lord in the case. He begins by reminding him of how God had exalted him by making him king and of the special command regarding the Amalekites, and then he directly charges him with disobedience. Before Samuel can proceed, Saul, evidently sensing what is coming, again tries to whitewash himself and puts the blame on the people. But Samuel justly holds him responsible and shows the absurdity of trying to please God by intending for Him a sacrifice from the results of disobedience, adding: "Behold, to obey is better than sacrifice and to hearken than the fat of rams."

This disobedience, which Saul considered a trivial matter, Samuel terms a rebellion, a sin as grave as witchcraft, a stubbornness as iniquitous as idolatry, as indeed it is since Saul thereby put himself above God.

And then Samuel pronounces the sentence of God: "Because thou hast rejected the word of the Lord, he hath also rejected thee from being king."

Saul is stunned. He sees his power and glory fading away, and in their stead there arises before his mind's eye impotence, shame, and disgrace.

In a last desperate attempt he tries to avert the impending

calamity. He says to Samuel: "I have sinned; for I have transgressed the commandment of the Lord and thy words." Did he mean it? Was he sincere? Alas, no. For in the same breath he again tries to excuse himself by saying: "because I feared the people and obeyed their voice." Consequently his plea to Samuel: "Now, therefore, I pray thee, pardon my sin and turn again with me that I may worship the Lord" was of a piece with his confession; it was not sincere; it was an external gesture in his desperate attempt to retain his throne, his power and glory.

Samuel therefore refused to return with Saul to worship and emphatically reiterated the judgment of the Lord: "Thou hast rejected the word of the Lord, and the Lord hath rejected thee from being king over Israel."

Saul became morose, melancholy. He became the plaything of an evil spirit. He resorted to witchcraft (Endor). Finally, wounded in a war with the Philistines, he fell upon his own sword and committed suicide, 1 Sam. 31.

Thus Saul lost not only his throne, but also his soul. The route he traveled was disobedience, lying, hypocrisy, impenitence, which resulted in death, temporal and eternal.

And now the warning to us.

2.

None of us was called of God to be a king, but all of us were called to a much higher position, honor, and glory. We were called by the Holy Ghost through the Gospel to be sons and daughters of God and heirs of salvation. We in no way deserved this calling to the sonship of God, no more than did Saul to the kingship of Israel. It was all due to the grace and mercy of God in Christ Jesus, even as Paul says: "God hath saved us and called us according to His own purpose and grace, which was given us in Christ Jesus before the world began," 2 Tim. 1, 9. Cp. also Eph. 2, 8. 9.

As unto Saul, so God has given also unto us His holy Word. And it is His holy and gracious will that we use that Word, the Gospel for the assurance of our forgiveness and the strengthening of our faith, the Law as a rule and norm of our life and conduct. A defection in either case is a rejection of God's Word.

It has come to pass in our day that many people no longer "tremble at the Word of the Lord." They believe such teachings of the Bible as appeal to their fancy; others they reject; and they obey such commands of the Lord as suit them and desregard others. In both cases they are rejecting the Word of the Lord. Many, e. g., no longer believe that God created the world in six ordinary days; they no longer believe the story of the Flood, the miraculous destruction of Sodom and Gomorrah, the passing of Israel dry-shod through the Red Sea, etc.; they no longer believe in the virgin birth of Jesus nor in His vicarious atonement on the cross; they deny His bodily resurrection and ascension into heaven and His actual, visible return to judge the quick and the dead; they do not believe in a hell of eternal punishment, saying man has his hell on earth.

All these evidently reject the Word of the Lord. And since they spread and broadcast their unbelief through many channels of publicity and try to support their position by "science" and other seemingly plausible arguments which appeal to our sinful reason, we are in danger of being infected by that same virus of unbelief, unless we take warning and remember the statement of Jesus, who said: "Heaven and earth shall pass away, but My words shall not pass away," Mark 13, 31.

Others, while not specifically denying the Lord nor any of the Bible doctrines, — Saul did not do that, — nevertheless actually reject them by conscious and wilful disobedience.

What good does it do you to recite the Apostles' Creed, if ever so unctiously and correctly, and then to show by your conduct that you do not really believe that Jesus is your Lord? What good does it do you to confess with your mouth: "I believe that Jesus Christ . . . redeemed me, a lost and condemned creature, purchased and won me from all sins, from death, and from the power of the devil" and then to continue to live in the slavery of sin and the devil? What good does it do one to bring his "sacrifice" to the Lord, as Saul intended to do, if he has obtained those very sacrifices in disobedience to God's Word? What good did it do Saul to ask Samuel to pardon his sins since he did not sincerely repent of them, but rather had a hidden desire and determination to continue in them? What good did it do Saul to ask Samuel to go with him to worship the Lord and then to blame others for his sins and transgressions? What good does it do you to go to church on Sunday and during the week to worship the golden calf, the god of the belly, or the god of fleshly lusts? In all such conduct man plainly shows that actually he has rejected the Word of the Lord.

Are we guilty in one form or another? Then, as we love our soul, let us not try to lie out of it, let us not blame others, but let us make a clean breast of it and with the publican say in all sincerity: "God be merciful to me, a sinner." Let us hie to the ever-outstretched arms of the merciful Savior, and we shall not be rejected as was Saul, but mercifully accepted by Jesus, "who sinners doth receive." Amen.

L. A. LINN.

Eighteenth Sunday after Trinity.
Ezek. 3, 17—21.

Our text reminds us of our duty to "warn the wicked" lest he "die in his iniquity." This is a disagreeable duty, and we usually try to shirk it. The ancient excuse "Am I my brother's keeper" readily suggests itself. We may fear that our words of warning may be resented, with bad consequences to us. Stephen met his death because of such testimony; so did our prophet Ezekiel and even our Lord. Such extremities may not be in store for us, but former friends may turn against us. But are we to prefer their friendship to Christ's? Matt. 10, 37—39.

The question is one of spiritual life or death to our fellow-being. Should we, then, not warn him of his danger? Could we ever rest quiet in conscience if we did not? And how could we then face the Judge of the quick and the dead, who holds us to a degree responsible?

For our own warning and also our encouragement let us ponder our text. May the Holy Spirit make our hearts receptive!

1.

We note the opening words of our text, where Jehovah says to Ezekiel: "I have made *thee* a watchman." The prophet was divinely commissioned to be a watchman when in Babylonian exile. This fact must have been a matter of great comfort and encouragement to him. When warning, he was doing the bidding of his Master, who would stand by His servant.

Your pastor, too, has been regularly called to this charge. He has been made a watchman unto you by that same Jehovah of old. So when the Law is preached from this pulpit, when perhaps a specific warning is given against erroneous deceptive doctrines or against a dangerous neglect of duty or against pandering to the world, then bear in mind your pastor is but attending to his plain duty of being God's watchman.

Your pastor's duty of being a watchman is *continual,* though it may be intermittent. Is. 62, 6: "I have set watchmen upon thy walls, O Jerusalem, *which shall never hold their peace day and night."* Warnings must often be repeated, "lest we forget." Both Law and Gospel are constantly in order, in their place. Is. 21, 8.

A sentinel, a watchman, cannot leave his post at will. A desertion of duty would imperil the safety of those in his charge and lay him open to penalties. (Jonah.)

His post is *needed and necessary;* or God would not have placed him where He did. Our God never assigns to us unnecessary or trivial duties, though they may seem so to us.

The faithful watchman *takes his directions from God.* He does not give warnings he himself has fabricated, perhaps omitting what God had told him to utter. ("Hear the word *at My mouth* and give them warning *from Me,*" v. 17.)

These words also give us the watchman's double duty of *detecting the danger* and *transmitting his discovery* promptly to those endangered. We find both thoughts in our text. In the first place, *"Hear the word* at My mouth." Your pastor must give time, and must be given time, to *search* the Scriptures, to delve in them. Our Synod very properly sees to the adequate training of her divinity students in the original languages of the Bible and in all branches auxiliary, so that they can intelligently hear the words at God's mouth.

In the second place, the watchman is to give the fruits of his Bible-studies to his parishioners, "give them warning from Me." This warning your pastor *dare not withhold,* but must give it as it comes from the Master, revealed in His Word. And you must come to hear the *message,* not the *pastor.* ("Blessed Jesus, at thy word We are gathered all to hear *Thee,*" Hymn 3.)

The *full message* of God is given you in the course of the church-year. Nothing is withheld of the rich provisions of God's house. Paul said: "I have not shunned to declare unto you *all the counsel* of God." No pet doctrines are continually harped on at the expense of the rest. But in order to get the full measure of God's blessings, you should strive to hear God's message *every* Sunday. And you should want to hear that message, both Law and Gospel, just as God intends it for you. No herald, soldier, or ambassador should think of modifying the terms in which his government makes a declaration of war or proffers terms of peace. The fact that your pastor wears the robe in the pulpit and at the altar indicates that he is acting not in a *personal,* but in an *official* capacity.

To whom is this message to be delivered? "Give them warning from Me." The whole congregation of Israel, then in captivity, was embraced. And so your pastor preaches to *all* — saint and sinner. You may invite, yea, you should invite, also the churchless to your services. The Maker of our frames, the Savior of our souls, the Comforter of our hearts, has teachings for the young and the adult, for the poor and the rich, for the wicked and the righteous. "I am a debtor both to the Greeks and to the barbarians, both to the wise and to the unwise," Paul says.

Our text, continuing, now speaks of the *individual,* the wicked and the righteous *man.* Before we enter upon this, let me remind you that, while the sermon is preached to the congregation as a whole, the *application* is to be made individually by each man, woman, and child. When the Law is preached in its severity, do not fail to apply it to yourself; *you* are meant. Then, too, you should not fail to apply the sweet and full comforts of the Gospel to yourself. Your dear Savior means *you,* as though you were the only person in church or on earth.

But at times, in accordance with the text, your pastor must apply Law and Gospel *individually, personally.* David's pastor, Nathan, came to him and told him to his face: "Thou art the man." You have pronounced sentence of death upon yourself. David did not cast Nathan into prison because of this, as King Herod did John the Baptist, but confessed: "I have sinned against the Lord." Then Nathan gave him the divine comfort: "The Lord also hath taken away thy sin," 2 Sam. 12.

Let us emphasize it is God's *will* that the wicked man be warned. God does everything possible to save his soul. If he is not warned, he cannot, 'tis true, make this his excuse. He "shall die in his iniquity." He had a knowledge of God's will, and his conscience will accuse him. The ungodly can clearly see the invisible things of God from the creation, "so that they are without excuse," Rom. 1, 18—20.

But also the best of Christians has occasional need of warning, v. 20. "Let him that standeth take heed lest he fall." A righteous man may turn from his righteousness and commit iniquity. When Christians desert the service of God, turn their backs on Him who saved them, crucify Him anew, and despite all warnings of men and conscience persist in this, even mocking God, then He may not only withdraw His grace and give them over to their perverse ways, but may even lay a stumbling-block before them, v. 20; He may place them into such circumstances as hasten their ruin. God's judgment has overtaken them while still in this life. Dreadful! When we see others fall, let us not "be high-minded, but fear," Rom. 11, 20—22.

V. 21. We praise God that, when the righteous is warned and cautioned not to sin or when, having failed to turn in repentance to God, as we daily should, he often heeds the voice of God's servant, the pastor. Then "he shall surely live"; there is no if or but in absolution. And he shall live a better, fuller life here on earth in the service of his Master. Our Lord stated, John 10, 10, He came that His followers "might have life and that they *might have it more abundantly.*" David had spiritual life "more abundantly" and served Jehovah more ardently after his pastor had spoken to him and he had been received back into grace.

2.

Perhaps the one or the other of you may think, "Well, I'm glad to be relieved of this disagreeable duty of warning the wicked. I'm glad the pastor is to attend to all this." But on second thought you would hardly repeat this. If you are seriously concerned about your own salvation and strive after holiness, the eternal fate of your fellow-being will be a matter of deepest concern to you. Our text is indeed directed primarily to the prophet or preacher, but it cannot be inferred that the admonitions must be strictly limited to him. Cain was not a preacher, but he was held to be his brother's keeper. The Bible abounds with exhortations, in precept, example, and parable, unto brotherly admonition. We shall dwell on only one injunction, that contained in Matt. 18. Our Lord addresses the church-member: If thy brother, thy fellow-Christian, trespass against thee, directly or indirectly, the latter by neglect of church duties (specify) or by falling into worldly ways, you are then your brother's keeper and must seek to approach your fellow-Christian. The *manner of approach* must be one which proves to your brother or sister your deep concern for his or her spiritual well-being. You may need the advice of your pastor on how best to proceed; but a fundamental rule is: Speak to thy brother *between thee and him alone*. This shows him, possibly more than anything else, that you desire his welfare. If in company, he will always be conscious of listeners and will adapt his words. Besides, the company may by interference neutralize the effect of your counsel.

He (or she) may "not hear thee." The case is too serious to give up. Ask other Christians to aid you. All efforts may prove futile. The offender may become manifest as a publican and sinner, and you may encounter his hatred. This you should gladly accept as the cross Christ lays upon you, Matt. 5, 10—12. And "thou hast delivered thy soul."

The "righteousness" of such a backslider "shall not be remembered," v. 20. Likely he banked a good deal on his "righteous" way of living, and at his funeral his "good deeds" may be extolled; however, all our righteousnesses are but as filthy rags, Is. 64, 6.

But quite often your admonitions prompted by love will be heeded. You will rejoice with the angels of heaven over one sinner that repenteth. The saved brother or sister "shall surely live" together with you and praise God to all eternity. Hymn 426.

A. W. MEYER.

Nineteenth Sunday after Trinity.
Psalm 37, 25—40.

A problem that has puzzled the children of God from earliest times is, Why do the ungodly often fare so well and the godly so badly? We see the worldly, even the scoffers, often rich and honored, perhaps enjoying the luxuries of life, while those who confess Christ are scoffed at and are often in poverty and sickness. Every pastor likely has had the experience of having the bed-ridden, the care-worn complain, I cannot see why God should visit us with sickness, unemployment, etc. We have always been faithful members of the Church and have made many a sacrifice for Christ's cause. Satan may even whisper to them, as he did to Job through his wife, I would not serve such a God any longer.

Very natural or "human" such thoughts are; for do not we, and men generally, act along such lines? If a friend favors us, we favor him. And our near relatives — do we not love them above others and show this love and affection in every way possible? Should not God do the same for us, His children? But now He seems to forget all we ever did for Him and His cause!

Our whole psalm treats of this problem and solves it for us. It is a psalm of particular comfort to God's children in distress. In it you will find our question approached from different points of view — apparently repetitions. Ideas are reiterated with emphasis. The psalm is like a necklace of pearls loosely strung.

We find the *life* of the godly and of the ungodly compared and the *end* of both.

Let us follow the line of thought our text gives us.

Vv. 25 and 26. The psalmist here makes the point that, speaking generally, it is not true that the righteous fare worse in this life and are unhappier than the wicked. Quite the contrary: "Godliness is profitable unto *all things,* having promise of the life *that now is* and of that which is to come," 1 Tim. 4, 8.

In the commonwealth of Israel the Mosaic provisions made begging very exceptional at least at the time of David. Yet David does not tell us that the righteous are *never tried;* but in their trials they are *never forsaken.* David himself was in sore straits when he asked bread of Abimelech; at another time he sent to Nabal for aid; when hounded by Saul, he was in extreme danger of life and no doubt often in dire want of the necessaries of life. But he was never *forsaken.*

Furthermore, the righteous are not perpetually in extreme want. The patriarchs, Job, the pious Jewish kings, and others in Holy Writ were men of means.

Besides, the Christians are happier because they have learned to *appreciate* the blessings they have. "God gives daily bread also to all the wicked, but He would lead us *to know it* and to receive our daily bread *with thanksgiving.*" I have seen a little boy of wealthy parents surrounded by expensive playthings, but disgruntled. How often you meet with the rich who are dissatisfied because they are not richer! The person who can appreciate the beauties of nature, who can rise with the poet above the commonplace, who is thrilled by the symphonies of masterly music, who can discern the intricate harmony and diversity of color and formation in flowers and plants, who can admire the multiform plumage of birds and the melody of their song, who is truly appreciative of health and ability to serve God and his fellow-beings, who can join in the uplifting chorals of our Church and is uplifted by them, and especially by the Gospel of Christ *is not poor*. And we have by no means exhausted the catalog of God's blessings.

The millionaire Carnegie once, when addressing a group of young men, said: "The greatest handicap a young man can have in making a success of life is to possess almost unlimited riches."

On the other hand, *poverty* has been praised by hermits and philosophers as the path to holiness and the mother of all virtues; but Solomon prayed, Prov. 30, 8. 9: "Give me neither poverty nor riches, feed me with food convenient for me, lest I be full and deny Thee and say, Who is the Lord? or lest I be poor and steal and take the name of my God in vain."

True, a man may live in a backwoods log cabin, be destitute of all comforts and social privileges, and still be content and happy. But pinching poverty usually implies that a person is undernourished, underclothed, haunted by the fear of want. It may mean foul air, unwholesome food, discomforts, and may tend to vice and crime, disease and death. Even a Christian may find himself in circumstances of extreme poverty; but the Holy Spirit will use that very cross to bring him nearer to God. Nearer my God to Thee, e'en though it be a *cross* that raiseth me.

What position did Christ take? He was neither a capitalist nor a Socialist nor a Communist. He did not have where to lay His head; yet He was not a beggar, nor did He make the appearance of one. His disciples, while with Him, never were in want, Luke 22, 35.

V. 26. It might appear that the righteous would lack because "he is ever merciful and lendeth." But he lendeth to the Lord — the safest investment; His bank has never been known to fail. Like the bounteous Giver of all good His children also delight in doing good. How the stingy, the covetous, when they read verses like this, can still hope for salvation is a marvel. How true the words: "It is more blessed to give than to receive"!

All has not been said. The seed of the righteous is blessed, v. 26. Such parents leave a rich heritage to their children as, though they have no earthly goods to divide, leave them their *blessing,* that of a godly example and training. When Christ was about to part with His disciples, He could not even leave them as much as His garments, but He said: *"Peace* I leave with you; my peace I give unto you." Their hearts, then, need not be troubled, neither need they be afraid, John 14, 27.

V. 28. *By way of contrast,* while the saints are never forsaken, but preserved forever, the seed of the wicked shall be cut off. Conclusion of the Ten Commandments. Consider the fate of the house of Saul, Jeroboam, Ahab. Even the world often quotes the saying that honor and wealth ill gotten seldom reaches the third generation. Be that as it may; the legacies of the wicked never include that peace Christ speaks of.

V. 30. How can you recognize the righteous? He *speaketh wisdom*. A man's tongue is an index to his character; the mouth portrays the heart. "Righteousness is wisdom in action." He *talketh of judgment*. He always favors strict obedience to the laws and impartial execution of them. (Capital punishment versus lynching.) He holds that God's judgments will come to pass as surely as God's promises, Final Judgment and the Flood. Matt. 24, 37—39.

V. 31. Furthermore there is no hypocrisy in the righteous, *for the Law of God is in his heart*. What he says he really means. His faith in God and the absence of guile secure an even tenor for life, for the Law of God in his heart is to him the pilot in days of depression as well as in days of prosperity.

Vv. 32. 33. On the other hand we find that *the wicked watcheth the righteous and seeketh to slay him*.

The Jewish leaders "watched" that Righteous One daily, trying to trip Him and to slay Him. This latter they were permitted to do. But Jehovah left Him not in their hands, but vindicated His innocense by raising Him from the dead. The same holds with all true followers of Christ. *Apparently* Christ was left in the hands of the wicked, for He suffered torments and a cruel death. Many were the martyrs in the history of the Church from Abel down.

But Jehovah *will not condemn the righteous when he is judged*, v. 33. Providence tolerates temporary injustices for purposes most wise, but the bitter shall not always be called sweet nor light darkness. On that Great Day the lying spirits shall be unmasked; the true shall be revealed. For the just shall then see how the wicked are cut off.

True, it may not so appear in this life; for *the wicked is seen in great power, spreading himself like a green bay-tree*, V. 35. He at times seems a veritable Caesar in power and a Croesus in wealth. He spreads himself like a green bay-tree, adding house to house and field to field.

The green bay-tree is taken to mean one ever verdant, luxuriant like a tree which prospers in its own native soil. *We* may think of the spreading beech or the wide-expanding oak. Thus we often see the wicked being rich, proud, and wanton in their prosperity, while the children of God may be tossed about by tempests of persecution and affliction. Yes, the Lord does at times permit the wicked to wallow in worldly wealth, but it is for their destruction. Take the case of Hophni and Phinehas. The Lord suffered them to prosper in their wickedness, "because He would slay them," 1 Sam. 2, 25. What a warning example!

But after all, this green bay-tree is a thing of the earth; its roots are in the clay of earthly things; its honors are as transitory as are its fading leaves. For a time it dwarfs by its shadow the lesser trees, but the woodman's ax will fell it. When you pass there again, the wood has been carried away, the very roots torn from the ground.

V. 36. *He passed away, he was not; yea, I sought him, but he could not be found.* The names and memory of the ungodly are soon lost and forgotten. How often we hear or read of riches' collapsing! We inquire for "the wicked in great power," him of green-bay-tree fame, and "he is not." Perhaps he has taken his life, perhaps he had trouble with the law, at any rate he has flown like a bird of ill omen. His name was in everybody's mouth yesterday; now "I sought him, but he could not be found."

This thought introduces the second and more important part of our text, in which we are told to look to *the end* of both the godly and the ungodly if we wish properly to evaluate their whole career.

V. 37 we are told to *mark,* observe, *the perfect man* for an ensample. Christ is the perfect model, 1 Pet. 1, 15. However, we should also remember them who have spoken unto us the Word of God, follow their faith and note their end, Heb. 13, 7. We should to the glory of God recount the services they have rendered and emulate their example, "follow their faith." Indeed, as God gives us grace, *we* should strive to be an example to others, 1 Tim. 4, 12; Phil. 3, 17; 1 Pet. 2, 12; for example is stronger than precept. We should "leave footprints in the sands of time, footprints that perhaps another, a forelorn and shipwrecked brother, seeing, shall take heart again."

It is the *perfect* man we should mark. God only is absolutely perfect. But the child of God is considered perfect also in God's sight through Christ's perfect work of atonement. True, also the Christian notices daily imperfections; he confesses, "We daily sin much and indeed deserve nothing but punishment." Therefore the Christian daily prays, "Forgive us our trespasses." And he knows from Scripture that God daily and fully forgives him and considers him "a perfect man" in Christ Jesus. St. Paul tells us, Col. 2, 10: "Ye are complete in Him."

That "perfect man," in setting out, may have encountered many obstacles, may have suffered many tribulations while on the way; but the *end* of that man *is peace* — a peace of mind, as opposed to doubting; a peace of security, having reached the goal; a peace of conscience, assured of the forgiveness of sins; a peace in death, falling asleep in Jesus, resting from all labors and tribulations; a peace which the world cannot give.

But if we want to die in Christ, we must live in Christ; we cannot die like Lazarus if we live like Dives.

The end of the wicked *shall be cut off,* V. 38, the time of grace shortened. "They live too fast"; sins shorten life. The end of the wicked is dismal, while that of the righteous is bright.

Why, then, envy the godless, even though for a season they have the acclaim of the crowd? Rather strive to be *lastingly* happy, taking as your guiding principle to fear, love, and trust in God above all things.

V. 39. The key to the whole situation is that the salvation of the righteous *is of the Lord.* The righteous lives the life he does and dies the death of peace and inherits life eternal — all *of the Lord.* This free grace is the very marrow of the Gospel. He is our "strength in the time of trouble." "A mighty fortress is our God," etc.

V. 40. Our text ends in the triumphant note of victory. If we but trust in Him He shall *help* us and *deliver* us and *save* us. "This is most certainly true." *   A. W. MEYER.

Twentieth Sunday after Trinity.
2 Kings 2, 6—18.

In our text we are permitted to witness the closing scene of a great life. It's like happened only once before, — and of that we have little record, — and it has never happened since. Only two men, Enoch and Elijah, went straight from earth to heaven without passing through the valley of death. It was true of Elijah as well as Enoch that "he walked with God." It is a solemn time, surely, in a man's life when he knows that his earthly journey is drawing to a close, when the scenes of earth are fading away, and when eternity is opening up before him. It is well then for those who, like Elijah, are ready to depart to be with Christ.

Elijah knows by divine revelation that he is soon to be taken away from the earth. Yet he wishes to spend his closing hours in busy activity and usefulness — visiting the schools of the prophets.

A lesson for us. Ought we not to imitate Elijah in redeeming the time, in working while it is day? Do you want to spend your last hours well? If so, you should spend your every day as you would like to spend your last. Hymn 25, 5. There are many whom God lays aside by age or infirmity or suffering for weeks or months or years before He calls them home. They cannot spend their closing hours in what is usually termed work for Christ, though they may really be work-

---

* Luther closes his exposition of this psalm with the words: "Oh, shame on our faithlessness, mistrust, and vile unbelief, that we do not believe such rich, powerful, consolatory declarations of God and so easily become disconcerted though there is but little cause, when we but hear the wicked speeches of the ungodly! Help, O God, that we may attain to right faith! Amen."

ing for Him by their patience in suffering, by their faith and hope, by their words of counsel to others, and by prayer of intercession. But as long as God gives us health and strength to work for Him, it is best to do as Elijah did, to live in the harness to the last.

Notice the busy activity of those last closing hours. He visited the schools of the prophets, where young men were trained for their future work of teaching others of the truths of religion. Elijah felt the importance of those colleges. He realized that these young prophets were the hope of the Church. Hence he would devote to them his last and perhaps his best hours. He would give them words of counsel and exhortation, words that under such circumstances few of them would ever forget. Our colleges and students.

Elijah's Ascension.

1. Elijah is Taken.

Having spoken his parting words of advice and instruction, he and Elisha set out from Bethel for the yonder side of Jordan. The students, a knowledge of what was about to happen having been divinely communicated to them, are deeply stirred. They know this meeting is their last. But their reverence forbids them speak to the prophet about his home-going. They have courage only to whisper to Elisha: "Knowest thou that the Lord will take away thy master from thy head to-day?" He, even more deeply stirred, cautions them to silence.

When they are about to depart from Bethel, the prophet requests that Elisha should remain behind. It is the natural craving of a man in his position. In this holy scene about to be enacted Elijah did not wish to have his private thoughts disturbed. But anxious as Elijah was to be alone, Elisha persistently determines to remain with him to the last. So on they went together to Jericho, where the students again spoke privately to Elisha of his master's departure and received an answer identical with that which had been given the students of Bethel. Again Elijah requests Elisha to remain behind, and the same reply of refusal was given with deeper and more earnest emphasis.

So out from Jericho, they went on. Fifty students followed them until they came to an eminence which overlooked the Jordan, and there they remained "to view afar off." The two pilgrims wend their way on toward the river; and when they reach the bank, Elijah, taking his mantle from his shoulders and wrapping it up into a roll, smote the waters with it, and immediately they were parted hither and thither, so that they went over on dry ground. Up from the opposite bank, they still held on their way; and now, breaking the solemn silence which they had both maintained concerning that which was so vividly before their minds, Elijah said: "Ask what I shall do for thee before I be taken away from thee," to which Elisha made the reply: "I pray thee, let a double portion of thy spirit rest upon me."

What a wise request! Solomon, 1 Kings 3, 5—13. He seeks not riches, nor worldly honor, nor power, nor anything that is in its nature earthly. He desires a double portion of his master's spirit. This does not mean that Elisha desires to be twice as great as his master had been. He wants the portion of the first-born in the family. "Thou hast been visiting thy spiritual sons at Gilgal, at Bethel, and at Jericho; let me be as the first-born among them. Let me by thy successor, the inheritor of thy spirit, and the continuer of thy work."

To this request Elijah replied: "Thou hast asked a hard thing; nevertheless, if thou see me taken from thee, it shall be unto thee; but if not, it shall not be so." And as they went on and talked one with another, a whirlwind came rushing up, a sudden change passed over the heavens, and, lo, in the bosom of the cloud there was, as it were, a chariot of fire and horses of fire. And so, "caught up to meet the Lord in the air," Elijah went up to heaven, while Elisha was left, exclaiming: "My father, my father, the chariot of Israel and the horsemen thereof!"

Who can imagine, who can describe, the transformation that took place in Elijah in that moment? In the twinkling of an eye the body of the prophet underwent that change which shall come upon the living on the day of Christ's appearing. Then, with every demonstration of welcome, he is ushered into the presence of Him whom he had served so lovingly and faithfully upon the earth. And as he is led on to his place of honor by the side of Enoch and Moses, there swells from the attendant throng the glorious chorus: "Well done, good and faithful servant; enter into the joy of thy Lord." Jesus' ascension.

2. The Lord Remains.

While Elijah goes into the realms of glory, Elisha is left exclaiming: "My father, my father, the chariot of Israel and the horsemen thereof!" Besides being a signal honor put upon a great servant of God and a striking Old Testament anticipation of the ascension of Christ, it gave to the Israelites in the midtime of their history a powerful confirmation of the fact of immortality. It is noteworthy that the immortality taught by Elijah's ascension is an immortality of the body. Elisha's lament at Elijah's parting does not in any way imply that he does not believe that his master is being taken up into heaven. It was the sense of personal loss and of loss to Israel that drew from him this plaint. And he did not overestimate the value of Elijah to Israel. He was more to Israel's defense than hosts of chariots and horsemen. We cannot overestimate the worth to a nation of the presence and labors of servants of God in it. Paul, Huss, Luther, etc.

Elisha, gathering up the mantle which had fallen from his ascending master, slowly retraced his steps; and when he came to the river, he smote the waters with the official garment, crying: "Where is the Lord God of Elijah?" As he called, the river was again divided, and he went over, as before, on dry ground. This was a sign to the students standing on the hill of Jericho that he had succeeded to Elijah's dignity, and they went forth to meet him and bowed themselves before him.

Elisha's request has been granted. He has been appointed as Elijah's successor. The Spirit of God, which had filled Elijah, has taken His abode in Elisha. Though the great prophet is removed, God still remains to bless His people. Elijah ascends, but God through Elisha is gracious as before. So to-day, when God takes away such great teachers and leaders as Walther and Pieper, He Himself is still left to His Church. These great and good men do not take Jehovah with them when they leave the earth. He remains with us and carries on His blessed work through other servants. This is true also in our homes. The head of the household may be removed; but the God of Elijah remains, who fed His servant by the ravens and made provision for the widow and the orphan in the home of Zarephath. He will provide for, and comfort, the bereaved who put their trust in Him.

Such comfort and hope is not the portion of those who grovel in doubt and unbelief, as we see in the case of the fifty students. Many are so slow to learn that the Lord remains. So much the worse for them. Those students knew from divine intimations that Elijah was to be parted from them, but they were too much blinded by grief at their teacher's parting to fully believe. They still felt that the parting might be only temporary, that, as on other occasions, the Spirit of God had caught him up and carried him away to some place where by searching he might be found. They therefore desired permission to send out fifty strong men to look for him among the mountains and valleys. Elisha knew better; but as they persisted, he allowed them, for the satisfaction of their own minds, to send out the searching-party. After three days of fruitless search they returned, and Elisha mildly rebuked them: "Did I not say to you, Go not?" But their search set their doubts at rest and confirmed Elisha in his position of authority.

How reluctant, like the students, are we oftentimes to submit to God's dispensations! Because we can not see the meaning of conditions which we consider unfortunate, we are slow to submit. Sickness, death in the family, present depression, etc.

Much more effective and God-pleasing service the students could have rendered by throwing themselves heartily into the work under Elisha. The Church of Christ best shows its regard for the workers of the past and their work not by standing still where they have left off, but by carrying forward and improving the work they have begun. There are ever new opportunities of service opening up, and these must be considered as well as the memories of the past.

W. A. SETZER.

Twenty-First Sunday after Trinity.
Dan. 3, 19—30.

The history of the Church of God has been written in the blood of the saints. Ever since man fell into sin and became allied with the Prince of Darkness, there has been one continual scene of conflict between the seed of the Serpent and the Seed of the Woman. Even when there was but one family upon earth, that family was divided between Satan and God. And in the first human family we are to find the origin of that stream which has flowed through all ages and all lands. Abel leads the van among the noble army of martyrs, and Cain appears as the first persecutor unto death of a saint of God. From that period to this the Church has been exerting her influence to subjugate the world; and the world has been laboring to destroy the Church. Our text presents to us one of the many instances of persecution appearing in its severest aspect, a persecution in which the faith of God's saints was tested to the uttermost. Let us give our devout attention this morning to this —

Fiery Trial of Faith.
1. The Circumstances.   2. The Principle Involved.
3. The Blessed Results.

1.

About 600 B. C. the kings of Judah, through long years of sinning, brought down upon themselves and upon the people the judgments of God. Jehoiakim had succeeded Jehoahaz; and Jehoiachin had succeeded Jehoiakim; and he again was succeeded by Zedekiah. Of each of these kings the record runs the same: "He did evil in the sight of the Lord." As punishment upon these wicked kings and the people who followed them in their wickedness, God sent Nebuchadnezzar up against Jerusalem to lay siege to it and overcome it. He burned the city with fire, broke down its walls, slaughtered many of the people, and numerous others he carried away as captives to Babylon.

Nebuchadnezzar commanded that a certain number of the most promising of the young Jewish captives be picked out and be instructed "in the learning and the tongue of the Chaldeans." Among the youths thus selected were the three young men of our text, Shadrach, Meshach, and Abednego. When the three years of preparation were over, during which these young men passed through numerous severe trials and tests, which time will not permit us now to mention, they were elevated to positions of trust and responsibility in the Babylonian empire. It was the Babylonian custom to appoint over conquered provinces princes frequently belonging to the vanquished nations, who, together with the people whom they governed, were kept under tribute to the empire.

This explains the motive for Nebuchadnezzar's setting up the image our text speaks of and his bringing together the officials from all parts of the empire and commanding them to worship that image. He wished to assert his sovereignty over them and, through them, over all his subjects in the most absolute manner. He feared that the worship of national gods would perpetuate nationality and the desire for independence in a conquered province. Therefore, wishing to weld the many kingdoms of his empire into one homogeneous whole, he determined to demand from all of them conformity to the idol-worship which he himself preferred. Unity of worship was sought that it might contribute to the unity of the empire. He was deter-mined to have a people loyal to one government, honoring one king and worshiping one and the same god. He therefore erected an image of immense size, sixty cubits high and six cubits wide, probably about ninety feet in height and nine to ten feet in breadth. It may have been constructed of wood and overlaid with gold. Some have thought that the image was designed to symbolize the king himself. The signal for the worshiping of this image was to be given by the sounds of music. The trumpet sounds, the herald shouts: "To you it is commanded, O people, nations, and languages, that at what time ye hear the sound of the cornet, flute, harp, sackbut, psaltery, dulcimer, and all kinds of music, ye fall down and worship the golden image that Nebuchad-nezzar, the king, hath set up; and whoso falleth not down and wor-shipeth shall in the same hour be cast into the midst of a burning fiery furnace." That was a punishment distinctly Babylonian, just as the placing of men in the dens of wild animals was a cruelty distinctly Persian. It was a fearful thing to face, but even with this dreadful fate before them, there were some who had the courage to refuse obedience to the king's command.

The order was given, very probably by the king himself, that the bands should strike up, just as on public occasions bands of music do now. The music could be heard afar off; and when the first notes burst forth, all were to bow down to the golden image. Satraps, princes, governors, counselors, high secretaries, judges, were ordered to be present at the dedication of the image. What a gathering that morning! All the rich and the great of the empire were there. Among this vast throng of dignitaries were the three young Hebrew officials of the text, Shadrach, Meshach, and Abednego. At the king's call they had assembled; there was nothing wrong in that. But when it was demanded of them that they worship the image, they refused.

Like all the servants of the Lord these three young Hebrews had enemies, Ps. 38, 20; 34, 19. There were some who bore them a bitter grudge. Possibly many thought that the king had favored them above others. Envy poisoned the hearts of their foes. So they wished to be rid of these hated Hebrews; they wanted their places; they were after their offices. So at the giving of the signal certain Chaldeans were watching these young men. These young men had so carried themselves and had so lived in Babylonia that their watchers felt sure they would not bow down. The watchers watched, and as they had expected, the young men did not bow. Away to the king they go with all haste to lay the information before him: "O king, live forever! Do you know that there are three men in your kingdom who will not obey your command?" "Three men in my kingdom who will not obey me?" roars Nebuchadnezzar. "Who are they? What are their names?" "Why, of course, these three Hebrew slaves whom you set over us, Shadrach, Meshach, and Abednego. When the music struck up, they did not bow down; and it is noised all around, the people know it; and if you allow them to go unpunished, it will not be long until your law will be worthless."

The king is speechless with rage, gesturing his commands that the men should be brought before him. "Is it true, Shadrach, Meshach, and Abednego, that you did not bow down and worship the golden image which I set up in the plain of Dura?" "True, quite true," comes the answer. The king's rage somewhat subsides. He has great respect for these young men. He wants to save them if it is at all possible. He determines to give them another opportunity before consigning them to the fire. Hence he issues anew the command that at the appointed signal they should prostrate themselves before the image. "If ye fall down and worship the image which I have made, well; but if ye worship not, ye shall be cast in the same hour into the midst of a burning fiery furnace; and who is that God that shall deliver you out of my hands?"

But those three young men were still unmoved, and with a heroic faith they said: "We are not careful to answer thee in this matter. If it be so, our God whom we serve is able to deliver us from the burning fiery furnace, and He will deliver us out of thine hand, O king. But if not, be it known unto thee, O king, that we will not serve thy gods nor worship the golden image which thou hast set up."

The answer, so calm, so dignified, so courageous, filled the monarch with such rage that he commanded that the furnace be heated seven times more than ordinarily; and after the three young men had been bound, he ordered that they should be cast into the fire, the heat of which was so great that the men who flung them into the furnace were themselves consumed. Have we such fortitude?

2.

Why did they act thus? Why did they run the risk of sacrificing their lives? Why did they not bow down and worship? Thousands of present-day professed Christians would have done that. Thousands are doing that to-day — lodges. But not these men. In all civil mat-

ters they were willing to be good, law-abiding subjects of Nebuchadnezzar; but they remembered that they owed allegiance to a higher
King, who had said: "Thou shalt have no other gods before Me."
"Thou shalt not make unto thee any graven image or any likeness of
anything that is in heaven above or that is in the earth beneath or that
is in the water beneath the earth; *thou shalt not bow thyself to them
nor serve them.*"

These young men would allow none but God to be the Lord of
their conscience. They believed that a man's faith and worship are
things to be controlled by God's Word and not by any man, be his
station what it will, Matt. 4, 10; Deut. 6, 13; Acts 5, 29. The Christian
regards himself as not his own; he therefore keeps his conscience for
Christ. Hence religious intolerance is to him not only an interference
with individual liberty, but also an infringement upon the right of
Christ to the absolute sovereignty of his soul. True, Christians are
commanded by God to be "subject to the higher powers," and they are
told that "whosoever resisteth the power resisteth the ordinance of
God." But when the higher powers interfere with our allegiance to
God, the principle is: "We ought to obey God rather than men,"
Acts 5, 29.

These three young men show us how a Christian should meet
persecution. They simply refused to do what Nebuchadnezzar commanded. The clear issue in their minds was this: "God says one
thing, but Nebuchadnezzar says another; whom shall we obey?" And
they did not hesitate a moment, but decided at once what they would do.
Many of our modern so-called Christians would have argued thus with
them: "You make too much of it; here is only a question of loyalty
to the king. Your bowing before the image is not understood as an
act of worship to it, but as an act of honor and obedience to the
king. And surely, after all he has done for you, it would be most dis-
courteous to refuse that." But they were not swayed by any such considerations. Nebuchadnezzar already knew their loyalty. They had
shown that in more ways than one. They saw clearly that to bow
before the image was simply and only idolatry; and they would not
dishonor God to show loyalty to the king. They took their stand for
the right, for the honor of God. Even if it cost their lives, what of
that? It would only hasten their promotion to glory, and they would
receive the greater reward, Matt. 5, 11. 12. The faithful three utterly
refused to bow before the god of gold. — How many to-day would cry
out: "Give me gold, give me money, and I will do anything." Money
is their god and social position their golden image. "Give me gold,
and you may have heaven; give me position, and you may have the
world to come. Give me worldly honor, and I will sell out my hopes
of heaven. Give me thirty pieces of silver, and I will give you Christ."
That is the cry of the world to-day.

O for a faith and courage such as these young Hebrews possessed! "If it be so, our God whom we serve is able to deliver us from the burning fiery furnace, and He will deliver us out of thine hand, O king. But if not, be it known unto thee, O king, that we will not serve thy gods nor worship the golden image which thou hast set up." They did not say absolutely that God would deliver them from the burning fiery furnace; but they declared that He was able to deliver them. They were sure that God would deliver them from the king either by death or by preventing the flames from touching them. If their deliverance should come by death, they were not afraid to pass from the presence of the king of Babylon to the presence of the King of kings. Could three such brave men be found to-day in our cities? O God, give us such courage, such boldness for Thy honor!

3.

Into the flames they went, bound hand and foot. From his royal seat the king peered forth, expecting to see the rebels burned to ashes. But to his amazement the bonds were loosed from these men, they arose, and now four men were walking about in the midst of the flames, — walking, not running, — walking as if in the midst of green pastures or on the margin of the still waters. There was no difference in them except that their bonds were burned off. The worst the devil is allowed to do is to burn off the bonds of God's children. If Christ be with us, the direst afflictions can only loosen our earthly bonds and set us free to soar the higher.

Four men were walking in the midst of the fire, although only three had been cast into the furnace. How was this? The Great Shepherd in heaven saw that three of His lambs were in trouble, and He leaped down, as it were, right into the fiery furnace. And so when Nebuchadnezzar looked in, a fourth form was to be seen. Imagine the king's consternation. "Did we not cast three men bound into the midst of the fire? Lo, I see four men loose, walking in the midst of the fire, and they have no hurt, and the form of the fourth is like the Son of God."

And it was the Son of God. There had been One watching the terrible scene of the king's attempting to turn the faithful. His tender pitying eye saw His loved ones condemned to death because of their loyalty to Him, and He sprang from His Father's presence, from His place in glory by their side, so that the fire could not come near them. Not a hair of their head was singed, their clothes were not scorched, and not even the smell of fire was upon them. True is He who has promised: "When Thou passest the waters, I will be with thee; and through the rivers, they shall not overflow thee; when thou walkest through the fire, thou shalt not be burned, neither shall the flame kindle upon thee." God will take care of us when we take our stand at His side, even if we have to go against the whole world. Dare to do right; dare to be true; dare to be honest, let the consequences be what they may. God give us courage to be men and women with the same faith, who are prepared to stand for the right, heeding not what the world may say or the world may think!

"Let your light so shine before men that they may see your good works and glorify your Father which is in heaven." This very thing these men did. "Then Nebuchadnezzar came near the mouth of the burning fiery furnace and spake and said, Shadrach, Meshach, Abednego, ye servants of the Most High, come forth and come hither." And they walked out untouched by the fire. They came out, princes of the Most High. Governors, counselors, and great men crowded around them. Nebuchadnezzar accepted his defeat. He had defied God and had been conquered. God had proved Himself "able" to deliver His servants out of the king's hands. And the king makes a decree "that every people, nation, and language which speak anything amiss against the God of Shadrach, Meshach, and Abednego shall be cut in pieces, and their houses shall be made a dunghill, because there is no other God that can deliver after this sort." And he promoted these three witnesses to a higher place and position and put greater honor upon them. God stood by them because they had stood by Him. Their light shone, and God was glorified. Let us so shine. (Hymn 354.) Amen.   W. A. SETZER.

Twenty-Second Sunday after Trinity.
Gen. 50, 15—23.

When Joseph revealed his identity to his brothers, he gave them ample assurance, by word and deed, that he had fully forgiven them the wrong which they had committed against him, Gen. 45, 1—15. His brothers, however, failed to make an open confession of their guilt and to discuss the whole matter frankly with him. And the result was that they remained in doubt as to Joseph's true attitude of heart towards them. The mere fact that Joseph was dealing so kindly with them could not be considered as conclusive evidence of his plenary forgiveness. Love for his aged father, whom he would not grieve by proceeding harshly against his brothers, could have been the motive for his kind words and deeds. If Joseph's brothers at this time only would have unburdened their conscience by an open-hearted confession, they would have received the positive assurance from their brother that he had heartily forgiven them all their wickedness and that he would no longer remember it against them. But as it was, there always remained that uncertainty whether Joseph was truly reconciled to them. Shortly before his death, Jacob commanded his sons to attend to this important matter, which they had put off for seven-

teen years. Obedient to the words of their now deceased father, they
came to Joseph with an unreserved confession and earnestly implored
his forgiveness. Thus a true reconciliation was effected, which gave
comfort and assurance to those who had offended as well as to the one
who had been offended. Further details are contained in our text,
to which we shall now direct our attention. Let us, guided by God's
Holy Spirit, consider: —

How Joseph and His Brothers Became Fully Reconciled.

1. Joseph's Brothers Made a Full Confession of Their Guilt;
2. Joseph Reassured Them of His Full Forgiveness.

1.

Joseph's brothers realized that their guilt was great indeed, v. 15.
They feared that Joseph would requite them all the evil which they
had done unto him. (Describe briefly the wicked deeds of Joseph's
brothers and Joseph's suffering in Egypt because of them.) They
could not deny their guilt nor offer any palliative explanation. Their
wrong against Joseph was not a rash act, but a premeditated crime,
Gen. 37, 18. 20. 27. They had planned to do him even greater harm,
for they wanted to slay the dreamer. They would have carried out
their wicked design if God himself had not turned their thoughts
into different channels. And the brothers of Joseph made no attempt
to evade the responsibility for all the evil they had inflicted upon
their brother nor to mitigate their guilt in order to escape punishment.
"He will certainly requite us," they say. They rather expected that
now, since their father was no longer with them, Joseph would repay
them their evil. And they knew full well what that would mean;
slavery, long prison terms, or even death. Joseph, being "ruler over
all the land," was in a position to impose any punishment upon them
that he might choose. Contemplating a punishment that would be
equal to their guilt only could fill their hearts with terror.

Deeply impressed by the magnitude of their guilt, they resolved to
confess their sins to Joseph. Fear, however, prevented them from
going themselves. Instead, they sent a messenger, v. 16. They informed Joseph that his father had commanded them to make this plea.
He surely would respect one of the last wishes of his beloved father.
They had the very words of their father repeated to him, v. 17.
A sincere confession. There is no toning down of their guilt. They
refer to it as sin and trespass. But they had truly repented of these
and all their other sins before God. They were no longer heartless
ruffians, but servants of God, serving the same God whom Joseph
served. Hence not only brothers after the flesh, but also spiritual
brothers. Their confession proceeded from a heart that was at peace
with God and that now sought peace with an offended brother.

A further proof of the uprightness of their confession, v. 18. — Deeply moved and encouraged by the information brought back by the messenger, v. 17 b, they now hasten to Joseph themselves, fall down before him, and offer themselves as his servants. Cf. Gen. 37, 7. 8. They are willing to submit to any punishment that Joseph might choose to impose if only he would forgive them the great wrong which they had committed against him. Luke 15, 19. Their acknowledgment of guilt bears all the marks of a true, God-pleasing confession.

Here we have an important lesson that we not only should study carefully, but also practise diligently. We sin often against our fellow-Christians. Often our tongue goes beyond that which is good and edifying, and before we fully realize it, we have probably belied, betrayed, slandered, or defamed our neighbor or inflicted some other injury. How easily are such sins committed! But how difficult is it to go to the offended brother and make a full confession and ask him to forgive us! We are tempted to think up all kinds of excuses that would tend to mitigate the offense. And when we have succeeded in toning down our guilt, we would make ourselves believe that it is such a trivial matter as requires no further consideration. So why stir up anything that is most likely forgotten? Yet all the while this supposedly small matter is burdening the conscience and disturbing the peace of the soul. No matter how small a sin is, it calls the curse of God down upon us. A truly penitent sinner will not only confess all his sins before God and ask for forgiveness for Jesus' sake, Ps. 51, 9. 10, but he will also confess such sins to his fellow-Christians as have offended them. Jas. 5, 16; Matt. 5, 23—26. Catechism, Qu. 316. — Following the example of Joseph's brothers, let us confess our sins to those whom we have offended, and let it be a true confession, calling the sin by its right name, and let us ask them to forgive us. Thus only a true and God-pleasing reconciliation can be brought about. But let us not put off this matter as long as possible, Matt. 5, 25.

2.

Joseph had truly forgiven his brothers when he first made himself known to them. Therefore, when he heard their confession and their plea to forgive their trespass and sin, he wept, v. 17 b. It grieved him that his brothers had put a wrong construction upon his kind words and deeds and that through all these years their hearts had been burdened with doubt as to the true attitude of his heart towards them. When they appeared themselves and proved the genuineness of their repentance, v. 18, Joseph spoke comforting words to them, v. 19. He does not minimize their guilt; but he assures them that there is no reason for their fear, as he was not in the place of God, i. e., "to judge, to condemn, and to punish. God had brought matters to pass in this manner, and it was not for him to change God's purpose." God had taken everything into His hand, even their evil designs, and had turned all for the best, v. 20. Their own wickedness, under the guiding hand of God, had so shaped matters that their lives were saved during the great famine.

Since God had turned evil into good, Joseph wanted to follow the example of the Lord; instead of repaying his brothers evil for evil, he wanted to reward them with good, v. 21. Joseph assured them of his continued favor and of his willingness to nourish them and their families as heretofore. He continued to comfort, and to speak kindly to, his brothers in order to convince them that he had fully and heartily forgiven them.

Joseph forgave his brothers because he knew that it was his God-given duty. We, too, must forgive our fellow-Christians if we wish to remain true children of our heavenly Father. It is not left to our choice whether we wish to forgive or not forgive. The Lord says: Matt. 6, 15; 18, 21. 22; Mark 11, 25; Eph. 4, 32. A Christian should forgive his fellow-men even before they have confessed their guilt and have asked for forgiveness. Yea, he should forgive them even if they do not confess, but rather continue their offenses, Matt. 5, 44. 45; Luke 23, 34. A true child of God will not say, "I will forgive him if he comes and asks me for forgiveness." "If thy brother trespass against thee, go and tell him his fault." Neither will a Christian say, "I will forgive, but I cannot forget." That is no forgiveness at all. We must forgive as God has forgiven us, Is. 38, 17; 43, 25; Jer. 31, 34; Rom. 4, 7. 8. That, however, does not mean that we should not concern ourselves about the faults of our fellow-Christians, but forget them. Matt. 18. But when truly penitent, they should be forgiven *heartily*. "So will we also heartily forgive, and readily do good to, those who sin against us."

Such forgiveness can be exercised by truly believing Christians only. Only he who has come to the full realization of what an abomination sin is in the sight of God and has obtained forgiveness of his sins through faith in Christ Jesus, will be ready and willing with the help of the Holy Spirit to forgive his fellow-men as God has forgiven him. True forgiveness for those that have sinned against us is a fruit of saving faith in Christ, the Savior, Col. 3, 12. 13.

God grant that we may take to heart the important lesson taught in our text! And as we, by the grace of God, confess our faults one to another and forgive one another our trespasses, may God graciously blot out all our sins and keep us in His grace, for the sake of our Lord and Savior Jesus Christ!   E. F. TONN.

Twenty-Third Sunday after Trinity.

1 Sam. 20, 27—42.

The friendship manifested by many in this world is not what that term implies. Many boast of having a host of friends. But if a real test of friendship should be applied to these friends, their number would dwindle down to a very few, if any at all would remain. Much of this friendship is nothing more than interest aroused by some advantages that may result from associating with a certain person. Some is Judas friendship, which may be purchased for thirty pieces of silver. And a great deal of it is plain hypocrisy. To the average person a friend means little more than an acquaintance. In fact, these two terms are often used as synonyms. Most people have a very hazy conception of the meaning of *friend* and *friendship*. It is therefore very necessary to study this subject in order to arrive at the proper understanding of these words. What is true friendship? The only correct answer to this question we find in Scripture. To God's holy Word, then, let us turn for instruction on this important topic. In our text we have —

An Example of True Christian Friendship.

True Christian friendship stands ready —

1. To Comfort a Friend in the Hour of Trial;
2. To Assist Him in His Needs;
3. To Bring Sacrifices for Him when He Is in Danger.

1.

In the hour of trial a true Christian friend is a great blessing. This, David experienced, as we are told in our text, vv. 41. 42. David had been anointed as the King of Israel to succeed Saul. But so far the way to the royal throne had been beset with difficulties and dangers. (Sketch briefly the jealousy of Saul and his attempts to put David out of the way.) And the future did not look any brighter. David had the definite assurance that Saul was determined to slay him, and the only way to save his own life was to flee. But where should he go so that Saul would not find him? Would he not become a victim of Saul's rage before his hope to rule over Israel would be realized? In this dark hour David needed a friend. And he found a *true* friend, strange to say, in a person who was considered to be his rival as prospective heir to the throne, Jonathan. The friendship that Jonathan manifested at this critical time stands out as a shining example for all time.

Jonathan assured David of his friendship, which was not merely a passing, but a soul-deep emotion, chap. 18, 1; text, v. 41b. The kiss always has been the sign and seal of true friendship, Gen. 33, 4; 48, 10. Jonathan proved the genuineness of his friendship further-

more by blessing David, v. 42.   Such blessings were not merely pious
wishes, but fervent prayers to God to bestow these blessings. Cf. Num.
6, 23—27 ("And I," the Lord, "will bless them"); Gen. 28, 1; 48, 15. 16.
Jonathan's wish and fervent prayer was that in due time the Lord
would subdue all the enemies of David and grant him peace.   Departing under the fervent prayers of his friend and the protecting hand of
the almighty God, David had nothing to fear.   The Lord would be
with him and direct his ways, and he would yet triumph over all his
enemies.   And the covenant that these two friends made, chap. 20,
14—16, "they would keep with all firmness; nothing should ever
persuade them to break it."   What a comfort it must have been for
David to find such a friend in this hour of trial!

Who would not earnestly desire such friends? But in order to
have such friends, you must be a true friend to others.   Let us therefore first examine ourselves before we subject our Christian brethren
to a scrutiny of their conduct as friends.   When you see some of your
fellow-Christians overtaken by reverses, do you listen to the voice of
the Old Adam, who whispers, "That is good for them; they were
getting altogether too proud; that will tone them down a little"?
Or do you act as a true friend and go to them, speak comfortingly
unto them, reassure them of your friendship, and thus let them know
that you are sympathizing with them and ready to assist them?
When your Christian neighbor is laboring under a heavy burden of
cross, when he is bowed down with grief and sorrow, do you try to
figure out for what sin in his life this is the well-merited punishment?
Or do you go to him as a true friend, comfort him with God's Word
as best you can, and thus strengthen him and help him to bear his
burden?   Or perhaps your Christian brother has been overcome by sin,
on account of which the world looks askance at him.   Do you then
also avoid him, as though you were ashamed of him?   Or do you
prove yourself a *true* friend to him? Matt. 18, 15 ff.; 2 Cor. 2, 7. 8. —
Let us be true friends to our brethren in Christ and not only comfort
them in the hour of trial, but also help them in their needs as the
example of Jonathan in our text teaches us.

2.

A friend in need is a friend indeed.   David was in need, and
Jonathan was to him a friend indeed.   After Saul had made several
attempts on his life, David escaped and fled to Ramah to consult with
his old friend Samuel.   Saul first sent messengers to Ramah, and
then he went himself to apprehend David and bring him back.   But
the Lord Himself intervened, chap. 19, 19—24.   It seemed as though
Saul's heart had changed toward David and that he would make no
further assaults on his life.   Yet David felt sure in his own mind
that the slightest provocation again would kindle the wrath of Saul

against him and that consequently there was but a step between him and death. But he did not want to act on his own conclusions; so he applied for help to Jonathan, his friend, whom he could trust and into whose hands he virtually placed his own life, chap. 20, 8. His friend was most willing to help him.

Jonathan suggested a plan to David that would not expose them to immediate danger, chap. 20, 11 ff. He spoke for his friend David at the table where the king and his courtiers sat at meat on the new-moon festival, vv. 28. 29. For David's sake he suffered the stern rebuke of his father, who accused him of being rebellious, of having joined himself to the rebellious son of Jesse, v. 30. For David's sake he suppressed the jealousy that his father wanted to kindle in his heart, v. 31. He defended his friend when the king's anger was kindled and he again threatened to kill David, v. 32. Jonathan did all he could to save his friend's life.

Here is a fine example for us. We have many opportunities in our every-day life to be of real help to our friends in need. How often are our fellow-Christians slandered or defamed in our presence! Then: Prov. 31, 8. 9. The command in the explanation of the Eighth Commandment. — Let your defense of your friends not be merely a half-hearted attempt, so that you can say afterwards, I did my duty according to the Eighth Commandment. But, like Jonathan, speak up courageously for them, "put up a fight," as it were, for them, even if you must incur the wrath and the rebuke of the slanderer. Perhaps your neighbor is in bodily need, Luke 10, 31. 32. Help and *befriend* him, Fifth Commandment, Luke 10, 33—37. — What a blessing such friends are!

3.

True Christian friendship finally stands ready to bring sacrifices for a friend in danger. Jonathan's friendship measured up to this requirement. He knew that David would succeed Saul as king over Israel, v. 31. He himself was the true heir to the throne. If David would have been out of the way, no one would have disputed his right to succeed his father; for he was popular with the people, and they would have acclaimed him gladly as their king. But instead of looking out for his own interest, Jonathan sacrificed his right to the throne and worked for the success of his rival. And this he did of his own free will, not being urged in any way. Consider what that means to sacrifice fame and fortune for a friend!

Jonathan even risked his own life for his friend, vv. 34—39. He warned his friend David regarding the real danger threatening him. He knew what that meant if Saul should find out, v. 33. His own life he did not prize too highly to risk it for his friend. Jonathan stepped between danger and his friend; he exposed his own life to extreme danger to shield and save his friend. John 15, 13. Truly, friendship supreme!

Would your friendship stand such a test? Would you step back for a friend and sacrifice a good position for him? Would you expose yourself to great danger, even the danger of losing your own life, in order to safeguard a friend? Your plea perhaps is not to be pressed for an answer to these questions, as such self-sacrifice seems humanly impossible. It is. Such friendship can be manifested by those only who by the grace of God know, love, and believe in, that great Friend regarding whom the poet exultantly exclaims: "What a Friend we have in Jesus, all our sins and griefs to bear!" This our dearest Friend sacrificed Himself for us, John 10, 11. 15. — Matt. 28, 20b; Heb. 13, 6; John 14, 18. If we are united with Christ Jesus, our beloved Savior in true faith, He will never be wanting when we are in need of a *true* friend: when the burden of our sins distresses us, Matt. 11, 28; 9, 2; when the shadow of the cross darkens our path, Matt. 11, 29. 30; Luke 7, 13; 8, 50; John 11, 25. 26. Hymn 395, 2. Under the guidance of this dear Friend and in the strength that He provides we can live up to all the requirements of true friendship.

May we by the grace of God always exercise a friendship that measures up to all the requirements set forth in our text! But above all, may we ever remain united in holy friendship with our dearest Friend, our Savior Jesus Christ, and enter with Him into His heavenly kingdom!   E. F. TONN.

CONFESSIONAL ADDRESSES.

Confessional Address on Ps. 51, 12 a.

Faith is a living thing. It is not such a dead possession like a precious stone or a lump of gold. Faith is rather to be compared to a plant which at one time may seem to be wilting, withering, dying, at another time, however, is growing, increasing, and bearing fruit. Our spiritual life of faith is like our physical life; at one time it is strong, at another time it is weak and ailing and in danger of perishing. The Bible therefore speaks of people who are weak in the faith. And then it speaks of people who are heroes of faith. That man knew something of this decreasing and increasing of faith who prayed: "Lord, I believe; help Thou mine unbelief." And the disciples knew something of this when they said: "Lord, increase our faith."

It is true, weak faith holds the same treasures which strong faith holds, but weak faith holds them in a weak hand and is in danger of losing them. Therefore we should pray to God for a strong faith. A strong faith increases our courage and our joy in the salvation of the Lord. That is what David also prayed for in this psalm, in which he prays so earnestly for forgiveness. That is what he meant when he prayed: "Restore unto me the joy of Thy salvation." To these words I would especially call your attention now.

"Restore unto Me the Joy of Thy Salvation."

1. How had David Lost This Joy?

a) Through his sin. David had borne much misfortune and sorrow. In the midst of all this darkness and tribulation he had clung firmly to God's Word. In it all he had had the joy of God's salvation, which made him strong, Neh. 8, 10. God's Word had supported and comforted him and had given him joy in the salvation of the Lord, 1 Sam. 30, 6. — But after he had become prosperous, after God had raised him to the throne of Israel, when he felt secure from temporal enemies and was enriched with wealth, comforts, and luxury, he became careless; he neglected God's Word, he despised the commandments of the Lord. His heart was filled with evil desires, and instead of fighting against these evil lusts with prayer and God's Word, he gave way to the sin of his heart and fell also into grievous iniquity. We are appalled to think of the sins which this man committed. To this day this sin of David's gives occasion to the enemies of the Lord to blaspheme. Thus David lost the joy of God's salvation. He fled from God.

b) David did not only sin grievously, but he continued in sin and was impenitent. He heard the Law of the Lord, which condemned him and his sin, but he refused to confess. He kept silence even though his bones waxed old through his roaring all the day long. God's hand was heavy upon him day and night; his moisture was turned into the drought of summer. He had lost the joy of salvation.

Application. — My dear communicants, that is the way we lose the joy of God's salvation — through sin.

And if one would say, But my sin is not as black as David's sin, to such a one I would say, It is God's grace which has preserved you. But remember, David did not at once fall into gross external iniquity. This sin entered his heart, polluted his soul. At first he thought little of it. But his evil lusts led him very far astray. Satan still goes about as a roaring lion, seeking whom he may devour. He is also seeking for you. And you have not remained sinless, and therefore through your sin of the heart you have in a measure at least lost the joy of God's salvation. Let no one think lightly of this. Let us rather pray: "Search me, O God, and know my heart," etc., Ps. 139, 23. 24. (Hymn 83, 10.)

2. How was the Joy of God's Salvation Restored to David?

David knew of the Fountain of Life; he knew the good Physician who could restore unto him the joy which he had lost. Therefore David prayed to God: "Restore unto me the joy of Thy salvation." And just so we are to be told that the joy of God's salvation may be restored. How is this done?

a) By forgiveness. Jesus purchased forgiveness. He is the Lamb of God that taketh away the sins of the world. — And this forgiveness is offered to us this morning in this Sacrament. As each of you receives the body and blood of Christ, God assures you of His pardon, of His favor, of His mercy and grace. How can it be otherwise than that through this assurance of your heavenly Father your heart should rejoice and the joy of God's salvation should be restored to you?

b) But this salvation is also increased by the strengthening of your faith. And again this Sacrament and the assurance of absolution are to strengthen your faith. How can you become right sure and confident that God has forgiven you, that you are at peace with God, that God has nothing against you, that His thoughts are thoughts of peace towards you? Not by staring at the sky, not by trying to read it in the stars, not by looking at your life, which is full of imperfection and sin, but *by listening to God's Word as He speaks to you here in absolution and by receiving the Sacrament* which God's messenger bestows upon you. By God's own command His minister assures you that God's gift of His Son and Christ's gift of His body and blood were all intended for you. Thus your faith is strengthened, you are assured of God's mercy, your confidence in His favor is restored, and thus the joy of God's salvation is restored to you.

c) Oh, how blessed are we that we have this opportunity to receive the Sacrament! We pray earnestly, "Restore unto me the joy of Thy salvation," and God hears and answers our prayer in this Sacrament.

Let us therefore gratefully determine with God's help to avoid that whereby this joy is destroyed and taken from us. Let us pray earnestly: "Lead us not into temptation, but deliver us from evil." "Lord Jesus, increase our faith." "I believe; help Thou mine unbelief." "Lead me in the way everlasting." Preserve me from Satan, strengthen me against the enticements of the world, help me in my battle against my sinful flesh and blood, that I may at all times retain the joy of Thy salvation. Let this be your prayer. Hymn 336, 1. 3.

S.

Confessional Address on Ezek. 16, 60.

God has forewarned us that it is possible so to partake of the Lord's Supper as to receive no blessing, but a curse.

It is my duty to tell you this (Ezek. 3, 17—19). I say it not to alarm you, but to help you to carry away from here the priceless treasures which your rich and gracious heavenly Father wants to give you in this Sacrament. A physician may prescribe a remedy which is to be used in one way, and in that way only; if used in another way — suffering and death. Such a physician must warn his patients to be careful. Even our ordinary daily food, if used in a wrong way, may prove harmful to us. However, we certainly do not cease to eat because our food, if improperly taken or eaten at the wrong time, may do us great harm. Neither say: "Because an unworthy partaking of the Sacrament is harmful, we prefer to remain away from this Sacrament." A suggestion to avoid this Sacrament comes from the old evil Foe. Let us not allow any enemy of ours to cheat us out of our inheritance. Let us rather be careful to partake of this Sacrament in a God-pleasing manner.

And we need not be in doubt about this. In our text God has given us explicit instruction. This text answers the question: —

How are We to Partake of This Sacrament in Order to Receive the Richest Blessings?

Note the first word of our text, "nevertheless." *

1.

This word calls our attention to what the prophet has just said. It points back to what immediately precedes our text. And what is that? That is one of the most scathing and galling denunciations of Israel that was ever uttered. God here tells Israel, especially the in-

---

* Let no one imagine that the translation of the Hebrew *vav* by "nevertheless" is not justified. The entire context here shows that this is the correct translation. Luther translated it by *aber*, and the French have translated it by *mais pourtant*. The LXX have *kai*, and that copula is also frequently used in an adversative sense.

habitants of Jerusalem, that He had found them in a most helpless, degraded, and repulsive condition. He compares their former condition to that of an unwanted girl baby which was thrown out on the rubbish heap to perish. He tells them: "None eye pitied thee," etc., vv. 5. 6. Thus God found them, and He alone pitied the poor, helpless, filthy, and disgusting waif, took it to His home, washed it, nourished it, clothed it, educated it, and gave it every advantage, and when this girl came to proper years, He betrothed her to an excellent Husband. And that girl became unfaithful to her Husband, unfaithful to her Savior and Rescuer, threw over all her blessings, played the harlot.

Could you describe sin in more lurid colors? Is such a person as here described worthy of any consideration? Would it not be perfectly just to cast her off forever? And now let us remember that, if we wish to partake of this Sacrament worthily, we are to see in this description our own picture. — Does this statement distress you? Do you think better of yourself than of the citizens of Jerusalem? Have you forgotten your sins? Then let me call your attention to them. God gave to you Paradise with all its riches and glory, and you lost it, and you were cast out. We dare not say, That was not my sin, that was Adam's sin. *Adam's sin is your sin.* God is even now dealing with you as if you had lived in Paradise and had lost it through your own wickedness. Through your sin you have become foolish, thoroughly depraved; your appetites are sinful, your very cravings are corrupt. And however much you may be able to hide your sin under a cloak of respectability before the world, God saw you, and saw you as an unwanted new-born child, thrown out in the field to perish. He had compassion upon you; He gave His Son to die for you; He called you by the Gospel; He made you the bride of the Lord Jesus.

But what did you do?

You did not love the Lord Jesus with all your heart; you were not glad to sacrifice all for Him; your heart went out after the beggarly elements of this world. That is the worst form of depravity to be found among men.

The thoughts and emotions of your heart are more clearly visible to God than any flagrant action is visible to mankind. We simply cannot, *we absolutely cannot,* deceive God. He knows our innermost thoughts; He knows them better than we ourselves know them. And now, what does He see in our heart? Unfaithfulness! How shameful is that sin! God seeth not as man seeth; God looketh upon the heart. And now, if we will just be sincere and honest, — and I hope that we all are, — we must confess that we have not feared God above all things. If we had, how could we so easily have excused ourselves for this or that neglect and sin? Have we reverenced God's Word? Have we stood in awe of everything that God tells us there? Have we trembled at the command, at the Law, of our jealous God? Our conscience tells us, No; in many cases we have feared men more than we feared God. And then, have we *loved* God as we should, above all things? Has He and His glory always been first in our thoughts? Who would dare to say that? Do you realize what a fearful spiritual harlotry that is to let any love come into your heart over and above the love of God? Oh, how shamefully our hearts have been polluted with the love of the world, with the lust of the flesh, with the pride of life! And, again, have we *trusted* in God above all things? If you had trusted in God above all things, not the least worry could have entered your heart, not the least misgiving, not the least trouble. If a person actually trusts in the almighty God, with whom nothing is impossible, trusts in Him implicitly and confidently, how could he worry or be troubled about anything? Every troubled thought, even the slightest worry, every anxiety concerning the future which has entered your heart, was a sign of unfaithfulness toward your God.

And do not imagine for one moment that God pays no attention to all this. He is deeply grieved over these sins. His anger is aroused. He sees the need of punishment and chastisement, and that is the very reason why you do not enjoy perfect happiness on this earth. God is chastising you because of your disloyalty, your lack of love and trust. And if these sins continue in us, if they grow and entirely possess our hearts, they will prove our final undoing. God will reject us then, cast us from His presence forever, there where there is howling and gnashing of teeth. And how much worse are these sins in your case! I am speaking to you who have enjoyed the blessings of the Christian Church. Your heavenly Bridegroom invited you to this feast, and you refused to come; your heavenly Bridegroom blessed you morning, noon, and night, and there were times when you gave very little thought to Him. Other thoughts, other loves, — carnal lusts, pride of life, confidence in your own strength, righteousness, ability, and means, — possessed you; and when these broken reeds began to shake and give way, you became alarmed and were filled with fear and misgiving.

See, my dear communicant, it is this to which this word *nevertheless* points, it points back to our sins in all their shame, in all their wickedness, folly, and repulsive uncleanness. Look back upon this and cry out: "O God, be merciful to me a sinner!"

2.

If that is the fruit of your hearing, then you may approach to this table to receive here the greatest blessings; for this word here in our text does not only point back, this word *nevertheless* also points forward to what God tells us in the words following this word *nevertheless.*

In spite of all that Israel had done, God tells them He is going to remember *not their sins,* but *His covenant.* "I will remember My covenant," etc. God had chosen these people at the beginning of their race and nation, that is, in their youth. And although they had sinned and had shamefully forsaken Him, He promises to forget all that and to be mindful only of the great promises made them, of His covenant relation to them. He had promised them a Messiah ("Seed of the Woman," "Lion of Judah," "Prophet like unto Moses"). For the sake of the Messiah and the Messiah's great work of redemption He promises this sinful Israel forgiveness.

That is exactly to what this word *nevertheless* also points us. The Israel of the Old Testament was a mere picture and type of ourselves, the Christians of the New Testament. God made a covenant also with us. In Holy Baptism, of which every one of us is partaker, His grace in its full mercy and kindness were showered upon us; in His great love for the sake of the Redeemer He there adopted us as His children. He has not forgotten that covenant which He made with us in Baptism, and if by our sins we have angered Him, offended Him, insulted Him, He still remembers His covenant of peace. He remembers the blood of Jesus Christ, by which we are cleansed from all this uncleanness, 1 John 1, 7b. And He calls our attention to this covenant and wishes us to return to Him and to His covenant by repentance and faith.

O what happy people we should be when we think of this, that, oft as we have left Him, He never left us! And in spite of our weakness, instability, carelessness, in spite of our sinfulness and wickedness, He calls to us, "Come unto Me." Let us be sure that we hearken to His invitation to-day and return to this our gracious Father.

Indeed, instead of abrogating and removing the covenant which He made with us, He tells us here in our text: "I will establish unto thee an everlasting covenant." Thereby He told Israel first of all of the wonderful covenant of the New Testament based upon the redemption of Jesus Christ, the Savior. That covenant is not to be a temporary arrangement and adjustment of relations between Him and us. No, it is to be a covenant which cannot be broken, which is to endure throughout all eternity. And it is this covenant which He wishes to strengthen and establish here in the Sacrament of the Altar, of which you wish to partake. To-day and here He wishes to assure you again that He is your Helper, your powerful Confederate, for the sake of Christ's body and blood, that very body and blood which you are to receive to-day. In this Sacrament God means to confirm in us the conviction that He has not turned from us, but that He will cling to us and support us against all our foes. What we lack He will supply. His mercy, His kindness, and His support shall not fail us throughout all the years to come. As a true heavenly Father He pledges His power and wisdom to defend us against Satan, the world, and the flesh. He will finally take us from this vale of tears to give us with Christ, His only-begotten, beloved Son, the inheritance of heaven, an inheritance undefiled, incorruptible, and that fadeth not away.

In order that we may have no reason to doubt this promise of His to which the word *nevertheless* in our text points, He in the Sacrament gives us the very treasure which was sacrificed for us, the body and blood of Jesus Christ. As true as it is therefore that here in the Sacrament you receive the body and blood of Christ, so true it is also that God does here and now forgive all your trespasses, whatever they may be, and does here and now receive you and adopt you again as His beloved children. Here and now He promises you to be with you throughout all the years to come, and finally to receive you from this earth to His heavenly glory.

Do you believe this? Satan would make you doubt it. He wishes to separate you from your good heavenly Father, like the prodigal son, whom he drove away from his kind, merciful father and from his home to the swine in the land of the heathen. Let us say "No!" to the evil spirit. "I am going to stay in my Father's house. God forbid that I should despise His precious gift, the Sacrament of the Altar!" The world laughs at your simple, childlike trust in your heavenly Father; but remember that he that laughs last laughs best. The laughter of the world shall be turned into wailing. They will be where there is weeping and gnashing of teeth. But of us who accept His mercy Christ says: "Your sorrow shall be turned into joy. . . . Ye now therefore have sorrow, but I will see you again, and your heart shall rejoice, and your joy no man taketh from you," John 16, 20. 22.

But haven't you in your heart some misgiving, some doubt? That may well be; remember, however, that this doubt comes from the flesh, from your corrupt nature. Crucify that, smother it, and ask God the Holy Spirit to fill your heart entirely with faith and confidence in your Savior, so that with believing and joyful hearts you may accept the gifts which that rich and gracious Father in heaven gives you in this Lord's Supper.

If thus you follow the pointing of this word *nevertheless,* first as it points back to your sin and then as it points forward to God's eternal and gracious covenant, you will receive in this Sacrament a treasure richer than any or all gold or silver in the world, namely, God the Almighty as your unfailing Confederate and Father.

Strengthened by such assurance and faith, you may go forth with confidence and joy to fight again the good fight of faith. Let this, then, be your prayer to-day: 344, 1. 7. 8. Amen.   S.

Confessional Address on 1 Cor. 11, 28. 29.

In the fourth chapter of the First Book of Samuel we are told that the children of Israel, having been defeated in battle by the Philistines, held a council of war and asked among themselves: "Wherefore hath the Lord smitten us before the Philistines?" Instead of remembering the sins they had committed under the leadership of Eli's wicked sons, instead of repenting of their wickedness and asking God to pardon their sins and restore His grace and favor unto them, they sent to Shiloh, where the Tabernacle then stood, and had the Ark of the Covenant brought into camp. This Ark they took with them into battle, hoping that the Lord God would now be with them and give them the victory. But when the battle was joined, the children of Israel met with a defeat more disastrous than before, and the Ark of the Covenant was taken by the enemy.

It is to be feared that there are some who think of the Sacrament as the Israelites thought of the Ark of the Covenant. They seem to think that, as long as they merely put in their appearance before the altar and partake of the Sacrament, they cannot fail to enjoy the grace and favor of God. Such impenitent, mechanical partaking of the Sacrament is not only futile, but it will result in disaster. For a heedless, impenitent communicant is an unworthy communicant. He indeed receives the very body and blood of the Lord Jesus Christ, as do all who partake of the Sacrament; but Paul says: "He that eateth and drinketh unworthily eateth and drinketh damnation to himself, not discerning the Lord's body."

St. Paul does not wish to discourage Christians from partaking of the Sacrament or to make their going to Communion a thing of fear and dread. The Lord Jesus instituted the Sacrament of the Altar for the comfort and strengthening in faith of all His followers. Here, too, the gracious invitation resounds: "Come unto Me, all ye that labor and are heavy laden, and I will give you rest." They are to come no matter how great or how many their sins, no matter how weak and halting their faith. He has grace and mercy for all. What Paul would do by impressing on us the necessity of a worthy partaking of the Sacrament is to guard us from harm and to help us gain the great blessings which Christ has in store for us in the Sacrament. For this reason He says: "Let a man examine himself, and so let him eat of that bread and drink of that cup."

Wherein does true worthiness consist? "He is truly worthy and well prepared who has faith in these words 'Given and shed for you for the remission of sins.' . . . For the words 'for you' require all hearts to believe."

Let us, then, briefly examine ourselves to determine whether we have that faith which alone makes us worthy communicants.

The first question which the communicant should ask himself is, "Why do I go to the Sacrament?"

When the Lord Jesus on the night of His betrayal instituted the Sacrament of the Altar, He said to His disciples: "This do in remembrance of Me." The Christian will partake of the Sacrament often, because it is the will of the Lord that he do so. When we partake of the Sacrament, we are, however, not so much doing the Lord a service as being served by Him. For in the Sacrament the Lord Jesus would give us to eat and to drink His very body and blood as a seal and pledge for the forgiveness of our sins and thus impart to us strength for our faith in the forgiveness of sins. This blessing the communicant must seek in the Sacrament. If he does not seek this blessing, he is unworthy and unprepared and eats and drinks damnation unto himself.

Before the communicant can seek that blessing, he must recognize himself to be a sinner who is in need of that blessing. He must ask himself whether he believes that he is in the sight of God a poor miserable sinner who has by his sins offended God and justly merited His wrath and displeasure, temporal death, and eternal damnation. He must ask himself whether he is truly sorry for having offended God by his sins, terror-stricken at their results, and therefore anxious to be relieved of the burden of his sin and guilt.

Such a confession will often be hard to make on the part of the communicant. It will take no great effort to join in the general confession "We are all sinners; none of us are without faults; to err is human." But to admit that we are poor, miserable sinners, richly deserving of God's wrath and punishment for time and eternity, that is something against which our natural pride revolts, something which the Old Adam cannot away with.

For this reason the communicant is not to consult with flesh and blood, not to heed the protestations of fleshly pride, not to listen to the excuses of the Old Adam. He is to examine himself according to the Ten Commandments and to invoke the aid of the Holy Spirit that his eyes may be opened so that he may see himself as the sinner he is and that he may give true heed to what God says of sin and its results.

When the Christian thus searches and proves himself, he will say in answer to the question "Why do I go to Communion?" I go because I feel the weight of my sin and guilt, because I am sorry for my offenses against the Lord, because I seek to be strengthened in the assurance that my sins are forgiven.

Moreover the communicant should ask himself whether he is sure of gaining the blessing which he seeks in the Sacrament. The benefit of partaking of the Lord's Supper, our Catechism says, is shown us by the words "Given and shed for you for the remission of sins."

"He that believes these words has what they say and express, namely, the forgiveness of sins." "He that does not believe these words or doubts is unworthy and unprepared."

In his self-examination as to his worthiness to partake of the Sacrament the communicant must ask himself if he truly believes that Jesus Christ is true God, begotten of the Father from eternity, and also true man, born of the Virgin Mary, and that the God-man, Jesus Christ, through His obedience, suffering and death, has won forgiveness, life, and salvation for all sinners. He must prove himself as to whether he believes that Jesus Christ and no other is *his* Savior and guard against the thought that he may receive forgiveness through his own merits or through the work of any other besides Christ. He must ask himself whether he believes the words of Jesus "This is My body; this is My blood" as they read, though he cannot understand them.

It may seem to the Christian that such self-examination on his part is superfluous and unnecessary since he has been taught, and has believed from his youth, that Jesus Christ is the Son of God and his Savior and knows that He who instituted the Sacrament of the Altar is Jesus Christ, the God-man, who is true, all-wise, and almighty. We are to consider well, however, that Satan, the old evil Foe, is ever on the alert, seeking to seduce us into doubt, misbelief, and unbelief, and that our Old Adam constantly is in rebellion against the mysteries of God's Word. The warning of Paul "Examine yourselves whether ye be in the faith; prove your own selves" is always in place, and particularly when we go to Communion.

Finally the communicant must ask himself if he really wants to be rid of sin, free from the dominion of sin.

There are certain sins for which individuals have a particular weakness. One may be given to pride, another to greed, another to anger, another to some other vice. They recognize these sins, are apparently sorry for them, and come to the Sacrament where the assurance of forgiveness is given. But they go forth, and after a short time they have fallen back into the same old sins, because they did not really repent of them and did not guard against them. There are others who have certain favorite sins. They recognize these as sin and go to Communion to receive forgiveness; but they do not want to forsake these sins, because they like them. What they really want is not to be freed from sin, but to live in sin without fear of punishment; and thus they would make Jesus a servant of sin.

Jesus gave His body and shed His blood for us sinners not only that we may be freed from the guilt, and spared the punishment, of sin, but that we may be freed from its dread dominion. When we, therefore, come to the Sacrament to be relieved of the burden of our sin and guilt, we must also have the desire to be freed from the dominion of sin and have the sincere intention to make use of the strength and power over sin which the Lord would impart to us by His Holy Spirit. Then, and then only, will our faith in these words "Given and shed for you for the remission of sins" be true faith. Then, and then only, shall we be worthy communicants.

"Let a man examine himself, and so let him eat of that bread and drink of that cup." May the Lord Jesus Himself give you grace so to examine yourselves that you may heartily repent of your sins, fully believe in Jesus Christ, and have the sincere and earnest intention henceforth by the assistance of God the Holy Ghost to amend your sinful life! Then yours will be that faith which alone is required for true worthiness. Then the Sacrament of the Altar will be to you a fountain of comfort and strength and salvation.

GEORGE WITTE.

Confessional Address on Heb. 12, 1. 2 a.

The Christian life is often described as "walking with God." Thus we read in Gen. 5, 24: "Enoch walked with God, and he was not; for God took him." This expression emphasizes the fact that Enoch lived as a true child of God. In a similar manner St. Paul exhorts his Corinthian Christians: "So run that ye may obtain." St. Paul thinks of the Christian life as a race and is anxious that his Corinthians might obtain the incorruptible crown of eternal life.

So also the writer to the Hebrews. He admonishes his Christian readers, and therewith also us, to "lay aside every weight and the sin which doth so easily beset us," so that we may also successfully "run the race that is set before us." Let us, then, ponder the admonition of our text —

"Lay Aside Every Weight and the Sin which doth So Easily Beset Us."

1. This Admonition Convicts Us of Sin.

2. It Urges Us, and also Shows Us How, to Lay Aside Sin and Its Weight.

3. It Warns Us against the Besetting Nature of Sin.

1.

The holy writer connects his admonition with the glorious examples of faith which have just been enumerated and pictured in the foregoing chapter. Being encompassed "with so great a cloud of witnesses" should urge us to follow their example and likewise to lay aside every weight and sin.

This very admonition convicts us of sin. For how can we be urged to lay aside what is not weighing us down or to abstain from that of which we are not guilty? Yes, the admonition of our text very pointedly accuses us: You are sinners. Is this accusation true? Can it be supported? Let us see. What is sin? "Sin is the transgression of the Law," God's Law. What does God demand of us in His Law? Jesus has summarized it thus: "Thou shalt love the Lord, thy God, with all thy heart, and with all thy soul, and with all thy mind," and: "Thou shalt love thy neighbor as thyself." Have we measured up to that demand? No. As we examine ourselves in the mirror of God's Law, we find that we have offended against every one of His commandments. These findings are in harmony with God's verdict: "There is not a just man upon earth that doeth good and sinneth not," Eccl. 7, 20. "There is none that doeth good, no, not one," Ps. 14, 3. So here is the situation: God demands: "Ye shall be holy; for I, the Lord, your God, am holy," and in response we bring a pack of foul, filthy, and corrupting sins. Sure "we are all as an unclean thing, and all our righteousnesses are as filthy rags."

There is a tendency in our days to belittle the nature of sin. Sin is looked upon as a mere defect in our human nature, something which we are all afflicted with and which must not be taken too seriously. Let us not be deceived. Sin is something devilish, deadly, and damnable. "He that committeth sin is of the devil," 1 John 3, 8. "The wages of sin is death," Rom. 6, 23. "Cursed be he that confirmeth not all the words of the Law to do them," Deut. 27, 26. Yes, the nature of sin is so devilish, so deadly, so damnable, that *one* unforgiven sin is sufficient to sentence a soul to eternal punishment. "Whosoever shall keep the whole Law and yet offend in one point, he is guilty of all," Jas. 2, 10. And so long as a person is guilty, he stands condemned by the curse of God's Law. Thus we stand convicted of sin. We deserve God's wrath and punishment, yea, eternal damnation.

Surely, realizing this our sinful state and condition, we shall be found willing to heed the earnest admonition of our text and shall also gladly receive God's instruction as to how we may lay aside our sin and its dreadful weight.

2.

When the holy writer urges us to "lay aside every weight and the sin which doth so easily beset us," he is thinking of the competitive games of his time. One who entered the stadium was careful to lay aside anything that might prove a hindrance. So we, as children of God, having entered the stadium of faith and sancification, thus running the race of life, are urged to lay aside everything that may tend to hold us back. The greatest hindrance in the race for the crown of life is sin. Sin distracts our attention from the goal; it leads us astray from the right way; it loads us down with a heavy weight, a heavy burden. Sin is always followed by the conviction, the consciousness, of guilt. This consciousness of guilt constitutes a weight which becomes heavier and heavier and will finally crush us unless we are enabled to lay it aside. Thus David in the knowledge of his sins exclaims: "For mine iniquities are gone over mine head; as an heavy burden they are too heavy for me," Ps. 38, 4. Therefore it is expedient that we follow the admonition of our text to "lay aside every weight and the sin." But how? Our text gives us the necessary information: "Looking unto Jesus, the Author and Finisher of our faith."

When the children of Israel murmured against God in the wilderness, God sent fiery serpents into their midst to punish them for their wickedness. When they cried unto God in repentance, Moses was directed to erect a brazen serpent. All who looked up to this brazen serpent believing God's gracious promise connected therewith were healed from the poisonous bite of the fiercy serpents and lived. We, dear friends, have been bitten by a poisonous serpent, the devil. The poison of sin has permeated our entire being. But as Moses lifted up a serpent in the wilderness, so the Son of God, Jesus, our Savior, was lifted up on the cross of Calvary to die as our Substitute, our Savior. "God hath made Him to be sin for us who knew no sin, that we might be made the righteousness of God in Him." In view of this glorious truth our text directs us, who have been infected with the deadly venom of sin, to look to Jesus the Crucified with the certain faith that God hath raised Him on the cross for our salvation, for the healing of sin's sores. If we follow this instruction, we shall be healed from the poison of the vile serpent, the devil. Our sins will be forgiven us in the blood of Jesus, the Lamb of God, and as a result the weight of our guilt will also be removed from our conscience.

Of this blessed truth we are especially assured in the Lord's Supper. Here Jesus Himself, who was crucified for our sins, invites us: "Come unto Me, all ye that labor and are heavy laden, and I will give you rest." Here Jesus Himself assures us: "Take, eat; this is My body which is given for you. Take, drink; this is My blood which is shed for you, for the remission of your sins." Come, then, with believing hearts, dear fellow-sinners, and be justified freely by God's grace.

But after having received so great salvation, it must ever be our most earnest concern to avoid sin and its besetting nature in the future. To this end let us also heed the warning of our text.

3.

The warning of our text is contained in these words: "which doth so easily beset us," referring to sin. We once saw the ruins of a latticed window which eloquently portrayed the besetting nature and the power of sin. A strong vine, several inches thick, had completely wrecked the once beautiful window and held a few remnants of the lattice-work in a vicelike grip. Can you not picture the encroaching, the besetting, the destroying work of that vine? At some time, when the window was in its original beauty, a tiny, tender tendril found its way into the lattice. Removed at that time, it would have worked no harm. It was delicate, soft, and pliant and could have been removed by the slightest touch of a finger. But it was not removed. It was permitted to stay and to twine itself through the lattice. The tender tendril, which looked so helpless and harmless, gradually developed into the strong vine, which completely shattered and destroyed the beautiful window. How aptly this describes the besetting nature and the power of sin! Sin also approaches us as something soft, sweet, most desirable. If met at once with the weapons God's Word supplies, it can be shaken off before it gains a deadly hold. But if left unmolested to stay, to grow, and to entwine itself into the heart of man, it grows stronger and stronger, until it thoroughly wrecks the heart and life of man and leads to eternal ruin. How aptly the Bible pictures this process: "But every man is tempted when he is drawn away of his own lust and enticed. Then, when lust hath conceived, it bringeth forth sin. And sin, when it is finished, bringeth forth death," Jas. 1, 14. 15. Let us not overlook the earnestness of this warning nor our need of being warned. "Let him that thinketh he standeth take heed lest he fall," 1 Cor. 10, 12.

Neither let any one imagine in his heart that he is strong enough to meddle and to play with sin with impunity. Sin is a dangerous playmate. A certain performer was wont to demonstrate his power over a boa-constrictor. In one corner of the stage there was an imitation jungle patch. From this seeming jungle the performer would call forth his large boa-constrictor and, keeping her head before him and under the constant control of his eyes, would permit her to coil herself around his body to the amazement of the onlookers. On one occasion, however, he made the fatal mistake of taking his controlling gaze from her before she had entered the "jungle" and the hidden cage. Thinking his "pet" safely in the cage, he turned to acknowledge the prolonged applause of the audience. The reptile, noting its opportunity, quickly and quietly returned and, taking the performer unawares, coiled herself about his body, this time free of the controlling eye of its master. The populace, thinking this a trick of performance, applauded and did not realize the seriousness of the situation until the agonizing outcries of the performer and the cracking of his crushing bones convinced them that he had fallen a prey to his "pet." Thus sin, petted and played with, seemingly under the control of the sinner, will eventually ensnare and crush its victim and drag him into the bottomless pit of hell. Again I say: "Let him that thinketh he standeth take heed lest he fall." Do not play with sin. Take sin seriously. Ask God to grant you His help and the Spirit's power to combat this besetting and destroying evil.

And may the God of grace and mercy bless our meditation and grant us the willingness and the strength of faith to follow its admonition and to accept its full comfort!

Come, then, dear friends, to the Throne of Grace and, acknowledging your sins freely and fully and without reserve, repent of them and, "looking unto Jesus, the Author and Finisher of our faith," accept God's own seal for the certainty of His grace and the surety for the forgiveness of your sins — the body and the blood of our Savior Jesus Christ.   W. H. HAFNER.

MID-WEEK SERVICES.

THREE ADVENT TEXTS.

God's Faithfulness.

Hab. 2, 1—4.

God keeps a waiting-list. He does not always respond to our call immediately, though it be based on His promise, Ps. 69, 3. He answers in His appointed time. For the insurance of temporal and spiritual success the Lord encourages us to enlist with the waiting, Ps. 27, 14. We find on His list all the faithful believers: Adam and Eve, waiting for the Messiah; Noah, for the subsiding of the waters; Abraham, for the son of promise; David, for the Deliverer. God's waiting-list of the Old Testament: Heb. 11 (cp. vv. 39. 40). The Church of the Old Testament waited for the great promise of God for 4,000 years, but the individual believer waited for the appearance of Jesus only a lifetime: Noah, 950 years; Joseph, 110 years; David, 70 years. The Lord placed more and more on His waiting-list, v. 3. Finally He fulfilled His promise exactly as given through the prophets. He is faithful. Luke 2, 25—28. 36—38; Ps. 69, 6. Then the apostles were added to the waiting-list, Acts 1, 4. At this time we wait, 1 Thess. 1, 10; Rom. 8, 23—25. Let us continue to wait, for: Is. 30, 18—21. God fulfils His promise, satisfies our desire, and finally delivers us. He is faithful. While He seems to tarry, and while blasphemers mock, He strengthens our faith.

God's Faithfulness.

1. It Appears in the Exact Fulfilment of the Old Testament Prophecy.

A) *The Situation,* v. 1.

1) Peering back into the past, we behold the prophet Habakkuk on the sentinel's post in watchful, prayerful, expectant attitude. To this service he had been called by the Lord. Many visions, prophecies, promises, had been given, preached, recorded. The prophets had bewailed the misery of the world and the suppression of God's chosen people. They had pointed to the Deliverer, the Prince of Peace, the Savior. In beautiful language they had pictured the relief which the Messiah would assure for soul and body, heart and mind, time and eternity. Their eloquence reached sublime heights when they spoke of the rest and liberty to be enjoyed under the New Dispensation. With them the people of God yearned and prayed, Is. 64, 1; Gen. 49, 18. Also the types encouraged to stronger faith and more ardent sighs. Still more prophecies were given, more promises proclaimed. The manner of the Messiah's coming, the place of His birth, His reception, His rejection, His message, His work, were foretold in minutest detail. The prophets reiterated the majestic word: "Thus saith the Lord."

2) But there seemed to be no fulfilment. In answer to their sighs

the hopeful received only new prophecies and promises. Jerusalem should flourish and shine like a light among the nations, but Jerusalem was reduced to ashes. Judah should be delivered from his enemies, but Judah was subjected to humiliation. The Temple should be built to greater splendor than Solomon's Temple, but the Temple was ruined and a habitat of owls. In the minds of the people, facts contradicted the prophecy; and confusion, doubt, disappointment, hopelessness, spread among the people. The derision and mockery of the faithless taunted the faithful.

3) Who would be a prophet at such a time as this? What courage to face the situation! What conviction of faith to meet and reprove the opposing rationalists! What a task to encourage and comfort God's people! What power further to proclaim: "Thus saith the Lord," as a thundering warning to the blasphemers and a soothing hope to the few believers!

4) The Lord does not forsake His prophet. He answers. Yet again not with immediate fulfilment of the prophecy, but with an additional word of hope. And this was about 630 years before Christ's appearance in the flesh!

B) *The Answer*, v. 2, is the command to write the vision in letters sufficiently large and attractive that a person passing by could read it on the run, similar to the size of letters on the bill-boards of to-day. What was he to write? The vision.

1) The word *vision*, here a collective term, refers to, and includes, all the visions of all the true prophets which pertain to the Messiah: His ancestry, virgin birth, place of birth, poverty, forerunner, all the steps in both His state of humiliation and of exaltation, His active and passive obedience, His entry into Jerusalem, suffering and death, His grace, mercy, love, peace, blessing.

2) The message announced that the time of fulfilment is not yet at hand, but approaching. While it tarries, further faith is required. God's faithfulness should not be questioned. Without delay He will deliver.

3) The answer of the Lord to the prophet's prayer for direction in his arguments with the mockers is the reproof, v. 4a.

4) To the reader the message further announced that patient faith in the vision justifies the believer, that the justified finds food for faith in the vision and is sustained by faith unto the end, and that by faith he enters eternal life. We repeat that this was about 630 years before Christ's appearance in the flesh.

C) *The Fulfilment.* — The last vision was given about 400 years before the appearance of John the Baptist. Then prophecy ceased. Yet the vision was fulfilled as prophesied, in every detail.

1) Believing Bible-readers have searched the Scripture to compare prophecy and fulfilment pertaining to the person, Word, work,

and blessing of the Savior. In adoration and admiration of God they closed the Book only to open it again and to begin anew this profitable study because of the overwhelming evidence of God's faithfulness, its refreshing comfort, its sustaining message that the just shall live by faith.

2) Unbelieving Bible-readers — their name indeed is legion — have perused carefully the Word of God to find a flaw in the fulfilment or to uphold, sometimes with tricky disregard of historical facts, their theory that the prophecies were written after Christ's death only to close the Book with the conviction that their soul is puffed up and not upright in them. Shame, confusion, punishment, will come to them as to their predecessors of Habakkuk's time. "Thus said the Lord": the study of prophecy and fulfilment, conducted in the pulpit, school, home, and chamber, especially appropriate in this Advent season, reveals to us God's marvelous faithfulness.

2. It Invites Us to Believe in His Existence and Urges Us to Accept His Mercy.

Text. The Lord spoke, and at the appointed time He wrought. We stand in awe of Him. For prophecy and fulfilment rests not with man. I challenge any person to make a prophecy and to fulfil it. I challenge any person to extend the fulfilment of his prophecy over a period of fifty or twenty-five or five years. I challenge him to live long enough to carry out his promise. I challenge him to display that degree of omniscience which will not make him ashamed. I challenge him to control all events to conform to his prophecy and to remain consistent even in the face of the opposition of the beneficiaries of his prophecy. Such faithfulness requires: a) Life, divine, eternal life: the nature, quality, ability to outlive the promise to the time of fulfilment; b) omniscience: full knowledge of the past, present, and future, of time and eternity; c) omnipotence: full control of all things, temporal and eternal, and government of all physical and political affairs from the time of the promise to the fulfilment; d) persistent love, divine love, which faithfully brings about the fulfilment, though forfeited untold times by the infidelity of the beneficiaries, of the promise. Prophecy and fulfilment belong to God only. God lives. He spoke, and it was done. His faithfulness causes us to believe in His existence, and it urges us to accept His mercy. Joshua's praise of God should issue forth from our hearts to His eternal glory. Josh. 21, 45; 23, 14.

Applications. — 1) A part of the vision remains to be fulfilled: Christ's last advent. Phil. 3, 20. 21; 1 Thess. 4, 13 f.; 1 John 3, 2; Rev. 21, 4. The faithful of to-day experience the same mockery and derision on the part of the world, and it is required of them to render reproof and to convict by their argument, and they are to display the same faith in the promise as Habakkuk, v. 4. 2 Thess. 2; 2 Pet. 3. —

2) Often we are also vexed by personal problems and afflicted by sorrows. We would rejoice in God's promises (Ps. 37, 4. 5; 1 Pet. 5, 7; John 16, 23) and in the fact of our justification (1 John 1, 7b; Rom. 8, 32), but physical facts seem to prevent or delay the realization of our faith and hope. — 3) The congregations, too, hear the Word of our Lord (Luke 12, 32; 1 Cor. 15, 58), but He seems to tarry with these particular Advent promises. — 4) But: v. 4b and v. 3; 1 Thess. 5, 24.

We believe. Help, Lord, our unbelief! We believe in the Triune God, who has revealed Himself in the Scriptures, which shall be a lamp unto our feet and a light on our path throughout this new church-year.   G. H. SMUKAL.

The Lord hath Sworn.
Psalm 89, 3—5.

God is a glorious mystery, Ex. 33, 20, and His essence, His greatness, His glory, is far beyond human understanding, Rom. 11, 33 f.; Deut. 3, 24 b. He has revealed Himself, but His revelation to us has only begun, Deut. 3, 24 a. The beginning is sufficient for this life, Ex. 34, 6. 7, and we have the promise of seeing Him face to face, 1 John 3, 2; 1 Cor. 13, 12. God moves in ways mysterious to us, and even His positive, transitive, operative attributes are a mystery to us in their perfection. And when we consider His works, which are beyond our comprehension, we fold our hands in prayerful meditation and in childlike trust, Ps. 143, 5. 6; 8, 3. 4. Our text speaks of an act of God performed in His love to man, which, though revealed, is a divine mystery, never fully grasped by our finite mind, but reverently accepted by faith. We cover our countenance in reverence and bend our knee in gratitude while we meditate on this act of God. What is this act of God?

The Lord hath Sworn
1. By Himself;   2. An Oath of Promise;
3. To Our Comfort and to His Glory.

1.

A) *God swears by Himself,* v. 3b; Gen. 22, 16; Ex. 3, 14.

1) By His attributes: a) His holiness (Ps. 89, 35), which is His absolute purity, unapproachable, glorious (Is. 6, 3; Ps. 104, 1. 2; 1 Tim. 6, 16); b) His righteousness (Is. 45, 23), also a transitive, operative attribute of God (Ps. 92, 15; Dan. 9, 7; Deut. 32, 4); c) His truth (Ps. 132, 11), He being the absolute Truth (2 Tim. 2, 13; Jer. 10, 10; Heb. 6, 18).

2) By His life (Num. 14, 21), of which no being can deprive Him (John 5, 26; 1 Tim. 1, 17).

3) By His solemn gesture, Ezek. 20, 5, which is significant of His

sincerity and determination to employ His power to execute His oath. Swearing by His attributes, by His life, by gesture, is the same as swearing by Himself.

B) *The Reason why God Swears by None Other than Himself.*

1) Man swears. God has forbidden man to swear by his own attributes, life, or self, Matt. 5, 33—37. Man has no control of heaven; he does not rule the earth; he does not own Jerusalem; the natural color of his hair lies not within his choice.

2) But man is told to swear, Deut. 6, 13; Heb. 6, 16. However, he is to swear by One greater than he, who is omniscient and almighty to confirm the truth. Because of the nature of the oath, which is a prayer to God to bear witness to the truth and avenge the falsehood, man's oath by himself has no value, but his oath by God has value.

3) God swears by Himself because He can swear by no greater, Heb. 6, 13. Thus God binds His word (promise or threat) to Himself. If He ceases to be, then His word ceases also, and if the word remains unfulfilled, then He dies. But He is the same, Ps. 102, 27, immutable, Heb. 6, 17 f.; and because He is and never changes, therefore His promise will be fulfilled and His threat executed. None can rightfully call Him a liar; none can discover a lie in His Word. His Word, now confirmed by His oath, is wrapped up in Him and endures. His enemies will never succeed in suppressing His Word because His Word, confirmed by His oath, is as strong as He, and they as weak over against the Word as against God. They would have to become greater than God and vanquish Him if they would muzzle His Word. God is oath-bound, and we rejoice to know that His oath is bound to Him.

4) God swears by Himself. We tremble. Heaven and earth must have shaken when He swore and gave oath by Himself in His wrath, Heb. 3, 11. We rejoice with thanksgiving. Heaven and earth must have rested in most serene peace and happiest solemnity when God confirmed by an oath by Himself His covenant of grace.

2.

A) God swears, but not for His own sake or benefit. The beneficiary of His oath is —

1) David the king, the successor of Saul to the throne of Israel, 2 Sam. 7, 11—13. The condescension of the Most High in binding Himself by oath to a mere human being is more than the proud mind of man can grasp. However, the solution lies in the fact that God's oath embraces His promise of the Savior. And the beneficiary of His oath is also —

2) The Messiah and Savior Himself. The portion of the psalm, vv. 18—37, is a promise of the Father given directly to His Son, the

Messiah, called also in the text, v. 3 a, "My Chosen." "David, My Servant," and "My Chosen" are names applied to the Anointed. Our psalm and text is Messianic.

B) This is evident also from the statement confirmed by God's oath. It is the covenant, the promise, v. 3 a, the nature, content, and extent of which is declared and published in v. 4. God makes the promise to His Son that He will grant prosperity and success to His plan and undertaking, permanence to His conquest, that He will gain and keep a following always, seed all His own, vv. 29. 36; Is. 53, 10. 11. While men die and their seed is intermingled and lost in the great mass of humanity; while kingdoms rise and fall and thrones topple and castles crumble and glories vanish, the Messiah's cause will prosper forever and to all generations, and His glory will endure. The heavens will proclaim the Messiah's praise, and the congregation of saints, above and here below, will publish the Lord's faithfulness. The cause of Christ will never fail.

3.

A) *God Swears to Our Comfort.* God swore and revealed to us His oath to convince us of His determination to save us, and to show "more abundantly" unto the heirs the immutability of His counsel, Heb. 6, 17. The statement of the text reminds us of the nature of Christ's kingdom. It is spiritual, a kingdom of grace and glory. And since we are one of the many generations and are individually, by grace, enrolled with the saints, therefore we, too, are affected by the oath of God: we are beneficiaries. The oath refers also to us, Micah 7, 20. It confirms to us the gracious promise of the Savior, the forgiveness of sin and eternal life by Him. God could not do otherwise than fulfil His promise of salvation. For our salvation, in our behalf, He swore. We rejoice because the oath was given to Jesus, our Savior. — Did God keep His oath? Yes, in every detail, Gal. 4, 4. 5; Luke 26, 26. 27. 44—47. He keeps His oath even to the present generation. By His grace and Word He has added us to the seed of the Messiah, and He celebrates His coming and the advent of His kingdom to this day. As the Lord has kept His oath, so He will keep His oath, fulfilling every promise to us for this life and for that which is to come, Rom. 8, 32. His second advent is as certain as His first advent. The Father cannot and will not retract any promise given to Jesus, and in Jesus to us. Hymn 306, 3; 314, 7; 317, 4; 505, 4; 506, 4. We love Him because He first loved us. Just so let us pay our vows to Him who has first kept His vow and oath to us, oath-bound to the oath-bound God.

B) *God Swears to His Glory.* When God, fulfilling His oath of promise, sent His Son into the world, the heavens declared His glory, Luke 2, 13. 14, and the saints extolled His faithfulness, Luke

1, 45—47. 54. 55. 68—75. This praise never ceases in heaven, Luke 15, 7. 10; Rev. 5, 11. 12; and as long as the earth remains, the whole family of God in heaven and on earth will jointly celebrate the faithfulness of God, Eph. 3, 21; Rom. 11, 36; 16, 25—27.

Conclusion. — By His faithful advent to us is our advent to Him, Heb. 12, 22—24.   G. H. SMUKAL.

A Division among the People Because of Christ.
John 7, 40—43.

Christ's advent to us is by means of His Word, Luke 10, 16; Rom. 10, 6—8. Therefore we must hear the Word, John 17, 17, and we must spread it, Rom. 10, 14. Sometimes we complain with the prophet: Rom. 10, 16. When Christ approaches us by His Word, the prophecy of Simeon is fulfilled, Luke 2, 34. Men express their opinions of Christ, and the Christian confesses His faith in Christ, John 1, 11. 12; Matt. 10, 34 f. One reason why we should test our present knowledge of the Word and improve it is indicated in the text: the enemy's endeavor to meet us on our own ground and his attempt to disprove Scripture by Scripture. Jesus' presence and Word provoked friends and enemies to express their opinions of Jesus.

"So there Was a Division among the People Because of Him."

1. *Each Party to the Division Claimed Scriptural Basis for Its Opinion.*
2. *Therefore the Division Was Inexcusable and Needless.*

1.

Each party to the division claimed Scriptural basis for its opinion. A) Text.

1) The first opinion expressed was the positive declaration uttered with a force of conviction that admitted no doubt and accepted no further argument: "Of a truth this is the Prophet." Cp. John 6, 14. 15. The fact was so well established in their mind that they felt constrained to publish it. In the previous chapter the people arrived at this conclusion when they witnessed Christ's miracle; now they state their conviction as a result of Jesus' word and promise; v. 37, f., in which He quoted Scripture and applied it to Himself, Is. 44, 3; 55, 1; Joel 2, 28. None before Him had identified himself by these prophecies and referred to them as fulfilled in himself, and none before Him had proved by word and work that he had such authority as He. Therefore these people, having and knowing the prophecy Deut. 18, 15, concluded that Jesus was most certainly that particular Prophet promised them, to whom they should hearken. What, then, was the basis of their opinion of Jesus? Holy Scripture.

2) Others heard the opinion and replied with the statement of another positive opinion, which expressed still greater respect and reverence for Jesus: "This is the Christ," that particular promised Messiah. They shared the conviction of the remaining disciples, John 6, 67—69, and of the Samaritans, John 4, 40—42. They arrived at this conclusion again when they heard Jesus' promise and the evidence to which He appealed, v. 37 f. What was the basis of their opinion? Holy Scripture.

3) Hearing these positive opinions stated freely and forcibly, some offered a third opinion, a negative and contradictory one. They did not go to the trouble of defining it, but entered into an argument immediately, advancing but two questions in support of their contradiction: vv. 41b. 42. To our surprise they quoted Scripture, Ps. 132, 11; Jer. 23, 5; Micah 5, 2, against Scripture, v. 37 f., prophecy against prophecy and referred to the fact that Jesus was a citizen of Galilee. Seemingly a most plausible and convincing argument — historical fact against prophecy. Hence the Scripture is not fulfilled in Him! And this proved to them that Jesus was neither the Prophet nor the Christ. But what was the basis of their opinion? Presumably the same Scripture.

4) Let us note that Christ referred to the Scripture to identify Himself and to implant in the hearts of the people the correct opinion regarding Himself. The first speakers refer to the Scripture as the basis of their opinion; the next speakers refer to the Scripture; the opponents to these opinions refer to the Scripture, — and there was a division among the people because of Him!

B) This is a rather common experience.

1) No person can ignore Jesus. He came into this world a person far too important to pass by. A general education requires some knowledge of Jesus. He changed the course of events. He is the most outstanding character in the history of the world. Time is reckoned from the date of His birth. Furthermore, He proclaimed in His Temple the Gospel of salvation by His merits, v. 37; John 3, 16; Luke 2; 1 Tim. 1, 15. 16. The hearers of the Gospel will call upon their intelligence to judge Christ, and opinions will be aired.

2) But there are no new opinions. The first is repeated by the Jews with a weakening change to the general assertion: This is a prophet. The second opinion is held and defended by the Christians, who insist on the emphatic declaration: "This is the Christ." The third is the opinion of the heathen and unbeliever and defended by the learned of this world, who also read the Scripture and from whom the less educated and the ignorant borrow their opinion: This is neither the Prophet nor the Christ. The division among the people because of Christ still exists.

3) Every one believes to have a right to his opinion. The ortho- dox Jew pores over the Old Testament prophecy and admits at first that Jesus is a great prophet in so far as He operated according to the Jewish interpretation of the Old Testament; but later he insists on John 19, 7. The reformed Jew is rather proud of Jesus and calls Him a prophet and condemns the action of the corrupt Council and of unjust Pilate. All Jewish teaching agrees that Jesus is not the Christ. The Christian searches the Scriptures of the Old Testament as we do this evening, guided by our text, and he insists that all prophecy is fulfilled in Jesus and that Jesus is the Christ. The heathen and the unbeliever appeal to the Old Testament prophecy and seek to find flaws in Scripture; they also consult history, some- times feign sincerity in making their researches, and finally announce that the opinion of unbelief is that Jesus is neither the Prophet nor the Christ. Their aim is to discredit the Old Testament prophecy and to dethrone the humble, meek, and loving Savior. All claim to have arrived at their conclusion on the basis of Scripture, and the division among the people because of Christ still exists. To some, all these opinions in their various shading are a perplexing con- fusion of contradictions which no guide can clear. The Old Testa- ment, the New Testament, history, mind, reason, intelligence, and science, all are set in operation, and the consequence is not an opinion, but opinions.

4) If Jesus is not the Christ, but only a prophet, then we must wait for another, then our faith is vain, and we are yet in our sins. If He is the Christ, then we have "found Him of whom," etc., John 1, 45. Who attempts to judge? Scripture is the witness, John 5, 39.

2.

Therefore *the division was inexcusable and needless.*

A) Let us confine our study to the prophecy cited in the text.

1) How careless and inconsistent of those concerned not to have approached Jesus Himself, who was so close at hand! He would have given all the information they desired on the question of His birthplace and His connection with Galilee. He would have proved that the prophecy of v. 42 was fulfilled in Him. But He would have referred them also to the prophets, whose prophecy, according to Matt. 2, 23, is fulfilled in Him. This suffices to convince us that the division among the people was needless and inexcusable.

2) The opinion expressed in v. 40b is insufficient. It does not embrace the high-priestly and kingly office of Jesus and does not express His full identity. It may be said to be based on Scripture in so far as it proposes a Scriptural passage as source and proof of the statement. But it is the result of insufficient Scriptural knowl- edge. We prove from Scripture that Jesus is true man; we dare

not, however, disregard the Scripture-passages which teach that He is true God. We have Scriptural basis for the fact that Jesus suffered and died; we dare not, however, avoid those passages of Scripture which ascribe vicarious merit to His suffering and death. There was no excuse for that insufficiency of Scriptural knowledge. There is no excuse for it now. Lack of Scriptural knowledge is dangerous and harmful. It causes division, and that division is also inexcusable and needless. Let us apply ourselves to the study of the Scriptures in this Advent season and during this entire new year of grace.

3) The opinion implied v. 41 b denies the true doctrine of the person and work of Christ. It would disprove Scripture by Scripture and fact by fact. It is quite hopeless. It will not consider the whole scope of Scripture. The proponents of this opinion can be given no better advice than Nathanael received of Philip, John 1, 46, that they may learn to join the officers in the confession, John 7, 46, and confess with Nathanael: John 1, 49; and with Peter: John 6, 68. 69. Their attitude toward Jesus and His Word is inexcusable, and the division which they cause is needless.

4) And what shall we say to the opinion given v. 41 a? It is the correct opinion. It is more than an opinion — true conviction, true faith. It embraces Christ with Scripture and Scripture with Christ. Hymn 120, 3. 4.

B) Lessons.

1) The division because of Christ, like unbelief, is unnecessary and inexcusable because the Scriptures settle every question and judge every opinion in favor of Christ. Therefore those Christians who in matters of faith and life adhere solely to the Scriptures are blameless in respect to the division existing now. Our text serves to show that the division between the Christians and the world is due to the unbelief of the latter and not to the faith of the former and that the divisions in the Church are caused by those who do not apply the complete Scripture. Without fear or favor the Christians should confess Christ and preach and live the Gospel and avoid those who cause divisions, Rom. 16, 17.

2) Christ and the Scriptures are inseparable. To know Christ one must know the Scripture, and to know the Scripture means to know Christ. However, see *Form. Conc.,* p. 55, § 23; p. 890, § 24.

3) In Paradise, after the fall of man, God identified the Savior by one prophecy and promise. One prophecy fulfilled in Christ is sufficient to identify Him as our Savior. However, our text convinces us that all Scripture must be studied. A true Christian will not be satisfied with meager knowledge, since God Himself added further promises later. There is no better and no more enjoyable Advent preparation than John 5, 39.   G. H. SMUKAL.

Christmas Eve.

John 3, 16.

Christmas Eve! What a happy, happy day this is! Especially to children. How their little faces beam with joy! Of all the days of the year this is the real children's day, Christmas Eve.

Why? What is it that makes you little ones so happy to-day? Is it Santa Claus? Jingle bells? Is it the fact that you receive all manner of gifts this day, many pleasant surprises? Oh, these things, too, stir your little hearts, make them beat faster. But these things are not the *real* cause of your happiness on this glad day. You are Christian children, and you know of something better than these earthly toys and joys. The little Christ-child is the real cause of your happiness.

Children love children, and the great God loves children, too. And what did He do but Himself become a little child this day? He wanted to be a little child with you children. Why? That He might enjoy you? Yes. But chiefly that you might enjoy Him.

You see, there is something in this world that takes the joy out of living. It is sin. You will understand this better as you grow older. But you know something about it now. You know the Old Serpent crept into Paradise, where Adam and Eve were happy, unspeakably happy. The Old Serpent, the devil, tempted them to sin, to disobey God's commandment. And they did so; they disobeyed, they sinned. And they were driven out of Paradise, their happy home, out into a dreary world, made dreary by sin. Instead of the sweet things of Paradise they now had to endure many bitter things. And the most bitter thing of all was death; they had to die. And if it were not for one thing, they would have had to die forever, — all because they sinned. How sad! How terribly sad!

Nor is this all. We, who are Adam and Eve's children, we, too, have sinned. We sinned when Adam and Eve sinned, and we have sinned many times since. Cain, Adam and Eve's first-born son, was born in sin, and he committed murder, murdered his own brother. And so it is with all of us; we all are born in sin, and we sin much every day. And the wages of sin is death, even everlasting death. Even little children have to die.

But, oh, the mercy of our God! God did not want us to die, He wanted us to live, to live in paradise, in a much better paradise than the one Adam and Eve were driven out of. He wanted us to live in heaven. So what did He do? He said: "I will save the people from their sins and from all their misery, even from death itself. *I* will live in this dreary world, and *I* will die *for them*." Oh, what love! And so God became a little child. He was born of the Virgin Mary, born a holy Child, born in great poverty, not in a paradise, but in a stable, among cattle. He was wrapped in swaddling-clothes and laid in a manger. "Away in a manger, where cattle were fed, the little Lord Jesus laid down His sweet head." And He lived in great poverty and suffered many things in this evil world, even death on the cross. Yea, He even tasted eternal death, — all that we might have forgiveness and live, live both in this world and yonder in heaven. And all who believe in Him, all who accept Him as their Savior, they all have forgiveness of their sins and live both here and yonder.

Life still has its problems, its sorrows, and its joys. Even little children have their troubles, their temptations, their annoyances and griefs, along with their joys. And in all these things the Christ-child is with them and shares their experiences. He comforts them in their troubles, helps them in their temptations, helps them say no when the Old Serpent tempts them to do wrong, lightens their annoyances and griefs, and heightens and hallows their joys.

Oh, what happiness Christmas brings! What great and holy joy! What a wondrous gift God has given us: His own dear Son and, in Him, eternal life! John 3, 16. The Son of God gave Himself, became a little child and grew up to manhood in this evil world, that we, both children and grown people, might be happy both in this world and the next.

Oh, let us who are grown be converted and become as little children that we may share in the little children's highest joy, that we may have part in the Christ-child. "Backward, turn backward, O Time, in your flight, make me a child again just for to-night" that I may enjoy to the full the pure joys of this holy night. But, oh, no, not just for to-night, but forever and aye.

And now let us all join with the children and sing that beautiful childlike Christmas hymn: "Let us all with gladsome voice," etc., vv. 1—3.   J. A. RIMBACH.

Christmas Day.

Is. 60, 2—7.

Christmas,—"what treasures untold reside in that heavenly word, more precious than silver and gold or all that this earth can afford!" The dearest memories are awakened by its sound; the most exalted truths cluster round its facts; the brightest hopes stream from its message; joys most noble and satisfying are identified with its observance.

We see the stable, the manger, the heavenly Child; we hear the angel's inspiring message, "Fear not; for, behold," etc. We go to Bethlehem with the shepherds to "see this thing which is come to pass," etc. We bring our gifts with the Wise Men, and in wondering faith we ponder as did Mary. A joyous, blessed day!

It has become a general custom to attach the sentiments of Christmas to certain objects, customs, or other symbols. There are Christmas-gifts, -trees, -ornaments, -colors, -carols, and the like, some of them so characteristic and intimately woven into the texture of the season as to bring Christmas to mind whenever we see or hear them. Perhaps the most general, expressive, and appropriate symbol of Christmas is illumination. The use of light at Christmas-time and in connection with the observance of this great festival, besides being unique and striking, is thoroughly Scriptural. In the text chapter before us Isaiah, the Christmas messenger of the Old Testament, foreseeing in a vision the coming of the Messiah, says, v. 1: "Arise, shine," etc. (See also vv. 2. 3 of the text.) The light seen by the prophet in his vision has become the light of Christmas in reality. There is much that is interesting and instructive in his comparison. In order that we may the more fully and deeply understand and enjoy this day and its message, we view —

The Light of Christmas.

1. What Is the Light of Christmas?

Christmas commemorates the birth of Jesus. Its story is told in detail by Luke, chap. 2. Its message and meaning are summed up expressively in John 1, 14 and 1 Tim. 3, 16. Isaiah foresees this day and its event. The coming of the light of which he speaks, vv. 2. 3, is the incarnation of the Son of God. Cp. Is. 2, 9, as referred to in Matt. 4, 12—16.

The light of Christmas is Christ Himself. He is spoken of in many places as a light, Is. 49, 6; Luke 2, 31. 32; John 1, 4—9; 3, 19; 5, 35. He refers to Himself in the same manner, John 8, 12; 9, 5. Note well that it is the *person* of Christ which is the light, not, in this case, His doctrine, etc. He therefore does not merely teach the light, He *is* the Light. He is the Light, first of all, because He is God, 1 John 5, 20 (hence the Author of light, Gen. 1, 3); He came from God, John 8, 42; cp. Jas. 1, 17. Then, too, He is the Maker and Bringer of light, of spiritual illumination. This is a dark world, v. 2a; cp. Is. 9, 2; Luke 1, 79. Sin has made it so, John 3, 19; cp. Eph. 5, 8. 11. There is the darkness of ignorance, of fear, of superstition, of sin, of death, of eternal doom. Into this darkness Christ came. He came to take sin away, the cause of all darkness, Is. 53, 5. 6. 10. 11; Matt. 1, 21; John 1, 29; 2 Cor. 5, 21; 1 Pet. 2, 24; 1 John 2, 2. Hence the poverty at His birth, the life of humility, ending in suffering and death. Compare a candle consuming itself to give light. On the manger falls the shadow of the cross. Compare the painting of the Child Jesus standing with outstretched arms, the sun causing His shadow to fall on the ground in the shape of a cross. — The taking away of sin meant the coming and bringing of light, the light of God's love shed on mankind; the light of spiritual knowledge, of faith, of

comfort, of courage, of hope, of deliverance from death, finally of
eternal life.

This is the light that Isaiah saw and Abraham (John 8, 56) and
all the other pious souls of old. The shepherds saw it, the Wise Men,
the venerable Simeon, the disciples, Paul. This is the light of Christmas. — Has it filled your heart with light?

2. The Christmas Light Shines To-day.

The light which Isaiah saw in the vision was not to be a mere
momentary flash, not a meteor or a comet. What is said vv. 2b—7
indicates that the light will go on shining in order that people everywhere may see the way to life. Cp. vv. 19—22; chap. 61; Mal. 4, 2;
Luke 1, 78 ("sun" and "day-star" indicating continued shining).
The Old Testament period was the dawning light of the coming new
day, Ps. 36, 9; Is. 58, 8; cp. 2 Pet. 1, 19.

Jesus, the Sun of Righteousness, has been shining ever since
His rising on that first Christmas Day. He shone in His personal
presence, in His words, in His works. Though temporarily eclipsed
in His death, He shone gloriously in His resurrection, also in His
ascension. His light has been shining in ever-widening circles since
Pentecost in and through His Gospel, in the growth and career of
His kingdom. Thus the prophecies in vv. 3—7 have been fulfilled and
are being fulfilled to-day. What a blessed, healing, saving light it has
been for all nations!

The light of Christmas has come to us, too. We still hear the
heavenly message, "Fear not; for, behold," etc. The Gospel word of
salvation is being preached and taught among us. Out of it, as from
a great lamp, shines the bright light of God's love for us poor mortals,
warming our hearts and showing the path of life paved with forgiveness of sins, comfort, help, hope, and victory and leading to the gates
of heaven eternal. On this very day of joy He who calls Himself the
Light of the world appears among us in the glad Christmas-story, and
the eyes of faith can see Him just as clearly as did the natural eyes
of the shepherds and the Wise Men of old.

Has this light of life come into your life and heart, my friends?
It is shining for you; its rays are reaching out toward you. Open
the doors and windows of your heart and let its beams stream in.
It will end the darkness of sin, sorrow, death, despair, and bring grace,
healing, assurance, joy, and peace. It will make this Christmas
season a time of real joy for you. (Hymn 90, 3. 2.) Happy are you
if you live in the light of Christmas to-day.

However, the light of Christmas does not merely bestow a blessing, it also conveys an obligation.

3. Help Spread the Christmas Light.

Our text chapter begins with a statement of that obligation, v. 1.
The text further develops the thought, vv. 2. 3. The prophet's ref-

erence to the darkness covering the souls of men and to the light of salvation that shall shine upon God's people clearly implies that the enlightened children of God are to be bringers of the light to the world around. Hence, too, in the subsequent verses the Gentile converts are shown as they gather in the city of God, attracted by the light streaming out of it. And this is corroborated by many other passages from the prophets. It also agrees with what the angel said, Luke 2, 10, and with the words of the venerable Simeon, Luke 2, 32.

The world around us needs the Christmas light to-day, needs the word of the redemption in Christ. The situation is as Isaiah saw it, v. 2. Three-fourths of the world know not the true God, are in the dark with respect to the way of life, have no real comfort in trouble, spend their lives in the fear and shadow of death. In our own country more than half the inhabitants are outside the churches. What is the situation in our community? in our neighborhood?

This is a challenge to the Church, to us individual Christians. We have been given the light not only in order that we may enjoy its possession ourselves, but especially also that we should cause it to shine upon the world around us. The Church has always answered that challenge with its missionary efforts at home and abroad. The prophet foresaw the success that God had in store for this work, vv. 4—7. Great would be the number of the saved in all nations, and wonderful has been the success of Christian missions. Let us continue in this work and become ever more active in it. It is the one great purpose for which the Church exists, for which we individual Christians are left to continue our sojourn on earth, and for which also our Christmas activity should serve. Cf. Matt. 5, 14; 1 Pet. 2, 9. "Shall we whose souls are lighted with wisdom from on high," etc. Compare the captain who was enabled to save his storm-driven vessel from being wrecked on a rocky cape by a light that shone from a cottage on the shore and who soon after caused a lighthouse to be built on that point for the guidance of navigators.

What a truly joyous Christmas Day you can make of it by bringing the light of Christmas to some troubled soul to-day, and how effectively the Christmas joy can be spread over the entire year to come through devouted soul-winning efforts! (Hymn 474, 3.)

God be praised for the light of Christmas! May it shine into our hearts and brighten our lives with its beams of grace and salvation! And may we continue to be bearers of that light to the world around us and bring its rays to hearts still languishing in spiritual darkness! And when the sun of our earthly day at last sinks beneath the horizon of death, may the light of God's saving love in Christ Jesus light our way to the glory and brightness of our eternal home!

K. KRETZSCHMAR.

New Year's Eve.

Psalm 90, 12.

How rapid is the flight of time! Like an ever-rolling stream the days and the weeks and the months rush away, to be swallowed up by the sea of eternity. Year follows upon year with almost astonishing swiftness. We are born to the world, pass through the years of childhood and youth into the prime of manhood and womanhood, enter old age, and arrive at the portals of death seemingly before we are aware of it.

> As the wingèd arrow flies
>   Speedily the mark to find,
> As the lightning from the skies
>   Darts and leaves no trace behind,
> Swiftly thus our fleeting days
> Bear us down life's rapid stream.

If ever the rapidity of time's flight forces itself upon our attention, it is when we, as on this night, come to the end of a year. The year 1935, with all its joys and sorrows, its weal and woe, its blessings and hardships, its successes and disappointments, is all but gone. In a few hours a new year will have been ushered in. Who knows but that it may be the last for one or the other among us, if not for all of us?

For the children of the world there is something baffling and disquieting in the thought of time's rapid flight. Even the world feels how time rushes ever onward and all things are hurrying toward the end. But not for long will worldlings allow their thoughts to dwell on the fact that with each succeeding year their time on earth is becoming shorter. They bid farewell to the old year and greet the dawning of the new with boisterous clamor, as if they would drown out every serious thought. They give the reins to their lusts and indulge their vices to unwonted excess, as if to bid defiance to God, to whom they must one day give account for the manner in which they have spent their days on earth.

It is not so with the Christian. He is not unimpressed by the rapidity of time's flight. He is not insensible to the seriousness of time and eternity. But this makes him all the more sober and thoughtful. For this reason he will, particularly at a time like this, when the old year wanes and a new year is about to dawn, pause and give serious thought to the lessons he is to learn from the rapid flight of time. His prayer will be that of Moses, the man of God, in our text: "So teach us to number our days that we may apply our hearts unto wisdom." Let us therefore to-night, as the old year is drawing to a close, prayerfully consider —

The Wisdom to which the Thought of Time's Rapid Flight Should Move Our Hearts.

1. The Wisdom Not to Set Our Affections on the Things of This World.

"So teach us to number our days that we may apply our hearts unto wisdom." Moses is prompted to make this prayer by thinking of the swift passing of time and of the short span of the life of men on earth. Ps. 90, 9. 10. He prays that the thought of time's headlong flight may move his heart to wisdom, that he may use the few days allotted to him in this life wisely and well. David utters a similar prayer, Ps. 39, 4. 5. That is the prayer of all true Christians.

We cannot number our days in such a way as to ascertain just how many years we shall live on earth. Our life may be cut short at any time. When that will be is known to God alone. But we can and should number our days in the sense that we consider that the years of our life are few and that they fly rapidly away. The best that we can expect is the threescore and ten or the fourscore years mentioned in our psalm. Man to-day has as much reason as did Jacob to say: "Few and evil have the days of the years of my life been," Gen. 47, 9.

Moreover we are to pray with Moses that we may learn so to number our days that we may apply our hearts unto wisdom.

The worldling does not like to think of the brevity of life here on earth. He shuns the thought of death. It is said that the great financier Andrew Carnegie would not permit any one to speak of death in his presence. Most unbelievers live and act as though they were going to continue in this world forever. With their whole heart they cling to the things of this world — its riches and honor and pleasures. What folly! How soon the riches and pleasures of this world become as ashes in the mouth. How short the time when even the richest man in the world comes to the bounds of life and must leave behind the world and all the things he held so dear. Suppose a man journeying through the trackless desert would, instead of pitching a tent or making a temporary shelter, laboriously dig a deep foundation and carefully build a solid structure, as he would if he were building a permanent home, only to leave it behind after a short sojourn with never a regret. Such is the folly of the worldling who sets his heart's affections on the things of this world.

In view of the brevity of our life on earth it is wisdom not to set our hearts' affections on the things of this world. That is wisdom which the Word of God teaches, 1 John 2, 15—17. The Christian is to regard his life here on earth merely as a brief sojourn. Gen. 23, 4; 1 Chron. 29, 15; Heb. 13, 14. Therefore he is to say: —

What is the world to me!
  It rapidly must vanish;
With all its gorgeous pomp
  Pale death it cannot banish;
Its riches pass away,
  And all its joys must flee,
But Jesus doth abide, —
  What is the world to me!

2. The Wisdom to Use Our Time Here on Earth to Prepare for a Blissful Hereafter.

The worldling does not like to think of the time when he will have to leave the world. Yet occasionally the thought of time's rapid flight will force itself upon him, as on this night. The death of a relative or friend will compel him to consider that some day, and that only too soon, he also must die. Then he, too, will number his days. But how? His numbering his days will move his heart not to wisdom, but to folly.

The worldling may hear the warnings of the Word of God. His conscience will tell him that he must one day give an account to God for his life on earth and that failure to stand in the Judgment will mean eternal damnation for him. But in his supreme folly he ignores the warnings of God's Word and throttles his conscience. He seeks to lull himself into the belief that there is no existence after death, no life beyond the grave, that death ends all. In order to bolster up this foolish belief, he will resort to scoffing at the Christians' belief in the coming of the Lord to Judgment, 2 Pet. 3, 3 ff. Wrapped up in the delusion that death ends all, the worldling is prompted by the thought of life's brevity to use the short time he has on earth in the enjoyment of all that the world has to offer. His watchword is "Let us eat, drink, and be merry; for to-morrow we shall die." Thus he will go through life consuming his days in a hectic chase after things with which to satisfy his fleshly appetites and lusts, utterly heedless of the future, until he is overtaken by death and meets the fate that befell Dives.

"So teach us to number our days that we may apply our hearts unto wisdom." Few and brief are the years that we have in this life before eternity is upon us. True wisdom dictates that we use them to prepare for a blissful hereafter.

Many a one thinks, There are so many things that I want to do here on earth, so many things that I want to enjoy; I shall put off preparing for yonder world till I am tired of what this world has to offer; time enough to prepare for heaven when I am older. Do not the hastening years show you what folly that is? The time is short, shorter perhaps than you expect. Wisdom tells you to prepare for eternity, for a blissful hereafter, now, now while you still have time. Ps. 95, 7b. 8; Is. 49, 8a; 55, 6; 2 Cor. 6, 2b.

We know that, if death finds us in sin and unbelief, ours will not be a blissful hereafter. Rom. 6, 23a; John 3, 36b; Mark 16, 16b; Ps. 1, 5.

Many are mindful of the nearness of eternity and strive to prepare for a blissful hereafter, but they try by their own efforts, through their own good works, to work out their own righteousness in which to stand in the Judgment of God. This is folly, because it is futile, Ps. 143, 2; Rom. 3, 20. 23; Gal. 2, 16b.

Only he is prepared for a blissful hereafter who has found Christ as his Savior and Redeemer. No one, nothing, else can help, Acts 4, 12; John 16, 6 b. Jesus is the true Savior, Matt. 1, 21; Luke 19, 10. Through His life and obedience and suffering and death He won pardon, peace, and grace for all men, Gal. 4, 4; Is. 53, 4. 5; Col. 1, 14; 1 John 1, 7; 2, 2; Rom. 5, 1. 2. He is still the Mediator between sinners and their God, 1 John 2, 1; Heb. 7, 25. The salvation which Christ won for all sinners is the gift of God to all that believe and trust in Him, John 3, 16; Acts 13, 39.

"So teach us to number our days that we may apply our hearts unto wisdom." It is wisdom to prepare for a blissful hereafter by using the brief time allotted to us here on earth to lay hold on Christ through faith and to become ever stronger in faith, Acts 16, 31; 2 Pet. 3, 18. By our own reason or strength we can neither believe in Jesus Christ, our Lord, or come to Him, nor can we abide in the faith, 1 Cor. 2, 14; Eph. 2, 1; Rom. 8, 7. God, who would have all men to be saved and is not willing that any should perish, would, however, through His Holy Spirit convert us, bring us to faith, and sanctify and keep us in the faith. In order that this may be done, we must make diligent use of the means of grace, whereby the Holy Spirit effects His saving work in us, Rom. 1, 16. 17; Rom. 10, 17; 1 Pet. 1, 5; Phil. 1, 6. This includes also that we, like Paul, make Christ our chief pursuit in life, Phil. 3, 7—11, and seek first the kingdom of God and His righteousness, Matt. 6, 33; that we fight against sin, 1 Pet. 2, 11, be on our guard against the temptations of the devil and the world, 1 Pet. 5, 8. 9; 1 John 2, 15—17, suppress the evil inclinations of our flesh, Gal. 5, 24; that we show forth our faith in a life of godliness and good works, John 15, 5; 2 Pet. 1, 10; and that we constantly pray God for the will and the strength to do all this, Phil. 2, 13.

May the thought of time's rapid flight remind us constantly to pray —

Teach me to live that I may dread
The grave as little as my bed;
Teach me to die that so I may
With joy behold the Judgment Day.

3. The Wisdom to Work while It Is Day.

Jesus came into the world to do the work which His heavenly Father had given Him to do, John 6, 38. Unremittingly He labored to carry out His tasks, begrudging Himself time for refreshment and rest, John 4, 31—35; Mark 3, 20. 21; 6, 31. Why this ceaseless activity? "I must work the works of Him that sent Me while it is day; the night cometh when no man can work," John 9, 4. God has placed us in this world not that we may pass our time in idleness or in pursuit of our own selfish devices. We have work to do for Him; we are to serve Him by being of service to our fellow-men. The fleeting years remind us that our time here on earth is limited, that

our day of life and opportunity is rapidly drawing to a close, that
the night of death is drawing near, the night when no man can work.
Is it not wisdom to work while it is day, before the night cometh when
no man can work?

We have work in the kingdom of God, the Church of Christ.
We must labor to foster and maintain the Gospel ministry in our
own midst as well as to extend the kingdom of Christ. John 20,
21—23; Luke 10, 7; 1 Cor. 9, 14; Gal. 6, 6. 7; 1 Tim. 5, 17. 18; Matt.
28, 19. 20; Mark 16, 15. How much there is to be done! How short
the time! The night is coming. Let us work while it is day.

We have duties toward our fellow-men. Second table of the
Decalog; Gal. 5, 13 b; 1 Tim. 5, 4; Prov. 19, 17. Note particularly
Matt. 5, 25. 26. Let us not neglect present opportunities. Now it is
day, but the night is coming. Our fellow-men will not long be with
us nor we with them.

Let us work while it is day, thus showing forth our faith in Christ,
so that, when He summons us from this world, we may hear the welcome words: Matt. 25, 21. 34 ff.

4. The Wisdom to Be Patient and to Rejoice amid Tribulations.

That this world is indeed a vale of tears, particularly for the child
of God, is borne out by the Scriptures, Gen. 47, 9; Ps. 90, 10; John
16, 20; Acts 14, 22 b, and by common experience. Not only is the
Christian reduced to sorrow and suffering by the ills to which all
flesh is heir, such as poverty, sickness, and death, but he must also
with Christ bear affliction, tribulation, persecution, and shame that
are heaped upon him by Satan and the ungodly world. 2 Cor. 12, 7 b;
John 15, 18—21; 1 John 3, 13; 1 Pet. 4, 12—14.

The rapid flight of time, however, teaches us that our life of
tribulation and sorrow in this world is not for long. In but a little
while: John 16, 16, God will in mercy make an end of all suffering
and sorrow by graciously taking us from this vale of tears through
death. It is wisdom to be patient. Jas. 5, 7. 8.

Not only is it wisdom to be patient in view of the brief duration
of our life in this vale of tears, but it is wisdom also to rejoice even
in the tribulations and sorrows of this present life. That the unbelieving child of the world will not and cannot patiently endure the
sufferings of this world, though they be of but brief duration, and will
often seek to end his misery by taking his own life is not to be
wondered at, for he has no hope to sustain him. But the Christian
has a hope for the future so great and so blessed that he cannot only
be patient, but will be able to rejoice in tribulation, Rom. 5, 3—5 a.
For after this brief life here on earth God will graciously take us
from this vale of tears to Himself in heaven. There will be perfect
rest and peace. Nothing that in this world gave us sorrow or pain

can reach us there, Rev. 21, 4. There will be joy unalloyed and unending. We shall see Jesus face to face and shall forever be with Him in whose presence is fulness of joy and at whose right hand there are pleasures forevermore, Ps. 16, 11 b.

"So teach us to number our days that we may apply our hearts unto wisdom." Make that your prayer to-night and every night of your lives. Let the thought of time's rapid flight keep you from setting your heart's affections on the things of this world; let it move you to prepare for a blissful hereafter; let it prompt you faithfully and diligently to do the work which God has given you to do here on earth while it is day, before the night cometh when no man can work. Just as an exile from home eagerly counts the days and months and years yet remaining before he can leave his prison and return to his home and loved ones and rejoices at the flight of time; just as a wanderer looks ahead over the way that lies before him and counts the days that yet remain before his arduous journey will be over and he will be at his destination, so do you also learn to number your days here on earth and rejoice that you are drawing ever nearer to the time when your journey through life will be done and you will at last be in your heavenly Father's home.   GEORGE WITTE.

New Year's Day.
Psalm 121.

In Jesus' name Christians to-day begin another year of grace. Without Him and all this sweet name implies it would be to all a year of unrelenting divine wrath and punishment; with Him it must needs be one of heavenly grace and blessings. For God, who loved His only-begotten Son, loved also this lost and condemned world and, prompted by His love, gave this Son to be the sinners' Redeemer, their Joy, and Delight.

Believing this, how happy and fearless Christians should be. At all times and places, under all circumstances, also to-day. How it grieves them that they want such abundance of joy, that not all fear has been banished from their hearts! Yet this is only natural, due to their sinful hearts, which are "deceitful above all things and desperately wicked," Jer. 17, 9. They also experience a measure of misgivings and fear when facing the hidden future, especially when in the judgment of men it presages much evil and but little good.

How necessary, then, and salutary that God's children give themselves to spiritual meditation at this time, so that they may enter the year prayerfully and confidently; for they have the most wonderful divine assurance that all will be well with them always. Oh, that such complete trust might ever be ours! May the Holy Spirit bless the study of the 121st Psalm to this end. We contemplate —

The Christian's New Year's Assurance "My Help Cometh from the Lord."

It is based upon —

1. God's Almighty Power;   2. His Constant Watchfulness;
3. His Earnest Desire that You be Preserved Forever.

1.

The psalmist here expresses confident assurance, vv. 1. 2. But also clearly implied we find an expression of need and of helplessness. His distress, his needs, might be many and manifold, of body, soul, property, honor; they might involve him, others, the whole nation. A number of these we find named by Solomon in his dedicatory prayer, 1 Kings 8, 31—53. Notwithstanding, David had that abiding assurance that at no time or place, in no situation, a need would arise when he could not confidently look to God for succor.

This is essentially a psalm of faith. Confidently the psalmist lifts up his eyes unto the hills "from whence cometh my help," v. 1. There rose the Holy City, stood the Tabernacle, later the Temple. In them God had established His holy name. There He dwelt among His people. There "have I set My King upon My holy hill of Zion," Ps. 2, 6. The meaning of this, David knew right well. For those hills every true Israelite yearned. How great his joy when privileged to worship there! Cp. Ps. 122. Well might David look thither for help.

Yet he does not expect help from those hills. While they were indeed symbols of strength and endurance, he knew well the truth of the words of a later prophet: "The mountains shall depart," etc., Is. 54, 10. His was not an idolatrous trust, found, by way of contrast, among the heathen, for he adds: "My help cometh from the *Lord.*" On Him David rests his confidence.

Nor could anything shake this faith; for had not this Lord "made heaven and earth"? V. 2. Here he sums up the whole work of creation as recorded Gen. 1, 1. The psalmist's faith was even as ours in the First Article: "almighty Maker of heaven and earth." "The worlds were framed by the word of God," Heb. 11, 3. "For He spake, and it was done; He commanded, and it stood fast," Ps. 33, 9. These undeniable truths come to David's mind and afford him the greater assurance that his trust in this Lord could not be in vain. He, the Almighty, and ever "the Same," Ps. 102, 27, could assuredly aid him, save him to the uttermost. His power undiminished and enduring. Again, well might he express his confident assurance "I will lift up . . . heaven and earth."

Is this faith and trust *your* happy possession to-day? It should be. You may have it for the asking and the taking. Do your many and perhaps sore needs trouble you? Your own helplessness? The futility of trusting in men, even in princes? Ps. 118, 8. 9. Friend, your grief and sorrow, your trials, tribulations, temptations, may reach mountainous proportions. But remember there are higher hills, whence cometh your help. "Let not your heart be troubled," John 14, 1. "Be not afraid; only believe," Mark 5, 36. Because of the Lord's almighty power you may rest assured that throughout the year your help, too, will come from the Lord. Ps. 46; Luke 1, 37; Rom. 8, 31 b.

2.

The psalmist's confident assurance is further confirmed by the consideration that this almighty Lord is *constantly watchful,* vv. 3. 4. What a sad situation if it were otherwise! Unspeakable fear would have shaken David's trust if Satan could have instilled this doubt: Perhaps, after all, your God may fail to watch over you. What if God could be justly mocked as Elijah once mocked Baal and his prophets, saying: "Peradventure he sleepeth"! 1 Kings 18, 27. How, then, could He keep watch? His children must in that case needs come to harm. However, the psalmist has no fear on this score.

The constant watchfulness of God embraces all. He is the Keeper of Israel, v. 4, of every one individually and of all collectively. Note the "my" and "thy" throughout the psalm. This word is ever true: "The Angel of the Lord . . . that *fear Him,"* etc., Ps. 34, 7. The psalmist was one of these.

God's constant watchfulness overlooks no detail in the life of His dear children, vv. 5—7. "He will not suffer thy foot to be moved." No foe, visible or invisible, great or small; no need, no peril, shall arise that is able to move thy foot, to do thee hurt. He keepeth careful, constant watch. He holds His foes and yours in leash. He is acquainted with all your ways and theirs, Ps. 139, 1—4; 33, 13—15. And why does He look from heaven? To thwart the evil counsel and will of the foes and to keep His beloved from harm. Experiences of Job, Joseph, Daniel, and his friends and of others clearly show this. From such a God, David could well expect help in time of need.

How well did David know the heart of God, how childlike his trust in His constant watchful care! The sun should not smite him by day, no foe, no force, be strong enough to overcome him; nor the moon by night, no foe subtle or intriguing enough to harm him. God, the ever watchful, would be his shade, his protection, upon his right hand, always near, always ready to guard and keep him. How like David's prayer, Ps. 55, 17: "Evening, morning, and at noon will I pray . . ., and He shall hear my voice"! Though it be but the "shadow of a rock in a weary land," Is. 32, 2; the protection of a gourd against the scorching rays of the sun, Jonah 4, 6; or that of a juniper-tree, 1 Kings 19, 5, this man of God in our psalm is confident that his God, who neither sleepeth nor slumbereth, knows his every want and will provide, knows his every peril and will deliver. Why, pray, should he not exclaim: "My help cometh from the Lord"?

Why not you, too, dear Christian? You should. All those wonderfully comforting truths set forth in this psalm are applicable to you. The psalmist's Lord is your Lord and Father in Christ. Even when you slumber and sleep, He keeps constant, perfect watch over you, all through the year. He it is who —

> Through all snares and perils leads us,
> Watches that no harm betides us;
> He cares for us by day and night,
> All things are governed by His might.

3.

The holy writer in our psalm looks beyond time, to eternity, vv. 7. 8. The Lord assures him by faithful promises that it is His *earnest desire to preserve him forever;* the more joyful and firm is his faith and trust "My help cometh from the Lord." How miserable he would have been if, although he could have trusted in God's almighty power to aid him, in His constant, perfect watchfulness to guard and keep him, this would have been limited to this short span of life! But his hope is a better one. He trusts in the Lord for time and for eternity, because he had God's promises for all of this.

Well did this man of God know that God had given him his body and soul not merely for a temporal possession. God would not give His all, Jesus Christ, to redeem his immortal soul, v. 7, together with the mortal body, only to forsake or destroy them in the end. All this to David was the perfect assurance that God earnestly desired to preserve his soul, to preserve all his going out and his coming in from that time forth, yea, even forevermore. Surely our psalmist's assurance was identical with that of the great Apostle Paul "The Lord shall deliver me from every evil work and will preserve me unto His heavenly kingdom," 2 Tim. 4, 18. Well might that ancient man of God declare: "My help cometh from the Lord," for He is almighty; He is ever watchful; He desires, and will grant me, full and final deliverance, eternal salvation.

You, friends, have the same grounds for an equal assurance on this day and every future day and year of your lives. God desires to preserve also your bodies and souls eternally. To this end He will be with you when you go out and when you come in, while you live and when you die, and through endless eternity. Look, then, to the hills whence cometh your help. Exclaim with joyful confidence: "My help cometh from the Lord!" Maintain in your homes the Word of God as your sanctuary. Keep God's faithful promises in mind. God cannot lie. Gather in this house of God, a true sanctuary, that the Spirit of God may confirm and preserve you in this faith until you shall be taken from this vale of tears to the Lord in heaven.

F. WESSLER.

THE TRIAL OF JESUS.

Six Lenten Addresses.

These addresses were delivered for the Detroit Lutheran Radio Committee during the season of Lent in the year 1933. On account of the brief time into which they had to be compressed and because the purpose was to present at least a part of the story of Christ's Passion, it was impossible to make detailed applications, as is generally done in Lenten sermons, except, as it were, to gather into a few focal points some scattered rays of light upon the way to the cross. A few things were kept in mind: a general audience and the story itself and its progress up to a certain point. There may be a little difference of opinion in places as to the order of events as presented. But we need not argue about that. A closer examination will show that the order as presented has much in its favor and that the natural order of the fourfold gospel record has been followed.

I.

"Whether Thou Be the Christ, the Son of God."

Matt. 26, 63.

"Let these sayings sink down into your ears; for the Son of Man shall be delivered into the hands of men," Luke 9, 44.

It is our purpose in this season of Lent to bring to you the story of the trial of Jesus, with particular reference to the narrative as contained in the gospel account.

On that Thursday night could be seen by midnight stragglers at the eastern gate of Jerusalem a procession issuing from the Garden of Gethsemane, down the Mount of Olives, across the brook of Cedron, and up the slopes of the city, with Jesus in the midst.

The agony of Gethsemane was over, the arrest had been made, and the Prisoner was conducted to the *palace* of the high priest, which at that time seems to have been occupied by the two prime movers of the black iniquity, Annas and his son-in-law Joseph Caiaphas.

For a better understanding of the following a brief account of the historical background must first be given before we can enter into the story itself. At that time Judea was under Roman rule and was administered by a governor, in this case Pontius Pilate, who usually resided at the seaport Caesarea, but during the annual Passover deemed it expedient to establish his headquarters in the ancient palace of Herod.

It was the policy of Rome to flatter the conquered territories with a semblance of self-government and especially to be tolerant in matters of religion. In general, there were but two rules which had to be faithfully observed: proper regard for the *pax Romana,* the Roman peace, and the payment of taxes. Thus in Judea the Sanhedrin, the ancient ecclesiastical tribunal, was still allowed to try all religious offenses as well as to punish offenders. Only if the verdict happened to be a sentence of death, the case had to be retried by the governor, and the carrying out of the sentence, if it was confirmed, devolved upon him.

In the present case it was at the instance of the Sanhedrin as led by Caiaphas that Jesus was arrested. But as a matter of fact his father-in-law, Annas, an old man of seventy, who had been high priest himself twenty years before and after him five of his sons and one son-in-law, was still the power behind the throne.

In ancient days the high-priesthood was an office for life, but ever since the days of Herod and the Roman rule the dignity had been degraded from a permanent and sacred religious office to a temporary secular distinction. No more did the high priests rule by the grace and in the fear of God, but by the grace of the Romans and in their own interest.

As to Caiaphas, it was he who as the strange tool of divine prophecy had given the counsel "that it was expedient that one man should die for the people." As to both Annas and Caiaphas and their whole family, they were cold, haughty, and worldly Sadducees, an able, but an ambitious and arrogant race. Jealous of their power and fearful of their security, they were filled with deadly hatred against the great Miracle-worker and popular Teacher, who had for the second time cleansed the Temple and interfered with their illicit and greedy gains.

And there was a good reason why Annas, who is remembered by his own people as the head of a viper brood, should strain to the utmost his cruel power to crush a Prophet whose actions threatened to make him and his family wholly contemptible and comparatively poor.

To him Jesus was brought first. This gave him a chance to subject the Savior to an initial investigation as well as to allow time to get the Sanhedrin together. Of course, it was not quite legal, but imagine what might happen if Jerusalem awoke in the morning and found the popular Teacher in the hands of His unpopular enemies! At all events, He had to be accused, tried, condemned, and delivered into the strong hands of the Romans before morning and before the multitudes had learned what it was all about. While messengers scoured the city for an urgent midnight meeting, Annas asked Jesus about His disciples and about His teaching.

Christian ministers complain that they do not gain enough disciples for Jesus; but the complaint of Annas was that Jesus Himself was making too many. And the purpose of the question was to ensnare Him into some incriminating statement and to advance some charge of secret sedition and unorthodox teaching.

Jesus replies, and for all His calmness His answer involved a stinging rebuke: "I have spoken openly in the world. Why ask Me? Ask them that have heard Me." If you really want to learn about Jesus, there is always plenty of chance. But the trouble with most is their lack of desire.

Upon this a miserable underling, probably seeing an indignant blush on the high-priestly face, clenched his fist and struck Jesus in the mouth. "Answerest Thou the high priest so?" Imagine, the face which angels behold in wonder is struck by a contemptible slave! And so often honest truth is met with unrighteous indignation. But without a trace of temper Jesus reproved this impudent transgressor: "If I spoke evil, bear witness of the evil; but if well, why smitest thou Me?"

In the mean while the Sanhedrin had been assembled. Into its august presence, the members seated in a semicircle around the high priest, Caiaphas, and his two clerks, whose duty it was to count the votes, Jesus was led. The seventy members themselves, with the high priest as the seventy-first, were made up of Sadducean priests, non-professional elders, and pharisaic Rabbis or scribes.

Ordinarily, in judicial trials, witnesses are on hand. But in this case witnesses had to be found. But, behold, their witness would not agree. Many witnesses were summoned, but the fiasco grew worse and worse. This would not do. If in no other way, incriminating evidence had to be extemporized and false witnesses sought against Jesus to put Him to death.

At length two witnesses were brought into approximate agreement, out of which it was hoped a charge could be constructed. It was a statement of Jesus' early ministry about destroying the Temple in three days and building it again. But while one witness twisted the words to refer to the physical Temple, the other testified that the reference was made to a temple built without hands. The fact of the matter was that the words of Jesus were neither a command to destroy, nor a promise to restore, the Temple of Jerusalem, but a reference to His death and resurrection. At any rate, it was as clear as day, even to the high priest, that out of these words a successful charge of blasphemy could not be constructed.

Jesus looked on in absolute silence while His disunited enemies confuted each other's testimony. Thus often guilt entangles itself in a net of noisy lies. The best kind of answer to shameless lies is often no answer at all. As the carefully prepared arrows of perjury fell at the feet of Jesus, as though blunted on the shield of His innocence, it looked as if the enemies would fail for the lack of a few consistent lies.

Overcome with a paroxysm of anger, lest after all his thirst of blood would go unslaked, the high priest sprang to his feet. "Answerest Thou nothing? What is it that these witness against Thee?" But Jesus answered nothing.

Reduced, then, to utter despair and fury, the high priest finally bethought himself of one more arrow in his quiver of unrighteousness, and this he now drew forth from it. It concerned not what properly belonged to the sphere of the court, what the defendant did, but what the defendant was. "I adjure Thee by the living God that Thou tell us whether Thou be the Christ, the Son of God."

As this question concerned a holy and eternal truth, it had to be answered. Apparently Jesus recognized the right of the high priest to put Him under oath. At least He saw that silence would have been construed into withdrawal of the assertion He had made regarding His person. Firmly and solemnly He answered: "Yes, I am." For the moment, He said, His accusers were His judges, but some day He would be theirs; for He adds: "Hereafter shall ye see the Son of Man sitting on the right hand of Power and coming in the clouds of heaven."

It has often been said that Christians claim for Christ what He never claimed for Himself. But here we have a straightforward, properly witnessed affidavit of the deity of Christ.

But what appears as the most glorious truth to the believing heart was as blasphemy in the horrified ears of the Sanhedrin. The cry of "Blasphemy!" reverberated through the hall of the ecclesiastical court. In holy horror the high priest rent his clothes. "What think ye?" he exclaims. "He is worthy of death!" was their impassioned reply.

The foul work of the night had been accomplished. It needed but the technicality of a few hours' adjournment to make the sentence entirely legal and binding. According to their law an acquittal could be immediately made; but a capital sentence could not be definitely pronounced until the following day. But that matter was easily taken care of. During the remaining hours of the night Jesus was left in the coarse and cruel hands of the guard. And after a brief reassembly of the Sanhedrin early in the morning the initial sentence was speedily confirmed. "What think ye?" The vote was taken and counted. And the result: "He is guilty of death."

And Jesus? The claw of the dragon was in His flesh and its foul breath in His mouth! He was not condemned for what He did or misdid, but for what He was: Christ, the Messiah, the Son of the living God, — that we might be made the children of God. 2 Cor. 5, 21; 1 John 1, 7.

O Christ, Thou Son of God, that takest away the sins of the world, have mercy upon us! Amen.   ADAM FAHLING.

II.

"This Fellow Was Also with Jesus of Nazareth."

Matt. 26, 71.

"And lead us not into temptation." And though we may be assailed by it, may God grant that we may finally overcome and obtain the victory!

To the ecclesiastical trial of Jesus there was an interesting side-issue, which is to occupy our attention to-day.

After the first panic of Christ's capture in the Garden of Gethsemane and the flight of the disciples, two of them, Peter and John, had so far recovered as to steal after the moving mass. It was only when the band was nearing its destination, the palace of the high priest, that they pushed forward, John entering with Jesus into the courtyard, while Peter remained behind until such time as admission for him could be procured.

Let us picture to ourselves the construction of such a house as the high priest's palace. Whereas our houses look out into the street, an Oriental house looks upon an open and enclosed inner court, reached through an arched passage, which is usually guarded and watched.

When the arresting party arrived with their Prisoner, the gate was opened and the whole party admitted, including John, who was acquainted with the high priest. But Peter was shut out. As the event shows, it would have been better had his exclusion been final.

It seems that John occupied a higher social level than the rest of the Twelve. Since the Gospel of St. John is rich with details of the Judean ministry of Jesus, it has been thought with a good degree of likelihood that he had spent quite a bit of his time previous to his discipleship in Jerusalem, perhaps as the representative of his father Zebedee's prosperous fish business in the capital city. At any rate, he was known to the high priest, also to the servants at the gate, because shortly he went out to the maid that kept the door and brought Peter in.

It was a friendly act. And still it was an ill turn. Neither of the two disciples had any business to be there. John did not enter as the disciple of Jesus, but as the friend of the high priest. And as to Peter, it was his purpose "to see the end," and he was led into temptation. Thus many Christians are not always quite honest in their confession with respect to their Savior nor entirely trustworthy with respect to the best interests of their friends.

After Peter had been admitted, John, it seems, hurried across the hall where Jesus was to witness the proceedings.

Not so Peter. He did not feel at home in that strange, big house. He felt more at ease among the servants, and even there he was out of place.

It was long past midnight by this time, and the spring air was cold and chilly. In the center of the court the servants had built a fire to warm themselves and were now standing with others around the coals of fire. It was this miscellaneous group that Peter resolved to join.

But Peter did not belong there. He was in danger, but in another sense than he supposed. It was not bodily peril. That would have been an eventuality which his fiery nature would have been equal to. But he did not anticipate dangers to his soul. Yet that was the very danger lurking in the shadows at the fire. No doubt the fireside was ringing with jests about the Prisoner who had been captured. Peter was silent. He did not interrupt the vulgar jesters. He simulated disinterest and indifference.

It is when least expected that temptation like a wild animal sneaks up and strikes a sudden blow. Already in the darkened arch-way Peter's pretended indifference and betraying restlessness had attracted the portress by whom he had been admitted. As a hypocrite he was a failure. When the gatekeeper was relieved by another maid, she stepped closer to the fire to verify her suspicious intuition concerning Peter. She fixed upon him an earnest gaze. No, she was not mistaken. With a flash of recognition she exclaimed: "Thou wast also with Jesus of Nazareth."

What an honor! To what greater praise could mortal man ever aspire? What better inscription could be engraved on the tombstone of a Christian's grave than the words: "He was also with Jesus of Nazareth"? At another time Peter himself would have desired none better. But here he was taken off his guard. A mask had been suddenly torn from his face. But instead of taking himself in hand, since the mask did not fit him anyhow, and confessing before all, he denied, lamely saying, "I know not what thou sayest."

How easily, how quickly, Peter glided and fell!

For a while Peter was at rest. None pursued, no one bothered him. But he felt uneasy and warm. There was a fire burning within him. Quietly he slunk away from the glowing brazier to the arch-covered entrance of the open court. He suddenly felt himself in need of refreshing air. Just then the crowing of a cock smote unheeded on his guilty ear. It did not occur to him that Christ had said: "Ere the cock crow twice, thou shalt deny Me thrice."

And not only that. If he had but heeded the warning! But he did not. That is the way of sin. You feel, you know, what you ought to do. But you don't do it. Such is our miserable human nature. You may talk all you want to about human nature, you will have to admit that it is corrupted, polluted, miserable. — A second maid replaced Peter's first accuser. At that moment she was standing with two or three men. Pointing him out to them, she came forward and said: "That is also one of the Nazarene's followers."

Poor sinful, fallen Peter! Again he is felled to the ground by the gentle touch of a woman's hand. And how often a woman's jeering laugh and saucy tongue have made a man feel ashamed of his highest and holiest possessions! This time it took more than a mere denial to set Peter straight. He flung an angry oath at her. He denied with an oath and said: "I am not. I know not the man."

This was the second denial.

By this time an hour had passed. Turning on his heels, he returned to the fire. He was now completely wild. He was boiling with conflicting emotions, and his mouth was out of control. Before he was silent; now he would talk. Assuming an air of defiance, he threw himself into the conversation, outdoing the rest in coarse and noisy talk. He would show them that he was not with Jesus of Nazareth. But before he knew it, he was fatally betrayed by his rough Galilean burr.

"Of a truth thou art one of them," the scoffing firesiders insisted; "for thy speech betrayeth thee." But Peter would show them! "When you are with the Romans, you must do as the Romans," is an old proverb. But the more Peter tried, the less he succeeded. Now that he tried to make good, he drew attention to himself.

In spite of his oaths and denials Peter was utterly despised. The devil hates man, and he hates him all the more for being a Christian. And then he hates him for having been a Christian. There was no hope for Peter to extricate himself. A kinsman of the wounded Malchus whose ear Peter had slashed off in the Garden confidently charged him with having been there with Jesus. In the face of such evidence, how could Peter deny? And still he makes one more effort. "Then began he to curse and to swear, I know not the man."

This was the third denial. How quickly and how deeply had Peter fallen! And immediately the cock crowed. The word of Jesus had been fulfilled: "Ere the cock crow twice, thou shalt deny Me thrice."

But repentance for Peter? Not yet. To his denials he added profanity and poured out curses and oaths. As far as he was concerned, Peter, that great disciple, had done his part, tried his best, to fill the whole courtyard with foul and infernal fumes. He was thoroughly lost.

But it is a good thing that our story does not end here.

There is a sequel. And thanks be to the merciful God that there is forgiveness for all sin! It was the Lord Himself who brought about Peter's return. "I have prayed for thee that thy faith fail not." Not even the second crowing of the cock, which ought to have shot into his conscience like a charge of dynamite, brought Peter to his senses.

It was merely a look which the Lord employed. "And the Lord looked upon Peter," probably as He was conducted across the court from Annas to Caiaphas.

But what a look! It was as if an arrow had pierced fallen Peter's inmost soul. Then he remembered, not before. There was pain in that look, disappointment and reproach, but also understanding, kindness, grace forgiveness, and unspeakable love. John 13, 1 b.

With his heart filled with unbearable pain, Peter cast down his tear-stained eyes and rushed out into the night. Gone, forgotten, was his foolhardiness, his enemies, his fears, denials, curses, perjuries, oaths. Something else had filled his heart. He rushed out into the night, but not into the unsunned darkness of miserable remorse, the midnight of hopeless despair, but by the grace of God into the sorrow of repentance. And he went out and wept bitterly."

God be thanked for the tears of Peter! They were better than his foul profanities and salvation-selling oaths. What a picture! And in the image of Peter every penitent sinner sees himself. For does not a sinner's salvation pass through the stage of sin, sorrow, contrition, and faith?

And what a sermon in that look of Christ! And with that same look the Savior views us: pain, reproach, disappointment, but also kindness, mercy, rescue, and undying love. 2 Cor. 7, 10. 11.

The Passion story does not need any oh's! and ah's! to stir the depths of the human heart. When hearing the story, examine yourself. What a powerful incentive to searching self-examination and unmerciful self-condemnation! But also what an invitation to accept the fruit of that self-sacrificing Savior love and to have it reflect in your life! 2 Cor. 5, 15.

This is most certainly true. Amen.   ADAM FAHLING.

III.
"What Is Truth?"
John 18, 38.

"What is truth?" Lord grant that we continue in the truth that Thy Son Jesus is our Redeemer and King. Blessed be His name!

"Suffered under Pontius Pilate." With these words the Creed forever stigmatizes the name of Pilate and at the same time fixes the approximate date of the suffering of Jesus.

The sentence of death had been passed on Jesus by the Sanhedrin, the highest domestic court in the land. Gladly would these judges have carried out their sentence, presumably by stoning, but it was not in their power. A capital sentence had to be confirmed by the provincial governor, in this case, Pontius Pilate. This he did in the end.

The governorship of Pilate coincided about with the beginning of the ministry of John the Baptist. He had been in office long enough to become thoroughly acquainted with the most difficult race which the experienced officials of Rome ever had to manage. There was no love lost between Pilate und the Jews. He despised them, and they hated him.

Pilate's usual residence was at sea-washed Caesarea, in itself a little Rome. But the pomp and the perils of the Passover Festival, when the heaving lava of glowing patriotism was ever apt to leap into flame, yearly summoned him to the capital of the nation.

At such times, especially when accompanied by his wife, he would occupy the gorgeous palace which the architectural extravagance of the first Herod had reared. It was a luxurious abode, overlooking Jerusalem, to the southwest of the hill on which the Temple was built. In front of it extended a broad pavement, locally called Gabbatha, flanked by porticoes and columns of marble. And here, in the open and from a raised platform the trials were conducted on account of the popular prejudice against entering the Gentile ruler's house. Besides, being in the season of the Passover, when every trace of leaven had to be removed, there was all the more reason to guard against ceremonial defilement. In this matter Pilate had to yield to his subjects' scruples, though he probably cursed them in his heart.

It may have been about six o'clock on that memorable April morning that a dignified procession, no doubt followed by a thrill-seeking throng, was seen approaching Pilate's palace. The matter was very urgent and had to be completely dispatched before sundown on the same day which had just begun.

The long-bearded and wise-looking judges, probably headed by Caiaphas himself, would not enter into the Pretorium or Judgment-hall and so Pilate went out to them. They were afraid of leaven which would be found in the Gentile's house, but they did not shrink from the shedding of holy and innocent blood. Thus there are many who are precise in observing propriety, but are utterly conscienceless in the violation of clear commandments of God.

Disturbed in that early hour, Pilate was in no pleasant mood, although he knew that disturbances might be expected in the Passover season. In a half-necessary condescension he had to accommodate himself to what he considered the ridiculous superstitions of a hated race. As he ascended the tribunal, no doubt accompanied by secretaries and guarded by bronzed representatives of the power of Rome, he cast one haughty look over the priestly notables and the turbulent mob. Noticing also a bound victim in their midst, he immediately demanded: "What accusation bring ye against this man?"

The question took them by surprise. It almost seems as if they expected Pilate to accept the verdict of the Sanhedrin and to sign the bill of execution as we would say "sight unseen." This manner of dispensing justice was sometimes observed by provincial governors, either out of indolence or in blind reliance upon the native courts. And especially, as in this case, in religious matters, which a foreigner was not expected to understand, it was not always the unreasonable course to pursue.

"If He were not a malefactor, we would not have delivered Him up unto thee," is the somewhat offended reply. But this morning Pilate was in no yielding mood. He would not give the sanction of his tribunal to their dark decree. He would not be the executioner where he had not been the judge. Very well, "take ye Him, then, and judge Him according to your law." If you do not want me to review the case, then you must be satisfied with what the law allows.

This meant that they would have to impose excommunication, fines, imprisonment, forty stripes save one, and the like punishments, which would not at all have satisfied their thirst for blood and would not be the sentence upon which they had agreed. They were forced into the humiliating confession: "It is not lawful for us to put any one to death," thus revealing their infernal desire as well as acknowledging the power of Rome. What fiendishness is revealed in these words! And even if they did have the right to inflict capital punishment, it was decreed in the counsel of God as well as foretold by His Son that Christ was to die not by stoning or by strangulation, but by the Roman mode of crucifixion. "And shall deliver Him to the Gentiles, to mock and to scourge and to crucify Him."

Therefore, since Pilate was determined to retry the case, the accusers were forced to formulate definite charges upon which they hoped that their sentence would be confirmed. A flood of vehement accusations unsubstantiated by witnesses is poured forth, out of which at last three distinct charges emerge.

First, that He was perverting the nation; secondly, that He forbade to pay the imperial tribute; thirdly, that He set Himself up as Christ, a king. Blasphemy, for which He was really condemned, is not even mentioned. They knew too well that, if they would advance this charge here, they would be sneered out of court.

The first vague charge, "perverting the nation," Pilate passes by. If they had told the truth, they would probably have stated that He was making too many disciples and that they were afraid that the whole nation would accept His teaching. Pilate understood perfectly well; he "knew that for envy they had delivered Him."

Likewise the second charge, "forbidding to give tribute to Caesar," Pilate passes by. Indeed, if true, that would have been a crime. But the government of Pilate was too well organized not to know that this accusation was a flagrant lie. The very opposite had been taught by Jesus. There must have been a smile on the governor's face at the prospect of this sudden zeal for Roman tribute.

It was the third charge which attracted his attention, "saying that He Himself is Christ, a king." Discounting the ungrasped Messianic reference for the present, — but if that was true that He was setting Himself up as a king, a possible rival to gloomy Tiberius, this certainly had to be investigated. Not as if there were any cause for particular worry, but it should not be said that he was "sleeping on the job."

Just how much Pilate was acquainted with the career of Jesus we do not know. It is certain that he was not altogether ignorant. On the evening before he had granted a Roman guard to assist in His arrest. Then there was the dream of his wife, Procula, which seems to show that there had been conversation in his house about that "young enthusiast" who was bearding the fanatic priests. Now the charge about saying that He was Christ, a king.

We assume that during these proceedings Jesus was, probably with a guard, within the walls of the Pretorium. Leaving the impatient Sanhedrin and the raging crowd, Pilate retired into the Judgment-hall.

In the silence of that interior hall Pilate stood face to face with Almighty Power. "Art Thou the king of the Jews?" he asked. That depends upon how the royalty of Jesus is understood. In His reply the Savior is cautious: "Sayest thou this thing of thyself, or did others tell it thee of Me?" "Am I a Jew?" is Pilate's disdainful reply. "Thy own nation and the chief priests have delivered Thee unto me. What hast Thou done?"

What a shame and what a charge! Israel's own people had rejected Israel's King! And what had He done? *Done?* "Done all things well," works of mercy, love, power, and still stands a prisoner at the bar.

But in His answer Jesus reverts to the first question of Pilate. Yes, He is a King. But no rival of Tiberius. For in that event His servants would fight. And still a King, but now His "kingdom is not of this world."

In making this explanation the word "kingdom" was used. At this point Pilate broke in and said: "Art Thou a king, then?" "Yes," Jesus answered, "thou sayest it, I am a King. To this end was I born, and for this cause came I into the world, that I should bear witness of the truth. Every one that is of the truth heareth My voice."

So that's it. A king. However, not a king of men, but a king of hearts and of the truth.

Truth! Truth? But "what is truth?" What has he, a busy, practical Roman governor, to do with such abstractions?

At this, almost persuaded, like Felix, Pilate rushed out. So near the fountain, and yet so far from the life-giving stream! This floating idea of unearthly royalty he set aside as completely unreal. Too bad! he thought. What a high-souled, but altogether impractical dreamer!

But this much was sure. Whatever He was, He was not guilty of death. Pilate went out to the impatient Sanhedrin and pronounced an emphatic and unhesitating acquittal. "I find in Him no fault at all."

Is Jesus a King? Yes, He is. And it makes no difference whether you believe it or not. He is a King. But is He your King, so that you may "live under Him in His kingdom and serve Him in everlasting righteousness, innocence and blessedness"?

And what is truth? It is this, — a divine, everlasting, unchangeable, gracious truth, —

"This is a faithful saying and worthy of all acceptation, that Christ Jesus came into the world to save sinners," to whom alone be all honor and glory forever and ever. Amen. ADAM FAHLING.

IV.

"And He Questioned with Him in Many Words."

Luke 23, 9.

God grant that we may always be glad to see Jesus as our Savior with the eyes of faith!

The examination of Jesus by Pilate resulted in an emphatic: "I find in Him no fault at all." Now what ought to have followed? The unjust verdict of the Sanhedrin ought to have been reversed, the prisoner released, and, if necessary, protected by a Roman guard. And why was this not done? Aside from the decree in the counsels of divine mercy that Jesus should die for the sins of the world, Pilate, with all his bold swagger, was a coward and did not have the nerve to resist. This the accusers knew. They were confident that, if they would persist, they would see the fulfilment of their foul design.

An incident in the previous life of Pilate may best explain. Some years before Pilate, recently arrived with a supply of new ideas, resolved to move the headquarters of the army from Caesarea to Jerusalem. Resolved and done. Roman legions with clanking swords, shining helmets, armored breast-plates, and military ensigns on which were affixed the Roman eagles and the effigy of the imperial master, were seen in Jerusalem. And who was there to resist?

But to the popular mind the images were idolatrous, and their presence in the Holy City itself was a gross insult and desecration. There was no objection to the image of Tiberius on the denarius or shilling, especially if sufficiently multiplied. Neither was there objection to the blades on the end of the hilt and the spears on the shaft. But there was serious objection to the gilded ornaments on the tip of the regimental standards.

Soon a noisy delegation rushed down to Caesarea with well-spiked protests against the introduction of idolatrous images into the Holy City. And besides, what is the idea of bringing them in stealthily in the night-time, as had been done? Furthermore, they reminded Pilate that, when former governors made their entry into the city, it was without those idols on the top of the poles.

Pilate refused. He was still a new governor, and he had to learn. For five days he refused. Finally he was so irritated that he gave the order to disperse the noisy mob and, if necessary, to cut off their heads, since there was no other way to silence their mouths. "All right!" they cried and stretched forth their necks, saying that they would rather die than have their city defiled. In the end Pilate had to carry out the images of his imperial master and store them in a warehouse at Caesarea.

Such was the governor, and such were the people with whom he had to deal. For the sake of the effigy of his master he could not afford to provoke a revolution and wreck the revenues of a tribute-producing province.

The word of Pilate "I find in Him no fault at all" was but a signal for the release of an angry clamor. Charges and accusations were hurled from every direction. The chief priests accused Him of many things. Pilate, hopelessly in the air, weakly turned to Jesus Himself. "Answerest Thou nothing? Behold how many things they witness against Thee." But Jesus, with His life at stake, was the only calm person in the assembly and answered nothing, so that Pilate marveled.

Suddenly, however, in the midst of the confusion a way out of the difficulty seemed to open itself to Pilate. He heard the word Galilee. "He stirreth up the people, teaching throughout all Jewry, beginning from Galilee, to this place." The mention of Galilee was intended to excite prejudice against Jesus, as Galilee was a hotbed of insurrection. But to Pilate's mind there was suggested a way to rid himself of the terrible responsibility and at the same time to flatter Herod, who was present in Jerusalem for the Passover. This he could do, in accordance with Roman law, by transferring to him the prisoner to whose jurisdiction, as a resident of Galilee, Jesus of Nazareth belonged.

Glad to rid himself of this detestable business, he sent the prisoner and His accusers down the hill to the near-by ancient Maccabean palace, in which Herod used to reside on his visits to the capital city.

In order to understand the following, we must briefly review a bit of Herodian history. After the death of Herod the Great his do-

minions were divided by Rome among three of his sons, in order to
facilitate keeping the country under control. Archelaus received
Judaea, soon to be taken from him at the request of the people themselves and to be administered by Roman governors, of whom Pontius
Pilate was fifth in line. Philip received Iturea and the northern
regions, while Antipas received Galilee and a strip of land east of
the Jordan; and at the time when Christ was brought to the latter,
after thirty years, both were still in the enjoyment of their possessions.

Like his father, Herod Antipas was a builder, and corrupt, but
in other respects he was very unlike his father — he lacked ability and
diplomacy. He took a fatal step when he entered into an adulterous
union with Herodias, his niece and another brother's, Herod Philip's,
wife, which brought about the death of John the Baptist. (A war
with Aretas of Arabia in the end cost him his tottering throne.)

When John the Baptist, that stern wilderness preacher of repentance, began to set the hearts of men afire, Herod Antipas was
interested and invited him to his palace and heard him gladly, until
John said: "It is not lawful for thee to have her." That was pressing
the matter of repentance too far. And especially did Herodias conceive a bitter hatred against him. We know what happened. On the
king's birthday Salome, Herodias's daughter by a former marriage,
danced before the drunken crowd. The king was pleased and promised
to give her anything that she might ask up to one half of his kingdom. "And he sware unto her." The young witch, well drilled by
her mother in the craft of hell, asked for the head of John the Baptist
on a charger, and she was not refused. The executioner was sent to
John in the dungeon. No time for preparation is given, nor needed.
A few minutes, and it is all over. The guard returns. And Herodias
receives her ghastly dish.

This awful crime filled the country with horror. Herod himself
was troubled by the accusations of his conscience. When the fame
of the great Galilean Prophet reached Herod, he thought it was none
other than John the Baptist risen from the dead. That is just like
many people who do not believe in God, but are foolish enough to
believe in ghosts. Or just like avowed and otherwise educated atheists
who are stupid enough to be deceived by fortune-telling frauds.

Feeling the hatred of his subjects, Herod Antipas, who was at
best only an Idumean Sadducee, turned more and more to foreign
customs. His court was distinguished for Roman and Greek imita-
tions. And especially were the professional conveyers of pleasure,
the charlatans and fakers of the day, jugglers, and the like, welcome
at his court. His annual visit to the Passover at Jerusalem was
altogether conventional and inspired not so much by devotion as by
the hope of amusement.

When he saw Jesus, he was exceeding glad. This appearance of Jesus promised excitement. And then what a compliment to have Pilate send him a prisoner! Indeed, we are told that as a result of this act of unexpected attention the erstwhile enemies became friends. But most of all his delight was increased by the hope that this great Galilean miracle-worker would entertain him with two or three choice miracles for his particular benefit. And why not? This was a prisoner's chance to turn influence in his favor. No doubt he thought that Jesus would grasp the opportunity to show His skill. Thus Herod reveals his estimate of the person of Christ. And it just about corresponds to what many still think of Christ. Thus Jesus is put down in Herod's mind on the level with a conjurer or dispenser of magic.

At once he addressed Jesus in the friendliest manner and questioned Him in many words. We can imagine the welcoming smile. In his eagerness he forgot altogether the purpose for which Pilate had sent Him. But Jesus answered him nothing. But Herod never noticed it and rambled on. He liked to hear himself talk. He himself in his day had done some strong theological thinking. He had views on religion and wanted to voice them. Even so to-day we have prominent manufacturers, scientists, and ex-rulers with insides on the hereafter, which they want their fellow-men to share. He had theories to ventilate, puzzles to propound, and remarks to make. Very often the unbeliever, the irreligious, the atheist, and the scoffer have a good deal to say about religion. "Then he questioned with Him in many words." Just imagine. The most shallow, silly chatter is poured into the suffering ears of the silent Son of God. "But He answered him nothing."

At last Herod had exhausted himself. He waited for Christ to speak. He waited. But Jesus never uttered a word. Silence continued. At last the old chatterer grew angry. But Jesus did not utter a word. He was silent that the word of John the Baptist might continue to ring in his ears: "It is not lawful for thee to have her." "Repent ye." "The tree that bringeth not forth good fruit is hewn down and cast into the fire."

The king is through speaking. And now the accusers begin. "And the chief priests and scribes stood and vehemently accused Him." The same old charges are poured out, and, it seems, this time into receptive ears.

Then the corrupt sattelites around the debased throne chime in. "And Herod with his men of war set Him at naught"; that is, they treated Him with the insolence of studied contempt.

Mocking His harmless innocence and ridiculing His candidacy for the Messianic throne, they throw a white robe over His holy shoulders. And midst ribald laughter and cruel insults, Herod sends

Him back to Pilate, with whom as a result he now again had become friends.

Thus in their common cause against Jesus Pilate and Herod became friends. But the records do not state that the friendship brought about by such unholy circumstances was very enduring. Nevertheless it is true that the cause against Christ and Christianity does make strange bedfellows and friends. But a thousand times better it had been for Pilate and Herod to have sought to retain the friendship of Jesus.

And are we friends of Jesus, and are we glad to see Him? And why? What are our views on religion, and what think we of Christ?

ADAM FAHLING.

V.

"His Blood Be on Us and on Our Children!"

Matt. 27, 25.

"What, then, shall I do with Jesus?" Lord, grant that we may accept Him as our Savior and Redeemer. Amen.

Pilate's hope in disposing of the case of Jesus by sending Him to Herod was in vain; before long the prisoner was brought back to the judgment-hall.

Herod treated Jesus with shameless disdain, while Pilate still treated Him with some respect. Yet Pilate could plainly see that the verdict of Herod agreed with his own, namely, that whatever views might be held as to the teaching and person of the Galilean Prophet, He at least was not guilty of death.

This point was now definitely established by Pilate's own observation and confirmed by expert advice, for as such, naturally, the action of Herod, as coming from a native prince, would be interpreted. There was now for Pilate absolutely no excuse for a delay of favorable action.

But what did Pilate do? He still followed the policy of all weaklings, that miserable policy of stalling for time. When the fate of Jesus was once more placed into his unhappy hands, he called together the chief priests and the rulers and the people for the purpose of making an important announcement, always hoping probably that something, he knew not what, might turn up.

At last he begins his speech. You have brought me this man as one that is perverting the nation. I have examined Him before you and have found in Him no fault at all. Then I sent Him to Herod. Herod examined Him. And the result is the same.

And therefore, he continues, still thinking hard, therefore—what? And therefore, you would expect him to say, I am going to release Him, and I warn you by the power of Rome and the terrible anger of

Tiberius not so much as to disturb a hair on His head. But instead he offers a proposition contrary to all logic and justice: "I will therefore chastise Him and release Him."

Was a more unjust proposal ever made? Inflict a cruel punishment, as a sop to their rage, and then release Him, as a tribute to justice! And yet this proposal was thoroughly characteristic of the man who made it as well as of the system which he represented. The spirit of imperial Rome ever was the spirit of compromise in order ultimately to gain the end. And nine times out of ten it worked. Scores of officials throughout the empire were even now successfully conducting their administration along these very lines. Only to Pilate fell the sad distinction of applying the base system to an altogether unexpected exception to the rule.

In proposing to have Jesus chastised though innocent, Pilate cut himself loose from all principles of justice. But he hoped thus to guide his course safely to the point at which he aimed. In this Pilate was fatally mistaken. The impulse of his own false beginning could only end in his own wreck and ruin. Only by means of right you can achieve right. You cannot do one thing wrong in the hope of making another thing right. It cannot be done.

Not that Pilate did not know better. Nor that he was unwarned. It was about this time that a distinct warning came to him from Procula, his loving wife. She sent to tell her husband of a painful dream she had just had about the prisoner and to warn him, not as governor, but as her husband, not to have anything to do with that just man.

And how did she know about Him? That is not stated. But we must remember that Jesus was nationally known, and no doubt He had been the subject of conversation in the palace. On the evening before, a Roman guard had been given to assist in His arrest. The matter was probably mentioned. And with the thought of Jesus she went to sleep.

Now, we are not going to talk about dreams. Many people are deceived by them. But God can make use of a dream. He has done that, and we can be assured that the hand of God was in this dream and that in the message both the hand of God and of a loving wife were outstretched to save Pilate from a doom to which he hastened.

Pilate, who as an educated Roman would have remembered Caesar's death and Calpurnia's dream, must have been impressed. Gladly would he have yielded and gratified both his nobler finer feeling and innate sense of justice, if it only would not have been for that secret streak of cowardice.

And it seems that in the eager pursuit of temporizing measures there was opened another avenue of hoped-for escape.

Up to this point the actors assembled on the stage of Christ's trial were still comparatively few as compared with the masses that now appeared on the scene. And it was just with this mob of Jerusalem as against the leaders with whom he had been dealing that Pilate hoped to find rescue. His knowledge that it was for envy that Jesus had been delivered to him by the leaders he hoped to turn to account.

It was the custom of the Roman governors as a contribution to the Passover joy to release a prisoner to the people whom they would. There were generally plenty of political prisoners on hand, rebels against the detested power of Rome, but for that reason popular heroes. And for once the annual demand to have a prisoner released was welcome to Pilate.

Here was the plan. He would give them the choice between a robber and leader of sedition, who in a late uprising had committed murder, Barabbas, and Jesus, who had a few days before been the hero of a popular demonstration. As an aspirant to Messiahship, he imagined, Jesus would be the very person they should choose.

It seemed to be a good plan. Why should it not work? Pilate at least thought he could not go wrong. And still, taking into consideration the person and the issue, failure is the only outcome in which this plan could result. Only by means of right you can achieve right. You cannot do one thing wrong for the purpose of making another thing right. You cannot gamble in the interest of justice. It cannot be done.

It was an utterly unjust thing for Pilate to do, because the proposal treated Jesus as if He were guilty and already condemned, which was not the case. And furthermore it staked the life of an innocent man upon the voice of the people, in the hope that the voice of the people is the voice of God, *vox populi vox Dei,* which is not always the case.

There was a brief interval, which was put to good use by the priests and elders. Since Pilate had appealed to the mob, they, too, would appeal to the mob. And they knew their mob better than Pilate. They persuaded and moved the people. All they had to do was to employ a simple political trick as old as politics, that is, pass the word around as to which of the two was Pilate's choice. And then, as far as the mob was concerned, the matter was safe.

Picture to yourselves the scene. The holy, undefiled, sinless Son of God standing with a scowling thug on that high tribunal! Words fail to describe the contrast: on the one side the King of Glory, on the other the minion of hell!

For the Holy, the Harmless, for Him whom thousands of hosannas had greeted five days before, not a word of pity is heard. And then, as the choice is made which is to decide the fate of the Redeemer and forever confirm the tragic truth of the natural depravity of the human heart, a thousand, ten thousand hands are pointed, and ten thousand voices raise the cry "Barabbas!"

And so, in spite of all manipulations, the matter had come to the worst. After a last brief moment of hopeful suspense the choice of Barabbas must have been a staggering blow to Pilate. He had staked all on the choice and lost. "What," he asked, "shall I, then, do with Jesus?" This is a question which every believer asks and answers. Probably Pilate had hoped for the answer "Give us Him, too." And how willingly he would have complied with the request! "What shall I, then, do with Jesus?" Quick as an echo the answer was flashed back: "Crucify Him!" As with wild vehemence the hideous yells rent the air, Pilate was made sensible that the accusers were in deadly earnest in their cry for blood.

What Pilate had considered a loophole for escape was a noose into which he had thrust his neck. He was lost. There was no use for him to plead any more.

When he saw that he could prevail nothing, he did a most silly and hypocritical thing. Calling for a basin of water, he washed his hands before them all and said: "I am innocent of the blood of this just person. See ye to it."

It was a most impressive act, and yet a solemn farce. Blood and guilt is not washed off so easily. And Pilate's hands were covered with blood.

Instead of washing his hands, he ought to have used them. He ought to have opposed the popular will at whatever risk. He ought to have refused to do the deed of which he himself disapproved. And so we could go on: Ought to have done this and ought to have done that. That is how the prisoner whiles away unmolested moments behind the iron bars: Ought to have done this; ought to have done that. But in back of the case against Jesus was the saving will of God.

Pilate, coward that he was, was afraid of guilt. But the people were not. His pitiful plea for mercy for Jesus — for that is what it was — is met with a hideous howl of hell. "His blood be on us and on our children!" Madder cries were never uttered, and profaner curses were never heard, and remembered, too, — with a vengeance.

And still, yes, His blood be upon us and on our children! The blood of Jesus Christ cleanseth us from all sin. "Who has redeemed me . . . with His holy, precious blood and with His innocent suffering and death."

> Yea, Jesus' blood and righteousness
> My jewels are, my glorious dress,
> Wherein before my God I'll stand
> When I shall reach the heavenly land.

ADAM FAHLING.

VI.

"Behold the Man!" "Behold Your King!"

John 18, 5. 14.

"Hosanna to the Son of David! Blessed is He that cometh in the name of the Lord! Hosanna in the highest!"

Accompanied by an outburst of joyful hosannas, Israel's true King made His triumphal entry into the city of David on that memorable Palm Sunday, but it is as the Man of Sorrows and thorn-crowned King that He is presented to our attention to-day.

Pilate's various attempts to save Jesus had come to naught. There was now no course open to him but to hand Him over to the executioners.

In presenting the intense suffering of our Savior, it is not necessary to linger over every detail until each sentence reeks with blood, as used to be the custom in a more realitsic age; as long as we remember that it was a real suffering, a vicarious suffering, and in true penitence are reminded of the cause: —

> Ah! I also and my sin
> Wrought Thy deep affliction;
> This the cause alone hath been
> Of Thy crucifixion.

The people had spoken. As we have pointed out, the voice of the people is not always the voice of God. And now Pilate yielded to the popular storm. He released Barabbas and delivered Jesus to be scourged. This terrible punishment, illegal for Roman citizens, was the ordinary preliminary to crucifixion and other forms of capital punishment. Woe unto him upon whom it was inflicted! It meant that he was doomed to die. It was a punishment so truly terrible that the mind revolts at its description. The victim was stripped and tied in a bent position to a pillar, and then blows were inflicted on the naked back with leathern thongs weighted with jagged pieces of bone or lead. The punishment was so hideous that the victim generally fainted and often died.

Pilate's purpose in tolerating this torture before the last and deciding word had been spoken apparently was to save Jesus from death by inflicting a punishment so cruel as to arouse the pity of the mob and then to let Him go. But if these were his hopes, they were as futile as his measures were heartless and unjust. —

Assuming that Jesus was condemned and that He was their victim, to be treated as they pleased, the soldiers now took Him in hand. In civilized countries all is done to spare suffering to a murderer condemned to death. But among the Roman soldiers, inured to bloodshed and delighted by the bloody sports of the arena, the opposite was the case. If there were no pain and bloodshed, they would consider themselves deprived of their chief amusement. The trial of Jesus was over. The Easter of Jerusalem meant nothing to them. And so they would make a Roman holiday of their own.

Somehow the fact had penetrated their barrack-schooled brains that the drift of the trial of Jesus was that He prentended to be a king, and so their horse-play took the form of a mock coronation.

In staging their heartless ceremony, the hardened ruffians treated Jesus as if they were creating a successor to the aged and suspicious incumbent of the purple who at the time was hiding his gloomy features at Capri. A king must wear the purple. And so they tore Herod's gift, a white robe, from His bleeding shoulders and threw over Him a cast-off officer's coat. He must have a crown. And so one of them pulled a few sharp-spined twigs off a near-by bush and plaited them into a crown of thorns. He must have a scepter. Thus a reed was thrust into His rope-tied hands. The royal outfit is quite complete. And now their newly made king must be duly saluted.

As to the proper royal address, the only time when they had seen that done was in Rome at a show, when they had seen gladiators approach the imperial presence with the greeting: *"Ave, Caesar, morituri te salutant."* And so they advanced, one after the other, and bending low, said: "Hail, King of the Jews!" And then, passing from unshamed mockery to savage cruelty, midst outbursts of coarse laughter they struck Him over the head with the reed which was in His hands. And (must we repeat it?) they covered His face with spittle. What a spectacle!

Putting an end to this misery for the present, Pilate led Jesus forth and burst out with that famous involuntary exclamation which has thrilled untold millions of hearts: "Behold the man!" Painters have chosen this moment of extreme humiliation when Jesus came forth bleeding from cruel stripes, wearing the scarlet robe and the crown of thorns, as the one to picture the Man of Sorrows. And many a canvas bears the title *"Ecce Homo!"* "Behold the man!"

Two words have fallen from Pilate's lips which the world will never forget: "What is truth?" and "Behold the man!" One may be taken as the answer to the other. "What is truth?" Heavenly truth, the will of the Father and the way of life, may be beheld only in the man Christ Jesus. "And no man ascended up to heaven but He that came down from heaven, even the Son of Man, which is in heaven. And as Moses lifted up the serpent in the wilderness, even so must the Son of Man be lifted up, that whosoever believeth in Him should not perish, but have everlasting life." Let the whole world turn to Him and with a truly penitent and believing heart "behold the man."

It was an outcry to move the hard hearts to mercy, but it only awakened a fierce uproar of bloodthirsty screams: "Crucify Him, crucify Him!" The sight of the suffering Jesus in these unspeakable depths seemed only to add fuel to the infernal flames. Pilate pleaded with them. But again he had missed his guess. There was no voice of compassion, but only the howling refrain of their wild liturgy of death. At his wit's end, Pilate cried out in utter disgust: "Take ye Him, and crucify Him; for I find no fault in Him." What an admission from a Roman judge, and what a wretched subterfuge to attempt to escape his responsibility by shifting the blame on others!

Now the enemies felt safe. They saw that they had the governor completely in their power. Now they could even come out boldly with their real charge against Jesus, which hitherto they had kept carefully concealed. "We have a law, and by our law He ought to die, because He made Himself the Son of God."

What was that? "Son of God"? When Pilate heard these words, terror filled his superstitious soul. Immediately he left the howling multitude and took Jesus with him to the inside of the judgment-hall. There he asked Him with awe-struck accents: "Whence art Thou?" For the fourth time since the trial began Jesus retired into majestic silence. We can but guess at the purpose. He could not say that He was not the Son of God. And if He had said it in this connection, it would have been understood by Pilate in a grossly pagan sense. So He said nothing. Besides, it was too late now. Pilate had heard enough.

Almost angrily Pilate breaks out: "Speakest Thou not to me? Knowest Thou not that I have power to crucify Thee and power to release Thee?" But Jesus soon set him straight on this point. Talking about power? Why didn't he show it? And what about justice, truth, innocence, and conscience? And as to power, in reality he had none except the governmental powers given to him from above. And he should be very careful not to abuse this power. Of course, Pilate thought that he had been forced into this present trial; yet he would not be excused for the miscarriage of justice. He would still be guilty, while the prosecutors, "he that delivered Me unto thee, hath the greater sin." Thus with infinite dignity, and yet with infinite tenderness, did Jesus judge His judge, who just a few minutes before had given Him over to torture.

Pilate returned. He was still intent upon releasing the prisoner. For the third and last time on that early Good Friday morning he ascended the tribunal erected on the pavement called Gabbatha. And this time he was determined at all hazards to carry out his purpose. A crisis had come, and the frantic rioters could plainly see that there was fire in his eyes.

But in his speech Pilate never got beyond the opening words. For once he was willing to connive at their cherished and ill-concealed royalistic aspirations. "Behold your King!" he said. But again he failed. For once the enemies of Rome would not have their disloyalty to the "dearly beloved government" of Rome flung into their face. Loyalty? Patriotism? Why, they even questioned Pilate's: "If thou let this man go, thou art not Caesar's friend. Whosoever maketh himself a king speaketh against Caesar." Pilate could not take the part of Jesus and retain the friendship of Caesar. There he had it. "Shall I crucify your king?" "We have no king but Caesar." If Tiberius had only heard! How was that for patriotism as coming from that hotbed of insurrection?

That settled it; for Pilate, for the priests, for the people, for all. Nothing would stop the crucifixion now. That was the last straw. "If thou let this man go, thou art not Caesar's friend." At that terrible name Pilate trembled. At all events there must be no complaint lodged against him at Rome. Rather the loss of an innocent life, yes, a thousand lives, than the loss of the friendship of Caesar.

And what about that hypocritical loyalty to Caesar "We have no king but Caesar"? Indeed, how true! Pilate took them at their word. Henceforth they had no Savior, no Redeemer, no Friend, no King, but Caesar.

"Behold your king!" And still He would have been their King, their Savior King. But with this rejection they flung into the winds every Messianic hope.

"Behold your king!" He is a King, your King! Thorn-crowned, rejected, but a King. Behold Him in faith. He cometh unto thee.

And with these words we conclude this address, this series: —

"Tell ye the daughter of Sion, Behold, thy King cometh unto thee! — Hosanna to the Son of David! Blessed is He that cometh in the name of the Lord! Hosanna in the highest!" Amen.

ADAM FAHLING.

Maundy Thursday.
Ex. 12, 11—14.

The feast of the Passover was one of the three major festivals of Israel; in fact, it was the principal annual feast of the Jews. It was celebrated in the first month of the Jewish ecclesiastical year, called Abib before and Nisan after the Exile. This month corresponds to the latter part of our March and the greater portion of April. In the New Testament no other festival of Israel is so frequently mentioned as this one. Our Lord, during His sojourn on earth, conscientiously observed the Passover. It was this festival which He celebrated with His disciples in the guest-chamber at Jerusalem in the night in which He was betrayed. Having celebrated the Sacrament of the Old Covenant for the last time, He instituted in its place the Sacrament which believers are to celebrate in the New Testament, the Lord's Supper, and which to us has such a deep, significant meaning and affords us so much comfort. As this day is Maundy Thursday, the day on which Christ instituted the Lord's Supper (of old it was called Day, or Birthday, of the Eucharist), it is only proper that we consider this Sacrament to-day.

The Old Testament Passover a Type of the Lord's Supper in the New Testament.

1. Its Essence;   2. Its Benefit;   3. Its Salutary Use.

1.

In the chapter of which our text is a part the institution of the Passover is recorded. As our text refers to the foregoing, let us recall the order of observance of the first Passover. On the tenth day of the first Jewish month every household in Israel had to take a lamb without blemish (without a defect of any kind) and a male of the first year. On the fourteenth day of the month the lamb was killed in the evening and its blood caught up in a vessel. (Here describe the manner of the celebration according to text.) This was, in brief, the order of observance of the first Passover. Later, especially when Israel dwelt in the Promised Land, certain changes in the order were made.

The main thing in the Passover was, of course, the paschal lamb. The paschal lamb was typical, pointing to the true Paschal Lamb of God, our Savior Jesus Christ. Of Him John says: "Behold the Lamb of God, which taketh away the sin of the world." Cf. Rev. 12, 11; 22, 1. That the paschal lamb was typical of Christ is also indicated by Paul: "For even Christ, our Passover, is sacrificed for us," 1 Cor. 5, 7. And as the paschal lamb was typical of Christ, so the whole feast of the Passover was a type of the Sacrament of the Lord's Supper in the New Testament. The memorable ordinance of the Old Testament is now abolished, and the Lord's Supper has taken its place.

The paschal lamb was killed, roasted, and eaten. That was a type of the nature and essence of the Lord's Supper. Just as the Israelites ate the paschal lamb, so Christ gives us His body to eat and His blood to drink in the Lord's Supper. When the Lord instituted this Sacrament, He said: "Take, eat; this is My body, which is given for you. Take, drink ye all of it; this cup is the new testament in My blood, which is shed for you for the remission of sins." These words, spoken by Him who is the Truth, cannot be misunderstood. They mean just what they say. These words cannot be taken figuratively, but must be taken in their literal meaning. In, with, and under the bread and wine we receive Christ's true body and blood, not types and emblems.

Neither does Christ say: "I give you My *changed* body and blood." The bread does not cease to be bread or the wine, wine, but in the Lord's Supper we receive the visible elements, bread and wine, and, in a supernatural way, the invisible elements, the body and blood of Christ. See 1 Cor. 10, 16; 11, 27.

Human reason cannot comprehend this; human philosophy cannot explain the mystery. But Christian believers trust the word of Christ. Faith takes the Lord at His word. This mystery is no greater than that of the incarnation. Without knowing how it may be so, it is enough for us to know from Christ's words that it is so.

2.

The Passover was a type also of the benefit we receive in the Lord's Supper. What benefit did Israel have from celebrating the first Passover in Egypt? That is stated in vv. 12. 13. It was a terrible night for the Egyptians when God through the angel of death executed judgment on them, from the proud monarch to the humblest citizen of Egypt. By nine successive plagues God had warned Pharaoh and the nation, but instead of bowing to the will of the almighty Lord and allowing Israel to depart, they hardened themselves more and more and defied Jehovah. But that night the angel executed God's judgment upon them. The first-born in Egypt of man and beast were slain, and, as our text states, "God executed judgment against all the gods of Egypt," so that the idols which the Egyptians worshiped were also demolished. The God of Israel proved that He is the omnipotent Lord.

But while the Egyptians felt the wrath of God descending upon them, the children of Israel were safe from the avenging work of the destroying angel. As the angel beheld the blood of the paschal lamb on the door-posts of their homes, he passed over them. Thousands fell at their side and ten thousands at their right hand, but Israel was secure, and no harm came nigh them. All this because the blood of the lamb was on their door-posts. This feast in later years commemorated God's mercy to them in freeing them from their bondage in Egypt.

This is a type of the benefit we receive from Christ's shedding His blood for us and of the benefit of the Lord's Supper. In the later history of Israel the Passover was observed with special reference to the Messiah and His redeeming work. Messianic psalms were sung, etc. — We are sinners before God; by nature we were in the bondage of sin and Satan and deserved the doom of eternal punishment. But Christ, the Lamb of God, shed His blood on the cross for us. Through His blood we have redemption, the forgiveness of all our sins.

And it is this blessing, the grace of God and our forgiveness, of which we are assured in the Sacrament of the Lord's Supper. This is stated by Christ in the words of institution: "Given and shed for you for the remission of sins." God assured the Israelites that the angel would pass over them if they sprinkled the blood of the lamb on their door-posts. He thus assured them of safety, of His love, grace, and mercy. In the Lord's Supper God assures us of forgiveness of our sins and that "there is no condemnation to them which are in Christ Jesus." In the Lord's Supper God says to every believing communicant: "You who have eaten My body and drunk My blood should now be absolutely sure that *you* have forgiveness of all your sins, that you have My love, grace, and mercy, that you are saved from the punishment of an eternal hell, and that you have life and salvation."

Again, let us remember that Israel was about to leave Egypt. The Passover strengthened the people for their journey through the wilderness. — Is not this a type of the strength our souls receive from the Lord's Supper? It strengthens our faith. On our journey through the wilderness of this world to eternity Satan will try to assail us with doubts concerning our forgiveness; but as often as we are guests at the Lord's Table, God assures us that our sins are forgiven. This repeated assurance cannot but strengthen our faith in the forgiveness of our sins through our Lord Jesus Christ. It will give us strength to strive against sin and to lead a godly life.

3.

The Passover is also a type of the salutary use of the Lord's Supper.

God gave Israel explicit instructions for the proper use of the Passover. V. 11 God commanded the people to eat the roasted lamb. They were not merely to look upon it or put it to superstitious use, but to eat it. — Neither are we to make a superstitious or idolatrous use of the Lord's Supper. (Adoration and Mass. A fortune-teller once offered ten dollars to a member of our Church for a Communion wafer with which to practise his nefarious trade.) We are to eat and drink the body and blood of Christ for the assurance of our forgiveness and the strengthening of our faith.

V. 14 God commanded Israel to keep the feast for a memorial, in commemoration of their deliverance from slavery in Egypt. — Christ says to us: "This do in remembrance of Me." In the Lord's Supper we believingly remember the great sacrifice of the true Paschal Lamb for our deliverance. If we believe what Christ says and commune with repenting and believing hearts, with faith in the promises made in the Sacrament, we receive all the great blessings. (The true worthiness of a communicant.)

Again, v. 14 God commanded the children of Israel to keep the Passover throughout their generations. — How typical of the Lord's

'Supper! (1 Cor. 11, 26.) This Sacrament should be celebrated by the Christians until Christ comes to judge the world. And Christ says: "This do as often," etc. Christians should commune frequently. See Christian Questions, Nos. 19 and 20.

V. 11 God instructs Israel to be fully equipped for the departure from the land of oppression and standing to eat the lamb. Israel did accordingly and was ready to leave. — Thus we, too, must partake of the Lord's Supper with the good and earnest purpose to forsake sin and to amend our sinful lives.

Lastly the Passover was instituted by God for Israel only, God's chosen people. No stranger was to join in the celebration, v. 43. — Christ instituted the Lord's Supper "for us Christians to eat and to drink." Notorious, impenitent sinners, heterodox, etc., are excluded from communing with us. (Close Communion, 1 Cor. 11, 27—29.) How conscientious must we, then, be in administering it!

If we thus use the Lord's Supper, we make a salutary use of it. May we treasure this Sacrament, etc.!   A. JORDAN.

Good Friday.
Is. 53.

To-day the attention of Christians through the world is directed toward Calvary. Some say that it was a skull-shaped elevation without the wall of Jerusalem. But it is not its location nor its peculiar shape that rivets our attention upon Calvary. It is the event that occurred there during that memorable Passion week, when Jesus of Nazareth was crucified. Every true Good Friday sermon to-day points to Calvary and proclaims: "Behold the Lamb of God, which taketh away the sin of the world."

It is one of the marvelous features of this great event on Calvary that we to-day, after the passing of nineteen centuries, with the aid of the Holy Spirit, have a more comprehensive view and understanding of it than those had who were eye-witnesses to the crucifixion. We understand its sorrow and its glory much better than the multitude which surrounded the cross of Christ on Calvary. But do you know that even before, long before, the actual occurrence there were men who with the eye of faith beheld the crucifixion of Christ? That vision was granted also to men who looked forward to it in the light of prophecy. Isaiah, in the 53d chapter of his book of prophecy, speaks of the death of the Savior and its significance in such a comprehensive and understanding manner that one not familiar with the facts would think the prophet had stood with John and Mary at the foot of the cross or mingled with the crowd that surrounded it. The eunuch of Ethiopia therefore thought Isaiah must be describing an event of his own experience or one to which he had been an eye-witness.

From olden times this chapter of Isaiah has been read in the Christian Church on the anniversary of the Savior's death. Let us to-day worship our Savior and strengthen our faith in Him by a devout meditation based upon this "Old Testament Passion-story," which presents to us —

Isaiah's Vision of Calvary.

Isaiah beholds —

1. Its Awful Solemnity;   *2. Its Transcending Glory.*

1.

Since the day when Adam and Eve brought the curse of sin upon themselves and all future generations, since Abel became the victim of his wicked brother's cudgel, tragedies have been enacted every day. If all the tragedies of mankind could be crowded into the lifetime of one man, no human being could endure them. Yet Isaiah in his vision of Calvary beholds One upon whom has been heaped all the suffering of the world, who is enduring the sum of all human tortures in a few hours.

Who is this person so smitten? "Of whom speaketh the prophet this?" is the question which the eunuch asked, Acts 8, 34. He is a tender plant; a root out of dry ground; one who hath no form or comeliness, v. 2. Isaiah had previously prophesied concerning the coming of this person: "And there shall come forth a rod out of the stem of Jesse," Is. 11, 1. Jesus, the Crucified, was a descendant of Jesse and David. But that once prominent royal family had lost all its prestige. The mighty family tree had been cut down, and only a dead stump was left. Jesus was born amidst poverty and lowliness. There was nothing in His appearance which seemed to distinguish Him from any of the other lowly and poverty-stricken of the land. Now Isaiah beholds a descendant of the mighty king David hanging on the accursed tree of the cross in the shadow of the city which was once His forefather's royal residence.

Furthermore, Isaiah sees the Crucified as one who was despised and rejected of men, from whom men hid their faces in disgust, v. 3. Think of the contempt in which Jesus was held by the leaders of the Jews throughout His ministry. Think of the manner in which He was treated by the mob which took Him captive in Gethsemane, by Annas, Caiaphas, and the Sanhedrin. Remember how the Roman soldiers mocked Him when they blindfolded and struck Him in the face and how they blasphemously pretended to worship Him. After the Savior had been nailed to the cross, the chief priests, scribes, and elders, the thieves who were crucified with Him, and the multitude which witnessed this awful spectacle on Calvary "reviled Him, railed on Him, wagging their heads and saying, Ah, Thou that destroyest the Temple and buildest it in three days, save Thyself."

Not only does Isaiah hear these expressions of contempt, but he sees the agony engraved upon the countenance of the Savior. The Crucified bore griefs and carried sorrow. He was stricken, smitten, and afflicted; He was wounded, bruised, and chastised. Stripes were inflicted upon Him, vv. 4. 5. From the time when He was manhandled by the mob in Gethsemane until He expired He suffered unspeakable tortures and agony in His body. The servants struck Him in the face. The platted thorns were driven into His brow with a rod. His bare back was lacerated with the dreaded Roman scourge. The heavy timbers of the cross rested upon His mangled back. The nails which held Him to the cross pierced His hands and feet, adding to the already excruciating pains, which increased in intensity until the climax was reached and He said, "It is finished," and, commending His spirit into the hands of His Father, bowed His head in death.

It was not, however, only a suffering in body that the Crucified endured. He made His soul an offering for sin, v. 10. His suffering included the travail of His soul, v. 11, and this suffering was even greater than that which He endured in His body. His suffering began in Gethsemane when His soul was "exceeding sorrowful, even unto death." The sneers of contempt of His accusers and judges, the deceitfulness of Judas, the Jews, Pilate, and Herod, and the denial and flight of His disciples caused the Savior anguish of soul throughout His Passion. The experience of man is that mental anguish and suffering of the soul may become more terrible than physical pain. The entire suffering of the Savior reached its climax when His soul experienced the tortures of the depths of hell, which caused Him to exclaim: "My God, My God, why hast Thou forsaken Me?" No human being on earth can imagine such agony or fathom such horror.

As man views this spectacle on Calvary, Jesus suffering the punishment which is accorded the lowest type of criminals, and sees Him numbered among the transgressors, v. 12, he draws the conclusion: Jesus must be suffering the curse and punishment of His iniquity. Man esteems Him stricken, smitten of God, and afflicted, v. 4, as a retribution for evil deeds. But Isaiah knows that all accusations made against the divine Sufferer were false, that He had not deserved this punishment, that He was suffering innocently the tortures heaped upon Him. He had done no violence, neither was any deceit in His mouth, v. 9. He was a righteous Servant, v. 11. During His life His greatest enemies could not convict Him of a single sin. Although the accusations had been manifold and bitter, His judges, Pilate and

Herod, confessed publicly that they found no fault in Him. The penitent thief on the cross confessed it as his belief that Jesus had done nothing amiss. Even the captain of the guard whose ghastly work it had been to crucify Jesus confessed: "Certainly this was a righteous man and the Son of God."

Man usually resents any indignities and any suffering which he must bear innocently. The convicted criminal goes to the electric chair scowlingly, even if he has fully deserved his fate. But Isaiah beholds the Christ enduring all this suffering with unparalleled patience. "He was oppressed, and He was afflicted; yet He opened not His mouth. He is brought as a lamb to the slaughter, and as a sheep before her shearers is dumb, so He opened not His mouth," v. 7. "When He was reviled, He reviled not again; when He suffered, He threatened not," 1 Pet. 2, 23. No word that indicated the slightest trace of anger passed His lips during the entire ordeal. There was no attempt at revenge. With calmness and self-possession did He bear it all. Rather did He pray for His tormentors: "Father, forgive them; for they know not what they do." Was there ever such patience and meekness as this?

Any hardships and suffering endured voluntarily for another commands our highest respect and sympathy. Judah was willing to become a slave or to suffer any punishment in order that his brother Benjamin might return home to his father. A loving mother will endure danger and hardships, even give her life, for her child. But how insignificant are such sacrifices when compared with the substitutional suffering of Jesus on Calvary! Throughout the chapter Isaiah emphasizes the fact that this suffering of Jesus was done for others, vv. 4. 5. 6. 8. 11. 12.

We say it was the bitter hatred of the Jews, the unjust sentence of an unscrupulous judge, and the cruelty of barbarian soldiers that caused the intense suffering and ignominious death of Jesus. Through these human agencies Jesus suffered the desperate assaults of the forces of hell. But man and the devil were not the final cause of the suffering and death of Jesus. It had been decreed from eternity by God Himself. So it is understood by Isaiah. He says: "The Lord hath laid on Him the iniquity of us all," v. 6. "It pleased the Lord to bruise Him; He hath put Him to grief," v. 10. It was God's decision that Jesus should suffer and die in order that His unfathomable counsel of love and mercy for the salvation of the human race might be accomplished, John 3, 16; Gal. 4, 4; 2 Cor. 5, 21. Did we not know that it pleased the Lord that Jesus should endure the suffering and death on Calvary in order that His gracious purpose to redeem the world might be accomplished, we should be bewildered and perplexed; for it would be utterly impossible for us to understand the tragedy

on Calvary. But knowing God's eternal purpose which He purposed
in Christ Jesus, our Lord, Eph. 3, 11, — though God's wisdom, counsel,
and grace are still beyond our understanding, — we glorify and praise
His boundless mercy and love manifested on Calvary. And therein
lies *its transcending glory.*

2.

The transcending glory of Christ's suffering is so intimately
fused with the tragedy that Isaiah sees both from the beginning
to the end in his vision. Constantly he has in mind the glorious
purpose and the blessed fruit of the crucifixion.

Isaiah again and again calls attention to the fact that the suffering and death of Jesus was of a substitutional nature. But why
was it necessary? It was because "all we like sheep have gone
astray; we have turned every one to his own way," v. 6. "All we,"
the entire human race, had strayed away from our Lord and God.
Instead of obeying the will and doing the pleasure of God, every
one had gone his own way, the way of separation from God, the way
of transgressions and iniquities. These transgressions and iniquities
brought upon us God's wrath and curse. Punishment is the inevitable consequence of transgression. We had fully deserved, and
were subject to, grief, sorrow, and chastisement. Sin is the cause
of all suffering, all sorrow, all tribulation, and pain in the world.
But all the suffering in this world is not sufficient to satisfy the
demands of God's holiness and justice. Sin had separated man from
God and had brought upon him the everlasting condemnation of
God and the punishment of hell.

But the grace of God that bringeth salvation hath appeared to all
men. "The Lord hath laid on Him the iniquity of us all," v. 6.
"Surely He hath borne our griefs and carried our sorrows. . . . But
He was wounded for our transgressions, He was bruised for our iniquities," vv. 4. 5. Look, then, toward Calvary and behold the Lamb
of God, which taketh away the sin of the world. All the suffering and
pain, the wounds, and the unutterable anguish of soul which Jesus
endured He assumed voluntarily that the wrath of God might be
appeased, that our punishment might be taken from us, that our sins
might be forgiven, that we might have peace with God and become
heirs of eternal life.

Isaiah knows that the purpose for which the Savior suffered and
died was fully accomplished. The offering which He made for our
sins was accepted by God; and accepting the sacrifice, God has turned
from His wrath and has forgiven our transgressions and iniquities.
"With His stripes we are healed," v. 5. Although the sacrifice was yet
to be made at the time when Isaiah spoke these words, he sees its
purpose achieved, and he accepts it as an accomplished fact. In His
supreme battle with sin and the devil Christ won a glorious victory.

Even the burial of Jesus foreshadowed His victory and glory. "And He [Am. R. V.: They] made His grave with the wicked and with the rich [Am. R. V.: a rich man] in His death," v. 9. Usually a dishonorable burial was accorded criminals. The Jews undoubtedly intended to give Jesus such an unceremonious burial. But God thwarted the design of the enemies and caused Nicodemus and Joseph of Arimathea, two honorable and wealthy men, to take charge of the body of Jesus and give it an honorable burial in Joseph's own tomb. But even an honorable tomb could not hold Him. "He was taken from prison and from judgment; and who shall declare His generation?" V. 8. The prison which the Savior had entered voluntarily to bear the punishment for the sins of men opened its doors. The judgment of God upon sinners had been satisfied, and He returned to the Father to be glorified also according to His human nature with the glory which He had together with the Father before the world began, John 17, 5. This was possible only because He had done no violence and there was no deceit in His mouth, v. 9 (text). Because He was without sin, He was able to take upon Himself the sin of the world. Because He who was made the Propitiation for our sins is God's own Son, He was able to bear the eternal punishment which the sinners had deserved and emerge gloriously as the Victor.

Finally Isaiah speaks of the blessed fruit of the sacrifice which the Son of God brought on Calvary. "He shall see His seed, He shall prolong His days, and the pleasure of the Lord shall prosper in His hand," v. 10. God Himself pronounces His "Well done, Thou good and faithful Servant," His "Amen," upon the glorious work of redemption. "By His knowledge shall My righteous Servant justify many. Therefore will I divide Him a portion with the great, and He shall divide the spoil with the strong," vv. 11. 12.

Though the focus of Isaiah's vision is Calvary, the vision extends far beyond, and merging with the vision St. John, the Seer, reaches the eternal throne of God. He sees an endless procession of sinners coming to the foot of the cross, there to cast down the burden of their sins and to be cleansed by the blood of Jesus Christ; then passing on to the eternal throne of the exalted Savior, giving glory to Him and saying: "Thou art worthy to take the book and to open the seals thereof. For Thou wast slain and hast redeemed us to God with Thy blood out of every kindred, and tongue, and people, and nation. Worthy is the Lamb that was slain to receive power, and riches, and wisdom, and strength, and honor, and glory, and blessing. Blessing, and honor, and glory, and power be unto Him that sitteth upon the throne and unto the Lamb forever and ever! Rev. 5, 9—12. 13. Amen.

OTTO C. MUELLER.

Ascension Day.

Psalm 47.

Ascension Day rightfully belongs to the festivals of joy in the calendar of the church-year. It is one of those sparkling gems in the ring of Christian festivals. Christmas proclaims "tidings of great joy." Easter declares in unmistakable language the message of triumphant victory which banishes every semblance of fear and sorrow. Pentecost, with its visible evidence of the outpouring of the Holy Spirit, resulting in that great transformation of cowardly disciples into fearless and heroic confessors of the crucifixion and resurrection of Christ for the redemption and justification of sinners, surely radiates genuine joy. Even Good Friday, with its terrors and darkness, has the bright lining of Christ's shout of triumph: "It is finished," and His lordly and majestic manner of dying to bring joy to the hearts of those who ascend Calvary's gloomy crest. To-day the Church rivets her eyes upon the ascending Lord, who after the completion of His momentous task ascended according to His human nature into the fullest use of divine majesty, yes, to be crowned amidst triumph and rejoicing of the heavenly hosts as Lord of lords. Bearing these things in mind, let us study the prophetic description of —

The Joy of God's People at the Coronation of Christ.

1. *Thereby He Entered upon the Majestic Reign over His Glorious Kingdom;*
2. *Thereby the Extension of His Marvelous Kingdom is Assured.*

1.

The psalm unquestionably invites unto jubilant joy and unbounded praise. The "clapping of hands" and the "shouting" with their voices indicate rapturous and tumultuous happiness. It was the Oriental way of expressing deep emotions of joy which could not be suppppressed. Undoubtedly the psalmist finds cause for such unbridled ecstasy in a very definite occurrence. Some suppose that he referred to deliverance from threatening destruction at the hands of Sennacherib's numerous and superior hosts. However, as McLaren puts it, the psalm "rises to prophetic foresight and by reason of a comparatively small historical occasion has a vision of the world-wide expansion of the kingdom of God." We need not surmise and guess. The psalmist mentions the reason for such a rapturous outburst of praise and exultation when he declares: "God is gone up with a shout, the Lord with the sound of a trumpet." He foresees the Messiah, who was always the center of prophetic joy, ascending on high "with a shout," and with the "sound of a trumpet." Note again that these expressions emphasize spontaneous outbursts of joy and praise.

The ascension of Christ is predicated upon His descension. The apostle states: "He that descended is the same also that ascended far above all heavens that He might fill all things." He asks: "Now, that He ascended, what is it but that He also descended first into the lower parts of the earth?" Eph. 4, 9. 10. He had come to earth for the express purpose of establishing His glorious kingdom and had filled the hearts of God's faithful people with fervent hope and intense longing and expectancy, Is. 9, 7; Jer. 23, 5—6, etc. This necessitated that Christ must overcome the hellish Foe, who had now become the "prince of this world," John 14, 30; "the ruler of the darkness of this world," Eph. 6, 12; "the prince of the power of the air," Eph. 2, 2, who had "the power of death" and was able to hold mankind in constant fear because he had subjected them unto this fearful bondage, Heb. 2, 14. The very first prophecy concerning the coming Messiah, Gen. 3, 15, foretold of the fearful combat which would take place between Christ and the devil, a fight to the hilt, a battle for possession. When the Redeemer appeared on earth, the devil sought to destroy the "new-born King of the Jews," Matt. 2, 16; for that blood-curdling slaughter of the innocents at Bethlehem could not have been conceived anywhere else than in the regions of hell. Again, when Jesus began His active ministry, the devil for forty days put forth every effort to frustrate the plan of God for the salvation of mankind and the establishment of the Kingdom by merciless onslaughts in the wilderness, Matt. 4, 1—11. Note also how often the demons of hell opposed Christ during His active ministry. When He entered upon His unparalleled suffering and death, Jesus understood full well that the battle would now rage in fiercest fury and that it would mean either the establishment of His kingdom or the continuation of the kingdom of Satan, John 14, 30.

Calvary's declaration of triumph from the lips of the conquering Combatant: "It is finished," to be followed on the third day by His victorious resurrection, corroborating every claim which Jesus had ever made, convinces us that He who had come to fight our battle for us in order that He might establish His kingdom and rule over us had accomplished every detail of His enormous task. We know that He employed the forty days after His resurrection to give final instructions to the heralds of His kingdom so that the work might go on after His ascension.

After everything had been completed, He was ready to return unto the Father, who had sent Him. Emphasize that also the human nature now entered upon the fullest use of divine majesty and glory. Such a thing was never known prior to this, that "our brother," "flesh of our flesh," should "go up with a shout and with the sound of the trumpet" to be "the King of all the earth, v. 7, and to "sit upon the throne of His holiness," v. 8. This, however, happened when the God-man Christ Jesus after His crucifixion and resurrection ascended on high, Luke 24, 51; Acts 1, 9, to sit at the right hand of God, Eph. 1, 20, and to take full control of the reigns of government. Cf. Ps. 110; Jer. 23, 5 f.; Luke 1, 33; John 18, 33—37; Eph. 1, 20—24; Acts 2, 36; 1 Cor. 8, 6; 2 Cor. 4, 5; Phil. 2, 11. With joyous acclaim the hosts of heaven greeted and welcomed the returning Conqueror. That accounts for the jubilation, the sounding of the trumpet, the going up with a shout, the exhortation to praise God, the clapping of hands, of which the psalmist speaks.

2.

The prophetic vision of the triumphant ascension embodies also the session. These two events are combined also in Mark 16, 19. One followed immediately upon the other.

The ascension, like unto the other features of Christ's exaltation, are to serve not merely for His glorification, but also for our benefit. Keep in mind the thought of His reign in the Kingdom which the psalmist emphasizes in vv. 2. 6. 7. 8. 9. The Jews, even the faithful disciples, entertained utterly false conceptions of this kingdom. They expected Christ to establish an earthly throne, John 6, 15; Luke 17, 20; Acts 1, 6, etc. The ascension, which included the withdrawal of His visible presence, disillusioned the disciples. They never asked such a question again, but realized that Christ's kingdom is spiritual. What a lesson for chiliasts!

The psalmist foresaw the tremendous power of the King. "He is a great King over all the earth," v. 2; "God is King of all the earth," v. 7; "for the shields of the earth belong unto God; He is greatly exalted," v. 9. Note also "the Lord most high is terrible." This holds true of Christ, Eph. 1, 22. 23. — The Church is safe under His wonderful protection. Nothing can withstand Him. Cf. John 10, 28; Matt. 16, 18; 1 Pet. 3, 22; Num. 23, 23; Is. 54, 17.

The real power of the Kingdom, however, is the Word, the Gospel, John 18, 19; Rom. 1, 16; Jer. 5, 14; 23, 29; Eph. 6, 17; Luke 2, 15. Heb. 4, 12. Thereby He subdues the people, v. 3. This is the power of divine persuasion, not of compulsion by His omnipotence. The entire work of the Christian Church, performed without armies, or navies or air forces, without earthly weapons or ammunition, without any temporal force whatsoever, merely by the proclamation of the truth, the preaching of the Gospel, bears witness to the marvelous efficacy of the Word. Whenever the Church resorted to the full use of the Word, it accomplished great things in the Kingdom; whenever it resorted to the use of temporal power, coercion, legislation, etc., it grew weak.

The prophetic seer beheld the vision of the kingdom as it extended beyond the boundaries of Israel. It should include both the Jew and the Gentile, vv. 4. 8. 9. In fact, it would extend over all the earth, v. 7. Since the ascension the work has been carried on effectively, and the King has been adding more and more people from all nations of the earth to citizenship in His wonderful kingdom.

"Sing ye praise with understanding." The deeper we enter upon an intelligent study of the fact and significance of Christ's ascension and session, the more fervently and intelligently shall we desire to sing praises unto our King. Hymn 235, 1.   J. W. BEHNKEN.

St. Michael and All Angels.
Psalm 103, 20. 21.

Sad to say, even we Christians must be constantly urged to bless the holy name of the Lord. — Just as slow as we are to glorify His name, so slow we are also to obey Him, to give heed to His Word. We should be servants who serve Him gladly, but we so often forget our high calling, and as a result our service of the Most High is sadly neglected.

There are, however, beings who do bless the name of the Lord joyfully and who follow His commandments with a will. By nature our will is not one with the Lord's will. Yes, even the will of the Christian is not obedient to the Lord's will as it should be. But there are beings, spirits, who need not be stirred up to bless His holy name, who do His holy will with joy. The angels are not beset with our frailties, and so when they raise their voices in praise, they do it with unmixed adoration of their Lord; and when they do His will, they do so without reluctance of any kind. The angels of the Lord, this powerful host, these invisible beings, are servants of the Lord who are perfect in their obedience and are unwearied in their praise of His holy name.

Strange to say, many people are inclined to doubt the existence of the holy angels of God, just as they doubt the existence of the devil and his angels. So the Sadducees at the time of Christ, and so to-day many modern theologians. Cf. Acts 23, 8. Yet it is a clear doctrine of the Bible that there are angels, holy angels, of the Lord, who are His ministers. And there is much comfort for the Christian in the thought that these ministers of the Lord are close to him, guarding and keeping him and finally carrying his soul into heaven. Although the doctrine of the angels is not a cardinal doctrine of the Bible, yet to deny the existence of the angels is not only a grievous sin, because thereby one contradicts the Word of God; but the neglect of this doctrine also robs us of very precious comfort. Our Church has therefore set aside a day for its study. For to-day I have chosen a very impressive text, which speaks to us of —

The Holy Angels of the Lord.

Let us from this text learn: —

1. *How the Holy Angels are Constituted;*
2. *How They are Employed.*

1.

In our text the angels are called "His angels," that is, angels of the Lord. They are therefore creatures which the Lord has created, beings which owe their existence to Him. The angels are not from eternity, as God is. On what day they were created we do not know. At some time, however, during the six days of creation the Lord called them into being. Being creatures, the angels are not to be adored, or worshiped. To worship angels is idolatry. Matt. 4, 10 we read: "Thou shalt worship the Lord, thy God, and Him only shalt thou serve." The angels themselves reject the adoration of man. Cf. Rev. 19, 10; 22, 8. 9. To pray to angels would furthermore be useless, since they are not omniscient nor almighty.

Together with the evil angels, the angels of the Lord are the handiwork of God. The evil angels however did not keep their first habitation, but rebelled against the Lord, who had created them, Jude 6. At the dawn of creation they all stood holy, sinless, before the throne of God. But whereas the evil angels fell away from God, the good angels abode with Him; they remained faithful to their Maker. And since they abode with the Lord, their will has remained one with the Lord's will. They are holy, without sin of any kind. They do not, as man so often does, turn a deaf ear to the Lord when He speaks; but they hearken to the voice of His word. It is the joy of the holy angels to hear the voice of the Lord and to heed it. They need in no way be urged to hear this word and to obey it. In no way do they feel any disinclination to follow the will of the Lord. Their will is in perfect accord with the will of their Maker.

The angels are spirits and as such invisible. Neither have they flesh and blood, Luke 24, 39. At times, however, God has allowed them to appear to men. With what kind of body they appeared to men it is idle to speculate. Angels appeared to Abraham, to Lot, to Zacharias, to Mary, to the prophets, to the women at the grave of Christ, to the disciples on the mount of ascension, to the shepherds at Bethlehem, etc. The angels ate with Lot when he made a meal for them. The angels have spoken with men.

One characteristic of the holy angels, which is brought out in our text, is that they are of great power. It is said of them that they excel in strength. They even have the power, given them of God, to perform supernatural things. They appear and disappear. They did this at the birth of Christ. The angel Gabriel appeared to

ST. MICHAEL AND ALL ANGELS.

Zacharias and Mary, and having delivered his message, he disappeared again. The angels are mightier than men are; they are mightier than the armies of men. They protected Lot against the rage of the men of Sodom. The angel of the Lord slew 185,000 men in the army of Sennacherib and caused that Assyrian king to abandon his siege of Jerusalem, 2 Kings 19, 35. Wild beasts have no power against them, as is shown when the angel of the Lord held shut the mouth of the lions, so that they could do Daniel no harm. They are able to unlock doors, to loose fetters, as was done by the angel who led Peter out of prison, Acts 12, 7—11. Cf. also Acts 5, 19. But all that they do they do by power conferred by God; they are not omnipresent nor omniscient. Ps. 72, 18. The power of the good angels is, however, never used for an evil purpose, as is the case with the evil angels, who strive only to destroy the works of God. They are also swift, carrying out the Lord's commands with speed, Dan. 9, 21.

As our Catechism states, the holy angels are confirmed in their bliss. Christ describes the holy angels as being holy angels still on the Day of Judgment, Matt. 24, 31. They, then, stand in no need of a Savior, as man does.

The angels are of great number. Scriptures speak of thousand thousands of angels, of legions of angels, of the heavenly host, of the innumerable company of angels. Cf. Heb. 12, 22. Names of angels are mentioned in Scripture, as Gabriel, Michael. Orders of the angels are: cherubim, seraphim, the archangel, etc. Like a well-organized army they are at the call of the Lord at all times. Cherubim and seraphim fall down before Him and worship Him and await His commands with joy and eagerness. When His voice sounds forth, they post over land and sea, faithful messengers of the King of kings.

2.

Being servants of the Lord, the angels have an occupation. In the text we read: "Bless the Lord, ye His angels." The holy angels need no encouragement in this, however, for they stand before the throne of God praising Him day and night. Thus did Daniel see the Lord in a vision on His throne and all the heavenly host worshiping Him, Dan. 7, 9. 10. At Bethlehem the hosts of heaven chanted forth the wonderful praises of God. Down through the ages their message has come to us: "Glory to God in the highest, and on earth peace, good will toward men." In a vision Isaiah saw the Lord upon His throne and heard the seraphim crying one to another: "Holy, holy, holy, is the Lord of hosts; the whole earth is full of His glory." And in Ps. 148 we read: "Praise ye Him, all His angels; praise ye Him, all His hosts."

The angels furthermore do the commandments of the Lord. And

they do His commandments not partially, but fully. Daniel saw how thousand thousands ministered unto the Lord. Gabriel tells Zacharias that the Lord had sent him to tell him those glad tidings, Luke 1, 19. After Jesus had victoriously resisted the temptations of the devil, behold, angels came and ministered unto Him. Again, when Jesus wrestled in prayer in the garden of Gethsemane, an angel came from heaven and strengthened Him.

The angels do the pleasure of the Lord especially when they serve mankind, above all, when they serve the Christians. In Ps. 34 we read: "The angel of the Lord encampeth round about them that fear Him and delivereth them." Heb. 1, 14 it is stated of them: "Are they not all ministering spirits, sent forth to minister for them who shall be heirs of salvation?" And in Ps. 91 the Christian has the comforting assurance that the Lord shall give His angels charge over him to keep him in all his ways. The angels, then, guard and keep the Christian so that no harm shall befall him. They often warn the Christian against danger and temptations. When Joseph was minded to leave Mary, the angel of the Lord urged him to take Mary unto himself as his wife and not to withdraw himself from her. Again, the angel warns Joseph to flee to Egypt since king Herod was seeking to kill the Child. Later on he reveals to Joseph that Herod is dead and that he should return to the land of Israel. Angels led Lot and his family out of the city of Sodom when that city was doomed. To assure Jacob that the Lord was with him the angels of God met him when he was on his way to Esau, and he exclaimed: "This is God's host." The same Jacob in a dream saw the angels of God ascending and descending the ladder which reached from earth to heaven. When Abraham sent his servant that he take a wife for Isaac from the kindred of his master and the servant was skeptical as to the outcome of his mission, Abraham said to him: "The Lord God of heaven shall send His angel before thee." It was an angel that led Peter out of prison. It was an angel that appeared to Cornelius and told him to send to Joppa for Simon Peter, who would tell him what he ought to do.

Angels take a great interest in the preaching of the Gospel and in the affairs of the kingdom of God. Stephen says that the Jews received the Law by the disposition of angels, Acts 7, 53, and in Gal. 3, 19 we read that the Law was ordained by angels in the hand of a mediator. The angels proclaimed the coming of the Messiah, who was to fulfil the Law and to liberate mankind from the curse of the Law. Angels were present at the resurrection of Christ and also at His ascension into heaven. In both instances they proclaimed wonderful news to the disciples and comforted their sorrowing hearts. The angels are present at the assemblies of the Christians, 1 Cor. 11, 10. They rejoice whenever a sinner comes to repentance, Luke 15.

On the Day of Judgment the angels will come with the Son of Man. The Lord shall send His angels with the great sound of a trumpet, and they shall gather together His elect from the four winds, from one end of heaven to the other, Matt. 13, 41; 24, 31. On that day the angels shall come forth and shall sever the wicked from the just, Matt. 13, 49. Angels carry the soul of the departed Christians into heaven, Luke 16, 22. The archangel Michael disputed with the devil about the body of Moses, which would seem to indicate that the angels keep watch over the graves of the Christians.

Who can be assured of the watchful care of the angels? In Ps. 34, 7 we read that the angel of the Lord encampeth round about them that fear Him, that is, the Lord. Therefore a Christian may only then comfort himself with the thought that angels are guarding him when he is walking in the ways of his duty as a Christian. In all other cases the word applies: "Thou shalt not tempt the Lord, thy God."

What should this doctrine of the angels of the Lord teach us? We should remember that the angels of God see every action we perform; hence we should fear to do evil before their pure eyes. By a wicked, godless life we drive the angels from us. Again, if a person does not fear the Lord, he cannot depend upon the guarding care of the angels. Furthermore, the presence of the angels in our services should induce us to conduct ourselves in a decent manner in the house of God, paying devout attention to that which is read and preached in the service. And since angels protect the children of God, we should be careful that we do not offend any child of God. Again, the conduct of the angels, their devotion to their Maker, should be an example to us. As they do the will of their Lord in heaven willingly and joyfully, so should we do His will here upon earth. As they are zealous in building the kingdom of Christ, so should we cheerfully and diligently engage in this work.

We should thank the Lord that He has given us His angels to guard and keep us. And if the angels have all cause to praise God, how much more have we cause to do so who are the redeemed of the Lord! Cf. 1 Pet. 1, 11. 12. What a comfort finally that the angels of God are with us in the last hour, ready to carry us home to the mansions of our Savior. If we are downcast, if the outlook in the kingdom of God is not very bright, let us remember that we do not stand alone. And may we with a devout heart pray every morning and evening: Heavenly Father, let Thy holy angel be with me that the wicked Foe may have no power over me. Amen.   P. SCHUMM.

Reformation Festival.
John 8, 31—36.

With praise and thanksgiving let us celebrate this year's Reformation Festival. The strokes of the hammer nailing the Ninety-five Theses, or sentences, to the church-door of Wittenberg resounded not only throughout all of Europe, but they were heard in other countries as well, and even to-day, after 418 years, they cause hearts to rejoice and to sing hymns of praise and thanksgiving to God for the blessings derived therefrom. The nailing of these Ninety-five Theses was the beginning of the Reformation, the first rays of a rising sun to usher in truth and liberty. To-day Christians assembled in their houses of worship, hearing again what great things God through the Reformation has done for us, seriously consider what all this meant for the true visible Church on earth. Luther, the great Reformer, brought the truth to light again and, with the truth, real liberty. Truth, liberty, what glorious words! Who does not strive and strain to secure and maintain these? Truth, liberty, are here used in the highest sense of these words. Christ says to His disciples: "If ye continue in My Word, then are ye My disciples indeed; and ye shall know the truth, and the truth shall make you free." He only has the truth, and remains in the truth, who has and remains with Christ's Word, and he only who has the truth, and remains with the truth, has and enjoys real liberty. This fact we clearly and distinctly see in the work of the Reformation. On the basis of our text let me speak to you to-day of —

Bondage and Liberty.

1. *Of Bondage wherever the Truth Is Missing;*
2. *Of Liberty which the Truth Brings.*

1.

Jesus in our text is speaking to the Jews which believed on Him, vv. 31 32. These people had the truth and were free, but did not understand the words of their Lord and Master and therefore asked: v. 33. Jesus explains: v. 34. Whosoever committeth sin is the servant of sin, is not free. He is a servant; he serves sin. He who serves sin does not know what liberty truly is. He is in bondage, in slavery. Sin rules over him, has dominion over him. That it is against which the Lord warns His followers. Continue in My Word, and ye shall know the truth ever better and be freed from the dominion of sin.

How necessary this warning and instruction of the Lord was history teaches sufficiently. As the years rolled by, the hearing and reading of God's Word was neglected, counted less and less, became of small importance, superfluous, and finally it was even forbidden to have and read the Bible in the home. And with the loss of the truth, darkness, bondage, and slavery filled the whole land. Emperors and kings became slaves; they feared to call down upon themselves the displeasure of the one who claimed alone to have the power and right to rule on earth. Officers and soldiers were afraid because they did not know the truth. Business men and laborers were under the rule of another. Priests did not dare to confess the truth without loosing their office. Yea, even in the homes bondage and darkness ruled. When a pious young man or a chaste virgin had the desire to enter holy wedlock, they were sent to the priest and had to confess their intentions to him and were often sent into the cloister. People who were troubled about their sins had to pay a fine in money. Those who were on their death-bed did not get to hear the truth "Repent and believe in the Lord Jesus Christ," and the angels will carry your soul into Abraham's bosom; but they were told that they would have to enter purgatory, where they would have to suffer until the mourning survivors would have seen to it that enough masses were read for them and had paid sufficient fees for an indulgence, and that thus after a long chastisement they would probably enter heaven.

Thus we could continue to speak of the darkness and wretched bondage. However, this will suffice. Where God's Word, the truth, is missing, there is bondage and darkness in the land, in the home, in the church. He who serves sin is the servant of sin. He who has not the truth is made a fool of by deceivers.

Luther, the sincere monk, in his despair looked and searched for truth. He found a Bible, but did not know the Bible. This Book was different from other books, and secretly he diligently studied it. He found the truth. "The just shall live by his faith," Hab. 2, 4. This quieted his troubled conscience, but as yet he did not know the whole truth. He continued his studies; the darkness disappeared more and more. What at first he could hardly believe the same Scriptures confirmed again and again, not only in one passage, but in many, e. g., Rom. 1, 17; 3, 28; Gal. 2, 16. 17. The Holy Ghost was working through the Word in his heart. Luther experienced the transforming power of the Gospel in his own heart. He experienced that the Gospel "is the power of God unto salvation to every one that believeth." Rom. 1, 16. With this knowledge of truth, he found liberty, liberty from the ordinances of man, liberty from sin, death, and the devil. Christ says: v. 36. If the Son of God makes us free, we are free indeed.

Thus Luther took courage to nail the truth which he had found and which had made him free in short, clear sentences to the church-door of Wittenberg to defend the same. He wanted to do his part as a soldier on the battle-field of his Lord, but never dreamed that God had chosen him to be the leader or captain to bring the truth to light again. Where God's Word does not reign, there is nothing but darkness and bondage; *the truth, however, brings liberty.*

2.

Jesus said to the Jews who believed on Him: vv. 31. 32. The Jews did not have the right understanding of these words and therefore asked: vv. 33—36. Jesus is speaking of the liberty which He Himself was to gain for them by His perfect obedience, suffering, death, and resurrection and now has won for us. This liberty becomes ours through faith. Faith, however, is wrought by the Holy Ghost through the means of the Word of God. Only if we continue in Jesus' Word, in the Word of God, we shall know the truth, and this truth which comes by the knowledge of the Word of God alone makes us free. Only he who believes in the Son of God, the Redeemer from sin, death, and the devil, is truly free.

By the grace of God we have learned this Word of God, most of us from our youth, and I hope to God that we all know the Son who really makes us free. But do we realize and appreciate what this means? Is this truth a treasure we would not lose for anything in the world? Or do we think lightly of it? Do we imagine that, because it has always been so during our lifetime that we could hear the truth without interference and were permitted to read the Bible in our homes and to instruct our children and have them instructed in the Word of God, it will always remain thus? Do we feel secure? Is there no danger, if we do not value this grace of God as highly as we should and do not defend the truth which makes us free nor use it deligently, if we do not watch and pray, that it might be taken from us, our country, and our children? Should there be such among us as say with the Jews: We always had the truth, we are the seed of Abraham, have never been in bondage to any man; how do you say: "Ye shall be made free"? v. 33.

The devil, with his evil spirits, always was and always will remain an enemy of the truth. Where he takes the truth away, there is nothing but darkness, and in the darkness he reigns with the evil spirits under heaven. He is never idle, but goeth about seeking to devour. And when those who have the truth and are free from his rule think themselves secure, become indifferent, do not watch and pray, the battle is half won for him. If he succeeds to take the Word of God, the truth, away, he has already won, there is no light from above, and he lords it over men, and they are his helpless slaves. "Verily," etc., v. 34.

We have already heard (in the first part) of the darkness and bondage everywhere, in state, home, and Church, where Antichrist ruled before the Reformation. God through his servant Luther brought light into this darkness. The truth became known, and by this truth thousands and thousands became free. They, and we with them, have found the Son, who indeed makes us free.

We, beloved hearers, are now enjoying the full blessings of the Reformation. And Jesus is to-day speaking to us through His Word (vv. 31. 32). Having obtained this precious liberty through the grace of our heavenly Liberator, let us awaken out of the sleep of indifference. "The old evil Foe now means deadly woe. Deep guile and great might Are his dread arms in fight; On earth is not his equal." "The Word they still shall let remain And not a thank have for it."

God grant us His Holy Spirit that we gratefully use the blessed fruit of the Reformation, and may He in His grace preserve it to us and our children!   O. C. J. KELLER.

Day of Repentance and Prayer.
Lam. 3, 40. 41.

Jeremiah weeping over Jerusalem, what a touching spectacle! The city once so glorious, chosen of God as His earthly abode, now trodden under foot, its Temple destroyed, its palaces consumed, its walls broken down, its strong men slain, its children dead of famine, its survivors led away into shameful captivity. All that because Jerusalem had grievously sinned, chap. 4, 11—16. Hence Jeremiah exhorts his countrymen not to complain because of the punishment, but to search and try their ways and turn again to the Lord.

God has visited our country also, yea, the whole world, in His wrath by a general depression and disturbance. The cause of that is sin, the sins of the nations, the sins of America, our sins. Let us not wait until God's judgments will become even severer, but let us to-day turn to God,

Making the Prayer of Jeremiah Our Own Prayer.

1. Let Us Search and Try Our Ways.
2. Let Us Lift Our Hearts with Our Hands unto God in the Heavens.

1.

Let us search and try our ways, trace them whither they lead, test them whether they have been good or evil. Let us be thorough in such searching and trying. The words used by Jeremiah indicate an all-including, careful search, a digging into them to find out their true nature; not a mere scratching at the surface, but a scrutinizing, painstaking investigation; not merely a passing look. Such a searching is necessary, and it is a good custom to observe a special day for such conscientious examination of our whole life. A merchant keeps his books in good shape all the year round, but at the close of the year he will make a special audit of them in order to see how he stands. A housewife sweeps and cleans every day, and still she finds it necessary to institute a special annual house-cleaning. In like

manner our whole life should and must be a constant searching of
our ways, and still it is necessary and profitable for us to set aside
a special day for special searching. So many at no time take trouble
to examine their lives. They are fully satisfied with themselves.
They have been baptized, confirmed, and partake of the Lord's Supper.
What can there be lacking? They forget that the Jews also were
externally members of God's people, that they brought their sacrifices
and that nevertheless the Lord said of them: Is. 1, 14. 15. So it is
possible to boast of one's Christianity and yet be an abomination
to God.

If we do not search our ways, God will, Ps. 139, 1. And He will
set our secret sins in the light of His countenance, Ps. 90, 8. Let us
not wait until that day, but let us *now* search and try our ways. We
know our home, every nook and corner of it. We know our business,
our sports. *Do we know ourselves?* Do we know what our relation
is to God?

Let us search our ways. Did they on Sunday morning lead to
church or to pleasure trips? Were they during the week ways pleasing or displeasing to God, ways of sin, leading to places where the
lusts of the flesh were gratified? Did our ways bring us nearer to
God or farther away from Him? Are you closer to heaven than you
were a year ago or closer to eternal damnation? Search your ways;
try them whither they are leading you.

Search your ways. Are they ways of progress or of retrogression?
Have you stood still or advanced in Christianity? Are you a better
Christian than a year ago? Have you succeeded in overcoming your
inclination to some pet sin, in getting rid of some bad habit? Or
have these sinful customs grown on you? Are you slowly, but surely
slipping back? Have you progressed in knowledge? Do you know
more than a year ago about the Bible, the Lutheran Church, its doctrines, its history, its missions, its needs, more about your congregation, its opportunities, its difficulties? You have had ample opportunity to increase your knowledge. Some seventy-five services were
held. You had your Bible at home. How often did you read it? Are
you a subscriber and reader of your church periodicals? You have
no excuse if you have not advanced in knowledge.

Let us search our ways. Have we let our light so shine before
men that they have seen our good works? Have we been shining
models of godliness? Cp. Dan. 6, 4. Does the world know you, and
must the world respect you as one who does not stray from the paths
of righteousness? Let us search our ways. God gave His Son, Jesus
gave His own life, Mary gave that precious ointment. Have you
given what you can? Is there one among us who has always done
what he could, who has never strayed from the right path, never
walked on ways displeasing to God and his Savior?

2.

Let us search our ways, and if we find that our ways are sinful, let us follow the second admonition of Jeremiah — let us "turn again to the Lord and lift our heart with our hands unto God in the heavens." We need not fear to confess our sins to Him. He, the Searcher of hearts, knows them, knows them better than we do. But ought not the very fact that God knows all our ways and knows that these ways are often ways of sin, leading us away from the Lord, — ought not this very fact drive us to despair? If God knows our sins, must He not punish them? Surely. If God were only holy and just, there would be no hope for us. But this God of holiness and justice is also the God of grace and mercy and loving-kindness, Ezek. 33, 11; John 3, 16. Come, let us go to Calvary, let us lift up our eyes to Him whose blood is being shed upon the cross. Let us lift up our hands to Him and implore His mercy and forgiveness. Let us lift up our hearts to Him, the Son of God, whose blood can cleanse us from all sins. (Hymn 325, 3.) And having been washed in this fountain from all our sins, let us turn to our God with the firm intention and the vow to avoid evil ways and to walk in the way everlasting. Let us turn to our God whole-heartedly, not only half-way, one eye toward heaven, the other looking longingly on the things of this world. Remember Lot's wife, Gen. 19, 26. Let us lift up not only our hands, but also our hearts. Let us not be satisfied with having appeared here, with having heard a sermon on the need of repentance, sung penitential hymns, prayed penitential prayers and then imagine we have done our duty. Such outward religion brought the judgment upon Jerusalem. And if God spared not His own people, but shut them out from His grace and pardon, Jer. 15, 1. 6; 1 Thess. 2, 16, how can we hope to escape His holy and righteous wrath if we commit the same sins, if we walk according to our flesh and expect God to pardon our sins merely because of a few hypocritical words or tears? Unless our repentance is a repentance of the heart, unless we sincerely purpose to turn away from all ways of evil, our very repentance will be an abomination to the Lord, our very tears will call down upon us His wrath and punishment. Turn, turn away, from all sin; turn, turn again, to the Lord. And since that is impossible in our own strength, let us ask Him, the God of grace, Him in whom we have righteousness and strength, to turn us, and we shall be turned, Jer. 31, 18. Then our very life and being will be consecrated to God, Rom. 12, 1 ff.; then Jer. 29, 11—13 and 1 Kings 8, 46—53 will be fulfilled. (Hymn 340, 1.)   THEODORE LAETSCH.

Thanksgiving Sermon.

Ps. 9, 1. 2.

Thanksgiving services are not of recent, but of ancient origin; they are, in fact, almost as old as the world. The first thanksgiving service recorded in the Bible was that of Cain and Abel, the eldest sons of Adam and Eve. "Cain brought of the fruit," etc., Gen. 4, 3b. 4a. Alas! Cain's thanksgiving was only outwards, while "the Lord looketh on the heart." So the inspired account continues: "And the Lord had respect unto Abel and unto his offering," Gen. 4, 4b. 5a, because he was a believing child of God. Other offerings in which the purpose of thanksgiving no doubt predominated were those of Noah after the Flood. As soon as this "preacher of righteousness" had gone out of the ark with the blessing of the Lord, he "builded an altar," etc., Gen. 8, 20. Of Abraham, Jacob, and many others Scripture makes similar statements. After the giving of the Law through Moses the children of Israel brought their special thank-offerings, generally called peace-offerings; as a nation they annually observed three great festivals, at which a very essential element was thanksgiving. In the course of time other nations, e. g., the Christian nations of Europe, celebrated thanksgiving days or seasons, regularly or otherwise. Coming to our own country and nation, it is possible that the first *Christian* thanksgiving service in America was held as early as 1000 A. D., *viz.,* by the Norsemen who reached our shores under Leif Ericson. We know definitely that Columbus and his crew conducted a thanksgiving service October 12, 1492, the day on which they discovered America.

In 1621, "after the ingathering of the first harvest in a new world," Governor Bradford of the Plymouth Colony invited the Pilgrim Fathers to keep "a day of prayer, praise, and thanksgiving." In 1789 George Washington, as President of the United States, issued the first *national* thanksgiving proclamation in this country. In 1863, after the bloody Battle of Gettysburg, President Lincoln urged the entire nation to observe a day of prayer and thanksgiving on the last Thursday in November. Since then this particular Thursday has been America's annual Thanksgiving Day. We Christians should certainly be glad to have an opportunity to gather in our house of worship to-day to give thanks to, and to praise, the God of our Salvation. Our text also encourages us to do this by presenting to us —

Three Important Thanksgiving Thoughts,

answering the questions: —

1. To Whom,   *2. For What,* and
3. How are We to Give Thanks and Praise?

1.

"To whom are we to give thanks and praise?" This, beloved, is
our first question. A rather superfluous question it may seem; but
is it? Of course, any little child, if it has learned to pray, can readily
give the right answer. Theoretically we all know that He who is
entitled to our praise and thanks, not only on our national Thanksgiving Day, but all the days of our life, is the Lord, our God. But
what practical use do we make of this knowledge? Do we actually
and always (Eph. 5, 20) give God all the glory and all the praise due
Him? Are we doing so to-day? The fact that we are saying and
singing "Lord, Lord!" may not mean anything at all. The Pharisee
in the Temple said: "God, I thank *Thee";* but did he thank God? It
is clear that he thanked and praised nobody but himself.

By nature all men are ingrates. A German proverb says truly:
"Ingratitude is the world's reward." Who has not learned this from
his own bitter experience? We Christians are not "of the world,"
but even we are often ungrateful, especially toward the Lord. In
the day of trouble even the weakest of God's children will call upon
Him. Then the smallest spark of faith will drive them to the Throne
of Grace, as Isaiah says: "Lord, in trouble," etc., Is. 26, 16. This is
their blessed privilege; it is right for them so to do. But thanking
God is also right. (As we confess in our communion liturgy: "It
is meet, right, and salutary that we should at all times and in all
places give thanks unto Thee, O Lord, holy Father, almighty, everlasting God.") Yet how many take time to thank and glorify their
divine Deliverer after the trouble, when He has heard "their cry"?
(Ps. 145, 19.) Alas! very few. Of the ten lepers whom Jesus cleansed
in answer to their pitiful prayer: "Jesus, Master, have mercy on us,"
only one "turned back," etc., Luke 17, 15b. 16a. Cf. 1 Sam. 1, 10;
2, 1 ff. There never were many thankful Samaritans and Hannahs.

"There is an old legend that tells of two angels sent to earth, each
with a basket, the one to gather up the prayers of the people and the
other their thanksgivings. When they returned, they were grieved to
find that the first basket was filled to overflowing while the other was
nearly empty." (*Holydays and Holidays;* Deems.) This is only
a legend, but what it illustrates is a sad fact, *viz.,* that true thankfulness is very rare here on earth.

The psalm before us, as so many of these psalms, expressly
mentions the rightful Recipient of our thanks and praises, saying
in the second verse: "I will sing praise to Thy name, O Thou
Most High," and in the first verse: "I will praise Thee, O Lord";
literally: "I will thank the Lord." (Cf. Luther.) In this text David
would encourage himself and others to thank as well as to praise God;
in other words, to speak and sing not only of God's goodness, but also
of His gifts, His "works," for the benefit of mankind.

2.

The second important Thanksgiving Day thought which we shall glean from our text answers the question: *"For what* are we to give thanks and praise?" This answer we read in David's words: "I will show forth *all* Thy marvelous works." What a picture is painted in these few words: "all Thy marvelous works"! The dark background for this most beautiful picture is man's sin. This background we may see in many psalms of thanksgiving and praise. Not in a penitential psalm, but in Ps. 106, the first and the last sentence of which reads: "Praise ye the Lord!" the words appear: "We have sinned . . . the multitude of Thy mercies," Ps. 106, 6. 7. On the one hand, "the multitude of . . . transgressions," Ps. 5, 10; on the other hand, "the multitude of Thy tender mercies," Ps. 51, 1. Even Jacob must confess: "I am not worthy," etc., Gen. 32, 10.

David, in this text, thinks of, and thanks for, the many "marvelous," *i. e.,* wonderful, works of God. Which are such marvelous works? In his explanation of the First Article, Luther gives us a long list of temporal blessings that we enjoy. If you should ever wonder whether you have any real reasons to be thankful, read or recite that explanation attentively. These blessings, like all of his doctrine, Luther found in his Bible. This you will see for yourself as you listen to a few sentences from the psalms: "Know ye that," etc., Ps. 100, 3 a. "I will praise Thee, for I am," etc., Ps. 139, 14. "He hath made His wonderful works to be remembered. The Lord is gracious and full of compassion. He hath given meat unto them that fear Him," Ps. 111, 4. 5 a. "I have been young and now am old; yet have I not seen the righteous forsaken nor his seed begging bread," Ps. 37, 25. "Commit thy way," etc., Ps. 37, 5. "There shall no evil," etc., Ps. 91, 10. "Like as a father pitieth," etc., Ps. 103, 13. "What shall I render," etc., Ps. 116, 12. "O give thanks," etc., Ps. 118, 1. 29; 106, 1; 107, 1; 136, 1.

For what shall we render thanks and praise to God to-day? For the many marvelous works of the Lord done and being done for our bodily welfare; in other words, for all our temporal blessings, including another "seed-time and harvest," Gen. 8, 22.

But not all our blessings are bodily and temporal; by far our greatest blessings are spiritual and eternal. This the psalmist knew very well, and we may rest assured that he thought of it when he spoke and sang about the marvelous works of the Lord. — When you "count your blessings one by one," which do you name first? The psalmist made a list of the blessings he had received in the 103d Psalm. At the top of that list he did not place health, which, so many will tell you, is the best thing any one may have. Wealth is not mentioned by him at all despite the almost general and uncontrolled "love of money." The psalmist thought first of his sin and his Savior; for these are his words: "Bless the Lord," etc., Ps. 103, 1—3 a.

Of all the marvelous works of God the most marvelous is the redemption, which Luther describes in that beautiful sentence: "I believe that Jesus Christ," etc. — Closely connected with God's "marvelous work" of redemption is His marvelous work of sanctification, described in Luther's catechism in the well-known words: "I believe that I cannot," etc. (1 Pet. 2, 9.) It was mainly of redemption and sanctification that the inspired apostles assembled in Jerusalem were speaking on the day of Pentecost, when devout Jews out of every nation marveled and said: "We do hear them speak in our tongues the *wonderful works* of God," Acts 2, 11. Friends, let us thank and praise God for *all* His marvelous works. (Ps. 98, 1 a.)

3.

"*How* are we to give thanks and praise?" Also this third question David answers in our text. First he says: v. 1 a. He is determined to thank and praise God with his heart, and with all his heart. Thanking God in any other way than with the heart is not thanking Him at all, but is committing the hollow mockery of a Cain and inviting God's righteous anger. Nor is a half-hearted thanksgiving acceptable to God. How God will finally deal with such as try to serve two masters and do not repent and amend we learn from Rev. 3, 16: "Because thou art lukewarm," etc. By the mouth of Solomon, God says to you and to me: "My son, give Me thine heart," and He does not mean only a part of the heart. Like David let us earnestly endeavor to thank and praise God with our whole heart.

But "out of the abundance of the heart the mouth speaketh." If we are grateful at heart toward the Giver of all good gifts, our lips will be opened, and our mouth will show forth His praise. Thus it was with David. How he delighted to speak and sing of all that God had done for him! In our text he says: vv. 1. 2.

And, friends, there is a "showing forth" of the "marvelous works" of God in deeds as well as in words. We here recall that general prayer in which we say: "And we beseech Thee, give us that due sense of all Thy mercies that our hearts may be unfeignedly thankful and that we may *show forth* Thy praise not only with our *lips,* but also in our *lives.*" The same thought is expressed by our blessed Savior when He admonishes: "Let your light," etc., Matt. 5, 16. This, of course, includes giving for church and for charity.

In conclusion, as "God loveth a cheerful giver," He loveth also a cheerful *thanks*giver. Such was David. And such was Pastor Martin Rinckart, who despite all his losses and crosses during the dreadful Thirty Years' War could give to the Church that matchless hymn of praise: Hymn 64.   ROBERT GROTE.

SUNDAY EVENING SERVICES.

THREE GREAT DOCTRINES.

The Holy Christian Church.

1 Pet. 2, 4—10.

"I believe in the holy Christian Church, the communion of saints." So the ancient Christian Church confessed, and so all Christians to-day confess; for the *Apostles' Creed* is an ecumenical creed and expresses the common Christian faith of all believers in Christ. In the *Nicene Creed* Christian believers confess: "And I believe one holy Christian and Apostolic Church." The words differ, but the confession is the same; the "one holy Christian and Apostolic Church" is the "holy Christian Church" of the Apostles' Creed. Which is that Church? It is not this or that Church which ordinarily we call a "denomination." When we say: "I believe in the *holy Christian Church*," we do not refer to any visible church organization on earth, but to "the communion of saints," that is, to the aggregate of all true believers in Christ, of whom many are in heaven, the Church Triumphant, and many on earth, the Church Militant, which is found wherever the Gospel is preached and the Sacraments are administered according to Christ's institution, the invisible Church, known only to God, the Searcher of hearts, Eph. 2, 19—22; Acts 2. This Church was called into existence through the Gospel, after the Fall, Gen. 3, 15, and has ever been preserved on earth, 2 Tim. 2, 19; Luke 17, 20. 21, in the Old Testament, 1 Kings 19, 18, and in the New Testament, Rom. 11, 4. 5; John 10, 27—29. "The saints on earth and those above But one communion make; Joined to their Lord in bonds of love, All of His grace partake. . . . One army of the living God, To His commandments we bow; Part of the host have passed the flood, And part are crossing now." (Hymn 463, 1. 3.)

It is well for us to consider the Scriptural doctrine of the holy Christian Church, for by many it is misunderstood, and by still more it is perverted; e. g., "The Church is a visible kingdom on earth." (Romanism.) "It does not matter to what local or visible Church we belong since only membership in the invisible Church matters." (Modern unionistic sectarianism.) "All churches point out the way to heaven, and so all are good." (Unionism.) It is true, no *visible Church* must be identified with the invisible Church of Christ; but God's Word demands that we should avoid all erring churches, Matt. 7, 15; Rom. 16, 17. 18. Our Catechism: "When do we properly use this doctrine of the Church? When we take heed to be and remain members of the invisible Church; when we to this end adhere to the Church of the pure Word and confession, contribute toward its maintenance and propagation according to our ability, and avoid all false churches, John 8, 31. 32; 1 John 4, 1; Matt. 28, 19. Let us, then, consider to-day —

The Holy Christian Church.

1. *Its Spiritual Nature;*   *3. Its High Dignity;*
2. *Its Divine Corner-stone;*   *4. Its Holy Purpose.*

1.

Our text is taken from an epistle that was addressed not to a church *at one place,* as, for example, Paul's Epistles to the Corinthians or his Epistle to the Romans, but to Christians "scattered throughout Pontus, Galatia, Cappadocia, Asia, and Bithynia," 1, 1. In all these provinces there were Christian churches, and in all these Christian churches there were true believers, who together form the holy Christian Church. From this the *spiritual nature* of the Christian Church is obvious. The Republic of Mexico comprises a certain territory; so does the Republic of the United States, and so do all kingdoms, empires, and dominions of this world. They have their boundary-lines, their definite confines, so that we can say: "This is France, and this is Germany, and this is Poland," etc. But of the holy Christian Church this is not true. The "strangers scattered throughout," as St. Peter writes, form the Christian Church, or to say it more directly, all true believers are the Christian Church, which is not earthly, but spiritual in its nature. In our text St. Peter states this truth very definitely. He says: "To whom [to the gracious Lord Jesus Christ] coming [by faith], . . . ye also as lively [*zoontes,* living] stones are built up a *spiritual house.*" What does the apostle mean by "spiritual house"? The antonym of "spiritual" is earthly, fleshly, in short, that which is of this world. The Christian Church is spiritual; for it lives, moves, and has its being alone in the *Holy Spirit.* It is of God, in God, and unto God, through faith in Christ. True, its builders on earth are ministers, 1 Cor. 3, 10; but they build with *spiritual means,* or the means of grace, Mark 16, 15. 16; Matt. 28, 19. 20. — The Christian Church is spiritual in its *foundation,* which is Christ Jesus, 1 Cor. 3, 11; spiritual in its *materials,* living stones, *i. e., spiritual persons,* or believers; spiritual in its *graces,* or the *gifts of the Spirit,* Eph. 4, 10—13; 3—7; 1, 21—23; spiritual in its *objectives,* "an holy priesthood to offer up spiritual sacrifices," etc. It has nothing to do with what is worldly. Reason disallows its Living Stone; the learned of this world, earthly builders, reject (vv. 4. 7) its divine Lord as a "stone of stumbling"; to them He is a "rock of offense"; for they are disobedient to the very Word by which the Church is called into being and exists, v. 8. *By nature* no one belongs to the Christian Church, v. 10. Even children of Christian parents are not lively stones in God's spiritual house unless they are born again of water and the Spirit, John 3, 5. 6. Members of God's spiritual house are only such as have "obtained mercy," have been made the "people of God," v. 10.

Everywhere the apostle thus stresses the *spiritual nature* of the holy Christian Church, the communion of saints. Whoever is not spiritual does not belong to it; whatever is not spiritual is foreign to it. The Jews at Christ's time misunderstood the spiritual nature of Christ's kingdom, or Church; hence Christ's instructions: John 6, 26—45; 8, 37—44; Luke 17, 20. 21. We must guard against that mistake to-day. Nothing earthly makes us members of Christ's Church — no external membership in a local church, no outward performance of ceremonies, no fleshly attempt at good works, no mumbling of prayers, no payment of money, etc. Only the coming to Jesus Christ by faith renders us living stones in God's spiritual house. By faith we become members; by faith we remain members; by faith we offer up spiritual sacrifices as members.

The question, then, is, Are *we* true believers and as such members of the holy Christian Church? This is a momentous question. (*Extra ecclesiam nulla salus.*) But, again, if we are believers in Christ, nothing and no one can annul our membership, no Pope, no unjust ban, no hatred of the world. — However, if you are lively stones in God's spiritual house, do you value this high prerogative? Do you *show yourselves* as such? When people see a beautiful cathedral, they say, "What a wonderful edifice!" When they see you, spiritual stones in Christ's spiritual house, can they say, "How wonderful is the Church of God!"? Consider the earnest admonition, vv. 11—25.

2.

The holy Christian Church is a *spiritual* house; so also its Corner-stone is *divine.* This is the second truth which our text teaches; in fact, it is the central truth of our text, as it is that of the whole Bible.

Of Christ, the divine Corner-stone of the Christian Church, the text speaks with great clearness and emphasis. *"To whom coming as unto a living Stone."* The reference is to the preceding verse, especially to the words: "The Lord is gracious." Christ is here called without any qualification "the Lord," or Jehovah (*kyrios*). The Church thus rests upon God Himself, John 10, 30. Its corner-stone is not any prophet or apostle, but the incarnate Word, who purchased and redeemed the Church with His blood, Eph. 2, 12—22; 5, 25—27. — Christ is called a "living Stone" after the manner of the prophets, Is. 8, 14; 28, 16, to denote His invincible power and eternal duration. He is the Rock of Ages that no man can remove. He stands forever and ever, Ps. 90, 1—4, the Joy and Crown of His believing followers, John 6, 68. 69; Phil. 1, 21, and the "rock of offense" to all who disobediently reject His Word, vv. 7. 8. Christ is called a *living* Stone, because He is the living Lord, who has eternal life in Himself, John 5, 26, and gives eternal life to His disciples, John 5, 24. — Though

His own people disallowed, or rejected, Him, as the majority of men do, John 1, 5. 10. 11, yet He was chosen of God, separated and foreordained to be the Fountain of the Church, 1, 18—20. Hence, whoever rejects Christ rejects God, 1 John 5, 1. 10; 4, 2. 3; 2, 22. 23. — Christ is a *precious* Stone both in the sight of God, Matt. 3, 17, and of His saints, v. 7 a; Rev. 5, 12. 13; most honorable and worthy to be the Corner-stone of the Church. This important truth was declared of Christ also in the Old Testament, v. 6; Is. 28, 16, and is here repeated in the New Testament because God is always the same and never alters His plans and purposes, 1 Sam. 15, 29. The Corner-stone, foreordained from eternity, *remains* the Corner-stone of the Church, though men reject Him (Pharisaism, Sadduceeism, Modernism). To these He is a "stone of stumbling" and a "rock of offense" because they stumble at God's Word and disobediently reject it, v. 8. Their ultimate damnation is their own fault, not Christ's, who desires that all men be saved, 1 Tim. 2, 4. The Corner-stone abides, for it is divine and eternal, 1 Cor. 3, 11.

Let us, then, love, honor, and follow Christ. He is the "chief Corner-stone in Sion." In Him we, as lively stones, are built up a spiritual house, v. 5. Whoever believeth on Him shall not be confounded, v. 6. Through faith in Him we are a holy priesthood, v. 5. Indeed, Christ is our All in all, our divine Foundation-stone. In Him is centered all our hope and happiness, John 14, 1—3. 6. Through Him we have true knowledge of God, Matt. 11, 27. In Him we have salvation, Matt. 11, 28. Through Him we are made partakers of all spiritual blessings, Eph. 1, 3 ff. — Do not mind the stubborn rejection of Christ by the world; to this "they were appointed"; that is to say, when they did not "retain God in their knowledge, God gave them over to a reprobate mind," Rom. 1, 28. The hardening of hearts has come upon them by God's righteous judgment, Rom. 11, 7—10. — "Believe on the Lord Jesus Christ," etc., Acts 16, 31; for He is God's own appointed Corner-stone of the Church, infinitely precious "in the excellency of His nature, the dignity of His office, and the gloriousness of His services." Come to Him again and again by a lively faith that as lively stones ye may be built up a spiritual house, that ye may remain members of His holy Church here and hereafter.

3.

The Christian Church has a divine, a precious Corner-stone; it has also a *high dignity*. The dignity of the Christian Church is described in our text in various ways. In the first place, its members are called *lively*, or living, stones; that is to say, they have new spiritual life through faith in Christ, the Corner-stone of the Church. By nature all men are dead in trespasses and sins, Eph. 2, 1—3; but through the work of the Holy Spirit in regeneration they have become alive to God, Eph. 2, 4—10. What high dignity! Christians are children of God and heirs of eternal life, Rom. 8, 15—18. — Again, in our text the members of the Christian Church are called a *"holy priesthood."* They are holy through faith in Christ, whose perfect righteousness is imputed to them, 1 John 1, 7. They are select persons, sacred to God, serviceable to others, well endowed with heavenly gifts and grace, so that they may serve God as priests, having access to His throne of grace in Christ. — Moreover, they are a "chosen generation," (*genos eklekton,* a chosen race), elected unto life eternal in Christ Jesus, Eph. 1, 3—7, God's holy family, ineffably dear to Him. They are a "royal," or *kingly,* priesthood, that is to say, kings and priests, who serve God with holy works and rule with Christ throughout eternity, Rev. 3, 21; 4, 4. They are a *"holy nation,"* consecrated and devoted to God, renewed and sanctified by His Holy Spirit. They are *"a peculiar people,"* or a people of His acquisition, choice, care, and delight (a people for a possession), who are God's own now and will be acknowledged as such in glory. The apostle here multiplies words to depict the high dignity of the Christian Church. Its glory is hidden now; it is now in its state of humiliation; but in heaven it will be glorified and exalted, Phil. 3, 20. 21; Rom. 8, 18—23; 38. 39.

Keep this dignity of the Christian Church in mind constantly and do not be offended at its trials and sufferings, Acts 14, 22; Luke 6, 22. 23. Some day the glory of the Church shall be revealed, Titus 2, 11—14. Follow Paul's example, Phil. 3, 7—15.

4.

Corresponding to the high dignity of the Christian Church is its *holy purpose.* This holy purpose is set forth in the words "to offer up spiritual sacrifices, acceptable to God by Jesus Christ," v. 5. These spiritual sacrifices are the Christian's own bodies and souls, Rom. 12, 1; their affections, Ps. 100; their prayers and praises, Ps. 103; and all works done in faith, Eph. 2, 10. They are *spiritual* because they are wrought by the Holy Spirit through the Word; they are *sacrifices,* or *offerings,* because they are consecrated to God through faith in Christ. The Church of Christ is to *serve Christ;* that is its holy purpose. This service is manifold and embraces uncounted things in the Christian's life, its standard being God's holy will, revealed in the Law, and its purpose the glory of God, 1 Cor. 10, 31. In our text the apostle thus summarizes the holy purpose of the Church: "that ye should show forth the praises of Him who hath called you out of darkness into His marvelous light," v. 9. To show forth the praises of God means above all to spread His holy Gospel, through which sinners are saved, v. 10. This paramount duty the Church must not neglect, Mark 16, 15. 16; Matt. 28, 19. 20. No true member of the Church will neglect it, 2 Cor. 5, 13—15. Every genuine believer is a missionary.

The Scriptural doctrine concerning the Holy Christian Church is most *important;* it is also most *blessed.* Let us therefore study it with great zeal and praise God for having revealed also this paramount truth to us in order that we may glorify Him here in time and hereafter in eternity.   J. T. MUELLER.

The Lutheran Church.
John 8, 31. 32.

What do we mean by "Lutheran Church"? The Church so called did not choose this name; it was thrust upon it by its enemies as a term of contempt. But the name which was intended to deter people from joining it has become one of dignity and attraction. The Lutheran Church is the Church of the Reformation, or the Church which holds and defends the Bible truths which Luther again taught when he purified Christendom from man-made additions and doctrines. No Church can truly call itself Lutheran unless it stands for that for which Luther stood — salvation by grace alone, revealed in Scripture alone, accepted by faith alone. And again, all true believers who maintain these principles are Lutheran in spirit, even though they outwardly do not belong to the Lutheran Church. — The Lutheran Church is not a sect, but the Apostolic Church, restored to its pristine purity in faith and life. Its creed is ecumenical; it accepts honestly and professedly the ancient creeds. It excludes and rejects all ancient and modern errors. — The Lutheran Church is rightly exclusive and antiunionistic, Rom. 16, 17; 2 John 10. — It is not the *una sancta,* — for there are true members of the holy Christian Church also outside the Lutheran Church, — but it is the orthodox Church on earth, the true visible Church of Christ on earth. It challenges all men to examine its teachings and to disprove its doctrines; but if these doctrines cannot be proved wrong, indeed, because they agree with Scripture, the Lutheran Church upholds the proud claim that it is the Church of the Bible, the Gospel voice. — All these facts we must constantly bear in mind to-day. There are so-called Lutheran churches which do not deserve this title of dignity. Within Lutheran denominations the demand is made that the Lutheran Church must become more liberal, more sectarian, more unionistic. On the other hand, the Papacy, the inveterate foe of true Lutheranism, is becoming increasingly aggressive and asserts its ancient claim with ever greater arrogance, namely, that the Reformation was the beginning of all evil things, such as atheism, Communism, Modernism, and the like. Again, the growth of the true Lutheran Church is not phenomenal; though it preaches the Gospel in its full truth and purity, its membership remains comparatively small. — So there are many things at which even Lutherans sometimes are offended. Should we, however, be offended? Luther said that all who are offended in him and his doctrine, are offended in Christ and His Gospel. No, we must not be offended at the Lutheran Church, but confess and defend its vital principles and its holy doctrines with ever greater fervor and zeal. Let us therefore examine this matter more closely.

The Lutheran Church.

1. Its Loyal Adherence to God's Word;

2. Its Clear Understanding and Profession of the Truth of Salvation;

3. Its Wonderful Freedom.

1.

The words of our text were addressed by Christ "to the Jews which *believed* on Him," who had definitely accepted Him as the "Light of the world," who were earnest and sincere in their profession of Him. They professed Him in opposition to the Pharisees, who hardened themselves against His Gospel, v. 12 ff. Their number was not small (v. 30, *"many"*); but they needed strengthening of faith, confirmation of their resolve to follow Christ, vv. 12. 28. What did Jesus demand of them? What rule of discipleship did He lay down for them? His words are simple: "If ye continue in My Word, then are ye My disciples indeed." Discipleship of Christ does not consist in outward things. Not the outward following of Jesus, not the calling of oneself by His name, makes a person a disciple of Christ. True discipleship is inward and spiritual; it presupposes true faith in, and abiding loyalty to, His Word. The disciple must learn the lessons the heavenly Teacher has taught us in His Word and cling and conform to them. In His school the rule is fixed and the doctrine established for all times; disciples must therefore accept unwaveringly this rule and doctrine. — When speaking of this, Christ had in mind not only the divine Law, He wished to be accepted and adored not merely as an "ideal" or "example," but as the "Light of the world," as the "Son of Man lifted up." He had in mind preeminently the Gospel of His atoning suffering and death, v. 28. In that Gospel, which is foolishness and an offense to the world, 1 Cor. 1, 23, His disciples must abide, continue, dwell. That must be the foundation of their faith and hope, the holiest truth in which all their religious thoughts center. Jesus demanded a Church that is abidingly loyal to His Word, His precious Gospel. — "My Word" (v. 31) is the whole Bible; for the Spirit of Christ spoke by the prophets and the apostles, 1 Pet. 1, 10—12. Discipleship of Christ means faithful adherence to the Bible and to nothing but the Bible. Christ's Church is a Bible Church.

The Lutheran Church is a Church of true discipleship. It continues in Christ's Word in doctrine and practise. It maintains as its basic formal principle the *sola Scriptura*. It stands four-square on the holy Bible. Whatever the Bible teaches the Lutheran Church teaches; whatever the Bible rejects the Lutheran Church rejects. It acknowledges no spurious sources of faith, no traditions, no decretals of Popes, no opinions of reason, no hypotheses of science falsely so called, no speculations of enlightened reason, — nothing at all outside the Bible. Our Small Catechism proves this: the Law, the Creed, the Lord's Prayer, etc. (Let the minister show from the Six Chief Parts of the Catechism how the Lutheran Church loyally adheres to God's Word.) Rationalistic Protestantism and rationalistic Papism refuse to continue in Christ's Word. In the denominations there are children of God, but these believing Christians really do not belong to these erring churches. They hold membership in them only outwardly. However, the Lutheran Church continues in Christ's Word also *in practise*. Christ in His Word demands a definite practise in conformity to it. Faith and practise must go hand in hand. The Word professed must be applied to life. (Let the minister illustrate this by adducing a few examples, such as the calling of ministers, unionism, close Communion, etc.)

Such, then, is the Lutheran Church, a Church of true discipleship of Christ, adhering to Christ's Word with sincere loyalty. In this it follows the ancient Apostolic Church, the members of which rather suffered martyrdom than deny Christ, Matt. 10, 31. 32. No, we must not be ashamed of our dear old Lutheran Church. If we are ashamed of its doctrines and the firm stand it takes in matters of doctrine and practise, we are ashamed of Christ. — Let us rather praise God that by grace He has made us members of this Church, and let us do all we can to uphold its dignity and truth, which the world needs so much to-day. Pharisees and Sadducees still oppose Christ; we must be loyal to Him.

2.

The Lutheran Church professes as its basic formal principle that every article of faith must be based upon an explicit word of God, and as its basic material principle it professes that we are saved by grace alone.

Let us now study its clear understanding and profession of the truth of salvation. — Agnosticism — and the spirit of agnosticism pervades all rationalistic and modernistic churches to-day — claims that the truth cannot be known. With Pilate it says: "What is truth?" Christ says: "And ye *shall know the truth.*" What did Jesus mean by "the truth"? He did not speak of that truth which lies within the domain of earthly things. That truth we know by reason, although on account of original sin, which has corrupted also our intellectual powers, this truth is not readily perceived (cp. modern science; the confusion of politics; modern ethics, etc.). Even the truth of the Law man by nature may somewhat perceive, Rom. 1, 19. 20. 32. However, man does not by nature know, and cannot know, spiritual truth, 1 Cor. 2, 14, the truth regarding salvation, of which Christ speaks in our text, vv. 12. 28. With respect to this truth all men by nature walk in darkness" and therefore do not possess "the light of life." But how different it is when men believe in Christ and continue in His Word! Then they *know* the truth, know it sufficiently, know it to their salvation. How well St. Peter knew this truth! Acts 2; 1 Pet. 1, 1—9. How well St. Paul knew it! Rom. 3, 20—28. Just so all believers *should* know the truth of salvation. All who do not know the truth are not Christians. The true Christian says: *"I know* whom I have believed," 2 Tim. 1, 12. Every true believer knows and professes the same truth.

This teaching, that we are saved by grace alone, includes the whole truth of salvation. It is the basic material principle of the Lutheran Church. How clearly and convincingly it knows and professes this divine truth! In this truth center the second and third articles of our Christian faith. Luther has written explanations of these articles, and how precious they are! (Show how in these articles Luther professes the doctrines of Christ's person and work and of the person and work of the Holy Spirit. Then show how the truth of salvation is set forth in the chief parts of the Sacraments and the Office of the Keys and Confession; also, how the Lutheran Church teaches the divine Law in all its severity in order that the Gospel may be preached in all its sweetness. The Lutheran Church knows the truth regarding salvation and professes it unafraid of any foes of the Gospel.)

Should we not praise God for having led us most graciously into a Church which knows the truth? Salvation is our uppermost concern, Matt. 16, 26. Let us value the truth of salvation, the *sola gratia,* with all that it implies.

3.

Of those who continue in His Word, Christ also says: "And the truth shall make you free," shall liberate you, free you. What did Christ mean by this? He referred to Is. 61, 1—3. Preaching good tidings to the meek, He proclaims "liberty to the captives and the opening of the prison to them that are bound." Christ here does not mean political or social and economic freedom, but freedom from our spiritual foes, freedom from the guilt of sin, Col. 1, 14; freedom from hell, Col. 1, 13; freedom from the accusations of conscience, Col. 1, 20; freedom from the dominion of wickedness, Col. 1, 21; freedom from the erroneous opinions of men, Col. 2, 8; freedom from ceremonies and external forms, Col. 2, 14; freedom from Satan, Col. 2, 15; freedom from man-made rules, Col. 2, 16; freedom from man-conceived worship, Col. 2, 18. 20. 21—23; freedom from the love of

this world, Col. 3, 1—3; freedom from the demand of the Law that
we must fulfil it before we may enter life eternal, Rom. 3, 28. What
glorious freedom! Justification frees us from the guilt of sin;
and "where there is forgiveness of sins, there is also life and salvation." Sanctification frees us more and more from corruption, Col.
3, 10; Eph. 4, 24. We Christians are free from the yoke of the
Ceremonial Law and the grievous burdens of human traditions. We
are free from spiritual bondage; we serve God, freely, willingly, Ps.
110, 3; we are free to use the privileges of the sons of God; free
citizens of the free Jerusalem, which is above, Gal. 4, 26. We are
free from all prejudices, mistakes, and false notions of men that
enslave and entangle the soul; free from the dominion of lust and
passion, 2 Cor. 3, 17; free to behold the glory of the Lord and to be
changed into the same image of glory, 2 Cor. 3, 18. Enemies of Christianity boast of their *free thinking* and their *free thought;* but they
are in the worst kind of servitude, the servitude of their reprobate
minds, of their Satan-controlled hearts. Free thinking is Christian
thinking, Gospel thinking. The only free thought there is, is found
in those whom the Gospel has made free. All thoughts that are
brought into obedience to Christ are free and glorious.

How wonderful is the freedom of our own dear Lutheran Church!
How beautifully it proclaims the freedom of souls through the
Gospel! How gloriously free it is from the traditions of men and
the bondage of ceremonial laws! The Gospel is the proclamation of
spiritual emancipation; and oh, how clearly, how forcefully, the Lu-
theran Church proclaims this Gospel with all its manifold freedom!
Gospel freedom made the Reformation; it is still the dynamic of our
Lutheran Church. Let the minister compare the Lutheran Church
with the papistic and Reformed churches. What slavery exists there!
Our Lutheran Church is the true company of God's kings and priests.

And what shall we say in conclusion? Continue in Christ's
Word. Only then are you His disciples indeed. Only then can you
know the truth. Only then shall you be free from all spiritual
bondage, children of God, and heirs of eternal salvation. May God
grant this! Amen.   J. T. MUELLER.

The Enemies of the Church.
Phil. 1, 27—30.

Enemies of the Church! Could there be a greater paradox than
this? We readily understand that there are, and must be, enemies of
what is evil, enemies of Satan and sin, enemies of wickedness; but
that the Church of Christ, which is of the greatest blessing to the
world, should have enemies, such as oppose and injure it, is itself
a mystery of iniquity. Our text does not speak of the devil, whose

enmity against the Church is not hard to understand, since Christ's kingdom displaces and destroys his own evil kingdom. But that men, originally created after God's image and now called by God through His Church to have that glorious image restored to them, should hate the Church for its mission of love is beyond ordinary comprehension. Men are enemies of Christ's holy Church only because they are enslaved by Satan and are used by this evil Foe to further his own destructive interests. Christ Himself was thus opposed and persecuted by Herod, Matt. 2, 12—18. St. Paul was opposed by the merchants at Ephesus who sold small models of the shrine of the goddess Diana, Acts 19, 19. 24 f. In all these cases there was a selfish motive; but Herod and the silversmiths at Ephesus arose in opposition to the Founder of the Christian Church and its chief promoter among the Gentiles because they assailed Satan's kingdom, whose interests these enemies of Christ and of St. Paul served. This fact we must bear in mind if we wish to understand the enmity of men against the Church of God. It is not natural, but demonic. In the enmity of men against the Church, Satan himself opposes the Christian Church, John 8, 44. This fact must also determine the Church's course and conduct over against the enmity of evil men. To-day many churches desire to conciliate their adversaries by yielding those truths which are essential to Christianity or by forsaking in practise the principles which the Bible inculcates upon Christ's followers. They either deny the saving truth of the Gospel altogether (Modernism) or, outwardly at least, hold fast to that truth to some extent and yet practise fellowship with the ungodly (unionism, lodgery), though this is forbidden by God's Word, 2 Cor. 6, 14—18. What, then, is the right course which the Church of God must pursue over against the enmity of ungodly men? Christ, St. Paul, and the entire ancient Church have shown us the way. The Reformation, too, points out the right way. In fact, no true Christian is ignorant of it, Matt. 10, 31—39. The main question is whether we have the strength and the devotion to Christ necessary to pursue this course, and then, how we may obtain the needed power, heroic testimony, even martyrdom, if God so wills, in the face of the enmity of the wicked. Our text instructs us on all these points. Let us, then, consider —

The Enemies of the Christian Church.

1. Our Text Instructs Us with Respect to These Eenemies.
2. It Tells Us What to Do in View of Their Enmity.

1.

The reference which we find in our text to the enemies of the Church is rather meager, but none the less satisfactory. As a matter of fact, the Philippians, to whom St. Paul first addressed the words of our text, did not require much information about their enemies. They knew them well enough; they were constantly battling against them. They were suffering persecution and therefore needed encouragement rather than information with regard to their enemies. They were exposed to false teachers and needed to be guarded against their wiles. How St. Paul fared at Philippi when he preached the Gospel there is recorded with great detail Acts 16, 16 ff. Similar hatred and persecution the Christians at Philippi suffered after Paul's departure. They were singularly devoted to the apostle and to the Gospel which he proclaimed, 2 Cor. 8, 1—5; Phil. 4, 14—18; 2, 25; 4, 10. 18, and suffered as Paul had suffered. This explains why the apostle did not say more about their enemies, who hated them because of their very devotion to Christ and His Word. He wrote all that was needed to encourage and console his readers. — And what did he write? He says: "In nothing terrified by your adversaries, which is to them an evident token of perdition, but to you of salvation, and that of God." (Being frightened in nothing by those who oppose, which to them is a demonstration of destruction, but to you of salvation, and this from God.) Let us glean from these words the various things which the apostle says of the enemies of the Church. In the first place, St. Paul admits the fact that there are enemies of the Church, men who oppose, and *habitually* so, those who are members of the Church. Literally, they "lie in wait against" Christ's followers, trying at all times to harm them, both *bodily* and *spiritually*. St. Paul himself suffered martyrdom at the hands of the enemies of the Church, and for almost three centuries persecution raged, there being at least ten major persecutions. The assaults and torments which the Christians sustained during these persecutions are almost incredible. The most horrible tortures were inflicted upon them, Heb. 11, 33—38. During and after the Reformation the same devilish tortures were inflicted upon those who accepted the Gospel and professed it before men. (Spanish Inquisition.)

But far worse were those adversaries of the Church who persecuted the Church by false doctrine. There were such enemies of the Church at Philippi when St. Paul wrote his Epistle to the Philippians, enemies who denied the Bible doctrine about the person and work of Christ, Phil. 2, 6—11; 3, 2. 4, and taught salvation by works. They were enemies of the Cross of Christ, 3, 18. 19. The first class of enemies destroyed the body, but those who taught false doctrine destroyed the immortal souls of those whom they misled. They were therefore much more dangerous than the first class. During the great persecutions many heathen were induced to adopt Christianity by listening to the glorious confessions of the dying martyrs; but false doctrines, such as the denial of the person and work of Christ and the teaching of salvation by works, make salvation impossible. Let us, then, note this fact: There are enemies of the Church who try to exterminate the Church by fire and sword and others who want to destroy it by means of false doctrine.

In the second place, the apostle informs his readers and us that the enmity of the Church's adversaries is to them "an evident token of perdition," or a "demonstration of destruction." "Those who oppose the Gospel of Christ and injure the professors of it are marked out for ruin." That means not only that God will finally judge and destroy them, but that they persecute the Church because they are condemned sinners, upon whom God's judgment has already come and who will experience it to the uttermost on the Day of Judgment and in all eternity (Luther: *"ein Zeichen der Verdammnis"*). In short, the enemies of Christ's Church, no matter whether they persecute by fire and sword or by false and pernicious doctrine, are reprobates, who will not escape eternal damnation. The divine verdict is already pronounced upon them, as it has been pronounced upon Satan, Jude 6—19. — "And that of God." God permits their enmity to rage against His Church, the same God who has already reprobated them. And why? "To you the persecution is an evident token of salvation." The Church suffers at the hands of its enemies because it is God's kingdom and people and has eternal salvation by His divine promise. The disciple must bear the shame of the Master, Matt. 10, 24. 25, in order that he may be crowned with Him, Matt. 5, 11. 12; 2 Tim. 2, 12.

How blessed we are for knowing all this about the enemies of the Church! There are enemies, and they exist not because God cannot control or hinder them, but because in His infinite wisdom He permits them for a while to carry on. Only let us not allow Christ's enemies to mislead us. Against this we are fairly safe when they attack us with fire and sword, with hatred and scorn, with bodily suffering and death; for their wrath drives us only the closer to our Lord. They are more dangerous when they transform themselves into angels of light, 2 Cor. 11, 13—15, and quote Scripture to support their erroneous doctrines, Matt. 4, 1 ff. Wolves appearing in sheep's clothing are nevertheless wolves, Matt. 7, 15, enemies of God and our souls, whom we must resist steadfast in the faith and with the Word of God, 1 Pet. 5, 8—11. To-day the enemies of the Church (Papacy, Modernism, rationalism, antichristian cults) have all but perverted the entire outward Christian Church. False doctrines are generally tolerated. Unionism is not regarded with horror, but is considered to be true Christian charity. Indifferentism is looked upon as a virtue. The Word of God is openly despised and blasphemed by those who call themselves Christian ministers. The enemy is within the Church, dynamiting the foundation upon which it rests (denial of the vicarious satisfaction of Christ, teaching of salvation by character, substituting for God's Word human speculations, etc.). Let us beware! Our text has been written for our warning.

2.

What, then, shall we do in view of the many enemies of the Church? The apostle's instruction is both positive and negative. In the first place, he says: "Let your conversation be as it becometh the Gospel of Christ." (Only worthily of the Gospel of Christ conduct yourselves.) Let your whole conduct be in agreement with the Gospel which you profess. Submit yourselves in all things to God's Word; be guided by His will; trust in the promises of the Gospel. Live always as Christians. Christians dare not sleep, but must be watchful, 1 Cor. 16, 13; Col. 4, 2; Matt. 26, 41. Christians dare not feel secure, but must incessantly be on their guard, 1 Cor. 10, 12. Christians must not love the world, but flee its lusts and pleasures, 1 Cor. 7, 31; 1 John 2, 15. How would we conduct ourselves if the enemy were at the gate? We would obey the orders of the commander; we would move about guardedly and keep our weapons of offense and defense ready at all times. It is war-time now, spiritually speaking. — In the second place, the apostle says: "Stand fast in one spirit, with one mind striving together for the faith of the Gospel." St. Paul demands true *unity* and *unanimity*. Christians must *stand fast* against all enemies on the secure foundation of God's Word; they must be united in spirit; with one heart and soul they must contend, fight (be athletes together) for the faith of the Gospel. The faith of the Gospel is the precious Gospel doctrine. All Christians (ministers, teachers, missionaries, laymen, presidents, visitors, etc.) must fight for purity of doctrine and not allow a single doctrine to be perverted, Matt. 28, 20. This they must do *together,* each contributing what he can, the minister in the pulpit, the teacher in school, the laymen in their meetings. Pure doctrine is the common possession; it must be fought for by all. How men strive together in a basket-ball game! What mutual protection! What unity of action and unanimity of purpose! Would that the Church were striving in that one spirit which the Holy Ghost brings about! Surely the enemy cannot overthrow the Church if all Christians are striving together. Oh, then, *strive!* And strive *together* against the common foe. Let there be no breach where the enemy may get in. Be *steadfast* and *immovable!* Let the minister remind his hearers also of the Macedonian phalanx or the Roman legion. There is much room in the text for detailed and practical application.

Negatively the apostle says: "In nothing be terrified by your adversaries." Christians are soldiers, and soldiers must have no fear.

The apostle uses a strong term, "frightened out of one's wits." Soldiers who are scared to death will never win victories. Of course, the enemy is strong, wily, inured to ceaseless battling; but Christ, the Captain of our salvation, has defeated Satan, and so he must yield. He has shown us how we may defeat him, Matt. 4, 1 ff. His Word is an effective weapon, Eph. 6, 10—18, mighty through God to the pulling down of strongholds, 2 Cor. 10, 4. "Be not afraid!" That very command takes away our fear; for it is the command of our divine Captain of salvation.

It is true, the fight against our enemies means suffering, vv. 29. 30. But as faith in Christ is a gift of grace, so also suffering for Christ is a privilege. It is a great honor and advantage to suffer for Christ; by it we glorify God and encourage others to fight the fight of faith. Blessed is the man who suffers for Christ, Matt. 5, 11. 12; 2 Tim. 2, 12. St. Paul suffered for Christ; so also the Philippians were to suffer for His sake, and we must do likewise. Only we must suffer in the same manner as Paul suffered. That is the meaning of v. 30: "suffering in the same manner as you saw and now hear of me that I suffer." How did Paul suffer? Not for any evil's sake or because he had done wrong, but for righteousness' sake, for the sake of the Gospel. Again, he suffered joyously, thanking God for the very sufferings he endured. He who murmurs in the fray is not a good soldier. Tears may be in our eyes, but there must be manly courage in our hearts nevertheless. Therefore regard the sufferings of your fight for the Gospel against Christ's enemies as your glory. God regards you as worthy of being His body-guard, His army, upholding the banner of His Gospel. Will you fail Him? He did not fail you in the fight in Gethsemane and on Calvary; will you fail Him in the lesser fight against a defeated foe? Surely not.

It is a wonderful text that we have considered, full of instruction, encouragement, and consolation. There are enemies, but enemies that we need not fear if we conduct ourselves worthily of the Gospel, strive together with one mind for the faith of the Gospel, and welcome the suffering which God's battle entails upon us. Of course, the text is not for unbelievers and spiritual stragglers; it is for soldiers of Christ who are with Christ in the battle for salvation. How splendidly it cheers them in their combat against Satan, the world, and their own flesh! May God inscribe His blessed Word into our hearts that we may defy the enemy of His Church and win the victory of salvation. Then our crown will be wonderful and our rest glorious.

J. T. MUELLER.

FOUR QUESTIONS OF JESUS.

"What Think Ye of Christ?"

Matt. 22, 41—45.

Many questions are recorded on the pages of history the answers to which have helped to mould the destiny of entire nations. Questions concerning the entrance of a nation into war, its alliances, its foreign policies, its commercial and industrial programs, usually leave an indelible imprint upon the hopes and happiness of millions. And in our individual lives there are personal questions which clamor insistently for answer and which place us squarely before great alternatives. A young man is asked to consider the ministry for his profession; a young woman's hand is requested in marriage; a father is offered a position in some doubtful venture; a mother stands before a decision which will help to shape her child's career. In these and in a thousand other issues of our daily lives the importance of the answers which we give to vital questions becomes apparent.

Yet our text introduces us to a question which is of infinitely greater and more personal importance than any question that deals merely with the issues of this life, of this body, of this world. It is a question asked by our Savior Himself — "What think ye of Christ? Whose son is He?"

This question confronts every one who has ever heard the Gospel, and it is the answer to this question that spells happiness or misery for time and eternity. A hundred other questions may loom up on the horizon of human experience as issues of surpassing importance; but here in these words of our Savior we are brought face to face with the supreme question of life. All other questions pale into insignificance when compared with this divine question to which we now direct our heart's attention: —

"What Think Ye of Christ?"

We dwell —

1. *Upon the Incorrect Answer of the Pharisees;*
2. *Upon the Correct Answer of Christ Himself.*

1.

When the Pharisees answered the question of Jesus "What think ye of Christ? Whose son is He?" by stating: "The son of David," they were, in accordance with current Jewish theology, placing a very high estimate on the person of the promised Messiah. In many respects David shared with Abraham the distinction of representing the greatest and highest and best of the Old Testament. It was under David that the kingdom extended its boundaries and the golden age of a united Israel was ushered in. It was under David, the sweet singer of Israel, that the Temple was planned; that the musical service and the liturgies were perfected; that psalmody reached its loftiest heights. Now, to say that the promised Messiah was of Davidic lineage, a descendant of this exalted sovereign, was to pay Him the highest imaginable tribute.

But besides being a very reverent identification, this designation of Christ as David's son was true. It was an old prophecy that the Messiah would come from the tribe of Judah, Gen. 49, 10. In the tribe of Judah it was the house of Jesse that was designated for this preeminence; and among the sons of Jesse it was David whose descendants were to constitute the Messianic lineage. In repeated and emphatic statements, notably in the seventh and twenty-third chapters of 2 Samuel, God Himself had told David that the promised Deliverer would be his son, in the larger sense of that term by which the Hebrew designates a descendant.

Yet, while correct, the answer is misleading. The Pharisees' answer admits only the humanity of Christ. The Messiah, they would say, will be a great man; even the greatest, they would readily concede, in view of His royal lineage and other distinctions. But their answer precludes any other possibility. He is, in their opinion a mere man.

Now, this answer was not in accord with the prophetic statements of the Old Testament that deal with the person of the promised Messiah. The response of the Pharisees betrays that blindness, misinterpretation of the Scriptures and lack of personal acquaintance with the basic truths of the Bible which have always characterized false leadership in spiritual affairs. If they had turned to the first of all Messianic prophecies, Gen. 3, 15, they could have realized that no mere man could crush the Serpent's head and perform the superhuman task of destroying Satan. If they had read David's own psalms, they would have known that the promised Deliverer was described in pictures and actions, with names and attributes, that imply more than human power, majesty, and glory.

Moreover, their answer was against their own theology, which appropriated the words of Ps. 49, 7: "None of them can by any means redeem his brother nor give to God a ransom for him." For in the reunion with God which the Messiah of prophecy was to establish, the best and finest human qualities were utterly inadequate. Christ, the Anointed of God, was to be the Son of Man, it is true; but according to the plain teachings of Scripture and according to the best of Jewish theology He was to be more.

Church history repeats itself. Our Lord Himself is no longer visibly present to throw this decisive challenge into the councils of men and to receive their deliberate answer. But with more books written about Him than about any other figure of history, with His name and His fame, His Word and His work, known to friend and foe alike through unprecedented distribution of the Scriptures and through the increasing range of the Church's work, the modern man, consciously or unconsciously, is put before the question of our text.

Unfortunately the spirit and substance of the Pharisees' answer has likewise perpetuated itself. Men are ready to concede that Christ was a great man. They do not hesitate to indulge in lavish superlatives as they describe His person and His work and His influence upon all subsequent history. Many indeed would not hesitate to acclaim Him as the greatest of all men, the most majestic figure that has ever graced the earth, the most influential personage in all human development. They not only parallel the carnal enthusiasm of pharisaical thought and concede that He was David's son; they also declare that in many ways He was David's superior and that in the sphere and permanency of His influence, in the dynamics of His teachings and ideals, His majesty has remained absolutely unattained.

But in all this they have not left the low level of pharisaical error. Modernism and skepticism still insist that Christ is only an exalted manifestation of the purely human. Now, if the Christ who was born at Bethlehem and died on Calvary is to us merely an innocent victim of unfavorable circumstances who lived many centuries before His time, merely a social revolutionist who had come to submit a new code of ethics to a hard, cold world, so set in its superstitions and bigotry that it killed Him; if He is to us, as the historian Froude designated Him, "the most perfect being who ever trod the soil of this planet" or, as Ralph Waldo Emerson described Him, "the most perfect of all men that have appeared," but only this, we lose the very essence of Biblical truth and Christian hope, just as modern unbelief, although it is enthroned in the stateliness of Gothic cathedrals, has sacrificed the very center and heart of Christianity. If Christ is a mere mortal, even though He personifies the greatest of all human greatness, then every word of His pledges and promises must be qualified by the weakness and inconsistency that marks every human utterance; then His redemptive efforts are woefully inadequate; then we shall still be harassed by an inescapable doom. Let us face this issue squarely. If the modern Pharisees and Sadducees are right in restricting Christ's nature and essence to the limitations of the human, then our Savior becomes an illusionist who crusaded for a lost cause and suffered the pangs of His crucifixion in a futile martyrdom. And we, with a staggering weight of human iniquity crowding down upon our hopeless souls, are the victims of the most cruel delusion conceivable, hopeless and helpless before the reverberating thunders of God's wrath that echo into a terrifying eternity.

2.

But perish that thought: With calm, but abrupt conciseness the Savior rejects the caricature of the Messiah that pharisaical unbelief has drawn. Without indulging in a formal rebuttal, He ironically defeats these churchmen of His day with facts drawn from their own science. He asks them, in effect, how Christ can be David's son, when David himself calls Him *Lord?* And to prove that David thus acknowledges the superiority and the divinity of the Messiah, he quotes the 110th Psalm, in the opening verse of which David writes: "The Lord [God the Father] said unto my Lord [David's Lord, God the Son], Sit Thou at My right hand, until I make Thine enemies Thy footstool." And the Savior draws the quick and irrefutable deduction: "If David, then, call Him Lord, how is He his son?" If, as the entire answer of our Savior implies, David in the 110th Psalm pictures Christ as his Lord (and, as the subsequent verses of that psalm show, as the victorious King who defeats all of His enemies, the unparalleled Priest after the order of Melchizedek, everlasting and divine), how can He be restricted to the limitations of the mortal?

It is significant that our Savior demonstrates His divinity from the pages of the Old Testament, for the doctrine that Christ is God is not "a New Testament development" nor a hidden, esoteric teaching of the Old Covenant. The Pharisees, who laid inordinate stress on the very letter of the Law, who were professionally occupied with the study of the Scriptures, should have known that the Promised One was to be God's Son, yea, God Himself. If they had read the Second Psalm, they would have heard the divine decree: "Thou art My Son; this day have I begotten Thee," v. 7. If they had studied the 45th Psalm, they would have heard the glorious Messiah addressed in this acclaim: "Thy throne, O God, is forever and ever," v. 6. If they had read the very psalm which Jesus had quoted, they would have been aware of the fact that Christ was there called *Adonai,* the All-sovereign, a title reserved for God. Had they but turned to Isaiah's pages, they would have read that the prophesied Conciliator was to be the mighty God (chap. 9, 6), Immanuel, that is, "God with us" (7, 14); that He was the God whose advent was announced by the voice of the Baptist crying in the wilderness (40, 3).

Now, if the divinity of our Savior is an emphatic and repeated doctrine of the Old Testament, how amazingly is this truth sustained in the more frequent and direct passages of the New Testament. On the day of His birth He is called "Christ the Lord," Luke 2, 11. John points to Him and asserts: "This is the true God and eternal Life." Paul calls Him: "God blessed forever,"Rom. 9, 5. And in His own direct words Christ insists: "I and My Father are one," John 10, 30.

These Scriptural claims for divine essence are supported by Christ's demonstration of divine power. When He restored the sick to health, fed famished thousands by divine means, resurrected the dead, and suspended the laws of nature to carry out His divine purposes, He offered a demonstration of His godhead so powerful that it stood unchallenged. And when, as the great climax to His life of love and death of substitution, He burst asunder the bonds of the grave, this victorious resurrection is the conclusive proof of the fact that Christ is God with all the divine attributes.

The implication of Christ's answer to the question "What think ye of Christ?" this basic doctrine of our Christian faith that Christ is both the Son of Man and the Son of God, "David's son, yet David's Lord," is no theological abstraction which can leave our lives cold and untouched. When we confess in the warm, pulsating words of Luther: "I believe that Jesus Christ, true God, begotten of the Father from eternity, and also true man, born of the Virgin Mary, is my Lord," we have been granted the basic promise upon which the great Reformer builds this conclusion: "who has redeemed me, a lost and condemned creature, purchased and won me from all sins, from death, and from the power of the devil, not with gold or silver, but with His holy, precious blood and with His innocent suffering and death"; then we know this absolutely essential truth of all human life, namely, the purpose of Christ's incarnation, that greatest love which made of God a man, that brought the Creator down into the form of His creature. We know that Christ had to be God to complete the superhuman task of appeasing the wrath of His Father, of accomplishing that which is humanly impossible, the vanquishing of sin, death, and the devil.

This paramount question of all human experience, "What think ye of Christ?" has brought us a twofold answer. The one is that which originates in the rationalism, the doubt, and the unbelief of the human heart and which is perpetuated, as we realize with increasing alarm, in many of the churches which dot our country, the fallacy that chains Christ to the weaknesses and limitations of frail humanity. The other answer comes from the lips of the Savior Himself as He cites the convincing statements of the Old Covenant and anticipates the many and convincing utterances of the New, the truth that changes human life from an uncontrollable puppet's existence to a divinely planned life hidden in Christ, a truth of truths, which will ultimately anchor our souls safely in the eternity of eternities.

What will your answer be? What else can it be, under the Spirit's blessing, but the confession of Thomas "My Lord and my God!" When gazing up to that Savior's cross and finding in that bleeding, wounded, dying Redeemer "the Lamb of God which taketh away the sins of the world," you join in the undying confession of Peter, given in answer to his Lord's question: "Whom do men say that I am?" "Thou art the Christ, the Son of the living God."   W. A. MAIER.

"Is Thine Eye Evil because I Am Good?"
Matt. 20, 15.

This text is chosen from the conclusion of the Savior's parable of the Laborers in the Vineyard. Jesus had just presented to His disciples the lesson of unmerited grace which that parable illustrates. He had shown that the householder had paid all who had labored in the vineyard the same wages, whether they had worked through the heat of the day or had started at the sixth, the ninth, or even the eleventh hour. And when those who had toiled from early morning murmured against the goodman of the house, he not only replied that he had maintained the terms of their agreement and that he could dispose of his funds as he pleased, but he also asked one of the dissatisfied laborers: "Is thine eye evil because I am good?" that is, Do you look at Me with evil in your eye because I have been generous to these last who have worked but an hour or two?

This question not only touches the very foundation of our Christian faith, but it also aims directly at envy and jealousy, sins prevalent even among Christians. And because our faith will be truer and our lives finer and nobler if we understand and follow the implication of these words, let us take as the subject for our study the question of our Savior —

"Is Thine Eye Evil because I Am Good?"

Under the enlightening guidance of the Holy Spirit let us put this question to ourselves —

1. *In Regard to Spiritual Blessings of Salvation;*
2. *In Regard to the Temporal Blessings of Life.*

1.

The great lesson of the parable of the Laborers in the Vineyard is that of the basic doctrine of our Church, that we are justified by faith, without the deeds of the Law. For the salvation of our souls and for our entrance into heaven even the aggregate of the best works of an entire lifetime are not sufficient. The ancients thought that they could purchase their way into heaven, as archeological research has repeatedly demonstrated; but the Christian knows that there is not money enough on earth to open the doors to a blessed eternity and that it is only in Christ that he has been blessed with the assurance of salvation. Let me repeat, "We are justified freely by His grace, through Christ"; not Christ in addition to our good resolutions, not Christ supplemented by our well-meant intentions, not Christ plus a lifetime of penance and multiplied virtues, but only, wholly, and unconditionally by the holy, precious blood of Christ, the sin-bearing Lamb of God.

Consequently, as the parable illustrates, the reward is of grace, not of merit. It does not matter how long the individual laborers have worked; those who have come in the last shifts receive, by the exhibition of the purest and most unmerited grace, the same penny that is paid to those who have borne the heat and burden of the day.

Interpreted in its spiritual significance, this parable implies that, while there are many who during their lifetime have been sincere and stalwart Christians, children of God who have come from Christian homes, who have borne the heat and brunt of the Church's tasks, who have worked tirelessly and incessantly for the advancement of the Kingdom, there will always be those who will come in the eleventh hour and with little exertion and less effort enjoy the full measure of blessings which Christian faith bestows. As the malefactor on the cross was blessed in his last moment with the promise of paradise by his Savior at his side, so throughout the history of the Church there have been those who have been plucked as a brand from the burning, saved in the last hour, brought to Christ even on their death-beds; and they, too, according to the immeasurable bounty of divine grace, are to receive the same salvation, joy, and blessing as has come to life-long Christians and their arduous, tireless labors in behalf of the Kingdom.

Swayed as we are by human impulses and instincts, this full, free, and unrestricted mercy of God in Christ often provokes our displeasure; and as the laborers murmured against the goodman of the house and looked at him with malevolent eyes, so we, God's children, weak and inconsistent as we all are, may be in danger of becoming displeased because God's mercy and goodness are so unfathomable and incomprehensible according to our human standards. It was this error which characterized the life of Jonah. He had been sent to Nineveh to call its hundreds of thousands steeped in the sins of degenerate paganism to repentance. But instead of fulfilling his divine commission, he endeavored to flee to Tarshish, in the very opposite direction, almost as far from Nineveh as the civilized world in his day extended. Why? As he himself confesses, he knew that by the preaching of this message from God that world metropolis would be converted from its sin and God, being merciful and compassionate, would forgive Nineveh. And this, his flesh told him, was directly contrary to the procedure that God should have followed. Why save the Ninevites and extend to them the blessings which he regarded as the peculiar heritage and property of the Jews, under which they had lived for centuries? He was bitter toward God and preferred to die rather than to live because the city repented. His eye was evil because God was good.

Now, it is a far cry from the Old Testament days of Jonah and the New Testament days of the parable of the Laborers in the Vineyard to the more modern church-life and the multiplied problems and opportunities of this new age. Yet we, too, are perpetually in danger of questioning or even indicting the gracious dispensations of God as we behold experiences in the smaller spheres of our own lives. Here is a doddering, decrepit drunkard who is reborn by the Spirit and who is brought into the Church in the eleventh hour. In too many instances there are glances of doubt, evidences of mistrust, questioning of motives, and particularly the suggestion of the pharisaical prayer of thanking God that we are not as other people. Here is a woman who has been converted to our faith and becomes a member of an older, established congregation. It often takes an inordinately long time before she is fully welcomed into our church circles or received as on a spiritual par with the older members, who may have founded the congregation and assumed the difficulties of its early and more trying years. Here is a hard-working, self-denying church-member, who shuns no task and refuses no responsibility when the welfare of his church is involved; yet in a dozen different ways he feels, and sometimes may even express the conviction, that, because he has distinguished himself in the service of his Lord, he should be preferred to others, particularly those whose zeal and labors have been more limited. And if this distinction is not accorded to him, and if perchance those who have played less important and less arduous rôles in the Church are signally honored, there is a danger that he, too, will look askance at God, because He is so good to the undeserving.

Now, it is a far cry from the Old Testament days of Jonah and mental truth of our faith. It takes for granted that there is something inherent in man and in his accomplishments which entitles him to recognition and distinction in the sight of God and that, the more pronounced and protracted the good works are, the greater should be his compensation. This the Scriptures emphatically and repeatedly deny, 1 Cor. 2, 14; Eph. 2, 1; Rom. 8, 7; etc. Indeed, the doctrine of *sola gratia* clearly separates Christianity from every other form or expression of religion. Therefore the person who seeks recognition and payment for services rendered in the Kingdom has made an altogether unchristian and anti-Scriptural approach to the greatest truth of saving faith.

But in addition to this fundamental misconception this idea of indicting God because of the extraordinary mercies which others experience is obviously a product of selfish motives, and selfishness is always the very antithesis to the spirit of Christ. The fact that others experience the blessings of Christian faith although they have not labored nor toiled in the Kingdom in no way detracts from our own ultimate joy and happiness. We have the seal and assurance of our faith. We receive what God has promised to us, just as the laborers who were first hired were given the contracted remuneration. Should we not content ourselves with this realization and be everlastingly grateful for these undeserved mercies?

Yet we are all prone to fall victim to this superiority complex. As long as we are in the flesh, those self-assertive emotions of ambition will whisper into our ears and tell us that God should show preference to us, and in moments of weakness our faith may ebb away to that low level in which we, too, will look to God with accusing eyes because He has been good to others. May we, led by the Spirit's guidance and fortified by a sense of our own unworthiness and a recognition of our many faults and frailties, be ready to fight against the encroachment of these unworthy and degrading impulses and, strengthened by Word and Sacrament, to cling with ever stronger faith to the central doctrine of our Church, the free and unmerited justification by faith!

2.

But, as many other statements of Scripture, these words of the Savior are capable of wider application. Men look askance at God not only because of His goodness in the spiritual blessings of His grace, but also because He often bestows His temporal benedictions contrary to their ideas. The sin of envy and the motive of jealousy have not only disfigured the pages of history as the prompting impulses to national tragedy, but they have also marred the happiness and serenity of many Christian lives.

This vice is found intimately associated with the first sin in Eden. Tempted by the delusion that they might "be as God, knowing good and evil," our first parents were brought to fall by their envy of God.

This sin expressed itself on the fallen countenance of Cain when his sacrifice was rejected because of his unbelief and that of his brother Abel accepted because of his faith.

Envy is still a besetting sin for the average man. It seizes the nations, as it seized the Philistines when they were overcome by their envy of Isaac (Gen. 26, 14). It comes into the Church, as it did in the days of Korah (Num. 16, 3), who in jealous ambition accused Moses and Aaron of assuming sacerdotal functions which he himself coveted. It invades the sanctity of the home, as in the case of Joseph and his brethren (Gen. 37, 11), where the second youngest of twelve sons became the object of envy on the part of his older brothers, or as in the case of the prodigal's brother, who could not tolerate the thought that his profligate, ne'er-do-well brother should be welcomed into the open arms of his father and be feasted with a fattened calf.

The more self-engrossed and ambitious the individual is, the more pronounced will be the inclination toward this sin. It held self-seeking Haman so tightly in its grip that in spite of his promotions he was disturbed by seeing a single Jew, Mordecai, sitting in the king's gate, Esther 5, 13. It takes Saul captive as he hears the women of

Israel sing the praises of David. It beckons to the high priests and the churchmen of the Savior's day.

Now, all this is not only contrary to the direct word of God which calls envy "the rottenness of the bones" (Prov. 14, 30) and which warns: "Let us not be desirous of vainglory, provoking one another, envying one another" (Gal. 5, 26); it is also against the second table of the Law: "Thou shalt love thy neighbor as thyself." And the picture of Christians moved by envy, with eyes of evil directed against God and their fellow-men, is one of the saddest of all spectacles. It is bad enough for men of this world, materialistic, self-seeking, and driven by thoughts of gain, to become enslaved to this relentless taskmaster. But to Christians, who know the love wherewith Christ has loved us and who have His new commandment "Love one another," to drop into these depths is to deny their high Christian calling.

But envy marked by the evil, covetous eye stands condemned in its own consequences. It never brings happiness; it always creates misery. Haman is hanged on the gallows he built for Mordecai; Saul is a suicide, while David is crowned king; Joseph's brothers are driven out of their homeland by hunger, while the "dreamer" becomes the food administrator of an empire. And in the repetitions of history to-day show me restless envy, and I will show you the blight of unhappiness.

Contrary to the divine injunctions, entirely opposed to the Savior's ideals and values, hostile to our own welfare, creating a shriveled soul and a dwarfed outlook on life, the sin of envy becomes the destructive force against which the Christian must daily battle with all his might. Because it so easily seeks and finds justification, because it so readily explains itself or minimizes its force and contention, it is one of the more dangerous and insidious of the sins that assail us. Let us, then, trusting not in our own strength, but in Him whose strength is made perfect in weakness, shake off all encroachments that would make us fall victim to that sin. Let us, looking ever to the Lord Jesus, to His life of humility and service, to the ceremonial of self-abasement in that upper chamber on the very night of His betrayal, and particularly to His cross as the symbol of Heaven's highest love, find there His holy ideal which we are to follow, strengthened by His Spirit, armed by His Word, purified by His Sacraments, fortified by prayer and victorious by faith.   W. A. MAIER.

"Which of You Convinceth Me of Sin?"

John 8, 46.

From their very first encounter with Jesus on through His entire ministry the enemies of our Lord met His claims of Deity with the one consistent legal charge "This man blasphemeth," Mark 2, 1 ff.; John 10, 33; Mark 14, 64. The four inspired Gospel records, especially the Gospel of St. John, inform us in detail how our Savior sought to convince His unbelieving enemies of the truthfulness of His claims. In our text we have the supreme challenge of the Son of God addressed to His opponents, a challenge that has stood in the sacred record these 1900 years for the serious consideration of every unbeliever: —

"Which of You Convinceth Me of Sin?"

This supreme challenge of our Savior involves a claim —

1. Of Sinless Perfection;   2. Of Absolute Truthfulness.

1.

Jesus during His earthly ministry repeatedly convicted His enemies of their sins. A brief glance at the instance described at the beginning of this chapter will suffice for our present purpose. When they brought the woman taken in adultery to Him for His legal judgment upon her, their one motive was to tempt Him, that they might have to accuse Him. Note that ignoble motive. But instead of succeeding in this evil design, Jesus completely routed these dastardly hypocrites by challenging them: "He that is without sin among you, let him first cast a stone at her." What happened? Were any stones cast? No; "being convicted by their own conscience, they went out one by one, beginning at the eldest even unto the last." Magnificent testimony to the great, fundamental doctrine of the Bible: "All have sinned and come short of the glory of God," Rom. 3, 23. To the wicked insinuation that Jesus connived at the woman's sin His final word is sufficient refutation: "Go, and *sin no more,*" John 8, 1—11. Convicted of sin, penitent, the woman was forgiven by the Friend of sinners. — That challenge also stands to this day: "Let him that is without sin first cast a stone."

In further debates with His enemies following upon this incident the Savior in sudden contrast challenges them in regard to His own personal record: "Which of you," etc.? As in the previous incident no stone was cast, so in this instance no answer was made to the bold challenge of Christ. No one was able to answer Him a word. And though many and bitter enemies have come and gone during the nineteen centuries following, not one of them has yet been able to find a single flaw, a single fault, a single sin in the life of Jesus. His moral purity, His sinless perfection, stands unassailable throughout the ages.

In order to grasp the importance of the sinlessness of Jesus, let us look at some of the testimonies given in the Bible. Does Jesus Himself positively claim that He is morally perfect? Indeed He does. Before these very enemies He had said: "I do *always* those things that please Him," *i. e.,* the Father, 8, 29. He sought not His own glory, but His Father's glory and honor, 8, 49. 50. And therefore He is true and no unrighteousness in Him, 7, 18.

And the Father, who sent Him, bears witness of His sinlessness, saying: "This is My beloved Son, in whom I am well pleased," 8, 18. Matt. 3, 17; 17, 5. And His disciples, who believingly accepted the evidence given them, testify to His sinless perfection: John: "In Him is no sin," 1 John 3, 5. "Jesus Christ the Righteous," 1 John 2, 1. "Full of grace and truth," John 1, 14. — Peter: "Without blemish and without spot," 1 Pet. 1, 19. "Christ did no sin, neither was guile found in His mouth, who, when He was reviled, reviled not again; when He suffered, He threatened not," etc., 1 Pet. 2, 22. 23. — Even Judas the traitor testifies to the sinlessness of Jesus: "I have sinned in that I have betrayed the *innocent* blood," Matt. 27, 4. — Paul was born out of due time, but he knows this important fact in the life of his Lord: "He knew no sin," *i. e.,* by act of commission or omission, 2 Cor. 5, 21. Jesus had no need to pray, as we do: "Forgive me my trespasses."

The Roman centurion at the cross exclaims: "This was a *righteous* man," Luke 23, 47. — Pilate, the pagan, convinced thoroughly of the innocence of the Man of Sorrows, testifies: "I find no fault in Him at all," Luke 23, 4. 14. 22; John 19, 6. And to Pilate's threefold witness his wife adds her testimony: "that *just* man," Matt. 27, 19. 24.

The author of the Epistle to the Hebrews adds weighty proof: "Jesus, our great High Priest, was in all points tempted like as we are, yet *without sin*"; "He is holy, harmless, undefiled, separate from sinners," Heb. 4, 15; 7, 26.

To quote but one Old Testament prophet, Isaiah in prophetic vision testifies: "He had done no violence, neither was any deceit found in His mouth," chap. 53, 9b. (Quoted 1 Pet. 1, 22.) Jer. 23, 5; 33, 15 are also important.

This veritable cloud of witnesses ought to be sufficient for any honest and candid seeker after truth that the Bible seeks to establish the sinlessness of Jesus; that Jesus Himself claimed absolute moral purity; that His disciples preached His sinlessness as an important Christian doctrine.

"Who art Thou?" the Jews ask Jesus in this chapter, v. 25. "Even the same that I said unto you from the beginning," answers Jesus. Who is this sinless One? we also ask. He is the Christ, the

Messiah, the Son of God, John 6, 69; 11, 27; 16, 30; 20, 31. His sin-lessness is an important proof of Jesus' deity, *His equality with God.* John 5, 18; Phil. 2, 6. Hence also the sacrificial death of Christ can be and is—there is no other mediator, no other sinless one—the effec-tive remedy against sin, the *only* remedy, Heb. 9, 14. 26; Acts 4, 12; 13, 38. 39; 1 John 1, 9.*

2.

Having established the sinless perfection, the unassailable moral purity of Jesus, let us look now at the other claim involved in His bold challenge to His enemies: "Which of you convinceth Me of sin," of a fault, a transgression, a violation of the Law, of unrighteous-ness? We have seen that no one was or is to-day able to take up the challenge. Now, if Jesus is sinless, that necessarily, yea, self-evi-dently, implies that He did not lie. To lie is a very serious sin, as you may see from Jesus' stern and severe statements about His ene-mies' being children of the devil, the Father of Lies, v. 44. To lie is a very grievous sin, because God is Truth and truth is the most precious possession any man can have. Therefore Jesus declares to His enemies: "Ye have not known My Father, but I know Him; and if I should say, I know Him not, I shall be a liar like unto you," v. 55. Jesus placing before His enemies the hypothetical case of His being a liar! How serious and zealous He must have been to safeguard the truth! Do you, dear friend, feel some of this zeal for the truth, divine truth, the truth as it is in Christ Jesus? His true Church is the pillar and ground of the truth, 1 Tim. 3, 15.

Accordingly, we hear Jesus again challenging His opponents: "And if I say the truth, why do ye not believe Me?" v. 46 b. Yes, if Jesus is absolutely sinless, then He self-evidently cannot be a liar; but if He speaks the truth, why do these enemies not believe His Word, His message, His teaching? Let us grasp Jesus' argument well. It runs thus: "If I am really without sin, — and none of you is able to convict Me of the contrary, — then am I also without *a lie;* but if I am without a lie, then do I speak the truth, and you on your part (the pronoun in Greek is emphatic) have no reason for not be-lieving Me. Thus we see how closely the guarantee of His veracity is bound up with our Savior's sinlessness and how both His sinlessness and His veracity *obligate us to believe Him.* But now I beg you to note that Jesus declares, v. 45: "Because I, on the contrary (the pro-noun in Greek is strongly emphatic, in opposition to the devil, v. 44), speak the truth, ye believe Me not." *"Because* I speak the truth" — what a thoroughly tragical "because"! What a terrible indictment of

---

* The notion of sin as a necessary transitional point in *human* de-velopment, a notion entertained and given publicity by some present-day writers, is shown to be groundless by the historic fact of the sinlessness of Jesus, who was *true man.*

unbelief, real unbelief! The unbeliever cannot find any flaw in Christ's character or life, he cannot charge Jesus with a single lie; and yet, when divine truth is proclaimed by Jesus, he rejects the message in unbelief. Unbelief, then, in its ultimate analysis is an insult offered to the divine veracity, in other words, to God, who, if He is at all worthy of being God, is above all *true,* 8, 26. God *cannot lie;* unbelief is an insult offered to His Son, Jesus Christ, who came into the world to *bear witness to the truth,* John 18, 37, and to His Holy Spirit, who is *the Spirit of Truth,* John 14, 17; 15, 26. This unbelief is the great sin which condemns and is the root of all other sins. Hence Jesus predicted that after His return to the Father, the Holy Spirit, whom He would send from the Father to *lead us into all truth,* is going to reprove (convict, same Greek verb as in our text) the world of sin "because they believe not" on Him, Jesus, whom the Father sent to testify, John 16, 9, who spoke to the world those things only which He heard of the Father and which the Father taught Him, 8, 28. (See also John 3, 19; 7, 7.)

Let us not fail to see the veracity of our Savior in its true light. The argument in all of chap. 8, yea, throughout the Gospel of St. John, is not based upon the position that "the Sinless One is the purest and surest organ of the knowledge and communication of the truth" or that "the knowledge of the truth is grounded in the purity of the will," which view presupposes a knowledge of the truth obtained by Jesus mediately or, at least, not acquired until He learned it in His human state; no, the argument of our chapter, as of the entire Gospel of John is that Jesus knew the truth immediately, that He possessed this knowledge before He became man, from all eternity, and that this divine knowledge of the truth was preserved and continued during His earthly life by means of constant fellowship between Himself and the Father, John 1, 18; 8, 26. 28.

Hence "he that is of God," the true Israelite, "heareth God's words; ye therefore hear them not because ye are not of God," 8, 47. 43. No wonder the unbelieving Jews replied to the Savior: "Say we not well that Thou art a Samaritan, *i. e.,* a heretic, and hast a demon?" v. 48. No true Israelite would indulge in such abusive language concerning his Messiah. No wonder that after these claims of Christ's they asked indignantly: "Art Thou greater than our father Abraham, who is dead? and the prophets are dead. Whom makest Thou Thyself?" v. 53. They felt that by His claim of absolute veracity and sinlessness Jesus was assuming a position of superiority far above the saints of the Old Testament. No wonder that they, who could not cast a stone at the woman taken in adultery because they were convicted of sin by their own conscience, now took up stones to cast at Jesus, the Sinless and Truthful One. It could not be otherwise, 2 Cor. 6, 14. 15.

To-day the Savior asks us also: "If I speak the truth, why do ye not believe Me?" He says: John 14, 6. This demands a great faith of each and every one of us. Let us continue in His Word and have faith in our absolutely sinless and truthful Savior, lest the sentence He pronounced on the unbelievers be spoken also upon us: "Ye shall die in your sins; for if ye believe not that I am He, ye shall die in your sins," 8, 24. — Close with John 8, 31. 32. 36.   O. W. WISMAR.

"Sayest Thou This Thing of Thyself?"
John 18, 34.

The death of Christ, the Messiah-King, lies at the very center of Christian truth. Hence also the causes which led to His death on Calvary are described for us in minutest detail by the sacred writers, every one of whom is very careful to emphasize the fact that Jesus was not guilty of the various charges preferred against Him.

While before the Sanhedrin the formal charge brought against Him was that of blasphemy, because He said He was Christ, the Son of God, the various accusations before Pontius Pilate finally resolved themselves into the single charge that Jesus said He was a *king*. It was at the very beginning of His trial before Pontius Pilate, when the procurator asked Jesus: "Art Thou the King of the Jews?" that Jesus rather abruptly interrupted the examination by asking the pointed and penetrating counter-question: "Sayest thou this thing of thyself?"

What is the exact meaning of this question of our Savior addressed to Pilate? Why did Jesus put this rather pointed question? What was Pilate's answer? What is the significance of the question if we address it to other Gentiles in Pilate's situation? What is the deepest significance of the question if we address it to ourselves and to Christians in general? What is our answer?

These searching inquiries at once arise in our minds as we face this question of our Savior.

Jesus' Pointed Counter-Question "Sayest Thou This Thing of Thyself?"

Let us consider it —

1. *As Addressed to the Gentile Pontius Pilate;*
2. *As Addressed to Us and Christians in General.*

1.

In keeping with Roman legal practise Pilate correctly opens the proceedings against Jesus by asking the plaintiffs: "What accusation bring ye against this man?" Lacking a *definite* charge, he advises the accusers to take their prisoner and judge Him according to their law, — which, note well, they have already done. Pilate's recommendation forces the Jews before the praetorium to confess that they seek the death of this man. He must die; nothing else will satisfy them. How the pagan procurator must have felt the hypocrisy of the plaintiffs, for he knew that for envy they, especially their chief priests, had delivered Jesus. Matt. 27, 18. We have here a striking example of religious hypocrisy: the same persons who went not into the judgment-hall of a Gentile governor lest they should be defiled, none the less stand with brazen boldness outside that judgment-hall and demand the death penalty for a prisoner whom they are falsely accusing and by their false accusation are unable to convict. Have you ever come face to face with this form of hypocrisy in so-called religious people? Blind guides, as Jesus in advance had characterized them and all their ilk, who strain at a gnat and swallow a camel! Matt. 23, 24. In the midst of their hypocrisy the accusers of the innocent Christ have to admit their political helplessness before pagan Pilate, conscious of his superior power, John 19, 10. Thus Jesus' repeated prediction as to the mode of His death, John 3, 14; 8, 28; 12, 32, moved toward fulfilment, 18, 30—32.

Having failed to shift responsibility and having received the definite charge, Pilate reenters the judgment-hall and, calling Jesus, begins the legal examination; for Roman law, like unto Jewish law, and unto any law worth the name, does not condemn a man unheard, John 7, 50—52. "Art thou the King of the Jews?" or rather, as in the original, with a sound of comtemptuous surprise: "Thou [thou emphatic] art the King of the Jews?" Thus, Pilate, baffled man of the world, introduces his personal examination of Jesus. We would expect him to begin: "Thou sayest that Thou art the King of the Jews?" But he does not. — There was something grossly wrong in Pilate's procedure. Not until the Savior reminds him of his unfairness as judge, does Pilate ask the legally correct question: "What hast Thou done?" v. 35. That is the question Pilate should have asked the accused at the very outset.

Accordingly, Jesus broke in upon the proceedings with the peculiar, penetrating, pointed counter-question: "Sayest thou this of thyself?" Pilate, though procurator of Judea from the very beginning of Jesus' ministry, Luke 3, 1, had never met the Lord face to face, had never heard of any political disturbance caused by Jesus, though Pilate had dealt summarily with other suspicious characters, Luke 13, 1. Then, why did Pilate give a band of men, troops, and officers (attendants) to the chief priests and Pharisees, John 18, 3, to come out as against a thief with swords and staves for to take Him? Matt. 26. 55. What had Pilate heard from the chief priests and Pharisees that caused him to deal thus with Jesus? They had undoubtedly told Pilate in advance that Jesus said He was the King of the Jews, a title that seemed to need investigation, though it did not perturb Pilate as badly as it had Idumean Herod thirty and more years previously, when the Magi came from the East to Jerusalem, saying, "Where is He that is born King of the Jews?"

"Thou — Thou the King of the Jews?" We can easily image Pilate's surprise, mingled with cynical contempt of all things Jewish, as he thus addressed Jesus, this meek, unassuming, self-effacing, solitary prophet of Nazareth, whom he did not even know to be of Galilee, Luke 23, 5; who had consistently shunned publicity, John 7, 1; 11, 54; and, who had never caused so much as a ripple of revolution against the government, though multitudes had often gathered around Him.

How, then, came Pilate to ask Jesus: "Art Thou the King of the Jews?" No wonder Jesus, conscious of His absolute innocence, counter-questions: "Sayest thou this thing of thyself or did others tell it thee of Me?" The Savior's question in other words was: "Are you saying this as Roman procurator and judge, of your own initiative, at your own instance and prompting, or did others tell it you of Me?"

Pilate, surprised and rather irritated at this unexpected dart, impatiently retorts: "Am I a Jew? Thine own nation and [especially] the chief priests have delivered Thee unto me." Thus the answer of the haughty procurator is an indirect denial of Jesus' first question and an affirmation of the second. Catch the proud, irritated emphasis of Pilate: "You do not suppose, I trust, that I, I, your procurator, am a Jew? How should I of my own judgment, at my own instance, think of trying Thee as king of the Jews? Nay, the opposite is the case: Thine own nation, the Jews, Thy fellow-citizens, more especially the highest of Thy fellow-citizens, the high priests, have delivered thee to me with this charge." And then only the proper legal question: "What hast Thou done?" or, "What evil hast Thou done?" (See Luke 23, 22.)

Now, what was Jesus' motive and purpose in putting this counter-question to Pilate? In the first place, Jesus wanted to impress upon Pilate the fact that he, the pagan Roman, the Gentile non-Jew, could of his own initiative impossibly have come upon the idea that Jesus, solitary and meek, was the King-Messiah of the Jews. His subjects, where were they at this crucial hour? Yea, and what could Pilate know about Jewish Messianic hopes — of himself, without hearing it from others, from the Jews? One thing only Pilate knew, that for envy they had delivered Him. — In the second place, Jesus by His pointed counter-question did not desire to gather the more exact sense of Pilate's question, whether it was intended in a Jewish and theocratic sense or in a Roman and political sense, a distinction of which Pilate, as Gentile, was not competent; but He, Jesus, simply claimed the right to know who was the author of the accusation contained in Pilate's words. Throughout the trial Pilate sticks to that charge. (See John 18, 39; 19, 14. 15. 19. 22.) The accusation *could* come only from the Jews. And while Pilate used the claim and the title in deepest scorn, sarcasm, and contempt, yet in God's government it stood unchanged: Jesus of Nazareth, King of the Jews, a title of honor, because He is the King of Truth, which is the glory of His people Israel, Luke 2, 32.

The attitude and answer of Pilate to our Lord's pointed question is of deeper significance than we might at first suspect. It proves that even the so-called historical knowledge of Jesus, the superficial acquaintance with Jesus as a historical personage, merely intellectual knowing about Jesus is derived from others, comes from without and does not originate in one's own mind and reasoning. Pilate, like the woman of Samaria, John 4, 9, could know of himself that Jesus was a Jew; but that He was and is King, Messiah-King, of the Jews, this Pilate could only learn by others' telling him of it, and those others in his case were Jesus' own contemporary fellow-Jews. When Jesus tells Pilate about His kingdom of truth, the Roman governor has heard the "good confession," 1 Tim. 6, 13, but does not accept the truth. Yet we must note that the truth was told him by another, was not discovered by himself; for the world by wisdom, by its own philosophy, knew not God, not the truth of God; for had they known it, the princes of this world would not have crucified the Lord of Glory, 1 Cor. 1, 21; 2, 8. Note that under God's providence even the enemies of Jesus must help to make Him known, Phil. 1, 16—18.

2.

Having considered the meaning and significance of Jesus' pointed counter-question in Pilate's case, let us now address the question to the believer, to ourselves as Christians.

If you declare in true faith: "Jesus of Nazareth, the historical Jesus, who stood before Pontius Pilate, is the King of the Jews, is the Messiah, the Anointed of God, is in verity and truth the Son of God," sayest thou this of thyself, or did others tell it thee of Him? What is your reply? In a far profounder sense than Pilate said it, you will gratefully and humbly confess: "Of myself, of my own thinking and reasoning, of my own judgment, I know nothing of saving truth, of Jesus as the King of Truth and of His kingdom of truth." Nor can I know. And I am convinced that I cannot by my own reason or strength believe in Jesus Christ, my Lord, my Savior, or come to Him. In a sense far nobler than Pilate said it, you will

readily admit: Others told it me concerning Him, Jesus. It may
have been your father or mother or both of your parents who first
told you of Him, in which case, lest you forget, you are under a debt
of eternal gratitude to them. Or the "others" who told you concerning
Him may have been your teacher, your minister, a friend, a stranger,
a professional or business man. Whatever the case may have been,
others, other believers, told you concerning Jesus. You did not of
yourself come to know Him. This you will readily admit. Andrew,
the fisherman, found his own brother and said to him: "We have
found the Messias, the Christ," and he brought him to Jesus. Philip
of Bethsaida found Nathanael and said to him: "We have found," etc.
"Come and see," John 1, 41. 45. 46. Andrew and John had heard the
message of salvation from John the Baptist, who said to them, looking
upon Jesus: "Behold the Lamb of God," John 1, 36. St. Paul in his
letter to the church at Rome gives the general rule when he says:
"How shall they believe in Him of whom they have not heard? And
how shall they hear without a preacher? And how shall they preach
except they be sent?" Rom. 10, 14. 15. The last statement reminds us
forcefully of the obligation of those who know toward those who do
not know Jesus. It is only when you have fully realized your in-
debtedness for the knowledge of your Savior to those who told you
of Him that you will be a witness to others who do not yet know
Jesus. The preacher, the servant of the Word, will ever and again
remind himself and his hearers of this truth of our religion in the
words of Paul to the Corinthian church: "Not that we are sufficient
[qualified] *of ourselves* to think anything as of ourselves; but our
sufficiency is of God, who also hath made us able ministers of the
New Testament," 2 Cor. 3, 5. 6.

The ultimate source of all true religious knowledge, accordingly,
is God, especially God the Holy Spirit. Hence we confess a clear and
incontrovertible truth of Holy Scripture when we sing: Hymn 3, st. 2.
Because of our utter ignorance of saving knowledge we must pray:
Hymn 259, st. 1. If we possess the true knowledge of Jesus, the light
of the glorious Gospel of Christ, this is due solely and alone to the
same God who commanded the light to shine out of darkness at the
creation of the universe. It is that same God who hath shined in our
dark hearts to give the light of the knowledge of the glory of God
in the face of Jesus Christ, 2 Cor. 4, 4. 6.

When Simon Peter answered the question of Jesus "Who say ye
that I am?" by saying: "Thou art the Christ, the Son of the living
God," what did Jesus say to him? "Blessed art thou, Simon, son of
Jonas; for *flesh and blood* hath not revealed it unto thee, but My
Father which is in heaven," Matt. 16, 15—17. Flesh and blood, men
following their own conjectures, were able only to say that the Son of

Man was John the Baptist, or Elias or Jeremias or one of the prophets; but to confess Him as the Christ, the Messiah, the Son of the living God, required a revelation of the Father of the only-begotten Son. Likewise John the Baptist testifies twice: "I knew Him not; but He that sent me to baptize with water, the same said unto me, Upon whom thou shalt see the Spirit descending and remaining upon Him, the same is He which baptizeth with the Holy Ghost," John 1, 31. 33.

This truth, that the ultimate source of true religious knowledge is the Holy Spirit, is further emphasized in such exceptional cases as Balaam in the Old Testament, Num. 22—24, and Caiaphas, the high priest, in the New Testament, John 11, 49—52, Balaam, the heathen soothsayer, the wicked unbeliever, and Caiaphas, the unbelieving, hardened political opportunist, are seized by the divine Spirit and compelled, against their own intention, to testify concerning the saving work of Christ. Of Caiaphas's prophecy we are told expressly: "This spake he not of himself." Another was witnessing through him on that occasion — the Spirit of Truth, the Holy Spirit.

Thus ultimately religious truth is traceable to God, so that no man can claim, I am saying this of myself; others did not tell it me. One human witness to Christ derives his knowledge from another human witness; the saving knowledge of all Christians is the gift of the Holy Spirit. The Holy Spirit glorifies Christ, whose are all things that the Father hath, John 16, 14. 15. That same Holy Spirit spake through the holy prophets who have been since the world began, Luke 1, 70, and through the apostles, who were eye-witnesses and ear-witnesses of Jesus' entire ministry of His divine words and works, from the beginning of His official life as Israel's Messiah-King until He was taken up into heaven, John 15, 27; Luke 1, 2; Acts 1, 1. 2. This prophetic and apostolic testimony is laid down in infallible, imperishable form in the Holy Scriptures, which are able to make us wise unto salvation through faith which is in Christ Jesus.

What, then, is your answer to the Savior's question, once pointedly asked of Pilate, to-day penetratingly addressed to you regarding your Christian profession: "Sayest thou this of thyself, of thine own wisdom and at thy own instance, or did others tell it thee of Me?" Let your answer be: 1 Cor. 2, 10 and John 1, 18.

O. W. WISMAR.

THREE PROMISES OF JESUS.

The Comfort and Prospect of Christian Faith.
John 14, 1—3.

"In this and the following two chapters," said Luther, "we have the best and most comforting discourse that our Lord delivered on earth." Nowhere will you find words so beautiful, so tender, so full of weighty thoughts, so charged with consolation, as these which our Lord spoke on that night in which He was betrayed, just before He and the Eleven broke up that private gathering in the upper room to go over the brook Kidron to Gethsemane. These chapters in John may be termed the consolatory part of our Christian religion, in which the Lord Jesus brings to bear on hearts filled with anxiety, perplexity, care, and trouble the tenderness of His Savior-heart. Marvelous words He speaks here to allay every fear, to silence every murmur, to calm the storms of doubt that may be rending the hearts of His disciples.

Our Lord speaks here exclusively to His disciples, to believers. He speaks to the Eleven not so much as apostles as to men, followers, friends, whom He loved and who cherished Him. But not only to these men who were with Him that night does he speak these words of our text. With prophetic eye He, the Son of God and the Son of Man, embraced in the Eleven all those who down the centuries would follow Him, accept Him as the Redeemer, and place their hope of eternal life in Him. To you and to me He speaks assuring words in our text.

The Comfort and Prospect of Faith in Jesus.

1. The Comfort of Faith.

"Let not your heart be troubled; ye believe in God, believe also in Me." There was much to trouble the Eleven that night. They had witnessed the sad disclosure of the traitor in their midst, a most disheartening, distressing, disturbing experience. And the Lord had not stopped the feet of Judas. He had let him go out into the night; He had even said to him: "That thou doest do quickly," John 13, 27. What ominous consequences lay in store for Him and them in that action! Moreover, the Master said that He would be with them only a little while longer. He had repeated these predictions; that, too, presaged something alarming. Yea, even Peter, despite all his protestations of loyalty, would deny Him thrice. Disaster was in prospect for all of them. Did the faces of the Eleven show their feelings? Their hearts were full of concern; fear laid hold on them. He spoke of laying down His life. They were to be left alone. What would the future bring? What would become of them? How could they face the world alone, without Him?

In this tense, foreboding atmosphere our Lord, seeing the events of the next day, the cruel, hard road which the Eleven would have to travel, even after they would see Him risen, even after their eyes would be opened and their hearts would be inspired with ardent faith in Him, the crucified and risen Savior and Lord, yea, seeing all they and many others after them would suffer for His sake and the Gospel's, Jesus says: "Let not your heart be troubled; ye believe in God, believe also in Me."

All Christians share in the experiences of the Eleven. Life is full of good and evil days, sunshine and storm, prosperity and adversity, health and illness, happiness and sorrow, affliction and persecution. Fear, anguish, worry, and care befall the Christian in this world no less than the unbeliever. Often the clouds of adversity and trouble and heartache seem to hide the face of God. Disheartening experiences with members of one's own family, with friends, with neighbors, with business associates, make the heart sick and cause our spirits to droop. Yet even through the clouds speaks the tender voice of our Savior: "Let not your heart be troubled; ye believe in God, believe also in Me."

In every circumstance and condition of life He is there to calm the troubled heart of His disciples. Are you poor, a child of toil? Do you eat your bread in the sweat of your brow? Does the heavy yoke of oppression gall your neck? Do you feel depressed and low, bow your head under a load of care for the wherewithal? "Let not your heart be troubled." See Him, how He fasted forty days, how He hungered, how He trod the weary road and, all athirst, sat down upon the curb of the well at Sychar. He, the Lord of Glory, who holds the clouds in the hollow of His hand, begs a drink of the Samaritan woman. And shall the disciple be above his Master? If He suffered hunger and thirst and had not where to lay His head, be of good cheer; He will not forsake you. Be not dismayed; He has compassion on your condition. In all these things you are a fellow-sufferer with Him, the Savior. You believe in God? Of course you do. Then believe also in Jesus. Let not your heart be troubled over these things, your condition. He suffered all for your sake. Follow Him.

Are you perhaps smarting under the sharp tongue of slander and bitter words? Is that adder embittering your life with evil words and wicked reports? Let not your heart be troubled by them. They can harm you none when He is your Friend. See, the King of kings was called a Samaritan, in which word a rock of contempt was hurled at His head. They said of Him that He had a devil. They called Him a wine-bibber. He was the pure Son of God, whom no one, not even His enemies, could convict of a sin, and yet they said that He cast out devils with the help of Beelzebub, the prince of devils. They mocked Him; they slandered Him; they contemned Him; they dishonored Him. "If they have persecuted Me, they will also persecute you," said Jesus to His disciples. Because you are not of the world, therefore the world hates you. "He who smites the Lord on the mouth," said Luther, "will certainly not honor the servant." Inasmuch as they slandered and reviled Him, think it not a burden that you should bear reproach for His sake. For He is with you. He carried His cross before you, and that cross was far heavier than yours will ever be. You believe in God. If God were not full of mercy and plenteous in compassion upon all them that love Him, would He have given His beloved Son to suffer, bleed, and die for you? Rom. 8, 32. Be not dismayed by these happenings to you. Let not your heart be troubled. Put your trust in the Savior, who will right all things in the end.

Do you have doubts you can be saved? Believe in the Lord Jesus, who died for you and rose again, as you believe in God the Father and let not your sins drive you to despair. But, you say, I can not be as holy as I want to be. I have tried very hard to get rid of my sins. I have labored to live a pure life, but wicked thoughts assail me again and again, and I find that my heart is a deceitful thing and desperately wicked. Surely I can not be saved while I am like this? Yes, you can. Let not your heart be troubled by such misgivings. Believe in Me, says your Savior. You are not to be your own physician and then go to Christ. You are to go to Him as you are, and He will heal your troubled soul. The only salvation for you or anybody is to trust implicitly, simply, wholly, in Christ. Believe that He died for you, purchased and won you from death and from the power of the devil. It is not your reformation, not your repentance, not your anguish over your sins and your imperfect life that saves you, but just the blood of Jesus Christ, which was shed for you for the remission of your sins. Let that cleanse you from all sin in the sight of God. As Moses lifted up the serpent in the wilderness, even so the Son of Man was lifted up, that whosoever believeth in Him should not perish, but have eternal life. Let not your heart be troubled, friend. You believe in God; believe also in Jesus as your Savior from your sin, and all is well.

Says another, I am weary of this world's din and clamor, of its iniquity and vice. You say that you have striven long to overcome evil. You have prayed and called on God for help in the struggle against an inquitous world. You have fought the good fight of faith for the good and noble, and yet the world sins blatantly; its plains are defiled with debauchery and shame, and its ear is polluted with filthy songs and foul oaths. God is not honored. Man is so vile. It is useless and futile to fight on. The kingdom of this world is too strongly entrenched. You seem to make no progress at all. You would say like Elijah: "It is enough, Lord; now take my life. I am not better than my fathers." You would sit under the juniper-tree and give up in despair. Come, friend, sit not under that tree. Let me show you a better tree. Sit here under the shadow of this one which outwardly, too, looks like a tree of defeat. But see on it nailed the Prince of Life and the Lord of Glory, who has honored you with the title of Christian. Evil men have nailed Him there. See how evilly He was treated. How He was bruised in the battle, the struggle, whose sole aim was to save, to rescue, to cure evil hearts from bitterness and hatred, from the emptiness of hypocrisy, from the sordidness of sin. See what sin did to Him. There they crucified Him. But did He despair? Ah, even there, even from His cross of anguish and sorrow, He spoke comforting words to a thief and promised him eternal life. Oh, if He had given up, if, when He bowed His head in death with a loud cry, it had been a cry of despair and defeat! Would you now bear the honored title of Christian? Would you now experience the blessed power of His words for your eternal salvation? See, this very cross, then the symbol of shame and crime, has become the sign of honor and glory and power and dominion and victory. Have you been treated worse than He was? Have you fought harder than He? Methinks this is enough for you to gird on your armor and to put on the helmet of salvation and to take up the shield of faith and the Sword of the Spirit and to fight the good fight of faith. Let not your heart be troubled that progress is so slow. You believe in God, believe also in Jesus. "Who is he that overcometh the world but he that believeth that Jesus is the Son of God?"

Yes, in every circumstance and condition of life, in every trouble, doubt, perplexity, and sorrow, hie yourself to this crucified Christ. Come, stand in the shadow of His tree and hear Him speak to you. Go to His Word and listen with what solicitude and love He watches over you. Gather from His cheering, comforting words strength, courage, and faith, and all your troubles will flee, your heart will lose its habit of complaint, the heavy burden will grow lighter, and suffering in body or in spirit, you will find peace in knowing His will, and in sorrow you will find balm for the smarting wound in the love He bears for you. Go to His Word ever. Let Him say to you: "Let not your heart be troubled; ye believe in God, believe also in Me." And with faith renewed, it will give new power to the opinions of hope to soar above this world and these little things. All these troubles will one day be ended for you when you come into the Father's house, when you arrive at your heavenly home.

2. The Prospect of Faith.

For the Lord not only asks His disciples to have faith in Him no matter what life may bring, but He also makes them a most wonderful promise. He opens to them a marvelous *prospect of their Christian faith*. In our text the Lord, turning the hearts of the Eleven away from the worries and perplexities of the world, gives them a glimpse of that yonder world of glory to which He is going. He said: "In my Father's house are many mansions; if it were not so, I would have told you. I go to prepare a place for you. And if I go and prepare a place for you, I will come again and receive you unto Myself, that where I am, there ye may be also." In other words: My beloved disciples, set not your heart on finding full happiness here in this world. If all that will happen to Me on the morrow meant a collapse of My whole work on earth, if My death meant disaster and defeat, I would have told you so. But that is not the meaning of it all. If I leave you now, it means something great and glorious. This life is not all. Death does not end all. I am going back to My Father's house, where are many mansions. There He will gather all His children in one great family around Me. I am going there to prepare a place for you. "And I will come again and receive you unto Myself, that where I am, there ye may be also."

What a wonderful prospect Jesus opens up to all believers! He has gone home to His Father's house of many mansions, whence He came. And we, His disciples, should also think that we are on the way home to the Father's house, that He, our Savior, is preparing a place for us, that God our Father is waiting for us to join the great family of the redeemed from every nation and kindred and tongue. God does not desire that any should perish in this world of tears, but that all should enter eternal life. What comfort is there not for the weary pilgrim, the stranger in foreign lands, that he is going home. Soon the last turn in the road will be reached and there — ah, blessed prospect — my home, happiness, rest, peace, surcease from the toil and the dust of the road! So Jesus bids all His genuine disciples lift up their heads and look forward to the end of the road of life not with fear and trembling, not with troubled hearts and perplexed spirits, but with joy and elation. There is the Father's house of many mansions, where they shall be with the Savior forever. Blessed heaven, to be where He is!

You who have wandered, perhaps far, from the path of life, who have lost sight of your baptismal vow, lost yourself in being too much occupied with the things of this world, do these words of the Savior call up memories when once you fellowshiped with Jesus, when once you wended your way to the house of God on Sundays, when you loved His Word, when you experienced the happiness of the child of God in the assurance of the forgiveness of your sins by the body and blood of the Sacrament? Do you look with wistful eyes on the happiness of the family of God, of which you once were a part? Do you groan in spirit over the disillusionment of your misspent years. Do you wish that you might share in this bliss of the believers once more? Let not your heart be troubled. "Him that cometh unto Me I will in no wise cast out," says Jesus to you. Come back. Repent sincerely. The

Father is waiting for you, my son, my daughter, in Christ. A contrite heart will He not despise. This prospect of heaven as the goal of life can also be yours by faith in the blessed Redeemer. "Believe in Me," says Christ to you.

And you who have wandered far in search of happiness in the ways of the world, do these words of our blessed Savior awaken in you a longing for this heaven which He promises to His disciples? You never shared in the fellowship of the believers. You have been disillusioned by the ways of the world, which are all vain. You have found this world's goods and glory to be nothing but tinsel and tinkling brass. Oh, if you could only find true lasting happiness like these Christians! You have tried to win it by prayer, by reading the Bible, by going to church; you have determined to lead a good life in order to win this precious prize. But the goal seems so far away. It seems to elude you. What lack I yet? you ask. Let Jesus answer for you. "Let not your heart be troubled. Ye believe in God, believe also in Me." Faith, that is all you need. "Without faith it is impossible to please God." Believe in the Lord Jesus Christ as your Savior, and you shall be saved. Jesus here assures you that He has a place for you. Heaven is yours by faith alone. Depend not on your good life; trust not in resolutions. Faith is of the heart. That is what God wants, that you present your body a living sacrifice, that you submit to His will; repent and believe. "The just shall live by faith." If God has opened your eyes to see that you are a sinner and has awakened faith in your heart to believe that Jesus died for your sins, then go your way comforted. You are on the way to heaven, on the way to the Father's house.

You fathers who have plodded along the dusty hard road of life, who have toiled year after year faithfully, who have borne with patience this burden of faith in your hearts as a precious treasure, lift up your heads, for your redemption draweth nigh. The prospect of the heavenly mansions, where Jesus dwells and waits to receive you — leave not that out of sight. Let not the trouble and weariness of life becloud the thought that you are on the way home. Keep the faith. He that endureth unto the end, the same shall be saved, shall receive the crown of life.

You mothers who have toiled and labored for your children, who have expended your love and care on your children in order to bring them up in the fear and admonition of the Lord, this comfort of Jesus is for you, too. Go your way cheerfully with a merry heart, warmed by the personal interest which Jesus has in you.

You young people in the vigor of youth, upon whom care sits lightly perhaps, whose eye is easily attracted by the tinsel and glamor of the world around you, let not the devil deceive you into unbelief nor trip you with his temptations and snares. Lift up your eyes and keep them fixed on that blessed prospect as the end of your life, the goal for which you are striving, to enter into the Father's house of many mansions. Jesus is waiting for you there. Keep yourselves pure and unspotted from the world. Remember how the Lord revealed unto you in His Word that He loved you and gave Himself for you. "He that believeth and is baptized shall be saved." Remember that Jesus said: "I am the Way, the Truth, and the Life; no man cometh to the Father but by Me." He is waiting for you at the end of the road. He is watching over your faithfulness to His truth. He is concerned that you live your life as in His presence, that you may obtain that everlasting life, the crown of glory at the end of the race. Always be reminded that you are on the way home to the Father's house. Let sin, the devil, your flesh, not rob you of this precious prize of the Christian faith.

And you, my aged friend, who have plodded down the dusty road of life; who are fatigued from long travel, scarred in the long struggle through life, head bowed and silvered, shoulders stooped, children gone from your home, friends passed long ago, sixty, seventy, even eighty and more years behind you; who live with your memories. Tired you wait for the end. Lift up your head! Let not your heart be troubled! It is not the end. Death does not end all in nothingness. Be not dismayed. Look beyond, to the bright prospect of home in the Father's house which our Savior here opens up to you. The way is not lonely, nor is it dark; for your Savior is with you. He upholds you with His right hand. Trust in Him; carry on in the faith once delivered to the saints. His rod and His staff, they comfort you down to that last turn in the road on the way home. He has prepared a place for you. See that you enter the great hall of the King with the wedding garment of His righteousness, which He has woven in the anguish of His suffering and death and dyed with His blood. Keep your lamp burning, the lamp of faith in Him. The long shadows of evening will fly quickly, and you will soon be home with Him in the great mansions of the Father's house, where there will be no more tears, nor sighing, nor pain, nor fear, nor darkness, nor hunger, nor thirst. There will be everlasting light and joy and peace before the Lamb of God, which took away the sin of the world. Ps. 16, 11; 17, 15.

O sweet and blessed country,
The home of God's elect!
O sweet and blessed country
That eager hearts expect!
Jesus, in mercy bring us
To that dear land of rest,
Who art, with God the Father
And Spirit, ever blessed.

G. E. HAGEMAN.

Jesus' Promise to Hear Our Prayers.
Matt. 7, 7.

Promises are made, and promises are broken. This is a common experience among men in all walks of life. Often with the best of intentions they pledge themselves to the performance or forbearance of a specific act and give the person to whom such promise is made a right to expect or to demand that it be carried into effect. However, as time goes on, the obligation very often becomes extremely irksome and from either weakness or malice the promise is broken. In proof of this we need only refer to the many broken marriage promises, the baptismal and confirmation vows, the promises of political leaders to their constituents and of business men to their patrons. Even entire nations repudiate their agreements with sister nations. Not so long ago it had become a common byword that the treaties of nations are nothing more than a mere scrap of paper. Such attitude breaks down confidence and works untold havoc among men. The world-wide depression, in no small measure, is due to repudiated promises.

Is there no one whom we dare trust? We Christians can challenge the world: Gen. 8, 22 f.; Josh. 23, 14, etc. This is particularly true of the many Gospel promises pertaining to our salvation and eternal happiness. Jesus, in His own person, is the very embodiment and fulfilment of God's promises, 2 Cor. 1, 20. (Amplify!) In our text we have one of the gracious promises of Jesus. We shall consider: —

Jesus' Gracious Promise to Hear Our Prayers.

By this promise He aims to make us —
1. Bold and Confident;   2. Insistent and Constant in Our Prayers.

1.

Text. Jesus is speaking of prayer. The words are taken from His Sermon on the Mount. Some time later we find that Jesus reiterated these very words. One of His disciples ("one of the later, ones, who had not heard the Sermon on the Mount"— *Pop. Com.*) had come to Him with the request: "Lord, teach us to pray." He again taught them the prayer of all prayers, the Lord's Prayer, gave them an instructive lesson, and then added the words of our text, Luke 11, 1—13. It is evident that Jesus attaches great importance and power to prayer and is very solicitous for the welfare of His followers, urging them to bring their requests before God in sincere and earnest prayer and supplication.

As a matter of fact, only Christians can pray properly and acceptably. Prayer is an act of worship which only such will and can perform as are reconciled to God through faith in Jesus Christ, as therefore are God's children and know God to be their loving Father. St. Paul says: "For ye have not received the spirit of bondage again to fear; but ye have received the Spirit of adoption, whereby we cry, Abba, Father." Without fearing or doubting Christians dare approach God's throne directly and need no mediator, John 16, 26. 27. Even when their pastor prays for and with them, he does not play the rôle of mediator, but of an assistant, aiding them to bring their needs to God in their own person, in the name of Jesus, their only Savior and Mediator. The veil in the temple was rent when our Savior had finished the work of redemption, Eph. 2, 14. 18. Heb. 4, 16 we read: "Let us therefore come *boldly* unto the Throne of Grace that we may obtain mercy, and find grace to help in time of need."

God's storehouse is full to overflowing with everything necessary for our own welfare; everything necessary to make us strong in faith and in the performance of our Christian duties, cheerful and zealous in laboring for His kingdom, kind and forgiving towards our neighbor, patient and resigned to God's will in trials and in the hour of death. It is all there for the asking, and God waits to be asked. It is free and at the disposal of all who ask it in Jesus' name and in firm confidence in His promise and power to give. The promise covers all needs, not only in general things, as "in the day of trouble," Ps. 50, 15, but it refers also to specific gifts, as wisdom (Jas. 1, 5), the Holy Spirit (Luke 11, 13); all things whatsoever we shall ask in prayer (Matt. 21, 22); "what ye will" (John 15, 7), etc. In addition we find that God is so desirous of hearing our prayers that He makes the astounding declaration, Is. 65, 24: "It shall come to pass that, before they call, I will answer, and while they are yet speaking, I will hear." Besides, we are assured of the intercession of the Son, Rom. 8, 34; Heb. 7, 25, and of the Holy Spirit, Rom. 8, 26. What a prospect!

Why, then, do we lack so many of the gifts which God in His kindness and grace puts at our disposal? Why is our life not so abundant as it ought to be? St. James gives the sad answer (4, 2): "Ye have not because ye ask not. Ye ask and receive not because ye ask amiss." Either we are too sluggish and tardy to pray, or when we do pray, our prayers never reach the throne of the heavenly Father because we do not pray according to God's will or we lack confidence in God's promise. The listless and doubting suppliant receives nothing of the Lord, Jas. 1, 6—8. Such attitude is a serious matter; in reality it makes God a liar. Of course, no Christian has such intentions; he rather deplores this most heartily when he becomes aware of it.

Jesus knows our weakness and yearns to come to our aid. He encourages us and pleads with us to cast off our natural slovenliness and tardiness, our fears and doubtings. "Ask, and it *shall be given you.*" This promise is as true as any other word that Jesus ever uttered. It is infallibly true and therefore forms a solid foundation for our faith in God's willingness and power to give us what we ask for. Jesus is so much in earnest to convince us as to the reliability of this promise that He seals it with an oath, saying, John 16, 23: "Verily, verily, I say unto you, Whatsoever ye shall ask the Father in My name, He will give it you."

Friend, do you trust Jesus' gracious promise? Do you pray? Remember: "Prayer is the Christian's vital breath, the Christian's native air." You are always breathing. If you cease breathing, you are dead. It is so with your spiritual life. For a person not to pray means spiritual death. To be a Christian means to pray. Who does not pray is not a Christian. This calls for an earnest spiritual examination on the part of all of us. This may prove that your spiritual breathing-power, your prayer, is defective and needs attention. The Savior is here to help you even now. He invites you to ask and fully to trust His promise. He is your best Friend, having given His life for you. True, you are not worthy of His love. He should come with threats and curses of the Law. But that is not the point at this time. He comes to you with His promise. Put your faith in it and join the full throng of His people who sing: "What a Friend we have in Jesus," etc. (Hymn 395.)

2.

Jesus continues in our text: "Seek, and ye shall find; knock, and it shall be opened unto you." Here we are called upon to be insistent and constant in our prayers. Note how Jesus pyramids the verbs to emphasize the importance of His promise: "Ye shall receive," "ye shall find," "it shall be opened unto you," provided you "ask," "seek," "knock." His aim is to have us continue in prayer, to be importunate in pleading, not to weary when at times it may seem that no results are forthcoming.

Friend, do you not see the interest Jesus takes in your welfare, how concerned He is that you have everything you need for your happiness here in time and hereafter in eternity? Do you argue: "This is all well and good, I hear this ever so often; but my experience does not always tally with Jesus' promise, for there are many things that I asked for but never received. Such promises seem at times a little too fantastic"? I answer: Have you ever considered where the trouble lies? In the first place, such language is the fruit of unblief. It questions God's veracity. It is the language of the devil: "Yea, hath God said?" But I take it that such intentions are far from you. The trouble with you is that you have not given proper attention to Christ's promise and have not carefully followed His instructions. The promise is made to the earnest seeker who approaches God with insistent and persistent pleadings, who continues his search in spite of all obstacles and adverse experiences, implicitly trusting in God's sincerity, truthfulness, and power. Nothing is promised to the sluggish, tardy, doubting suppliant, who prays half-heartedly and list-lessly. No wonder that we lack so many things necessary for our sanctification, for a spirit of consecration to fulfil our Christian duties, and everything that makes for an abundant life. We fail in earnest and insistent seeking, and so the Savior's promise does not apply to us.

Again, the promise reads that the door to God's heart and trea-sury is opened only to those who knock. In our prayers we stand at the door of God in due humility, fully conscious of our unworthiness, wholly trusting in the merits of our Mediator. We come in Jesus' name; in fact, He goes with us and tells us to knock at God's door. He tells us, Take courage, don't be afraid, and knock. He does not say that the door will open at the first rap. God often tests our faith by letting us wait. It is not His purpose that we should earn the gift and the hearing of our prayers, but rather that we may more fully realize and appreciate both the Giver and the gift. For this reason Jesus urges us as He is standing at our side to knock and keep on knocking till the door swings open, as it surely will if we only persist. His promise will not fail. It is backed up by His great love and faith-fulness. When faith holds God to His promise, it must prevail; for God will not be made a liar.

This is divinely attested by many instances recorded in Scripture and on the pages of the history of the Church. The Syrophenician woman, e. g., knocked at the Lord's door till it opened. Like Jacob she wrestled with God and would not let Him go until she received the desired blessing. That is written for our learning.

May we learn the lesson! God grant us boldness and confidence, insistance and constancy, in praying, and grace to put our trust in the unfailing promises of Jesus. May the Holy Spirit grant us ever more the gift of a praying heart, so rare in these latter and perilous days, and fill us with ever greater faith in the gracious promises of Jesus! To this we add our Amen. (Hymn 396, 9.)

C. J. BEYERLEIN.

Jesus' Promise to Be with His Christians to the End of the World.

Matt. 28, 20 b.

In moments of deep emotion when our hearts are stirred by the trouble or distress or sorrow of a friend, we often make promises of fidelity and aid in all sincerity, trustfully expecting to keep our word. But man proposes, and God disposes, as we know, or as the Scottish poet says: "The best-laid plans of mice and men oft gang aglee." God in His wise providence frequently overrules us or makes it exceed-ingly difficult for us to keep our promise or prevents us altogether from fulfilling it. We discover that our human efforts are far too feeble to do even the half that we promised. Life and its problems are too much and too hard for us.

In our text we have a promise that has all the earmarks of being impossible of fulfilment. It is an amazingly sweeping statement, covering not merely a lifetime, but all time, to the end of the world. Yet it has found its fulfilment in the lives of His disciples in a most remarkable manner and is as true to-day as the day it was uttered. It has given comfort and strength to all who have trusted its message.

1. Note the Person who Speaks These Words.

What is the aim of every religious teacher worthy of that name? Is it not to bind men to God and to obliterate himself? "We preach not ourselves," wrote St. Paul. And he spoke for all true religious teachers of every age. Each servant, each minister, each evangelist, each prophet, of the most high God who can rightfully lay claim to these designations, preach Him whom he serves and not himself. He is content to be the voice, the messenger, the agent, of God. Moses, Samuel, David, Isaiah, John the Baptist, the apostles John, Peter, and Paul, to mention some of the great servants of God, never exalted themselves, never attracted men to their persons, but directed their hearers to God. "Therefore let no man glory in men," declared St. Paul. "He that glorieth, let him glory in the Lord." When Luther struck the fetters of Rome from the souls of men, did he proclaim himself? No, on the contrary, he shouted from the house-tops that he himself was nothing. "With might of ours can naught be done," is his frank confession before the world. If those preachers, evangelists, prophets, reformers, had set themselves up as standards around which men should rally, their names and their work would long ago have been submerged in derision, contempt, and oblivion. Their promises would soon have been proved to be vain and empty.

Now by comparison turn to Him who made the promise of our text: "Lo, I am with you alway, even unto the end of the world." What makes His words so different? When He spoke, men were "astonished with astonishment," as Mark says. They were amazed at the language He used. Yet all who heard Him felt that He spoke with authority, not like the scribes and the Pharisees. He said what no man dared to say without making himself ridiculous and the object of scorn. He made *Himself* the burden of His message. "Lo, *I* am with you alway." Not My fame, not My example, not merely My words, but I Myself, My presence, will be with you. In fact, I will be with you in person, is the burden of His promise. To whom did He bid men come? To Himself. Take that familiar invitation, one of the most touching of His many sayings, "Come unto Me, all ye that labor," etc. Who is it that ventures to say, "I will give you rest"?

Who is it that says here in our text, "I am with you alway"? Who is it that offers Himself as the haven for the storm-tossed soul? Who is it that demands allegiance to Himself? Is it a mere man? Indeed not; it is the Christ, the Anointed One, the Son of God, to whom is given all power in heaven and in earth. That is what gives power to this promise of our text. It is the almighty Son of our heavenly Father who here speaks to us. That is what makes these words so different. As He stands here in the midst of His disciples for the last time on Mount Olivet, He takes in the whole sweep of the centuries, yes, to the end of time and gives them the promise of His presence with them here on earth. He will be with them unfailingly. There will never be a time, no matter how desperate the occasion may be, how pressing, how dark the hour, when He will not be present personally with those whom He loves and who love Him. It reminds us of that other comforting promise of His: "Where two or three are gathered together in My name, there am I in the midst of them." Only God can speak so, and we truly believe that this Christ who speaks to us in this text is the Son of the living God. That means that Jesus with His Gospel of grace and power will always be with us to pardon and to bless us.

2. Note Also the Personal Address of Jesus' Promise.

When Jesus spoke these words, He stood before a large group of men and women, all of them His disciples. But each and every one of them felt that He was addressing each one individually. The words went directly to each soul. — It is this direct attention which Jesus gives to each one of His disciples that makes our relationship to Him so intimate, so endearing and enduring. Remember that just previous to this promise Jesus had given His disciples the command to go out into all the world and preach the Gospel of Him, the risen Savior. That was a large order for these humble, uninfluential, unlettered people. It was an undertaking that might make anybody quail and hesitate. "The world!" Even if we take in only the Roman Empire, what a vast enterprise it was that He laid upon their shoulders! They were to scatter to the four corners of the world, go out alone, at best in twos, as Peter and John did in the beginning. But Jesus makes them aware that He knows what is in store for them in a hostile world. So He assures them not only that He in whose name they were to go forth and witness to Him possessed almighty power to bless their witness with results, but that He would go with them to the uttermost parts of the earth; though His visible presence would be removed from them, He would be invisibly present with them to guard and protect and lead them. "Lo, I am with you alway, even unto the end of the world." No matter where you go to witness for Me, there I shall be.

Visitors to Switzerland who plan to climb the Alps are always warned by the natives that it cannot be done without a guide. To the uninitiated this seems a needless precaution; but very few ever set out without a guide. And as the party gets under way, it soon becomes apparent how necessary the guide is for the undertaking. The presence of the guide spells safety and confidence. When they reach a fork in the road, every one looks to the guide for instruction. When the path leads by a steep precipice, around the side of a mountain, each one gladly grasps the guide's hand and passes safely by the dangerous corner. When the path becomes very narrow and stony, the guide warns each one to follow closely in his footsteps, step by step. When a member of the party tires and wearies of the burden of the knapsack, the guide willingly lends a hand and takes over part of the load. When some tremble with fear at the height, the reassuring words of the guide sound like music to the ears. And when finally the summit of the mountain is reached, the magnificent view is ample reward for all the toil and hardship of the climb.

And so it is with our journey through life. Jesus warns us in His Word: "Without Me ye can do nothing." And after a few attempts many soon learn to appreciate the kind warning; they entrust their lives to His competent guidance and leadership. They feel safe with Him at their side who said, "Lo, I am with you alway, even unto the end of the world." He is the Way, the Truth, and the Life. He guards and protects us when dangers hover round. He urges us, "Follow Me," when the path is stony and narrow. And when the burden of life would become too heavy, He comforts us with the kind words, Come unto Me, and I will give you rest for your souls. He leads us in the paths of righteousness for His name's sake. When Dame Care presses us hard and we are close to the precipice, we can gratefully seize on this promise: "Lo, I am with you." Fear not, be not dismayed. Yes, life to a disciple of Christ is always an upward climb, up to the heights where is our home. And when finally we shall reach that goal, eternal life, what a magnificent view will stretch before our eyes, the glories of His grace and mercy and peace and salvation. Yes, to you, even to you, He makes this promise. In the power of this promise His first disciples went out into the world and preached and lived the Gospel and conquered. So can you if you carry in your bosom faith in this promise of His presence.

Think of the heroism of soldiers when they are aware that they are fighting under the eyes of their leader and general. A man will perform almost superhuman tasks in the presence of his wife and children. How much more should not this promise of the Lord's presence do for us? Think of Peter and John before the council of the Jews, which threatened them with death if they would continue to "teach in the name of Jesus." Think of Stephen, who under a hail of stones could pray for his enemies just as his Master had done. Think of Paul and Silas, who, though their bodies were bruised and though they were confined in the deep of the dungeon, with their feet in the stocks, could sing songs of praise and thanksgiving for the grace of God in Christ Jesus. Think of a Chrysostom, hounded to death by his foes like a beast of prey, praying as he dies, "Thanks be to God for everything!" Think of Elizabeth Fry, who visited the prisons and jails of England like an angel of mercy, dispensing cheer wherever she went. Think of the missionaries who have been sent to the far-distant countries of the world, into strange lands, among hostile people, to preach the Gospel of salvation and to fall early victims to an unhealthy climate. Think of the many patient sufferers tied to sick-beds for years, with no hope of relief or release for long periods, preserving a calm and patient and cheerful spirit under most adverse circumstances. Ask these where they obtain the strength and forti-tude to endure, and every one of these disciples of Jesus will con-fess:—

> Whatever I need for my journey to heaven
> In Thee, O my Savior, is unto me given.

Yes, every genuine disciple of Jesus knows the truth of the words of that hymn:—

> I need Thy presence every passing hour:
> What but Thy grace can foil the Tempter's power?
> Who like Thyself my Guide and Stay can be?
> Through cloud and sunshine, O abide with me!
>
> I fear no foe, with Thee at hand to bless;
> Ills have no weight and tears no bitterness.
> Where is death's sting? where, grave, thy victory?
> I triumph still if Thou abide with me.
>
> G. E. Hageman.

THREE PETITIONS OF JESUS.

I.

Mark 14, 36.

In response to their petition Jesus had taught His disciples the Lord's Prayer, Luke 11, 1 ff., teaching them both what to pray for and how to pray. The opening words indicate the proper spirit, "as dear children ask their dear father." Jesus not only taught us so to pray, He Himself as our Savior and as our Example practised what He taught.

Let us go to dark Gethsemane and—

Learn of Jesus Christ to Pray—

1. With Childlike Trust; 2. With Childlike Frankness;
3. With Childlike Submission.

1.

"Abba, Father." Here is a Child speaking to His Father, a unique Child to a unique Father, that Child of man who is at the same time the Son of God. So God Himself calls Him, Ps. 2, 7. This relation did not cease after He had assumed the human nature, John 1, 14. Then also God acknowledged Him as His Son, Matt. 3, 17; 17, 5.

In this sense none but Jesus could call God Father. Yet for Jesus' sake every believer may, like a dear child, call God his dear Father. In our day we hear Modernists making much of the universal fatherhood of God and the universal brotherhood of man. But their implications involve a fallacy. Though created in His image and as His child, Adam fell away from God, and all the offspring of Adam have like him left their Father's home, are outcasts, exiles, aliens, Eph. 2, 2. 12; 4, 18; Col. 1, 21. Through faith in Christ, the Son of God, we have again become children of God, children of Him who through Christ has become our reconciled Father, Eph. 2, 19; Gal. 3, 26; John 1, 12. 13. As such children we may like Christ turn to our heavenly Father and with childlike trust in His almighty power ask Him as dear children ask their dear father. This is what Christ does in our text: "Abba, Father, all things are possible unto Thee." He does not doubt in the least God's ability to help. He knows that God could, if He so determined, remove that cup, deliver Him from suffering and death. Why should anything be impossible to Him, the Creator and Ruler of the universe?

God has not changed since Christ spoke this prayer. He is to this day, and will forever remain, the eternal, unchanging, omnipotent God. Knowing that, ought we not without fear and doubt turn to Him in all our trials with the firm conviction that He can help? If we believe that He whom we call Father is the almighty God, why should we ever hesitate to ask Him for His help? Shall there be anything impossible to Him? Ps. 33, 9. 10; Is. 40, 25—31. Why, then, not call on that almighty God who through Christ has become your Abba, Father? "Abba, Father, all things are possible unto Thee." So the harassed preacher may and should speak when opposition raises its voice against the Word of God, when worldliness and unionism and lodgery demand toleration or else threaten to ruin the congregation. "Abba, Father, all things are possible unto Thee"; Thou surely canst fulfil Thy promise that Thy Word shall not return unto Thee void, that Thou wilt bless the efforts of Thy faithful pastors. — "Abba, Father," so may the parent pray at the sick-bed of his child. "The doctor tells me there is no more hope for my child. Father, all things are possible to Thee; remove this cup, let my child live." — "Abba, Father," so may the worried business man pray. "They tell me that it is impossible to save my business, that there is no escape from bankruptcy. All things are possible unto Thee; help me! They tell

me that in order to be successful in my profession, I must join sinful societies, make use of dishonest practises, dare not live up to Thy
Word and will. Father, Thou canst prosper my business even if all
the world is against me. Father, help!" — "Abba, Father, that child,
that friend of mine, tells me that it is impossible for him to believe
the Bible; it is so utterly unreasonable to him. Father, all things are
possible to Thee. Remove his unbelief. Thou alone canst create
faith. Save him." If we Christians would but with such childlike
trust in the omnipotent power of our heavenly Father turn to Him in
all our needs, how much useless worry would we be spared!

2.

"Abba, Father, . . . take away this cup from Me." With absolute
frankness Christ nestles close to His loving Father and pours out
into His loving heart all that troubles His own, laying bare His very
soul, not withholding one single wish or desire. "Take away this cup."
That was the cup of suffering and death, for the drinking of which
He had come into this world, Heb. 2, 10. 14. 15. The drinking of this
cup was part of that eternal counsel for the redemption of mankind on
which He Himself, with the Father and Holy Spirit, had determined.
The drinking of this cup He had in mind when in the word of
prophecy He had exclaimed, Ps. 40, 7. 8. Yet when this cup was
actually pressed to His lips, He shuddered, Matt. 26, 37. 38; Luke
22, 44. If the first drops of this cup were so bitter, how horrible must
it be to drain that cup to its very dregs! What shall He do? With
utter frankness He turns to His Father and pleads with Him, Must
it be? May I not be spared this bitter cup? Is there no other way of
redeeming mankind? While perfectly willing to submit to the will
of His Father, while not the slightest dissatisfaction with the Father's
will marred the perfection of His obedience, still in marvelous frankness He plainly states to His heavenly Father what was the inmost
wish and desire of His human heart.

Let us learn such frankness from Christ. There is much in our
human, sinful nature to hinder such openness and sincerity. It may
be a sense of pride, which does not wish to confess its own weakness,
or a sense of shame. We may have come to the Throne of Grace so
often that we are ashamed to come again; or we may fear that ours
is too daring a petition, or that our prayer is of too little importance
as to make God willing to listen to us. Just these little daily worries
and anxieties, how they do mar the peace and harmony of our lives,
simply because we do not like Christ, as God's children should do, turn
to our heavenly Father and frankly and openly tell Him all that burdens us! No matter what it may be, nothing is so important and
nothing is so small and insignificant that your heavenly Father will

not with equal interest listen to the worries and anxieties that trouble and harass you, His beloved child. He is never too busy. He told you: Phil. 4, 6. Your household worries and your business troubles, that gnawing anguish over a wayward member of the family, those anxious thoughts at the sick-bed of your friends and relatives, come, tell them to your Father, tell them, one and all, openly, frankly, talk them over with your God, withholding nothing from Him. So Jesus prayed, and He thus gave you an example which you should follow. Learn of Jesus Christ to pray with childlike frankness.

3.

"Abba, Father, . . . not what I will, but what Thou wilt." What marvelous obedience, submitting His own will completely to that of His God! Heb. 5, 8. Even if Thou dost not fulfil My wish, Thou shalt remain My Abba, Father. I know that all things are possible to Thee; I trust Thee to make it possible that, even if not My will, but Thine be done, I shall not want, I shall not perish; for Thou art Abba, Father, My loving Helper, My gracious Preserver. In answer to this submissive prayer an angel came from heaven to strengthen Him, Luke 22, 43, and He found strength to meet His enemies and to finish the work allotted to Him.

Let us learn childlike submission to God's will from our Savior. Not only that is obedience if a child does the will of his father whenever this will agrees with his own. Obedience implies and requires much more. The test of true obedience comes when God's will differs from our own, runs counter to our desire. We have made up our minds to enjoy years of health, happiness, wealth, honor; God's will may be to take away one or all of these gifts and instead give us to drink the bitter cup of trial and tribulation. It is then that we should prove our obedience to our heavenly Father by willing submission to His counsel. "Not my will, but Thine, be done," we must say then. "If I must drink this cup, bitter though it be, I know all things are possible unto Thee. Thou wilt give me strength to bear my cross. I shall not perish, nor shall I despair. Thou art and shalt remain ever Abba, Father. I am, and ever will remain, Thy child, weak, feeble, doubting mayhap, yet Thy own for Jesus' sake in time and eternity. Thy will, not mine, be done."

Learn of Jesus Christ to pray. He is not only the perfect Example, He is our Savior, our High Priest, standing in Gethsemane in our place. He is willing to cover up our imperfections, daily of His grace to give us strength that our prayer may become ever more childlike, so that we firmly trust in our Father's power, frankly tell Him all our troubles, and obediently submit to His good and gracious will.   T. LAETSCH.

II.

John 17, 17.

Christians are often called saints in Holy Scripture, 1 Cor. 1, 2; Eph. 1, 1; 2, 19. Such they have become through faith, which accepts the righteousness procured by Christ for all sinners, Eph. 5, 26. 27; Heb. 10, 22. Why, then, does Christ in our text pray that God would sanctify those who are already holy in His sight? Let us look a little closer into this matter as we consider —

Christ's Prayer for the Sanctification of His Believers.

He prays for this gift
1. *Because Sanctification Is Necessary;*
2. *Because It Is Impossible without God's Almighty Grace;*
3. *Because It Is Wrought Only by Means of the Word of God.*

1.

Christ asks His father, "Sanctify them." He has in mind His own disciples; not the unbelieving world, which still hated Him because it knew Him not, vv. 9. 25. Here He prays for believers, who are no longer of this world, v. 16, who know Him, v. 8, who are God's own, v. 6, kept in God's name. These disciples He had on this very evening declared to be holy, clean, John 13, 10; 15, 3. Yet Christ asks His Father to *sanctify* them. Evidently He feels that they are in need of sanctification. That righteousness which made them children of God and clean and pure and holy in His sight was an imputed righteousness, not in their own nature, Phil. 3, 9; 2 Cor. 5, 21. Being children of God, it is self-evident that they should walk and live as it behooves children of the heavenly Father, in other words, that they live in holiness and sanctification of life. That does not merely mean that they shun that which is evil, that they no longer run to the same excess of riot with the children of unbelief, 1 Pet. 4, 4, that they no longer lie and steal, no longer contaminate themselves with crime and vice. Surely all that is necessary, and a Christian who does not abstain from sinfulness and worldly lusts is a standing offense, will not inherit eternal life, Gal. 5, 21, and ought to be put out of the Christian congregation, 1 Cor. 5, 15. Yet shunning evil is only one side of sanctification, the negative side. God demands more. A Christian should *sanctify* himself, dedicate, consecrate himself, body and soul, all his faculties and powers, to the service of the living God.

Such sanctification was the will of God already in the Old Testament, Lev. 19, 2; Deut. 27, 26. Christ had repeated this demand frequently, Matt. 5, 15—19. 48; 7, 24. 25; had uttered the threat: Matt. 5, 20; 7, 26. 27. And by His apostles He admonishes Christians of all times and places, 1 Pet. 1, 14; Rom. 13; etc. For this purpose He has redeemed them, 1 Pet. 2, 24; Gal. 6, 14; called them, 1 Pet. 2, 9; united them with Himself, Rom. 6, 4; granted them the gift of the Holy Spirit, Rom. 8, 11—13. If anything is clear, it is this, that this is the will of God, even our sanctification, 1 Thess. 4, 3. That is the first reason why Christ prays that His believers may be sanctified.

Now the question arises, Why, then, does Christ ask His Father to sanctify them? Why does He not rather admonish His disciples to lead a life of sanctification? We have seen that Christ does admonish His Christians and demand of them that they lead a holy life. Still He knows that His prayer that God sanctify the believers is necessary. That sanctification which He, together with His heavenly Father, demands, for the accomplishment of which He redeemed and called and regenerated and keeps His believers, without which they would not see the Lord, Heb. 12, 14, this sanctification would be an utter impossibility were it not for the Father's continuous, almighty power and grace.

2.

Christians are regenerated, new creatures. The Holy Spirit dwells in them. Their new nature is holy, a creation of God, 2 Cor. 5, 17; Eph. 2, 10. If a Christian were only spirit, then all his works would be holy and perfect; for the spiritual nature, the new man, cannot sin, 1 John 3, 9. Yet as long as we live in this world, Rom. 7, 15—23 applies. Hence the enemies of our salvation, Satan, Eph. 6, 12; 1 Pet. 5, 8, and the world, John 17, 14; 16, 1—3; 1 John 2, 16, succeed time and again in seducing us to that which is sinful and displeasing to God and repugnant to our own new nature. And in our flesh they have a most powerful ally, who finds no greater pleasure than doing the will of sin and Satan. Christ, having been tempted in all points like as we are, yet without sin, Heb. 4, 15, knows how fierce the attacks of the enemies are. Cp. Heb. 5, 7. 8. He knows how impossible it is for His Christians in their own feeble strength to resist, and hence He pleads with His heavenly Father that He would sanctify them, He, the God of grace and power, yea, omnipotence. Give them strength not only to overcome the manifold temptations, not only to shun sin and evil, but to do only, and to do it willingly, what pleases Thee, that they consecrate themselves ever the more completely and perfectly to Thee, their Father in heaven.

Let us learn to pray in like manner. Self-reliance spells ruin and disaster, Ps. 30, 6. 7; 1 Cor. 10, 12. Hymn 316. Hence: Ps. 51, 10; 84, 5—7.

3.

Such sanctification is wrought only by the Word of God, and hence Jesus prays in our text: "Sanctify them through Thy truth. Thy Word is truth." In the Word the true nature of our enemies is revealed to us. Sin and its pleasures are so alluring to our flesh until we read Rom. 6, 23; Ezek. 18, 20; Deut. 27, 26. The world knows how to paint its gaiety and vanities in such pleasing colors that our flesh is at once ready to join with them, to seek its amusements on the dancing-floor, at other questionable places, until we read 1 John 2, 16. 17. Self-righteousness appears in so respectable a garb that we are very often deceived as to the utter depravity of every unbeliever, until we read the word of Him that searches the heart of man, Matt. 5, 20. The age-old temptation voiced in the lament of the psalmist, Ps. 73, 12—14, will lose much of its force when we do as the psalmist did, v. 17.

In the Word of God we are also told what are works that please God. He has described those works which He has foreordained that we should walk in them, Gal. 5, 22; Eph. 5, 9; etc. The Word of God not only warns against sin, not only points out good works, it also gives us strength to overcome the temptation to sin and to walk in the path of holiness; for it is the Word of the living God, like Him spirit and life, John 6, 63. We have already experienced the living power of the Gospel in our regeneration, 1 Pet. 1, 23. And the power of the Word is not exhausted after having converted us. That Word, the Word of the eternal, unchanging God, as unchanging and eternal as God Himself, is the means of our sanctification. Having given us the knowledge of how we ought to live and please God, it at the same time gives us strength to abound more and more in these good works. As we learn to know better the wickedness of sin, we are enabled in turn to hate with a truly divine and heaven-born hatred all that is sinful. With every day the loathing and dislike of worldliness, of sinful, doubtful pleasures, increases. Every day we learn the better to exclaim with the psalmist: Ps. 119, 10. 14—16. 103, and to follow the admonition of Paul: Phil. 4, 8. 9.

While, on the one hand, we humbly beseech God, "Sanctify us," let us, on the other hand, diligently make use of the only means through which God works such sanctification, His Word, which is eternal truth. Then Ps. 1 and Jer. 17, 7. 8 will be fulfilled in our lives also.   T. LAETSCH.

III.

John 17, 24.

A remarkable prayer! A prayer of our Lord not only for His apostles, "but for them also which shall believe on Me through their word," v. 20. May we be numbered among these truly blessed people! True, Christ's followers are still in the world, v. 11, where evil surrounds them, v. 15; the world hates them, v. 14; in which they have sorrow, chap. 16, 20, and tribulation, v. 33. The hatred of the world in addition to their sharing in the sorrows common to all men often depress the Christians. Cf. Ps. 73, 2. 3; Job 2, 9. Christ knows the weakness of His brethren and comes to their aid. To comfort and strengthen them in their hour of need was one of the reasons why He offered up His sacerdotal prayer, v. 13.

Christ Fulfils His Joy in Us by His Prayer for Our Glorification.

1. It Is Joy to Visualize the Glory for which He Prays.
2. It Is Perfection of Joy to Know that This Glory cannot Fail Us.

1.

In pleading for His followers that they might have His joy ful-filled in themselves, Christ asks His Father "that they may behold My glory." Christ's glory is seen in the mighty works of nature, all of which are His handiwork, John 1, 3, and all of which show forth His glory, Ps. 19, 1—3. This glory of their Savior as revealed in nature already fills the heart of the believer with holy joy. (Expand.)

Yet it is not the creative majesty and glory of Christ which He has in mind when He pleads with His Father to fulfil the joy of the believer by granting them a view of His glory. Christ Himself defines this glory by calling it *"My glory, which Thou hast given Me."* Cp. v. 5; John 1, 14; 10, 30; Heb. 1, 3; Col. 2, 9. What a joy for the apostles to be privileged to behold this glory! Luke 10, 23. 24. Even in his old age John with holy rapture remembers those years of bliss and happiness, 1 John 1, 1—3. And now Christ asks His Father that His followers, even after His return to His heavenly home, shall be privileged to behold His glory. On that very evening He had promised His disciples: John 14, 18. And only forty days later He gave His parting promise: Matt. 28, 20. Accordingly we read: Mark 16, 20; Acts 4, 30. And to the end of days His believing followers shall behold His glory in that peace of God, that heavenly joy, which Christ gives to all His disciples. Cp. Rom. 8, 31—39.

Nor is this all that Christ asks of His Father in His remarkable prayer. Not only during their life in this world shall they see His glory. He says to His Father: "Father, I will . . . which Thou hast given Me."

Christ was standing in that upper room where He had eaten the passover with His disciples and had instituted His Holy Supper when He spoke these words. Yet He was not only in that room in this hour. He says: "I am no more in the world. . . . I come to Thee," v. 11. And in v. 12 He says: "While I was with them ["those whom Thou hast given Me"] in the world, I kept them in Thy name." He speaks as one who has already left this world and has returned to His heavenly Father. To this Father He says: "Father, I will." No longer does He speak with the Father as the humble servant sent by Him to accomplish the work of redemption and as one who was willing to do that work, Ps. 40, 7. 8. No, He speaks as God, the equal of His Father, who has like majesty and power; He expresses His own divine will. There, standing before the face of His Father, in whose very presence He had dwelt before the foundation of the world was laid, He says: "I will that they also whom Thou hast given Me be with Me where I am," that with Me they may behold Thy countenance, participate with Me in that fulness of joy in Thy presence, in those pleasures forevermore at Thy right hand. And being with Me in Thy presence, I will that they shall behold *My* glory which Thou hast given Me, behold that glory not as they beheld it on earth, veiled and hidden by poverty and lowliness, but in its fulness and perfection as I had it with Thee before the world began, v. 5.

What an amazing vision is opened to the eye of our faith in these words! We shall — that is the will of our Savior — behold the King Messiah in His beauty. No longer need we be satisfied with beholding Him in His works of nature. No, we shall behold Him in His glory, shall see Him, the Creator Christ, who spoke and it was done, whose mind conceived, whose words called into being, whose omnipotent wisdom shaped and formed, all those wonders of nature which surround us at every step. And He is not as human artists very frequently are, far inferior to His works. He is perfection, and His perfection, His fulness of glory, we shall behold.

No longer need we turn to His Word, our Bible. In that Word we indeed beheld His glory, that was indeed a lamp unto our feet and a light unto our path. Still, in His Word we saw His glory only as through a glass, darkly, 1 Cor. 13, 12. When with Him we shall stand in the presence of His Father, we shall see Him face to face in the fulness of His divine glory, a glory so great that mortal eyes cannot see it and live, Ex. 33, 20; a glory so great that human language is insufficient to express those things which human ear has heard while in the presence of this glory, 2 Cor. 12, 4; a glory so great that even cherubim and seraphim cover their face at the sight of it, Is. 6, 2. This glory we shall be privileged to see. We behold that fulness of the Godhead which was His from eternity and which now dwells in His glorified human body as its temple. We shall bask in the sunshine of His grace, His truth and mercy encompassing us round about, His loving-kindness and never-ending goodness surrounding us at every step, He Himself, our glorious Savior, being with us world without end. The Savior in His glory, that shall be the vision greeting our astonished eyes as, raised from grave and corruption, our bodies and souls reunited, we stand before His throne of glory. What happiness, what heavenly bliss, will overwhelm us! And as, enraptured at this vision, we turn about to behold our fellow-Christians, we shall behold in them so many images of that glory which is Christ's; for like ourselves they shall have been fashioned like unto

His glorious body. We shall know them. There is father and mother, and husband or wife, and brother and sister, and son and daughter, and friend and acquaintance, yet no longer in the body bearing the image of sinful Adam, but in a spiritual, glorified body, shining as the stars, yea, as the very sun of heaven. And though all the glory that we behold in our fellow-Christians flows from that Fountainhead of glory, our Lord and Savior Jesus Christ, yet His own glory is not in the least diminished, its perfection not lessened. And—O glory!— as our astonished eyes look farther, they shall behold a new earth, a new heaven, not sin-stained, not burdened by the curse, not marred by unrighteousness and iniquity, but gloriously perfect and beautiful, surpassing infinitely in glory and beauty even this present earth as it issued forth from the creative hands of God. In us glory, above us glory, round about us glory, and every whit of that glory is the reflection of that Fountainhead of glory from which all glory flows, our glorious Lord and Savior Christ Jesus. Ah, happy day of our glorification! Then indeed shall our mouth be filled with laughter and our tongue with singing. Then shall rise from pure lips and glorified tongues that hymn of unending praise: Rev. 5, 13.

Child of God, child of glory, ought you ever to be sad? Ought the trials and sorrows of this present world to grieve us and, painful though they be, serve to drive out of your heart and mind that joy and peace which is the privilege of justified brethren and sisters of the Lord of Glory?

However, there is one thought which might, and often does, mar the perfection of our joy and peace in this world. Can we be sure of this glory? Many a human promise has failed of fulfilment. We have been told that better days were just around the corner; we have looked for them; we have confidently expected them, but time and again our hopes were blasted. Is the promise of future glorification a promise of this kind? Shall we, after all, be doomed to bitter disappointment? No, never! Christ fulfils His joy in us by giving us the assurance that the glory for which He asks in His prayer cannot fail us.

2.

Let us once more turn to our text: "Father, I will," etc. Christ is speaking with His Father as being on equal terms, as the Son of God, who is one with the Father, one in essence and being, and hence one in will. Father, I Thy Son, begotten of Thee in eternity,—*I will!* My divine, unchanging, and unchangeable will it is that My own shall be with Me and see My glory. No longer does Christ in humble obedience submit His will to that of His Father, as He did in Gethsemane, Matt. 26, 39. No, as the eternal God standing in the presence of His Father, He issues an unalterable decree, "Father, I will!" He knows that what He wills will not be denied Him, that His Father's will will not run counter to His own; for is He not One with His Father? Is His will not God's will?

Believing child of God, Christ wills, the Son of God Himself wills, that you be with Him where He now is to see His glory. If God wills your everlasting glory, who shall deprive you of it? Why doubt your glorification? Why be sad even though your present life may not reveal so much of the glory as of the sorrow and tribulations through which Christians must pass? Hymn 335, 1.

"Father, I will." Thus speaks He who was standing in the upper room, ready to finish that work which the Father had given Him to perform in order that He might give eternal life to as many as God had given Him, John 17, 2. He was ready to sacrifice Himself for the sake of His own, for the propitiation of their sin. He was now ready to take up the battle with the enemies of mankind. And because He foresaw the glorious, victorious outcome of that fierce contest, John 14, 30, because He is the Eternal, to whom the future is as yesterday and yesterday as to-day, therefore He could say: "I have finished the work which Thou gavest Me to do." He knew that through His suffering and death the enemies would be shorn of their power; He knew that through His vicarious atonement God would be reconciled to the world. And on the basis of His finished work of redemption He turns to His Father and says: "Father, I will that these My redeemed, believing disciples shall be with Me where I am to see My glory."

Surely, my dear friend, the hope of your glorification rests on a firm foundation. What though you are a sinner? What though you have transgressed time and again, transgressed daily, the will of God? What though you here on this earth can never attain to perfection? Read Rom. 8, 34. And this Christ, thy Savior and Redeemer, thy Righteousness and Justification, tells His Father: Father, I will that this believing Christian shall be with Me to see My glory.

"Father," so says Christ and adds another stone to the firm foundation of your glorification by continuing: "I will that they also whom Thou hast given Me be with Me." The Savior here refers to the promise which the Father Himself had already in the Old Testament given to His obedient Servant, Is. 53, 10—12. In accordance with the promise which Thou hast given, yea, in accordance with Thy determinate counsel and will from eternity, Thou, Father, hast given Me these My believing followers as My own. And therefore I will that they be glorified with Me. — That, my dear Christian friend, includes you also. You, too, are pledged and given to Christ by the everlasting counsel of God Himself. How do I know that? you ask. Why, you believe in Christ, do you not? You accept Him as your Savior, do you not? Then listen to what your Savior tells you. He says in the 20th verse: "I pray for them also which shall believe on Me through their word." That certainly includes you, does it not?

And what does He pray for those who believe in Him? What does He pray for you? "Father, I will that they also whom Thou hast given Me," all those who believe in Me, "be with Me where I am, that they may behold My glory which Thou hast given Me." That includes you, does it not? That includes every believer. Why, then, be sad and despondent? Hymn 335, 2. 3. T. LAETSCH.

TWO SERMONS ON THE HOME.

The Ungodly Home.
Esther 5, 9—14.

We are interested in the home. A home may be either godly or ungodly. The godly home is a haven of happiness, the bulwark of the Church, and the corner-stone of the State. The home of the ungodly, no matter how peaceful it may appear for the time being, is the very gate of hell. In this age of wrecked homes it is well to examine for our own warning —

The Home of the Ungodly.
1. It may at Times Appear as a Haven of Happiness.
2. It Is in Reality a Hotbed where Disaster is Bred.

1.

Haman, the notorious satrap at Shushan, apparently had a happy home. He had just returned from a banquet in the palace where he and the king were the private guests of beautiful Queen Esther. "Then went Haman forth that day joyful and with a glad heart, . . . and when he came home, he sent and called for his friends and Zeresh, his wife. And Haman told them of the glory of his riches and the multitude of his children and all the things wherein the king had promoted him and how he had advanced him above the princes and servants of the king." Certainly this coddled prince enjoyed honor and social distinction. His seat was set above all the princes that were with him. All the king's servants that were in the king's gate bowed before Haman and reverenced him; for the king had so commanded concerning him. This prime minister was immensely wealthy. He had flocks of friends whom he invited into his home. His wife Zeresh graced these gatherings with her presence. A multitude of children completed this apparent family happiness. "Haman said moreover, Yea, Esther, the queen, did let no man come in with the king unto the banquet that she had prepared but myself; and to-morrow [!] am I invited unto her also with the king." As it is to-day, so it shall be to-morrow.

Such is the "ideal" home of the ungodly. No matter what spiritual corruption and moral baseness nest in foul hearts, if they had what vain Haman brags of, that would satisfy them. To sit about a cheering fireplace in a pretentious living-room and boast to a host of friends of being a self-made man, of having climbed from one rung of the ladder to a higher one, of holding down a remunerative executive position, with cowed inferiors bowing before them; to tell of their smart speculations and sound investments,—what a home, sweet home, that would be! To-day the standards of the modern Hamans are not quite so exacting as to the "multitude of children." They could get along with fewer. You are familiar with such princely homes in your suburban Shushan. The outward glitter and glamor of such homes has perhaps even caused the thought to steal into your heart: "Behold, these are the ungodly, who prosper in the world; they increase in riches. Verily, I have cleansed my heart in vain and washed my hands in innocency." It does appear that the ungodly homes of the Hamans and Zereshes, of the Ahabs and Jezebels, of the Herods and Herodiases, have the advantage over the humble roofs that shelter a Mordecai, an Elijah, and a John the Baptist. It seems that ungodliness with earthly advancement is great gain.

But listen to Haman's confession while his boastful words are still reverberating in his palace: "Yet all of this availeth me nothing." Royal station and honor, wealth and riches, wife and children, have absolutely no charm or satisfaction for him so long as he sees "Mordecai, the Jew, sitting at the king's gate." Haman is frankly confessing the total bankruptcy of his godless heart. Deceitful riches often prove to be thorns that choke the soul. A dollar, whether sound or inflated, whether gold or silver, whether one or a million, has never brought really abiding peace and contentment to a home. Bricks are not made for the stomach nor dollars for the human heart. We may harbor the persuasion when we see Haman with wife, children, and friends in his Shushanite home that "they are not in trouble as other men, neither are they plagued like other men." Nevertheless Haman assures us that despite all his envied glory he is a most miserable and unhappy man. The tinseled splendor of an ungodly home is a deception and a snare.

2.

If it is an ungodly home, be it a palace or a hovel, it will inevitably prove to be a den of iniquity and a foul nest where disaster breeds. Such a home is a menace to the State, to the Church, and to its own occupants.

Haman's home was a liability to the Persian empire. This fawning scoundrel was a political leech, while the honest and God-fearing Mordecai was the real loyal patriot. This Jew was of princely descent. In his youth he was ruthlessly carried into the Babylonian captivity by Nebuchadnezzar's armies. Nevertheless he was loyal to his new government. Though in a strange land, he conscientiously followed the Word of God that had been spoken by one of the great prophets of his nation, Jeremiah: "Seek the peace of the city whither I have caused you to be carried away captives and pray unto the Lord for it." In those days, while Mordecai sat in the king's gate, two of the chamberlains of the king, Ahasuerus, sought to lay hands on him. Mordecai discovered the plot and saved the life of the king. Such was the attitude of the Jews in Persia. Yet because Mordecai would not cringe before the vain Haman, he swore as a bloody vengeance the total extermination of all the loyal Jews in the land. By bald lies and satanic intrigue this godless monster had a law written in the name of King Ahasuerus, and sealed it with the king's ring, "to destroy, to kill, and to cause to perish, all Jews, both young and old, little children and women, in one day." A million faithful Persian subjects was a small price in Haman's estimate to appease his little grudge. There was no consideration for the welfare of the empire as long as his own base and selfish desires and greed had to be pampered.

Homes where men take counsel with friends and family to despoil the government for their own selfish advantage are a menace to the State. Yet just such homes are all around us. Christless, godless, prayerless homes, plotting tax exemption, seeking special favors, privileged class distinction, and the like, are found everywhere. The fatted fledglings that take wing from these foul nests are the grafters, the corrupt politicians, the dishonest financiers, the racketeers. Then there is the class of patriots that waves the flag only when their own selfish greed is being served. The backwash of these homes is lawlessness and crime, the wrecking of banks and of commerical institutions, depressions and national distresses, the undermining of governments and revolutions. The home of the ungodly is a menace and a heavy liability to the State.

Certainly the Church of Christ does not look for any encouragement from the ungodly home. The issue between Haman and Mordecai had a religious implication. The kings and Oriental satraps had the affront to demand divine honor and worship for themselves. Nebuchadnezzar and Darius of that country are examples. Not much over a century before, three men of Mordecai's religious convictions had refused to bow before Nebuchadnezzar's golden image, yet were miraculously delivered from death in his fiery oven. Daniel, the president of all Persian princes, had refused to pray to King Darius, yet was providentially delivered from the lions' den. These kings, astounded at these divine deliverances, had made public proclamation to every province of the realm that men tremble and fear before the Lord God; "for He is the living God, because there is no God that can deliver after this sort." Haman was an avowed enemy of that religion and of its devotees. As an Agagite he thoroughly despised the descendants of Jacob. By hook and crook he convinced the king that "there is a certain people scattered abroad and dispersed among the people in all the provinces of thy kingdom; and their laws are diverse from all people, neither keep they the king's laws; therefore it is not for the king's profit to suffer them." We have heard that sort of language elsewhere. When Ahab saw Elijah, he snorted: "Art thou he that troubleth Israel?" The whole multitude of our Savior's enemies rose and led him to Pilate. "And they began to accuse Him, saying, We found this fellow perverting the nation." At Philippi, Paul and Silas were dragged to the magistrates by their religious enemies and falsely accused: "These men, being Jews, do exceedingly trouble our city and teach customs, which are not lawful for us to receive, neither observe, being Romans." This was the stereotyped accusation against the Christians during the bloody persecutions. That is the attitude of mind in the homes of the Christless to-day. They have no use for the Church of Christ. There are millions of them in our beloved America. May God continue to protect His Church and deliver His children from the enmity of these breeding-places of disaster!

Incredible as it may seem, these homes breed their own ruin. Haman had called his wife and his friends together to remove the last barrier from his happiness. It is well to take important family affairs to God in prayer, to be guided by His Word. Of course, such a procedure would have been ridiculed in that home in Shushan. As far as family worship, Bible-reading, family prayers, are concerned, many a supposedly Christian home is little better than that of pagan Haman. In his family council the fatal plan was concocted which blasted that home. We read: "Then said Zeresh, his wife, and all his friends unto him, Let a gallows be made of fifty cubits high and to-morrow speak thou unto the king that Mordecai may be hanged thereon. Then go thou in merrily with the king unto the banquet. And the thing pleased Haman; and he caused the gallows to be made." That night, in the lurid light of torches, hammer and saw could be seen busy in the erection of the grim gallows. Haman went to bed well pleased. But what happened on the next day? You know how Haman was ordered by the king to honor Mordecai. The proud Haman was utterly disgraced. "But Haman hasted to his house mourning and having his head covered. And Haman told Zeresh, his wife, and all his friends everything that had befallen him." What comfort, consolation, or encouragement did his wife and friends offer in that bitter hour of doom? "Then said his wise men and Zeresh, his wife, unto him, If Mordecai be of the seed of the Jews, before whom thou hast begun to fall, thou shalt not prevail against him, but shalt surely fall before him." What black despair stalks in such homes when the shades of misfortune darken their threshold! When these icy words fell from those unhallowed lips, Haman had reason to say, "Miserable comforters are ye all. Shall vain words have an end?" When he had been thus advised, "while they were yet talking with him, came the king's chamberlain and hasted to bring Haman unto the banquet that Esther had prepared." There Haman was unmasked as the monstrous assassin and murderer of the queen's people. At the king's command "they hanged Haman on the gallows that he had prepared for Mordecai." "Woe to them that devise iniquity and work evil upon their beds! When the morning is light, they practise it because it is in the power of their hand. . . . Therefore, thus saith the Lord, Behold, against this family do I devise an evil, from which ye shall not remove your necks."

Let us beware. There is too strong a tendency among Christians to pattern their homes after those of the ungodly. Jeremiah writes: "Pour out Thy fury upon the heathen that know Thee not and upon the families that call not on Thy name!" Those Israelites who adapted themselves to the paganism about them God warned: "I will set My face against that man and against his family and will cut him off." Think of Ahab dying in his chariot and Jezebel's miserable end, being eaten of dogs. Herod and Herodias wrecked their home and their lives. The ungodly home may for the time being appear to be a haven of happiness. Sooner or later, however, it is bound to be revealed as a den of iniquity, as a hell of despair and of broken hearts, as the shambles of damned souls.

Whither are we and our families drifting? Are the musty and dusty Bibles, the prayerless lips and unfolded hands in our homes pointing to the rocks of disaster? Too much is at stake. "Behold, I set before you this day a blessing and a curse: a blessing, if ye obey the commandments of the Lord, your God, which I command you this day; and a curse, if ye will not obey." God loves us. His Son laid down His life to redeem us. His Spirit has sanctified us to be His temples. Let us lay up His Word in our hearts and in our souls and do according to God's command: "Ye shall teach them [these My words] your children, speaking of them when thou sittest in thine house, . . . that your days may be multiplied and the days of your children . . . as the days of heaven upon the earth." Let us take a strict inventory of our own individual homes.

> O blest the house, whate'er befall,
> Where Jesus Christ is all in all;
> Yea, if He were not dwelling there,
> How poor and dark and void it were!
>
> O blest that house where faith ye find
> And all within have set their mind
> To trust their God and serve Him still
> And do in all His holy will.

H. W. BARTELS.

The Godly Home.
Josh. 24, 14—18.

A historian and philosopher wrote a book in recent years on *The Decline of the West.* The book predicts the utter collapse of our Western civilization. America is doomed to go the way of ancient Babylonia. The prediction will come true as soon as America becomes a nation of godless homes. A godless home is the breeding-place of vice and crime, of Russian atheism and Communism, of Hollywood infidelity and immorality. The ungodly home is America's greatest menace.

Our own homes are in danger. The light of high Christian ideals is flickering down on the candlestick. It is well to hold godly homes before our eyes for serious thought and for ready emulation. Such a home was that of Joshua, the son of Nun. The motto that was the guiding principle in his home was: *"As for me and my house, we will serve the Lord."*

The Motto in Joshua's Godly Home

served notice that this home was —

1. Dedicated to the Lord;   2. Pledged to Serve the Lord;
3. United in Its Loyalty to the Lord.

1.

Joshua at a very solemn occasion made this famous declaration: *"As for me and my house, we will serve the Lord."* The Land of Promise was now in the possession of the chosen race. Joshua gathered all the tribes of Israel to historic Shechem and called for the elders of Israel, and for the heads, and for their judges, and for their officers; and they presented themselves before God. He reviews the marvelous history of Israel and the gracious blessing that a kind God had showered upon them. Then in a most impressive way he places the momentous choice before them: "Choose you this day whom ye will serve." It was a choice between "other gods" and the Lord God.

It is an indication of man's depravity that he is inclined to serve "other gods." When Abraham was still in Ur of the Chaldees, his family worshiped the idols common to that pagan civilization. Those were the "gods which your fathers served on the other side of the flood and in Egypt." The descendants of Jacob were misled into Egyptian idolatry. Joshua also mentions "the gods of the Amorites in whose land ye dwell." Did the gods of the Chaldees save their devotees from utter destruction? Did the idols of Egypt save Pharaoh and his horsemen from drowning in the Red Sea? Could the dumb idols deliver the Amorites from the conquering armies that came on their triumphant march under the guidance and protection of the Lord Jehovah? Indeed, "their idols are silver and gold, the work of men's hands. They have mouths, but they speak not; eyes have they, but they see not; they have ears, but they hear not; noses have they, but they smell not; they have hands, but they handle not; feet have they, but they walk not; neither speak they through their throat. They that make them are like unto them; so is every one that trusteth in them." Nevertheless these Israelites were inclined to worship these dumb idols.

When Laban had overtaken Jacob on his flight from Mesopotamia, he confronted his son-in-law with the question: "Wherefore hast thou stolen my gods?" At this very spot, Shechem, their patriarch Jacob said unto his household and to all that were with him: "Put away the strange gods that are among you and be clean." When the people saw that Moses delayed to come down from Mount Sinai, they gathered themselves together unto Aaron and said unto him: "Up, make us gods which shall go before us." After he had made a molten calf, they said: "These be thy gods, O Israel, which brought thee up out of Egypt." Joshua had been with Moses on the mount and had been an eye-witness of this degrading scene. Israel throughout its history had an astonishing weakness for pagan idols.

There seems to be a satanic charm and deception which draws men to worship false gods. We have the false gods of Judaism and Modernism to-day. The Christless religions of secret societies are dedicated to idols. In many homes these gods are tolerated and glorified. There are homes where Mammon is adored, where the dollar is worshiped. Your heart because of its natural depravity is not proof against these wiles of the devil.

The choice that Joshua placed before Israel was whether they and their houses would dedicate themselves to these "other gods" or cast their lot with the Lord God.

In speaking of the God to whom he and his house dedicated themselves, Joshua uses a word for God in the plural form and yet employs the pronoun "He" in the singular. Joshua refers to the Triune God, three distinct Persons in one divine essence. Unto this same Lord God, Abraham reared an altar at this very place when he entered the Land of Promise. The gathered assembly refers to this God in our text: "And the people answered and said, . . . The Lord, our God, He it is that brought us up and our fathers, . . . which did those great signs in our sight and preserved us . . . and drave out the Amorites which dwelt in the land," vv. 17. 18. That same God has created and preserved and blessed us. That Lord loved us and gave Himself into death to redeem us. That God called us with His Gospel, enlightened, sanctified, and kept us in the true faith.

At our baptism and at our solemn confirmation we vowed to consecrate ourselves to the one true and only living God, the Triune God. The question is, Will you dedicate your home to this God completely, entirely, exclusively?

This is a matter of free choice. There is no duress or constraint. Joshua is not a Hitler, nor was Elijah in his day when he said: "How long halt ye between two opinions? If the Lord be God, follow Him; but if Baal, then follow him." Weigh the evidence for the Lord God carefully, conscientiously, and likewise the arguments that speak in favor of "other gods." With your conscious, sincere, deep, and determined inner conviction you must dedicate your home either to "other gods" or to the true God, who has revealed Himself in His Word. "Ye cannot serve two masters." Who shall be the God of your home? The motto in Joshua's home served notice that his home was dedicated exclusively to the Lord God.

2.

The motto in the godly home of Joshua was not an empty phrase. The dedicating of himself and his house to the Lord was no meaningless ceremony. Joshua pledged himself and his household to a constant and devout service of the Lord God.

The act of serving the Lord is emphasized and stressed in the text. "Now, therefore, fear the Lord and *serve* Him, . . . and *serve* ye the Lord," v. 14. "And if it seem evil unto you to *serve* the Lord. . . . But as for me and my house, we will *serve* the Lord," v. 15. "Therefore will we also *serve* the Lord, for He is our God," v. 18.

The Hebrew word for "serving" employed in the text implies worship. The repeated demand made on Pharaoh by God was: "Let My people go that they may serve Me." Israel was warned not to "serve other gods and worship them." The two and a half tribes of Israel east of the Jordan purposed to build an altar as a witness that they might do the service of the Lord before Him with burnt offerings and with sacrifices and with peace-offerings. In later years when the godly king Hezekiah restored the true Temple-worship, he solemnly charged the Levites: "My sons, be not now negligent; for the Lord hath chosen you to stand before him, to *serve* Him, and that ye should minister unto Him and burn incense." In the home of Joshua there would be full compliance with the divine command: "Thou shalt worship the Lord, thy God, and Him only shalt thou serve."

Our homes should be sanctuaries. Such things as obscene pictures, salacious literature, filthy conversation, impure religious literature, or anything that would tend to desecrate our homes must be barred from under our roofs. There must be no compromise with error, no insincerity and hypocrisy, no religious indifferentism, no toleration of a false worship. *"Now, therefore, fear the Lord and serve Him in sincerity and in truth,"* is Joshua's demand. The family altar should have a prominent place. There must be regular Bible-reading. In this age of both physical and spiritual danger there should be daily prayers for guidance, for protection, for strength to resist the wiles of the devil. May our homes be houses of prayer, temples of worship!

The word *serve,* however, has another implication. It is used in the sense of working as a slave or as a servant for a master. Thus David charged his son Solomon: "And thou, Solomon, my son, know thou the God of thy father and serve Him with a perfect heart and with a willing mind." St. Paul sums up his life-work when he confesses to the elders of Ephesus: "Ye know, from the first day that I came into Asia, after what manner I have been with you at all seasons, serving the Lord with all humility of mind." Joshua's household was pledged humbly and willingly to comply with God's will in every detail of their daily life and conduct. Where all members of a family truly believe God's holy Word and lead a godly life according to it, there will not be found the Hollywood type of relation between husband and wife. There prodigal sons and daughters will not leave the home fires to waste their goods, their bodies, and their souls in riotous living. In such homes the fathers will be patterns of godly living. The virtuous mothers will grace their homes and not eat the bread of idleness. "Her children arise up and call her blessed; her husband also, and he praiseth her." Blessed is every home that fears the Lord, that walks in His ways! Happy shalt thou be, and it shall be well with thee!

You are to choose this day whether you care to pledge your home to be ever more a place where God is worshiped in spirit and in truth and where His sovereign and His good and gracious will are carried out with all humility of mind.

3.

The motto in Joshua's home, moreover, told the world that his family was *united* in its loyal service to the Lord. The members of this family were a unit in their faith. Worshiping and serving God was a family affair.

This is not often the case. The very first family on earth was torn and tortured by Cain, the fratricide. Ishmael brought heartache to the family of Abraham. Esau with his Hittite wives was a grief of mind unto Isaac and to Rebekah. The family of Jacob had its bitter dissensions. David wept over his wayward son Absalom. Where hatred smolders in the bosom and hot words shoot their poisoned arrows into broken hearts, there family peace and happiness is forced to take wing. The fires of discord turn homes into hells of un-happiness.

Many fathers to-day have themselves to blame for torn family ties. Religion to their mind is good for wife and children. They are too busy. They need their Sunday mornings for sleep or for golf. Joshua certainly was a busy man. He ministered to Moses on Mount Sinai. When twelve spies had to be chosen, Joshua was one of them. Ten of the spies were cowed down with fear, but Joshua and Caleb courageously stood up and said: "If the Lord delight in us, then He will bring us into this land and give it us. . . . Only rebel not ye against the Lord, neither fear ye the people of the land, for they are bread for us." Joshua, as Moses' successor, conducted the entire conquest of Canaan. Indeed, he was a busy man. But when it came to serving the Lord, he put himself down as first of his family: *"But as for* ME *and my house, we will serve the Lord."* This attitude towards God had a most wholesome influence on the rest of his family.

Furthermore, Joshua was not indifferent as to the spiritual life of his entire household. The courageous and busy man of affairs considered himself the spiritual priest of his family. He and his house were bound together in the service of God. "WE *will serve the Lord."* Joshua believed: "Train up a child in the way he should go; and when he is old, he will not depart from it." In the godly home, parents will take time and every opportunity to bring up their children in the nurture and admonition of the Lord. Such families are the sunlit garden spots of God on this sin-cursed earth. Such families dwell not merely under roofs, but under the sheltering wing of the Almighty. God, who has our welfare at heart, tells parents the formula for a contented and peaceful family life: "These words which I command thee this day shall be in thine heart; and thou shalt teach them diligently unto thy children and shalt talk of them when thou sittest in thine house." Such parents are assured "houses full of all good things." And children who respect and honor their father and their mother are given the promise that it shall be well with them. Would to God that every home were so knit together in the ties that bind every heart to the Lord Jesus!

What a wholesome influence does such a home exert! The power of Joshua's example brought the entire assembly to their feet and caused them as one man to vow: "God forbid that we should forsake the Lord to serve other gods. . . . Therefore will we also serve the Lord; for He is our God." From such homes flow rivers of blessings. The most honest, the most dependable, the most successful business men come from the godly homes of the land. They send forth the most consecrated clergymen, the profoundest scholars, the most altruistic statesmen. The godly home is the greatest asset to a nation and the strong bulwark of the Church of the living Christ.

How about our homes? What shall we make of them? Shall we say: "As for me and my house, we will have a good time"? or: "As for me and my house, we will choose the dollar"? or is our motto: "As for me and my house, we will aspire to social distinction"? Can it be: "As for me and my house, we don't care"? Joshua evidenced a firm, resolute, and consecrated determination when he said: "As for me and my house, we *will* serve the Lord." Blessed are you members of this congregation if every one of you will dedicate his home to the Lord, if furthermore every family will pledge itself to serve the Lord in spirit and in truth, and finally, if every household, with all the power at its command, will be a family united in the service of God. May each of us go home with the firm determination: "As for me and my house, we will serve the Lord"!

> Then here will I and mine to-day
> A solemn covenant make and say:
> Though all the world forsake Thy Word,
> I and my house will serve the Lord.

H. W. BARTELS.

THREE LOVELY THINGS.

The Love of Jesus.
1 Pet. 1, 8a.

It is noteworthy that the Bible does not speak nearly so much of the love we owe Christ as of the love which He manifested toward us. There is a striking difference in quantity when one compares the two sets of respective passages. This is as we should expect it. Upon the love of Christ everything depends that we are religiously. What should we be at present without the redemption of Christ? What kind of future would be in store for us? What of the human race without the love of Christ? It is hence most natural that the love of Christ toward us is made far more prominent than the love which we should entertain toward Him.

This is an important hint for all our religious thinking and teaching. The most exalted place must always be given to what Christ has done for us; never should we put the chief emphasis on what we must do for Him. Here is where much of modern theology is making its most serious mistake.

While all this is true, we must not be understood as saying that love of, or to, Christ is not clearly inculcated in the Scriptures. A passage that will at once come to mind is John 21, 15 ff. Aside of it we may put the beautiful statement of St. Peter in our text. Our theme is: —

The Love of Christ.

It is something that certainly deserves the epithet "lovely." We note two points concerning it: —

1. *It is Not Based on Our having Seen Christ in the Flesh, but on the Gospel-message about Him.*

2. *It Is a Natural, Spontaneous Feeling for Christians to Entertain toward Christ.*

1.

When love of Christ is spoken of as one of the characteristics of a Christian, some person might think that such love constitutes a difficult requirement because we have not seen Him. Nineteen hundred years separate us from the time when He appeared on this earth. We are inclined to think that such love was easily rendered by those who heard Him every day and saw His miracles of mercy. But consider the text.

The Christians addressed had not seen Jesus in the flesh. They lived in Asia Minor, far away from Jerusalem. At the time when Jesus walked on earth, most of them, it seems, were heathen, if they had been born at all.

How did they get to love Jesus? He had been preached to them. Paul and Barnabas and then Paul and Silas and others had been the messengers of the Lord. It is not impossible that Peter himself preached to some of the congregations addressed. These men had painted Jesus in all His loveliness as the great Friend of sinners, who gave His life to redeem the world. Hence, while these people had never seen Jesus with their bodily eyes, they had come to see Him with the eyes of faith. Having never met Him, they nevertheless were well acquainted with Him.

It is true, we are still farther removed from Jesus' life here on earth than they were. That is no reason for us to lament. We have the Word. There Jesus is pictured to us in all His beauty. In the Word He comes with His saving grace. What the people in Palestine heard, we hear, too. The great truths about Him that they knew, we likewise know. Hence let us not think that love for Jesus on our part is without a proper foundation.

See how the Scriptures enforce this truth, Rom. 10, 6 ff. It is not necessary for us to go into heaven or into the world of the dead to become acquainted with our Lord. Jesus, says Paul, is near to us in the Word. Cf. also the words of the Savior spoken to Thomas, John 20, 29.

2.

St. Peter tells the Christians that they love Jesus: "whom ye love." You observe that there is no command here in the text that Christians entertain love to their Savior, although at other places this is definitely inculcated, for instance, Matt. 10, 37. In the text

Peter speaks of love of Christ as something that is found in every Christian.

It is a great truth that every Christian loves Jesus. It is something that cannot be divorced from his status as a Christian. While it is very true that it is not love of Jesus which makes one a Christian, but faith in Him as the only Savior, it is a fact nevertheless that no one will believe in Christ without loving Him. We might say that with the Christian love of Christ is something spontaneous, inevitable.

Whoever realizes what Jesus in true love has done for him will love Him in return. Think of how tenderly St. Paul speaks of the love which Jesus showed to him, Gal. 2, 20. Since he saw the meaning of the work of Jesus, there was in him a powerful motive to devote himself entirely to the service of Jesus and to undergo the greatest sacrifices while thus engaged. Love of Jesus is one of the fruits of faith. Having arrived at the assurance of redemption through the blood of Christ, a man will consider Him his dearest and best Friend, his highest Possession, the Source of his purest joy.

Jesus is pictured in the Scriptures as the Bridegroom; the Church, that is, the believers, as His bride. That He loves us is an assurance which rests not merely on words, but on His deeds, His bitter suffering and death. Contemplating what He has done, the bride will not withhold from Him true affection and devotion. This love, too, must not be one consisting merely in an outward profession. How we should love to converse with Jesus in prayer! How much we ought to occupy ourselves with Him in our thoughts! How we should endeavor to please Him in all of our deeds! When the question arises, What kind of deeds will bring out our love? the Savior Himself answers: John 14, 15. 21.

This is a beautiful, lovely subject, on which poets have expended their talents. Cf. "Jesus, Priceless Treasure"; "O Jesus, King Most Wonderful"; etc. Let us endeavor to rise to the heights so vividly indicated in these hymns.   W. ARNDT.

The Love of the Word of God.
Ps. 119, 140.

Nearly every Bible-reader knows that the 119th Psalm is the longest psalm. There are other features of it which are more important. It is divided into twenty-two sections, of eight verses each, according to the number of letters in the Hebrew alphabet; every one of these sections is so arranged that in the Hebrew each one of its verses begins with the same letter. What is still more striking than this outward form is that each verse speaks of the Word of God called

by various names (testimonies of God, the Law, commandments,
statutes, etc.). Hence the whole psalm exalts the Word of our great
God. If one reads it with this in mind, it will be found very beautiful.
The text speaks of —

The Love of the Word.

Hearing the term "Word of God," we think of the Scriptures.
That is right; there God speaks to us. Love of the Word is certainly
something which we may well call lovely. Studying this love on the
basis of the text, we see —

1. Who It Is that Manifests Such Love;
2. An Inherent Quality which Makes the Word Lovely.

1.

Love of God's Word would seem to be something that might be
expected of every one. Does it not seem very natural for a child to
love the word of its father and mother or for a poor person to love the
word of his benefactor? Alas! love of God's Word is, ever since the
fall of man, not a natural trait of the human race. Think of how
Adam and Eve, after they had sinned, endeavored to avoid hearing
that Word.

What the natural attitude of man now is toward the Word of God
we see from Jer. 36, 23 (Jehoiakim destroying the prophecies of Jeremiah), from Acts 22, 22 (the outburst of rage on the part of Jews at
Paul's speech).

There are people who in their natural condition take an interest
in God's Word and read it assiduously. They do it because of the
language of the Bible or the history related there, possibly also because of the morality which it teaches. They are not attracted by the
revealed truths on its pages.

Natural man hates the Word because an altogether different way
of salvation is set forth there from the one he himself approves. What
he wants is a way consisting in his own virtue and good works. What
the Word of God sets forth is a way consisting in the merits of Christ,
which are appropriated by faith.

If a person is really to love God's Word, he must first become
a different being. While by nature we are all the servants, or slaves,
of sin, we must become the servants of God to have such love. Note
the text. The great change is accomplished by the Holy Spirit, working in the Word and the other means of grace. It is the transition
which Paul describes, for instance, 1 Cor. 6, 11 and Rom. 6, *passim.*

Visualize the man in whom the great change has been effected.
Having become the servant of God, he ardently loves His Word. If
there is anything in which he rejoices, it is the voice of the Master
to whom he has now dedicated himself. The Word has rescued him.
When he was rushing toward the brink of destruction, it called him

and placed him on the road that leads to the heavenly home. How
could he do otherwise than love this Word? Are you surprised that
Mary Magdalene was ever anxious to hear the voice which had ex-
pelled seven demons from her? Think of the example of the first
Christians, Acts 2, 42. 46.

2.

The Word has inherent qualities which make it lovely apart from
the wonders it accomplishes. It is conceivable that a voice which
brings you a much-coveted message is harsh and grating; and if you
nevertheless find it sounds like sweet music, this is merely on account
of the good news it has conveyed and not on account of any quality
of its own.

The text stresses one of the great inherent qualities of the divine
Word. It is very pure. We may compare it to pure gold, in which
no refining fire will reveal the presence of base metals. What does
the psalmist mean? In the Word of God, the Holy Scriptures, there
is no foreign admixture. From beginning to end it is God Himself
who is there speaking to us. It is very true that He employed
prophets and apostles to give us this marvelous Word; but what they
proclaimed and wrote was not the word of man, but the Word of God,
1 Thess. 2, 13. The process which is here involved we call inspiration.
What a grand quality of the Word: every part of it comes from the
Creator and Father of all, whose Son is sent for our redemption. It
is deserving of our love.

The Word of God is very pure; that signifies that there is no
error in it. Whenever human writings are produced, be they ever so
splendid, there is a likelihood that they will contain errors. Even the
wisest and most learned of the human race are fallible beings. Who
would say that President Lincoln's speeches, which are among the
most famous compositions written on American soil, contain no erroneous statements? With respect to the Word of God we have the
assurance that no error will be discovered in it.

Human books, even if they do not misrepresent facts, are often
marred by sentiments which are not entirely proper, verging perhaps
on what is lascivious or frivolous. It is doubtful whether any human
book has ever been produced whose every judgment we unqualifiedly
endorse. In the Word of God we have nothing but purity, perfection,
holiness. In fact, how could it be otherwise, since it in its entirety
comes from the holy, perfect God?

That the Word is very pure is borne out by experience. Critics
have not been able to point out a single error in it. Scoffers have
attacked this or that section, but always it has been found, upon close
investigation, that they were unable to prove their point.

If the Word, then, is entirely pure, without error, without taint, it can accomplish that for which it was given. It makes us wise unto salvation through faith in Christ Jesus, 2 Tim. 3, 15. How we should love it, prize it, exalt it!

Remember, this whole discussion is worthless if we do not make the proper application. If love of the Word remains a matter with us which we endorse in theory, but do not put into practise, then our situation is sad indeed. What we must do is hear, read, and ponder the Word. Will you avoid the company of a person whom you love? God exhorts you to give your attention to His Word: "Blessed are they that hear the Word of God and keep it." Will you acknowledge that the Word has a claim upon you? Will you let your love of it be real and live, issuing in constant contact with it and loyal adherence to its grand truths? Hymns 111; 117.   W. ARNDT.

The Love of the Neighbor.
Lev. 19, 18.

One of the glories of the Christian religion is that it not only makes him happy who espouses it, but tends to bring about the happiness of others. When the apostles preached the Gospel of Christ Jesus, the people who accepted it entered into great joy and experienced the peace of God which passeth all understanding. But at the same time happiness and joy was brought to others. Not only did these early Christians, after having received the Gospel, endeavor to acquaint others with the blessed news, but in other respects, too, they radiated sunshine upon those that surrounded them. See what a change came over the Roman Empire through the spread of the Christian religion — the sick and the orphans were cared for, hospitals were erected, slavery was checked and began to disappear, the poor and the downtrodden were befriended. The Christians manifested love to the neighbor, which became a mighty factor in the victory of Christianity. It is a very lovely thing —

Love of the Neighbor.

Let us discuss it on the basis of our text, which informs us —
1. *It Is God's Will that We Love Our Neighbor;*
2. *This Love Must Not Be a Weak Sentiment, but We Should Love Our Neighbor as Ourselves.*

1.

Love of God is the highest duty. Think of Luther's explanation of the First Commandment. How strongly is not this taught in the words of the Savior Himself, Matt. 22, 37 f.!

But in addition we must love the neighbor. The text is very plain. The Savior teaches the same thing Matt. 22, 39. It is interesting to see that even in the Old Testament this commandment was taught. It reminds us that Jesus did not teach any new laws in His message. The view of Him which is current in some circles, that He was a new Law-giver, is not in keeping with the Scripture testimony.

The usual rule for people with respect to love is to love those that love them. Everybody is willing to do that. No special command is needed to enforce that rule. The love of parents for their children need not be especially inculcated; it can be taken for granted. Cf. what the Scriptures say of a mother's love, Is. 49, 15. Likewise is it natural for children to love their parents. If a child does not manifest affection for its parents, we speak of it as exhibiting an unnatural wickedness. Cf. 2 Tim. 3, 3a. To this category belongs love of relatives in general. Everybody loves his family. It is certainly not wrong to harbor such feelings, but we can all see that no special commandment is required to urge that such an attitude be adopted. It is a give-and-take relation, and there is no special merit in it. Cf. Matt. 5, 46 f.

Love thy neighbor as thyself, says the text. That is especially commanded because it is not something which we naturally do, although the justice of it is recognized by our conscience. Our selfishness militates against the universal love of the neighbor.

Who is our neighbor? It is the one who is near enough to us so that we may know him and can help him in his distress. Speaking simply, our neighbors are the people that we come in contact with.

We are to love them all. They should be dear and precious to us, and we should endeavor to further their interests. Especially close to us are, of course, those that are of the household of faith, Gal. 6, 10.

But what are we to do if the neighbor is very unattractive in his person and his appearance or if his standards of bodily cleanliness are deficient or if he belongs to a different race, etc? He still is our neighbor and entitled to our love.

2.

Our text further mentions the degree of love which we are to manifest toward the neighbor: love thy neighbor as thyself.

God must be loved above everything. In His case the highest degree of love possible is demanded of us, and considering that we owe everything to God, we have to admit that the requirement is not too high. With respect to the neighbor the Law says, Love him as thyself. He must not be put on the same level with God. It would be idolatry if we placed a dear friend or relative aside of the Creator when the degree of our love is considered.

What does it mean to love the neighbor as ourselves? It means that we treat him as we should like to be treated ourselves. Cf. the Golden Rule, Matt. 7, 12. It means that, when he is in want and suffering, we assist him as we should like others to assist us, if we were in his situation. In our wishes, in our strivings, we are not to put him beneath ourselves, but aside of ourselves. Think of what a paradise this earth would be if this commandment were obeyed! How the strife between capital and labor, between the various classes of our population, the many social problems that are confronting us, would vanish! Instead of the application of complex remedies, what we need is obedience toward the law: Love thy neighbor as thyself. If that were accepted and followed universally, how quickly wars would disappear!

On account of our inherent selfishness this is a very difficult thing to do. As we contemplate this commandment, we become aware of our imperfections, of our coming short of the obedience we owe God. Let us here, too, repent and go to God for forgiveness, which He freely offers on account of the work of His dear Son. After we have again received Christ into our hearts, we shall have new strength to overcome the evil tendency in us militating against the love of the neighbor and shall be making progress along this path.

A study of the Holy Scriptures will help us to understand and to practise love of the neighbor. Think of the story of the Good Samaritan, Luke 10, 30 ff. We may think, too, of the help the congregation in Antioch furnished the church in Jerusalem, Acts 11, 27 ff.

Especially the example of Jesus, who laid down His life for us, will be potent in making us love our neighbor. Cf. 1 John 4, 10. 11.

W. ARNDT.

GREAT HYMNS OF THE CHURCH.

A Hymn for Missions.
"JESUS SHALL REIGN WHERE'ER THE SUN."
(*Ev. Luth. Hymn-book*, No. 483.)
Ps. 72.

Christian missions are the perennial task of the Church. No matter what the conditions of the times are, the Great Commission must be held up before us as the high privilege of all who have accepted the Lord Jesus as their Savior and Lord. "Go and tell" is the constant command of our Master.

With Modernism taking a bold stand against the fundamental truths of the Gospel and undermining the Church's work both in the homeland and in the mission-fields, we who have been graciously blessed with the Gospel in its purity and fulness have an increasing obligation devolving upon us. Are we aware of it?

The consideration of the great missionary hymn of Isaac Watts offers much for edification and inspiration in this connection. Let us consider: —

A Prophetic Vision of the New Testament Church.

1. The Nature and Extent of the Church.
2. The Blessings Bestowed on the Church.

1.

Before the days of Watts the English Church was fettered to the metrical version of the Psalms, especially Francis Rouse's version. This usage was in conformity with the Reformed theory that none other than inspired hymns should be used in the church services. The metrical psalms were for the most part clumsy, rough, and stilted; nor did they interpret the psalms in the light of the New Testament. Watts wished to make better verses, divest the psalms of their Judaic character, and to "present them in the sunlight of the Christian dispensation." He said of his work: "I have expressed as I may suppose David would have done had he lived in the days of Christianity."

The hymn before us is typical of Watts's work. He gives us the 72d Psalm from the Christian viewpoint, the only correct one. James Montgomery based his hymn "Hail to the Lord's Anointed" on the same psalm.

The kingdom of our Lord, which is described in our hymn, is of course not a temporal, but a spiritual kingdom, John 18, 36 f. Many of the statements in the hymn emphasize the spiritual nature of Jesus' reign, especially those that refer to the blessings.

All chiliastic notions must therefore be discarded, even though they are widely held to-day, because they are based on misinterpretations of the Scriptures.

If we confine ourselves to the points stressed by the hymnist, we learn that the extent of Christ's kingdom, the Church, shall be worldwide. (Stanza 1.) It will last here on earth as long as the world stands, Ps. 72, 8.

To give to these statements a chiliastic interpretation will lead to falsehood; for although we believe that there are Christians in all parts of the earth where the Gospel is preached, it would be foolish to claim that the authority of Christ as King of kings is everywhere acknowledged. Nor need we look forward to such a consummation before Judgment Day. Cp. Luke 17, 26; Luke 18, 8.

It is inspiring nevertheless and a constant proof of the power of the Gospel that Christ has made His spiritual conquest among all

nations, kindreds, tongues, and peoples; that our Lutheran Church
has had the privilege to participate in its spread (polyglot character
of our work here in America); that the Gospel has its believers among
high and low, rich and poor, old and young. (Stanzas 2 and 3.) Is
it not a remarkable kingdom? Shall we not labor to advance it in
our day? Are the many millions at home and abroad who do not
recognize Jesus as Savior and Lord not a mighty challenge to us to
help spread His kingdom?

2.

The blessings of Christ's kingdom are described in detail by the
poet in Stanzas 4 and 5. He refers to a number of statements in
Ps. 72, *e. g.,* in vv. 2—6. 12—14. Cp. also Is. 61, 1—3.

His blessings are the result of His atoning work. His blood
cleanses us from sin; His death brought our salvation; His resurrection means our life. Through Him (John 3, 16) we are no longer in
the power of Satan (Gal. 4, 4 ff.), no longer burdened (Matt. 11, 28),
no longer famishing (Is. 55, 1. 2), no longer sick and sore (Matt. 9,
12. 13), and no longer under the curse (Gal. 3, 13 ff.). Cp. Luther's
explanation of the Third Article.

These are blessings no earthly king or ruler can give. What are
fame, wealth, power, position, and worldly wisdom compared with
these? Matt. 6, 33. 19 ff.

Here is a kingdom in which the Lord of Love reigns supreme.
No earthly monarch ever established a domain like it. Napoleon the
Great on St. Helena truly said: "You speak of empires and power.
Well, Alexander the Great, Julius Caesar, Charlemagne, and myself
founded empires; but on what did we found them? Force. Christ
founded His on love, and at this moment there are millions ready to
die for Him. It was not one day nor one generation that accomplished the triumph of religion in the world. No. It was a long war,
a war begun by the apostles and continued by successive generations.
In this war all the kings and armies were on one side, but on the
other I see no army, no banner or battering-ram; but yet a mysterious
power is there, working in the interests of Christianity—men secretly
sustained here and there by a common faith in the great Unseen.
I die before my time, and my body will be given to the earth as food
for worms. Such is the fate of him called Napoleon the Great. But
look to Christ, honored and loved in every land. Look at His kingdom, rising over all other kingdoms. His life was not the life of
a man; His death not that of a man, but of God."

This King, the Great Head of His Church, has entrusted us, His
followers, with the task of extending that kingdom and its blessings,
Matt. 28, 19. 20.

As we join in singing the last stanza of this hymn, as we pray the Second Petition of the prayer He taught us, let us not forget that we cannot do so acceptably unless we are active in His behalf, remembering also the promises He has left us for our encouragement: Is. 55, 10—13; 1 Cor. 15, 58.

Biographical Notes. — Isaac Watts (1674—1748) is known as the father of English hymnody. He published his *Hymns and Spiritual Songs* in 1707 and his *Psalms of David Imitated* in 1719, thus beginning a new epoch in English church-song. The present hymn is found in this collection. By the second half of the eighteenth century Watts was an institution. No doubt his extraordinary success was due to his ability to reach the heart of the average Christian. It was his inspiration that underlies the work of other well-known hymn-writers of that century, *e. g.,* Philip Doddridge, John Fawcett, Anne Steele, and Samuel Stennett.

W. G. POLACK.

A Hymn of Joyous Faith.

"NOW I HAVE FOUND THE SURE FOUNDATION."

(*Ev. Luth. Hymn-book,* No. 312.)

2 Cor. 5, 19 and 1 Tim. 1, 15—17.

One of the marks of our age is the lack of true and saving faith. It is a time of "falling away." The "faith once delivered to the saints" is cast aside as out of date and insufficient for the needs of our "enlightened" generation. The old paths which the fathers trod are too strait, too narrow, for those who seek to make a heaven out of this earth.

By the grace of God the Lutheran Church has not sunk to the level of our time. It still holds aloft the banner "Justified by Faith." It still preaches salvation by Christ the Crucified. How is it with the members of the Lutheran Church, pastors and people? Are they whole-heartedly in accord with the Church's doctrinal position? Pray God that every one who calls himself a Lutheran does so out of a firm and heartfelt conviction. Then we Lutherans can fervently sing this grand old hymn (see above), which for more than two hundred years has been a favorite. May we consider: —

The Grace of God the Comforting Foundation of Our Faith.

We shall note: —

1. *Where This Grace as the Foundation of Our Faith is to be Found* (Stanzas 1—4);
2. *How This Grace Offers Comfort in All Stages of Life* (Stanzas 5—8);
3. *That We should Resign Ourselves to God's Will and Faithfulness* (Stanzas 9. 10).

1.

The natural, unconverted man may be likened to a ship on the sea, tossed about by the storms and tempests of life, doomed to destruction on the rocks and cliffs that line the shore, without being able to cast an anchor that will save it. The believer, however, has found a place where the anchor of his ship will hold securely. He has a foundation, a rock, that has been provided for him in eternity — "before the world's creation" (1 Pet. 1, 18—20), on which he may rely, even if heaven and earth pass away (Matt. 24, 35).

Where is this foundation? The poet answers: "Where else but in my Savior's wounds?" He can say in the words of another hymn: —

> On Christ, the solid Rock, I stand;
> All other ground is sinking sand.

By the wounds of Christ our salvation was accomplished. (Stanza 1.)

In the work of atonement we have the foundation in which our anchor may rest securely because it is the evidence of that endless mercy "which all conception far transcends," *i. e.,* which our human reason can in no wise grasp; and because it is the proof of the everlasting love of God to sinful man; for thereby God "with love's arms extending, to wretched sinners condescends" (Jer. 31, 3), and the wilful waywardness of those whom He loves causes Him anguish and pain (Jer. 31, 20; Is. 65, 1. 2). (Stanza 2.)

This condescending mercy of our God shows that He does not will the damnation of the sinner (2 Pet. 3, 9), but rather his salvation (1 Tim. 2, 4). For this reason God sent His Son to redeem us, and the Son, after completing this work, returned to heaven to govern His Church and to be our Intercessor. Furthermore, in order that we may accept Him, He knocks at our heart's door (Rev. 3, 20) insistently. Every one who by contrition and faith makes this redemption his own has found in the mercy of God through Christ the only real foundation of faith. (Stanza 3.)

The realization of this blessed truth, that Christ's blood washes away all sins, that there is now no condemnation for them who believe, that the wounds of our Lord continually plead for us, as it were, — all this is marvelous and beyond understanding, Heb. 12, 24; Rom. 8, 1. 31 ff. (Stanza 4.)

2.

The foundation of our faith serves our spiritual welfare continually and provides enduring comfort in all conditions of life.

a) *When our sins trouble us.* We are frequently in distress over our transgressions. The more we realize the viciousness and damnableness of sin, the more anguish and sorrow we feel on account of them, Ps. 38, 1—8. At the same time, faith turns our eyes to the mercy of God, and we behold ever-growing beauty and sweetness therein, Is. 1, 18. (Stanza 5.)

b) *When body and soul must endure tribulation.* How comforting is this great truth, too, when by God's permission all sorts of bodily and spiritual trials afflict us. How priceless when we are forlorn, forsaken, friendless, etc., are the promises of grace, such as Is. 49, 14 ff.! (Stanza 6.)

c) *When earthly cares and wants oppress us.* Very often it is these things that cause some to suffer shipwreck of faith. They are like those who in the parable of the Sower are likened to the seed which fell on stony and thorny ground, Luke 8, 13. 14. Let us pray diligently that this may not be our lot; let us pray with the poet: Stanza 7.

d) *When we are conscious of our own imperfect sanctification.* In this point the poet directs our attention to a common Christian complaint. Though we may strive ever so hard, we are far from being perfect in our life and conversation, Phil. 3, 12. At the same time the acknowledgment of our imperfection makes us realize that it would never do to put our trust in our own works. From the beginning to the end of our Christian life we can hope only in mercy. (Stanza 8.) Summarize!

3.

The hymn, in conclusion, stresses two things that follow from the foregoing. First, since God's grace in Christ is so comforting, we should gladly resign ourselves to His will and guidance. Commit thy ways unto Him, faithful Christian; He will lead you to the glorious goal; the Word of His mercy will be your rod and staff even through the valley of the shadow of death, Ps. 130, 7. 8. (Stanza 9.)

Secondly, we should remain faithful, Rev. 2, 10; Rom. 5, 1 ff. (Stanza 10.)

Biographical Notes. — John Andrew Rothe (1688—1758), the author of this hymn, was a native of Silesia. He studied theology at Leipzig, but could not at once upon graduation make up his mind to follow his father's example and become a minister. In 1722, however, he accepted the call to Berthelsdorf at the invitation of Count Ludwig von Zinzendorf. He also served the Moravians at Herrnhut. Later in life he held several other charges. He was a gifted, learned man, an effective preacher, and a good hymn-writer. Of the forty-five hymns written by him the one before us is the best and has found general acceptance in German hymnals. According to Nelle this hymn was not written, as some authorities say, in 1728, on the occasion of Zinzendorf's birthday, but first appeared in the second edition of the *Berthelsdorfer Gesangbuch*, 1726—27.

W. G. POLACK.

A Hymn of Explicit Trust.

"WHATEVER GOD ORDAINS IS GOOD."

(*Ev. Luth. Hymn-book*, No. 507.)

Deut. 32, 4.

In our days of economic distress and religious disintegration it is necessary for us Christians not to overlook the many promises of the Scriptures given to sustain and comfort us. If it were not for these, we should be the most pitiable of men, Ps. 124, 1—7. But with the truth of the Lord's unceasing loving-kindness impressed on our hearts, we may and should always be able to say with David: "Our help is in the name of the Lord, who made heaven and earth."

The hymn selected for our meditation, one of the old Lutheran gems, is a beautiful expression of Christian trust. We should sing and pray it often.

Let us consider the truth it expresses: —

"Whatever God Ordains Is Good."

We note the reasons advanced by the poet to demonstrate this fact and make his resolution our own to hold fast to it at all times.

"Whatever God ordains is good," this brief sentence enfolds a wealth of truth. God is good, righteous, just, benevolent. Every good and perfect gift emanates from Him. He sends, or permits to come, good and ill fortune, life and death; but whatever He does for the Christian is well done, even though we cannot always understand His dealings with us, even though He "works in a mysterious way His wonders to perform."

Why is everything good that God does? *Because His will abides holy, just.* Whatever He does or plans regarding us, He will always be just, fair, and loving. He could not be true to Himself if He were to act otherwise, Deut. 32, 4; Job 34, 10—12; Ps. 111, 2—4.

Therefore "I will be still whate'er He doth," patient, resigned, without complaint, "follow where He guideth." He is our God, our Father, in Christ. He knows how to shield us, so that no real harm can befall us, 2 Pet. 2, 9; Ps. 91, 1—7. He *knows,* according to His omniscience; He *can,* according to His omnipotence and omnipresence; He *will,* according to His love, Ps. 37, 5. (Stanza 1.)

Why is whatever God ordains good? *Because He leads us in or "by the proper path."* Man may deceive us, God is not deceitful, Num. 23, 19. The paths on which He leads us are always the very ones on which we ought to go, for our own good, Ps. 23, 3, *i. e.,* those best suited to promote our eternal welfare. Therefore let us be content and be patient under the cross, 2 Cor. 12, 9. Everything that seems to be "ill" can by Him easily be turned into "well," Ps. 77, 5—14, and "sadness" changed into "gladness," Rom. 5, 4. 5. Ex.: Joseph; Daniel; wedding at Cana; Elijah and the widow. (Stanza 2.)

Whatever God ordains is good *because He is the Good Physician.* His medicine may be bitter, but the cure is sure. He makes no mistakes, as other physicians sometimes do. Cf. Ex. 15, 23—26. All His medicines are administered by a loving hand, which is never careless, indifferent, inattentive, hurried. He does not have to grope in the dark when a particular specific is needed. He who was able to work out a certain cure for the most grievous ailment, sin, surely will not be puzzled or deterred by our lesser troubles. Shall we, then, be filled with doubt, misgivings? Nay! Cf. Ps. 84, 11. (Stanza 3.)

Whatever God ordains is good *because He is our Life and Light.* He has graciously dispelled the darkness of sin and tribulation, Ps. 27, 1; 1 John 1, 5—7. He gives the true life, Ps. 36, 9. He can intend no harm, Rom. 8, 28. We may give ourselves into His care implicitly; for one day "we shall see clearly that God did love us dearly," Ps. 43, 5. (Stanza 4.)

Whatever God ordains is good *because He will turn our cup of bitterness into sweetness.* No one can escape from tasting this cup of bitterness at some time or other in this life, Matt. 26, 39. However, since it is the hand of divine love that puts it to our lips, we should bravely "take it all unshrinking." In due time, "when His hour comes," He will impart the balm of healing, Micah 7, 9; Ps. 94, 19; Heb. 12, 11. (Stanza 5.)

The only proper conclusion to be drawn from the strengthening and comforting facts mentioned above is to resolve to take our stand on the truth *Whatever God ordains is good.* We may suffer need, bear a cross, be afflicted with trials like Jacob, David, and other children of God, aye, even death may lay his cold hand upon us, yet He will never leave us nor forsake us, Ps. 91, 10 ff. (Stanza 6.)

Biographical Notes.—The author of this hymn, Samuel Rodigast (1649 to 1708), was born in Groeben, near Jena. He studied at Weimar and then at Jena, where he later became member of the philosophical faculty. He wrote this hymn at Jena. From 1680 on he served at the *Gymnasium zum Grauen Kloster* in Berlin. It is his only hymn; but who can measure the breadth of its influence since its first publication in 1676?

W. G. POLACK.

FOUR CHARACTERS
OF THE NEW TESTAMENT.

Lazarus.
John 11.

In perusing Holy Scripture, we are often introduced into private life, called upon to observe individuals who make no great showing in the eyes of mankind. But a character may be important and interesting without possessing social distinction. Many persons of eminence who once lived in Judea are now forgotten; their names, their places of abode, their connections, all have perished from the earth. But one family is transmitted down to our times with peculiar marks of regard, a family that will be had in everlasting remembrance. It resided at Bethany and consisted of a brother and two sisters. These three persons lived together in harmony and in piety; and what crowned the whole matter was this: "Now, Jesus *loved* Martha and her sister and Lazarus."

Of Lazarus we have but a few incidental touches to guide us in giving individuality to his character. That he was a loved brother, the object of tenderest affection, we may infer from the grief that came over the sisters when he was so suddenly taken from them. Included, too, was he in the love which the divine Savior bore to the household, which leads us to think that his spirit was cast into much the same human mold as that of his beloved Lord. We can think of him as gentle, amiable, forgiving, heavenly-minded; an imperfect and shadowy characterization it may be, but still a faithful reflection and transcript of our Master's loveliness. May we not venture to use regarding him that eulogy which Jesus pronounced on another: "Behold an Israelite indeed in whom is no guile"?

1.

There is one thing we may learn from this — *the partiality of friendship.* God would not have us to shut up our bowels of compassion against any of our fellow-creatures; we are to do good, as we have opportunity, to all men; but our Lord, who was a true man in this respect also, teaches us by His example that we are at liberty to choose and select. He had an ardent affection for all His apostles; but among them there was an inner circle of holier attachment, Peter and James and John; and out of this sacred trio again there was one preeminently beloved. He was kind to all His followers, but it is said: "Now, Jesus loved Martha and her sister and *Lazarus.*"

But to know Christ after the flesh and to enjoy His peculiar effection when He sojourned on earth was a privilege confined to but few. There is, however, a sense in which He loves us as ardently as He loved the members of the family in Bethany. He loves us with the divine love of a Savior, a love which existed long before we had a being, a love which sprang from no excellency in us, but was entirely self-derived, a love not only the most undeserved, but the most costly and powerful. It led Him to undertake our cause, to assume our nature, to suffer and die for us. "He bare our sins in His own body on the tree that we, being dead to sin, might live unto righteousness; by whose stripes we are healed." "Greater love hath no man than this, that a man lay down His life for his friends." But He has discovered a greater; He laid down His life for enemies, He died for "the ungodly"; "while we were yet sinners, Christ died for us." The same love gave us the Gospel, called us by His grace, and pardoned all our sins, for His name's sake."

And the same love will manifest itself to us in the same manner in which He expressed it to these three favored persons. His love admitted of their suffering affliction. Disease invades the family — "Lazarus is sick." The sickness of the brother is the distress of the sisters; they are filled with anguish, anxiety, and alarm. Jesus' love could have hindered all of this; and probably we should have thought that it would have done it. Surely He will exempt friends He so highly regards from everything trying and disagreeable. But His thoughts are not our thoughts, neither are His ways our ways. His love is wise; it seeks our everlasting welfare; it does not take pleasure in our pain, but it does delight in our profit; and though "no chastening for the present seemeth to be joyous, but grievous, nevertheless afterward it yieldeth the peaceable fruit of righteousness unto them that are exercised thereby." You may therefore share in His affection and be severely tried, relatively or in your own persons. Lazarus, beloved of Jesus, takes sick and dies.

His love suffered Him in their distress to treat them with apparent neglect. As soon as Lazarus was seized with an ailment, "his sisters sent unto Him, saying, 'Lord, behold, he whom Thou lovest is sick.'" Yet, instead of sending an answer or instantly repairing to Bethany, it is said: "When He heard therefore that he was sick, He abode two days still in the same place where He was." And before He set off, Lazarus was dead. A friend is born for adversity; then we peculiarly need his presence, his assistance, his counsel, his sympathy. And Jesus was the Friend of those three in Bethany. How, then, is this indifference to be accounted for? It was *not* indifference. So indeed it appeared to Martha and Mary, and no doubt it was very discouraging and perplexing. It gave rise to many unkind thoughts: "What can be the reason of this? Surely He has relinquished His regard; we have presumed too much upon His friendship." But He was not indifferent. He was only waiting to be gracious. His delay was no refusal. He knew that "His time was not yet come." Our ex-

tremity is His opportunity. He indifferent to their case! All the
time He was thinking of them and caring for them. He entered into
all their feelings, and He said to His disciples, "Our friend Lazarus
sleepeth; but I go that I may awake him out of sleep. Let us go unto
him." Then follows the account of His visit to Bethany and His raising of Lazarus. Thus did He give undeniable proof of His affection
and of His power. Thus all was overruled, not only for the glory of
God, but for the good of Lazarus, the good of his sisters, the good of
the disciples, the good of many who in consequence of the miracle
believed.

2.

Two thoughts are suggested for profitable reflection.

a) *Jesus is our true Source of consolation in time of deep affliction and sorrow.* Mary and Martha were not altogether friendless in
Bethany. The narrative shows the reverse. They and their brother
were held in high esteem. We do not doubt that during their brother's
illness and after his death many tendered their loving services and
did what they could to mitigate their sorrow. Nor would we undervalue such sympathy. There is a deep-felt anguish when in times of
bereavement no word of tender concern, no token of kindly feeling, is
offered us and we are left to mourn alone. But those afflicted sisters
were accustomed to the tender tones of a nearer and dearer Friend
than could be found among the circle of their relatives. — So it is
with God's children everywhere. There is One that knows us as no
one else can, knows the precise condition of our minds, knows what
truths and promises are best fitted to restore us to calmness and to
bind up the bleeding wounds. True, He no longer visits our homes in
the flesh; but did Hc not ere He left the world promise the disciples
that He would send the Comforter, who in periods of despondency and
grief would minister to their wants? Have we not all felt how certain passages of God's Word, brought home to us in a moment of
heaviness, have exercised a power, singular and inexplicable, banish-
ing our doubts and our fears and mitigating our sorrows? We may
have been familiar with the same truths for years and have heard
them repeated again and again by ministers and friends, but never
before have we grasped their full meaning. In the light of our affliction they possess a sweetness, an adaptedness, a wealth of comfort,
never before understood.

b) *Jesus is the Resurrection and the Life.* Lifting His eyes in
prayer to His Father in heaven, He cried with a loud voice, "Lazarus,
come forth." Straightway the dead came forth; the blood began to
circulate in his veins, the eyes beamed with intelligence, the tongue
spoke. Lazarus, leaving behind the gloomy prison of the grave, was
restored to his sisters.

Similar manifestations of Jesus' almighty power await us. He does not literally before our present eyes bring back our loved ones to life; but He does what is of equal value — He tells us that we must not regard them as dead, but as living, as only removed from this sensual vision, but still real to the grasp of faith. And what wonderful relief it is to the stricken soul to realize that, though His visible presence is withdrawn from us for a while, He is still with us.

And that manifestation at the grave of Lazarus in Bethany is a faint prelude of what is going to happen on that great and glorious day when the voice of the Son of God shall resound through the resting-places of the dead and the long-tenanted forms of the children of men shall rise, and death shall be no more. Oh, what an omnipotent Friend we have, what strong hope and consolation in the doctrine: "I believe in the resurrection of the body"! L. BUCHHEIMER.

Joseph of Arimathea.
Matt. 27, 57—60.

There are very few Bible characters more striking than this noble man. Each of the four evangelists gives us an account of him. He was "of Arimathea," probably Rama, or Ramathaim, in Ephraim, where Samuel was born. He was rich; from the emphasis placed upon the word, probably immensely so. He was a man in very high position, a member of the Grand Council, the Sanhedrin, the supreme court of the land. He was "just," righteous, famed for his faithful observance of the Law toward his fellow-man. More than that, he was "good," that is, pious, devout. And (records the evangelist St. Luke) he was waiting for the kingdom of God, the coming of the Messiah. Representative man that he was, he had watched the ministry of the youthful Rabbi of Nazareth, had studied His words and actions, had compared them with the Scriptures, and had reached the conclusion that He was none other than the promised Messiah. Two points stand out most prominently in meditating upon his conduct, the *one reprehensible,* the *other* highly *commendable.*

1.

He was a disciple of Jesus secretly. So great was the hold which caste and position had upon him that he did not manfully declare his conviction. Such a step involved so much self-denial that he did not see how he could take it. He was in all probability present at the trial of Jesus; he did not sympathize with the malice of his fellow-councilors nor give consent to their wicked verdict; possibly he ventured to advance some cautious protest. Yet he did not take the side to which in his heart he belonged, for fear of the Jews. In this particular his course was faulty, most unsatisfactory and inconsistent.

For three considerations ought every disciple of Christ be an open, avowed confessor: for Jesus' sake, for the sake of others, and for his own sake.

For Jesus' sake. He is your Lord and Savior. To secure your soul's salvation and immortal glory, He made the most stupendous sacrifice of love. He has laid you under the greatest possible obligations. He is the Lover of your soul. He left heaven to win you. You have no other such friend, never will have, never can have. Not to come forward and own Him is shameful ingratitude.

You owe it to others. Associated with Joseph is a man in the same station in life, named Nicodemus, who also had been deeply interested in Jesus. Perhaps not so much as Joseph of Arimathea, to the extent of being His disciple even secretly. He must, however, have been convinced that Jesus was a prophet. In a night interview which he had with our blessed Lord in the early part of His ministry, Nicodemus confessed that our Lord was a teacher sent from God and that no man could do those miracles unless God was with him. But such was his constitutional timidity that he never publicly acknowledged that conviction. When the Sanhedrin was unjustly seeking to destroy Jesus, without even the show of a trial, Nicodemus interposed a few feeble words, uttering a general principle, but was immediately silenced by a sneer. If Joseph of Arimathea had not espoused the cause of Jesus when he afterwards did, it is very improbable that Nicodemus would have done so. The confession and action of the one inspired the other. It is so to-day. It is contrary to all Bible directions to bury one's convictions and allegiance in one's bosom, Matt. 10, 32; Rom. 10, 10. When Charles G. Finney was holding evangelistic services in the city of Rochester, in the fourth decade of the last century, he gave a series of lectures to lawyers. He had himself been a lawyer before his conversion, and the lawyers of Rochester and the surrounding country flocked to Finney's lectures. One night there was a great company of them in the church, and a justice of the Supreme Court of Appeals of New York State sat in the gallery. This justice had taken a strong stand against Finney and his teaching, but as he listened to Finney's tremendous logic that night, he became convinced that Finney was right and he was wrong. He said to himself: "That man is right, and I am wrong. But it will not do for me to confess it. I hold one of the highest positions of honor in this State, indeed, one of the highest positions of honor in the judicial world in the United States, and it will not do for me to rise up with the ordinary run of men." Then the voice of God spoke in his heart, "Why not? If you are convinced that that man is right and you are wrong, the very fact that you hold so exalted a position of honor and influence lays upon you all the more responsibility for taking your stand for what you believe is right." So the justice arose quietly from his seat, passed out of the gallery, went outside the church, and came in the back door. Mr. Finney was preaching from a high pulpit that one ascended by a flight of stairs. The justice of the Court of Appeals went up the stairs behind the preacher, pulled at his coat, and said: "Mr. Finney, if you will make a call for confessors, I will come forward." Mr. Finney turned around and faced that great crowd of men and said: "The justice of the Supreme Court of Appeals of New York State says that if I make a call for confessors he will come forward." The justice immediately responded, and lawyers sprang up all over the building, following suit.

And *we owe it to ourselves.* It is a shame for any man to be married to a woman and to wish to keep the marriage a secret. It is not honorable to belong to a society or organization membership in which he must conceal. For any one to be convinced of the truth as it is in Christ, to possess love to Christ, to regard His religion and Church as the means of salvation to a fallen, sinful world and not to espouse the cause of Christ is a shameful, ungrateful attitude. Such a one is in danger of losing his discipleship.

2.

The burial of the Savior by Joseph. When the final catastrophe had come and Jesus had expired on the cross, when the danger arose of Christ's body being thrown unburied into a trench with the corpses of the crucified thieves, his convictions broke through all barriers; no fear of the Jews deterred him from saving our adorable Lord's body from indignity and a felon's fate. Reads the account: "He went in boldly" and asked Pilate to be permitted to give the body honorable burial. That act was a striking illustration of faith. Christ was numbered with the transgressors. In the opinion of the multitude His character as an impostor was proved by His inability to deliver Himself from His enemies. "He saved others, Himself He cannot save." "If Thou be the Son of God, come down from the cross." Little did they know that He bore their insults in silence because He was in that hour making atonement for their sins. The popular fury had not affected Joseph's faith. He knew whom he believed. The sight of the Savior, blindfolded, spit upon, arrayed in mock royalty, and finally bearing the accursed cross, then nailed to the tree, the taunts of the priests and rabble hurled at Him, did not shake the faith of the man. It seems as though his faith had rather increased than decreased amid the terrible events of that day. Though he must have been aware that by his act he imperiled his all, that he would forfeit his position as a member of the Sanhedrin, and that his great wealth was placed in danger of confiscation according to a Jewish law, Joseph made a public confession of his faith. Before the whole people of the Jews and in the presence of the Roman governor he, like his divine Master,

witnessed a good confession by taking the dishonored form of Jesus
from the cross and giving it honorable committal. So, when we believe with all our heart, we shall not be hindered by trifles or great
difficulties from professing Christ. The grace of God can make any
one so strong in faith that he will rise up in avowal of his divine and
crucified Redeemer.

The conduct of Joseph is an illustration of the power of ardent
love for Christ. Here was the secret of his courage. He loved Christ.
The Savior's rejection and suffering had raised his affections to their
highest pitch, and he bestowed upon the dead body of his Redeemer
the utmost proofs of love. He had prepared for himself a tomb. No
price could have purchased interment there. He, too, might have said
to himself, "It is my family tomb." But now, behold, the first occu-
pant is taken from what we should call the scaffold, from between two
thieves, amid the execrations of a great city, and in the face of contempt and scorn without measure. What made it? Love. Love can
do great deeds; love regards not human opinion, numbers, influence;
intent on its object, it heeds no difficulties, feels no burden, 1 Cor. 13.
It was love for his and our Savior by which Joseph prepared a place
in his own new tomb.

As to Joseph's reward. On the third day Joseph's tomb became
the scene of an event second only to the scene on Calvary in importance to the human race. There, in that tomb, life and immortality were brought to light. Never had man a house or palace so
honored as Joseph's tomb. The armies of Europe and Asia have done
battle for it. The wars of the crusaders were waged to rescue it from
the infidels. To Joseph and his household what associations must
have been connected with that family tomb, and with what peace must
he and they have buried their dead to sleep in the Savior's own bed
of death! All the Church of God thanks and loves thee, Joseph, for
thy love and service to its Lord. Forever in the history of redemption
this man will be remembered in connection with the Savior's death.

Every one of us has his own peculiar opportunity of showing to
Christ his attachment to Him. Joseph had his; that act of burial
was his profession of faith and piety. There is something for each of
us to do to test and show our love for Christ. It may not be published,
but Christ, who sees in secret, will know it, and that will be sufficient
reward. If, then, we wish for enduring honor and happiness, let us
connect our names and influence with Christ and His cause. To be
the builder and owner of all the pyramids, mausoleums, and obelisks
of Egypt and to have your names and deeds emblazoned there is not
to be compared with being Joseph of Arimathea and the owner of that
tomb in his garden. So the most desirable reputation will at last be
comparatively or wholly lost unless it is in some way connected with
Christ's cause. Matt. 19, 29. Hymn 353, 3. 4.   L. BUCHHEIMER.

Onesiphorus.
2 Tim. 1, 16—18.

At the time when St. Paul wrote the words of the text, he was undergoing his second imprisonment. During his previous detention he occupied his own hired house, with no other restriction than having a soldier of Nero's guard to watch him. Now, however, the case was altered. The indulgence which had been granted him during the first captivity was at an end. The reason we know. The city of Rome had been set on fire by its emperor, Nero; for six days and seven nights the conflagration had raged without intermission. The damage was incalculable, and the sentiment of the people rose high. To avert from himself the odium of the crime, Nero, the guilty perpetrator, laid it to the charge of the innocent Christians. They, he said, had started the blaze. The falsehood was successful, too, in rousing the popular indignation against the sect of which Paul of Tarsus was the acknowledged leader. Furious, history records, was the assault made upon them. Some were covered with the skins of wild beasts and left to be devoured by dogs. Others were nailed to the cross; numbers were burnt alive; and many, covered with inflammable substances, were lighted up as torches during the night. For the convenience of seeing this tragic spectacle, the emperor lent his own gardens, and to their sufferings Nero added mockery and derision. That the leader of such persecuted people should suffer with them is evident. We have good reason to infer that he was arrested on the charge of being implicated in the incendiarism and treated no longer now as an honorable state prisoner, but as a common criminal; he was subjected to a strict military custody, placed in a dungeon. So rigid was his confinement that only occasional visits of former friends and associates were permitted, and then the allowance was made only at the imminent personal risk of those who were impelled for love's sake to make the venture. Onesiphorus, a Christian of Ephesus, was one of those visitors. We cannot tell what it was that took Onesiphorus to Rome. Perhaps he was a merchant and went there to buy and sell. Perhaps he was a scholar and went there to listen to its poets and orators and to acquaint himself with its works of art. But whatever he went for, he resolved to see his friend. It is possible that he was not at once successful. To find out the prison where Paul was confined and to obtain permission to visit him may not have been easy, and a man only half in earnest would have given up the search. But he grudged no time; he spared no effort. And at length he succeeded. He found Paul. The latter, in writing to Timothy a short time before his martyrdom, thus pours forth the language of a grateful heart: "The Lord have mercy unto the house of Onesiphorus; for he oft refreshed me and was not ashamed of my chain. But when he was in Rome, he sought me out very diligently" — the expression used in the Greek denoting alike the difficulty and danger which beset the effort — "and found me. The Lord grant unto him that he may find mercy of the Lord in that Day." This prayer of the apostle is a striking and solemn one. Let us, with the divine blessing, dwell upon a few of those lessons with which it is so full.

1.

First we would emphasize, as a general truth, the *power and value of human sympathy*. It was so with our adorable Savior. Time and again during His life upon earth, and specially towards its close, we are called to note His yearning for fellowship and sympathy. When He called His disciples, it was, we are told, that they might be "with Him." What was the Mount of Transfiguration but a scene of exalted sympathetic communion? Representatives alike from the Church Militant and the Church Triumphant gathered to solace and sustain Him in the dread anticipation of His approaching suffering. As that hour approached and the shadows were more densely falling, His longings for personal fellowship with His disciples seemed to deepen and intensify also. "With desire have I desired to eat this passover *with you* before I suffer." In the climax of His woe in Gethsemane He sought to alleviate its insuppressible bitterness by having close at His side the sympathy of those earthly friends He deemed most reliable: "Tarry ye here and watch *with Me*." St. Paul was in this as in other respects endowed with all the nobler and finer feelings of human nature. How he mourns being "left at Athens *alone*"! What a new man he was when rejoined by Timothy and Silas! How a former visit to the city of Troas was saddened because an expected fellow-laborer and friend had not been found! "My spirit had no rest because I found not Titus, my brother." When the brethren came to meet him at Appii Forum after the shipwreck, how his soul revived! He "thanked God and took courage." If he felt thus dependent on human support even in the years of manly vigor, how genial and gladdening must such sympathy have been to him at this period of his history, when that buoyancy and gladness which characterized the period of his first imprisonment must necessarily, from various causes, have undergone diminution. His energies could not possibly have been what they once were now that threescore winters were whitening his locks and furrowing his brow and that in the dampness and in the chilliness of that dungeon he felt chilly and cold. Then, what added to his dejection was that in his case, too, as with his Lord before him, many had grown faithless. 'Tis ever so. When honors are flowing in upon us and we have little need of kindness, many will make expressions of regard for us; but when the tide has gone down and things are at the ebb with us, we shall discover that most of these professions have been forgotten and that we are forsaken

and almost alone. Those who, like swallows, come twittering around
us in the summer of our prosperity will mostly leave us in the winter
of our affliction. But all are not of this fair-weather sort. Some, like
Onesiphorus, will be faithful to the very last and will come only closer
to us because of our chain. These are friends indeed, because they are
friends in need. Nothing winnows our friendships like a gusty trial;
but, blessed be God! it is the chaff which is blown away. The wheat
remains, to be to us the type and similitude of Him who is a "Friend
that sticketh closer than a brother." Such was Onesiphorus. We may
think of the two in that Roman prison: Paul, the aged and home-
less; Onesiphorus, the friend. What glorious themes warmed their
hearts, tuned their lips, and evoked their prayers and praises in that
lonely cell! Their Master's name, His cause, His kingdom, His
matchless love, His upholding grace, His coming glory; talking about
their common trials, perplexities, solaces, hopes. When Onesiphorus
left Rome for Ephesus, the remembrance of his visit lingered in the
apostle's heart a long time afterward. The unbefriended prisoner
dwells on it as a bright spot in his captivity. And as he now writes
a letter to his beloved Timothy, asking from him a similar boon, that
he would hasten to see him before he dies, he cannot resist telling, in
a parenthesis, of this ray of kindness. Nor is there anything more
powerful and valuable still than tender sympathy. Whose heart has
not been kindled under its tender offices! Who has not felt in deso-
late moments, amid trials and life's bitter reverses, how it soothes,
braces, and gladdens, dries the flowing tears, and stops the bleeding
wounds! Oh, that we may exercise it more amid this cold, selfish,
unsympathetic world! That, like in Onesiphorus' case, shows true
nobility of character and conduct and the mind of Him who is a
Brother born for adversity.

2.

In the second place, we would note from this reference of the text
the sublime *recompense of prayer*. St. Paul could not in any wise
remunerate his friend when it meant material things. Silver and gold
he had none. Yet one recompense he had. Rome and Ephesus were
geographically far distant. The Great Sea lay between them. But
a wire and electric sound waves more wondrous than discovery in our
day has dreamt of united the two. It connected both with the throne
of God. As the memory of his friend's sympathizing visit moves before the eyes of the apostle, he must interrupt for a moment the
thread of his epistle to breathe a passing prayer: "The Lord give
mercy to the house of Onesiphorus! The Lord grant that he may
find mercy of the Lord on that Day!" That prayer, we may affirm,
ascended not unanswered. Blessings innumerable fell on the distant
household, though we are not told of them. It is well worth observing
that it is "the house of Onesiphorus" (not Onesiphorus personally)

for which the prayer is offered. The question has been raised: What are we to understand from this? The first and natural interpretation is that the apostle's large heart embraced the whole household of his friend, that he prayed God to bless that Ephesus home as the house of Obed-edom was blessed on account of the Ark or as the family of Saul was dealt with kindly because of Jonathan's sake. But a deeper interpretation has been made by some commentators. The name of Onesiphorus is mentioned by St. Paul once more, in the close of this epistle; and again, though it occurs among the greetings to individual friends, not Onesiphorus is mentioned by name, but "the household of Onesiphorus," making it appear very probable that Onesiphorus had died, very likely had suffered the death of a martyr for Christ's cause even before St. Paul. If so, it gives affecting interest and beauty to this Bible incident. Be that as it may, the apostle bestows upon his family the only recompense and withal the noblest and best of all returns for earthly kindness. Let us note it. We can give this when we can give no other. Prayer is still the golden key by which we can unlock for others as well as for ourselves the treasury of heaven and "move the arm of Omnipotence." As we heard, it annihilates space; it knows nothing of distance. That friend, that child, that brother, the companion of your youth, may be far separated from you; his place is vacant in the pew, his chair is empty at the table, his voice is missed at the home hearth. But you *can* be present with him. Prayer can bring you to his side. Prayer can fetch the angels of God around him as a guard, his shield in danger, his defense in trouble. Oh, for the power and value of prayer! What we owe, on the other hand, to the prayers which have hovered over our cradles will never be known until that Day, when the secrets of all hearts shall be revealed.

3.

Observe next the special boon desired. It is *mercy*. "The Lord give mercy." "The Lord grant that he may find mercy of the Lord." There is perhaps at first sight something strange in this request of the apostle's prayer. It is not what we should have looked for in the circumstances. When the apostle prays for him, we almost look for some such petition as this: "The Lord reward him for his deeds. Great has been his faith, his devotion, his unselfishness, his considerate sympathy to me, Thy prisoner. Recompense his kindness according to its deserts." Not so. What he invokes for his sympathizing visitor is mercy. Now, mercy is a sinner's word. It is the pity which God shows to the undeserving. There is deep significance in this. St. Paul would remind us here of the one and only ground of hope and confidence we have in the sight of a holy God. He was indeed the last to undervalue the precious fruits of the Spirit as manifested in the heart and the life of the true believer, and well did he know that at the Great Day they will draw from the lips of the righteous Judge His divine approval: "What ye have done to the least of these My brethren, ye have done it unto Me"; but, after all, he also knew that at that final bar of unswerving rectitude and equity nothing would avail as the sinner's plea but what he here prays upon the household of Onesiphorus: the mercy of God in Christ Jesus. You will find, as you carefully study the letters of the apostle, that, the more mature he grew in grace and holiness, the nearer he approached to God, the more deeply did he feel his need of mercy. Yes, come and lern from this giant in grace, standing on the borders of the grave, the only unfailing anchorage of a sinner's, or rather a believer's, hope. With all the memories of his apostleship behind him, a thousand battles of the faith in which as a spiritual champion he had fought and bled and conquered; with the remembrance of Jewish hate and Gentile scorn, of the buffeting of winter tempests he had braved by land and sea, of the sacrifice of home, country, friends, now that the executioner's sword was hovering over his head, he closes the drama of a consecrated life with the plea "I obtained mercy" and wishes it as the dearest, most appropriate blessing for his friend and his beloved ones. God grant that we and ours may be the recipients of it!

4.

Once more, and finally, would we observe the *great day of recompense.* "The Lord grant unto him that he may find mercy of the Lord in that Day." *"That* Day." We are not told what day it is to which reference is made. But we are in no doubt in the matter; neither was Timothy, to whom the epistle was written. And it shows us this, that the Great Day, the Day of the Lord, the day which gives consequence to all other days, was to Paul and to his friends a familiar matter of thought and speech. And what connection was there between those visits paid by Onesiphorus to a lonely man in irons in a gloomy prison and the transaction of that Day? The same that exists between the seed and its appropriate crop. The chained, lonely captive in this gloomy ward, with the tear of gratitude in his eye, could picture Onesiphorus among the multitude who are then represented as thus disavowing the good deeds with which the great Judge has credited them: "When saw we Thee in prison and came unto Thee?" receiving the gracious reply: "Inasmuch as ye have done it unto the least of these My brethren, ye have done it unto Me."

Let us be wise; in the Gospel of salvation and the Sacraments seek the same rich grace and mercy which St. Paul sought for Onesiphorus. It's our one and only hope and confidence now and in that momentous hour when the Lord shall arise in the glory of His majesty, when that throne shall be set before which the gathering myriads shall hear their final and eternal retribution.

L. BUCHHEIMER.

Phebe.

Rom. 16, 1. 2.

If upon a certain morning in the spring of the year 58 after the
birth of Christ we had stood as observers in the spacious harbor of the
city of Corinth, in Greece, we should have witnessed a scene which at
the time looked quite commonplace. Beside one of the wharves lay
a ship just on the point of sailing for Italy. The sailors are hustling
about in obedience to their captain's orders, while the passengers are
taking leave of their friends on shore. Of the various groups gathered there our attention is riveted upon one. The central figure
is a middle-aged woman, evidently one of the intended passengers.
Around her are assembled several friends, who have come down to the
harbor to see her off. Among these is a man insignificant in general
appearance, but with a face of deep intelligence and resolute will. As
he bids farewell to the woman just mentioned, he draws from beneath
his arm a roll of parchment, which he gives to her with careful instructions as to its delivery. Then the last farewells are spoken, the
passengers step on board, and the vessel, with hoisted sails, glides
slowly from the shore, cutting her way across the blue waters of the
Gulf of Corinth. What was the name of that vessel and what kind of
cargo it carried little interests us; but this would we note, that, unknown to the captain and the crew, it carried on board a treasure more
precious to the world than a shipload of the purest gold. That man
with the striking face, referred to as standing on the wharf, was Paul,
the great apostle of the Gentiles. The woman to whom he spoke was
Phebe, the deaconess of the church at Cenchreae, while the roll of
manuscript which Paul handed to *Phebe* was the epistle which Paul
wrote from Corinth to the church which was in Rome, an epistle so
important to the future of Christianity that Phebe, as she sailed from
Corinth, as one writer says, "carried beneath the fold of her robe the
whole future of Christian theology."

It will be remembered that Paul on his second missionary journey
stopped at Corinth for an evangelistic campaign of a year and a half.
There were many converts to show for it; among them such notable
ones as Aquila and Priscilla; Crispus, the ruler of the synagog, and
Sosthenes his successor; Justus, in whose house Paul preached after
being driven out of the synagog, and Gaius, "mine host," evidently an
influential man. Just across the narrow isthmus, not ten miles from
Corinth, lay the busy seaport town of Cenchreae, where Paul probably
preached as in other suburban places. Presently a church was organized there, and Phebe became a member of it. A few years later Paul
was again in Corinth and, while there, wrote his Epistle to the
Romans. It chanced that Phebe was just then meditating a journey
to Rome, and the conveying of this epistle was entrusted to her.

The last chapter of the epistle is devoted to salutations; it begins thus: "I commend unto you Phebe, our sister, which is a servant of the church which is at Cenchreae, that ye receive her in the Lord, as becometh saints, and that ye assist her in whatsoever business she hath need of you; for she hath been a succorer of many and of myself also."

By this is would appear, *first,* that Phebe was a woman of some consequence, since she had planned a long journey on business of her own. *Secondly,* that she was prominent as "a servant" in the affairs of the Cenchrean church. *Thirdly,* that she held an official position of some sort connected with the relief of the poor. It would involve a discussion too lengthened for our limits and somewhat foreign to our purpose did we enter into the question of deaconesses, such being the English form of the word by which she is here designated, an order of church helpers now being revived in our midst. Such an order we regard as eminently qualified for usefulness and as fitted to render a very important service and to supply a want which has frequently been felt. By this present reference to Phebe we are moved to a consideration of —

Woman's Work in the Church.

Christianity, the religion of Christ, is not a religion of works, but of grace and of faith, as the apostle says: "By grace are ye saved, through faith"; yet does it free no one from the necessity to work as a proof of that faith. On the contrary, clear and authoritative are the injunctions which direct us to work. And this work pertains not only to our worldly, secular callings, — that woman should be a diligent, painstaking housewife, the conscientious helpmate of her husband, an attentive, loving mother of a family, looking well after their needs and comforts, — but it means work in the kingdom of Christ, His Church. A lady who was once asked to unite with a society of the church, no circumstances or other consideration preventing, declined, replying that she had a society to look after with which none compared. "Which is that?" "That society is my family." There was truth in that. The family is the chief society. Christian discipleship and example and work, like charity, begins there. But it does not end there; nor is it restricted to there. No man and no woman liveth unto himself and herself, neither alone unto his family.

Time was when there was little evidence of woman's work in the Church. The words of St. Paul: "Let your women keep silence in the churches," were construed to mean that the women should not only refrain from publicly preaching and teaching the Word of God, but that they likewise refrain from taking an active part in other church activities. This, however, is a misinterpretation of the passage. As to teaching, this and other passages certainly exclude any public preaching on the part of women. They do not, however, say that women dare not give any instruction whatever. Thus Timothy was taught by his pious mother, Eunice, and his grandmother, Lois. In the ancient Church, women taught women and children, preparing them for baptism. It is not contrary to God's Word that women teach our children in Sunday-school. As to church activity, there is no lack of examples in Scripture. Think of those Galilean women who followed Jesus and ministered to His wants. Think of busy Martha in Bethany, of Dorcas in Joppa, of Lydia in Philippi. We read in this same sixteenth chapter of Romans of "Tryphena and Tryphosa, who labor in the Lord," and of "the beloved Persis, which labored much in the Lord." So to-day. This is one of the most hopeful, encouraging features of present-time church-life, that on all sides men and women are recognizing that they are called to do church-work. Opportunity is certainly not lacking. To indicate briefly some of the modern channels for women's activity, the supplying of articles of furniture and decorations to beautify the house of God, the response to the many and repeated calls of the various charities — orphanage, hospital, homes, and asylums. How well qualified from nature and how more readily able to devote themselves to such enterprises from considerations of time are women! Another feature is the missionary, especially as our city churches are constituted. Another is the social. It is necessary that the members become acquainted, that they be urged to help in the work. This end is admirably attained by means of such organizations as our ladies' aid society. (Cf. previous volume of Concordia Pulpit.)

Enough has been said to show that there are various ways in which the Christian women may become servants of the Church. The great thing wanted is that women should be willing to do whatever work they are qualified for and that every woman who is a member of the church should be determined to do something. Cf. example of Mary, John 2, 5. Thank God, there are already many noble workers among our Christian women. Our prayer is that many more may be raised up, resembling that one whose name has been preserved to us in the apostolic commendation: Phebe.   L. Buchheimer.

THREE SINS OF PETER.

Peter's Rash Impulsiveness.
Matt. 16, 21—23.

We have considered Peter's cowardice and his hypocrisy. If now we speak of another fault of Peter, it may seem as if we undertook to belittle Peter, perhaps in order to satisfy our own vanity. That would be an ignoble undertaking. But the Bible throughout does give us this comfort that it truthfully pictures the saints of God as mortals of like sins and failings with the rest of us. They became saints only through the forgiveness of their sins and through the sanctifying influence of God's Holy Spirit, to whose discipline they penitently submitted.

The failing which we will consider to-day and which sometimes sorely threatened his spiritual life is —

Peter's Rash Impulsiveness.

We say "rash impulsiveness," for we do not wish to appear to condemn all impulsiveness. A mind well grounded on God's Word may well be impulsive, may on occasion very quickly, instantaneously, and sharply resent an evil that is asserting itself. God give us such men and women! Such a mind is better than the mild disposition which is ever slow to speak out against an evil. And a mind that spontaneously leaps to assistance when confronted with real need, is it not better than the one that hesitates and calculates? But we speak of an impulsiveness not well grounded and informed in God's Word.

1. Let us Consider an Occasion in Peter's Life that Illustrates This.

Peter had one day made a fine confession. He had said: v. 16. Thereupon Jesus had praised him and said: v. 17. Note well that Jesus said: v. 17 b. Jesus' kingdom is not of this world, nor is Jesus of this world. Hence He cannot be recognized by any of this world's means of perception. Pilate could not recognize Jesus though He stood visibly before him. No height or depth of man's thinking will avail. 1 Cor. 1, 21 a. (Matt. 11, 25; 13, 13.)

"From that time forth," etc., v. 21. The disciples had confessed that Jesus was the Son of God, and now they must also realize that He must suffer and die most cruelly and shamefully. Jesus taught them this repeatedly and insistently and showed them that all this was in agreement with Scripture. (Luke 18, 31.) When Peter heard this, he yielded to a rash impulse. Perhaps the praise he had just received made him rely on his own judgment, which, he thought, in this instance was better than that which Jesus had just displayed.

He took Jesus aside to speak to Him privately. And he spoke earnestly, zealously, vehemently. He rebuked Jesus for entertaining such thoughts of shameful suffering. He wanted to give Jesus some good advice, wanted to keep Him from going to extremes, wanted Him to spare Himself. And was it not pious concern that motivated Peter? Was it not love and veneration that bade him speak thus? Did he not speak as a friend speaks to a friend?

We say Peter *wanted* to give such advice. He did not get very far. The text says: "He *began* to rebuke Jesus." But Jesus at once, instantly, turned His full face upon Peter and sharply said unto him: v. 23. Again, note well v. 23 b. When Peter had made the good confession, v. 16, that was in conformity with God's Word, and Jesus said: v. 17 b. But this present advice of Peter was contrary to the Word of God, v. 21, and hence proceeded from purely carnal impulsiveness and was altogether devilish and evil. It is idle to say that Peter meant well, which of course he did. It is beside the point to say that he was honest and sincere, which, humanly speaking, he was. But what he said was in disobedience to God's Word, and that is altogether evil and the source of all evil. One time, in the desert, Satan had similarly tempted Jesus to spare Himself in disobedience to God; and now the temptation returned, and this time it came from a friend, which made it worse. How easily we yield to a friend who tempts us to avoid a cross that God has laid before us! But Jesus' mind was fully entrenched in God's Word. He did not toy with the temptation and waste time over Peter's good intentions. At once and without a moment's hesitation and with an unsparing sternness, which emphatically cut off all thought of hedging and shifting, Jesus said: v. 23. Thus did Jesus deal with Peter's rash impulsiveness.

2. *We Find Much Rash Impulsiveness in the Religious Thinking of To-day.*

a) The wicked basis for such sinful impulsiveness is systematically laid wherever the Bible is no longer regarded as the infallible Word of God and the unerring guide of faith and morals. Sad to say, this faith in the Bible has commonly been discarded in Protestantism. It follows that men must seek other guides. Protestants will not accept the Pope's authority, and so they must look for other authority. They find this authority within themselves. Rarely will they say this in so many words. Instead, they speak of the "spirit" within them, of their Christian ego, of their regenerated mind, of their religious feeling, or of scores of other things which all are but other names for their own judgment and authority. For every spirit or impulse which is not in agreement with the express teaching of God's Word is only wrong and evil. Such people govern their religious thinking by their own wicked mind. (Example. The fanatics of Reformation time who smashed the furniture of churches, closed schools, and wrought all manner of violent disturbances, professing to be led of the "Spirit." They denounced Luther as cold and carnal and unspiritual, for he abode only by the Word of God, staunchly testifying against whatever was contrary to the Word of God, but permitting whatever did not conflict therewith.)

b) But also they who profess to accept the authority of the Word of God easily depart from it with rash impulsiveness, as Peter's example teaches. The old sinful flesh, the mind of the flesh, ever seeks to assert itself, pretending to be so pious. Does not St. Paul say (2 Cor. 11, 14) that the very devil likes to transform himself into an angel of light? Surely you do not expect the devil to appear to you visibly in that form; do you? But you will do well to be on your guard against temptations and thoughts and impulses arising within you or others with ever so pious an appearance, but contrary to the Word of God. (Example. The Galatians yielded to false teaching that seemed so good, so pious, so zealous, and even Scriptural. But it was not Scriptural and hence not good and pious. Paul said to them: Gal. 3, 3.) Was not that the temptation when the devil suggested to Jesus to leap from the pinnacle of the Temple? Jesus had just shown firm trust in God; now the devil flatteringly sought to prompt Jesus to make an exhibition of His great trust in God. And he even quoted the Bible. But the Bible quotation was brought in a muddled form. Do not accept every teaching for which men seem to bring Scripture-proof, even much Scripture-proof. "There are many false prophets." You actually reject the Bible and substitute your own notions when you do not apply the Bible accurately as it speaks concerning the matter in hand.

Let us beware of all emotionalism, of every pious feeling, of every religious impulse, though it be ever so well meant, that is not in true conformity with God's Word. It is a delusion and a snare. Though the person that promotes it seem ever so well intentioned, honest, and sincere, it may be the very devil, as Jesus said when Peter impulsively urged Him to spare Himself and not to suffer and die. Jesus says: John 8, 31. 32.   H. M. ZORN.

Peter's Cowardice.

John 18, 25—27.

Cowardice is a vice that is universally detested. And yet how much of it is in the hearts of all of us! St. Peter's inborn cowardice came to light when the vulgar servants in the high priest's palace challenged his faith. Peter lost courage, yielded to fear; he did not confess his faith, but denied his Savior. He was a coward. For what is cowardice but a lack of courage and a yielding to fear in the face of duty?

The Shame of a Christian's Cowardice when He Should Confess His Savior.*

1.

Jesus and His small band of disciples leaving the silent, sleeping city. Eastward, through the dark shadows of the rugged Kidron ravine. Jesus' warning: The Shepherd shall be smitten, flock scattered. All shall be offended. Peter especially is warned. Satan has desired to sift, but Jesus has prayed. Peter's violent and repeated avowal of faithfulness, ready to enter torture, dungeon, death. Though all should be offended, not I. But — O Peter! It is near midnight; soon the approaching day will cause the cocks to crow, and before that happens twive, you will have three times utterly denied Me.

The garden scene. Jesus' amazing, growing anguish. His lowly entreaty to remain with Him and watch. Ever such a request before? But not for His sake only. Their own safety requires it: "Watch and pray!" But sleepiness, reenforced by opinionated self-confidence, brushes aside all those tremendous things that take place in the Garden. Only a drowsy impression of that most eventful struggle in prayer. Jesus needs it. But the disciples, Peter —?

The midnight raid. Peter's dash of courage, flourishing a menacing, cruel sword. Jesus' gracious providence prevents murder. When Peter is sternly corrected, and when the unbelievable, though oftforetold, happens, when Jesus yields to shameful, cruel arrest, then Peter's courage vanishes. There seems to be no use for it. He takes to his heels. Later, in retrospect, Peter saw the utter folly and shame of his behavior. Jesus all along was Master of the situation, protecting His disciples, yielding not to force, but obediently going the path of duty that the Scriptures be fulfilled. But now Peter is blind to

---

* Especially if this sermon is to be preached in Lent, there should first be a vivid presentation of Peter's denial. A new and prayerful study of the synoptical account will supply the inspiration. Faithful to the text, one must visualize the event and be intensely alive to convey the picture so obtained. Let the aim be not so much to present each detail of the synoptics as rather to show up Peter's cowardly denial on the background of his boastful courage before the event.

that. His flight and spiritual collapse. Then, at a safe distance, there is a return of courage, but of the old, foolish, vainglorious kind. Wants to see. No true repentance. Not to stand at the side of Jesus, but to see, at a distance.

The courtyard, the fire, the soldiers, servants, maids. The story of the denial. The hasty first denial. Mixing with the vulgar mob, chameleonlike. The second denial. The hour of uneasiness in retreat of the dark doorway. But conscience is slugged, prayer forgotten, Jesus' words out of mind. Return to the fire. The utter and blasphemous denial. How quickly, how completely! Did he really forget Jesus? Had he not come into the courtyard for the love of Jesus? No; his own self was in the foreground of his thoughts. Jesus, the True, the Loving, so full of grace and truth, was forgotten and denied. Jesus, the Christ, the Son of the living God, was forgotten and denied. Forgotten completely were the eyes of Jesus, the kind Savior, ever upon him.

2.

The shame of it! But it is a true picture of human weakness, of our own cowardice.

Peter's situation in the courtyard was so unspectacular. At the time of his boastful assertions he doubtless pictured himself in some dramatic pose, which never materialized. Compare Jesus' steadfast and obedient courage without any thought of spectacular effect. (In the desert. In the garden.) Learn here.

Physical courage is much more common. Many brave women in hospitals. Many brave soldiers, though their position in foul, neglected, seemingly forgotten trench is not at all spectacular. — Moral courage is more rare. The most death-defying soldier may be of low moral type. Blood-thirstiness, beserker rage. Really something different from determination to be faithful to duty regardless of danger. — Spiritual courage, faithfulness in confession of Jesus, most rare.

But just this, faithful confession of Jesus, is all that the Savior asks of His disciples. Without it true faith is impossible. To continue with Jesus, Peter must confess Him. And you. And I. But that requires courage. (Compare Daniel, chap. 6. — We have young converts in the Foreign Mission fields who exhibit such courage. Often they must face the hatred of men in a very real way. Ostracized by society; village well forbidden; merchants refuse to sell; thatch roofs burned down; men beaten almost to death, thrown into cactus hedge. A young Mohammedan at Vellore, India, in 1930, confessing Christ before Mohammedan throng though his people had shattered his arm so completely that it had to be amputated.)

But why be afraid "when the chief Captain takes the lead"? when His protection is assured? when He bids us not to be afraid? Matt. 8, 26; Luke 12, 32; Acts 18, 9. — Examine. Why are you afraid?

Is it because you do not really believe? Still entertain doubt?
"Perhaps our fathers were wrong"? 2 Tim. 3, 7.

Faithful witnessing requires *determination*. (Compare Spaniards
burning their ships, others burning bridges, resolutely cutting off
retreat. The commanders of this world require resolute obedience
and faithfulness. Woe to those who fail! And what reward can they
bestow?)

Behold our Lord and Savior. He is seeking only our own eternal
salvation. He has obtained it at the extreme cost of His own life.
Now He points out the way for us. It is the way of faithful confession. Be undismayed, says He. I am with you. My eyes see you.

Lord Jesus, forgive us our cowardice, keep us faithful! Make us
faithful witnesses to Thee!   H. M. ZORN.

Peter's Hypocrisy.
Gal. 2, 11—13.

Last Sunday we heard of Peter's cowardice; to-day, of an occasion when he became guilty of *hypocrisy,* which was closely related
to, and a result of, his inborn cowardice. The word *hypocrisy* is not
found in our English text, but it is found repeatedly in the original
language of these verses. Our English version instead uses the words
dissembled and *dissimulation*. Indeed, what is hypocrisy but dis-
sembling, dissimulation?

Peter's Hypocrisy.
1.

Let us first acquaint ourselves with the story of the occasion when
Peter became guilty of hypocrisy.

Paul and Barnabas had in perfect harmony been serving the
church of Antioch, which consisted of Gentile Christians. Then it
happened that this fine congregation was seriously disturbed by certain Jewish Christians who came from Jerusalem. These men had
formerly been Pharisees and had stood high in the esteem of the
church at Jerusalem; but they were zealots for the Law of Moses,
and they were in the grip of old prejudices. These men said to the
Christians of Antioch: "Except ye be circumcized after the manner
of Moses, ye cannot be saved." That had created a great disturbance;
but all this had now long since been corrected. St. Peter, who also
had at one time been laboring under similar prejudices, had been
taught otherwise by God Himself, as chapters 10 and 11 of Acts
tell with considerable detail. And when there had been a special conference at Jerusalem about this question, Peter had been particularly
cordial in the support of the teaching of Paul and Barnabas. Now,
upon a later occasion, Peter also came to Antioch, and, true to his

teaching and conviction, he associated freely with the Gentile Christians as with brethren, and he ate with them, which was a particularly convincing proof that a Jew had discarded his former prejudices. Naturally, there was great rejoicing. The former disturbances were thoroughly allayed.

Then, for some reason or other, there appeared again at Antioch a delegation of Jewish Christians, sent by James, who headed the Christian church at Jerusalem. What their business was we do not know. St. James had emphatically agreed with the teaching of Paul and Barnabas. But these men were full of the old prejudices, and evidently they were men of strong will-power. And now the congregation of Antioch was shocked to note that Peter was seen to waver, not in his teaching, but in his behavior. Gradually he withdrew from intimate association with the Gentile Christians, and presently he was seen to eat only with Jewish Christians. He feared the Jewish zealots, just as once he had feared the servants of the high priest. And his behavior belied his teaching, his profession. He dissembled. He acted like a hypocrite, says St. Paul. He "walked not uprightly according to the Gospel," v. 14. His behavior condemned him. He stood convicted by the contradiction between his profession and his behavior. This was a very serious thing. Actions speak louder than words. In spite of his correct teaching this behavior of Peter seemed to brand the Gentile Christians as unclean after all and inferior to Jewish Christians and not ripe for salvation.

This behavior of Peter had so strong, so powerful, an influence that even Barnabas, beloved Barnabas, that dear Barnabas who had sold all he once owned and had given it to the church; that steadfast companion of Paul, who had fought the battle with Paul at Antioch and had maintained with him at the conference at Jerusalem the truth of the Gospel for the freedom of the Gentile Christians — even he was carried away, swept from his former steadfastness, and he, too, became guilty of shameful dissimulation, or hypocrisy, denying by his behavior what his lips professed and taught. Lack of moral courage again showed itself and resulted in a behavior out of harmony with Peter's and Barnabas's convictions. And that is hypocrisy.

2.

We see here how easily this sin is committed and how the hypocrite is his own greatest dupe.

The self-deception of it! It is not to be supposed that Peter was conscious of his hypocrisy or that he was maliciously intent upon deceiving the church at Antioch. Is not hypocrisy for the most part an unconscious sin? There are some malicious and intentional hypocrites, as were those who spied upon Jesus and "feigned themselves just men," Luke 20, 20. He who wants to deceive his fellow-man may well be conscious of this and malicious in his hypocrisy. But how foolish is any one who goes to the trouble and expense of serving God while living in hypocrisy. How could one hope to deceive God, or what could one hope to profit by such deceit?

And yet there is much hypocrisy in the service of God. They say: "Lord, Lord," but their heart is far from Him. On the Last Day they will say: "Lord, Lord, have we not prophesied in Thy name and in Thy name done many wonderful works?" But the reply will be: "I never knew you; depart from Me ye that work iniquity," Matt. 7, 22. 23. The Pharisee who stood in the Temple and thanked God that he was not as other men are and boasted of his many good works, was he conscious of his hypocrisy? It is unthinkable. See how the very murderers of Jesus deceived themselves; they were too scrupulous to enter the house of Pilate. We can plainly see their hypocrisy, but they could not. Many that killed the Christians thought they were doing God a service, John 16, 2. What stupendous blindness to the discrepancy between profession and behavior! But for all that it is untruthfulness. They who glory in their alms-giving, and like to be seen praying, and wish to have it known how they afflict themselves in the service of God, and are zealous to correct their neighbor while they are blind to their own faults, all these are called hypocrites by Jesus, Matt. 6. Their stupid conceit makes them hypocrites.

But although hypocrisy is often such an unconscious and such a common fault, it is a most grievous and detestable sin. All the world detests a hypocrite, although it is plain that others see the hypocrisy far better than the guilty one does. It is a grievous sin, for it is untruthfulness; and what hope is there for the entrance of the truth where one stubbornly is untrue? There is indeed more hope for publicans and harlots than for the foolishly conceited hypocrite.

It was a necessary act of kindness on the part of St. Paul to face Peter and charge him with this duplicity energetically and effectively, at once, and in the presence of the entire congregation. Nor can there be any doubt that Peter here again, as in the high priest's palace, repented at once. Peter and Paul continued their work in perfect harmony, and the Acts pass this event over with complete silence, as befits such a merely momentary weakness of Peter and Barnabas.

Does not this lesson contain for each and every one of us an earnest admonition to examine himself in the mirror of God's Law and to judge himself lest he be judged? 1 Cor. 11, 31. Ah, indeed: Jer. 17, 9. Hence pray: Ps. 19, 12; 139, 23. 24; 51, 10. And in the strength of such prayer let us confess Christ, let us confess our faith before men, by word and by deed, lest our behavior convict us of hypocrisy.   H. M. ZORN.

FOUR COMMON SPIRITUAL AILMENTS.

Lukewarmness.

Rev. 3, 15—19.

"Deep guile and great might Are his dread arms in fight; On earth is not his equal." If Satan cannot seduce the Christians in one way, he will try it in another; if not to-day, then to-morrow. He will try to lead them on to *doubt* the Word of God. "Yea, hath God said?" Gen. 3, 1. He will try to induce them to believe *false teachings*. If they have the Word of God in truth and purity, he will endeavor to distract their attention by introducing all manner of diversions into the activities of the congregation (*worldliness*). He will even dare to lead the true followers of the Master into *gross sins,* strife and hatred, dishonesty, shame, and vice.

The chief temptations with which he approaches the youth are worldliness, pride and lust of the flesh, while older persons he tempts principally with care, greed, and avarice.

But if he does not succeed in this manner, he will endeavor to lead both young and old astray by lukewarmness, lack of interest, and indifference in spiritual matters. This is a course which he has always followed, even of old.

Lukewarmness caused the holy writer to admonish the congregation of Laodicea. We cannot deny that —

Lukewarmness Is an Alarming Malady of the Present-Day Visible Church.

1. *The Symptoms of Lukewarmness within the Church are Pronounced, and the Consequences are Disastrous.*
2. *The Remedy Offered will Effect a Lasting Cure to Such as Are Willing to Accept It.*

1.

What is lukewarmness? Vv. 15. 16. He that is A and O, Amen, "the faithful and true Witness, the Beginning of the creation of God," He who speaks to the congregation at Laodicea, well knows. True, within this congregation there were faithful, loyal Christians; but upon the whole the conditions in this congregation were deplorable; the majority of the members were lukewarm, neither cold nor hot. They had no real interest in their own salvation, no interest in the welfare of the congregation. They still desired to be numbered among the Christians; with their mouths they still confessed the name of Jesus, Matt. 15, 8, but within their hearts there was no real love and zeal for Christ and His cause.

Whence lukewarmness? The lukewarm lack understanding. They have never seriously examined themselves according to the Law of God. They are satisfied with themselves; they say: "I am rich and increased with goods and have need of nothing," v. 17. They have never considered and grasped the true meaning of the Law of God. They feel secure and do not realize how "wretched, and miserable, and poor, and blind, and naked" they are, v. 17. They do not realize that they are children of wrath and have deserved eternal damnation. They do not realize the seriousness of sin. Because of this they do not understand and grasp and believe the Gospel.

Prosperity another reason for lukewarmness. The lukewarm say: "I am rich and increased with goods and have need of nothing," v. 17. Thus they spoke at Laodicea. Their city afforded them many opportunities to accumulate riches. — We ask, Was not the prosperity of a few years ago a reason why so many became lukewarm? Many felt like those of Laodicea: "We are rich." And because they received a rich measure of temporal blessings, many believed that this was a real indication that God loved them. They failed to realize, however, that "the goodness of God ought to lead them to repentance," Rom. 2, 4. Blindness filled their hearts to such an extent that they believed "they had need of nothing," v. 17. — That is a trait of natural man.

The fearful consequences to the lukewarm person himself. Lukewarmness is a grave condition, not to be trifled with. One who is lukewarm is ever on the downward path. Since he takes little interest in things pertaining to his eternal welfare, he will but seldom come to the house of God, to Holy Communion, and only rarely will he read the Word of God at home. And even if he attends public worship, his thoughts are elsewhere; he is making plans for his business or thinking of some amusement in store for him. And if he does listen to the sermon, how often is he inclined to criticize! For the same reason he is ever unwilling to give toward the support of his own church and for the furtherance of the work of the Church at large. Gradually he is drifting on the broad way, drifting into all manner of sin, shame and vice, dishonesty, etc.

Lukewarmness is exceedingly dangerous also to the congregations in which the lukewarm still hold membership. The evil example will be soon followed by others, and many in the midst of a congregation already afflicted with lukewarmness will be more and more confirmed in their attitude. The congregation will soon notice the evil consequences. The attendance at public worship decreases, the voters' meetings are not so well attended, brotherly admonition is not practised, unified, concerted, energetic effort is no longer put forth in the interest and welfare of the home congregation. Missions and the work of Synod receive little or no consideration. Contributions decrease.

Grave are the consequences to the world at large. How shall the children of the world be interested in the cause of the congregation and the work of the Church if the lukewarm members of the Church show no interest in their own congregation and no zeal?

Such lukewarmness rouses the wrath of the Lord. He who is Amen, the omniscient God and the Creator of all things, says, vv. 15. 16: "I know thy works," and in v. 17 He discloses the hypocrisy of the lukewarm: "Thou sayest . . . naked."

Lukewarmness is a great offense to the Master, gross ingratitude toward Him who gave His all whole-heartedly. It calls forth His wrath: "I will spue thee out of my mouth," v. 16.

2.

The Lord Himself first makes the *diagnosis*. This, above all, is very necessary; for only then can a *cure* be effected. But it was necessary that He Himself make the diagnosis; none other than He, the Omniscient, is able to do so. And therefore He who alone can know can prescribe the remedy.

The *remedy:* "Anoint thine eyes with eye-salve that thou mayest see," v. 18. By nature we are blind, 1 Cor. 2, 14; Eph. 4, 18; we cannot see or understand our true condition. Therefore He counsels to buy eye-salve with which to anoint the eyes. The ointment, the salve, is none less than the Holy Ghost. Read and hear the Word of God, and you will receive the Holy Ghost, who will open your eyes that you will see your deplorable condition, that you are not rich, as you surmised, but "wretched, and miserable, and poor, and blind, and naked"; that it is not true, as you thought, that you "have need of nothing," but that you need everything.

Having anointed the eyes and now realizing your utter helplessness, also the fearful consequences of sin, you will be ready to follow further counsel given: "Buy of Me gold . . . do not appear," v. 18. With gold we can buy many things we need. Gold is the most precious metal. It is a symbolic expression for faith. By faith we come into the possession of things that will really make us rich, happy, and blessed, v. 18. "Buy," each one for himself. Read the Word of God, ponder upon it, and accept in true faith what it offers. "Buy white raiment." Grasp that beautiful garment of salvation purchased by Christ's innocent suffering and death. Put it on, *i. e.,* believe. That garment will cover your "nakedness," v. 18, the multitude of your sins. In it you will be able to stand before the omniscient and holy God.

After the Master has diagnosed the malady and uncovered the fearful consequences of the cankerous growth, He speaks of a *remedy* and *cure* and offers it. How does He do it? He first tries to gain your confidence. It hurt you that He so rudely uncovered the malady, that He so earnestly admonished you, so bluntly made known to you His disgust, and so openly pronounced His wrath. But He said: "As many as I love," etc., v. 19. He now explains how the wretched, etc., v. 17, may be healed. "Be zealous therefore and repent," v. 19b.

Repentance is the only cure for lukewarmness. Daily repentance is necessary because daily we are prone to drift to lukewarmness. "Godly sorrow worketh repentance to salvation," 2 Cor. 7, 10. None will regret this godly sorrow. It will be a sorrow unto salvation. "Anoint thine eyes with eye-salve." Examine yourself according to the Ten Commandments, and you will detect that you are a sinner and possibly afflicted with dangerous symptoms of lukewarmness. If you are lukewarm, do you feel sorry that you are neither warm nor cold, that you have no earnest desire to grow in the knowledge of the Word of God, to come to a better understanding of your sins, and to come closer to Christ, your Savior? Do you regret that you so often have no desire to hear the preaching of the Word, that you are unwilling to conform your life to the will of God, that you so seldom pray earnestly and fervently, not only not for temporal, but particularly not for spiritual things, and that you are more and more loving the world and the things the world offers? How foolish! The world and its pleasures pass away; but the Word of God with its blessings abide forever. How dangerous! Here in time you will in your opinion enjoy life, but in the hereafter —?

Do you regret that your conduct has given offense to your congregation, so much so that others have been led to follow in your footsteps; that because of your attitude you in a measure are at fault that brotherly admonition is not so fully practised, that so many are not interested in the welfare of the congregation and of Synod nor in the great work entrusted to their care; that you and like you many others are so unwilling to help promote the cause of the congregation and the Church at large? Are you mindful of it that you are your brother's keeper; that it is your duty to lead your brethren on to salvation through faith in Christ Jesus? What must the Master think of you for not only not doing this, but being even a positive hindrance to your brethren?

Be *zealous* to repent, v. 19. Repent to-day; do not postpone repentance. It might be too late. And the Church needs you, needs you now, needs your active cooperation. The revival of interest in the work of your congregation and of the Church at large grows out of sincere repentance and a living faith.

Remember, the Master looks to your return. He therefore concludes this chapter by saying: "Behold, I stand at the door," etc., vv. 20—22.   F. C. STREUFERT.

Discouragement.
2 Tim. 1, 7—9.

What is wrong? This is the cry of the nations of to-day. Fortunes have been lost. Business is at a standstill, and in spite of all efforts on the part of the powers that be the situation has not changed perceptibly.

What is wrong with the Church at large? Never in the history of our Church have there been times like these. The work as such is almost at a standstill. Few new missions are organized, though the doors are wide open everywhere, and souls are perishing every minute. Numbers of graduates stand idle in the market-place. Contributions have decreased. Officials of Synod and members of mission boards are troubled, and grave fears fill their hearts.

What is wrong with our congregations? Present-day conditions are reflected in the work of the home congregation. Our work is seriously impaired. Has the former love and zeal vanished? Is the Church growing apathetic, lukewarm, indifferent? Some are still faithfully following the Master, but they are *discouraged;* the future fills them with grave concern. Such discouragement involves a great danger. Our text is written for just such conditions.

The Warning of Paul to Timothy against Discouragement an Admonition to the Christians of To-Day.

Paul reminds us —

1. *That Fear and Anxiety Are Indeed Dangers Threatening the Progress and the Very Existence of the Church;*
2. *That Fear and Anxiety Are not Compatible with the Spirit of God Given Us.*

1.

Timothy was afraid and discouraged. — "God hath not given us the spirit of fear," v. 7. What moved Paul to address Timothy in this manner? What did he mean? Paul stood very close to Timothy. Since the day when Timothy entered the ministry he was in close touch with him. He closely followed him in his work. Doing this, he noticed that he still loved the Master and firmly believed the Gospel of Jesus Christ, which until now he had presented in spirit and in power, but that for the time being he was in need of encouragement.

Why was Timothy so fearful and discouraged? The continued opposition, animosity, persecution and, no doubt, also the present developments, the hatred displayed toward his spiritual father, the Apostle Paul, who now was a prisoner, filled his heart with deepest gloom. And then, too, Timothy was still young and inexperienced.

Paul realizes the dangers threatening Timothy because of this fear and anxiety.

There are dangers ahead for Timothy himself. These fears will interfere with his pastoral duties. Being fearful, he will not properly profess and confess the sacred truths. Does not this fear and anxiety in reality involve a denial of the truth, disobedience to God?

Dangers ahead for Paul, now a prisoner, should Timothy weaken in his testimony. What a sad spectacle: Timothy too fearful to confess the truth and to defend it boldly! It would indeed be disloyalty to his spiritual adviser and teacher, the aged missionary, should he, the youthful coworker, not carry on, not boldly preach and teach.

Dangers ahead for the faithful few, the local congregation, and for the Church at large. Being fearful and discouraged, Timothy could not lead the flock boldly. Not a half-hearted presentation of the sacred truths, of sin and grace, but a whole-souled, cheerful, convincing testimony was demanded. How pertinent therefore the admonition of the Apostle Paul!

Fear and anxiety are also a danger threatening the progress and the very existence of the Church of to-day.

Fear and anxiety lie heavy upon the Church of God throughout the world as also on the Church in our midst. We thank God that the Gospel is still proclaimed in truth and purity among us. We are as yet fully convinced that it is even to-day a power of God unto salvation. But have not the days of "the first love" passed? Oh, for the time when all with one accord fearlessly, joyously, zealously, and loyally stood side by side with one another to perform the work the Lord had entrusted to His Church! "There is no fear in love," 1 John 4, 18. (First love in the home congregation.) To say the least, the Church of to-day is fearful and alarmed.

But why this fear and anxiety? There is the continued opposition on the part of the sinful world. Ungodliness is on the increase; the sins of the country cry to heaven. Opposition on every side, not only on the part of the unbelievers, but also on that of Lutherans falsely so called. Lodges. Increasing worldliness. Such difficulties are confronting us within the home congregations and within the Church at large, in Synod. The number of such within the congregation as are lukewarm is alarming. While struggling with the difficulties of the present economic era, many have become so engrossed with their own personal needs, problems, and difficulties that they consciously or unconsciously exaggerate their own plight and thus lose sight of their spiritual needs. The selfish materialism has begun to stifle the spiritual life and the interest in the spiritual welfare of others. — We meet with unwillingness to contribute to the Lord's cause, to contribute as the Lord hath prospered our people.

The fearful consequences of such fear and anxiety. It spells neglect of the work of the Lord in the home congregation and in the Church at large. Brotherly admonition is neglected. Work in the

Lord's vineyard is slighted. Missions are at a standstill, graduates are standing idle in the market-place. All in all, timidity is interfering with, and hampering, bold testimony. Truly, the Church of to-day needs this admonition of Paul!

2.

Paul reminds us, however, that fear is not compatible with the spirit which God has given us. "For God hath not given us the spirit of fear," v. 7. Let us note how the apostle endeavors to strengthen Timothy that the work of the Church might not suffer.

He does not stimulate Timothy by external means (though he commends him for his "unfeigned faith," v. 5), but directs him to the real source of encouragement, the Word of God. Even so to-day purely external measures, campaigns, etc., alone mean little. Note how lovingly the apostle accosts Timothy, vv. 3—6. Because of his youth, inexperience, and natural timidity he does not treat him roughly, but with all consideration and tender love. Nevertheless he reminds him most earnestly that God has not given us the *spirit of fear,* that God never intended us to be fearful. Such an attitude is not in harmony with the preaching of the Gospel. He reminds him that the spirit which we received from God is a *spirit of power.* With God and the Scriptures on his side he need fear nothing, because the power of God then dwells within him. Ps. 46, 2; cf. 2 Cor. 12, 7—10; Phil. 4, 13. True, the enemies within and without may heap on him all manner of sorrow, but "if God be for us, who can be against us?" Rom. 8, 31 b; Luke 21, 15; Is. 40, 31 c. — Paul reminds him that the spirit given us is a *spirit of love.* True love, which is a fruit of true faith and is given by the Holy Spirit, enables us to bring the greatest sacrifices. "Perfect love casteth out fear," 1 John 4, 18. Cf. Rom. 8, 15. Such love overcomes all fear, and he in whose heart this love reigns sees in his fellow-men, even though they be his greatest enemies, pitiable creatures that he must take care of and lead to Christ, his Savior.

The apostle further reminds Timothy that the spirit given a child of God is a spirit of *a sound mind.* This spirit enables him to see how to conduct himself in order that he may attain the goal which the Lord has set him. Consequently he overcomes fear, trembling, and timidity. Even though his heart trembles at times, all fear must nevertheless vanish. This "spirit of a sound mind" will enable him tactfully and joyfully to perform the task given him, will make him judicious, careful, and courageous to confess and profess the truth before friend or foe, whether he will be lauded or criticized, loved or persecuted. Paul admonished Timothy: "Be not thou therefore ashamed of the testimony of our Lord," v. 8. Paul is truly a master in admonishing his spiritual son. How lovingly does he speak: "Be not thou therefore ashamed of the testimony of our Lord"! Cf. Rom. 1, 16. How carefully does he choose his words! He means to say: Timothy, you will not think of withholding the testimony to avoid affliction. Cf. Mark 8, 28; Heb. 11, 26. You will not be ashamed of the Gospel nor of me because I am a prisoner. You know that I am in prison not because of any crime committed, but that I am suffering for the sake of the Gospel.

In other words, if Timothy now withdraws from Paul, he therewith withdraws from Christ. "But be thou a partaker of the afflictions of the Gospel according to the power of God." Be unafraid and endure patiently the hatred and animosity, the persecutions and sufferings, which we must endure because of the Gospel. All this will not really harm us. 1 Cor. 10, 13; 2 Cor. 12, 9a. The Gospel will prove to be a "power of God," v. 8.

"Who hath saved us," v. 8. How, therefore, can Timothy or any Christian upon whom the Lord has bestowed such blessed things be ashamed of the Gospel, be fearful and afraid? Our salvation, the salvation of the world, is complete, purchased by Christ, 1 John 2, 2. 4—9; Gal. 1, 13. God has "called us with an holy calling" through the Gospel, v. 9 a. He invites us and all sinners to accept the salvation prepared by Christ Jesus *before the world began,* v. 9 b; hence works are excluded.

Thus Paul strengthens Timothy. In spite of all afflictions Timothy should courageously, earnestly, and continuously "stir up the gift of God which was in him."

Let us examine ourselves. Are we at all times filled with zeal, full of courage to follow the Master's bidding? Are our hearts filled with fear, anxiety, and grave concern? Are we discouraged as we think of the future?

We ask, Dare we permit the hatred and animosity of the sinful world, the difficulties confronting us, the world-wide financial depression or anything else deter us, fill us with grave fears and discourage us? — Dare we weaken? Dare we perform the work of the Lord slothfully if we remember that the Lord has "not given us the spirit of fear, but the spirit of power, of love, and of a sound mind" and that God "hath saved us and called us with an holy calling, not according to our works, but according to His own purpose and grace, which was given us in Christ Jesus *before the world began"?* Should we not be filled with joy, courage, and zeal? Should not this "spirit of love given us" constrain us to do all in our power to rescue the perishing souls, those near and dear to us, yea, even the souls of such as hate us and persecute us? And if we consider that the spirit "of a sound mind" has been given us, we shall work while it is day, trusting that the Lord will guide us in all our endeavors. Let us think on the gracious blessing which the Gospel of Jesus Christ conferred upon us. Heb. 6, 9—12.

The spirit of fear is indeed not compatible with "the spirit of power and of love and of a sound mind." In the name of the Lord we must go forward, ever onward, within the church at home and within the Church at large, in Synod. Heb. 12, 12. 13; 13, 20. 21.

F. C. STREUFERT.

Faultfinding.

Matt. 7, 1—5.

The man without a fault has not yet been born. Even the great heroes of the Bible had feet of clay. "There is not a just man on earth that doeth good and sinneth not," Eccl. 7, 20. We readily agree to this when we think of others, for their shortcomings are always before us. It is more difficult when we think of ourselves; for we carry the pack of our sins on our back, where others see them, but we march on in ignorance of their number and magnitude.

If we could see ourselves as others see us and as God sees us from heaven, perhaps we should not be so hasty and harsh in our condemnation of others. We might even ask ourselves the question "Does the Bible anywhere make it my business to spy out the faults of my neighbor and pounce on him in a loveless manner?" And the answer would come to us: By no means, but search out your own heart and repent. Jer. 17, 9.

The divine Law, of which our text is a part, humbles our proud spirit, tears up the ground like the pointed share of the plow, the cutting wheel of the disk, and the sharp tooth of the harrow. You may sow good seed in a field year after year; but if you fail to use the plow in season, you will reap a poor harvest. So the divine Law must tear up the hard, callous places of the heart that the Gospel may sink in and bring forth fruit a hundredfold. To-day we shall devote our attention to the common spiritual ailment singled out in the text —

Faultfinding.

1. *Its Prevalence.*

A) *The Warning against It Is General.* "Judge not," v. 1. "Condemn not," Luke 6, 37. This warning is addressed to Christian people, to followers and hearers of Jesus, to believers in His person, His Word, His redeeming work. It implies the possibility, the ever-present temptation, and, in a measure, the existence of faultfinding among Christians of all times and all places. It is a wide-spread evil, this habit of finding and forging and telling of faults, not your own, — oh, no! — but your neighbors, a habit stirred and fostered by the devil and thoroughly enjoyed by our old sinful flesh.

B) *It Mars the Pages of Sacred History.* Cain, even while he worshiped, found fault both with God and His own brother, who was so much better than he. Dissatisfied spirits in Israel found fault with Moses and Aaron. Their rebellious attitude was contagious, until the whole congregation murmured and that long judgment came over them in the wilderness. The Pharisees, master faultfinders of their day, criticized everything that Jesus did, His teaching, His preaching, His healing, His condescending mercy, His eating, His drinking, His toil and His rest. They watched and waited and sought occasion against Him, ostentatiously holy, yet at heart more like jungle beasts disturbed in their lair, ready to pounce on their prey. They plotted to entangle Him in His talk. They had the effrontery to lay their unbelief at His door and say: "How long dost Thou make us to doubt?" John 10, 24. And when He permitted His disciples to pluck corn on the Sabbath-day to satisfy their hunger, they were exasperated enough to kill. Some of the disciples, especially Judas, found fault with Mary's offering of love, condemning it as waste and prating of the poor, until Jesus intervened and said: "Let her alone . . . ," Mark 14, 6. 9.

C) *It Is in the Air To-day.* We are living in an age of restlessness and change. The Church has not remained untouched by present-day conditions. The stress of the times rather has tended to bring out all the flaws in human nature, also among the Christians. There are those who have given themselves to an orgy of faultfinding, becoming sin-seekers, judging motives, magnifying faults. By mysterious nods, innuendos, and half-truths they make mountains out of molehills, and in their opinion nothing that is done is done right.

Moreover, those who do the least are often the most exacting. Those who complain about lovelessness in the congregation are often the most uncharitable; those who critize the sermon, the most irregular and inattentive; those who find fault with the choir, the ones who never come to sing; those who berate the Sunday-school, the ones who have never done anything for it; those who least appreciate the church-building and property, the ones who made no sacrifice in acquiring or improving it; those who watch and wait and judge most unkindly, the ones who are idle in the Lord's vineyard, out of step and out of sympathy with those who bear the heat and burden of the day. When such faultfinding became prevalent in his day, Paul hurled this challenge at all his critics: "With me it is a very small thing" etc., 1 Cor. 4, 3. 4.

2. *Its Destructive Nature.*

A) *It Has a Baneful Effect on Human Happiness and Progress.* It is always easier to tear down than to build, to destroy than to create, to be critical than to be correct. For this reason faultfinding is as dangerous as it is easy. "Judge not, that ye be not judged . . . measured to you again," vv. 1. 2. Any one, with or without talents, may rise to heckle and plot and accuse as the Pharisees did; but it takes a courageous, patient, faithful soul to rise above it and carry on as Jesus did. Faultfinding as a diet may please the flesh for the moment, but it will surely leave a bitter after-taste. Like cursing, it will fall back on those who indulge in it.

For the newly married we pray: "Enable them in wisdom and meekness to bear with patience each other's infirmities." Many a home has been broken, many a business wrecked, many a neighborhood feud started, many a church split to its foundations and made a house divided against itself, because people have not been willing to bear with patience each other's infirmities. George Washington, at thirteen, compiled a list of maxims for the guidance of youth; among them these: "Speak not injurious words, neither in jest nor in earnest. Be not hasty to believe flying reports to the disparagement of any. Be not apt to relate news if you know not the truth thereof." Think of the injury done to the kingdom of God, of the energy lost to the Church, because of hasty and unwarranted judging. You know, when a horse starts to kick, it ceases to pull. The devil is always best served, human happiness is marred and progress arrested, when Christian people, in public or private, pause to fall upon each other.

B) *It Tends to Destroy Faith and Humility.* Can any habitual faultfinder be a Christian? Can he love God? Does he love his neighbor? Does his religion mean anything to him? Jesus said: "Judge not," v. 1. (Cf. John 14, 15.) To do it nevertheless may at first be a weakness, but eventually it may become a chronic spiritual ailment and deliberate disobedience that will drive out Christian faith and humility and let pride and unbelief ride in. Ps. 50, 19—22.

To pay tithe of mint, anise, and cummin and omit the weightier matters of the Law, judgment, mercy, and faith (Matt. 23, 23) will bring down upon our heads the sentence: "Thou hypocrite," v. 5. When people work themselves into a rage to set others right, it is not probable that the spirit of Christ is in them. They may be hunting down in others the very sins they shelter in themselves, Rom. 2, 1. They shall not stand in the Judgment, Ps. 1, 5. They shall be judged without mercy, having showed no mercy, Jas. 2, 13; Matt. 18, 32—34.

3. *The Divinely Appointed Cure.*

A) *Rigid Self-examination.* V. 3: "Why beholdest thou . . . , but considerest not the beam that is in thine own eye?" "The greatest of faults," said Carlyle, "is to be conscious of none." If you do not know from the divine Law that you are a sinner, you will not see the need of, or believe in, the Savior. Accordingly, the Lord here turns the search-light of our faultfinding gaze from others upon

our own breast, where it may do some good. Christian Questions,
1—3. Catechism, Qu. 318. An ancient Greek temple bore the inscription: "Know thyself." A celebrated Persian writer said: "It was
my custom in my youth to rise from my sleep to watch and pray.
One night as I was thus engaged, my father awoke. 'Behold,' said
I, 'thy other children are lost in irreligious slumbers, while I alone
wake to praise God.' 'Son,' was the solemn answer, 'it is better to
sleep than to wake and find fault with thy brethren.'" The Pharisee, Luke 18, 11. "Examine yourselves," 2 Cor. 13, 5.

B) *Sincere Repentance.* V. 4: "Let me pull out . . . ." The
word "mote" denotes a particle of dust or other matter, troublesome
to the eye, it is true, but as nothing compared with a "beam," a
plank or joist, which would obstruct your view altogether. If a fault
is to be removed, a sin forgiven, be it mote or beam, it must be
repented of, confessed, and forsaken, Jas. 5, 16; 1 John 1, 8. 9; Prov.
28, 13. The faultfinder, too, must go that divinely appointed way.
The publican: "God be merciful to me, a sinner," Luke 18, 13. Peter
"wept bitterly," Matt. 26, 75. Paul, "chief of sinners," 1 Tim. 1, 15.
David: "Cleanse Thou me from secret faults," Ps. 19, 12.

C) *Faith in Christ.* Christ is the Way, the Truth, and the Life,
the Sin-bearer of the world, the divinely appointed sacrifice and cure
for all sin, also for the sin of faultfinding. There was no fault in
Him, Luke 23, 14; Is. 11, 3. He willingly endured the contradiction
of sinners to atone for our sins of the tongue and teach us patience,
Heb. 12, 3. "When He was reviled, He reviled not again . . . healed,"
1 Pet. 2, 23. 24; John 12, 47. 48. By faith we are all patterned after
Christ. We are likeminded, but not alike. You may pluck a hundred
leaves from the same branch and not find two alike. They will all
follow the same general pattern, but differ in size, and vigor, and
shade, and shape, and bent, and curl, and not one will be geometri-
cally perfect. Yet on the bough they looked graceful and symmetrical
enough. We sometimes forget that Christians retain their individuality, that, though they all have the same Spirit, they differ in the
degree of gifts, knowledge, love, labor, talents, responsibilities, and
temptations. We cannot establish a rule of uniformity. All the saints
are led in a right way, but no two of them in precisely the same way.
If we were to reject all believers who labor under infirmities, who are
marred with faults, or who do not think and act precisely as we would
under like circumstances, our fellowship should be scant indeed.

D) *The Observance of Matt. 18.* V. 5: "Then shalt thou see
clearly . . . ." When a brother's faults assume such serious proportions that charity cannot cover them and you cannot conscientiously
ignore them, you may protect yourself against the charge of faultfinding by adhering gently, but firmly to the rule laid down by our

Lord: "If thy brother . . . alone . . . gained thy brother," Matt. 18, 15, and he may be eternally grateful to you.

Parents must train and correct their children. Teachers must judge the work of their pupils. Evil-doers must be sentenced by the courts. Sound doctrine and practise must be upheld. False prophets must be exposed by the Word. Manifest and impenitent sinners must be excluded from the Christian congregation. But "brethren, if a man be overtaken in a fault . . . restore . . . meekness . . . tempted," Gal. 6, 1. Remember, the darkest night the world has ever seen did not put out the stars. The burden of this world's sin did not put out the love of God. His mercies to us have been new every morning. "Where sin abounded," etc., Rom. 5, 20. "As far as the east is from the west," etc., Ps. 103, 12, that we, the redeemed, might stand without fault before His throne, Rev. 14, 5. Hymn 306, 4.

WALTER F. TROEGER.

Busybodies.

2 Thess. 3, 11—13.

The Scripture urges us to improve, redeem, conserve, the time, to meet the challenge of our opportunities while we may, because the days are evil and our time of usefulness is short, Eph. 5, 16. "Go to the ant, thou sluggard, consider her ways, and be wise," Prov. 6, 6. Or let us think of the bee and the fly. The bee is always busy. It works to a purpose, moves with direction, seeks out the sunshine, the fragrance and sweetness of the garden and the field, gathering honey while it may, to the glory of God and the welfare of man, never meddling, avoiding things unclean, and using its sting only in self-defense. As for the fly, it, too, is always busy. But it is a busybody, serving no good purpose, always a bother, if not a menace. It has no reverence for the infant's slumber, the mourner's tears, the thinker's brow. Men everywhere resent its intrusions and are bent on its extermination. Yet we have these little busybodies always with us in our communities and in our homes. In our text the apostle applies the name "busybodies" to some of the Thessalonians. May we all profit by His timely censure and His stirring exhortation spoken in the name of the Lord Jesus.

Busybodies.

1. They Exalt Idleness, v.11.

A) *Living Disorderly.* When Cecil Rhodes, who added Rhodesia to the British Empire, was about to die at forty-nine, he said: "So much to do; so little done." If we must give account for idle words, how much more for idle lives! The apostle here is not speaking of the aged, the infirm, the involuntarily unemployed who sadly tramp the streets for work. He is addressing those who are idle by choice. There was a tendency among the Thessalonians to shrink from honest toil and look with covetous eyes upon a life of ease and indolence. But that was a mistake. It was disorderly, *ataktos,* used of soldiers who desert their ranks. Idleness does not fit into the divine plan and is contrary to the example of Jesus, who taught and preached till tired and worn and marched many a weary mile in search of souls gone astray. To curb the evil tendency, Paul branded them "busybodies," who walked disorderly, working not at all. Yes, in vv. 6 and 14, he urged the brethren to withdraw themselves from all such and have no company with them.

B) *Inviting Temptation.* Idlers are always bad company, not only because of their slothful example, but because they deliberately invite temptation and multiply the opportunity for mischief. "The busy man is plagued with but one devil, the idle man with a thousand." Cf. "industry," Cat., Qu. 54. David, 2 Sam. 11,1—3. Because of this ever-present danger it is a mistake, even for a man of means, to glory in idleness, to be served only by others, to pamper his body. Let us thank God for many duties also in the Christian congregation; for the better the sheep are fed, the greater will be their need of exercise. They who stand all the day idle, assuming no duties or responsibilities, are courting trouble.

C) *Meddling in Other People's Business.* Jesus would not be a busybody in other men's matters. He declined to be crowned a king, John 6, 15. He refused to serve as an earthly judge, Luke 12, 14. He said: "My kingdom is not of this world," John 18, 36. His is the kingdom of mercy and truth, in which He was ceaselessly active. It is a mistake for churches to-day to be busy in politics, dissipating their strength and prestige in all manner of civic, social, and economic reforms. It is a mistake for clergymen to neglect their Gospel ministry and tell public officials, legislatures, business men, farmers, laborers, how to run their affairs. It is a mistake for those not specifically trained to try to give advice to those who are trained and whom God has called. It is a mistake for idlers to give uncalled-for advice to busy people, to be so officious, exacting, garrulous. The thorns of idle gossip they sow will surely hurt both them and others. Of certain wanton young widows, Paul wrote: 1 Tim. 5, 13.

When Korah and his company of 250 princes rebelled against Moses and Aaron and meddled in the affairs of the priesthood, the earth opened up and swallowed them, Num. 16. When the five old pine-trees in Kensington Gardens, London (famed in Matthew Arnold's verse), died one by one, investigation revealed that a busybody had made it a habit to come there and sweep the ground clear of the needles that fell, which the trees needed for their existence. 1 Pet. 4, 15.

2. They Undervalue Honest Toil, v. 12.

A) *Ignoring a Divine Command.* During the war an order was issued for all able-bodied men to work or fight. Christians did not need this order to work. It was established long ago by God. Even in Paradise our first parents had a definite assignment of work. It was their joy and pleasure to dress the garden and keep it, Gen. 2, 15. The command in the Old Testament was: "Six days shalt thou labor and do all thy work," Ex. 20, 9. While the New Testament does not specify any number of days and hours, the command to work remains. It is always a sin to ignore a divine command, but "in keeping of them there is great reward," Ps. 19 11. Therefore Paul says to the busybodies: "Them that are such we command and exhort . . . work!" v. 12. Cf. Eph. 6, 5—7; Rom. 12, 11; 1 Thess. 4, 11; Col. 3, 23. "Let him that stole . . . labor, working with his hands . . . needeth," Eph. 4, 28.

B) *Neglecting Their Own Welfare.* After the Fall sorrow and fatigue were added to labor, Gen. 3, 17—19, but much of the original blessing remained. *(Arbeit macht das Leben suess.)* Labor is a natural exercise that enhances our physical, mental, and moral well-being. It builds health, develops strength, colors life, keeps the mind alert, and fills us with a sense of usefulness, the joy of cobuilders, having a definite part in the development and progress of our age. Even children are happier, healthier, and more content for having something to do, something to occupy their little hands and minds.

> For labor, the common lot of man,
> Is part of a kind Creator's plan.
> And he is king whose brow is wet
> With the pearl-gemmed crown of honest sweat.

Busybodies, meddlers, drones, and idlers injure themselves as well as their neighbor, cheating themselves out of much of the happiness of life and out of the fruits of labor. Ps. 37, 25; 128, 2; Luke 10, 7. In their shiftlessness, indolence, and desolation they remind you of rows of vacant houses with broken windows and stolen fixtures.

C) *Eating Other People's Bread.* In the city of Ghent a beggar collected alms for years on the pretense that he had a secret disease of the bones, which made it impossible for him to work. Yet he became such a busybody that one in authority insisted on a thorough examination, and the only disease found in his bones was laziness, habitual disinclination to work. We sympathize with the truly unfortunate, the underprivileged, the handicapped, who have had no fair chance, and the wreckage and driftwood that has lost the battle of life. But surely the burdens of the tax-payers, of the relief agencies, of business in general, of the church and the home, are great enough without having busybodies sitting on top of the load as parasites and leeches, dictating to others, sapping their strength, and eating their bread. By a glib tongue, fraud, and deceit they may succeed for a time, but they are treasuring up unto themselves wrath, Rom. 2, 5. And it is written: "If any would not work, neither should he eat," v. 10; "eat own bread," v. 12; "worse than an infidel," 1 Tim. 5, 8.

3. They Grow Weary in Well-doing, v. 13.

A) *Their Misspent Life.* "But ye, brethren," etc., v. 13. Here is an appeal to your heart and conscience. Has yours been an empty life, without proper direction, without real purpose, void of charity perhaps, but full of criticism and needless imposition on others? Has there been a certain grasping at shadows, a waste of effort, a putting of money into bags with holes, Hag. 1, 6, a spirit of indifference and weariness in well-doing? If so, consider the vanity and uselessness of it all.

> An idler is a watch that wants both hands,
> As useless if it goes as when it stands. — Cowper.

Is it not better to wear out than to rust out? The magnet, unused, loses its power. The man who sits and whittles away a stick at least can get another stick; but the man who whittles away his life has his whole life to account for. Oh, the world is in such dire need of good cheer, constructive leadership, and pure religion! Pray God this day that Christ may come into your empty life and fill it with the assurance of forgiveness, the riches of His love, the power of His Spirit, the fulness of His grace, that you may be of some use to Him and to others.

B) *Their Lost Opportunities.* The life of a busybody will be void of well-doing like that of the priest and the Levite who saw their countryman in his need and passed him by or like that of the nine lepers who, when they were cleansed, plunged into so many other activities that they forgot to return and give glory to God. "But ye," etc., v. 13. Be not like the horse in the fable that ran away in the morning and returned at night, saying: "Here I am, my master." "Yes," said the master, "but the field is not plowed." Jas. 4, 17.

C) *Their Scant Harvest.* Blessed are they who see their many faults, repent of, and acknowledge, them, and find forgiveness in the Savior's wounds. But the final mistake of busybodies is that they are prone to continue blindly in their ways. Certainly, confirmed busybodies have buried their talents, sown to the flesh and fallen from the faith, and are therefore wicked servants. They will never hear the gracious welcome: "Well done, thou good and faithful servant," etc., Matt. 25, 21. "Be not deceived . . . reap corruption . . . reap everlasting life," Gal. 6, 7. 8; "sparingly . . . bountifully," 2 Cor. 9, 6.

Whatever our duties in business, at home, or at church may be, let us look to our Lord Jesus Christ, remembering how He labored for our redemption, bearing the cross, and for His sake "let us not be weary in well-doing," etc., Gal. 6, 9. 10; 1 Cor. 15, 58; Heb. 6, 10. The greatest good that we can do to honor God and help our neighbor is to spread the Gospel. May all our labor and a just portion of the fruits of our labor be consecrated to this end.

WALTER F. TROEGER.

FOUR WOES OF JESUS.

Woe unto Those Who Spurn God's Grace!
Luke 10, 13—15.

In the days of Christ, according to estimates of authorities in Palestine, there was living around the Sea of Galilee approximately a million of people. These were inhabitants of rather busy, prosperous cities. Galilee represented the hub of activity, the productive source, the busy market, of Palestine.

To-day you look in vain for such activity. The cities of those days are gone, there is no longer a dense population in that section of Palestine, business has vanished, and the glories of yesterday are mere names to-day. There is only one town, Tiberias, now called Tubariya, on the western shore of the Sea of Galilee, with approximately 5,000 inhabitants. Ruins mark the sites of those prosperous centers of Jesus' day. We must necessarily think of the similarity of this condition with that of those places mentioned in the seven letters of the Book of Revelation. They, too, have disappeared through the ages.

What has brought about this sorry condition? Where shall we seek the cause of this desolation? What were the sins of these cities that brought down such destruction upon their heads? We find the answer in the woes of Christ which we have in our text as well as in the parallel passage, Matt. 11, 20—24. Our Lord shows us that He observes the attitude the people assume over against His Word and call them to account if they despise it. Privileges bring responsibilities. We consider: —

Woe unto Those who Spurn God's Grace!

1. To Whom did Jesus Address This Woe?

"Woe unto thee, Chorazin! Woe unto thee, Bethsaida!" etc. "And thou, Capernaum," etc. These three cities were singled out by the Lord Jesus at this time and the curse was pronounced over them.

What were these cities, and why should Christ single them out before others? These were three of the cities located immediately on the shores of the Sea of Galilee. There is some dispute even now about the exact location, and men are hoping that further excavations on the west shore may settle some of the doubts. However, this much is certain, that all these three cities were in the immediate vicinity of the Sea of Galilee.

This, too, is true, that they were cities which the Lord had visited frequently and in which He had performed many of His miracles, alleviating suffering and want and showing forth His divine glory. Some of these miracles are recorded in the gospels; however, many more were performed. This we see from John 20, 30. 31. We may recall several of the major works of Christ in these cities. We think of the nobleman's son at Capernaum, of the centurion's servant, of those possessed with devils, of Simon's mother-in-law, of the feeding of the five thousand, and of the many summarized in Matt. 15, 29—31. All of these and many more divine signs Jesus performed in these centers and round about them. Besides, His miracles were only accompanying phenomena, introductory, as it were, to His principal work as Prophet, the preaching of His Word. He first preached and then showed signs and wonders. Signs and wonders without the Word He objected to.

Now, those greatly favored cities were unappreciative of what Christ did in their midst; they rejected Him and His disciples. He spoke the words of our text in connection with the sending out of the Seventy. From His own experience He knew what their reception would be in some of the cities He mentioned, and therefore He warned them and told them what to do if they would meet with the same treatment as He. And then He proceeded to utter the cry of woe and to curse those cities, which had had more reason than others to listen to His Gospel and to love Him for the many kindnesses shown them.

We also have received gracious gifts. Do we show our appreciation?

2. What did Jesus Expect of Those People?

Since much had been given the inhabitants of those three cities, much was also expected of them. Jesus shows this by comparing these cities with localities that had not been so highly favored as they. V. 13: "If the mighty works had been done in Tyre and Sidon which have been done in you, they had a great while ago repented, sitting in sackcloth and ashes." Tyre and Sidon were ancient Phenician strongholds and ports of Mediterranean trade; they never had enjoyed the privilege of having the Lord reside in their midst, nor had He visited their region for any length of time. They must nevertheless, despite their very limited knowledge, have shown themselves more appreciative, more thankful, than the cities He was now condemning. Besides, Jesus spoke contingently, showing what might have happened under given circumstances.

The Lord expected repentance in sackcloth and ashes. Sitting on the ground in sackcloth and ashes was the Oriental way of showing great grief. Cf. Job; also Nineveh in the Book of Jonah. This was not expecting too much, Ezek. 3, 6. The grace of God calls to repentance; hence those three cities should have been a shining example of this very thing. Surely the Lord had not preached among them to be ignored, nor had He performed His miracles to have them so easily forgotten.

Repentance, however, was totally lacking in them. The Lord was persecuted; His disciples had to shake the dust off their feet, being treated no better than the Master. Therefore the Lord pronounced His withering curse upon these cities. They were to be cast down to hell, that is, rejected for their unbelief and sin. We may compare here John 12, 48; 1 Pet. 2, 11; Jer. 51, 53; Ezek. 26, 20.

3. The Consequences of Christ's Curse.

It will be more tolerable for those cities that have not received such great grace than for Capernaum, Chorazin, and Bethsaida. Here the Lord indicates that their punishment will be greater than that of Tyre and Sidon or of Sodom and Gomorrah. He does not herewith mean to say that Sodom and Gomorrah or Tyre and Sidon will be saved despite their sins, but He says these Galilean cities are more reprehensible, their sins are greater; for they knew better; they sinned against better knowledge and neglected wonderful opportunities.

People sometimes ask, Will there be degrees of punishment in the hereafter? Even reason dictates that there must be since the subjects for punishment are so different. The Bible also points to this fact, as Jesus does right here. Cf. Luke 12, 47. 48; John 9, 41; 15, 22; Rom. 2, 12; Matt. 5, 22; 10, 15.

Terrible are the consequences, and that the pages of history have amply shown. Those three cities were cast down to hell after having been exalted to heaven, that is, highly favored. As Sodom and Gomorrah were totally destroyed in the day of Lot, Gen. 19, so these cities met the same fate of extinction and decay. The Lord did not speak in vain; He is not to be trifled with. He spoke through the prophets, Deut. 1, 28; Ezek. 32, 18; Is. 14, 13—16. None of these words lost its truthfulness and force. All has been fulfilled. So also everything concerning Capernaum, etc. They are mere names now, and the place thereof shall know them no more.

We cannot help but think of the warning Dr. Luther gave his beloved Germans in his day for fear that they might reject the Word of God. His classic dictum regarding the Gospel's departing from one place and going to another is well known. Was he not a prophet when he spoke those words?

What would Jesus say of our cities and hamlets to-day and of many country communities? Does not this saying apply with equal truth? The Gospel has been preached for many years, great wonders, granting forgiveness of sins, have been performed, the disciples have labored, — yet where are the results? Have we appreciated the Gospel of Jesus as we ought? Who must not hang his head in shame? Let us beware of the sin of ingratitude lest the curse of Capernaum, of Bethsaida, and of Chorazin strike us. To lose salvation means to lose everything.

The Lord grant that we repent in sackcloth and ashes and turn to the Savior, who still receives us as He would receive Tyre and Sidon. Hymn 318, 7. 8.   O. KRUEGER.

Woe unto Those Who Hinder Others from Obtaining Salvation!
Matt. 23, 13.

Leadership among men is certainly a privilege, but a privilege coupled with grave responsibilities. People often think only of the honor and forget the responsibilities. This is always commensurate with the honor, yea, it often outweighs the latter by far and makes the recipient of the honor wish that others might take the honor and relieve him of the responsibilities.

This is true of leaders in Municipal, State, and Federal Government, in the school, but especially in the Church. In the Church the leaders deal with immortal souls which are at stake, and they are of far greater importance than the issues in other walks of life. Whoever accepts the position of teacher, leader, guide, instructor, in the Church must be conscious of the tremendous moral obligation attached to such prestige. This is brought out strikingly in the words of Christ, the first of the eight woes addressed to the scribes and Pharisees. We consider: —

Woe unto Those who Hinder Others from Obtaining Salvation!

1. For He who Hinders Others from Reaching Heaven Thereby Loses His Own Salvation.

Text. This is surely severe, uncompromising language. Men to-day are not accustomed to speak thus, and the multitudes do not care to listen to such strong denunciations unless some one else in general disfavor is meant, in which case they may enjoy it. We must remember that we have here the plain statement of the Lord Himself, that He passes judgment and not we. We cannot and dare not change an iota of the words here spoken. Truth must remain truth. The withering denunciations of this whole passage, vv. 13—39, remind us of some of the Old Covenant prophetic utterances, cf. Is. 5, 3 ff.; chap. 10; Hab. 2.

The Lord accuses the scribes and Pharisees of being hypocrites, which means that they were not what they pretended to be. Their whole life and conduct showed this. (Here may follow a description of the historical development of the Pharisees and scribes and of their man-made precepts.)

Worse than this, however, was their rejection of the salvation God had prepared in Jesus, the only Savior. They had substituted the traditions of men for the Law of Moses. Jesus on several occasions showed them the hypocrisy of their hearts evidenced by their doctrines and actions in this very respect. Trifles were made to appear of enormous importance, while God's commandments were lightly set aside.

They would not receive the Lord as the promised Messiah, but acted as though they had superior knowledge and were far above the lowly carpenter's son of Nazareth. What good could come out of Nazareth? "Is not this Joseph's son" of Galilee? We think of their attitude towards Christ as they displayed it when Christ healed the man who had been blind from his birth, John 9. They rejected the counsel of God against themselves, being not baptized of Him.

They thus kept themselves out of heaven. Many of the common people would gladly have permitted themselves to be led aright; but these scribes misled them by not going the prescribed way to heaven. They would rather perish in their own false conceits than to accept the salvation through Christ. They stood in their own light. How stubborn and stiff-necked they were and thus brought on their own perdition and destruction.

Jesus therefore condemns the scribes and Pharisees in our text. He was speaking to the multitude specifically about them, vv. 1. 2. These words were to serve the people as a warning and the scribes and Pharisees as a call to repentance. They should humble themselves immediately and seek salvation while the day of grace still continues. Soon it would be too late for repentance. Should not such cutting words have rung in their ears and pierced their hearts and consciences?

May all false teachers of our day listen to the earnest warning of their Savior and teach His Word truthfully! If they will not, they will forfeit their salvation by misleading others.

2. He Causes Others to Lose Their Salvation.

Text. This verse twice accuses the Pharisees and scribes of doing this very thing: "Ye shut up the kingdom of heaven against men"; "neither suffer ye them that are entering to go in." For this sin the Master condemns them.

Our text indicates that heaven is really open for all men. God's will is that all enter and be saved. This is a well-established fact, Ezek. 33, 11; 1 Tim. 2, 4; 2 Pet. 3, 9.

The office of the ministry, the duty of the spiritual leaders and teachers, is to lead people through this open door to heaven. Now, when men who are the reputed leaders do the opposite, namely, close the door of the Gospel to the sinners, they are perverting their holy office and calling.

How do they shut the door; how do they hinder others from obtaining salvation? By false doctrine and ungodly example. In Luke 11 the Lord speaks of the lawyers as taking away the key to salvation. This key can be none other than Jesus and His Word. Thus Jesus speaks of Himself and His Word in John 17, 3; 5, 39; 14, 6. Take Christ away, and the key to heaven is gone, the door is closed. The angel once more guards the way to the tree of life, and paradise is lost to that particular person.

This hindering others, *tous eiserchomenous,* those about to enter, or in the act of entering, wanting to enter, to lose their salvation, is surely the greater sin, and for that the false leaders must suffer the greater damnation. How shall they stand before the Judge who condemns the giving of offense? Matt. 18, 7; Rom. 16, 17.

The Lord here answers the age-worn question of these people, heard already out of the mouth of the first murderer, "Am I my brother's keeper?" Yes indeed you are. What a privilege to lead your brother aright and to assist him to obtain salvation! But how damnable to hinder him in his search for eternal life or from entering the door of heaven.

This second portion is again both a warning and an encouragement to all pastors to be careful of their leadership. Preach the entire Gospel; conceal nothing; obscure nothing. Throw wide the doors of heaven that all repentant sinners may enter. May many come through our preaching and sit down with Abraham, Isaac, and Jacob!

This should be addressed also to all Christians. They must watch their words and lives lest they become an offense in the eyes of others who would enter. Otherwise the Lord will say of them what we read Rom. 2, 23. 24.

The Christian congregation prays and sings: Hymn 485, 2.

O. KRUEGER.

Woe unto Such as Strain at a Gnat and Swallow a Camel!

Matt. 23, 23. 24.

In warning His hearers against sin, the Savior did not generalize. He preached in such a manner that His hearers were led to single themselves out as the people who were guilty of sinning. Whenever He discovered sin, He condemned it, in the case of hardened sinners in thundering terms, no matter how prominent the persons were in whom the sin was found. In the text before us He condemns in sharpest terms the proud and haughty Pharisees, that prominent Jewish sect noted for its strict formalism and pretensions to superior sanctity, and sternly He pronounces upon these hypocrites an awful, withering woe. (Text.) There is a great deal to be learned from this text, and we shall proceed at once to the study of it. Our subject shall be: —

Straining at a Gnat and Swallowing a Camel.

Let us see —

1. How the Pharisees Did This in Their Day;
2. How Men Still Do This in Our Day.

1.

The Savior first reminds the Pharisees of something that in itself was not wrong: "Ye pay tithe of mint and anise and cumin." Practically the law of tithe was enforced only in the case of the produce mentioned in Deut. 14, 23 — corn, wine, and oil. But the Pharisees, in their overstrained scrupulosity, interpreted the law of tithes, Lev. 27, 30: "All the tithe of the land, whether of the *seed* of the land or the fruit of the tree, is the Lord's," so strictly as to include the smallest pot-herbs and vegetables, even their leaves and stalks. (See Edersheim, *The Life and Times of Jesus,* Vol. II, p. 412 f.)

Mint is here mentioned. Of this well-known sweet-smelling plant several species grow in Palestine. It was one of the ingredients of the sauce of bitter herbs eaten at the Passover-feast, Ex. 12, 8, and was hung up in the synagog for its fragrance.

Anise, the second herb mentioned, is known to us as dill and is much used in medicines and for seasoning.

Cumin, the third herb here spoken of (cf. Is. 28, 25. 27), is a plant which seeds something like caraway and like it is used for medicinal purposes or to give relish to food. With respect to all three of these herbs the Pharisees were conscientious tithers.

But while affecting a scrupulous conscientiousness in things infinitely little, these Pharisees omitted "the weightier matters of the Law." Their religion consisted in small outward observances. They were so busy with the fussy trivialities on which they prided themselves that they had no time to attend to more important duties. But while they were so scrupulously intent on observing minute forms, there was at the same time found with them a demoralizing indifference toward moral purity. Very carefully they avoided small formal improprieties, but in their general conduct they indulged in the grossest and most abominable license. Without compunction the greatest sins were committed, and the most important duties were omitted.

In our text the Lord particularizes the weighty duties which the Pharisees neglected, duties unspeakably more important than the details of mere outward ordinances. And which are they? "Judgment, mercy, and faith." These three are named in contrast to the three petty observances mentioned before, "mint, anise, and cumin." The Savior, in speaking of judgment, mercy, and faith, seems to refer to Micah 6, 8: "What does the Lord require of thee but to do justly and to love mercy and to walk humbly with thy God?" (See also Hos. 12, 6; Zech. 7, 9. 10.)

"Judgment" implies justice in principle and practise, acting equitably toward one's neighbor, harming no one by word or deed. Thus in Jer. 5, 1 a man is sought "that executeth justice." Such impartiality is specially enjoined in Deut. 16, 19. 20: "Thou shalt not wrest judgment; thou shalt not respect persons," etc.

But also "mercy" is here spoken of. "Mercy" is loving-kindness in conduct, pity in the heart, love toward those in need of compassion.

And "faith," the last quality here mentioned, means sincerity, faithfulness, fidelity to God first and then also to man, works of faith. The exactest ritual and the strictest orthodoxy are of no value without these three great virtues: justice, mercy, and faith.

We see from our text that Jesus does not criticize the Pharisees for being conscientious in small duties, but that He finds fault with them for that expenditure of zeal on trifles which stood in the place of, or left no strength for, higher duties. He tells them: "These," judgment, mercy, and faith, "ought ye to have done and not to leave the other," the tithing of herbs, "undone." It took a very elastic conscience to pay the insignificant tithe on common garden herbs, but to neglect judgment and mercy in dealing with some poor Lazarus. Such a practise Christ condemns and says: "Woe unto you, scribes and Pharisees, hypocrites!"

The reason Jesus pronounced so many woes on these people was that they were straining at a gnat and swalling a camel. What does it mean to strain at a gnat, or, as Trench reproduces the words, to "strain out the gnat"? The stricter Jews were extremely particular in straining their wines and liquors before drinking them lest they inadvertently swallow some unclean insect and so be defiled. The wine gnat was easily caught when strained through linen. This practise, which was in a sense a religious act, is still found among the Buddhists in Hindustan and Ceylon and elsewhere, who thus endeavor to avoid pollution. A traveler in North Africa reports that a Moorish soldier who accompanied him, even when he drank water, always unfolded the end of his turban and placed it over the mouth of his *bota,* drinking through the muslin, to strain out the gnats, whose larvae swarm in the water of that country.

The Pharisee indeed strained out the gnat carefully. But while concerned about the gnat, these hypocrites were perfectly satisfied to "swallow a camel." The gnat and the camel, both of which were considered unclean, stand at the extremities of the scale of comparative size. The proverbial saying among Hindus is "swallowing an elephant and being choked with a flea." Jesus in our text speaks as He does to denote the inconsistency of the scribes and Pharisees, who would avoid the smallest ceremonial defilement, but would make light of the gravest moral pollution. The Pharisees strained out the gnat, the small ritual offense, but swallowed the camel, the huge uncleanness of soul-defiling sin. Unblushingly they practised the greatest iniquities. They swallowed the camel when they gave Judas thirty pieces of silver for promising to deliver over to them "innocent blood"; they strained out the gnat when they had scruples about putting the returned pieces of silver in the Temple treasury. They strained out the gnat when they would not go into the judgment-hall for fear of being defiled; yet they swallowed the camel when they stood at the door, crying out against the holy Jesus, "Crucify Him! Crucify Him!"

By their conduct and corrupt living these Pharisees were heaping up woes unto themselves; for the word *woe* is repeated again and again in this chapter. Great humiliation, hopeless ruin, would overtake them, Jesus warned them. "Woe unto you, hypocrites! Ye blind guides, which strain at a gnat and swallow a camel!"

2.

Even to-day we find this attitude among people. Vast multitudes still strain at a gnat and swallow a camel. People are very scrupulous about points of politeness, but very negligent of real kindness. They will not offend an acquaintance with a harsh word, yet they will ruin him if they can outwit him in a business transaction. They forbid innocent forms of amusement to others, yet they themselves are self-indulgent, ill-tempered, uncharitable, and covetous. The greatest care in correctly observing a ritual; yet the spirit of true devotion is neglected. A rigid standard of orthodoxy is insisted upon; yet the plain will of God is disregarded. Labors of mercy, if done on a Sunday, are damning sins in the esteem of many modern hypocrites; yet they themselves cheat and lie and grind the poor. Such people are particular about the mint and anise and cumin, but they omit the weightier matters of the Law. They see the gnat, but they do not perceive the camel.

Just a few examples. Many liberal churches permit agnostics and infidels to hold membership and even to occupy high positions, while they deny to the Christians some things which they may well enjoy in evangelical liberty, opposing in some quarters even such harmless things as congregational singing and organ music in connection with worship. It is certainly a case of straining at a gnat and swallowing a camel.

In a recent issue of the *Christian Century Pulpit* (Nov., 1933) the Rev. M. E. Bollen, pastor of the University Baptist Church at Seattle, Wash., criticized congregations and pastors for "building cathedral-like churches, robing their choirs and gowning the pastor, working out elaborate rituals, and rivaling in their services the priests and Temple of Solomon's time." And yet in the same article this man insists that the kingdom of the Messiah must be pushed ahead until it "includes all industrial affairs and dominates all international relations. . . . Not until then will the world behold the dawn of that era for which Jesus taught His disciples to pray, 'Thy kingdom come.' " What a warped conception of the kingdom of Jesus! Might we not call this a straining at gnats, insignificant things, and a swallowing of camels, gross error?

Several years ago the Latter-day Saints' School of Music, which is an official part of the Mormon organization in Salt Lake City, sent out letters to interested parties in that city in which the management emphasized that they had "one of the most elegant ball-rooms in the West," which was described as being particularly attractive. What an insult to clean-minded young people! Yet how representative of the terrible deception which "the Church of Jesus Christ and the Latter-day Saints" operates! "Twentieth-century Pharisees" would be a better designation for these people, who rave against coffee-drinking and the use of tobacco, but cast aside the commandments "Keep thyself pure" and "Flee youthful lusts" to "hold" their young people. Blind guides, which strain at a gnat and swallow a camel!

Friends, we have all on this or that occasion strained at a gnat and swallowed a camel. We are all more or less cramped by our own pettiness. We must be lifted out of ourselves. We need the awakening of our higher spiritual powers. Jesus alone can effect this change in us. When He pronounces a woe, it is not merely an expression of holy wrath, but also an exclamation of sorrow. Because He loves us and cares for our immortal souls, He uses cutting words, as a surgeon uses the knife to save the life of his patient. He leaves nothing un-

tried to turn our hard hearts to repentance, to take us out of our sinful ways, and to bring us to the knowledge and confession of the full
truth. 1 John 1, 7. Oh, let us permit Him, our dear Savior, to take
possession of our soul, and He will set all things in their true light.
With Jesus we shall be able to strive for great objects, fight great sins,
win great victories, and because of the magnitude of the camels we
shall forget the gnats.   ALBERT J. KORRIS.

Woe unto Those Who Are Outwardly Clean, but Inwardly Polluted!

Matt. 23, 25. 26.

Recall the foregoing "woes." This text is one in a series of most
startling pronunciations from the lips of Jesus. Some contend that
Christ will not punish, that He is Love, and that it is altogether incompatible with love that He should inflict punishment. Let them
study these "woes" and note how terrible they really are. They speak
for themselves. They are directed sharply and pointedly against
hypocrisy. Jesus, who can discover hidden hypocrisy, enumerates
various phases and features of such hypocrisy. In this section He
deals a telling blow to those who look to the external appearance without giving due thought and attention to the inward condition.

Christ's Woe upon the Outwardly Clean, but Inwardly Polluted.

1. The Outward Cleanliness;   2. The Inward Corruption;
3. The Folly of Such Hypocrisy.

1.

"Ye make clean the outside of the cup and of the platter." The
scribes and Pharisees were scrupulously conscientious about outward
ceremonies. The washing of their "cups and platters" is a matter to
which Jesus referred also in Mark 7, 4. They had "received these
things to hold." God's Ceremonial Law contained certain definite
commands regarding cleansing and purification: Lev. 8, 6; Ex. 30,
17—21; Lev. 12—15; Deut. 21, 1—9. To these they had added many
more. In the course of time greater attention was given to man-made
laws than to those which God had prescribed. Hence Jesus complained
that they "teach for doctrines the commandments of men," Matt. 15, 9.
Even through the prophet Isaiah, chap. 29, 13, God had complained:
"Their fear toward Me is taught by the precept of men." St. Paul
urges Titus to teach that there should be no "giving heed to Jewish
fables and commandments of men, that turn from the truth," Titus
1, 14. Cf. also Col. 2, 20—22. There was evidently much of this practised. So here; the scribes and Pharisees gave full attention to the

thorough cleansing of the dishes; at least they cleaned the outside of the cups and of the platters.

Undoubtedly Jesus is addressing Himself to these hypocrites in the matter of attempting merely to give thought to the outward appearance of things. They were conducting themselves in such a manner that men would be impressed with their actions. Cf. vv. 5—7. To them reputation meant more than character. The outward cleansing, the washing and ablutions, were all things which men could see and about which they would speak. Hence they were so extremely careful about them.

This is not at all unusual to-day. Our real character cannot be seen by men, but our reputation is something about which they speak to one another. Our reputation, in fact, is built upon that which men can see us do or upon that which they hear us say or hear about us. Hence people are very careful to safeguard their reputation and put on outward appearances. Many want to be considered honest and upright, kind-hearted and charitable, peaceable and friendly, moral and clean, in their community and in their circle of friends, etc.

2.

"But within they are full of extortion and excess." With these words Christ uncovers the real trouble. The inside of the cup and of the platter present an entirely different picture. That which is hidden from the eyes of men is fully visible to the eyes of God, and He beholds "extortion and excess." The things which their cups and platters contained were gotten in a sinful manner and were serving a sinful purpose. These leaders belonged to the wealthier class of people, but much of their wealth and possession had been obtained wrongfully. Jesus accused them of devouring widows' houses, v. 14. They had deprived the poor, even the widows. Briefly stated, they were thieves. Though men did not suspect them of such wickedness, though they were generally regarded as ideal citizens and noble and trustworthy children of God, the Lord had an open view of the inside of the cup and of the platter. That which He saw was all filthy and corrupt, because it was permeated with sin. The account of St. Luke states "ravening and wickedness," Luke 11, 39. God saw more than this. He mentions "excess." There appears to have been much of "society life" among the Pharisees, "feasts," v. 6. There they not merely vied with one another for the most prominent places, but they also became guilty of excess, of too much eating and drinking. Gluttony and drunkenness were all too common then, as now. That accounts for so many Scriptural warnings against such sins, Deut. 21, 20; Prov. 23, 1—3; 23, 21; Luke 15, 13; Gal. 5, 21; Eph. 5, 18; 1 Pet. 4, 3; 2 Pet. 2, 13.

What a lesson for our day and time! We passed through a period of unparalleled prosperity. There was an almost unbelievable amassing of fortunes. Many grew abnormally wealthy. Much was obtained by "extortion." How many people "gambled" in the stock market, put over a "sharp deal" in business, enriched themselves by oppressing the poor! How many have taken advantage even of the "depression" to enrich themselves by inflicting even greater suffering upon the unfortunate! And how many of these people claimed to be church-members! Oh, what shocking and startling revelations were made during the past few years! The depression, with resultant investigations, exposed so much of dishonesty and corruption. Even such filth was revealed as members' of the church "keeping the outside of the cup and of the platter clean" for the express purpose of practising "extortion and excess."

What a detestable character: proper, and even punctilious, in outward behavior and within lovelessness, envy, hatred, covetousness!

Again, we have passed through an awful period of feasting and drinking. "Prohibition" did not prohibit. The charge has repeatedly been made that such as claimed to be members of the Church in good standing were regular customers of the bootleggers. Think of the wild parties at Christmas and New Year, etc. Gluttony and drunkenness have certainly been common sins in our land. Wherever they have been practised by church-members, let us remember that God knows what has been happening on the "inside of the cup and of the platter."

3.

The Savior points out the utter folly of this action. "Thou blind Pharisee, cleanse first that which is within the cup and platter, that the outside of them may be clean also." How foolish for a person to wash the outside of a dish and then be unconcerned about the filth that is on the inside! Will it not contaminate and harm if the dirt and corruption within is eaten? Of course, Christ refers here to the condition of the heart. If that be corrupt, will it not render the entire person filthy, and will it not bring harm and destruction upon him though there be ever so much "outward polish" in a seemingly splendid conduct by the outward fulfilment of the commandments? God looks to the heart, 1 Chron. 28, 9; Jer. 17, 10; Rom. 8, 27. Unless that be clean, unless that be filled with the proper motives to prompt the outward conduct, everything about that person is filthy and corrupt.

This necessitates that the "inside" must be cleansed first. This was the very thing which the Pharisees were not merely omitting, but refusing to do. The only cleansing of the heart can come through the meritorious work of Jesus Christ, through the precious blood which He shed for us, Rom. 3, 24. 25; 1 John 1, 7; Eph. 1, 7; Heb. 9, 14; 1 Pet. 1, 18—19, etc Only if we accept the forgiveness which Christ wrought for us, can we be cleansed. Hence the importance of faith, Acts 13, 39; Rom. 3, 22. 24. 28; Gal. 2, 16, etc.; for by faith we accept Christ's accomplishments.

Jesus does not mean to teach that we should not look to the "outside of the cup and of the platter," to the outward appearance of our life and conduct, to our reputation. If any person should watch his conduct and reputation, then surely the Christian should do so. What Christ would impress is that we attend *first* to the "inside," and then the "outside" will take care of itself. A clean spring will bring forth clean and wholesome water. A justified Christian will be concerned about his sanctification and will succeed, by the grace of God, to lead a godly life. If we follow Joel 2, 13 and Prov. 23, 26, then will follow Matt. 12, 34b.

God grant us the grace to put first things first! Any other course will result in hypocrisy, and hypocrisy leads to ruin.

J. W. BEHNKEN.

THREE HATEFUL THINGS.

That Hateful Thing — Slothfulness.
Rom. 12, 11.

Rom. 12, 1. We are God's own both by creation and by redemption. Therefore we should willingly and gladly present our bodies, ourselves, a living sacrifice to Him who has made us and sustains us and who has redeemed us from the power of darkness and called us into His wonderful light. His should be every thought, every heartbeat, every act of our will. Every member of our body should at all times be eager to do His will.

But the very fact that the holy writer finds it necessary to exhort us shows that there is a shortcoming. Indeed, every pastor knows this to his sorrow. Every true Christian is painfully aware of a strange apathy over against this presenting of our bodies a living sacrifice to God. The holy writer himself deplores it, Rom. 7, 24. He hates it. That we may also hate it, let us view carefully —

That Hateful Thing — Slothfulness.

1. It Is Hateful in Its Nature;
2. Hateful because of Its Consequences.

1.

Spoude means zeal, eagerness. *Okneros* means lazy, indolent, slow, slothful. Be not lazy in zeal. The English Bible has "Be not slothful in business." The German rendering is clearer: *"Seid nicht traege, was ihr tun sollt."* The context shows to what our zeal should be directed. It is summed up in v. 1 of this chapter. There are many things in which we should be active, things that concern God and our fellow-men, according to the first and the second table of the Law.

The negative form of this exhortation indicates that we Christians are prone to be just that — slothful, lazy, in regard to what we should do. And that is a hateful thing.

Slothfulness is hateful in every man, but especially in a Christian. It is a mean disposition of mind, will, and heart. It reveals a contempt for God's innumerable temporal and spiritual blessings. It has its source in a lack of appreciation of God's wonderful mercies. It reveals a heart in which there is very little love of God and man, small consideration of what pleases God and contributes to man's welfare. It disregards the example of faithful leaders, even of the Son of God Himself. No wonder the holy writer warns against it. Be not lazy in what you should do; do not neglect your duties to God and man. It is a hateful thing, that slothfulness.

Note the neglect of duty which is spoken of Matt. 25, 41—45. How hateful this vice is to God we see from Matt. 25, 26—28.

2.

Slothfulness has many evil consequences. For the slothful himself. It weakens still more his already feeble spiritual life. Exercise is good for the body. (Explain.) Exercise is good also for the spiritual life. If a Christian keeps on training, if he persists in his efforts to present his body a living sacrifice to God, he will thereby grow stronger spiritually, 2 Pet. 1, 5—8.

But the opposite is also true. Inactivity, laziness, in spiritual duties will weaking a Christian's spiritual life. God views this with displeasure. Remember the parable of the Fig-tree, Luke 13, 6 ff. Slothfulness makes for spiritual poverty and ends in death. See also Luke 19, 12 ff.

Slothfulness has evil consequences for others. Slothful members are extremely harmful to a congregation, to its well-being. It is irritating to the active members, retards or stops all progress, dampens the zeal of others, discourages the pastor.

Slothful congregations hinder the work of our Synod. Witness the empty treasuries, the great number of candidates that have not received a call. Slothfulness causes our officials grief and worry. It is a great offense and stumbling-block to unchristians.

The slothful will lose those precious rewards of grace, Gal. 6, 9; 2 Cor. 9, 6.

Slothfulness retards all mission-work. Millions may perish because many Christians are too lazy to take an active interest in the soul-saving work of the Church. Oh, the crushing accusations the slothful will have to face on Judgment Day!

Therefore beware of that hateful thing, slothfulness. Apply the cure, Law and Gospel. Do you see the significance of the words in St. Paul's exhortation "by the mercies of God"?   H. J. BOUMAN.

Sinful Pride.

Jas. 4, 16.

Ps. 139, 14; Luke 18, 11. 12. Here are two prayers, one by David, the other by a Pharisee. The first prayer comes from a humble heart; the second is uttered in a proud spirit. Admiration of our body, its symmetry, its manifold functions, and of our soul with its wonderful faculties, need not be pride, and it is not pride if such admiration goes side by side with the humble knowledge that everything we have is a gift of God, and not merited at that. And if we take care of these gifts of God, that is respect for God's temple, our body, and not pride. Such respect is a God-pleasing virtue; pride, however, never. Pride is a hateful thing, against which our text warns us.

Sinful Pride.

1. It Is a Common Sin.   2. It Is Foolish.   3. It Is Disastrous.

1.

Text. Study the context. It explains "your boastings." The holy writer speaks of such as plan for the future without taking into consideration the will of God and their own utter dependence upon Him. Their proud spirit makes them believe that they themselves are the lords of their destinies. That is sinful pride, for which they are here rebuked.

But such pride lives in the heart of all men. Ever since Satan ensnared Adam and Eve with the lie "Ye shall be as gods," Gen. 3, 5, man is proud. Believing this lie and acting accordingly is the root of all sinful pride, of the desire to be as gods, to be masters of our lives, our destiny, to build our own system of religion, to lay down our own rules of behavior and to be unwilling to be dictated to by any one, not to be dependent on a higher power.

Therefore the rejection of the true God and of His revealed truth, the many forms of idolatry, the idea that man can save himself by good conduct, by character, by the deeds of the Law; therefore his idolatrous admiration of human wisdom, his worshipful praise of human achievements, achievements of the mind and the body. His philosophical systems praise man; man himself is the central figure upon the throne. His books, his works, his speech, all his actions, reveal that man is by nature the slave of pride. He is born with that sinful pride. If it were not so, natural man would not laugh to scorn the wonderful story of God's divine love in Christ. Just because salvation by Christ demands the humble confession of guilt and help-lessness, man calls it foolishness. There are many examples in Bible history: Saul; Benhadad, 1 Kings 20, 1—21; Peter, Matt. 26, 33.

Although so common a sin, such pride is *very foolish.*

2.

The holy writer points to the foolishness of pride in v. 14 of this chapter. History itself should teach man that he is utterly unable to control all the forces that are to be met. He does not and cannot know what the next hour may have in store for him. He is not the master of his days. He knows all that, and yet he acts as though he were the lord of it all. That is foolish.

He is surrounded everywhere by evidences of God. Nature declares the existence of an almighty God, and yet the fool says in his heart: "There is no God," Ps. 14. His pride makes him deny God and refuse Him obedience and service. Note also man's vain attempts to fight Almighty God. How foolish his worship of idols, which he himself manufactures: idols that have ears and hear not, eyes and see not, mouths and speak not, hands and cannot help. Such idols man worships!

Man knows his sinfulness, his helplessness; his heart, his con-science, tell him. But his pride attempts to explain it away. Foolish. How Satan must enjoy these foolish antics, these senseless vagaries, to which that pride leads man into which Satan's lie betrayed him "Ye shall be as gods!" Of a truth the arch-enemy has made a fool out of man. Luke 12, 14—21. But do not take that lightly; for such foolish, sinful pride is *very disastrous.*

3.

Text. All rejoicing in one's boastings is evil. Pride is an evil thing and must of necessity have disastrous consequences. National pride has caused terribly bloody wars and has thus brought untold misery upon millions. It has destroyed entire nations. (Napoleon I; Rehoboam.)

Individual pride prevents reconciliation and causes endless strife with untold heartaches. It has wrecked families, torn asunder con-gregations. Who can tell all the disastrous consequences of sinful pride?

Pride is above all disastrous for man's soul. It prevents man from acknowledging his sinfulness and from accepting salvation by Christ. Witness the Pharisees and scribes, who in their pride opposed the Savior of mankind, the Son of God, and waxed so bitter in their opposition to Him that they became His murderers. It always has been thus.

The Old Adam of the Christians has also inherited such sinful pride. And it shows its hideous face in many ways. Christians therefore should take heed of the warning contained in our text and seek to beat down that pride of their flesh by the divinely instituted means lest it lead them into spiritual death and eternal destruction, Prov. 16, 5; Rom. 11, 20. Cling to your Savior; in His strength you will conquer. Heed the admonition of your God: 1 Pet. 5, 5 b. Jesus Himself is presented to us as our Example, Phil. 2, 5—8. Remember the parable: Luke 14, 7—11.   H. J. BOUMAN.

Unbelief the Greatest Evil.
John 3, 18—20.

In order to cure a patient, the conscientious and intelligent physician first of all tries to discover the nature of the ailment.

It is even so with this sin-cursed world. If we are to help the world (men and women and children), we should know what is its chief ailment.

That is the reason why so little progress is made in improving conditions on this earth. The would-be physicians of this earth, the would-be saviors, do not know what is the matter with the patient.

Now, what is the chief evil from which man is suffering? God Himself tells us in our text. Let us give earnest heed; for no wisdom of this world can teach us what God teaches us in these words.

Unbelief the Greatest Evil.
1. It Rejects Salvation.   2. It Plunges Man Deeper into Sin.

1.

V. 18. *The name of the only-begotten Son of God.* Here our attention is focused on God's unfathomable love in planning sinful man's salvation. Describe briefly man's fall, his separation from God, the Source of life and happiness, his pitiful helplessness, his utter hopelessness, his fearful destiny. In contrast to this describe God's divine pity, His wonderful love of unworthy sinful man, His plan of salvation, which transcends all human understanding; the sending and sacrificing of His only-begotten Son, the atoning work of this Son, whose name therefore is Jesus, Savior, Redeemer; the wonderful results of Jesus' work: forgiveness, life, and salvation. Tell what all that means for sinful man, what heavenly happiness is now in store for him.

And unbelief rejects it all; it frustrates the work of Jesus, over-throws the plan of God. Can there be a greater evil than unbelief?

And do not forget that Jesus is the only Savior. There is none other. There is salvation in Jesus or none at all. It is true, man has tried, and still tries, to find another way, the way of conduct, of works; but such trying avails as little as trying to go north by traveling south. Thus by rejecting salvation by Christ, unbelief for-feits the only chance man has. He is therefore "condemned already." The full and terrible force of God's eternal judgment strikes him not only on Judgment Day, but already in this life. Cp. John 16, 8—11. Conscious rejection of salvation by Christ, conscious, persistent un-belief, carries the sting of rightful condemnation. Indeed, unbelief is the greatest evil.

2.

Vv. 19. 20. The moral condition of man is love of sin, enmity against God. But this is not always clearly apparent, until the light strikes him. Witness the scribes and the Pharisees. Not until Jesus, the Light of the world, came and lived among them and preached to them the Gospel of salvation for sinners, was it revealed to what depths of evil they were capable of descending, to what extremes their enmity of God could go — from haughty pride of self-righteousness to horrible deceit and murderous brutality. Witness Pontius Pilate. Confronted with Jesus, the Witness of the truth, this seemingly bland, tolerant heathen revealed a glaringly unjust, cringing, unfeeling, despicable spirit. It cannot be otherwise. The more consciously man rejects God's love in Jesus, the farther he separates himself from life, and the farther down he plunges into sin and into its power. It, then, becomes increasingly clearer, also to himself, that his rejec-tion of God's love in Christ is not based on the supposed incredibility of salvation by Christ, not on an honest conviction that the story of Christ's substitutionary death is foolishness, but upon man's love of sin, upon his unwillingness to give it up; and this increases his resent-ment, his enmity against God. Nothing makes greater and more determined sinners than conscious and persistent unbelief, the rejec-tion of salvation by Christ. Such unbelief is stepping toward that dread judgment of obduration, when man becomes hardened and irrevocally confirmed in his opposition to the merciful endeavors of the Holy Spirit, 1 Cor. 1, 18; 2 Cor. 2, 16. Is unbelief therefore not the greatest evil?

The preacher will close with a fervent plea against unbelief. "Lord, I believe; help Thou mine unbelief!" H. J. BOUMAN.

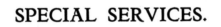

SPECIAL SERVICES.

Christian Education.

Ex. 2, 9.

The superintendent of a State penal institution for women once said: "Few come here that have had a good Christian home and thorough religious training." If we want to stem, in a measure at least, the godless spirit that otherwise threatens to engulf our country and break down the fiber of our national integrity; if our youth is not to be tainted with gross materialism, which desires but a boundless freedom to enjoy this life, which is impatient of any restraint and will tolerate no restriction to the reckless quaffing of the frothy cup of this life's dissipations; if any remedy is to be found for the crowding of our juvenile courts and penal institutions, for the mounting contempt of all law and order, for the drunkenness and immorality that are spreading like rank poisonous weeds among our young people, to counteract the indecency that flaunts its brazen face in the floods of questionable literature and amusement and that likes to parade under the guise of art, to serve as an antidote for the selfishness and self-interest that threatens to corrode the fabric of our commonwealth, it is thorough Christian training at home and by the Church.

Moreover, this is a task given to the Church by her Lord. "Feed My lambs." Nor is it to be considered an unwelcome, irksome task, but one so rich in promise and so well calculated to return great blessings that our congregations will be eager to devote their best efforts to it.

A Profitable Task: Nursing the Children of the Church.

1. The Nature of This Task;   2. The Profit which It Brings.

1.

Our text takes us back to Israel's sojourn in Egypt. The descendants of Jacob become populous tribe. Pharaoh, ignorant of the service of Joseph, anxious lest Egyptians be outnumbered and overpowered, sets about to suppress Israel by ever more arduous labor, then by the monstrously cruel and wicked edict that all boys born to Israelites be destroyed. Moses born; parents hide; when no longer feasible, a basket is plaited of bulrushes, the child placed in reeds at the brink of the river at the time when Pharaoh's daughter is wont to come to bathe; Miriam stationed near to observe.

Basket noticed, retrieved, child cries, heart touched, wanted to keep child alive. At this opportune moment Miriam comes forward, offers to find nurse, brings own mother. To her, unwittingly, the child is entrusted, text: "Take this child away and nurse it for me, and I will give thee thy wages." Even this pagan woman knew that a child needs nursing and bringing up; how much more should we Christians know!

What this princess said to Jochebed, God says to us Christians: Eph. 6, 4. Children a gift from Lord. Given into our care, but really His, by right of creation and redemption; taken into His family through Baptism, precious to Him. Job knew something of this, Job 1, 21 b. Christian parents and Christian churches now to nurse them for Him, in His interest, so that His plans for them are carried out. Well to remember in our day that children are heritage of Lord, a precious talent; many God-forgetting parents and careless congregations, selfishly intent upon own ease or amusement, consider children a bore and nuisance, accept them very unwillingly, and neglect them shamefully.

Take child away and nurse it for me; what a stupendous task, tremendous responsibility! To raise children for the Lord, in such a way that they remain the Lord's, in this day and age, with its mounting godlessness and bewitching deceits, enticing glamor of the world, pressure of worldly interests, insidious temptations, and suffocating mists of doubt and unbelief that rise from the miasmic swamps of modern theater and literature and the so-called higher learning of the world, is a task of terrifying difficulty; and every Christian couple and every Christian congregation that takes the matter seriously would shudder to think of facing that responsibility if they could not turn to the Lord, draw strength and wisdom from Him, and receive from Him the means of nursing those children for Him.

For the Lord does supply the means. "Nurse." To us Christians this means more than to that pagan. Makes us think of verse: "As new-born babes," etc. The milk whereby children are to grow in knowledge and love of Christ would be simple catechism-teaching, Bible history. From early childhood, as indicated by the word "nurse." "From a child" Timothy was instructed.

Where is there a better medium for that than the Christian day-school? Whole course of instruction is orientated upon Christian standpoint; Christian viewpoint obtains; Christian principles are instilled, Christian views implanted in tender and impressionable hearts, the fundamentals of Christian knowledge imparted, and the whole course of training, instruction, and discipline are held in Christian attitude; Christian atmosphere surrounds whole school-life of child. This should go far towards raising the children for the Lord. If day-school not possible, a Christian congregation will try to have well-organized Sunday-school. And it will have such a Sunday-school as missionary agency in addition to its day-school. Christians will also give much thought to higher education under Christian control and from Christian viewpoint. Christian congregations will go to all possible lengths in the interest of Christian education, primary and higher; nor will outward difficulties be permitted to deprive the young people of the church of the benefits of a thorough Christian training. We will try to make our schools, Sunday-schools, instruction periods, as efficient as possible, constantly bent upon improving them.

2.

Christians will attempt all that with all the greater eagerness because from text it is plain that this is a very profitable investment. Let that cheer you under grind, in the face of obvious difficulties connected with work of Christian education.

Text: "Wages." No doubt the daughter of Pharaoh paid the mother of Moses quite liberally, in money, perhaps relief from most bruising labor. Greater reward: satisfaction of keeping son alive, able to rear him in faith of fathers. Finest wages: Son at heart remained true to religion of Israel even when at court, looked upon as prince, and seemingly in line for position of great honor in Egypt; he willingly shared humiliation, poverty, exile. Surely, result of earlier home training and religious instruction; must have been great reward to mother. Who can express what this child and its training meant to the Church of God? Should that not encourage us to do our duty toward the children entrusted to us?

Similar reward and recompense in prospect for Christian congregation that is intent upon Christian education and nurses her children with the milk of the pure Word. Affords best hope of keeping children later, keeping them loyal to their Church. To be sure, it does not work out that way in every case, but to achieve that object is possible much more regularly in this way than in any other manner. Entire history of Synod demonstrates that Christian day-school, properly handled, efficient and thorough instruction in the Word of God, is a most profitable investment, that God does give wages in every department of Christian education.

So, then, in your own interest, for the continued blessed existence of your congregation, foster the Christian training of the children. Your reward: a continued stock of well-indoctrinated members, Lutherans by conviction, to whom their Church means so much, and a well-developed *esprit de corps* among the members, a highly valuable feature. Such a membership should also be wide awake to mission possibilities in its own neighborhood and in more distant fields, be able to speak for their Church, and its life should be a standing testimony to the power of the Gospel.

Reward also: to be able to furnish many fine, well-grounded members to sister congregations and new mission-places; to be in a position to furnish much fine leadership material for the Church among the lay members and also to send many boys to our seminaries and to supply, in an outstanding manner, the financial backing for Synod's work. There is a great reward also for the state, since children fitted for life by a thorough Christian education should make the best sort of citizens.

Best reward: see many in heaven. The final aim of all church-work "to present every man perfect in Christ Jesus," Col. 1, 28, laboring with an eye to that Great Day; also final object of Christian education to present the children before the judgment-throne "perfect," clothed in the spotless robe of Christ's righteousness accepted by them in faith.

May God bless the work of Christian education so that children may be led to the saving knowledge of their Redeemer and after a life of usefulness here may attain the eternal kingdom of heaven!

O. H. SCHMIDT.

Confirmation Address.

Is. 45, 24.

What a solemn hour does this day mark for you! What a momentous day, which finds all eyes focused upon you and on which prayers on your behalf ascend to the Throne of Grace! What an impressive service that sees you kneeling at the altar, with a fervent confession of loyalty upon your lips! The Savior said: "Suffer the little children," etc. In obedience to this divine command you were in earliest infancy brought to Baptism and through this Sacrament received into the Kingdom of Grace. To-day you appear in the sanctuary of the Lord solemnly to repeat and confirm your baptismal vow, joyfully to confess your faith, and to rededicate yourselves to your Redeemer for time and eternity.

We rejoice in this your resolution. But though your determination be ever so firm, yet we dare not forget the dangers, etc. Therefore turn to the Source of life and power and say: text.

A Blessed Confession: "In the Lord Have I Righteousness and Strength."

1. What does This Confession Mean?
2. What does It Require of You?

1.

"In the Lord have I righteousness and strength," that is the confession of the believing confirmand as he renews his baptismal vow, pledges loyalty, faces life with all its battles, thinks of the future, and girds his loins for the struggles life will bring. Let other young people rush heedlessly into the future, with careless disdain of facts and thoughtless disregard of realities, or scatter-brained frivolity, as though life were nothing but rosy foam and a series of pink-tinged dreams; let others, who realize that life will call for sterner stuff and make demands for strength, depend in rash youthful self-confidence upon their own prowess; let those who do serious reflecting and recognize accountability before God put trust in good intentions, strength of character, and purposes of righteousness, — *you,* privileged to receive thorough instruction in God's Word, will not rashly depend on your own strength, but confess: "In the Lord," etc. (text).

What a glorious Lord. He is the Right One to turn to when looking for righteousness and strength. He created the heavens and formed the earth, as this chapter declares. Testimony of the immeasurable power of God; but still more the Lord's goodness and benignity gleams and shines out of this great work; for He prepared the earth to be a good place to live for man; fitted it up so wonderfully and adorned it so magnificently that all creation is an eloquent witness to the Lord's kindliness and goodness.

Just as the earth was formed for a purpose, to be inhabited, not for a vain show, so also the Word of God is spoken for a purpose. It is not uttered in secret, in a dark place; God is not tricking us when He tells us to seek Him and in Him to find righteousness and strength. In contrast to heathen teachers, who pretend to mumble secrets, claim to deal in mysteries and to have contact with spirits, God has not spoken in secret; His Word has nothing in common with mysticism, secretism, Spiritism, and all cryptic delusions. God's Word is always proclaimed freely, openly. God never disappoints, as is the manner of false religions and heathen delusions, which lead men to base their hopes upon vague phrases. The Word of the Lord is right; all His works are done in truth. We can rely upon God and His promises, find in Him righteousness and strength.

In the Lord we have righteousness and strength. Isaiah draws the sharpest possible contrast between God and the impotent idols of heathen. Blessed they who know the true God. Poor heathen, who drag about wood of their idol statues and pray to gods that cannot save, have no knowledge, the prophet says. How sad that people should put their trust in things of no value! How blessed you who have learned to say: "In the Lord," etc.

Indeed, in the Lord we have righteousness and strength. From ancient times God raised up His covenant, the glorious promise of salvation. In the glamorous days of David, Israel was given a small foretaste of the greatness of God's Kingdom of Grace. In the dreary days of the Exile the promise seemed to have fallen to the ground. But it was only a time of trial and purification. The promise, proclaimed before all the world, could not fail. Isaiah again proclaims the greatness of the realm of God as it was to be in the days of the New Testament. God is the Lord of the covenant, and He fulfils His promises.

And this promise involves particularly righteousness and strength, that righteousness by which we can stand before God and gain heaven. In ourselves we have no such righteousness; but God sent the Savior, who supplied our deficiency, in whom we have righteousness and strength. A verse before this text declares that God is "a just God and a Savior." The same thought in the prophecy of Zechariah, who calls upon Zion to rejoice at the advent of the promised Messiah, who is a King "just and having salvation." The holiness and flaw-less purity of the Savior, His perfect fulfilment of the Law, and His expiation of all our guilt through the shedding of His innocent blood is our cover and our wedding-garment. The righteousness of Christ is imputed to us as our own through faith. For Jesus' sake the eternal Judge pronounces us righteous. In the Lord we have righteousness, or, as the very next verse has it: "In the Lord shall all the seed of Israel be justified." Cf. 2 Cor. 5, 21.

"And strength." In the Lord, believing in His promises, trusting in His mercy, resting our hope on God's grace, do we find strength to serve Him, to run in the paths of His commandments, to fight the good fight of faith, to bear our cross, to withstand the onslaughts of the enemy, to cling to our crown. If you wait on the Lord, He will always renew your strength, Is. 40, 31; if you rely on yourself, you will faint and grow weary. Remembrance and appreciation of God's grace will give you strength to serve Him and supply determination to resist temptation. Phil. 4, 13; 1 Cor. 10, 13 b.

What a fine start for a Christian life if you begin this way: "In the Lord"! Then you have a sure foundation. God has sworn by Himself; and this word, gone out of His mouth in faithfulness, shall not return void, shall not fail. This great God, before whom one day every knee shall bow, whether gladly and in faith, as with be-lievers and the holy angels, or unwillingly and grudgingly, as with unbelievers and evil spirits, this great God is your Righteousness and Strength. That is a very humble confession, disclaiming all reliance upon yourself, but also a supremely confident, gloriously defiant con-fession. Blessed children, what will you lack if this is your con-fession on confirmation day: "In the Lord have I righteousness and strength"?

2.

And now, in order that this may remain your confession and your trust, your shibboleth and watchword all through life, seek righteous-ness, the righteousness of the Lord, not, as the world does, riches, honor, pleasure, gratification of self. Righteousness exalteth a nation. This is one thing that will give you true satisfaction now and for the life to come. Seek first the kingdom of God and His righteousness, and you will find that all other things necessary for your wellbeing will be supplied by the Lord, Matt. 6, 33. Seek the righteousness of God, abide in the faith in your Savior Jesus Christ, build your trust and hope solely upon His blood and merit. That alone will stand you in good stead on Judgment Day, when it will become evident to those who trusted in riches in this life that they were but transitory and cannot avail them before the Judge of the world, indeed that because they made them their gods, they will be plunged into everlasting doom and despair. Make that your first business, the main concern of your lives, to have and retain the righteousness of the Lord, to serve Him in the strength that He is ever ready to supply.

To that end remain in close contact with the Word of God. Wend your way diligently to the house of God. Appear frequently at the Communion table; for there you will receive ever new assurance that the righteousness of God is yours through the blood of Christ; there you will obtain ever new strength to continue your pilgrimage in the name, the fear, and the joyous service of your God. At all time give your heart to this great God, in whom you have righteousness and strength. We pray the Lord that, as He gives you the strength and courage to-day to make a good confession of your faith and as He renews to you the promise of grace which He made at your baptism, He may continue to kindle in you anew the fire of His Holy Spirit and endow you with constancy and faithfulness unto death.

And we, dear friends, who are assembled here to-day, who have seen the good work accomplished which the Lord had begun in these children, a work in which angels take delight; we who have witnessed the confession of these confirmands, let us open the circle of Christian fellowship and receive them. Remember they have dedicated themselves to the Lord, and He gives them into our safe-keeping and solicitous care; He binds them upon our heart and conscience. Do not offend them; give them no cause to lose their faith or to leave the Church. Lead them, assist them upon the narrow way. By example teach them to believe and to love, to confess and to suffer, to battle and to conquer, even as we all to-day quietly, in the fastnesses of our hearts, renew our baptismal and confirmation vow, having been inspired to new loyalty where we may have grown lax and enkindled to zeal where we may have become cold and indifferent, so that we may all in the end overcome and gain the everlasting victory in the Lord, our Righteousness and Strength. Amen.   O. H. Schmidt.

Reunion Service.
2 Thess. 2, 13—17.

This is a day of memories, memories sweet and sacred. It is our desire to make it such. With that objective in view this present service has been planned. We want to recall this evening a most solemn day and hour, the day and hour when you, after a long period of instruction in the fundamentals of the Christian religion, at this altar made public confession of your faith and vowed loyalty to Jesus Christ. (Point out how all the features of the service are meant to serve this purpose.) It is my sincerest hope that you are in memory living over again that blessed experience.

In order to make the most of the present occasion, to utilize your present frame of mind to the fullest extent, and to make this sacred hour redound to your spiritual benefit, permit me to direct your undivided attention to the words of our text and with the gracious assistance of the Spirit of God to impress upon your mind and heart the great fact that —

God has Called You by the Gospel to the Obtaining of the Glory of Our Lord Jesus Christ.

My purpose in reminding you of this great fact is: —

1. *That You may be Led to Consider the Wonderful Grace which Is Yours;*
2. *That You may be Filled with a Deep and Abiding Gratitude to God;*
3. *That You may be Inspired with a New Determination to Stand Fast;*
4. *That You may be Prompted Earnestly to Call upon God for His Continued Grace.*

1.

The apostle in the words of our text reminds the Thessalonians of their wonderful state of grace. Marvelous are the things which God has done for them.

A) "God hath from the beginning chosen you to salvation," v. 13. They are the elect of God. From eternity they have been the objects of divine mercy.

B) To accomplish the purpose of this election, God redeemed them in the fulness of time through the work of His incarnate Son. This He did that His Holy Spirit might sanctify them, might bring them to believe in the truth, and thus lead them to salvation, v. 13.

C) Finally God had in time brought them to this saving faith. This He had done through the Gospel. "Whereunto He called you by our Gospel," v. 14. He had sent Paul to preach the Gospel to them,

Acts 16, 7—10; 17, 1—4, and by it the Spirit had sanctified them, brought them to a firm belief in the truth of the Gospel-message.

D) Thus God had called them "to the obtaining of the glory of our Lord Jesus Christ," v. 14. The purpose of all God had done for them was ultimately their final salvation. The faith which God had wrought in them by the Gospel and which they now possessed was the assurance, the pledge, of the heavenly inheritance. By it they were made God's children and as such heirs of God and joint-heirs with Christ, sharers of His eternal glory, Rom. 8, 17.

E) All this without any merit or effort on their part. It was entirely a work of God, a gift of His grace. What might have been their lot, what would have been their lot if God had left them to themselves, is pictured in the contrast, vv. 10—12.

No wonder the apostle calls them the "beloved of the Lord," v. 13. What favor God had showered upon them! What grace was theirs! How plainly they were the objects of God's love!

But, my friends, when I say to *you* to-day: "God has called *you* by the Gospel to the obtaining of the glory of our Lord Jesus Christ," I want to remind you that you are as richly blessed as the Thessalonians and with them the "beloved of the Lord." I ask you to consider the wonderful grace which is yours. God sent His Son into the world for the redemption of all men, John 3, 16. 17; 1 John 2, 2, and therefore also for your redemption. That this redemption might be brought to you and be made your very own possession, He brought you under the influence of His Gospel. Through the means of grace He called you.

By the Sacrament of Holy Baptism you were brought to the saving faith. By the instruction from His Holy Word which was given you in your youth, especially in the catechetical instruction which preceded your confirmation, He led you into a deeper knowledge of His grace to you and established you more and more firmly in the faith. Since that time He has continued to strengthen that faith by the reading and the hearing of His life-giving Word and by participation in the holy Sacrament of the Altar. Thus by His grace you are to-day still the possessors of that faith.

This faith which is in your heart is the earnest of your glory. It assures you that "God hath from the beginning chosen you to salvation through sanctification of the Spirit and belief of the truth," v. 13. From eternity you also have been the objects of His mercy, Eph. 1, 3—10. (F. Pieper, *Christliche Dogmatik,* III, 544. 546.)

This faith is also the guarantee that God has called you by the Gospel "to salvation," "to the obtaining of the glory of our Lord Jesus Christ," vv. 13, 14. (Answer and passages to Qu. 207 in Catechism. Also Eph. 1, 13. 14. 11; Phil. 1, 6. 7.)

All this by pure grace, without any worthiness or effort on your part.

Oh, consider the wonderful grace which is yours! Truly, you are the "beloved of the Lord." You might have been one of them who are haunted by strong delusions, who believe a lie, who, because they believe not the truth, because they have pleasure in unrighteousness, are traveling to damnation, vv. 10—12. But thanks to the grace of God you are the chosen children of God and heirs of that glorious eternal life.

2.

We do not ponder often and deeply enough what it means that God has called us, etc. Go to your Catechism and study diligently once again Luther's explanation of the Third Article. You will surely be filled with a deep and abiding sense of gratitude to God.

When contemplating the wondrous grace which God has bestowed upon the Thessalonian Christians, the spiritual gifts which He has given them, Paul is constrained to give thanks to God: "We are *bound* to give thanks always for you," etc., v. 13. (1 Thess. 1, 2—10; Col. 1, 3—6; Phil. 1, 3—7; 1 Cor. 1, 4—9; Rom. 1, 8; Eph. 1, 17.)

Paul does not write this to them merely to show them how concerned he is about them. Paul desires to be their example. They are to conclude: If the apostle gives thanks to God for our state of grace, how much more ought we who are the recipients of these spiritual gifts be filled with a deep and abiding spirit of thanksgiving!

All this, v. 13, is written in Scripture not merely as a matter of historical record, but for our learning. We are to make the same conclusion. We are to say: Eph. 1, 3. (Col. 1, 12—14.)

We are so thankless. We do not even thank God for earthly gifts, for the gifts which the senses can perceive, much less for spiritual blessings. How often have you thanked God that you were made His child by Holy Baptism, that you were brought up in the nurture and admonition of the Lord, that you were instructed in the great truths of His holy Word, that you have been received into membership with a Church which adheres strictly to that Word, that you can read that Word and hear it preached, that you may partake of His holy Sacrament for the strengthening of your faith, that you are not a slave of sin, but a servant of God, that you have the certain hope of eternal life? How often have you thanked Him because you can say: "The Holy Ghost has called me by the Gospel, enlightened me," etc.?

Oh, thank God that He has called you by the Gospel to the obtaining of the glory of our Lord Jesus Christ. Thank Him with all your heart. Thank Him every day of your life. Thank Him with words of praise. Ps. 100, 3. 4. Thank Him by proclaiming His mercy to men. Thank Him by a holy life. Eph. 4, 1. You are *bound* to do that (*opheilomen*). Hymn 349, 5.

3.

After reminding the Christians that God has, according to His eternal counsel, called them by the Gospel to eternal life, the apostle continues: "Therefore, brethren, stand fast and hold the traditions which ye have been taught, whether by word or our epistle." "Therefore," because of their election in eternity, their calling in time, and the wonderful goal God has set before them, they should stand firm in spite of all attacks on the part of the enemies and keep a strong hold on the truths the apostle has taught them both by word of mouth and by means of the first epistle addressed to them. This would be the only course a child of God could pursue. It alone would be in keeping with their election to grace and their high calling.

This admonition is addressed to the elect of all times. If you count yourself among them, you, too, must hear and heed it. I remind you to-day that the Triune God has chosen you to salvation and called you by the Gospel to the obtaining of eternal glory in order that you might be inspired with a new determination to stand fast. It would be folly to argue that, because we are heirs of life by God's election and calling, we need not be concerned about our faith, need not feed and nourish it, need not bother about the dangers which threaten it nor concern ourselves about its enemies, need not be careful how we act and live. The very opposite is true. The very knowledge that men are God's children only by the election and the calling of God will cause us to make sure of our election and calling by daily looking in our hearts and lives for those things which mark a chosen child of God. Knowing that God saves His elect by faith in Christ and that he creates and sustains this faith by His Word, we shall be zealously watchful that we possess and retain that saving faith, and we shall diligently use the written and spoken Word. A steadfast faith which flourishes by the constant use of the means of grace is the distinguishing characteristic of God's elect. As the elect of God we shall stand fast, be firm in faith, hold tenaciously to the inspired Word, which alone is the reliable foundation of faith and hope, and shun every word and work which wars against the Spirit. (Pieper, *Christliche Dogmatik* III, 558. 559. 2 Pet. 1, 10.)

Hence, if you this evening realize the full import of the fact that God has called you by the Gospel to the obtaining of the glory of our Lord Jesus Christ, you will be, you must be, inspired with a new determination to stand fast, to remain in your baptismal covenant, to keep your confirmation vow.

4.

However, since salvation is, as our text so definitely affirms, only and altogether a work of God, since it is God who elects, redeems, and calls by the Gospel to salvation, it is also God's work to lead to salvation's final consummation. (Pieper, *Christliche Dogmatik*, III, 111.)

Realizing that God alone could keep the Thessalonian Christians in faith unto the end, until they would reach their goal of glory, the apostle closes our text with the fervent wish and prayer "Now our Lord Jesus Christ and God, even our Father, which hath loved us and hath given us everlasting consolation and good hope through grace, comfort your hearts and stablish you in every good word and work," vv. 16. 17.

The God who has loved them in eternity, who has saved them through Jesus Christ, who has by His Spirit called them by the Gospel and thus has by sheer grace given them an everlasting consolation and the good hope of eternal life, He must give them the necessary steadfastness. That He may do so is the apostle's earnest prayer. He prays that God may establish them in every good word and work, in those external evidences which are the unfailing signs of a steadfast faith. Thus Paul reminds the Thessalonian Christians that they must look to God for the carrying out of the work which He has begun in them. Phil. 1, 6. They must know that He is not only the Author, but also the Finisher of their faith. He would have them look to Him for that steadfastness which will lead to the ultimate goal. And hence he would have them do what he has done. He would have them pray most earnestly to God for that steadfastness.

This is also a lesson for you. Looking upon your state of grace, considering that it is God who has, according to His eternal decree, called you by the Gospel to the obtaining of the glory of our Lord Jesus Christ, who has made and kept you His child and heir, you, too, must realize that what remains to be done in the matter of your salvation must be done by Him. 1 Pet. 1, 5. Then you will confidently look to Him for the final achievement of the purpose of your election and calling, and you will be prompted earnestly *to call upon God for His continued grace.* John 6, 37; Ps. 31, 22—24. Hymn 349, 6. 7.

Thus this day becomes for us a day of earnest reconsecration to the God who called us by the Gospel to the obtaining of the glory of our Lord Jesus Christ. We are His. By His grace may we remain His! Jude 24. 25.   ARTHUR E. NEITZEL.

Children's Easter Service.
Luke 24, 45—48.

When something unusual happens at home, at school, at Sunday-school, you children can barely wait until you can tell your parents and friends. When God sends a baby brother or sister into your home, it does not take long before the whole neighborhood knows about it. If you happen to bring home a report card on which there are only E's or a report card that shows that you were promoted, skipping an entire grade, your parents find out about it very soon. You just bubble over with the good news. You simply cannot stop speaking about it.

Something very unusual happened in Jerusalem some 1900 years ago. Jesus, the Son of God, suffered in a most terrible way. He was nailed to the cross; He died and was buried, and on the third day He rose again. The disciples who saw all these wonderful things happen could not stop speaking about these matters in later life. John and Peter talked so much about the fact that Jesus suffered and died and rose again that the enemies of Jesus put them into prison. They threatened Peter and John and tried to scare them into silence, but the apostles said: "We cannot but speak of the things which we have seen and heard," Acts 4, 20.

This is the way all of us, children and adults, should feel about the wonderful things that happened on Good Friday and Easter so many years ago. We should always be ready to bear witness for Jesus. But we are not always ready to do this. Jesus had to encourage the disciples, and He still has to encourage us. Let me do this for Jesus this evening as on the basis of our text I speak to you on the subject —

Little Witness-Bearers.

A) Refer to context. Happenings of the first Easter, especially the appearance in that room where the disciples had gathered behind locked doors. While Emmaus disciples were telling them about their wonderful experience with the living Lord, He appeared to them. They were afraid. Thought Jesus was a ghost. Jesus had to convince them. Told them to touch Him, to bring something to eat. Still seemed to be hesitant. Jesus had to open their hearts.

B) V. 45: "Then opened He their understanding." Most people have trouble to understand religious matters, trouble to understand the way to salvation. Disciples had had Jesus for their Teacher for three years, but still on the evening of Easter they needed special instructions from the risen Lord before they could really become witness-bearers. Even so to-day children need teachers before they can see Jesus and before they can be real witness-bearers. For this reason you children come to Sunday-school, to the Christian day-school, to confirmation instruction, to Bible class, and to the church services.

Only in this way can Jesus open your understanding. But not only the children need to have their understanding opened by Jesus. The disciples were grown men. Grown men and women, your fathers and mothers, need to have eyes opened. So many people are like oysters. When these are disturbed, they crawl into their shell. So many people, when they happen to come to church, when the Word of God disturbs their conscience, they also crawl into their shell, they shrink back from proper understanding of Christian religion. Jesus has to open their hearts as He opened the hearts of the disciples, as He must open hearts of little ones to-day.

C) What did Jesus tell His disciples to make witness-bearers of them? He pointed to the Bible. V. 46: "Thus it is written." We point people to God's Word to-day. We do not teach all kinds of non-essential things in Sunday-school, but use the time for teaching the Word of God. In our day-school we have secular branches, but we give the best hour of each day to seeing Jesus in His Word. Before we can be witness-bearers, we must know the Bible, learn it, memorize it, quote it. And then we shall know that Jesus had to suffer, to die, and to rise again *for us*. You boys and girls know this. You know that this was all done so that we might receive forgiveness of sins and be saved. Now, certainly you will be anxious to tell others, to be little witness-bearers for Christ.

D) Just this, Jesus expects of you. V. 47. You are to be little preachers telling people that they are sinners and have deserved damnation, but that by believing in Jesus Christ they can receive forgiveness of their sin. Peter did this on the day of Pentecost. That same Peter who so shamefully denied Jesus, who said that he did not even know the blessed Savior, stood there before many thousands and said: Acts 2, 38. 39 a. The disciples were to tell this good news in all the world, "among all nations," but especially in Jerusalem. So you little witness-bearers are to tell about Jesus, who suffered and died and rose again, who is anxious to give forgiveness to all who believe, especially at home. Speak to your fathers and mothers, sisters and brothers, uncles and aunts, about Jesus and His Word and work. Then tell others. Share also by your gifts in missions in far-away lands.

E) V. 48. Disciples actually carried out command of Jesus. Great things happened. Thousands accepted message; thousands became Christians in Jerusalem and elsewhere. You are to be witnesses unto the resurrected Savior. As the Savior blessed disciples, so He can and will bless you. Often you children can do more than adults. Often the Savior can use you when even your pastor and teacher fail. [Tell the story of 2 Kings 5, 1—19.] Encourage them to go out quickly and tell. Be ye witnesses unto Jesus, your Savior.

E. L. ROSCHKE.

Walther League Rally.

Gen. 3, 1 b.

"All men are liars." Does this statement startle you? Does it offend your pride and tempt you to challenge its truthfulness? Nevertheless, these words are true and stated repeatedly in Scripture. Ps. 116, 11; 62, 9; Rom. 3, 4. By nature all men have turned from God to vanity, lies, and deceits. The facility with which man violates truth is readily seen from the mountains of false testimony offered in court, from statements in tax returns, and from the lying propaganda that was carried on during the late World War. The harm of such falsehoods, in part, affects temporal affairs. But there are other falsehoods emanating from the father of lies, the devil, which aim to destroy both body and soul in hell. The favorite lie of the arch-deceiver, the lie of the ages, he utters here in our text —

"Yea, hath God Said?"

Let us now see —

1. How Satan Tries to Implant This Lie into the Hearts of Men;
2. How We can and must Resist Satan.

1.

God had created Adam and Eve perfect and holy. They were in full possession of perfect mental, physical, and spiritual powers. They knew the will of God perfectly and had the power to live up to that will, and it was a pleasure for them to live up to that will. Had the devil openly declared his purpose of leading them to disobedience toward God and finally plunging them into eternal ruin and despair, he would not have had such easy work. No doubt, Eve would have been appalled. So, in diabolical cunning, the Temper insinuates himself gradually and insidiously into the confidence of Eve, posing as a benefactor, whose sole purpose is to give even greater happiness and ability than she now possessed. V. 1: "Yea, hath God said, Ye shall not eat of every tree of the garden?" "Eve," he means to say, "are you sure you have understood God right? Did not God create this garden with all its trees for your enjoyment? Why should He deny you any of its fruits?'" Thus the devil tries to instil the poison of doubt into the heart of Eve, knowing full well that this is the first step of unbelief. Doubting the infallible Word of God ever so little is a powerful entering wedge into the heart of man.

And the devil distorts and exaggerates. "Hath God said, Ye shall not eat of every tree of the garden?" This sounds as though God had forbidden to eat the fruit of all trees, whereas they were to avoid only the one tree, the tree of the knowledge of good and evil. The insinuating words of Satan take root in the heart of Eve. She begins to ponder whether perhaps, after all, there may not be some truth in them. The Tempter now follows with the bold declaration: "Ye shall not surely die; for God doth know that in the day ye eat thereof, then your eyes shall be opened, and ye shall be as gods, knowing good and evil." The devil is trying to make Eve entertain ill thoughts against God, to make her think that God is not so concerned about her complete happiness, that He has some selfish motive in withholding the fruit of this one tree. What harm could there be in knowing what good and evil is?

Then, again, mark the great promise he makes to the woman: Ye shall be as God Himself; ye shall have and know and enjoy everything that God now enjoys. As the desert traveler follows the deceptive mirage that lures him to destruction, so Eve is led onward by the devil, away form God and His word, to ultimate ruin and disaster.

The Tempter used the same tactics on Jesus in the wilderness: "If Thou be the Son of God, command that these stones be made bread." Christ should doubt that God is His loving Father because He is asking Him to fast and hunger so long. "Cast Thyself down from the pinnacle of the Temple" he further demands, at the same time distorting and falsifying the Word of God to prove that God would protect Jesus in the foolhardy attempt of leaping to the ground. And as Satan had promised Eve wisdom and knowledge unlimited, so he offers Christ all the riches and glory of this world.

When the Lord tells the disciples that He soon would go up to Jerusalem to suffer and die, Satan fills Peter's heart with the same doubt as to the need of such suffering. Peter takes Jesus aside and bluntly tells Him: "Lord, this shall not be unto Thee." Christ, knowing who prompted Peter to speak thus, offers the stern rebuke: "Get thee behind Me, Satan, for thou mindest not the things that be of God." Not only was *Peter* tempted here by Satan, but *Christ Himself;* for that is the aim and purpose of the devil to hinder man's salvation wrought by Christ Jesus.

The devil is the same even to-day. He tries to lead man away from his God through doubt, exaggeration, falsification, and denial of God's Word. As he used the serpent, a creature of God, to serve his wicked ends, so to-day he uses the ungodly world and insincere show-Christians as his dupes and tools.

In your Christian day-school and confirmation instruction, my dear young friends, you have learned the way and will of God. You were taught that the Bible is the infallible Word of God, that God created the world in six days, that man fell into sin and is now under the wrath of God, that Jesus Christ, the Son of God, born of the Virgin Mary, is our only Savior, who lived, suffered, died, and rose again for fallen man. You were shown that the Bible teaches us to avoid sinful companions, flee youthful lusts and fornication, keep ourselves pure, earn our daily bread at some honest occupation, be regular in hearing and using God's Word, and hold fast to every word of God that has been entrusted to us. But going out into the world, you met with vast numbers whose standard of living is not the Word of God, which you have learned to follow. As temptation was flung into your path, did you follow the course of Joseph or of Eve, of Jesus or of Judas? Blessed indeed are you if in sin's sweet siren voice you detected the muffled tones of the roaring lion of hell and sought protection and guidance in God's Word.

But alas for the many who no longer keep themselves separate from wilful sinners, who no longer strive to keep themselves pure and flee youthful lusts. With increasing worldly-mindedness their interest in church-work and God's Word wanes and lags. We are told that a snake is able to hypnotize and fascinate small birds till they become its easy prey. So the hellish serpent enthralls many by his arts and blandishments, paralyzes their spiritual power of resistance, till they follow him like a Pied Piper into haunts of sin and destruction.

Such seduction does not happen overnight. In the flush of their first love many a young man and woman heeds the voice of parents, pastor, and conscience for a time. But the tempters are persistent and resourceful. Gradually the poisonous darts of doubt and ridicule are brought into action. And so, with loudly beating heart and guilty conscience, the young Christian nibbles at the forbidden fruit. A second bite, then again and again. Each succeeding time the warning, accusing voice of conscience grows fainter and duller. Ere long another promising member has become a typical worldling, though still nominally a Christian. And now he has the feeling that this matter of being a Christian is not nearly so hard as was pictured. Ah, that is the devil's favorite bait, that one can serve the world and still preserve a faith unsullied, though the Savior expressly says: "No man can serve two masters."

The devil is still ready in our day to exaggerate and to distort God's Word. He tries to make Christians believe that it is impossible in our modern time to lead a life strictly according to God's Word. That was easy enough in days gone by, when families were more for themselves and church-members associated only with their kind. But in our day of intermingling with the world in a business and political way, it just can't be done. God is asking too much, or rather the Church and the preachers are interpreting God's Word too strictly.

Opportunities for sinning have been multiplied greatly in these modern times. And Satan knows how to paint the pleasures and enjoyments of sin in most alluring colors, showing by contrast what a drab, gloomy life the way of God is. Who knows what eternity may bring? But the enchantments of this physical, temporal life are realities to those who reach out and indulge. And, ah, the lure of gold and wealth — how it stifles the nobler instincts in the human breast and drives men to sell their very souls! So successful is this lure that Satan had the brazen audacity to try it on the very Son of God.

If men would only meet the Tempter as Jesus did! Alas, too many succumb to his deceptions. A Christian's occupation should be one in which he can glorify his God and truly benefit his fellow-man. But too many chose their trade or occupation regardless of whether it redounds to the glory of God or whether it tempts the fellow-man to sin. Too often the only determining factor is the money to be gained. Many a Lutheran business man contributes indiscriminately to every drive and collection in the community, including the charity ball and community dance, simply because he thereby hopes to keep and increase his trade. Many men remain members in the lodge solely because of the insurance money. They realize that Scripture says: "Be not unequally yoked with unbelievers . . .; be ye separate," but they cannot bear losing hundreds and thousands of dollars of eventual insurance. Thus the devil constantly goads men on to continue the dance around the golden calf, assuring them that God Jehovah is still their God, Jesus is still their Savior, that all is well with them. What a terrible deception!

Having been confirmed, perhaps a majority of our young people attend high school, the old Gospel-truths still fresh in their mind and heart. During the course of the year, from somewhere, the devil is likely to whisper in this strain, "Is that all really and literally true about God's creating the world and man in six days only about six thousand years ago? How can that be since modern science claims that it took hundreds of millions of years to perfect this world as we see it to-day? What material evidence is there that *God* created this world, when text-books offer abundant evidence that the world and human life slowly evolved and developed out of itself from the lowest or primal cell to the present highly developed type of man? Did man really come into existence as you were taught in church and Christian school?" And as these shafts slowly sink in and take hold, Satan becomes more bold and insistent in his argumentation.

And so our boys and girls graduate from high school and some enter college, and again Satan is there with them, as he was with the sons of God at the time of Job. Now he no longer shyly *questions* the truthfulness of the Bible, but through the mouths of learned professors openly brands it as a book of myths, in which truth is largely mixed with error. "The Bible the complete revelation of God? Preposterous! Who would take his whole faith and religion from a book that was finished 2,000 years ago! What intelligent man will close his eyes to the ever-progressing revelation of God and His will as it is brought to us in the findings of a never-resting science! Christianity is not a cut-and-dried creed or a system of theology taken from any one book, but

rather the essence of all that man has found good in this earthly life."
And so with persistent effort the father of lies tries to impress this
destructive lie of the ages upon the hearts and minds of our young
men and women, sweeping aside God, our Creator, Jesus, our Savior,
and placing on the throne *reason,* sinful, depraved, self-righteous
reason.

Eve sought wisdom which God had wisely withheld from her, and
through her disobedience she received God's curse and eternal woe
and misery, losing all her holiness and perfection. The young men and
women throwing off the restraining influence of God's Word for the
easy morality of modern Liberalism will, like the foolish moth flitting
about the burning flame, eventually find themselves not only seared
and ruined in body, but more so in soul, often so far gone as to be
beyond redemption. The modern philosophy of life leads to atheism,
infidelity, and hopeless despair. A confession by a skeptic (taken
from *Literary Digest,* July 19, 1924) is to the point: Brought up in
the Calvinistic faith, this man at his majority began reading such
avowed agnostics as Spencer, Huxley, and Tyndall. These men convinced him, he thought, that the theology of Christianity was a fallacy,
chiefly of legendary origin. But after following the philosophy of
reason and the religion of unbelieving science for years, he lost all
certainty as to the hereafter. He writes: "I crave the faith of my
parents, who seemed to feel as certain of a life hereafter, of a personal
God, and a personal devil as they were of what had happened yesterday. But that sort of faith has been made impossible for me by the
scientific philosophy of the day and by my inability to reconcile the
pain and suffering and brutality of humanity with the Christian
theory of an omnipotent, omniscient, and benignant God."

If this is the state of mind that religious and scientific philosophy
of our modern higher education creates while life is at its best, what
a cheerless and terrible prospect in the hour of death and never-ending
eternity! Behold what a hopeless derelict man becomes when he casts
aside the guiding rudder of God's saving Word! Let us watch and
pray that God may grant us power to overcome the temptations of the
devil, and let us beware lest any man spoil us "through philosophy and
vain deceit, after the tradition of men . . . and not after Christ,"
Col. 2, 8.

2.

How can we resist Satan's attempts to bring us away from God?
By taking heed unto God's Word and following it implicitly. Eve
was fully equipped to overcome the temptation of the devil. She had
a full and perfect knowledge of God's word. The fact that the serpent
spoke to her should have caused her to think that this was something
unnatural, God not having given the serpent the power of speech. She
should therefore have been on her guard at the start.

And when the Serpent suggested that perhaps, after all, God wanted her and Adam to enjoy the fruits of the tree in the midst of the garden, the woman should have repeated God's express command "Thou shalt not eat of it, for in the day that thou eatest thereof thou shalt surely die." This should have ended the discussion. Eve should have turned away and left the Serpent to his own musings. Instead she lends a willing ear and begins to wonder just how much of the Serpent's words may be true. Her reason begins to crowd out the word of God. True, she answers: "Ye shall not eat of it . . . lest ye die." But she weakened the force of the word of God, who had said to her: "Ye shall *surely* die." Again, she doubts while she should have implicitly believed. That was the beginning of the Fall. She tampers with God's word and tries to shape it to suit her own desires. From desire to consummation was but a short step.

God wants the fall of Eve to be a warning to us not to take the temptations of Satan lightly. When his tools, the ungodly, tell us that a few sins do not matter, that God's Word must not be taken too literally, let us say, Thus said the Lord: "The soul that sinneth, it shall die." If we are asked to adopt a free and easy morality, let us remember the words of St. Paul to Timothy: "Flee youthful lusts." "Keep thyself pure." The strength of a Christian does not lie so much in entering temptation and overcoming it as in the avoidance of sin and its enticements. "My son, if sinners entice thee, consent thou not," warns the prophet.

When temptation unexpectedly confronts us, then let us follow our Savior's example. He overcame all doubt in the providence of God by quoting the proper word of God and trusting in it. Jesus countered the devil's false use of the Word of God with God's Word as it reads and stands true. Each time he meets Satan with Scripture. He does not reason with him, does not consider his arguments, just puts His implicit trust in the Word. Thus He overcame the Evil One and obtained the victory.

If we would triumph over Satan's wiles, we must trust in Christ and His Word. "He that abideth in Me . . . without Me ye can do nothing." Jesus Christ came into this world to suffer, die, and save us from sin, death, and damnation. There is salvation in none other. Let the superrefined world turn from us in disgust because we believe in this medieval "blood theology." We are content, for we know that this blood of the Lamb of God alone can cleanse us from all sins. Let the multitudes ridicule us because we refuse to believe the lie of the ages, *viz.*, that the Bible is not the infallible Word of God and the only guide to salvation; we know it to be true, for from its pages we have learned of our Savior, who lives and reigns in our hearts and lives and makes us strong to overcome all onslaughts of the wicked Foe. May the multitudes discard the Gospel of Christ Jesus and trust in a man-made science, philosophy, or religion of reason, we know that on that great Last Day all these new systems shall crumble and fall, and with them all their supporters, while, towering high over these wrecks of time, the cross of Him who died on Calvary shall stand, rugged and alone, surrounded by those who washed their garments clean in the blood of the Lamb.

My dear fellow-believers in Christ, let us beware of the monstrous delusion that has become a snare to untold numbers, the lie of the ages: "God has not said." Let us heed the admonition of St. Paul to Timothy: "O Timothy, keep that which is committed to thy trust, avoiding profane and vain babblings and oppositions of science falsely so called, which some professing have erred from the faith," 1 Tim. 6, 20. 21. Hymn 550.   G. A. TROEMEL.

Young People's Sermon.
Text: "Learn of Me," Matt. 11, 29.*

The Bible is the most catholic, that is, the most universal book in the world. It appeals to all men, young and old, rich and poor, educated and ignorant, high and low. Its poetry, its histories, its doctrines, its prophecies, are intended for all human beings without distinction.

But it is true that there are certain portions which were written for certain classes. In the 31st chapter of Proverbs we have the description of a model woman. In the letters of St. Paul God addresses some words specifically to fathers, other words specifically to children, again others to servants. The Bible gives instruction to those who are rich in earthly goods, 1 Tim. 6, 17; it gives instruction to the poor, Matt. 6, 19. There are in these sacred pages words directed to congregations, words directed especially to pastors, appeals directed especially to believers, and words intended especially for the impenitent.

Among these specific portions of Scripture we have a large number directed especially to young people, to the youth. Perhaps all of you will recall those words of Solomon's: "Rejoice, O young man, in thy youth," Eccl. 11, 9. And the same writer tells the young people: "Remember, now, thy Creator in the days of thy youth."

However, it is a mistake to imagine that each class is to heed only what is said specifically to it. Every one rather is carefully to note also what is said in God's Word to all men, without distinction. Such a word is that of our text, wherein Jesus says to

* We realize that the context could easily be utilized, but in order to impress these three words of Jesus all the more, we used them alone.

every one of us: "Learn of Me." And yet, while these words are
spoken to every one, they have a peculiar emphasis and appeal for
young people, because youth — that is universally admitted — is the
time for learning and study. True, "we are never too old to learn,"
but certainly there can be no question about this, that youth is
the time to learn.

The Words of Jesus: "Learn of Me."

1.

The *meaning* of these words.

a) Some of you may be surprised that I am to speak of the
meaning of these words. You may say, Are they not very clear?
To hear them is to understand them. It is well that you think
them clear. Let me impress upon you right here that the Scripture
is not a puzzle of all manner of perplexities; it is very clear.
The Bible is not a dark book, difficult to understand. Remember
what God says: "But if our Gospel is hid," etc., 2 Cor. 4, 3. 4. As
long as St. Augustine followed the great philosophers, he was perplexed, muddled, and in despair. As soon as he began earnestly
to study the Bible, he discovered the truth of these words: "The
entrance of Thy words giveth light; it giveth understanding unto
the simple," Ps. 119, 130. And he chose the Word of God as his
guide, taking as his motto: "Thy Word is a lamp unto my feet
and a light unto my path," v. 105. As long as Luther followed the
Church Fathers and the priests, he walked in darkness and practised
all manner of folly. As soon as he studied the Bible, heavenly light
illuminated his mind and his soul. It could not be otherwise; for
Jesus said: "He that followeth Me shall not walk in darkness, but
shall have the light of life," John 8, 12. Paul and untold others
have had the same experience.

b) But it is true that through our own carelessness and in-
attention we may overlook the length, the depth, the breadth, and
the height of these precious words. The words of Scripture are not
only clear; they are very rich and full of meaning. They require
and are worthy of the most careful attention and consideration.
This is not slight chatter by vain and irresponsible talkers. No;
God's words are weighty words, to which we are to give closest
heed, with fervent prayer to God: "Open Thou mine eyes that I may
behold wondrous things out of Thy Law," Ps. 119, 18. That is one
reason why many get so little out of reading, repetition, and hearing of God's Word — they read, hear, and repeat, but do not give
sufficient attention to the precious content of these words of heavenly
wisdom. Let us not be guilty of such heedless hearing in this hour.
Let us follow the example of Jesus Himself, of whom it is said that
at twelve years of age He was in the Temple. He heard the doctors

with attentive, questioning mind, Luke 2, 46. Let us be about our Father's business in real earnest. Let us determine to take with us something worth while.

c) I call your attention, first of all, to this word "learn." You have all, even now, learned many things. I need not fear that there is any one here who does not believe in learning. No doubt every one of you is glad that he has learned and is only too willing to learn more. You want to learn; but be careful what and how you learn. There are not a few who, after they have learned, must unlearn, and that is a very painful process. They have learned a bad habit. — Physically it is painful to retrace our steps, but in the realm of the mind and spirit and habit it is far more painful to unlearn what we should never have learned. It is so easy for us to learn that which is wrong, foolish, and perverse because our nature is inclined to this. Even now we hear complaints that young people at the schools and colleges and universities have learned that which bewilders their mind, misleads their judgment, and corrupts their morals. Be sure of this: also in learning there is right and wrong. Therefore the Word of God warns us against the teachers who would mislead us and deceive us, Matt. 7, 15; 1 John 4, 1.

We need not believe that all the teachers who mislead their pupils are insincere. Some of them may be very sincere. Many of those who cried: "Crucify Him! Crucify Him!" over Jesus thought that they were condemning a genuine criminal. When Saul of Tarsus consented to the death of Stephen, he thought that he was doing God a service. Jesus forewarned His disciples that many very sincere people would go about to kill them, thinking that thereby they served the God of their fathers. We need not in all cases decide whether those who wish to lead us are sincere or not; we are to make sure that they lead us aright.

d) It is for this reason that Jesus has given to us an *infallible Teacher*. In our text He tells you: "Learn of *Me*." This same Teacher tells us: "No man hath ascended up to heaven but He that came down from heaven, even the Son of Man, which is in heaven," John 3, 13. And again God's Word tells us: "No man hath seen God at any time; the only-begotten Son, which is in the bosom of the Father, He hath declared Him," John 1, 18. If we would know the truth and be led aright, no one may lead us but Jesus Himself. Therefore our text insists: "Learn of Me."

That does not mean that we are to run about in this world seeking to find Jesus in the flesh. Jesus has given us His Word in the Holy Scriptures, and He has given us many faithful teachers who teach us God's Word. To these He has said: "He that heareth you heareth Me, and he that despiseth you despiseth Me," Luke 10, 16. By these words, therefore, "Learn of Me," Jesus would have every one of us never to cease to be a learner in His school; and that means, a learner, a reader, a student, and a pupil of the Bible, faithful in private reading, faithful in public worship, that we may learn, — learn more about Jesus, learn of Him; learn from His Old Testament, learn from His New Testament; learn the truth concerning His person, concerning His work as our Savior and Redeemer; learn the Law that He has given, learn especially the precious Gospel that He has proclaimed; learn from His teaching, learn from His life, learn from His prophecies.

And note one thing about this learning of Jesus: it is to be not only intellectual learning; it is to be a learning which enlightens our whole soul, it is to bestow upon us also heavenly *abilities*. We should learn to believe in His atonement; we should learn to follow His footsteps; we should learn of Him to increase in wisdom and knowledge, in godliness and self-sacrifice, in love for the brethren.

We should learn *to know;* we should learn *to do;* we should learn *to be.*

And this learning is to continue throughout our entire life. As Christians, we rejoice to learn of a Savior from sin, but we are not to stop there. Having learned about the Savior, we are to continue to learn from Him; we are to continue to pray that He would not only teach us to know God's will, but teach us to do it, to be patient, to bear the cross, teach us to pray, teach us to be courageous, teach us to suffer, teach us to hope, teach us to conquer. That is what these words mean. Their appeal is to all men, but to you young people their appeal is to be particularly impressive. Be and remain a pupil, a disciple, a scholar, a learner, a student in the school of Jesus Christ.

2.

Here any one of you may ask a natural question: Of what *benefit* is such learning? It is true that in our brief text this question is not answered; but in connection with these precious words and at many other places of Scripture very good reasons are urged for heeding these words of our Lord Jesus, for the benefits of heeding them are so many and so great that I must limit myself to the mention of just a few.

a) The first benefit is this: "This is life eternal, that they might know Thee the only true God and Jesus Christ, whom Thou hast sent," John 17, 3. Jesus teaches us of the love of God; from Him we learn that God so loved the world, etc., John 3, 16. And should not such learning fill our souls with a flood of light and move our tongues to praise God? Is not the learning of this Gospel the power of God unto salvation to every one that believeth? Rom. 1, 16.

b) But from Jesus we learn also the right understanding of God's will, the right understanding of the Law of God. We Christians, who want to do God's will, are certainly thankful that we know this will of God, that we know that it does not consist in all manner of rules of church etiquette, genuflections, fastings, tortures, starvations, and the like, but that it consists in the love of God (and all that this implies) and the love of our neighbor, Rom. 13, 10; Matt. 22, 37—40. If you do not learn what Jesus teaches of the Law, you cannot but live in all manner of foolish and vain practises, Matt. 15, 9.

c) Because by learning of Jesus, and in no other way, we become world-conquerors, as He was, Phil. 2, 9—11; Acts 2, 36; Rev. 1, 18. — "Without Me ye can do nothing," John 15, 5b, but through Him we can do all things, Phil. 4, 13. Examples: Moses, Joshua, Rahab, Samuel, Paul, etc.

Should this not induce every one of you young people now again and now forever to determine to learn of Jesus? Because, by learning of Him, you will receive the Kingdom and the crown that He has intended for you. Think of the many who are striving in higher schools to obtain the prize of a degree or a title. And how long will their victories last? Their learning and their titles, their positions and their prestige, and the honor which they derive from them will soon be taken from them again. But in this school of Jesus we are to gain titles, degrees, nobility, which no man can take from us: we are to have an eternal inheritance, riches incorruptible and that fade not away. As the days pass, we are drawing closer and closer to the hour which will take all earthly goods, honor, position, from us; but all that we learn and all that we receive in the school of Jesus Christ is continually becoming greater and greater, and its full enjoyment is coming closer and closer and is never to be taken from us.

God grant that every one of you may join in the words of the poet: "Wisdom's highest, noblest treasure, Jesus, lies concealed in Thee," etc. Hymn 83, 5.   S.

Mission Sermon.
2 Kings 7, 9.

This text takes us back in spirit to a dark period in the history of the Jewish nation. Under the reign of the kings the people of Israel, from king down to peasant, became more and more godless. On account of their chief national sin, idolatry, God sent grievous and sore afflictions. Thus, in the days when Elisha was prophet and Jehoram was king of Israel, Benhadad, the king of Syria, mustered his armies against Israel. In a battle Jehoram was thrown back and compelled to withdraw his troops to the city of Samaria, which was surrounded by walls. The Syrians forthwith laid siege to the city.

Our chapter tells us of four lepers who kept themselves near the city gates during the siege. According to Jewish law the men were not permitted to enter. Driven by hunger, these lepers finally resolved to go to the camp of the Syrians and surrender themselves for better or for worse. When they approached the lines of the enemy, they were surprised not to be halted; as they came nearer, lo and behold, they found the camp deserted. No soldiers were in sight; instead, they found a vast quantity of provisions and spoils of war. Overjoyed, they helped themselves in a liberal manner. By and by, however, they realized that their action was selfish and dangerous. They thought of their famishing countrymen in Samaria. They resolved to return to the city and report the good news to their fellow-men. By this action they saved thousands of their countrymen form death by starvation.

This incident can well be applied to the great work of the Church under consideration to-day, mission-work. Let us note some of the striking truths suggested by this text and thus warm our hearts and fix our purpose for the great work of the Christian Church. May God bless our speaking and hearing!

1.

You have a picture of the situation portrayed in our chapter. Let us note these lepers. The position of lepers among the Jews in those days was a pitiable one. They were ejected from their communities; they were compelled to live with their like in the uninhabited wilderness. They were social outcasts. And taking into consideration their loathsome disease, we in a measure understand their tragic situation.

I hope it will not startle you when I say that in these lepers we have a picture of ourselves, as we are by nature. Yes, we are by nature sinful and unclean before God. In consequence of sin we are outcasts. God cast out the first sinners from His holy presence, and the descendants of the first sinners have inherited the disease and must share the disgrace of their ancestors. By our daily sins we aggravate our condition and compel God to deal with us as with rebels and outcasts. In this terrible condition we should meet an awful doom away from God here and away from God throughout all eternity. Luke 16, 23—26; Matt. 25, 26—30.

2.

These lepers came upon an unexpected find. Death, either by starvation or by the sword, stared these men in the face. They chose to risk the latter. They resolved to go to the camp of the Syrians. Approached with fear and trembling. Finding themselves unchallenged, they went into the very midst of the camp and found it abandoned. How did this happen? Our chapter relates: vv. 6—8.

In this remarkable manner they came upon a find by which their lives were saved.

Similarly we, too, have come upon a rich find. Infected with the leprosy of sin, cast out, we have found treasures of far greater value than all the riches of this world. We have found Jesus, our Lord and Savior, forgiveness of sin, peace of heart and mind, a sure foundation of hope, a reliable, satisfying Gospel. Like these lepers, we have come upon these treasures unawares. As little as these wretched men expected to find those provisions in the camp, so little aware were we of the riches of the treasures of the grace of God in Christ Jesus. The Holy Spirit opened our eyes, enlightened our understanding, and led us to recognize the riches of God's love and grace. As these lepers did nothing to produce those vast quantities of provisions, as they were in no wise responsible for their being there, so we, too, have done nothing to produce the rich spiritual treasures of which we have become partakers. They have been given to us without money and without price. Jesus, the Son of God, came into the world; He fought and overcame Satan, the enemy of God and man, and by His life, suffering, and death procured for us all these spiritual spoils, which God in His mercy has permitted us to find, to possess, and to enjoy. Truly, when we consider all this, must it not awaken in us an earnest resolution?

3.

The unexpected finding of those rich supplies awakened an honorable resolve in these lepers. Having fully satisfied their present wants and having hidden some supplies for future use, they said one to another: v. 9.

They realize that their actions were selfish. They were in possession of food, and their countrymen in the city were starving. In addition, they conjectured that their selfishness and delay might prove disastrous to them. The watchmen on the walls would have observed that the enemy was inactive and would cause spies to be sent to find out the reason. Had they been caught indulging in these rich supplies, it would have gone hard with them. Realizing this, they hastened to tell of their wondrous find.

Precisely the same reasons should urge us to do mission-work. By the grace of God we are Christians. We enjoy extraordinary advantages. In our dear Lutheran Church we have and enjoy the pure Gospel and the unadulterated Sacraments. How richly are we blessed with spiritual blessings! Shall we be selfish? Shall we indulge in the enjoyment of these blessings while so many others lack them? We should not be Christians if we kept all these blessings to ourselves. It is wicked to ignore our neighbor's physical needs, but it is infinitely more sinful to pass by our neighbor's spiritual needs.

To say in the language and spirit of Cain: "Am I my brother's keeper?" is a sin against which God and His Word solemnly protest.

Moreover, if these lepers feared trouble in case they delayed in reporting their find, we have all the more reason to fear for our delay and indifference in spreading the Gospel. We know that a day is coming when God's holy Son will return in order to hold judgment. We must give an account of our stewardship. If we be found slothful, selfish, and indolent, He will frown upon us and give us our desert. Let us make the cry of the lepers our own: "This day is a day of good tidings." We are living in the time of grace. Who knows how long it will last? All signs point to the approaching end of the day of grace. Let us work while it is day. Let us be active, for the need is truly great.

4.

The lepers thought of the great need in the city. There, within the walls, were thousands of men, women, and children suffering extreme want in consequence of the siege. All food supplies from without had been cut off, and the supplies in the city had been consumed. The famine was so great that the vilest morsel was sold at the highest prices, chap. 6, 25. For want of food mothers slew their children and ate their flesh, chap. 6, 29. The situation was terrible.

This besieged city is a type of the people and nations that have not yet received the Gospel of Christ. Samaria is a type of this ungodly world, where sin and sorrow and suffering, vice and crime, death and desolation, abound. Oh, there are many Samarias! The thousands of people that are surrounded by thick walls of superstition, idolatry, worldliness, sensuality, and lust; the countless numbers of heathen in India, China, Africa, and in other countries, surrounded by almost impenetrable walls of foul and vile Buddhism and low Mohammedanism. To come closer, the countless number of people in so-called Christian lands who have no spiritual knowledge, who live for this world and for its pleasures and treasures; the large numbers of our fellow-citizens that are being led and fed by false prophets, who deprive them of the wholesome Bread and Water of Life and give them the husks of perverted human reason. What are all these conditions else than spiritual Samarias? In view of the deplorable state of unconverted men here and abroad how can we stand aloof and be selfish? Surely the great need on all sides should cause us to hasten and spread the good tidings of salvation from shore to shore, from pole to pole.

5.

We should be all the more zealous because we have that which is able to supply the needs.

The message those lepers brought to the city was indeed a good message. They informed the watchmen that the enemies had fled and had left their provisions and equipment behind. They informed them that vast quantities of foodstuffs were to be gotten in the camp. What welcome news! Could anything have been more timely and necessary? By this message the poor lepers saved the lives of thousands.

Similarly we are in a position to bring good tidings to our fellow-men. The Church of which we are members has a great message to proclaim. The pure Gospel has been given to us. We are not better than others. It is a blessing of God. But great privileges imply corresponding responsibilities. It is our duty to let the light of the holy Gospel shine. We must carry this light into the dark places of the world. It is our duty to proclaim to the Samarias of the world that Jesus Christ came into the world, fought and overcame the enemy; that He has established a camp where people of all lands may go and where they can find great spiritual supplies. This camp is the Christian Church, in which God richly and daily forgives all sins and where He bestows those things upon men that really satisfy even the innermost desires of the soul.

The watchword of the day is "recovery." Yes, our country, the whole world, is in need of recovery and reconstruction. But no real reconstruction and recovery is possible without the spiritual factor. Men need the Gospel of Christ, which reconstructs the heart. Only when the hearts of men are reconstructed, can there be a true recovery of the social structure.

As we do our part in the program of recovery, let us not forget that the missionary enterprise challenges our very best efforts and our fullest cooperation. Through the channels of mission work souls, blood-bought souls, are recovered for time and for eternity. Let us not stand aloof from this spiritual recovery program which the Savior of the world has laid upon our hearts.

If the pastor chooses to preach on this text according to stated theme and parts, the following brief outlines may be found useful: *This Day Is a Day of Good Tidings.* 1. Why is this certainly true? 2. To what should this induce us? — or: *Aloofness from Mission-work.* 1. This is a selfish attitude. 2. This is a dangerous attitude.

W. F. LICHTSINN.

Initial Sermon.

Phil 1, 3.

A spirit of thankfulness is a tonic in life. It lifts the soul from the drudgery and humdrum of the daily toil to the fresh, pure air of the mountain-top and gives us a clear vision, a new courage, a fresh impetus, a richer character, a sunny disposition.

Having accepted the call to the pastorate of this congregation, I come to you, brethren, happily as a thankful servant of Jesus Christ.

Thankful Ministers of Jesus Christ.

1. Thankful for the Office into which God has Led Them;
2. Thankful for the Success which God Gives;
3. Thankful for the Trials which the Lord Sends.

1.

With reference to his work the pastor says with Paul: text. Paul speaks in the most glowing terms about his work and his people. At the beginning of this epistle he calls himself and Timothy servants, bond-servants, of Jesus Christ. Paul was no servant of man, no men-pleaser; he stood in the direct service of Jesus Christ, from whom alone he was willing to receive orders and accept commands concerning the proper discharge of his work. What greater privilege could come to a man of clay and dust than this, that Jesus Christ, God's only-begotten Son and the sinless Son of Mary, the resurrected, glorified Christ, would take him into His direct and immediate service.

Men take pride in the firm in which they have found employment, in its founder, its long and useful history, its volume of business, its service. The Founder of the firm for which a Christian pastor works is Jesus Christ, the same yesterday, to-day, and forever, the Creator and Preserver of the world, the Author of life, the Alpha and Omega, the Beginning and End of our salvation, the Prince of Peace, the Atoner for the world's sins, the Way to eternal glory, the Anchor of our hope, the King of kings and the Lord of lords.

The firm which Jesus has founded, has a brilliant history. It was founded after the Fall in the Garden of Eden and numbers among its members the patriarchs and prophets of old. It was gloriously reestablished on Pentecost, and the apostles of the Lord were the builders and defenders of the New Testament Church. Luther brought it back to new life and again placed it upon the firm foundation of the apostles and prophets. Dr. Walther and other faithful pastors were helpful in establishing this firm of divine origin on the hard soil of free America. What a privilege to be in the direct service of Jesus Christ for a firm which has such a glorious history!

But we could say much more about the Christian Church. Calvary is the center of its history. Golgotha, "the place of a skull," was the kernel of all Old Testament prophecy, the fulfilment of the hope of God's people, the realization of God's eternal plan for the redemption of a sin-laden, sin-cursed race by the vicarious atonement for sin through the sacrifice of the guiltless Son of God.

And what a sublime business the Founder of the firm, the Master, has for His bond-servants! Paul exults in grateful strains about the privilege of doing the work of the Kingdom upon the hearts of men. Text. Gal. 1, 14. 15; Eph. 3, 8. What, to go out as representatives, ambassadors of Christ, and preach Jesus, ask sinful, mortal men to be reconciled to God, who through Christ is reconciled to men, to bring to poverty-stricken men "the unsearchable riches of Christ," to bring to men groping in the darkness of human vagueness and falsehood "the Word of Truth," to men struggling for rest of soul "the Gospel of peace," to men groaning under the weight of soul-torturing sin the "Gospel of salvation," is not this a service for which angels may well envy us?

God help me in the midst of my toil and trials among you always to see the greatness of my calling and to thank Him that He has separated me for this wonderful work and that His providence has made me a bond-servant of Jesus Christ, a messenger of truth in a world of doubt, a bringer of peace in a world of unrest und strife, an evangelist of hope in a world of hopelessness, a torch-bearer of life in the valley of death. Text.

Oh, it is only when men's hearts have been hardened by the love of money, fevered by the business of the world, excited by its pleasures, petrified by its materialistic maxims, that they cannot see the glory of the Christian ministry. But if the eyes of the understanding are opened by the Spirit and they can form judgment not on the dead level of business, money, worldly honor, but with spiritual discernment, they will find no more noble, no more useful, no more glorious work than the work of the Christian minister. Brethren, together with me thank God for the office of the holy ministry.

2.

Grateful to be your minister, I wish to be grateful also for the success which God in His grace will give me in my ministry among you.

Paul says: Phil. 1, 3 ff. These are not the words of false optimism, which is ignorant of the facts. Paul knew the facts in the case. There was room for improvement at Philippi, although things were in a much better state there than at Corinth. But the Philippians were not perfect Christians. Paul prays to God that their love may yet abound more and more in knowledge and in all judgment. He had reason to admonish them to be humble, to warn them against false teachers, the enemies of the Cross of Christ. Euodias and Syntyche are admonished to be of the same mind in the Lord. Yet in spite of their weaknesses Paul loves the people at Philippi. He has them in his heart. He longs after them all in the mercies of Jesus Christ. The preaching of the Gospel has not been in vain among them. He thanks God for their faith, their good works, their kindness and love to him, the aged apostle in bonds. And as to the future, Paul is buoyant with hope. "Being confident of this very thing that He which hath begun a good work in you will perform it until the Day of Jesus Christ."

Brethren, a faithful pastor dare not be blind to the faults and shortcomings of his people, but must ever try to deepen the faith of those given into his care and increase their fruits of righteousness, warn them against falsehood and moral dangers, privately warn and exhort those that are not walking uprightly in the Lord. But his work must be done with Christian assurance of the power of the Word.

To-day, then, as I begin my ministry among you, I thank God for the success which the ministry of the Word and the Sacraments has had among you, and I am joyfully confident that also in the future the Word of the Lord will not return void. God has done great things among you. There are in this congregation precious souls whose Christianity is not a mere matter of the lips, but also of the heart and life, who have not bowed their knees to the Baal of mammon and pleasure, but who, as the hart panteth after the waterbrooks, thirst after God, the living God; souls who pray for their pastor, deeply appreciate his spiritual ministrations, and are willing to labor and sacrifice for the extension of the kingdom of our Lord. Yes, there are also in this congregation living monuments to the converting and sanctifying power of the Gospel of the crucified, but now exalted Jesus. And I am gratefully confident of the fact that the preaching and teaching of the Word of God will be blessed among you, even though it is preached and taught by such a weak vessel as I am. Yes, my weaknesses, my shortcomings! Which pastor can be satisfied with the earnestness of his prayers and supplications in behalf of his people? Who can be satisfied with the form and delivery of his sermons? Who is a perfect master in the supreme art of pastoral care and missionary endeavor? Who is without fault before his Master? With my weakness vividly before me and my deficiencies keenly felt in my soul, I am thankful that God's grace is made perfect in our weakness, and we have the assurance, given us in the Bible, that He will bless the preaching of His Word in our midst.

3.

Finally, like Paul, grateful ministers of the Lord ought to thank God even for their trials. Such sacrifices of thanksgiving are the hardest to offer. The evil things that happened to Paul, he says, had "fallen out rather unto the furtherance of the Gospel."

I do not know what difficulties and setbacks the Lord has in store for me during my ministry among you. Loyalty to the Bible and its principles bring conflict with the self-righteous and the worldly. When a Demas forsakes the ranks and goes over to the world, a faithful pastor's heart is deeply grieved. When a soul he hoped to win for Christ remains in unbelief, he is keenly disappointed. When faithfulness to duty brings unmerited criticism, a pastor's heart is cut to the quick. When a spirited call to missionary activity is met with cool indifference, courage is likely to wane. To outward conflict may be added inner struggles.

God grant to His servants the ability to bear hardness with grateful cheerfulness, as good soldiers of Christ. Has He not given the promise, which cannot fall to the ground, that *all* things work together for good to them that love Him? We must have not only sunshine, but also rain to make the crops grow and mature. Often the cloud we feared "breaks in blessings o'er our head." God help me in every evil day that may come to sing hallelujah and to trust the Savior's guiding love. God grant that in a dark hour I may be and do like that man who wrote this text: Acts 16, 25.

Brethren, faithful to the Word of Truth and the Savior, whose I am and whom I serve, certain of your love and cooperation, I shall, with God's help, endeavor to be among you a faithful and grateful servant of Jesus Christ. WALTER E. HOHENSTEIN.

Church Anniversary.
Rev. 3, 7—12.

"This is the day which the Lord hath made; we will rejoice and be glad in it," Ps. 118, 24. These words of the divinely inspired psalmwriter fitly express the sentiment in your heart as you gather in festive assembly on this joyous occasion. Out of the fulness of the heart the mouth speaketh. As your mind goes back and you review the experiences of your congregation during the past —— years, you cannot but exclaim with David: 2 Sam. 7, 18, or in the words of Jacob: Gen. 32, 10. If you have never felt moved to do it before, then surely this anniversary day must teach you to realize how boundless God's blessings are, how little you have deserved them, and how important it is that you come into the Lord's presence with thanksgiving and with vows of renewed devotion and consecration.

However, while appropriate expressions on your part are essential to a fitting observance of this anniversary, it is even more important that you ask, "Is there not some word for the Lord for us on this occasion?" Permit me to answer, "There is." Not only is the Lord pleased to *hear* you on this your day of rejoicing, He also has something interesting and instructive to *say* to you. May I present the text as —

A Message from the Lord for This Anniversary.

This message contains: —

1. A Reminder; 2. A Commendation; 3. An Admonition;
4. An Assurance.

By way of introduction we must first of all justify the statement that the text before us is a message from the Lord for this anniversary. Though originally intended for, and addressed to, the congregation at Philadelphia as a general letter without any reference to a special occasion, this passage is at the same time part of the Holy Scriptures, which are given by inspiration of God to all people (including this gathering) and which at all times (including this day and occasion) "are profitable for doctrine," etc., 2 Tim. 3, 15. In addition, it may be truthfully said that all those parts in the Bible that can be applied to certain people and are found suitable for certain occasions are intended for such people and occasions. We may therefore very properly consider the text before us a message for to-day's anniversary because it so well fits this congregation and the present occasion.

We shall also find it profitable to get the connection. The text is the sixth of the seven messages entrusted by the Lord to John to be delivered to the pastors of the seven leading churches of Asia Minor and through them to their congregations. It was addressed to the pastor and congregation at Philadelphia, the city of brotherly love, in Asia Minor. It is a most beautiful and appealing message and evidences a high degree of affection on the Lord's part for the Philadelphian congregation. And now the text.

1.

The message before us, first of all, *presents the Author* of its contents in striking terms, v. 7. It is the great and holy Son of God, the Source of all truth, who, as the spiritual David, has the key to the Kingdom and who, as the world's Redeemer, alone possesses the power to say who shall and who shall not come into that kingdom. A message from so exalted a personage is a distinction to this congregation, constitutes the noblest feature of this anniversary, and deserves an attentive hearing.

The message contains a brief *reminder* of privileges and blessings enjoyed in the past, v. 8 a. Verily, the Lord has known you, has been with you, according to His promise, Matt. 28, 20, these —— years. Sympathetic knowledge; loving, helpful presence! During this blessed era of divine favor the doors have been constantly open — the doors to the merciful heart of God, to the abundant stores of God's Church on earth, to many rooms of fruitful and successful endeavor, to the safe, eternal refuge of heaven; opened even when you, perhaps, were not interested enough to enter, but chose rather to stray about in the byways of self-love and indifference; opened through the redeeming sacrifice of God's Son on Calvary and kept open by faithful Gospel-preaching and -teaching. Is not your experience that of the disciples, Luke 22, 35, as you contemplate the untold blessings you, your fathers, and your children have enjoyed in this sacred place during the past —— years? Every grateful Christian among you may fittingly express himself in the words of David: Ps. 103, 1—4.

2.

We also find in this message certain expressions of *commendation*. We read: vv. 8 a. 8 c. 10 a. These statements are similar to such as occur in other letters, chap. 2, 1. 2. 9. 13. 19. What a fine record has a church of which such things can be said! Numbers and size, representative standing, costly buildings and furnishings, are not to be ignored in writing a church's story. But divine appraisal attaches far greater importance and places higher value upon the features mentioned in the text. The latter make a church great even in the absence of the former, and without them even a Solomonic Temple is but an empty shell. Applying the text to the present occasion, we may say, without giving undue glory to man, that much faithful work has been done in and by this congregation. You have prayed, labored, and brought gifts in order that the preaching and teaching of the Word might continue and that old as well as young might have a constant supply of the Bread of Life. Leaders have come and gone, but you have kept the Word. You have been faithful in the midst of difficulties and discouragements, and though surrounded by erroristic organizations on every side, you have not denied your Savior's name and cause. Many of you have borne mockery and contempt and have brought real sacrifices as evidences of your interest in, and loyalty to, the Lord's church. And your labors have not been in vain. Compare present conditions in your church with things as they were in the past.

Though you are what you are alone by the grace of God; though what you have done has been done only by His help and was not always done as efficiently and joyously as it might have been; though much was left undone and such success as attended your efforts is an entirely undeserved blessing from above, yet the Lord has graciously kept the record of your achievements and on this festive occasion lovingly acknowledges your work and rewards it with His divine favor. If what your friends are saying and the newspapers are printing concerning the record of your church means anything to you, God's own personal commendation should be to you a source of the deepest gratification.

3.

You will therefore also give heed to the Lord's well-meant *admonition*. The Philadelphians are reminded of the door set by the Lord, still open, v. 8 b, a door not merely to the privileges of God's kingdom, but especially a door of opportunity for greater service and increased efficiency in church-work. Also they are admonished to keep what they have and thus become confirmed in their status as God's people, in their efficiency as service units in the Kingdom, and in their prospective possession of the crown of glory, v. 11.

You have in the past been active in the work of "bringing in the sheaves"; you have to this day kept the faith and loyally defended the

truth. But the time has not yet come to rest on your laurels. There
is still work to do, and opportunities are calling. There are souls to
be won for the Kingdom all around you. Unchurched adults and
children can be found everywhere. The world at large is still three-
fourths pagan. These conditions can be met only through the saving
Gospel, which you possess and in which alone there is hope and help.
These circumstances constitute an open door and challenge you to
enter and take possession. If your anniversary is to serve its purpose
best, it must inspire you to renewed consecration and devotion for
the great task of maintaining and extending the Kingdom of Grace
in the territory which you occupy.

To this end it will be important that you keep what you have.
The forces of doubt, error, denial, and unbelief, all the powers of
darkness, seen and unseen, are more than ever determined to destroy
the truth that you confess, overthrow the Church of Jesus Christ, and
bring the work of your congregation to naught. They are active
without as well as within Christianity. This church is one of the
few that still contend for the truth of every Bible word; the full
and free salvation of sinners by the grace of God, for Christ's sake,
through faith; the regenerating and preserving power of the Sacraments; the liberty of God's children from the yoke of man-made laws;
and other vital teachings of Christian truth. For your own sake as
well as for the sake of your continued successful activity hold fast
the spiritual assets that you have enjoyed these past —— years. Hear
the Word diligently in this house of God and search it earnestly in
your homes; keep up the family altar and see to it that the little ones
are given the best possible bringing up in the nurture and admonition
of the Lord; work with your church, pray for it, give to it; what
it stands for is your crown, the most valuable treasure you will ever
possess. Gal. 6, 9; 2 Cor. 9, 6.

4.

In conclusion, the Lord's anniversary message to you contains
words of cheering *assurance*. The Christians of Philadelphia lived
in times that tried their souls, and the future offered no prospects of
peace and relief. It must have heartened them greatly to hear the
divine promises conveyed to them in John's letter, v. 8b, 9. 10b. 11a. 12.
These words assured them that their labors would not be in vain;
even enemies would be converted to their Gospel; strength would be
given them to resist every temptation and attack; the Lord would
soon deliver them from all evil and signally honor them with a crown
of life.

For you to-day all this implies that success will continue to
attend your faithful work and crown your conscientious efforts, and
this in the very face of those influences that oppose your church
policies, your missionary activities, your school-work, and thus seek
to close the door of opportunity and achievement before you. The

experiences of the past show that the future is safe for you. Luke 21, 15. You will find that the Gospel will win victories even among those who now are alined against you. And when in the years to come temptations and trials, like angry waves, will toss the vessel of your church about and threaten to swamp it, you will have nothing to fear, for: Ps. 46, 1—7. Only keep "the Word of His patience" and "hold that fast which thou hast." Remember, there will not always be labor, conflict, sacrifice. For those who persevere and remain faithful unto death, God has prepared a crown of life. Many who have during these past years gone on before are now members of the Church Triumphant. Pray God to-day that in the final resurrection you will be reunited with and counted among them.

This, then, is the Lord's anniversary message. To impress it on your memory, we close with the words of the text: "These things saith," etc.   K. KRETZSCHMAR.

Church Music.
(Anniversary of a Church Choir.)

Ps. 98, 1.

You are in the midst of your various celebrations, commemorating the fiftieth anniversary of your church. All your services in this connection are services of praise, in which you are expressing your humble and heartfelt thanks to God for the many blessings bestowed upon your congregation and its various agencies in the past. It is entirely fitting and proper that you should do this. The inspired psalmist said: "It is a good thing to give thanks unto the Lord and to sing praises unto Thy name, O Most High; to show forth Thy loving-kindness in the morning and Thy faithfulness every night. . . . For Thou, O Lord, hast made me glad through Thy work," Ps. 92, 1 ff.

As the service this evening is the anniversary service of the choir, we thank the Lord especially for the gift of sacred music and song and express our gratitude for having blessed the cultivation of it by the choir and the congregation.

In this service it will be proper and edifying if we turn our attention for a few moments to consider, under the guidance of God's Holy Spirit, the subject of *the song of the Church,* to which the psalmist encourages us with the words: —

"O Sing unto the Lord a New Song; for He Hath Done Marvelous Things!"

1.

When the ancient Greek philosopher Aristotle was asked what he thought of music, he replied: "Jupiter does not sing, neither does he play the harp." He seemed to infer that music is unbecoming to deity and therefore also unprofitable to man. The true God, on the other hand, before whom the morning stars sang together at the creation and around whose throne the cherubim and seraphim sing their glory-songs, is a Lover of music. The harps of music belong to Him, and His children on earth have their hearts set to singing, inspired by His great works.

Music has therefore always had a home in the Church of the Most High, and the children of God have from time immemorial expressed their religious emotions through music.

It seems to lie in the very nature of music that this should be so. Man's deepest being is moved by the sweet concord of sound. Of all the arts, music is most delicate, most ethereal, most spiritual, most divine, and it reaches its loftiest heights when employed in the cause of true religion. It is for this reason that Luther placed music of the last-named kind next to theology and said: "Music is the highest art, the notes of which cause the words of the text to live." And again: "I long to see all the arts, especially music, in the service of Him who created them."

The Old Testament early speaks of music. Jubal is mentioned as the father of all those that handle the harp and organ, Gen. 4, 21. Moses and the children of Israel, after their deliverance from Pharaoh, sang a song in praise of Jehovah, a song of triumph and victory (Ex. 15, 1) : —

> I will sing unto the Lord, for He hath triumphed gloriously:
> The horse and his rider hath He thrown into the sea.

The Sacred Record makes repeated mention of music and song in the service of the Lord. King David, the sweet singer of Israel, took a leading part in appointing the Levitical chorus and orchestra for the song of the Temple to be built, 1 Chron. 15, 16—24, and wrote many psalms to be used for that purpose; and when his son Solomon dedicated the Temple with appropriate ceremonies and the sons of Asaph, of Heman, of Jeduthun, and others, to the accompaniment of a great orchestra, sang: "Praise the Lord, for He is good; for His mercy endureth forever," the house of God was filled with the glory of the Lord, 2 Chron. 5, 12 f.

That was no doubt *the most impressive event in the Old Testament era.* There were other outstanding occasions, as when the angel of the Lord appeared to Abraham as he was about to sacrifice Isaac; or when Moses received the tables of the Law on Mount Sinai; or when Elijah called down the fire from heaven that devoured his sacrifice on Mount Carmel; or when Elijah was translated into heaven on a chariot of fire; but none of these approximate that event when the singers, the players of instruments, and the priests, arrayed in white linen and in wonderful harmonies of sound praising and thanking the

Lord, saw this manifestation of His glory. There we see music put to its loftiest service and the Lord manifesting His pleasure by according His benign presence to His chosen people in the cloud that filled the Temple.

But, my friends, as we close the Book of the Old Covenant and turn to the Book of the New Testament, we hardly open its pages before a still more striking and impressive event meets our gaze. It is over the fields of Bethlehem on Christmas night that we see the heavens open and emptying themselves of their heavenly host, which sings the most glorious song that has ever ravished human ears: "Glory to God in the highest and on earth peace, good will toward men!" It is there that we hear the new song, the song that was to be sung by the New Testament Church, the song that surpasses in theme and completeness all the songs ever uttered under the Old Covenant.

In the Old Testament we have types and symbols, the foretelling and the foreshadowing; in the New Testament we have the fulfilment and the fruition — the body itself, in Christ Jesus. What the Old Testament enfolds and conceals the New Testament unfolds and reveals. In the Old Testament we have the longing for, and the looking toward, the Promised One; in the New Testament we have the actuality, the completion of the great work of redemption planned in the eternal counsels of our God. And so in the song of the Old Testament Church there is an incompleteness that is not made perfect until the coming of the Christ.

> What the fathers most desired,
> What the prophets' heart inspired,
> What they longed for many a year,
> Stands fulfilled in glory here.

The new song of the Church of Jesus Christ has therefore the most exalted theme imaginable. It has rightly been said: "You cannot sing a great song about something trifling or frivolous. To have great music, you must have a great subject. Love is a great theme, and love claims some of our greatest songs. Beauty is a great theme, and some of our most stirring songs sing of beauty. Victory is a great theme, and some of our best songs sing of victory. But the greatest theme of all is glory, the glory of God." That is the theme of the New Testament song. Thus the angels as they sang before the wondering shepherds, thus Mary in her *Magnificat,* thus Zacharias in his *Benedictus,* thus Simeon in his *Nunc Dimittis,* and thus the angels before the throne of the Lamb echo and reecho the theme of glory to God. Thus the Church in her liturgical services constantly repeats the theme in the *Gloria Patri,* in the *Gloria in Excelsis,* in the *Te Deum Laudamus,* and in the doxologies, never tiring of offering glory and praise to the Most High for His gracious works, particularly the work of redemption.

Everything centers in that. We praise God for the wonders and beauties of creation and declare His glory for His wise providence and untiring preservation; but it is the song in praise of His grace and mercy through Jesus Christ that accords Him the highest glory, as St. Paul says: "For God, who commanded the light to shine out of darkness, hath shined in our hearts to give the light of the knowledge of the glory of God in the face of Jesus Christ." There we see our God in His most wonderful manifestation.

> It is God; His love looks mighty,
>   But is mightier than it seems;
> 'Tis our Father; and His fondness
>   Goes out far beyond our dreams.

Isaac Watts, the father of English hymnody, therefore correctly gave the New Testament interpretation to the psalm from which our text is taken when he sang the "new song" in the fitting words: —

> Joy to the world! the Lord is come;
>   Let earth receive her King;
> Let every heart prepare Him room
>   And heaven and nature sing.

> No more let sins and sorrows grow
>   Nor thorns infest the ground;
> He comes to make His blessings flow
>   Far as the curse is found.

And every repentant sinner who by faith has found forgiveness of his sins in Christ Jesus joyfully sings this new song to God's glory and exults: —

> O may Thy love inspire my tongue!
> Salvation shall be all my song,
> And all my powers shall join to bless
> The Lord, my Strength, my Righteousness.

2.

It follows that the Church of Christ must cultivate this new song unto the Lord. The early Church was a singing Church. The testimony of St. Paul and the history of the Church are sufficient basis for that assertion. The great apostle wants the Church to sing, saying: "Let the Word of Christ dwell in you richly in all wisdom, teaching and admonishing one another in psalms and hymns and spiritual songs, singing with grace in your hearts to the Lord," Col. 3, 16. The ancient Christians, even in the trying days of the persecution, met together and sang hymns to Christ as God. The oldest hymn, outside of the New Testament, that has come down to us is one that honors Christ, our Lord. Later when error, superstition, and unchristian practises crept into the Church and checked the flow of the Gospel-stream, the new song of the Church was often corrupted or at least limited in its use; but even then the song of faith was not silenced altogether, and we have such hymns as St. Bernard's "Jesus, the Very Thought of Thee with Sweetness Fills the Breast" with its matchless stanza: —

> Nor voice can sing, nor heart can frame
> Nor can the memory find
> A sweeter sound than Thy blest name,
> O Savior of mankind!

In the Reformation Age, Martin Luther led the way to a renewal of sacred song. Luther's hymns all exalt the grace of God through Christ, who died to make us heirs of heaven. He wanted the Christians' faith in Him to be so vital and vibrant in the heart that it would spontaneously break out in song. His hymn "Dear Christians, One and All, Rejoice" is still a clarion call to all evangelical Christians to "sing unto the Lord a new song." His vision of the evangelical Church was that of a happy body of believers, who have found forgiveness of sins, peace of conscience, and the hope of heaven through faith in Christ, who now travel the road of their earthly pilgrimage in spite of all hardships, burdens, crosses, and trials "singing and making melody in their hearts to the Lord," like the man described by Clinton Scollard in the words: —

> I met a traveler on the dusty road
> Who bravely bore a heavy load.
> "Stranger, how fare you mid life's toil and smart?"
> "Comrade," he said, "I have a singing heart."

By his work of Reformation, Luther freed the Church from the papal yoke, and music also became free. It was taken out of the hands of the monks and restored to the people. Then, as a free art, it spread its wings and developed its powers in a natural manner. The hymn of the Reformation became a powerful witness to the great truths which were the corner-stone of the Lutheran doctrines, and the wealth of Lutheran song developed under Luther's impetus in the next two centuries following the Reformation, constitutes, next to the open Bible and the Confessions of our Church, the finest heritage that we possess. The Protestant world and even the Roman Catholic Church have learned congregational singing from Martin Luther, and the greatest musicians of the world received their highest inspirations from him. "If they had not been inspired by the grandeur and beauty of Lutheran church music, Bach, Mendelssohn, and Brahms could not have written their great choral and organ works in which they glorify the doctrine of Scripture," says one authority (Reuter), and another declares: "Much of the wealth and depth of modern music may surely be traced in a large measure to the mental and spiritual stimulus accompanying the rise of Protestantism" (Waldo Pratt, in *History of Music*).

This is also your precious heritage, dear friends. Ever since the founding of your church Lutheran song has been fostered in your midst. Your services have been enhanced by proper and dignified congregational singing, and who can measure the influence for good that has been exerted by your song? For years it was in German, in the very language of the Reformation. In late years it has become more and more English, with the attendant temptation to follow in music the customs of the English-speaking churches surrounding you. Be it far from me even to intimate that the English-speaking Protestant churches have brought forth no worthy church hymns and church music. Our own hymn-book bears testimony to the fact that we gratefully accept the best that has been produced in this field. It is to-day universally acknowledged, however, that nothing can supersede the Lutheran choral, and many outside of our Church are learning to prize it highly. Even the Anglican Church, which, no doubt, ranks highest in the field of English hymnody, does not claim to have surpassed the Lutheran choral. "We have not one composition corresponding with the earliest burst of German song," says one of the Anglican authorities. "This primary formation with its massive strength and its mountain ranges, upheaved by the great inward fire of the Reformation, is with the Church of England altogether wanting." (*Christian Life in Song.*)

The Lutheran choral, churchly, dignified, reverential, is preeminently the song of faith, glorifying God for His redemption in Christ; and if the best that others have produced dare not supplant this treasure among us, how much less the light and trivial and emotional! The so-called Gospel-hymn is altogether unworthy. It too often emphasizes man instead of glorifying God and deals with things that are merely sentimental. The modern social-service hymns also cannot be classed with the "new song" of the Church. They lack the theme of God's glory. "That is why they are," as one authority states, "so heavy-hearted, so argumentative, and drop earthward. It is difficult to sing about ourselves. It is difficult to sing about society." And "ecclesiastical jazz or ragtime" may be fitting in a revival service, but it is not suitable in a service which is characterized by solemnity and dignity and in which everything is done unto edifying.

What has just been said about congregational singing in your church may be said also about the singing of your choirs. Since the founding of your church, choir music has been cultivated, and to-day you have three choirs that take turns in helping to beautify your services. But has the attempt been made to supplant the song of the congregation by thrusting the choir into the foreground? Your choirs have had in the past, and have to-day, only this aim, to aid in worship and edification. To help in developing an appreciation of the art and beauty of Christian hymnody, to assist in increasing the religious knowledge and consciousness of the people, that is and must remain the sphere of the choirs. It has truly been said: "Music is a fine servant, but a very poor master. Whenever music is used in a worship service, it should be the outcome of a conscious purpose, since not a note of music is *necessary* to the performance of our church service." "Mere esthetic delight, although worthy in itself, must not be mistaken for worship."

May this ever be the function of your choirs and of all the music used in your church services, and may your congregational singing in the future remain on the high plane which it has had in the past, so that all the harmonies of sound, all the anthems and hymns will repeat again and again the great theme of the "new song," the glory of God, for the redemption of man through the cross of Jesus Christ!

In conclusion permit me to say that in order to have singing Christians and a singing Church, the true doctrine of salvation by faith in Christ must be preached. That has been the great work of your congregation in the past; may God in His grace keep it so in the future! Where the pulpit proclaims the Gospel in its purity and the people in the pews accept it with believing hearts, it is there, and there only, that the mouths will be filled with laughter and the hearts with singing.

Go forward, then, my friends, in God's name and in all your work as Christians praise the Holy One, the God who created, redeemed, and sanctified you, until there shall come the final glorification, —

Where saints find full employ,	They who are most beloved,
Songs of triumphant joy	They who are tried and proved,
Ever upraising;	Together praising

before the "grandest of all masters of harmony," joining in the rapturous songs of the angelic choirs, "Blessing, and honor, and glory, and power be unto Him that sitteth upon the throne and unto the Lamb forever and ever!" Amen.   W. G. POLACK.

NB. The material in this sermon may be used for other occasions, such as National Lutheran Music Week, dedication of an organ, and Cantate Sunday.

Wedding Address on Rom. 12, 12.

"Ye have not passed this way heretofore." Thus Joshua — all the children of God in the Old Testament. Just before they entered Canaan, the — promise. Come from their wanderings of forty years in wilderness. There — born. There received the oracles of God. There told that going to a land of promise. Now arrived at the borders —. Only Jordan separating —. Joshua, God-appointed leader, in their midst. He would lead —. New experiences, new joys, new conflicts, and new victories awaited —. They had not passed this way before.

You, — , in similar situation to-day. True, not come up from wilderness, but brought up in God's own garden, where the milk and honey of His Word do flow. But — mile-post of human experience, a new boundary on your earthly pilgrimage. From to-day onward — together. United in holy wedlock. New experiences, new joys, new conflicts, and, we hope, new victories are awaiting you. You have not passed — before. And you desire to be consecrated, hallowed, and sanctified by the Word of God, by prayer, and benediction. You have selected the passage given to the bride as a memory verse on the day of confirmation: Rom. 12, 12. This passage is to guide you on your way of wedded life.

Three Inscriptions on the Guide-Post Directing Christians to a Life of Wedded Joy and Happiness: —

1. Rejoice in Hope!   *2. Be Patient in Tribulation.*
3. Continue Instant in Prayer.

1.

Rejoice in Hope. So reads the first —. I say advisedly that this is advice to guide Christians —. Others cannot be urged to rejoice in hope. Have no hope. Paul, Eph. 2, 12: Aliens from the commonwealth of Israel, strangers from the covenants of promise, no hope, without God in the world. To be without God surely means to be without hope, for — no God, is godless, ungodly. "The way of the ungodly shall perish," Ps. 1, 6. But Christians have a hope. What —? It is God. But not any god. The Hindu, too, has a god, the Mohammedan —, the societies with Christless religions —, but not the true God. Only a figment of the imagination. Who is the true God? The God of the Bible, the God who has revealed Himself through Jesus Christ, who has said: "I am the Way," etc. "No man cometh unto the Father but by Me." "All men should honor the Son," etc. This God, the true God, the Bible God, is the hope and joy of the Christian. God revealed in Jesus Christ. The Chistian —: "I will greatly rejoice in the Lord; my soul shall be joyful in my God. For He hath clothed me with the garments of salvation; He hath covered me with the robe of righteousness, as a bridegroom decketh himself with ornaments and as a bride adorneth herself with jewels." Is. 61, 10. In this God the Christian hopes that all things must work together for good to him. And this hope and joy in God goes even beyond the life that now is; it reaches into the glories of the world to come. 1 Pet. 1, 3. 4. and 2 Cor. 1, 20.

But if God is the hope and joy of the Christian, then why put up this sign with the inscription, Rejoice in *hope?* The reason is this: Christians still in the flesh, and the flesh is apt to become absorbed with, and entangled in, the affairs of the world so much that they will forget about their God and their hope and joy in God; in good days they pride themselves with their successes and deny God, and in evil days they take the name of God in vain. Therefore remember the inscription: Rejoice in hope. Hope in God. Let God be the health of — countenance, and in good and evil days — truly happy.

Yes, there will be evil days also. Therefore—second inscription—.

2.

Be patient in tribulation. Yes, Christians — tribulations. The Savior: "In the world ye shall have tribulation," John 16, 33. It is part of God's dispensation of mercy that we must through —. Those who have already reached that blissful goal described as "they that have come out of great tribulation." Suffice it to say there are crosses, losses, and reverses of all kinds. "No cross, no crown." Christians apt to become impatient. Especially when cross grievous and lasting. Then Job. 7, 14. But — should be patient even in tribulation. "Tribulation worketh patience; and patience, experience; and experience, hope; and hope maketh not ashamed; because the love of God is shed abroad in our hearts," Rom. 5, 3—5. Remember that the Gospel which brings tribulations also supplies the strength to overcome them. It teaches us not how to get rid of —, but how to bear patiently.

Therefore look often to the inscription: Be patient in tribulation. Let this direction lift your hearts heavenward and Christward, who is the true Model and Example and by whose power, through faith, you will be enabled —. Heb. 12, 2.

However, all these things, hope and joy and patience, are not of our own making. The Holy Spirit must work and supply them.

3.

Therefore continue instant in prayer. What is more natural than that children should look to their father in all their wants! Let it be so with you. You are the children of God by faith in —. God is your Father. "Like as a father pitieth his —." God, your Father, has promised to hear your —. "It shall come to pass that, before they call," etc., Is. 65, 24. One of the uses of adversities is to make us more diligent and more fervent in prayer. "Call upon Me in the day," etc., Ps. 50, 15. There is much to hinder —. The devil with his fiery darts, the world with its silly derision, the flesh with its foolish doubts, all work together to rob the Christian of his joy in paryer. But the Lord wants His children to pray. Here is His command: Continue instant in prayer. "Pray without ceasing," 1 Thess. 5, 17. And listen to the Savior's direction in the Sermon on the Mount, combining both command and promise: "Ask, and it shall be given," etc. And if it seems as though your prayers are not heard, "be clothed with humility; for God .... Humble ..., that — exalt — time, casting all," etc., 1 Pet.

5, 6. Continue instant in prayer. Continue your importunity as did the woman of Canaan. And Luke 11, 5—13. Say with Daniel: "O my God, incline Thine ear and hear; open Thine eyes," etc., Dan. 9, 18. Continue instant in prayer. That will make and keep you truly happy. God, your Father, has promised to hear you.

God never will forsake in need
The soul that trusts in Him indeed.

A. C. KLAMMER.

Wedding Address on Eph. 5, 22—33.

The Bridegroom and His bride — that is the theme of the apostle in our text. This is also our subject on this happy occasion. However, I do not mean the bridegroom and the bride who have come before us, that their vows to each other may be sanctified and solemnized with God's Word and prayer. *"I speak concerning Christ and the Church."* I am speaking of the Bridegroom of us all, dear fellow-Christians, and of His bride. That is what you are, every one of those of you who have learned to say yes to His wooing voice.

But our text and theme for this occasion are well chosen especially for your consideration, dear bridegroom and bride. You wish to remain happy. "They lived happily ever after" or words to that effect form a phrase common in fiction. But such enduring earthly bliss is becoming more and more rare in every-day life. *"Our* marriage will be happy," so you think and dare to say. However, if we consider the troubled seas where innumerable others are suffering shipwreck, we may well pause and pray. Happiness in married life is based upon mutual love and respect, and such mutual love and respect must be based upon that love which truly never knows doubt or change, the love of the Savior, and then, too, on the love of both the man and his wife for the Bridegroom of their souls. Therefore on this day, when you will publicly plight your troth to each other, —

Give Your Promise of Love and Obedience Also to Jesus, the Heavenly Bridegroom.

1. Hear and Accept Your Savior's Offer of Love To-day and Every Day.

2. So will You Also Learn to Be for His Sake Ever More Loving, True, and Kind to Each Other.

1.

The words of our text are in part found also in the wedding service provided by our Lutheran agenda. As the sainted Dr. Stoeckhardt at one time said, "This admonition of the apostle could at no time be more appropriate than at a wedding." And so to-day you shall not merely hear it read, but I beseech you also to ponder these precious words with me very carefully.

The great love of Jesus, what it is and what it does, this is to be our first meditation. Ah, "very pleasant hast Thou been unto me; thy love to me was wonderful, passing the love of women." Why do we say so of Him? Because "He loved the Church and gave Himself for it," etc. (Text.)

In these beautiful words St. Paul shows forth the divine love of our Bridegroom as it was, is, and ever shall be world without end. Of eternity He chose us to be His bride. Few are chosen. Just why He who loves all chose you and me, who can tell? Truly, what I am saying concerning Christ and the Church "is a great mystery." You, dear bride, may wonder just why the bridegroom chose you. And for you, her lover, it is a mystery that she preferred you to others. But, lo, I speak of a far greater mystery when I speak of Christ and His Church. There was neither in me nor in you aught of form or comeliness or beauty, that He should desire us; naught did His pure eyes see in you of all that you to-day admire in each other. Instead, He saw in us much sin and great ugliness, spiritual sickness and death. Yet He loved us — wondrous thought! O unspeakable mystery, He "chose us before the foundation of the world, having predestinated us unto the adoption of children"!

And what we so sorely lacked He of eternity resolved to supply "that we should be holy and without blame," "without spot or wrinkle or any such thing." For the sake of those whom He loved, us sinners, He had to become poor, had to give Himself a ransom for us. There was no other way. He died for us. He gave all of His heart's blood, and into the fountain filled with it He dipped our filthy rags and brought them forth again pure and whole, a glorious wedding-garment, graciously with it to cover all our sins. This is that garment of which faith sings: —

> Jesus, Thy blood and righteousness
> My beauty are, my glorious dress.
> Midst flaming worlds, in these arrayed,
> With joy shall I lift up my head.

To be sure, you must put this garment on if it is to adorn you. You will offend your Lover mortally if you refuse to do so, if you despise it. It is not customary for an earthly bridegroom of our time to supply his bride's wedding-dress. But he does buy her flowers. What would he say if she should spurn his gift and choose a bouquet out of another garden? Do not, then, hurt the loving heart of Jesus by ever daring to come to Him cheaply adorned with the flowers of your own righteousness. Wear only the wedding-garment of His righteousness. As early as when you were baptized, at "the washing of water by the word," He Himself clothed you in it. Put it on daily as you hear His offer of love. Let each of you always be His lover. No man, no woman, should ever be permitted to cast their shadow between Jesus and His own.

Let Him daily have His good way with you. He will then make you, His bride, ever more beautiful, a glorious church, one to whom He can direct the attention of even His holy angels, saying, "This is my beloved. See how glorious!" Grow in grace and in favor with God, your Lover, and on the Last Day, when He will come for you as never before, He will in the power of His love remove from you all that still is unfair, and you will be forever without spot or wrinkle or any such thing, altogether holy and without blemish, young and beautiful without ceasing. This He will do for all who hear and accept His offer of love.

Husbands and wives often have an altogether wrong conception of their duty toward each other. Some consider it praiseworthy to leave their own Church merely because this will please their spouse. Let me tell you, men and women who deliberately undermine each other's loyalty to Jesus will at the same time be digging the grave of their own marital happiness. But on the other hand, those who to-day and every day truly say yes to the wooing voice of Jesus, who learn to know His Word and command, will then also learn to be, for His sweet sake especially, ever more loving, true and kind to each other.

2.

What I have just said is most certainly true. Love and faithfulness to Jesus demands of us love, faithfulness, and kindness to our spouse, which in the case of the woman will manifest itself even in obedience. The apostle says: "Wives, submit yourselves unto your own husbands as unto the Lord; for the husband is the head of the wife, even as Christ is the Head of the Church. Therefore as the Church is subject unto Christ, so let the wives be to their own husbands in everything." Those things alone are excepted which loyalty to Jesus forbids. This sounds as if it were too old-fashioned. Equal rights for men and women is the cry of the times. Some churches, in their pitiful endeavor to be found up to date, no longer ask the bride whether she will also promise to obey. Affected by the rebellious spirit of the day, some Lutheran women have gone so far as to ask their pastor not to request such a promise; and, alas, how many who have promised to obey have never seriously tried to keep their vow! The Christian pastor has no right to change the marriage vows. You might as well ask him to take away from the words of the Bible. And if he does, God shall take away his part out of the Book of Life.

But why should the woman obey the man? She may well wave the question whether there is any natural superiority in him. Christ is her superior in every sense. It is He who asks her to obey. And she is willing to do it, gladly, lovingly, for His sake. She does it "as unto the Lord." That means it is really He to whom she renders obedience, and she knows that He will consider it as done unto Him. So you see that the Christian woman who is really loyal to Jesus will for His sake be loving, true, and kind to her husband.

Nor ought this to be at any time an irksome duty. It will not be if the husband, too, loves and obeys the Savior. It takes two to make a success of marriage, and it requires the obedience of two, the obedinece of both the man and the woman to their Bridegroom Jesus. He says to the man: "Husbands, love your wives, even as Christ loved the Church. . . . So ought men to love their wives as their own bodies. He that loveth his wife loveth himself; for no man ever yet hated his own flesh, but nourisheth and cherisheth it, even as the Lord the Church." Here we are taught to see in our marriage a type of the tender relation between Christ and His Church. To be sure, it is at best, as everything earthly, a faint image.

> For the love of God is broader than the measure of man's mind,
> And the heart of the Eternal is most wonderfully kind.

Nevertheless the unspeakable love of Christ is and should be for the Christian man his shining example for his daily conduct toward his wife. He will not make her obedience a grievous burden. Even as Christ came not to be ministered unto, but to minister, he will give himself for his wife in deeds of loving-kindness, so that her own reso- lution to do him good and no evil all the days of her life will grow firmer in her, not be weakened by his bitterness. Behold, then, how good and how pleasant the home is where a man and a wife and their children dwell together in Christian unity, love, and peace! Hymn 445, 1. 2. 5. KARL H. EHLERS.

Mother's Day.
Matt. 15, 21—28.

This is the Gospel for the Second Sunday in Lent. However, since we are this year using a series of Old Testament selections in our morning services, we are afforded the opportunity of employ- ing this text in our Mother's Day celebration. The combination of this day and this text gives us occasion to view this story from the life of our Savior from a somewhat unusual angle. This portion of the Scripture is eminently appropriate for the observance of Mother's Day because —

The Story of the Syrophenician Woman
presents to us —

1. A Mother's Sorrow;
2. A Mother's Love;
3. A Mother's Faith;
4. A Mother's Joy.

1.

This mother's sorrow was the distress of her daughter. Her bitter complaint is: "My daughter is grievously vexed with a devil." She makes her daughter's sorrow her own. "Have mercy on me." "Lord, help me."

The affliction of a child always brings heart-ache to a true mother. This is true of physical distress and temporal misfortune. For her children's sake every mother spends anxious hours and sleepless nights. To a Christian mother, however, the spiritual affliction of a child is especially grievous. She sorrows because her child is flesh born of the flesh, a sinner. It causes her anguish and anxiety when she thinks of the seriousness of this ailment, of the danger of eternal death, to which it exposes her child. And when her children, ignorant of their sad plight, continue in their sin, wander from God, walk the road to perdition, her sorrow is boundless. We have caused our mothers much grief. Some of it we could not avoid. But are we perhaps wilfully causing her grief by our godlessness and sin, our spiritual negligence and indifference? (Read Augustine's regrets when thinking upon his early sins and the tears and grief of his mother Monica.)

2.

This mother's love is revealed in her anxiety for her daughter's welfare and in the efforts she puts forth in her interest. Nothing is too much for her. Nothing discourages her. Nothing is beneath her. She is willing to spend and to be spent for the benefit of her child.

Think over your life. Is not this the portrait of your mother? Thank God for mother's love. Remember she loves you when she pleads with you to remain true to your Savior or to return to Him. *E. g.*, Hannah. Ruth's attachment to her mother-in-law Naomi. Ruth 1, 14—17.

3.

This mother's faith shines forth beautifully. She goes to the proper source for help, to the Lord, the Son of David, v. 22; Mark 7, 24—26. To her Jesus is the Lord, the Almighty, who can help when all other helpers fail. To her He is the Son of David, the promised, gracious Savior, who will help, who cannot deny her plea. In spite of all appearances to the contrary she believes in His mercy, vv. 23—27. Her faith makes her persistent in prayer and intercession. Jesus gives her the beautiful testimony: "O woman, great is thy faith." And the faith of this mother is the blessing of her daughter.

This story has repeated itself over and over (Monica). Many are the children who have been blessed by a mother's faith temporally, spiritually, eternally. Thank God for a *Christian* mother.

What a beautiful example this mother gave to her daughter in her faith! If you have a godly mother, let her faith and piety inspire you.

4.

This mother's joy is found in the welfare, the health and happiness, of her daughter. It filled her heart with an ecstasy of joy when Jesus announced to her burdened heart: "Be it unto thee even as thou wilt," v. 28; Mark 7, 29. 30.

You know that your mother's joy is wrapped up in your welfare. For her sake you ought to cultivate a cheerful disposition. Let her hear something besides complaint. And by all means, for your own sake and her sake, let her have joy in the knowledge of your spiritual well-being. And if you have strayed away from your God and Savior, for your own sake heed her admonition and cheer her heart by a return to God. Then she will share the joy of the angels over one sinner that has repented.   ARTHUR E. NEITZEL.

Harvest Home.
Deut. 8, 6—18.

A Harvest Home festival we celebrate in keeping with an old custom to offer up thanks and praise to God at the close of the harvest.

In the Old Testament such harvest festivals were commanded by God. The children of Israel were obligated to bring in the first sheaves at the beginning of the harvest during the Passover Festival, about the end of March or the beginning of April, as a thankoffering, Lev. 23, 10—14. But the principal Harvest Home festival was celebrated fifty days later, on Pentecost Day, also called the Feast of Harvest, Ex. 23, 16. This was the season of the year when the grain, especially the wheat, was harvested and a "new meat-offering," an offering of the new crop, was presented unto the Lord, Lev. 23, 16. 17. That was a day of great joy, Deut. 16, 11, on which also a free-will offering was brought into the sanctuary, Deut. 16, 10. The third great festival, the Feast of Tabernacles, in the fall of the year, after the wine and olive harvest, was the Thanksgiving Festival of the Israelites.

In the New Testament, God has commanded no special days of worship or festival days. The choice of such days and festivities is left to us. But Christians are always grateful people. Christians recognize the grace and love of God, who out of fatherly goodness and mercy, without any merit or worthiness in them, so bountifully provides for the support of their body and life through the blessings of the field which He gives. New Testament Christians therefore, according to a custom of long standing, also joyfully celebrate a Harvest Home festival at the close of the harvest. At this time we love to appear in our house of worship, which is often beautifully decorated for this occasion, and to encompass the altar heavily bedecked with fruits and products of the field, to offer up to the Lord our praise and thanks for the bountiful harvest which He has given us. And so to-day also we raise our voices to Him, the Giver of all good gifts, and sing Hymn 291, 1. (Here the congregation may arise and sing this verse or the whole hymn.) Being thus moved to gratitude, let us consider: —

"The Bounteous Hand of God."

1. How It has Again Blessed Us; 2. How We may Keep Its Blessing.

1.

A) God has blessed us in our native land. Vv. 7—9: description of the Promised Land, its fertility, natural resources; "the glory of all lands," Ezek. 20, 6. See Schaller, *Book of Books,* p. 146, § 151. — Our country similar with its variety of climate and soil, grain and fruits, natural resources. (Describe in general and refer to local industries, mines, agriculture, etc.)

B) In this year. Crops, economic conditions, industry, employment, etc. If favorable, what a blessing from the bounteous hand of God! If unfavorable, remember what advantages we still have compared with other countries: the starving millions in China, slave conditions in Russia, etc.

C) From the hand of God, v. 10. All these blessings come from God. The farmer prepares the field, cultivates it, reaps a harvest, but God gives the seed, the air, the rain, the sunshine, the fertility of the soil, without which the harvest would be impossible. No one, not even the greatest scientist, though he may know all the ingredients of seed and soil, has ever invented a living seed, a breath of fresh air, a drop of rain, a bit of sunshine. It is all the handiwork of God. So also the coal and iron, oil and gas, copper and zink, gold and silver, which we get from the earth. God alone has placed them there, and by His grace we are able to use these natural gifts for our earthly life and comfort. No one else has created a living being, given him strength, intelligence, ingenuity, and skill to make these various, countless gifts of God useful and serviceable to man. Each one must confess that "God has made me and all creatures," etc. Explanation of the First Article. We all are moved to render praise and thanks unto God, Ps. 117.

2.

A) But how may we keep these blessings? The children of Israel are warned in the text against loss of their blessings by forgetting God, v. 10—14, by boasting of their own power and ingenuity, v. 17. Curses are threatened unto them for ingratitude, chap. 28, 15—68. These were literally fulfilled when the Israelites became disobedient, idolatrous, ungrateful. Terrible punishments were visited upon them. Fall and destruction of Jerusalem and the Temple. — So we are warned by God against forgetting Him and abusing His blessings. "Be not deceived; God is not mocked," Gal. 6, 6—8. God has blessed us with food that we may have to eat and that the poor may also live. If we hoard it, squander it, waste or destroy it in order to keep prices high and to satisfy our greed, or otherwise abuse it, we call down upon us the wrath and punishment of God. The economic condition in the civilized world of to-day is the result of reckless and godless use of the blessings of God. And unless such misuse of the gifts of God is curbed, worse punishments will follow.

B) Therefore the caution of the Lord, v. 6. Israel should remember who brought them out of Egypt and led them through the wilderness, v. 15—17, should remember the true God, from whom all blessings flow, v. 18, that the people of God may at all times have and enjoy the blessings sworn unto the fathers. — Do we desire to be blessed? Shall God continue to us His blessings? Oh, then let us in faith and in the fear of God preserve them! We are not absolute owners of the blessings of God. We are only His stewards. He has given these blessings of the earth to us to be used according to His will. He will call us to account for the use of His gifts. How shall we use them? For our own support, 1 Tim. 5, 8; Prov. 12, 11; to help the poor and needy, Eph. 4, 28; Matt. 5, 42; Prov. 19, 17; Heb. 13, 16; to support the kingdom of God, Matt. 25, 14—30, the parable of the Pounds.

C) Let us Christians, then, as we thank God for the harvest, show and prove our gratitude. He has done great things for us, whereof we are glad. He has brought us into His kingdom and made us His own through faith in Christ Jesus. We are His children, and He desires to bless us richly and daily by providing us with all we need for the support of this body and life, by forgiving us all our sins and healing all our diseases, Ps. 103, 3. He has opened unto us heaven and prepared for us eternal life through Jesus Christ, our Savior, and during our life here on earth He "openeth His hand and satisfieth the desire of every living thing," Ps. 145, 15. 16. Let us with grateful hearts conserve these blessings by remaining true to Him in faith and walking in His ways. Let us pray that He in His mercy and grace may never withhold them from us. Let us learn ever more from His Word to look up to Him in faith and say: Hymn 298, 4.

TITUS LANG.

Memorial Sunday.
Rev. 7, 15.

America is celebrating another Memorial Day. At first set apart in honor of the soldiers who died in the Civil War, it has to-day come to include the soldiers of all wars who have fallen in the service of our country. And it is proper that we who enjoy the fruits of their sacrifice should honor their memories. It is a laudable custom for our nation to visit the silent cities of the dead on Memorial Day and by the monuments marking the resting-places of our soldier dead to be reminded of the price which they paid. Let the flowers with which we decorate their graves be placed there in token that they and their sacrifice shall not be forgotten.

At the same time let us dedicate ourselves to live for our country with the same loyalty and devotion with which our soldiers who are sleeping beneath the sod died for it. Nor let us forget to send an earnest prayer to the throne of the Ruler of nations for the land we love. "God bless our native land . . . by Thy great might."

Now, it is but natural, that the observance of the annual Memorial Day by our nation should cause our thoughts to turn to all our loved ones, especially to those who, having lived for Christ, have entered into the better land. On the basis of our text I would direct your attention to —

That Better Land.

Not one of us but has a personal interest in *that better land;* for there are within the jasper walls of the mansions in that better land those who once bore our names. It may be grandparents whose heads were silvered as we laid them in the grave; it may be parents who seemed indispensable to the comfort of the home; it may be a husband or a wife who was dearly loved; it may be a child who was called away in the springtime of life. The silent moments bring memories of loved ones; and because we loved them, we sit and wonder what are their experiences in that unseen country beyond the stream called Death.

And we have a very deep interest in that eternity; for we know that *shortly* we, too, shall stand on its limitless shore. No fact is so sure as death. It is one event that will come whether we wish it or not; and it may come at any time. "There is but a step between me and death," 1 Sam. 20, 3. To a man who was anticipating a visit to Europe a friend said: "Before you go abroad, read about the countries you expect to visit, so that you will have some knowledge of what you are to see." Good advice, to be sure. And why should not we who must make the crossing over the ocean between time and eternity earnestly study what the Word of God tells us concerning the better land and especially about the way to reach it? It is quite true that where one neglects this preparatory study, there is, if not wilful unbelief, at least a shrinking from an earnest consideration of a matter which some day must be faced and for which no time like the present may be better suited. Ps. 90, 12.

But what do we know of the better land? Is there anything about it that we can know with any degree of certainty?

There are certain evidences of the immortality of the soul which point to a possibility, perhaps probability of a life beyond the grave. Men have argued the immortality of the soul from the fact that in this life goodness is often unrewarded, sin goes unpunished, and that a just and holy God has in His infinite wisdom only delayed the hour when in another existence He will reward the good and punish the evil. Or men have argued the immortality of the soul from the well-nigh universal belief in immortality; from the historical fact that people generally, whether civilized or not, have believed in the existence of life after death. Then, again, there is that innate longing for immortality, which shrinks from the very thought of annihilation, which hopes for the reunion of loved ones in a better land with an eagerness that no philosophy can dampen. And yet, all such evidences can at best point only to a probability; they can never establish that certainty and positiveness of belief which we desire so much. That can come only if we take our stand on Olivet and gaze heavenward through the telescope of the inspired Word.

And what do we see? To begin with, the divine Word reveals to us most positively that there is a heaven, a better land, a place, which Jesus has gone to prepare for His people, John 14, 2; Ps. 16, 11; 17, 15.

To be sure, our vision of the heavenly Canaan, even through the telescope of God's Word, is not such that every question which arises in our mind concerning it is fully answered. For life in the better land is so far above us here upon earth and our understanding that there would be much we could not comprehend. The all-wise God has properly limited His revelation of the better land to our present ability to understand heavenly things. Here, too, applies the word of the Lord: "What I do thou knowest not now, but thou shalt know hereafter."

Nevertheless God has given us many a precious revelation concerning the better land. In the chapter from which our text is taken St. John sees the saints of God who "have come out of great tribulation and have washed their robes and made them white in the blood of the Lamb" as now "standing before the throne of God and serving Him day and night in His temple." What blessedness to have a place before the majestic throne of our great God! What joy divine to spend time without end in perfect service and worship of God! What bliss to have God dwell in the midst of His people! The original text has it: "He that sits upon the throne shall overshadow them." "Just as the Shekinah, the cloud of the covenant, hovered over the Taber-

nacle and over the mercy-seat in the Old Testament with intimate
care, thus the presence of God will overshadow the elect in heaven
in order to be united with them in intimate fellowship and to satisfy
them with the rich gifts of His house." This intimate, perfect communion with God is the very summit, the pinnacle, of the blessedness
of the saints of God in the better land.

Our text mentions and emphasizes one activity in particular —
service. The holy writer tells us that there in the happy abode of the
blessed, in heaven, God's people will *serve Him* day and night. It is
true, we cannot enter upon details of this service; but we may be
sure that our service there will glorify the Father, who has loved us,
will exalt the Son, who has redeemed us, and will express the mind of
the Spirit, who has sanctified us, and that, free from sin, corruption,
worldly ambition, selfishness, or worry, we shall be given whole-
heartedly and with utmost joy to the service of Him who has loved us,
who has redeemed us, and who has bestowed upon us this eternal
happiness.

Life in the better land will be the perfection of all that in its
transitoriness gladdens this earthly life. Our joys, our pleasures, our
associations with those we love, our tasks, our service to the Kingdom,
our communion with God, indeed, everything that makes life here
worth while, is marred by sin and its dire consequences, manifested
in so many different ways. Up yonder, however, in the better land, —
this we can see clearly through the telescope of the Word, — there will
be no sin, no sickness, no death, no grave, no tears, no sorrow, but only
fulness of joy, rivers of pleasure, perfect rest, heavenly peace, full
knowledge, blessed communion with God. Truly, here, too, applies
that "eye hath not seen, nor ear heard, neither have entered into the
heart of man the things which God hath prepared for them that love
Him." Does it surprise us that St. Paul said he had "a desire to depart and to be with Christ," and that he added: "which is far better"?

In view of all this there should be a joyous note in our memorial
service this morning. We may look upon the silent face and say:
"Death, thou art but the stream which my loved one has crossed to
enter into the better land." We may go out to the cemetery, and as
we place the beautiful flowers upon the grave of one whom we loved
and who loved the Lord, we may whisper: "Not here, not here, but
with Jesus." And as the days pass by with their lonely hours, instead
of brooding over our loss, let us rather think of their gain, rejoicing
that the hands which here below held the sword in the battle of life
now bear aloft the victor's palm; rejoicing that their faith has now
given place to sight; rejoicing that their love to God, no longer chilled
by sin, is casting its crown at the pierced feet with one eternal question: "What shall I render unto the Lord for all His benefits toward
me?" Aye, rejoicing, we say with the poet: "O how blest are ye whose

toils are ended, Who through death have unto God ascended! Ye have arisen From the cares which keep us still in prison. . . . Christ has wiped away your tears forever; Ye have that for which we still endeavor; To you are chanted Songs that ne'er to mortal ears are granted."

We cannot conclude this memorial meditation without earnestly asking ourselves this question: Am I on the way to the better land? Do I know the way? There are but few who do not entertain the hope of some day enjoying life in the better land. Most men, too, some time or other, give thought to this question, Which is the way? Men have answered that question differently. The savage in the wilderness asks the way, and he answers it by worshiping ugly idols and making hideous sacrifices; the philosophers ask it and answer it with their vain speculations; the Pharisees, old and modern, ask it and answer it by pointing to their good works and own righteousness. But Jesus answers the question by pointing to Himself: "I am the Way. . . . No man cometh unto the Father but by Me." The holy apostle said emphatically: Acts 4, 12. Is Jesus your Way to the better land? With all the power at my command and with the divine Word to give emphasis I say to you: There is no other way; it is either by Jesus or not at all. John 10, 7. 28.

By the blood which has opened the door of mercy; by the crown of thorns which has bought our crown of life; by the hope of seeing Him face to face who, even through the dim glass of faith, we see as "One altogether lovely"; by the memory of those whose faith and piety were their precious legacy to us; by the glad reunion by and by in the better land, I urge you this morning henceforth and forever to live in "Him who loved you and gave Himself for you." Let this be your motto and inspiration: If I live, I live unto the Lord; if I die, I die unto the Lord, so that, living or dying, I am the Lord's.

WILLIAM H. EIFERT.

Funeral Sermon on 2 Sam. 12, 16—23.

A Christian minister is permitted to penetrate more deeply into the homes, aye, into the very hearts, of the members of his church than others. When winter comes and sorrow, doors now barred even to familiar friends, still open quickly to his knock. He knows as few others how those who dwell under one roof fare with one another, how they love one another, how cruel the blow that falls to separate them. I know how you now grieve. But it is not my business in this hour to rend your hearts by picturing for you the great loss you have suffered. The Spirit of the Lord is upon me. He hath anointed me to preach good tidings unto the meek. He hath sent me to bind up the broken-hearted, not to wound them. He has sent me to comfort all that mourn, to give them beauty for ashes, the oil of joy for mourning, the garment of praise for the spirit of heaviness, that they might be called trees of righteousness, the planting of the Lord, that He might be glorified.

Yes, that He might be glorified by you also on this day. Our text for this occasion is a chapter out of the life of David the king. David, so the Bible tells us, was a man after the heart of God. No, not perfect. A sinner even as you and I. But a child of God just the same, trying to do God's will. But to be a Christian does not bring with it that we always get what we want, even though with tears we pray for it. There came a time when David's beloved, the child Bathsheba had given him, became sick. Yes, and he was plainly told that this child would surely die. Then David's heart was overcome by sorrow. He fasted. He lay all the night long upon the earth in prayer and lamentation. And though the elders of his house, alarmed for his own well-being, after a while went to him, though they endeavored to raise him up from the earth, he would not, neither did he eat bread with them. And this continued for seven days and nights, seven long days and nights of prayer, seven long days and nights of fasting, prayer and fasting, by a sinner forgiven, a man after the heart of God, who delights in the sacrifice of a broken heart, a humble and a contrite spirit. And yet — after these seven days the child died. You, my friends, are Christians, men and women forgiven. You have fasted and wept and watched and prayed, hoping even against hope that it would please God to restore your beloved to health. But it was not His will. She has fallen asleep in Him. And now, as Daniel said, so it is: "God doeth according to His will in the army of heaven and among the inhabitants of the earth, and none can stay His hand or say to Him, What doest Thou?"

And so your beloved died despite all your prayer. What shall we, then, do, I and you? Let us do what David did, who rose up from prayer at the couch of death to worship and to praise the Lord, to eat bread also that he might gain strength for life's burdens.

Let Us in This Hour Rise Up to Worship and to Praise Our God.
And why?

1. Because of God's Gracious Dealings with Your Beloved;

2. Because of God's Gracious Purpose with You.

1.

The servants of David had been witnesses of his grief as I have been of yours. Long before the child was dead they saw him lying seven days and nights on the ground in fasting and lamentation. Then his child died. Now his servants lacked the courage even to tell him. They thought this blow must absolutely crush him. Even so we fear to inform men of the impending death of their loved ones and know not how to speak when death has finally come. But love has sharp eyes, keen ears. A faltering, evasive answer from our lips to a searching question, the slightest hesitancy, a grave and sorrowful expression on our faces, then love knows. So, when David saw his servants whispering to each other, careful that he should not overhear, he said to himself, "My beloved is dead." He asked them to their faces as love must, "Is the child dead?" To so direct a question we must give a plain answer. They said, "He is dead."

And then and there, lo and behold, a remarkable thing took place. To the astonishment of his servants David arose from the earth; he washed; he anointed himself; he changed his apparel. He went into the house of the Lord to worship. Then he returned to his house, and when he had requested it, they set bread before him, and he did eat. In amazement his servants looked on. At last they felt they had reason to question him about this strange change in his behavior. They said, with some reproach I am sure: "What thing is this that thou hast done?" etc. They could not understand it. It seemed to them a lack of proper grief, callousness. But no accusation against David could be more unjust. This man had wept and prayed and fasted seven days and nights. Later in life when Absalom, another son, a traitor against his own father, had been slain in his rebellion, the father cried: "O my son Absalom, my son, my son Absalom, would God I had died for thee!"

What, then, explains David's fortitude when his child had died? Let him give you the explanation. He tells us: "While the child was yet alive, I fasted and wept, for I said, Who can tell whether God will be gracious to me that the child may live? But now? Can I bring him back again? He shall not return to me." Yes, he now knew beyond the shadow of doubt what was the good will of God in his child's sickness. He now knew that there was nothing else that he could do about it. Therefore he bowed his head before the sweet will of God to worship Him still, to praise Him for His goodness. Then he went home to eat; for there was a great nation dependent upon him, a nation in need, surrounded by foes, which for seven days and nights had been like sheep which have no shepherd. To care for them, to lead them, and to guide them was a duty God had laid upon him. Parental duty ended, he must now give his attention anew to his needy children in the nation.

Such is the behavior of truly good and great men. Let fools and sinners curse their God and die. Let them vow to forsake His Church and His altar with execrations because their prayers were not heard in their own way. You, my friends, shall be like David. You, my friend, upon whom this blow fell hardest, acted like David on the day when your beloved was taken. With quivering lips and a heart struggling for strength you cried, "I had hoped and prayed that it would be God's will to heal her. But — His will be done." God give you strength to say so ever more bravely, to say: Not my will, but Thine, O Lord, be done.

> My eyes see dimly till by faith anointed,
> And my blind choosing brings me grief and pain.
> Choose for me, Lord, nor let my weak preferring
> Cheat my poor soul of good Thou hast designed.
> Choose for me, God; Thy wisdom is unerring,
> And we are fools and blind.

My friends, as David was the leader of a great people, so many are dependent on you. They need your wisdom, your counsel, your guidance, in these troublous times. Dry your tears, eat, and with renewed strength take up anew life's duties and burdens. She whom you loved so ardently cannot be benefited by aught you could do. It was God's good and gracious will to give her the life that is fuller, freer, happier, from which she will not return to you.

2.

But you can go to her. And this is indeed, in the second place and, in a way, in the first place, the reason of our courage and the source of our consolation. David was not so readily as it may seem reconciled to the loss of his child. Loss? He knew that his child was not lost, that his beloved was with God in heaven, and that the way thither was open before himself, that he, too, would some day enter there. "I shall go to him," he cried in holy determination, "though he shall not return to me."

Dear friends, of this we all are confident, that our friend is happy with God. She trusted in Jesus. How eagerly she again partook recently of the holy Sacrament, in which He feeds us with the body that He gave and the blood that He shed for the remission of our sins. All her trust was placed in Christ alone. It pleased Him to test her faith severely, to make true His prophecy: "We must through much tribulation enter into the kingdom of God." Her lover, her friends, her physician, and her nurses could ease her pains, but could not cure her. But in these long hours of trial and pain she learned to endure hardness as a good soldier of Jesus Christ, uncomplaining. And as a veteran in his noble, but arduous service, she went into the last battle with the grim foe of God and man and obtained a glorious victory. I need not and I shall not rehearse for you how she in many ways proved her faith with good works. She never wanted these things to be made known, and we shall respect her wishes even in death. Only this much we who were the beneficiaries of her kindness must be permitted to say, that we see in also these good deeds nothing but evidences of her sincere affection for the greatest Benefactor of us all, the only Savior, Jesus, who bought her, too, with His blood, washed her clean in the saving waters of Holy Baptism, anointed and confirmed her with His Spirit through His life-giving Word, and kept her steadfast in the true faith unto her blessed end. Now she has gone to be with Him. And we can go to her. We have not lost her, only sent her before.

> We cannot say, and we will not say, that she is dead;
> She is just away.
> With a cheerful smile and a wave of the hand
> She wandered into heaven's land
> And left us wondering how very fair
> It needs must be since she's dwelling there

and especially also our Lord Jesus, the Fairest among ten thousand, our most beautiful and adorable Savior. — He is anxious to bring us also to the place of bliss. He is Himself the ladder reaching from the earth to the land of the sky; He said: "I am the Way and the Truth and the Life. No man cometh unto the Father but by Me." Friends, cling to Him, to His Word, to the holy Sacrament, in life and in death. So you, too, shall at last go to Him and be reunited with all your loved ones who have fallen asleep in His arms.

Abide with us, dearest Lord, that we may abide in Thee. Fast falls the eventide also of our life's little day. Hymn 40, 2. 6. 8.

KARL H. EHLERS.

Funeral Sermon on Ps. 90, 5. 6. 12.

We are living in the coldest and dreariest season of the year — winter. This period of the year is not the time of harvest. There is, however, a reaper that pays no attention to times and seasons of the year.

This reaper cares not for fields of golden grain and gardens of beautiful flowers, but for men and women, young and old.

This reaper, death, has come into our midst and with his gleaming scythe has cut down one who was in the very flower of manhood. However, in the opinion of the Creator the time had come for him to be harvested, and so He sent His reaper.

Now, friends, every time this reaper makes his appearance and with his shining scythe cuts down one after another of the children of men, it ought to teach us that sooner or later we, too, shall be visited by him. Blessed is the man who takes this lesson to heart and like the psalmist of old turns his eyes unto the hills from whence cometh his help and prays: "Lord, teach us to number our days that we may apply our hearts unto wisdom."

That is what we are to do now as we give attention to the words of our text and learn for our consolation and admonition: —

1. That Our Days are Numbered by an Infallible God;
2. That We are to Apply Our Hearts unto Wisdom.

1.

The psalm from which our text is taken is the oldest that has been preserved in the Psalter, the occasion for its writing probably being the incident recorded Num. 14, 23. 29—32. (Relate the incident.) The deep impressions which those years of wandering made upon Moses he by inspiration of God penned in the psalm before us.

The inspired author, with a few strokes of the pen, depicts the brevity and transitoriness of life. Text, vv. 5. 6. Human life he compares to a flood whose swiftly rushing stream carries mortals away into the sleep of death. Then he likens life to a sleep or dream which is past and gone before a person fully realizes it. Again, he says that our days are like the grass which grows up in the morning and in the evening is cut down and withers. The history of a blade of grass has been summed up by one writer into five expressive words: "sown, grown, blown, mown, gone." Considered from a purely physical side, the history of man is much the same. Compare Ps. 103, 15. 16; Is. 40, 6—8; Jas. 1, 11; 4, 14; 1 Pet. 1, 24.

Yes, dear friends, brief indeed are the days of man. In vv. 9 and 10 of our psalm the sacred writer says: "The days of our years are threescore years and ten; and if by reason of strength they be fourscore years, yet is their strength labor and sorrow; for it is soon cut off, and we fly away." And how soon it will be cut off no one knows; for there is nothing more uncertain than the hour of death.

Let us, however, bear in mind that it is the wisdom of God that calls us from this world. This truth is repeatedly emphasized in our text and in other places of the psalm. V. 3 we read: *"Thou* turnest man to destruction and sayest, Return, ye children of men." V. 5: *"Thou* carriest them away as with a flood." All these expressions emphasize the truth that God numbers our days, in fact, numbers the very hairs of our head, Matt. 10, 30. Our times are in His hand, Ps. 31, 15.

Our days are numbered by God. What a consoling truth to contemplate! That truth ought to cheer and console you, my dear mourners. Think of it — God called the departed away. His days were in God's hands. God was the Harvester of that life. Bear in mind the wisdom of God. He makes no mistakes. He knows when our life is ready for harvesting, and then He sends His reaper. Surely, dear friends, you would not want it otherwise? Would you with your finite and faulty wisdom, with your ignorance of what the future has in store for you, want it otherwise? Surely not. Let us, then, thank God that His infinite love and wisdom set the bounds of our life on earth.

2.

And now turning to v. 12, we read: "So teach us to number our days that we may apply our hearts unto wisdom." After speaking of the brevity and transitoriness of life, Moses prays for a proper understanding that he and Israel may fully realize the uncertainty of human life, namely, that every day may be their last day on earth in order that they may apply their hearts unto wisdom, *i. e.,* be prepared for death at all times.

Like Moses we, too, should plead with God to grant us grace to realize the uncertainty of our life in order that we may be prepared for death at all times.

To be always prepared to meet our Redeemer is indeed wisdom, true wisdom. But in what does true wisdom consist? Some there are who think that true wisdom consists in crowding our days and nights with the maximum of earthly joys for ourselves and with the minimum of concern about any one else and about eternity and where they shall spent it. That, however, is not the wisdom of a child of God, but of a worldling. The Preacher in Ecclesiastes shows us the folly of such wisdom. After having experienced what this world has to offer, he comes to this conclusion: "Vanity of vanities; all is vanity."

There are others who labor under the impression that true wisdom consists in doing the best we can, and if we do that, no one, not even God Himself, can expect more. But, dear friends, if we build the hope of our salvation on what we do and on what we are, then our life must be perfect, so that no one, not even God, can point to a sin that we have committed. "Be ye perfect, even as your Father which is in heaven is perfect." If we do not live a perfect, sinless life, then we are under the curse of God; for it is written: "Cursed be he that confirmeth not *all* the words of this Law to do them," Deut. 27, 26. "The wages of sin is death," Rom. 6, 23. But who is there in this wide world that can live a perfect life? Not one. Is. 14, 3; Eccl. 7, 20; Is. 64, 6. It is therefore evident that no one can be saved by his own good character or works since God demands perfection, and that is out of the question for sinful man. (Hymn 325, 2.)

To the question, Wherein does true wisdom consist? there is only one correct answer, and that the child of God, the Christian, knows. He takes an entirely different attitude toward life than the worldling and the self-righteous. He realizes that the only hope of salvation lies in Jesus Christ, whom God has sent into the world to become humanity's Redeemer. Like the wise man he acknowledges "that the fear of the Lord is the beginning of wisdom." Like St. Paul the Christian, applying his heart unto wisdom, takes as the motto of his life: "I determined not to know anything among you save Jesus Christ and Him crucified. To know Jesus, to put one's trust in Him as the only Hope of our salvation, that is true wisdom, Acts 16, 30. 31; John 3, 16.

Our departed brother was fully conscious that his days were numbered, and he made good use of the time of grace still allotted to him in preparing for eternity. During the last few months of his life it was my privilege to assist him in preparing to meet his Maker. In all my visits I found him to be of a humble and contrite spirit, finding peace and consolation in the forgiveness of sins won for him by the death of his Savior on Calvary's cross. Twice during his illness he received Christ's body and blood as a seal that his sins had been forgiven. He prepared for eternity. He applied his heart unto wisdom.

Dear friends, as a dying man speaking to dying men, may I plead with you daily to bear in mind that our days are numbered by God; and may we, like the departed, apply our hearts unto wisdom, firmly believing unto our end in Jesus Christ as the Lamb of God, that taketh away the sin of the world.   C. J. KILLINGER.

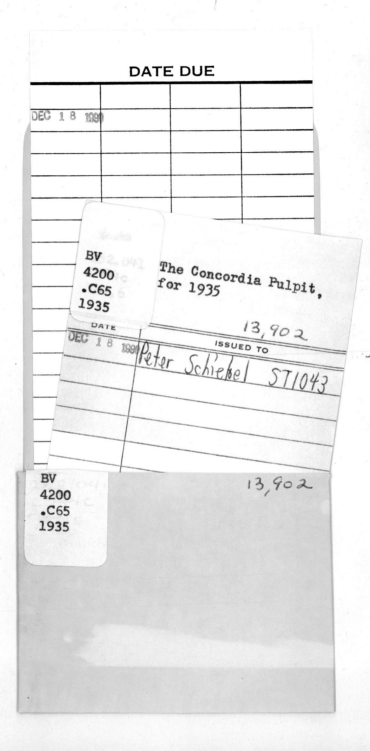

DATE DUE

DEC 18 1990			

The Concordia Pulpit,
for 1935

13,902

DATE	ISSUED TO
DEC 18 1990	Peter Schiebel ST1043

13,902